Loma Linda Messages (Unabridged)

Ellen G. White

2023

Contents

A Great Work 9
Instruction to Secure Loma Linda 11
    Answered to Former Representations 11
    To Become an Educational Center 12
    Action of Pacific Union Medical Convention 13
    For the Training of Physicians 14
Resolutions 16
    Cautions Against Premature Growth 16
    March 24, 1908, Sister White wrote further 20
Action of General Conference Committee 23
To be Separate from the World 27
Endorsement by the General Conference Committee 30
Endorsed by the Pacific Union Conference 33
An Important Council 39
Prospects 41
Our Needs 42
Testimonies and Experiences in Connection with the Glendale Sanitarium 44
Established Prosperity 53
"Christ's Object Lessons" 69
Extracts from Letters and Mss., on the Training and Work of Medical Missionaries 73
To Stand as God's Witness 76
The Truth, Practiced and Taught, Will Lead to the Conversion of Some 77
To Engage in Soul-Saving in Our Sanitariums 78
God Invests with Holy Dignity Those Who Go Forth in His Power to Heal the Sick 80
In the Early Days, The Workers Were Medical Missionaries, and the Power of God was Manifest in the Healing of the Sick 83
Medical Missionaries and Ministers to Meet Together to Study Bible 85

To be a Medical Missionary, Means to be a Laborer Together with God	86
The Training of Medical Missionaries, Not Properly Understood	88
The Training of Medical Missionaries	89
Privileges and Opportunities of a Gospel Medical Missionary	92
Medical Missionaries to Unite with Ministers	94
Every One to Work as Christ Worked	95
Every One to Work as Christ Worked	97
Every One to Work as Christ Worked	99
Medical Missionaries to be Thoroughly Educated in Bible Lines	100
Medical Missionary Work as a Door to Large Cities	101
The Purpose of Medical Missionary Work	102
Labor in Connection with the Gospel Ministry	103
Make the Bible Your Man of Counsel. Your Acquaintance with it Will Grow Rapidly If You Keep Your Mind from Rubbish	104
Nurses as Missionary Evangelists	107
Physicians and Nurses to Unite with Ministers in Soul-Saving Work	108
Companies Organized and Educated Most Thoroughly to Work as Nurses, as Evangelists, as Ministers, as Canvassers	110
Plans for Medical Missionary Work	111
To Our Brethren and Sisters in Southern California	125
To the Workers in the Glendale Sanitarium	134
The Loma Linda Sanitarium	154
Loma Linda Meeting	163
A Reform Needed	174
To the Executive Committee of the Southern California Conference	175
Notes Of Travel (E. G. W.)	211
To Ministers and Physicians	215
To Elders Reaser, Burden, and the Executive Committee of the Southern California Conference	236
The Workers in the Paradise Valley Sanitarium	248
An Open Letter	254
Individual Responsibility	261

God's Wisdom to be Sought	263
A Change of Heart Needed	265
Jehovah is Our King	272
A Constant Peril	273
An Exalted Privilege	274
Paul's Experience	276
Extracts from Letters to Mrs. S. M. I. Henry	278
The Work to be Done for the W.C.T.U	283
The Temperance Work	286
To Elder Geo. W. Reaser and the Ministers in Southern Calif	291
Arise Shine	294
Extracts with Explanatory Notes on the Training of Medical Students	301
To the Workers in Southern California	313
To Ministers, Physicians and Teachers in Southern California	325
Provision for our Schools	327
In Humility and Faith	332
To the Workers in Southern California	341
The Responsibilities of a Conference President	349
The Management of Conference Affairs	359
The Work Hindered by Lack of Faith	366
Report of the committee on Suggestive Plans and Resolutions Pacific Union Conference Medical Convention	369
The Work In Southern California	372
Elder J.A. Burden and Others Bearing Responsibilities at Loma Linda	378
To the Leading Men in the Southern California Conference	386
Reformation Needed in the Churches	388
The Conference President	388
The Work in Southern California	393
(601) Not for Publication	402
A Collection of Extracts from the Testimonies on the Medical Missionary Work	403
1. Our Work—To Preach the Everlasting Gospel. Matthew 28:19, 20. Revelation 14:6-11	403
2. To Every Man His Work. Ephesians 4:11-13	404

    3 Medical Missionary Work a Part of the Gospel. Mark
        16:17, 18 405
    4. Medical Missionary Work to Prepare the Way for
        Gospel Workers 406
    5. Union of Medical Missionary and Gospel Work 407
    6. High Calling of Medical Missionaries 410
    7. Every Church Member to Engage in Medical
        Missionary Work 411
    8. The Training of Physicians and Nurses 412
The Medical Missionary Work 421
Elder J.A. Burden and Others Bearing Responsibilities at
    Loma Linda 426
To the Brethren in Southern California 431
Deeper Consecration 434
    The Teacher and Evangelist 435
Instruction to Sanitarium Workers 438
A Plea for Medical Missionary Evangelists. Importance of
    the Work 444
The Training of Workers 447
Nurses to be Evangelists 449
Portion of a Letter from J. A. Burden to W. C. White, Nov.
    18, 1908 455
A Plain Statement of Facts Regarding the Establishment of
    the Paradise Valley Sanitarium 458
    It is Plain from These Facts, That 460
Medical Missionary Work in Southern California 463
The Proposed Transfer 466
A Summary of Facts 468
In Conclusion 470
To the Teachers in Union College 472
Passed by the Southern California Conference 479
Talk by Mrs. E. G. White before the General Conference
    Committee, June 11, 1909 486
The Relation of Loma Linda to Medical Institutions 487
    The Medical Student 491
    Importance of Bible Study 497
Memorial 499
Condensed Memorial 511

Loma Linda College of Evangelists	511
Extracts from Testimony	518
To the Leading Ministers in California	521
A Message for Our Time on Medical Missionary Work	527
To Our Sanitarium Workers in Southern California	529
"A Statement Regarding the Training of Physicians"	540
A Statement Regarding the Training of Physicians	542
Interview Between Mrs. E. G. White and W. C. White	546
Words of Counsel	547
"A Statement Regarding the Training of Physicians	549
Talk to the Students at Loma Linda, Calif. April 5, 1910. By Mrs. E. G. White	550
A Statement Regarding the Training of Physicians	566
To Those in our Sanitariums	570
Remarks of Mrs. E.G. White Regarding Aggressive Moves at Loma Linda	572
Our Duty to Reach Out	574
Unity Among the Workers	575
Not Amusements but Consecrated Work	576
Regarding the Purchase of Land Adjoining Loma Linda	586
An Appeal in Behalf of our Medical College	588
Loma Linda	591
A Statement Regarding Some Interviews With Mrs. E. G. White	592
The Purchase of Land at Loma Linda	593
The Work Before Us	596
Be of Good Cheer	606
Words of Encouragement	607
Perplexities	607
An Important Interview Regarding Physicians' Wages	610

(Consecutive parenthetically enclosed numbers of this copy indicate the paging of Elder Burden's original compilation of "Loma Linda Messages", divine instruction, the "blue-print" through the inspired pen of Ellen G. White.)

A Great Work

In the messages that have been sent through the Spirit of Prophecy to the workers in Southern California, great emphasis has been placed upon the advisability, because of the great tourist traffic in that section, of establishing strong institutional work in various important centers. In a letter written November 1, 1905, Sister White said: "The matter was presented to me that many sanitariums would have to be established in Southern California, for there would be a great inflowing of people there. Many would seek that climate."

Bearing this in mind as a part of the Lord's purpose for the carrying forward of His work in Southern California, we can better understand the calls that have been made for extraordinary movements in this field. In 1904 the Paradise Valley Sanitarium was secured, and early in 1905 the conference purchased the sanitarium at Glendale. Yet notwithstanding the financial burdens necessarily connected with the purchased and equipment of these two institutions, a call was made to establish a memorial for God in another important center.

In a letter written in February, 1905, to a brother living in Redlands, Sister White said: "I hope that when you find a suitable place in Redlands, which could be used as a sanitarium, offered for sale at a reasonable price, you will let us know about it. We shall need a sanitarium in Redlands. Unless we start an enterprise of this kind, others will...

"I merely mention this matter so that you may keep it in view. We shall not take any steps to establish a sanitarium in Redlands until we can be assured that we are doing the right thing."

Two months later she wrote: "Redlands and Riverside have been presented to me as places that should be worked. These two places should not longer be neglected. I hope soon to see an earnest effort put forth in their behalf. Will you please consider the advisability of establishing a sanitarium in the vicinity of these towns, with treatment rooms in each place, to act as feeders to the institution?"

[2]

In this same letter we find this statement: "Our people in Southern California need to awaken to the magnitude of the work to be done within their borders." And further: "I have a message to bear to the church-members in Southern California: Arouse, and avail yourselves of the opportunities open to you."

Instruction to Secure Loma Linda

Following the telegram sent to Elder J. A. Burden from Washington, D. C., asking him to secure the property at Loma Linda, "without delay", Sister White wrote:

"Your letter has just been read. I had no sooner finished reading it than I said, "I will consult no one; for I have no question at all about the matter." I advised Willie to send you a telegram without spending time to ask the advise of the brethren. Secure the property by all means, so that it can be held, and then obtain all the money you can and make sufficient payments to hold the place. This is the very property that we ought to have. Do not delay; for it is just what is needed. As soon as it is secured, a working force can begin operations in it. I think that sufficient help can be secured to carry this matter through. I want you to be sure to lose no time in securing the right to purchase the property. We will do our utmost to help you raise the money. I know that Redlands and Riverside are to be worked, and I pray that the Lord may be gracious, and not allow any one else to get this property instead of us."

The letter from which the foregoing paragraph is quoted was written May 14, 1905. Between that time and the end of the month four other letters were written to Elder Burden, emphatically urging the purchase of Loma Linda, and giving strong assurances that it was in the purpose of God that this property be secured. "Be assured, my brother," Sister White wrote in a letter dated May 26, "that I never advise anything unless I have a decided impression that it should be carried out, and unless I am firmly resolved to assist..... By all means secure the property if you can; for I believe it to be the very place the Lord desires us to have.

Answered to Former Representations

Those who, in harmony with these directions, took steps to secure the property, were further assured by statements made by

Sister White after she had visited Loma Linda on her return from the General Conference, that it answered fully to representations of places she had been shown should be secured. In a letter written from Glendale, June 23, 1905, to a brother in the South, she wrote regarding the property:

"Until this recent visit, I had never before seen such a place with my natural eyes, but four years ago such a place was presented before me as one of those that would come into our possession if we moved wisely. It is a wonderful place in which to begin our work for Redlands and Riverside. We must make decided efforts to secure helpers who will do most faithful missionary work. If God will bless the treatments given, and Christ will let His healing power be felt, a wonderful work will be accomplished."

On another occasion Sister White wrote: "The buildings are all ready, and work must be begun as soon as we can secure the necessary physicians and nurses. I am anxious to see the work started. For some time I have been looking for just such a place as this, with buildings all ready for occupancy, surrounded by shade-trees and orchards. When I saw Loma Linda, I said, Thank the Lord. This is the very place we have been hoping to find.

"The character of the buildings, the terraced hill covered by graceful pepper trees, the profusion of flowers and shrubs, the tall shade-trees, the orchard fields,—all combine to make this place meet fully the descriptions that I have given in the past of the place presented to me as the most perfect for sanitarium work. Everything at Loma Linda is fresh and wholesome and attractive."

To Become an Educational Center

Thus it is evident that the counsels of the Spirit of Prophecy were very clear and positive regarding the securing of the property. But the question will arise, has the growth of the work been guided and directed by the same counsels?

Clear intimation of an important educational work to be carried forward at Loma Linda is indicated even among the first communications that were sent by Sister White after the property was secured. In a letter written to Elder Haskell, inviting him to labor in Southern California, she said:

"We must soon start a nurses' training school at Loma Linda. This place will become an important center, and we need the efforts of yourself and your wife to give the right mold to the work in this new educational center."

The following written November 1, 1905, is also to the point: "A school will be established as soon as possible, and the Lord will open the way... With all the buildings in connection with the main buildings, we have great advantages. If we will walk humbly with God, and do according to that which He hath prospered us, we will have Christ as our friend and our helper. "If any man will come after Me, let him deny himself and take up his cross, and follow Me." These are the terms of our discipleship. Will we comply with them?"

Action of Pacific Union Medical Convention [4]

October 28 to 31, 1907, there was held at Loma Linda a medical convention for the Pacific Union Conference, at which were present the president and the vice-president of the General Conference, and the secretary of the medical department of the General Conference. At this convention, Sister White, in a talk given October 31, spoke thus of the educational work at Loma Linda:

"Here we have ideal advantages for a school and for a sanitarium. Here are advantages for the students and great advantages for the patients. I have been instructed that here we should have a school conducted on the principles of the ancient schools of the prophets. It may not be carried on in every respect, as are the schools of the world, but it is to be especially adapted for those who desire to devote their lives, not to commercial pursuits, but to unselfish service for the Master.

"We want a school of the highest order,—a school where the word of God will be regarded as essential, and where obedience to its teachings will be taught. For the carrying forward of such a school, we must have carefully selected educators. Our young people are not to be wholly dependent on the schools where they are told, 'If you wish to complete our course of instruction, you must take this study, or some other study,'—studies that perhaps would be of no practical benefit to those whose only desire is to give to the world God's message of health and peace. In the education that many receive there are not only subjects that are non-essential, but much that is decidedly objectionable. We should endeavor to give instruction that will prepare students quickly for service to their fellow-men.

"We are to seek for students who will plow deep into the Word of God, and who will conform the life-practice to the truths of the Word. Let the education given be such as will qualify consecrated young men and young women to go forth in harmony with the great commission, 'Go ye therefore, and teach all nations, baptizing them in the name of the Father, and of the Son, and of the Holy Ghost: teaching them to observe all things whatsoever I have commanded you.'

For the Training of Physicians

In answer to a question, "Is this school that you have spoken of simply to qualify nurses? or is it to embrace also the qualification of physicians?" Sister White replied:

"Physicians are to receive their education here. Here they are to receive such a mold that when they go out to labor they will not seek to grasp the very highest wages, or else do nothing."

As early as December 10, 1905, Sister White had written to Elder and Mrs. Burden, "In regard to the school, I would say, Make it all you possibly can in the education of nurses and physicians."

But it was difficult for us to grasp at once a clear comprehension of the magnitude of the work to be accomplished in the training of medical missionaries for the world-wide work. All could not see alike as to how much might be involved in the training of physicians. Some felt that we could not hope successfully to give a complete medical course; others thought that we might give a special course that would enable our students to be recognized as practitioners of some system of healing, as are osteopaths, chiropractors, etc; while others thought that we might give two or three years of the medical course, sending the students to some other institution to complete their medical studies, where they might be granted degrees.

Feeling that careful study should be given by the General Conference Medical Department to the training of physicians and to the development of the educational work at Loma Linda, and believing also that the magnitude of the work called for the world-wide support of our people, the convention voted unanimously the following resolutions:

* * * * *

Resolutions

"Whereas, the Loma Linda School of Evangelists has been established for the education and training of those who shall go forth into home and foreign mission fields to teach the gospel and to heal the sick: and,

"Whereas, In these home and foreign mission fields there is need of thousands of medical missionary evangelists, thoroughly qualified to carry the gospel message and to minister to the sick, laboring as nurses who through diligent study and experience have acquired extraordinary ability; therefore,—

"1. Resolved, That we approve of the efforts of the founders and managers of the Loma Linda School of Evangelists, to equip and conduct a school in connection with the Loma Linda Sanitarium; and we encourage them to strengthen its faculty, and to continue to give its students a thorough education and training in those practical lines of work in which the medical evangelist is called to engage.

"2. Resolved, That the General Conference Medical Department be requested to give most careful study to the question of providing for our young people the most favorable opportunities for them to secure the qualifications that they must have in order to carry forward the medical missionary work of our cause.

[6] "Whereas, The financial burden of so conducting the Loma Linda School of Evangelists that the very best work shall be done in training workers for home and foreign mission fields is more than the Loma Linda Sanitarium and the Southern California Conference can carry unaided; therefore,—

"3. Resolved, That we ask the Pacific Union Conference and the General Conference to assist in bearing the expense of this school.

Cautions Against Premature Growth

It must be evident to all that, in order to undertake such an enterprise as the establishment and maintenance of a medical college, there must be, among our leading brethren, a united belief that God is calling for such an enterprise, and a faith that He will enable His people to make it a success. With this thought in mind, we may now understand counsel that came early in 1908 urging caution in the matter of making large moves in this direction prematurely.

In February of 1906 there met at Loma Linda a council consisting of the faculty of Fernando Academy, the faculty of the Loma Linda school, and the executive committee of the Southern California Conference. It should be especially noted that this council was wholly composed of persons living in Southern California, and connected with the work located in one local conference, the membership of which was only about two thousand.

In a letter to Mrs. E. G. White, written February 14, after mentioning the assembling of these brethren, Elder J. A. Burden wrote:

"There was perfect agreement among all present in the conclusions reached and the plans laid. It would have done you good, Sister White, to see the spirit of unity, and the desire of all that the work at Loma Linda should be made just what the Lord designed it to be.

"After carefully considering the light that has been sent to us, and the counsel that has been given with reference to the school at Loma Linda, all were unanimous in their decision that it must be the Lord's plan that a medical missionary school should be carried forward here, with a course sufficiently complete to thoroughly qualify nurses for their professional duties, and to work as educators in medical evangelistic work; and also to qualify certain ones to stand at the head of our medical evangelistic work; and also to qualify certain ones to stand at the head of our medical institutions as fully accredited physicians.

"As we studied over what would be necessary for the school to accomplish this work, it seemed to us it would be necessary to employ two physicians as teachers in the school, a Bible instructor, and one other general school man. These four instructors, with the three physicians employed by the Sanitarium and such practical instructors as those qualified to teach practical hydrotherapy, practical nursing, healthful cookery, etc., would be a strong educational faculty for the qualifying of the two classes of workers, one as nurses, and the other as physicians to engage in evangelistic medical work...

[7]

"Now in order to give these evangelistic physicians standing in the world, it was thought we should secure a charter for the school, which would enable it to grant degrees to all who finished the prescribed course of study. Many, no doubt, would enter the field without waiting to secure a degree, possibly after studying one or two years, as there are many fields in which they could labor freely as medical missionary evangelists without a degree. But from the instruction in the testimonies, we understand that some should qualify as fully accredited physicians, hence the school should plan its course accordingly.

"In planning what would be necessary for a school of this character, to afford facilities for the training of say twenty-five to fifty, it was thought that we would need to erect buildings and equip them with proper laboratory facilities, etc., at a cost of from ten to fifteen thousand dollars. Possibly we would not need all of this at once, but our plans ought to be laid to embrace that amount when completed. This seems like expending a good deal of means in addition to what we have already expended at Loma Linda; but all who were present were unanimous that if such a school were to be carried forward, not simply for the local interest, but for the many who are appealing to us for education in these lines, the expenditure named would be about as little as we could consider....

"The amount named, of course, would not include rooming facilities for the students, but only the school recitation building and necessary equipment in the way of laboratories, etc. for the school work. It certainly would be a great relief and help to the sanitarium work at Loma Linda if sufficient funds could be raised to meet a portion of the indebtedness represented in the buildings occupied by the students for rooming, which would mean at least another ten or fifteen thousand dollars. But as matters now stand, of course we have these, although we are obliged financially for them.

"The committee present felt that these matters should be laid carefully before you before we proceeded further, with the request that if it seemed good to the mind of the Lord for us to move forward, a special call be written by yourself and Brother White through the Review and Herald, that the people may know the real aims and purpose of the school, and the way be opened to call for means everywhere from those who are interested in such an enterprise.

"All through the United States there are young people writing to us, inquiring what the outlook is for the medical school at Loma Linda, and whether it aims to qualify accredited physicians, or only to give a medical course of study for those who want to do missionary work along with their other Bible work. We always answer that the aim and purpose of this medical school is not for professional work, but to qualify consecrated persons with medical ability to labor in evangelistic lines; but that it is the intention of the school that those who finish the course will be credited with degrees as physicians....

"Now, Sister White, we have tried to lay before you these plans as best we can, and are praying the Lord that if He has any more light for us, He will be pleased to reveal it to us, as we do not want to make a mistake in undertaking anything that the Lord has not planned should be carried forward at this place.

"Praying the Lord that He will give you special light on these matters, and that we may be able to cooperate with Him in carrying out His designs in this place, we beg to remain,

Yours,

J. A. Burden."

* * * * *

While these brethren in the Southern California Conference had, after a study of the needs of the field and the instruction found in the testimonies, reached the above conclusions, yet the brethren upon whom must ultimately fall a considerable part of the burden of supporting and maintaining a medical school, had not given to this matter the study and thought that would lead them to unite heartily and courageously in making a success of such an undertaking.

Evidently it would have been unwise "at this time" to hasten the launching of large enterprises, for which our people generally were not prepared, and to which only a portion of the brethren in Southern California were ready to give their approval.

After reading the foregoing letter from Elder Burden, Sister White addressed a letter to the Physicians and Manager at Loma Linda, dated February 20, 1908, in which she said:

"I dare not advise you in such large plans as you propose. You need to make the Lord your wisdom in these matters. I do not feel that you should plan for such large outlay of means unless you have some certainty that you can meet your obligations. I would caution you against gathering a large load of indebtedness. There is the food factory to be completed and set in operation. I call your attention to this enterprise, that you may not lay more plans than you can well carry out.

"You are men of varied talents, and you are right on the ground. The Lord will be your instructor in all matters if you will seek His counsel in faith. If He gives you light in the matter, then you can move with assurance. Now is the time for you to ask of the Lord wisdom, and submit your plans to Him. It is an excellent opportunity for you to receive an individual experience. Plan wisely; move guardedly; and the Lord will certainly be your helper.

"I feel a deep interest in the work at Loma Linda. The plans you suggest seem to be essential; but you need to assure yourselves that they can be safely carried. You should not make hasty moves that will involve heavy indebtedness.

"The work which you propose will require wise business men and efficient physicians. If you had the talent and means to carry such responsibilities, we should be glad to see your plans carry. But the sanitarium must be your first consideration. May the Lord give you wisdom and grace to bear these responsibilities as He would have you. This institution must have all the talent that is needed to make it a success."

March 24, 1908, Sister White wrote further

"I have clear instructions that wherever it is possible, schools should be established near our sanitariums, that each institution may be a help to the other. But I dare not advise that steps be taken at this time to branch out so largely in the educational work at Loma Linda that a great outlay of means will be required to erect new buildings. Our faithful workers at Loma Linda must not be overwhelmed with such great responsibilities that they will be in danger of becoming worn and discouraged.

"I am charged to caution you against building extensively for the accommodation of students. It would not be wise to invest at this time so large a capital as would be required to equip a medical college that would properly qualify physicians to stand the test of the medical examinations of the different State (s).

"A movement should not now be inaugurated that would add greatly to the investment upon the Loma Linda property. Already there is a large debt resting upon the institution, and discouragement and perplexity would follow if this indebtedness were to be greatly increased. As the work progresses, new improvements may be added from time to time as they are found necessary. An elevator should soon be installed in the main building. But there is need of strict economy. Let our brethren move cautiously and wisely, and plan no more than they can handle without being overburdened.

"In the work of the school, maintain simplicity. No argument is so powerful as is success founded on simplicity. And you may have success in the education of students as medical missionaries without a medical school that can qualify physicians to compete with the physicians of the world. "Let the students be given a practical education. And the less dependent you are upon worldly methods of education, the better it will be for the students. Special instruction should be given in the art of treating the sick without the use of poisonous drugs, and in harmony with the light God has given. Students should come forth from the school without having sacrificed the principles of health reform.

"The education that meets the world's standard is to be less and less valued by those who are seeking for efficiency in carrying the medical missionary work in connection with the work of the third angel's message. They are to be educated from the standpoint of conscience; and as they conscientiously and faithfully follow right methods in their treatment of the sick, these methods will come to be recognized as preferable to the methods of nursing to which many have become accustomed, which demands the use of poisonous drugs.

"We should not at this time seek to compete with worldly medical schools. Should we do this, our chances of success would be small. We are not now prepared to carry out successfully the work of establishing large medical institutions of learning. Moreover, should

[10]

we follow the world's methods of medical practice, exacting the large fees that worldly physicians demand for their services, we should work away from Christ's plan for our ministry to the sick.

"There should be at our sanitariums intelligent men and women who can instruct in Christ's methods of ministry. Under the instruction of competent, consecrated teachers, the young may become partakers of the divine nature, and learn how to escape the corruptions that are in the world through lust. I have been shown that we should have many more women who can deal especially with the diseases of women, many more lady nurses who will treat the sick in a simple way and without the use of drugs."

* * * * *

Action of General Conference Committee

"The matter of broadening the scope of the school at Loma Linda was largely held in abeyance until the matter could be carefully considered by the General Conference. Feeling that the school should be general in its character, the Executive Committee of the Southern California Conference and the Board of Trustees of the Loma Linda Sanitarium met in March, 1909, and prepared a memorial to be presented to the General Conference which was to convene in May in Washington, setting forth in brief the steps that had been taken and the counsels that had been given. This memorial concluded the following request:

"We respectfully ask the General Conference to recognize the Loma Linda College of Evangelists as an institution for the education and training of both nurses and physicians in harmony with the testimonies above quoted. Second, that it assist the management in arranging the curriculum, and planning for the future development of the school." [11]

The Committee on Plans did not bring this memorial before the Conference, but left it in the hands of the Executive Committee, and at a meeting of this committee, held in June, a few days after the close of the conference, this matter was considered. The action taken by the committee at this time, and what was done in harmony with this action, are set forth in a letter from Elder J. A. Burden addressed to Mrs. E. G. White under date of Sept. 20, 1909. In order that Sister White's response to this may be fully understood, the letter is here given in full:

Sanitarium, Calif.,
Sept. 20, 1909.
Dear Sister White,

"You will recall that at our last talk at the General Conference concerning the medical educational work at Loma Linda, you suggested that notwithstanding the failure of the General Conference to take any action encouraging us to go ahead with the advanced medical training, you advised us to go forward, following the instruction you had formerly given regarding the medical school.

"The points that perplexed me at that time were, first, what liberties our students would finally have to do real medical work other than nursing or such work as could be carried on by nurses without the qualifications of physicians; second, what plans should we lay that our students might become recognized as physicians, qualified to practice our healing art. You stated that God would give us recognition when He saw it was necessary. Thus the matter dropped.

"After this, ... The General Conference Committee met and considered at some length the question of the Loma Linda College of Evangelists, and passed the following recommendations.

"'The Loma Linda Sanitarium is an important institution, having a splendid location, and is capable of doing a great amount of good in the development of workers. It should be not only a sanitarium of the first class, but a training center for young people who can enter service for foreign fields.

"'While the General Conference is not in a condition to render financial aid to Loma Linda Sanitarium (beyond the salary of a Bible teacher), it is still in fullest sympathy with the principles for which it stands and the work which we believe it is appointed to accomplish; Therefore,—

"'We recommend, That the Pacific Union Conference cooperate with the trustees of the Loma Linda Sanitarium in carrying forward the work which the institution should accomplish.

"'(a) By helping along such financial lines as are mutually agreed upon the trustees of said institution and the Pacific Union Conference Committee.

"'(b) By aiding the institution to secure the best possible help in the way of teachers, and aiding in the payment of their salaries.

"'(c) By encouraging our young people to take training at this institution.

"'Resolved, that we recommend the Loma Linda College of Evangelists as a special training school for medical missionary workers for the world-wide field, and encourage it to maintain and strengthen its efforts to provide a course of study for the training of workers combining the qualifications of the highly trained nurse with those of the practical evangelist; and, further, that, before giving counsel as to the suggested plan of adding to their faculty and equipment so as to give one or two years medical study that would be accepted by a recognized medical college as a part of a regular medical course, we request definite information concerning the changes involved in adapting their course of study to this purpose, the requirements of such colleges as would affiliate on this basis, and as to what such a plan would involve financially."

"You notice there are four points in the above resolutions: First, the question of strengthening the faculty and equipment so that the work done by the college would be recognized in other medical schools, giving students who might want to finish their course of study in regular schools, advanced standing for (because of) the work done at Loma Linda. Second, the Conference desires to know what changes would be necessary in our present course of study to give students this advantage in entering other schools. (The following words, not on my enlarged photographic-print copy, probably due to printing difficulty, seem necessary: Third, Names of schools) that would recognize the education given at Loma Linda, if such change were made in its course of instruction. Fourth, What additional expense would be involved in fitting the Loma Linda College to do a complete work that would be recognized in other medical schools.

"Since receiving the communication of the General Conference we have gone into the matter as fully as time and opportunity would permit, to obtain definite information on these four points. First, we find that the way is open for the students of Loma Linda College to take advanced standing in other medical schools, provided we secure a charter from the state, which would cost us about $75. Second, That in order for our students to enter other medical colleges after the charter is secured, we would need to strengthen our course of study in the first two years about three hundred hours, or one hundred and fifty each year. The students would have to meet the State requirements for entering the College, which is at present a high school education or its equivalent. Third, almost any regular medical college in America would receive our students for advanced work if these requirements were met. Fourth, in reference to the outlay financially, to do this work acceptably to the State, about $3000. Then, to meet what we feel is necessary to give practical work, we

[13]

should have a small sanitarium, costing not more than $6000 or $7000. This would make an outlay of about $10,000.

"Perhaps you are aware that our medical course of study covers three years. The medical schools used to require a three year course, but recently they have raised it to four years. Inasmuch as we give in our medical course not only the scientific training, but the Bible and our methods of treatment as well, we could not cover the first two years of a regular medical college course in the same time; but our three years course we find will be readily accepted for two years of a regular medical course.

"Now as to the question involved. Would there be danger, first, in securing a charter for the school that would open the way for the Loma Linda students to secure this advantage in worldly schools of completing their course, and becoming accredited physicians? Would such a plan lead away from the purpose of the school—to qualify large numbers with the ability of physicians to labor as evangelists? The brethren generally seem to feel that it would be out of the question for us to think of equipping the Loma Linda College with facilities for giving a full medical course to qualify students to receive recognition by the State. Hence the suggestion of this compromise plan, which would keep the students under right influences for three years, while becoming well grounded in Bible study along with their scientific preparation. Then it is thought that if only the most capable were encouraged to go on and complete the full course as accredited physicians, and all others were encouraged to enter the work as evangelists, all might work out satisfactorily.

"Without going further into detail, we desire to lay the matter before you for your consideration, to see if the Lord has any light for us.

Yours truly,

J. A. Burden.

* * * * *

To be Separate from the World [14]

Sister White read this letter carefully early in the morning, and later in the day, in an interview with Elder Burden and Elder W. C. White, which was stenographically reported, she expressed herself as follows:

"We want none of that kind of 'higher education' that will put us in a position where the credit must be given, not to the Lord God of Israel, but to the God of Ekron. The Lord designs that we shall stand as a distinct people, so connected with Him that He can work with us. Let our physicians realize that they are to depend wholly upon the true God.

"I felt a heavy burden this morning when I read over a letter that I found in my room, in which a plan was outlined for having medical students take some work at Loma Linda, but to get the finishing touches of their education from some worldly institution. I must state that the light that I have received is that we are to stand as a commandment-keeping people, and this will separate us from the world. The Sabbath is a great distinguishing line. As God's peculiar people, we should not feel that we must acknowledge our dependence upon the transgressors of God's law to give us influence in the world. It is God that gives us influence. He will give us advantages that are far above all the advantages we can receive from worldlings....

"If we follow on to know the Lord, we shall know that His going forth is prepared as the morning. There are some who may not be able to see that here is a test as to whether we shall put our dependence on man or upon God. Shall we by our course seem to acknowledge that there is a stronger power with the unbelievers than there is with God's own people? When we take hold upon God and trust in Him He will work in our behalf. But we are to stand distinct and separate from the world.

"I feel a decided interest in the work at Loma Linda, and I desire that it shall exert a powerful influence for the truth. Your success depends upon the blessing of God, not upon the views of men who are opposed to the law of God. When they see that God blesses us, then people will be led to give consideration to the truths we teach.

'We need not tie to men in order to secure influence. We need not think that we must have their experience and their knowledge. Our God is a God of knowledge and understanding, and if we will take our position decidedly on His side, He will give us wisdom. I would that all our people might see the inconsistency of our being God's commandment-keeping people, a peculiar people zealous of good works, and yet feeling that we must copy after the world in order to make our work successful. Our God is stronger than any human influence. If we will accept Him as our educator, if we will make Him our strength and righteousness, He will work in our behalf...

"You have the Word, which tells you that God's commandment-keeping people are to have His special favor, and that they are to be sanctified through obedience to the truth. Shall we unite ourselves with those that are full of error, who have no respect for God's commandments, and shall our students go forth to obtain the finishing touches of their education from them?"

W. C. White: "What is to be the final outcome? Will all our medical missionaries be simply nurses? Shall we have no more physicians? or shall we have a school in which we can ourselves give the finishing touches?"

E. G. White: "Whatever plan you follow, take your position that you will not unite with those that do not respect God's commandments."

W. C. White: "Does that mean that we are not to have any more physicians, but that our people will work simply as nurses? or does it mean that we shall have a school of our own to educate physicians?"

E. G. White: "We shall have a school of our own. But we are not to be dependent upon the world. We must place our dependence upon a power that is higher than all human power. If we honor God, He will honor us.

J. A. Burden: "The governments of earth provide that if we conduct a medical school, we must take a charter from the government. That in itself has nothing to do with how the school is conducted. It is required, however, that certain studies be taught... Would the securing of a charter for the medical school, where our students might obtain a medical education, militate against our dependence upon God?"

E. G. White: "No, I do not see that it would. Only see that you do not exalt men above God. If you can gain force and influence that will make your work more effective without tying yourselves to worldly men, that would be right.....

(See Loma Linda Messages or this copy, pages 754-759 [original page numbers]

E. G. White: No, it is not. I have had very distinct light, however, that there is danger of our limiting the power of the Holy One of Israel. He is the God of the universe. Our influence is dependent upon our carrying out the word of the living God. We weaken our powers by not placing our dependence upon God, and taking hold of His strength. This is our privilege.

* * * * *

[16] # Endorsement by the General Conference Committee

Soon after this the General Conference Committee met in College View, and the question of establishing a medical college at Loma Linda received careful consideration:

Among those who took their stand strongly in favor of the plan called for in the communication from Sister White, were,

Elder G. A. Irwin,	Dr. D. H. Kress,
Elder I. H. Evans,	Dr. W. A. George,
Dr. W. A. Ruble,	and Prof. Griggs.

Elder Evans, then treasurer of the General Conference, made a thrilling appeal in behalf of the value of such an institution for the training of workers for the mission field. Prof. Frederick Griggs, secretary of the Educational Department of the General Conference, made a strong appeal in behalf of our young people who wish to study medicine. Dr. W. A. Ruble, Secretary of the Medical Department, gave a logical and candid review of the serious objections to our undertaking such a great work, and then clearly presented reasons why we should attempt the work, expecting by united effort and the blessing of God to make a success of the enterprise.

Some came to this meeting with serious misgivings as to the wisdom of undertaking such a large enterprise, but the Spirit of the Lord witnessed convincingly to the words spoken by various ones, showing the necessity of providing facilities in Christian schools for the qualifying of our workers as physicians the same as we had to prepare our other missionary workers for the cause. The brethren were convinced that the Lord was calling for the establishment by us of a medical college, and after the discussion the following action was taken:

Resolved, That we recommend the Board of Management of the Loma Linda College of Evangelists to secure a charter for the school, that it may develop as the opening providences and the instruction of the Spirit of God may indicate.

After this action had been taken a communication was received from Sister White, dated October 11, 1909. The principles therein laid down strengthened the brethren in their belief that the Lord had led them in the step they had just taken. Following is a portion of this letter:

"I am instructed to say that in our educational work there is to be no compromise in order to meet the world's standards. God's commandment-keeping people are not to unite with the world, to carry various lines of work according to worldly plans and worldly wisdom.

"Our people are now being tested as to whether they will obtain their wisdom from the greatest Teacher the world ever knew, or seek to the God of Ekron. Let us determine that we will not be tied by so much as a thread to the educational policies of those who do not discern the voice of God, and who will not hearken to His commandments...

Shall we represent before the world, that our physicians must follow the pattern of the world before they can be qualified to act as successful physicians? This is the question that is now testing the faith of some of our brethren. Let not any of our brethren displease the Lord by advocating in their assemblies the idea that we need to obtain from unbelievers a higher education than that specified by the Lord.

"The representation of the great Teacher is to be considered an all-sufficient revelation. Those in our ranks who qualify as physicians are to receive only such education as is in harmony with these divine truths. Some have advised that students should, after taking some work at Loma Linda, complete their medical education in worldly colleges. But this is not in harmony with the Lord's plan. God is our wisdom, our sanctification, and our righteousness. Facilities should be provided at Loma Linda, that the necessary instruction in medical lines may be given by instructors who fear the Lord, and who are in harmony with His plans for the treatment of the sick.

"I have not a word to say in favor of the world's ideas of higher education in any school that we shall organize for the training of physicians. There is danger in their attaching themselves to worldly institutions, and working under the ministrations of worldly physicians. Satan is giving his orders to those whom he has led to depart from the faith. I would now advise that none of our young people attach themselves to worldly medical institutions in the hope of gaining better success or stronger influence as physicians."

In view of such definite encouragement, our brethren hearing the burden of the work at Loma Linda felt free to go forward, and on December 9, a charter was secured under the laws of the State of California, enabling the College of Medical Evangelists to grant degrees in the liberal arts and sciences, dentistry, and medicine.

* * * * *

Endorsed by the Pacific Union Conference

The next great question for consideration was, Who shall bear the burden of providing funds and directing the management of the college? Thus far the members of the General Conference Committee had looked upon it as very largely a Pacific Coast enterprise. The Pacific Union Conference had treated it as a Southern California affair. The Southern California Conference knew that it was a work too large for them alone, and believed that it should be supported by our people throughout the world.

[18]

This led to a review of the whole question at the session of the Pacific Union Conference held at Mountain View, January 25-30, 1910. Especially thorough was the questioning as to the character of the work to be done by the College of Medical Evangelists. A committee consisting of I. H. Evans, E. E. Andross, and H. W. Cottrell, was appointed to interview Sister White. This committee submitted to her in writing the following questions:

"Are we to understand, from what you have written concerning the establishment of a medical school at Loma Linda, that according to the light you have received from the Lord, we are to establish a thoroughly equipped medical school, the graduates from which shall be able to take State Board examinations, and become registered, qualified physicians?"

In response to this question, Sister White wrote:

"The light given me is, We must provide that which is essential to qualify our youth who desire to be physicians, so that they may intelligently fit themselves to be able to stand the examinations essential to prove their efficiency as physicians. They are to be prepared to stand the essential tests required by law, and to treat understandingly the cases of those who are diseased, so that the door will be closed for any sensible physician to fear that we are not giving in our school the instruction essential for the proper qualification of a physician. Continually, the students who are graduated are to advance in knowledge; for practice makes perfect.

"The medical school at Loma Linda is to be of the highest order, because we have a living connection with the wisest of all physicians, from whom there is communicated knowledge of a superior order. And whatever subjects are required as essential in the schools conducted by those not of our faith, we are to supply, so that our youth need not go to these worldly schools. Thus we shall close the door that the enemy would be pleased to have left open; and our young men and young women, whom the Lord would have us guard religiously, will not need to connect with worldly medical schools conducted by unbelievers."

The foregoing statement was so definite and emphatic that the Committee on Plans and Recommendations reported, and the Conference passed, the following recommendations, outlining a plan for the establishment of a medical school on a broader and firmer basis:

"We Recommend (1) That, in harmony with the above instruction, we favor the establishment and maintenance of a medical school at Loma Linda, California.

"(2) In order that this medical school may meet the mind of the Lord in doing the work appointed for it by the Spirit of Prophecy, we invite the General Conference of Seventh-day Adventists, the Lake, Northern, Central, Southwestern, and North Pacific Union Conferences, and the Southern California Conference, to unite with the Pacific Union Conference in establishing and suitably equipping and maintaining this school.

"(3) That a board of control, for directing the management of the school, be appointed as follows: (a) Two members to be appointed by the General Conference; (b) One member by the Lake Union Conference, one by the Northern Union Conference, one by the Central Union Conference, one by the Southwestern Union Conference, one by the North Pacific Union Conference, and one by the Pacific Union Conference; (c) two members to be appointed by the Southern California Conference.

"(4) That the school be maintained by Funds obtained as follows: (a) Tuition; (b) Donations; (c) Deficit, if any, to be met annually by the General Conference, the Lake, Northern, Central, Southwestern, North Pacific, and Pacific Union Conferences, and the Southern California Conference, all sharing equally.

"(5) That each of the above mentioned organizations be requested to raise one thousand dollars, in behalf of the equipment and maintenance of the school for the calendar year 1910.

"(6) That a separate set of books be kept, carrying all accounts of the school, so that the same can be audited, and full knowledge of the cost of operating the school can be submitted to the constituency annually.

"(7) That a committee, consisting of the incoming president of the Pacific Union Conference, the president of the Southern California Conference, W. C. White, and J. A. Burden, be asked to present this entire question to the General Conference and the Union Conferences referred to, and to lead out in the establishment of this medical school."

The action of the Pacific Union Conference was communicated by the committee appointed for that purpose to the conferences mentioned in the recommendation. Each of these Union Conferences took the matter up and gave it favorable consideration and appointed a person to represent them on the board. The General Conference at their spring council in Washington, in April, 1910, took the following action on the invitation of the Pacific Union Conference:

"Whereas, It is advised that a medical school be equipped and conducted at Loma Linda, Calif.; and, [20]

"Whereas, The Pacific Union Conference of Seventh-day Adventists had petitioned that the General Conference join it in this undertaking; therefore;

"Resolved, (1) That the General Conference unite with the Pacific Union Conference (and other union conferences) in establishing a medical school at Loma Linda, California.

"(2) That we authorize the officers of the General Conference to appropriate one thousand dollars, or any fraction thereof, for the above purpose, during the year 1910.

"(3) That A. G. Daniells, W. A. Ruble, and H. R. Salisbury be the General Conference members of the board of control of the said school."

May 6 to 12, 1910, there was held at Loma Linda, Cal., a council composed of the following: Three representatives from the General Conference, one each from the Central, Lake, Northern, North Pacific, Southwestern, and Pacific Union Conferences, and two from the Southern California Conference, besides the Executive Committees of the Southern California Conference and the Pacific Union Conference and the incorporators of the Loma Linda Sanitarium and of the College of Medical Evangelists. The council was the outgrowth of an invitation extended by the Pacific Union Conference at its session in January to these conferences to join with it in establishing and suitably equipping and making provision for maintaining a denominational medical school at Loma Linda, Cal.

Early in the progress of the council it was made very clear to all that it would be unwise to have two corporations operating upon the same ground and doing a work that the testimonies clearly implied should be one. For this reason, one of the first definite actions was the passage of a resolution to consolidate the sanitarium corporation and the college corporation into one, to be known as the College of Medical Evangelists, thus making the medical school the main feature, and the sanitarium work a branch, or auxiliary of the same. By this action, the whole of the sanitarium plant, with its facilities and equipment, would become of great service to the medical college, thus making it possible to begin at once to operate a medical school, allowing the work of providing other necessary appliances to follow later, as the wants of the school should demand.

By resolution of the council, the constituency of the new corporation is composed of the following:

(1) "The members of the executive committee of the Southern Calif. Conference of Seventh-day Adventists.

(2) "The members of the executive committee of the General Conference of Seventh-day Adventists resident in the United States.

(3) "The members of the executive committee of the Pacific Union Conference of Seventh-day Adventists.

(4) "The original incorporators."

The consolidation of these two corporations entailed some minor changes in the articles of incorporation, and made it necessary to elect a board of twenty-one members. The following persons were elected to this board:

A. G. Daniells, G. W. Watson, J. R. Leadsworth,
Allen Moon, G. A. Irwin, J. J. Wessels,
R. A. Underwood, E. E. Andross, J. W. Lindsay,
E. T. Russell, W. C. White, W. A. Ruble,

C. W. Flaiz, Luther Warren, J. A. Burden,
Q. K. Abbott, T. J. Evans, R. S. Owen,
Julia A. White, H. F. Rand, and F. G. Lucas.

One third of this number serve for one year, one third for two years, and one third for three years; so that at each annual election, the members elected will serve for a term of three years. This board was organized by the election of the following persons as officers:

G. A. Irwin, President: John A. Burden, Vice-President; Dr. W. A Ruble, Secretary; S. S. Merrill, Treasurer; John J. Ireland, Auditor.

A curriculum, outlining the entrance requirements and fees and courses of study, was, after very careful consideration, adopted, and a faculty of teachers selected.

Looking forward to the needs of the college, it was voted to authorize the expenditure of $25,000 in buildings and appliances for the ensuing year, and to receive such students as could furnish evidence of sufficient preliminary education to enter the course.

The most pressing needs were found to be laboratory, and dormitories for the young men and young women. Soon after this meeting, work was begun on a dormitory for the ladies. This is a four-story cement building, one hundred eight feet long and thirty-six feet wide. It contains sixty rooms, and will accommodate more than a hundred.

With the opening of the College in the fall of 1910, the most advanced class of medical students were to enter upon their third year; and in order to conform to the requirements of the State, it was necessary to provide them facilities for thorough laboratory work. A laboratory building was therefore erected and is well equipped with the essential appliances.

During the year 1911 steady progress was made in the work at Loma Linda. The various departments were strengthened. Twenty-four students entered the medical course, and twenty the nurses' course. The patronage of the sanitarium increased, and notwithstanding the expense of maintaining the educational departments, there was a profit in the operating expenses for the year, of $5,795.41. The expenses of erecting the girls' dormitory and laboratory building, and providing the facilities that were necessary, were heavy; yet the present worth of the corporation increased from $27,650.00 in 1910 to $61,892.34 in 1912.

* * * * *

An Important Council

A constituency meeting of the College of Medical Evangelists was held at Loma Linda, March 27 to April 1, 1912. At this meeting were present the president, the treasurer, and the medical secretary of the General Conference; the president of the Pacific, North Pacific, Columbian, Lake, Northern, Southern and Southwestern Union Conferences, and four other members of the General Conference Committee. The executive committee of the Pacific Union Conference, and the executive committee of the Southern California Conference.

In his address to the constituency, Elder G. A. Irwin, president of the Board of Trustees, referred to the launching of the medical college as "one of the most important moves made by this denomination since the removal of our General Conference headquarters from Battle Creek, Michigan, to Washington, D. C. He spoke of three things as being "positively necessary in order that the school may be successful and meet the mind of the Lord in its establishment: (1) Money with which to erect and properly equip the necessary buildings; (2) The hearty cooperation of the entire denomination through its recognized leaders; (3) Steadfast adherence upon the part of the directors and medical faculty to the principles contained in the instruction upon which the institution was founded...

"When we ask young men and women to come to Loma Linda, to take a medical course, we must have buildings where they can be comfortably housed. If we expect these students to successfully pass their examination before the State boards at the close of their term, we must provide the necessary facilities to enable the teachers properly to instruct them.

"If this constituency does not want to see the indebtedness of the institution increased, then it must provide a plan whereby the necessary means can be raised to do what of necessity must be done if we proceed with this undertaking.

"On the other hand, even though we might obtain all the means necessary, a few men and a small constituency could not make a success of this work; it must have the hearty support and confidence of the whole denomination...

"I have placed adherence to the principles upon which the institution is founded last, not because in my judgment it is least, but because I wish to give special emphasis to the fact that we might have both money and influence in abundance, and yet fail because we lose sight of the fact that this enterprise is but a part of a great movement in which there must be perfect union between the medical and the Evangelical departments of our work...

"The possibilities before such a school as this are very great. Hundreds of medical evangelists could be used today by this denomination to good effect, not only in heathen lands, but in the cities and densely populated districts of the civilized nations of the earth. May our faith lead us to grasp these possibilities and cause us to lay broad plans and to act promptly in view of the limited time which yet remains to do the work allotted to us as a people."

Dr. W. A. Ruble, president of the medical College, reported 237 students as being in attendance at the college and allied schools. These are grouped as follows:

College: 1st. year, 24; 2nd. year, 23; 3rd year, 9; Medical Evangelistic Course, 1. Nurses: 1st year, 19; 2nd year, 21; 3rd year, 20. Special, 5; Preparatory, 26; Church school, 87.

Speaking of the Laboratory, Dr. Ruble said: "This building is perfectly adapted to the purposes for which it was constructed; thanks to the counsel of those who knew what they needed and have worked to produce it. Already courses have been conducted in the respective laboratory rooms in histology, embryology, bacteriology, chemistry, and materia medica. Just the apparatus for these courses that was required has been provided. The line of demarcation between economy and efficiency has been carefully guarded."

* * * * *

Prospects

"When the proposition to found a Seventh-day Adventist medical college began to be considered seriously, two or three years ago, it seemed an impossibility. The lack of means and men was apparent. The fulfillment of the promise, God shall supply all your needs, has certainly been verified to us. The very best apparatus, facilities, and appliances have been provided as needed, and we are not a whit behind the most up-to-date school as far as we have gone. Instructors have been provided as required, and are conducting strong courses in every department of the college. Surely we might almost begin to walk by sight, but we shall not. What we do see and have seen certainly strengthens our faith to believe that we shall be able to provide whatever is necessary to make a strong, first-class medical college.

* * * * *

Our Needs

"As has been pointed out already, whatever has been required by medical boards, or of necessity has been provided for the school. The medical inspectors have been satisfied in the matter of entrance requirements, curriculum, faculty, laboratory and equipment, library, and medical periodicals. Emphasis was laid by each of the inspectors upon the necessity for a clinical hospital. This is our great and immediate need, and demands attention at once...

"A proper dormitory for a home for the young men is greatly needed. Housed as they are in three or four cottages scattered over the grounds, it is impossible to give them the supervision that would be given in a Christian home...

"If the College of Medical Evangelists has any mission scientifically and medically, it is in emphasizing and advancing physiologic therapeutics. Of all departments in the school, this one should be the best equipped. If we are to educate away from drug medication, it must be by demonstrating a better way of treatment. Provision must be made that will enable us to secure the best possible results in the treatment of disease."

Careful consideration was given to the necessities that must be met. There was a general feeling that the indebtedness must not be increased, yet it was evident that the work demanded additional facilities. It was voted,—

1. That a central heating plant be installed according to the plans submitted, with two one-hundred-horse power boilers and direct connected dynamo and engine, with a probable cost of $15,000. It is with the understanding that the means be secured for the same by the time the plant is completed.

2. That we proceed to raise, by solicitation, $15,000 for the beginning of a clinical hospital.

By the few present at this meeting, pledges to the amount of $3,375. were made, toward the fund for erecting these buildings.

The following were elected to act on the Board of Managers for three years: W. A. Ruble, J. A. Burden, G. K. Abbott, J. A. White, T. J. Evans, W. A. George, W. D. Salisbury. Careful study was given to the matter of dividing the heavy responsibilities of the many departments.

Brother W. D. Salisbury, who has spent a number of years in Australia as manager of the Echo Publishing Company, and later the Signs Publishing Company, was asked to act as general business manager, It was also voted to request Elder J. A. Burden to act as Treasurer of the corporation, and as chaplain and business superintendent of the Sanitarium. Assistance was provided for Elder Burden, so that a portion of his time may be spent in the solicitation of means that must be raised in order to carry forward this great work.

Surely a study of the providences that have marked the beginning and growth of the work in Loma Linda must lead to the conviction that this institution is designed of God to act an important part in the training of efficient workers for the world-wide field. May we not expect a general rally in behalf of this great enterprise, the success of which is dependent largely upon the support of every loyal believer in the third angel's message?

*****

Testimonies and Experiences in Connection with the Glendale Sanitarium

Early in 1903, while I was in Australia, Sister White forwarded to me a large bundle of manuscript concerning the medical work in southern California, and a little later she wrote me concerning the reverses that were coming to the medical work in Los Angeles, asking how I would feel about returning to America to help in the work.

The communications sent were most carefully read, as I had been connected with the starting of the Vegetarian Cafe and Los Angeles treatment rooms before I left for Australia. At that time I felt no desire to return to America, and so wrote her. The Lord, however, was evidently preparing my mind for the work in this field, although at the time I did not know it.

On returning to America in February, 1904, I was again solicited by Sister White to come to southern California to assist in the medical work. Just then there was considerable agitation concerning the purchase of Paradise Valley Sanitarium. When it was learned that I was thinking of coming to southern California, several took occasion to warn me against being foolish enough to connect with such a hopeless enterprise.

I had, however, read too carefully the communications sent me concerning the prospects of the work to be discouraged by any such representations. After listening again to Sister White's account of what had been shown her concerning the work, and of the providences of God that had led to the purchase of the Paradise Valley Sanitarium, I was convinced that the hand of the Lord was in it, hence I consented to come down and spend a month in looking over the situation.

At this time such a strong sentiment had been worked up in the Conference against incurring any further indebtedness in advancing the medical work that from a human standpoint it seemed impossible to do anything.

After looking over the ground carefully, visiting a number of places that looked hopeful for sanitarium work, and attending a number of councils of the committee, it was very clear to me that the brethren would feel relieved if I did not stay, and if I did remain, they would rather I would drop the agitation of securing the sanitarium.

I therefore returned to northern California and wrote Sister White that, while I could see a need and many opportunities for carrying forward the work, I did not feel that I was the one to undertake it. I was therefore planning to turn my attention to something else. Her reply was brief, but right to the point. I was instructed to return to Southern California and stay there, with the intimation that I did not know what was before me; that if I failed in getting something started, I could at least look over the field, and she herself would join me in the fall and would see that something was accomplished; that the time had come that something must be done.

With these instructions, we decided to return with a determination to do everything in our power to carry out the instruction concerning the medical work in southern California. By this time, a change had come, and the brethren invited me to take hold with them. Our first work was to plan for the work in Los Angeles, where the lease was about to expire, and to try to unload the work in Pasadena, which was running behind quite heavily, and had continued to do so ever since it was started.

At both of these places, we found conditions perplexing, and it took some time before the tide could be turned so that the work as a whole was making a small gain. During this time, we also spent much time and thought in planning for a sanitarium outside of Los Angeles. From the very first, our convictions rested down upon the Glendale building, and the more we looked over the field, the more satisfied we were that the Glendale property, all things considered, was the best thing in sight. In counsel with Brother and Sister Simpson, and the conference committee, we worked away at the Glendale proposition until we got it down to a cash proposition from seventeen thousand five hundred to twelve thousand dollars. Many hours of counsel were then spent with the committee as to what action we should take, but they found themselves bound by certain resolutions of the Conference, which forbid their making an investment of over three hundred dollars without the sanction of the conference, hence nothing could be done until the conference could convene in September.

Business, however, could not wait in an indefinite way for the pleasure of the conference, so it became necessary for some one to assume responsibility if anything was done. Two or three of us, therefore, undertook the preliminary work of contracting for the purchase of the Glendale Sanitarium. A number of things arose which held the matter in abeyance until about the middle of the camp meeting, which we felt was very fortunate, as it would give us opportunity to counsel with the delegates before we would have to make the first payment. As soon as the conference convened, several meetings were held with the delegates, but without favorable results. At each meeting the proposition was turned down. Various testimonies were read concerning the general outline for the medical work in this field, and also specific statements recently received, such as the following, addressed to the southern California Conference, dated April 26, 1904:—

"Dear Brethren",

"I have always looked with great interest upon the work in Los Angeles and San Diego, hoping that right moves would be made, and that the sanitarium work might be established in these important places. Every year a large number of tourists visit these places, and I have longed to see men moved by the Holy Spirit, meeting these people with the message borne by John the Baptist.

"The Lord has ordained that memorials for Him shall be established in many places. He has presented before me buildings away from the cities, and suitable for our work, which can be purchased at a low price. We must take advantage of the favorable openings for sanitarium work in southern California, where the climate is so favorable for this work.

"It is the Lord's purpose that sanitariums shall be established in southern California, and that from these institutions shall go forth the light of truth for this time. By them the claims of the true Sabbath are to be presented, and the third angel's message proclaimed.

"There is a special work to be done at this time, a work of great importance. Light has been given me that a sanitarium should be established near Los Angeles, in some rural district. For years the need of such an institution has been kept before our people in southern California. Had the brethren there heeded the warnings given by the Lord to guard them from making mistakes, they would not now be tied up as they are. But they have not followed the instruction given. They have not gone forward in faith to establish a sanitarium near Los Angeles.

"The buildings secured for this work should be out of the city, in the country so that the sick may have the benefit of out-door life. It is the purpose of God that a sanitarium shall be established at some suitable place near Los Angeles. This institution is to be managed carefully and faithfully by men who have clear spiritual discernment, and who have also financial ability, men who can carry the work forward successfully, as faithful stewards."

Another communication, dated April 27, 1904, addressed to the President of the Conference and associate member, reads as follows:—

"There is a special work to be done just now. A sanitarium should be established near Los Angeles. My brethren, will you not remember that it is the expressed will of God that this shall be done? Why this work should be delayed from year to year is a great mystery. This is a matter that has long been kept before you, my brethren. And again and again sanitarium work has been pointed out as an important means of reaching the people with the truth. Had the light given by God been followed, this institution might now be in running order, exerting a strong influence for good. Arrangement could have been made to utilize for sanitarium work buildings already erected.

"It has been a lack of harmony, a lack of determination on the part of the workers to lift with one purpose in view, that has delayed the establishment of a sanitarium in southern California. There has been so much variance that means that should have been invested in sanitariums have been turned into other channels.

"The idea that a sanitarium should not be established unless it could be started free from debt, has put the brakes upon the wheels of progress. In building meeting houses, I have had to borrow money, in order that something might be done at once, I have been obliged to do this, in order to fulfill the direction of God. For the past twenty years I have been borrowing money and paying interest on it, to establish schools and sanitariums and to build meeting houses. The institutions thus established and the churches built have been the means of bringing many to the truth. Thus the tithe has been increased, and workers been added to the Lord's forces.

[29] "Will my brethren consider this, and work in accordance with the light God has given us? Let that which should be done be done without delay. Do your best to remedy the neglect of the past. The word has come once more that a sanitarium is to be set in working order near Los Angeles. If this sanitarium is conducted in harmony with the will of God, it will be a means of great blessing, a means in the Lord's hand of leading souls to the truth.

"From the light given me when I was in Australia, and renewed since I came to America, I know that our work in southern California must advance more rapidly. The people flocking to that place in search of health must hear the last message of mercy.

"For years the work in southern California has needed help, and we now call upon our brethren and sisters who have means to spare to put it into circulation, that we may secure the places so well suited for our work. God has not been pleased with the way in which this field has been neglected. From many places in southern California the light is to shine forth to the multitude. Present truth is to be as a city set on a hill which cannot be hid.

With all this definite instruction outlining just what should be done, strange as it may now seem, when the hour arrived to close the bargain on the Glendale Sanitarium property, no favorable action could be secured from the conference. Two or three had to advance a thousand dollars and assume the whole responsibility. Later, after the place had been purchased, it was brought before the entire conference, and after considerable opposition, the conference voted to purchase the Glendale Sanitarium property, and raised a little over five thousand dollars in donations and pledges. Donations for furnishings were secured from individuals and churches amounting to nearly two thousand more. In a few months the institution was furnished and ready for work. Its history since then is known to you all.

Writing from Washington, July 15, 1904, when Sister White had learned of the prospect of securing the Glendale property, she said: "I am very grateful to my heavenly Father that you have secured a building near Los Angeles for sanitarium work. Your description of the building shows the truth of the testimonies that I have borne, that buildings suitable for our work will be offered to us at a low price. We must make earnest effort to improve the opportunities that God sends us, that His work shall advance as rapidly as possible. Let us have faith that we shall have special help from God. Let us not talk unbelief, but be cheerful in the Lord.

After visiting the Glendale Sanitarium, December 21, 1904, she writes: "We feel very grateful to God that our brethren and sisters in southern California have secured a property near the city of Los Angeles, which is well adapted for sanitarium purposes."

"We hope that our people in southern California will come heartily to the support of the Glendale Sanitarium, so providentially placed in our hands, and that it may be fully equipped to do its blessed work.

"The Lord has not been honored or glorified by the past showing of the sanitarium work in southern California. This work has been greatly hindered because men have relied upon human devising instead of following the Lord's leading. Dependence has been placed upon human wisdom, and failure has been the result."

"One night we seemed to be in a council meeting and the question was being considered, how can the sanitarium work in southern California be best advanced? One present proposed one thing, and still another proposed something entirely different. One of dignity and authority arose and said: "I have some words of counsel for you. Never, never repeat a mistake of the past. Men have placed too much confidence in themselves ... You have, said our instructor, come to an important place in the history of your work."

Again, in a letter dated February 4, 1905, she writes as follows:

"The remark is often made, by one and another, why depend so much on sanitariums? Why do we not pray for the miraculous healing of the sick, as the people of God used to do? In the early history of our work many were healed by prayer. And some, after they were healed, pursued the same course in the indulgence of appetite, that they had followed in the past. They did not live and work in such a way as to avoid sickness. They did not show that they appreciated the Lord's goodness to them. Again and again they were brought to suffering through their own careless, thoughtless course of action. How could the Lord be glorified in bestowing on them the gift of healing?"

"When the light came that we should have a sanitarium, the reason was plainly given. There were many who needed to be educated in regard to healthful living. A place must be provided to which the sick could be taken, where they could be taught how to live so as to preserve health. At the same time, light was given that the sick could be successfully treated without drugs. This was the lesson that was to be practised and taught by physicians and nurses, and by all other medical missionary workers. Drugs were to be discarded because when they are taken into the system, their after effects is very injurious. Many suffering from fevers have died as the results of the drugs administered. They might have been alive today had they been given water treatment by those competent to administer it.

"Great care should be shown in choosing young people to connect with our sanitariums. Those who have not the love of the truth in the soul should not be chosen. The sick need to have wise words spoken to them. The influence of every worker should make an impression on minds in favor of the religion of Christ. Light has been given me that the young people chosen to connect with our sanitariums should be those who give evidence that they have been apt learners in the school of Christ.

"It is to save the souls as well as to cure the bodies of men and women that our sanitariums, at much expense, are established. God designs that by means of them, the rich and the poor, the high and the low, shall find the bread of heaven and the water of life.

"I will thus explain the reasons why we have sanitariums. It is to gather in a class of people who will become intelligent upon health reform, and will learn to regain health and how to prevent sickness by following right habits of eating and drinking and dressing. As a part of the treatment, lectures should be given regarding the right choice and preparation of foods, showing that foods may be prepared so as to be wholesome and nourishing, and at the same time appetizing and palatable. These lectures should be diligently kept up as a means of instructing the patients how to prevent disease by wise foresight. By means of these lectures the patients may be shown the responsibility resting on them to keep the body in the most healthful condition because it is the Lord's purchased possession.

"The sick may look to the great Healer as they do all that is possible to be done on their part, cooperating with Him who so loved the world that He gave His only begotten son, that whosoever believeth in Him should not perish, but have everlasting life. He who would be healed must cease to transgress the law of God. He must cease to lead a life of sin. God cannot bless the one who continues to bring upon himself disease and suffering by neglecting and violating the laws of heaven. But the Holy Spirit comes with a healing power to those who cease to do evil and learn to do well.

"I think I have answered the question, why do we not pray for the healing of the sick, instead of having sanitariums? The education of many souls is at stake. In the providence of God, instruction has been given that sanitariums be established, in order that the sick may go to them, and learn how to live healthfully. The establishment of sanitariums is a providential arrangement, whereby people from all places are to be reached and made acquainted with the truth for this time. It is for this reason that we urge that sanitariums be established in many places outside of our cities."

Again, in a communication to the Glendale workers, dated March 14, 1905, we quote the following:—

"We are glad that, notwithstanding some delay, the property at Glendale has been secured for a sanitarium. Years ago the Lord gave me instructions that there should be a sanitarium near the city of Los Angeles. Instruction was also given that we should find properties for sale on which there would be buildings suitable for sanitarium purposes, and that we might secure such properties at a very low price. The location of the Glendale Sanitarium meets the representation given me of places God has reserved for us.

"Let all connected with this sanitarium keep in mind the purpose for which this property has been secured. The institution is to act a special part in bringing souls to Christ, leading them to love God and keep His commandments. Unless the workers have a living connection with God, unless there is seen in the institution a spirit of kindliness and compassion which will recommend Bible truth and win souls to Christ, the establishment of the sanitarium will have been in vain. Spiritual as well as physical healing is to be brought to those who come for healing."

In a communication addressed to the brethren and sisters in southern Calif., dated Dec. 12, 1904, I read again:—

"I am instructed to bear a message to you. You have a great work to do in soul-saving, but you cannot accomplish this work by following man-made plans and human devisings.

"Special light has been given me regarding the character and magnitude of the work to be done in Los Angeles. Several times messages have been given regarding the duty that rests upon us of proclaiming the third angel's message with power in that city.

"For a long time our people in southern California have had messages from the Lord that there should be sanitariums near Los Angeles. For want of means the work has been delayed. But not long ago a building at Glendale, eight miles from Los Angeles, was purchased and is now being fitted up for the work. I visited the building, and can say that it is beautifully situated and is well adapted for sanitarium work.

"We hope that our people in California will come quickly and heartily to the support of this sanitarium, so providentially placed in our hands that it may begin without delay to do its work."

* * * * *

Established Prosperity [33]

Text: 2 Chronicles 20:20.

"Believe in the Lord your God, so shall ye be established; believe his prophets, so shall ye prosper."

Isaiah 8:20. "To the law and to the testimony; if they speak not according to this word, it is because there is no light in them."

Two texts are here set before God's people: two conditions for success. The law spoken by Jehovah himself, and the spirit of prophecy, are the two sources of wisdom to guide His people in every experience. Deuteronomy 4:6. "This is your wisdom and your understanding in the sight of the nations, who shall say, Surely this great nation is a wise and understanding people."

The law of God and the Spirit of Prophecy go hand in hand to guide and counsel the church, and whenever the church has recognized this by obeying His law, the spirit of prophecy has been sent to guide her in the way of truth.

Revelation 12:17. "And the dragon was wroth with the woman, and went to make war with the remnant of her seed, which keep the commandments of God, and have the testimony of Jesus Christ." This prophecy points out clearly that the remnant church will acknowledge God in His law and will have the prophetic gift. Obedience to the law of God, and the spirit of prophecy has always distinguished the true people of God, and the test is usually given on present manifestations.

In Jeremiah's day the people had no question about the message of Moses, Elijah, or Elisha, but they did question and put aside the message sent of God to Jeremiah until its force and power was wasted and there was no remedy but for God to carry them away into captivity.

Likewise in the days of Christ the people had learned that Jeremiah's message was true, and they persuaded themselves to believe that if they had lived in the days of their fathers they would have accepted his message, but at the same time they were rejecting Christ's message, of whom all the prophets had written.

As the third angel's message arose in the world, which is to reveal the law of God to the church in its fullness and power, the prophetic gift was also immediately restored. This gift has acted a very prominent part in the development and carrying forward of this message.

[34] As differences of opinion have arisen in reference to interpretations of Scriptures and methods of labor, calculated to unsettle the faith of believers in the message and lead to disunion in the work, the spirit of prophecy has always thrown light on the situation. It has always brought union of thought and harmony of action to the body of believers. In every crisis that has arisen in the development of the message and the growth of the work, those who have stood firmly by the law of God and the light of the Spirit of prophecy have triumphed and the work has prospered in their hands.

The question naturally arises: Whence comes this wisdom revealed through this gift, which is more than the combined wisdom of all the church besides?

As the message developed and grew, it was this gift that urged the extension of the work, and from that day to this has done more than all other influences combined to push the message into the regions beyond. In every development of the message—evangelical, education, medical, and publishing, the spirit of prophecy has not only led the way, but given light on how to conduct these different departments in such a way as to bring success in the spread of the message.

Again and again as the wisdom of men has failed and the work became hedged about or tangled up in any of its departments, the wisdom of this gift has always been shown in setting it free. The clear-cut missionary policy laid out for all departments of this great work by the spirit of prophecy in contrast with the mercenary policy oft times worked into it by men to whom the care and keeping of the message has been entrusted, shows that the wisdom of this gift is from above.

When our educational work, under the fostering care of this gift, first developed the Battle Creek College, it was a power for good in fitting men and women to carry this message to the world.

Many of those now bearing responsibility in the cause received their early training at that place. The same is true of the early days of Healdsburg College, which was fostered and molded by the same gift. But a change came over all our educational work. The wisdom of men molded it after the wisdom of the world until the schools, instead of sending forth laborers into the missionary fields, were turning the minds of the young to worldly avocations, many of who were losing their love for the truth.

Whence came the wisdom to correct this wrong and turn our schools again into the pathway of life? Who is responsible for the great wave of Christian education that has molded the entire denomination and multiplied our Christian schools by the score, enabling them to send forth hundreds of young people as missionaries into the home and foreign fields? Shall we not learn to esteem more highly, and follow more closely a gift that can bring such blessing and prosperity to the cause of God?

At the beginning of this message believers were few and widely scattered. There was no definite organization for the direction of the work, but as believers came into the truth and companies were formed, it was manifest that some organization was necessary. But strange as it may seem, the wisdom of man led them to oppose all organization. Again light was shed upon the perplexing situation by the spirit of prophecy, which resulted in a simple form of organization for the protection and furtherance of the work; and peace, harmony, and prosperity came out of confusion. This same form of organization continued until the wisdom of men, to whom the care of the organization had been committed, began to plan for a centralizing power at the head of the work, which resulted in retarding rather than fostering it. Missionaries in the field felt their hands were tied, and mission fields were languishing, and the resources were drying up. Where was the wisdom of men in this perplexity?

Again the spirit of prophecy shed light upon the situation, pointing out the difficulty and the remedy. As the light has been followed, relief has come, the message has gone with leaps and bounds, and the resources have increased wonderfully. The great need of the hour is consecrated men and women whose faith and experience has grown strong in grappling with difficulty and in undertaking great things for the cause of God.

The object and aim of every organization and institution connected with third angel's message is missionary, and when it fails in this, its usefulness is gone.

The publishing work, like every other department of the message, was started under the light and fostering care of the spirit of prophecy. Its aim was missionary, to disseminate the light of present truth. But as the work enlarged and the publishing work was committed to the wisdom of men, it grew into a great commercial machine that was working more for the world than for the spread of the message. Men conceived the idea of centralizing our publishing work under one great combine to be ruled by the great men at the head of the work. High wages were paid, and the missionary spirit left the work as the spirit of the world came in. The spirit of prophecy called for a change of plans in our publishing work, it called for a distribution of the abundant facilities established at Battle Creek to assist plants in more needy fields, but called in vain. The wisdom of men, which was the wisdom of the world, could see no light in distributing. There seemed to be no remedy for God to correct the evils in this department of His work but to let His judgments fall upon the institution. From a communication written from Australia, I quote the following:—

"The God of Heaven has been dishonored. You have found a place to invest means in various enterprises as though it were a virtue to leave my work in other lands to struggle in poverty and nakedness. You have not shared your abundant facilities as you might have done, even (though) the sacrifice required might appear large to you. Nothing that earth has given is of sufficient value to recompense the travail and burden of soul, the agonizing of mind that has been felt in seeing the people working at cross-purposes with God, hindering the work, and making it necessary for God to withdraw His prospering hand from the publishing association and from the conference."

Had the light given this department been followed, how different might the results have been today! Note the result when men did turn to follow the light. The prosperity of God has been seen all through our publishing work. Instead of today running them simply for commercial ends, every publishing house is crowded to its utmost capacity, publishing the truth, and more than fifty thousand copies of books are being published in outside printing houses because our own publishing houses cannot turn them out fast enough. The canvassing work is renewed, and hundreds of young people from our schools are carrying the pages of truth to the homes of the people. Such has always been the prosperity of God's people as they have believed his prophets.

All who are acquainted at all with the medical work know that it was the testimonies that first turned the attention of this people to the importance of establishing medical institutions, and as the years have come and gone, the same gift has led out in establishing sanitariums and medical missionary enterprises all over the world.

Wonderful light has been given in every detail of the various departments, and as the light has been followed, success has attended the work. The policy outlined for this branch of the cause, like every other, has been missionary, educational, and evangelical. And when our medical work was in danger of being swayed into wrong lines, message after message was sent to the head of the work to save it from ruin. A centralizing power had also entered the medical work, which was seeking to gain control, the sanitarium was losing sight of the regions beyond, the real object of this department of the message. In this case communication from Australia from (Sister White came) I quote further:—

"Then the test came upon the sanitarium. God has given them prosperity, not to be a means of self-exaltation, but that they might impart of their substance. When His servants were sent to Australia, you should have understood that God would work through them, and you should have exercised liberality in appropriating means to advance the work. The medical missionary work should ere this have been established upon a solid foundation. There should be no withholding of means. The Lord has let His chastening hand fall upon the Review and Herald office because they would not heed His voice. Self-sufficient managers hedged up the way that His work should not advance. The Lord calls upon the Battle Creek Sanitarium to extend her work and to place the health institution here upon a proper basis. This should have been done two years ago. The withholding tends to poverty."

The result of failing to heed the light sent by the spirit of prophecy is now manifest in the destruction of that institution, and the present situation at the head of our medical missionary work. Could the brethren at the head of the department have accepted the light that was given through this gift, we should today see the same prosperity attending this department that has come to the others as the light has been followed.

God has permitted all these things to come upon His people that they might see the folly of trusting to men, however great their power or influence, and that His people might learn to believe in the Lord their God and in His prophets that established prosperity might follow their efforts to advance His cause.

The message from the spirit of prophecy today to this people is a call for a reorganization of the entire medical missionary work, the key of which is unity. It would seem that this particular phase of the message is to be so blended with every other part that the entire message is to stand out before the world after the similitude of Christ's work that every individual member of the church—layman, canvasser, Bible teacher, school teacher, institutional worker, and minister is to stand in Christ's stead before the world with His message of teaching and healing. The nurse or physician is no longer to content himself to simply minister to men's physical necessity, but is to perform a double ministry. The minister and missionary worker are to minister alike to soul and body in their need, and thus the entire work is to become one united medical missionary evangelistic work.

"We have come to a time when every member of the church should take hold of medical missionary work." "Christ is no longer in this world in person, to go through our cities and towns and villages, healing the sick. He has commissioned us to carry forward the medical missionary work that He began."

"If ever the Lord has spoken by me, He speaks when I say that the workers engaged in educational lines, in ministerial lines, and in medical missionary lines must stand as a unit. "Medical missionary work is yet in its infancy. The meaning of genuine medical missionary work is known but by few. Why? Because the Saviour's plan of work has not been followed."

"Christ, the great medical missionary, is our example. He healed the sick and preached the gospel. In His service, healing and teaching were linked closely together. Today they are not to be separated.

The nurses who are trained in our institutions are to be fitted up to go out as medical missionary evangelists, uniting the ministry of the Word with that of physical healing."

"There should be companies organized, and educated most thoroughly to work as nurses, as evangelists, as ministers, as canvassers, as gospel students."

"From the instruction that the Lord has given me from time to time, I know there should be workers who make medical evangelistic tours among the towns and villages. Those who do this work will gather a rich harvest of souls, both from the higher and lower classes."

"Let our ministers who have gained experience in preaching the Word, learn how to give simple treatments, and then labor intelligently as medical missionary evangelists. Christ stands before us as a pattern man, the great medical missionary, an example for all who should come after."

"The Lord calls upon our young people to enter our schools, and quickly fit themselves for service. In various places, outside of cities, schools are to be established, where our youth can receive an education that would prepare them to go forth to do evangelical work and medical missionary work."

From the above quotations and the experiences rehearsed, is it not clear to all that (the) Lord, through the spirit of prophecy, under whose fostering care the entire message had developed, and through whose influence each department—publishing, evangelical, and educational, has been reorganized and restored to its original purpose after the wisdom of man have turned them aside, is not calling for a reorganization of our medical missionary work in all its departments,—educational, institutional, and evangelical?

What is our individual responsibility in this matter? When God moves forward in His work, it divides men into two classes, those who follow in the way He leads, and those who turn aside. Are not the words of Mordecai to Esther applicable to each of us today: "For if thou altogether holdest thy peace at this time, then shall there enlargement and deliverance rise to the Jews (the work) from another place, but thou and thy father's house shall be destroyed: and who knoweth whether thou art come to the kingdom (the work) for such a time as this?" Esther 4:14. Or shall the prophetic words of Christ as He wept over Jerusalem, Matthew 23:34-39 describe our attitude and our condemnation at last?

* * * * *

[39] **April 17 - May 7, 1904-7**
"Elmshaven", Sanitarium, Cal.,
April 14, 1904.
My dear Brother,

I wish to write you a few lines regarding the work in San Diego. We have long desired to see sanitarium work established in this place, not that we ourselves may be benefited, but that those who have never heard the truth may have an opportunity of hearing the last message of mercy to be given to the world. If you have known and enjoyed the comfort of the Holy Spirit, the assurance of the grace of God, the hope of the gospel of Christ, your heart must be drawn out in earnest longing that this work may extend rapidly, while mercy's sweet voice is still heard inviting perishing souls to come to the Saviour.

I have always looked with great interest upon the work in Los Angeles and in San Diego, hoping that right moves would be made, and that the sanitarium work might be established in these important places. Every year large numbers of tourists visit these places, and I have longed to see men moved by the Holy Spirit meeting these people with the message borne by John the Baptist: "Repent ye; for the kingdom of heaven is at hand."

"This is he that was spoken of by Esaias, saying, The voice of one crying in the wilderness, prepare ye the way of the Lord; make His paths straight."

"Jerusalem and all Judea, and all the region round about Jordan," went out to hear John the Baptist, and were baptized of him in Jordan, confessing their sins." Just such a work as this can be done today in Southern California.

The Lord has ordained that memorials for Him shall be established in many places. He has presented before me buildings away from the cities, and suitable for our work, which can be purchased at a low price. We must take advantage of the favorable openings for Sanitarium work in Southern California, where the climate is so favorable for this work.

There are many other places in Southern California, besides Los Angeles and San Diego, in which sanitarium work could be started. To sanitariums in Southern California, people will come from far and near, because the fame of the climate is world-wide.

It is the Lord's purpose that sanitariums shall be established in Southern California, and that from these institutions shall go forth the light of truth for this time. By them the claims of the true Sabbath are to be presented, and the third angel's message proclaimed.

Institutions in which medical missionary work can be done are to be regarded as especially essential to the advancement of the Lord's work. The sick and suffering are to be relieved, and then, as opportunity offers, they are to be given instruction in regard to the truth for this time. Thus we can bring present truth before a class of people who could be reached in no other way.

The buildings secured for this work should be out of the cities, in rural districts, so that the sick may have the benefit of out-door life. By the beauty of flower and field, their minds will be diverted from themselves, from their aches and pains, and they will be led to look from nature to the God of nature, who has provided so abundantly the beauties of the natural world. The convalescent can lie in the shade of the trees, and those who are stronger can, if they wish, work among the flowers, doing just a little at first, and increasing their efforts as they grow stronger. Working in the garden, gathering flowers and fruit, listening to the birds praising God, the patients will be wonderfully blessed. Angels of God will draw near to them. They will forget their sorrows. Melancholy and depression will leave them. The fresh air and sunshine, and the exercise taken, will bring them life and vitality. The wearied brain and nerves will find relief. Good treatment and wholesome diet will build them up and strengthen them. They will feel no need for health-destroying drugs or for intoxicating drink.

The workers connected with our medical institutions should have the full confidence of the patients. Let them remember that this will be gained, not by elegant dress or by smartness of speech, but by living the life of Christ. Warm-hearted, unselfish workers are needed in our sanitariums,—workers who can speak words of tenderness and compassion to the sick and suffering. The physicians and nurses are not to be stiff and unsocial, neither are they to be light and trifling. They are to be bright and cheerful, bringing sunshine to the hearts of the sick. They are to talk of the Saviour and His power to save. In Him there is healing for soul and body.

In the establishment and carrying forward of sanitarium work, and strictest economy is ever to be shown. Workers are to be employed who will be producers as well as consumers. In no case is money to be invested for display. Gospel medical missionary work is today to be carried forward in simplicity, even as it was carried forward by the Majesty of heaven, who, seeing the necessities of a lost, sinful world, laid aside His royal robe and kingly crown, and clothed His divinity with humanity, that He might stand at the head of humanity. In His way of working, He has left us a perfect example. "If any man will come after me," He declared, "let him deny himself, and take up his cross, and follow Me." The true medical missionary will obey these words. He will not strain every nerve to make a display, thinking thus to win souls to the Saviour. The Son of God left His heavenly home to come to a world all seared and marred by the curse, that He might seek and save the Lost. Ought we not, His followers, to show the same self-denial and self-sacrifice that His life revealed? For us He endured the privations of poverty. Shall we refuse to deny ourselves for His sake?

Christ gives to all the invitation, "Come unto Me, all ye that labor and are heavy laden, and I will give you rest. Take my yoke upon you, and learn of Me; for I am meek and lowly in heart, and ye shall find rest unto your souls. For My yoke is easy, and My burden is light." If God's people will wear Christ's yoke, if they will learn in His school the lessons that He teaches, there will be sufficient means to establish gospel medical missionary work in many places.

Christ might have come to this world with a retinue of angels; but instead, He came as a babe, and lived a life of lowliness and poverty. His glory was in His simplicity. Shall we refuse to engage in medical missionary work unless we can follow the customs of the world, making a display such as worldlings make? To one who asked if he might follow Him, Christ said, "Foxes have holes, and the birds of the air have nests, but the Son of man hath not where to lay His head." Shall those who profess to be His followers refuse to engage in the work of helping their suffering fellow-beings unless they can be placed where their dignity will not be lessened?

In no other way can we do the work of God successfully than by following in the footsteps of the One who gave up His high command to come to our world, that through His humiliation and suffering, human beings might become partakers of the divine nature. For our sake He became poor, that through His poverty we might come into possession of the eternal riches.

It is not being rich in the wealth of this world that increases our value in God's sight. It is the meek and contrite that the Lord acknowledges and honors. Read the fifty-seventh of Isaiah. Study this chapter carefully for it means much to you. I will make no comments upon it. If you will study it carefully, and prayerfully, you will become wise unto salvation.

"Thus saith the high and lofty One that inhabiteth eternity, whose name is Holy; I dwell in the high and holy place, with him also that is of a contrite and humble spirit, to revive the spirit of the humble, and to revive the heart of the contrite ones."

My brother, we need means to advance the work of the Lord in many places. We must firmly establish the work at the capitol of our nation. Do you not wish to have a part in the work that God has given us to do there? Will you not do your best to help us to secure the facilities that we must have in order to advance the work in Washington, D. C. and in Southern California?

[42]

At San Diego we have made an advance move by purchasing the Potts Sanitarium in Paradise Valley, near National City and about six miles from San Diego. We hope soon to be able to furnish a part of the building, and to open its doors to those for whom it was purchased.

The building was erected for a sanitarium by Mrs. Mary Potts nearly twenty years ago. It is a fine, three-story structure, built on a rise of ground, and commanding a view of a beautiful valley. It has about fifty rooms, many of which are large and airy. The building is in very good condition, considering that it has stood idle for about fifteen years.

Three years ago light was given me that our people in Southern California must watch for opportunities to purchase such properties. I told our brethren that they would find all ready for use, and for sale at reasonable prices, just the buildings they would need for their work. And thus it has proved. In a most remarkable way the Lord is preparing the way for the advancement of His work in Southern California.

For two years I have been interested in the Potts Sanitarium property, and have advised and urged our people to secure it. Two years ago we thought it could be secure[d] for $12,000. One year ago it was offered for $8,000, and this spring it was offered for still less. I advised those having in charge the medical work in Southern California, to purchase the building, and when they hesitated, because of a lack of funds, I persuaded Sister Josephine Gotzian and Brother J. F. Ballenger to join me, and we have purchased the Potts Sanitarium, and eight acres adjoining for $5,000.

Something similar can be done in the neighborhood of Los Angeles, if wise plans are adopted for the carrying forward of the work, and if the men to who the Lord has entrusted His talent of means will put their money into use for the honor of God and the blessing of humanity.

We have not purchased the Potts Sanitarium to gain advantage for ourselves, but to help in carrying forward the work that Christ has given us to do,—the work outlined in the following scriptures:—

"Go ye therefore, and teach all nations, baptizing them in the name of the Father, and of the Son, and of the Holy Ghost, teaching them to observe all things whatsoever I have commanded you." These signs shall follow them that believe: In My name they shall cast out devils; they shall speak with new tongues; they shall take up serpents; and if they drink any deadly thing, it shall not hurt them; they shall lay hands on the sick, and they shall recover." "Ye shall be witnesses unto me both in Jerusalem, and in all Judea, and in Samaria, and unto the uttermost part of the earth. "And, lo, I am with you alway, even unto the end."

From the light which was given me when I was in Australia, and which has been renewed since I came to America, I know that our work in Southern California must advance. The people flocking there for health must hear the last message of mercy.

God has not been pleased with the way in which this work has been neglected. From many places in Southern California the light is to shine forth to the multitudes. Present truth is to be as a city set on a hill, which cannot be hid.

Southern California is world-renowned as a health resort. Every year many thousands of tourists go there. They must hear the last warning message. We are called upon by God to explain the Scriptures to these people. We are not to build hotels for the accommodation of tourists, and we are not to establish sanitariums in the cities. We are to establish our work where we shall be able to do the most good to those who come to our sanitariums for treatment.

Workers who can speak to the multitudes are to be located where they can meet the people where they are, and give them the message of truth.

What will you do to help, my brother? Will you put the Lord's money into circulation to advance His work? Will you respond at once to this appeal? We so greatly desire that these favorable openings may be taken advantage of. If we do our duty, the Lord will give us many souls for our hire.

The aim and burden of our work is to show that the truth uplifts and saves. Missionary work must be done. The world is our field of labor, and we must meet the people where they are, and give them the message. God desires his workers to develop the capabilities and powers that He has given them. It is His purpose that they shall constantly increase in usefulness, ever gaining greater ability to win souls to Christ.

* * * * *

.H.
Nashville, Tenn.,
June 30, 1904.
To the Ministers in Southern California:
Dear Brethren,

I have no desire to hurt the soul of any one, but I must bear the straight testimony given me. Some of the ministers and leaders in the Southern California Conference need to realize the necessity of counselling with their brethren who have been long in the work, and who have thus gained a valuable experience. Their disposition to shut themselves up to themselves, and to feel competent to plan and

[44]

execute, according to their own judgment and preference, brings them into financial embarrassment. Then, when the embarrassment bears heavily upon them, they are tempted to think that the Union Conference or the General Conference should help them out. This independent way of working is not right, and should not be followed. The ministers and teachers in our Conferences are to work unitedly with their brethren of experience, asking them for advice, and paying heed to this advice.

Earnest work should be done in Southern California in carrying the Fernando school forward successfully, and earnest work should be done in establishing a sanitarium near Los Angeles. Several buildings have already been offered for sale. If these are not suitable, or if they cannot be purchased for a reasonable sum, land should be purchased and buildings erected.

Our small conferences should be careful not to create burdens of debt for the General Conference to carry. At times inconsiderate moves are made, buildings are put up without sufficient thought as to their use, and responsibilities are assumed where there is not ability to carry these responsibilities. Thus, money is absorbed that brings no returns. Enterprises are started which consume without producing. This is not as it should be.

Diligent efforts should be made to lessen the debt resting on the school, but these efforts should be made by all. I have supposed that "Christ's Object Lessons", handled discreetly, would do much toward relieving our schools from debt, and I believe that this book will yet be the means of doing much to help the Fernando School.

I do not see the wisdom of the school depending on the second tithe to meet so much of its expenses. I fear that if the brethren rely so much upon this that difficulties will rise. You should labor patiently to develop those industries by which students can partly work their way through school.

Let each family try to pay the expenses of the students that it sends to school. Some families, in which there are several children attending school, will be hard pressed. Would it not be wisdom to create a fund by the sale of "Christ's Object Lessons" for the assistance of such ones? There are many young people who desire to be in school, and who ought to be, but who have no means. These young people can be helped through school, if our people will do their duty in handling "Object Lessons".

The purchase of the school buildings at Fernando was in the order of God. Valuable property was obtained at a price far below its original cost. The brethren did right to buy it, and the school can be sustained if the families of believers in Southern California will do their best to make it a success. The young men and women who expect to attend school should do all in their power, before entering the school to earn money to meet their expenses.

A Special Work.

There is a special work to be done just now. A sanitarium should be established near Los Angeles. My brethren, will you not remember that it is the expressed will of God that this shall be done? Why this work should be delayed from year to year, is a great mystery. This is a matter that has long been kept before you, my brethren. Again and again sanitarium work has been pointed out as an important means of reaching people with the truth. Had the light given by God been followed, this institution might now be in running order, exerting a strong influence for good. Arrangements could have been made to utilize for sanitarium work buildings already erected.

In order for successful work to be done in the field or in our institutions, workers with harmonious elements of character are needed. The work can be carried forward only by patience and harmony of action. It has been a lack of harmony, a lack of determination on the part of the workers to lift with one purpose in view, that has delayed the establishment of a sanitarium in Southern California. There has been so much variance that means which should have been invested in a sanitarium has been turned into other channels.

The idea that a sanitarium should not be established unless it could be started free from debt, has put the brake upon the wheels of progress. In building meeting houses we have had to borrow money, in order that something might be done at once. We have been obliged to do this, in order to fulfill the directions of God. Persons deeply interested in the progress of the work have borrowed money and paid interest on it, to help establish schools and sanitariums and to build meeting houses. The institutions thus established and the churches built have been the means of winning many to the truth.

Thus the tithe has been increased, and workers have been added to the Lord's forces.

[46] Will my brethren consider this, and work in accordance with the light which God has given us, regarding the work in Southern California? Let that which should be done be done without delay. Do your best to remedy the neglect of the past. The word has once more come that a sanitarium is to be set in working order near Los Angeles. If this sanitarium is conducted in harmony with the will of God, it will be a means of great blessing, a means in the Lord's hands of leading souls to the truth.

* * * * *

"Christ's Object Lessons"

I wish to say a few words more about the circulation of Christ's Object Lessons. My brethren, show our people what they can do in handling this book. As tourists from all parts of the world flock into Los Angeles and other parts of Southern California, let there be those who can call their attention to this book. It is full of precious truth, and as it is presented to unbelievers, angels of God will impress many to buy it. Let those who do this work keep in mind the words, "As unto the Lord". The purpose for which it is done will invest this work with a dignity that will improve the habits, the manners, and the address of the workers. By this effort the poorest, humblest worker is linked with the great Master Worker.

In order to be ready to receive the impressions of the Holy Spirit, in order to advance in harmony with the will of the Lord, we need consecrated minds and hearts. Let not human beings seek to put their own plans and preferences in the place of God's plans. Those who do this will hinder the Lord's work. Let no one say or do anything that will discourage Christlike effort. To each one God has given his work. If every one would be zealous to do that which will increase his ability to labor, how much would be accomplished.

The Lord wants you, my brethren, to arouse to action the minds of those who do not realize that God is calling them to active service. Tell them that their obedient love, in willing effort, is to flow forth as streams in the desert. Day by day what they accomplish is to give evidence that they are laborers together with God. The work that the Lord places before them may be dreaded, but they will gain courage as they advance.

Let all do something. All can do much more than they have done. Let parents and children help. The consciousness that they are co-workers with Christ will give the workers a joy and assurance that they could gain in no other way. And not only will relief be brought to the schools, but the light of truth will be widely diffused.

The experience gained by the youth who engage in this work will be of great value to them, teaching them to improve every God-given opportunity to labor with diligence and fidelity, and with perseverance under disappointment. The Lord makes a way for all who employ the means He has provided for the accomplishment of certain objects.

My brethren and sisters in Southern California, educate yourselves to work for the Master. Remember that in helping to circulate "Object Lessons", you are placing before others truths which cannot fail of being a blessing to them. Each one of God's people has a part to act in the work of the Redeemer. Those who receive Christ are to prove the sincerity of their love for Him by earnest, self-sacrificing efforts in His service. No opportunity for helping to advance the Lord's cause is to be allowed to pass by. In meekness and lowliness, yet with an earnest determination to accomplish something for the blessing of others, God's children are to take hold of His work.

Only a small part of that which may be accomplished has yet been done in circulating "Christ's Object Lessons". Let not our people think that their duty is done, their work finished. This book is still to be taken out by God's people, and is to find its place in many more homes. Let the same territory be gone over and over again. In this there will be a blessing for the one who sells the book and for those who buy it. Let us take hold of the work with renewed courage. Let God's people consecrate to His service the time and tact that He has given them. O, what a blessing many will obtain from the consciousness that they are working for God. This thought will help them to do their work intelligently.

My brethren and sisters, by earnest prayer brace yourselves for duty, and then expect the help of the Lord. Prove yourselves to be laborers together with God. As you go forth to sell "Object Lessons" repeat again and again the words, "Not slothful in business, fervent in spirit, serving the Lord." With this as your motto, press on with the work.

With humble hearts begin afresh, and by your words and example encourage those who have never tried to sell the book to make an effort. Let all that you do be done gracefully and cheerfully and well. Learn to ask the Lord to help you and believe that He surely will. The work that is undertaken in the name of the Lord and for the purpose of placing the light before the people will be blessed by Him. What is needed is workers who are humble and contrite. He who lives near the Saviour will reveal in his life that he has held communion with Him.

Ellen G. White.

* * * * *

July 15, 1904-7
Takoma Park, Washington, D. C.
July 15, 1904.
Dear Brother Burden,

Last night I was unable to sleep past twelve o'clock. I was given an important message to bear. I have been writing out the instruction that was given me, and will send you a copy of this when it is ready. I shall no longer hold my peace. I am bidden to cry aloud, and spare not. I have tried in every way to bring about the needed reformation, and save the souls of those who are following a wrong course. But I cannot go on as I have been going. When every effort has been made to save their souls, and yet all is in vain, we must cry aloud and spare not, lest our silence be interpreted to mean consent. The time has come when each one must stand in his lot and place, prepared to call sin, sin, and righteousness, righteousness.

I am very grateful to my heavenly Father that you have secured a building near Los Angeles for sanitarium work. Your description of the building shows the truth of the testimonies I have borne,—that buildings suitable for our work will be offered to us at a low price. We must make earnest efforts to improve the opportunities that God sends us, that His work may advance as rapidly as possible.

If it is at all consistent with our work, we shall attend the Los Angeles camp-meeting. At present I am not at all strong. But I am praying to the Lord to strengthen me.

For several months before I left California, I was engaged in work that was terribly wearing. At last my strength gave way, and for two or three weeks I wrote hardly anything. I feared that my brain power was seriously impaired. One day, just before leaving home, I was alone with God in my room, praying for His healing power to come upon me. All at once a change took place. The difficulty in my head left me instantly, and I was made whole. My head has endured the strain of the meeting here and the one at Berrien Springs. At Berrien Springs my work was exceedingly difficult. It was terrible to see the blindness upon minds. But the Lord gave me special victories; angels of God stood by my side, and His spirit rested on me.

Let us have faith that we shall have special help from God. Let us not talk unbelief, but be cheerful in the Lord. Let us be one in Christ. Unity is strength. Christ's last prayer with His disciples, shows the importance of unity.

My brother, have constant faith in God. Every day comes to us weighted with important responsibilities, which God alone can give us strength to fulfill. Be not weary in well-doing. Be always abounding in the work of the Lord. Walk and work by faith.

Ellen G. White.

* * * * *

Extracts from Letters and Mss., on the Training and Work of Medical Missionaries

(Files of 1902-1905 drawn from)

H. 291'04 (Oct. 12, 1904)

If the Lord has ever spoken by me, He speaks when I say that the workers engaged in educational lines, in ministerial lines, and in medical missionary lines must stand as a unit, all laboring under the supervision of God, one helping the other, each blessing each...

Those connected with them (our schools and sanitariums) are to labor with earnest alacrity. The work that is done under the ministration of the Holy Spirit, out of love for God and for humanity, will bear the signature of God, and will make its impression on human minds.

We do not look upon you, my brother, as a man who has put only half of his heart into this grand work. We take the opposite view of this, knowing that you put heart, mind, soul, and strength into your work. The only fear that I have had in regard to you is that you will try to carry too heavy a burden.

Those who put their whole soul into the medical missionary work, who labor untiringly, in peril, in privation, in watchings oft, in weariness and painfulness, are in danger of forgetting that they must be faithful guardians of their own mental and physical powers. They are not to allow themselves to be overtaxed. But they are filled with zeal and earnestness, and they sometimes move unadvisedly, putting themselves under too heavy a strain. Unless such workers make a change, the result will be that sickness will come upon them, and they will break down.

While God's workers are to be filled with a noble enthusiasm, and with a determination to follow the example of the divine worker, the great Medical Missionary, they are not to crowd too many things into the day's work. If they do, they will soon have to leave the work entirely, broken down because they have tried to carry too heavy a load. My brother, it is right for you to make the best use of the advantages given you of God in earnest efforts for the relief of suffering and for the saving of souls. But do not sacrifice your health.

We have a calling as much higher than common, selfish interests as the heavens are higher than the earth, but this thought should not lead the willing, hardworking servants of God to carry all the burdens they can possibly bear, without periods of rest.

[50] How grand it would be if among all who were engaged in carrying out God's wonderful plan for the salvation of souls, there were no idlers. How much more would be accomplished if every one would say, "God holds me accountable to be wide-awake, and to let my efforts speak in favor of the truth I profess to believe. I am to be a practical worker, not a day-dreamer." It is because there are so many day-dreamers that true workers have to carry double burdens.

It is the part of a medical missionary to minister to the needs of the soul as well as to the needs of the body. The precious truth of Christ's power to save, spoken in season, will give hope and courage, and may save both soul and body. The Lord waters and watches over the seed thus sown. The promises of the Bible, repeated to those who are sick and discouraged, will be the means of saving many souls. The Holy Spirit cooperates with the worker who labors in the fear and love of God. God gives such workers wisdom and success.

We need as workers to keep looking unto Jesus, the author and finisher of our faith. As workers together with God, we are to draw souls to Christ. We are to remember that we each have a special part to act in the Master's service. Oh, how much good the members of the church might accomplish if they realized the responsibility resting upon them to point those with whom they come in contact to the Redeemer. When church members shall disinterestedly engage in the work given them of God, a much stronger influence will be exerted in behalf of souls ready to die, and much stronger efforts will be put forth in medical missionary lines. When every member of the church does his part faithfully, the workers in the field will be helped and encouraged, and the cause of God will move forward with power. Let the ministers of the gospel and the workers in medical missionary lines labor in perfect harmony.

May God help you, my brother, to be cheerful, to look on the bright side. Study the twelfth chapter of Romans. It points out the unity, the sympathy, the kindness, the unselfish love, that is to exist amongst God's workers.

"As we have many members in one body, and all members have not the same office; we, being many, are one body in Christ, and every one members one of another." "Let love be without dissimulation. Abhor that which is evil; cleave to that which is good. Be kindly affectioned one to another with brotherly love, in honor preferring one another; not slothful in business; fervent in spirit; serving the Lord; rejoicing in hope; patient in tribulation; continuing instant in prayer; distributing to the necessity of saints; given to hospitality. Bless them which persecute you; bless, and curse not. Rejoice with them that do rejoice, and weep with them that weep." Be not overcome of evil, but overcome evil with good."

* * * * *

[51] **To Stand as God's Witness**

W. 105'04 (March 1, 1904)

Definite instruction has been given concerning the part that medical missionary workers are to act in the work of God. They are to stand as God's witnesses, to represent the work of the great Medical Missionary, Jesus Christ,—God's Gift to our world to save men from the very mistakes that have brought the rebuke of God upon this people. Not a thread of selfishness is to be woven into the web.

* * * * *

The Truth, Practiced and Taught, Will Lead to the Conversion of Some

G. 33'05 (Jan. 23, '05)

---seeking to treat the sick by correct methods, and to impart to those coming to the institution the sound doctrine of the gospel. Under the hallowed influence of such teachings souls will be converted. The truth practiced and taught by medical missionaries will be received in the heart of some, and will lead to conversion and the establishment in the heart of the true principles of righteousness.

* * * * *

To Engage in Soul-Saving in Our Sanitariums

B.97'05 (March 14 '05)

Let all connected with this sanitarium (Glendale) keep in mind the purpose for which this property has been secured. The institution is to act a special part in bringing souls to Christ, leading them to love God and keep His commandments. Unless the workers have a living connection with God, unless there is seen in the institution a spirit of kindness and compassion, which will recommend Bible truth and win souls to Christ, the establishment of the sanitarium will have been in vain. Spiritual as well as physical healing is to be brought to those who come for healing...

You... may do a precious work in letting the light of present truth shine forth in clear rays. Remember that you are doing a work for time and for eternity. You should have an ever-increasing faith in the promises of God's Word. It is your privilege to seek wisdom and help from God. Come to the Saviour in humility, confessing your sins, and seeking for strength and grace.

The Holy Spirit enlightens the mind of the one who depends on the merits of a crucified and risen Saviour, and indites a prayer of confession and repentance that is acceptable to the Lord. "We know not what we should pray for as we ought; but the Spirit itself maketh intercession for us, with groanings that cannot be uttered." "He that searcheth the heart knoweth what is the mind of the Spirit, because He maketh intercession for the saints according to the will of God."

In every sanitarium there must be kept before all in the institution the principles of true service. From the institution is to go forth light and knowledge. All connected with it are to act their part intelligently, as representatives of the truth for this time. It is that they may be trained to do true missionary work, that young people are brought to our sanitariums.

If you will cooperate with God, He will go before you, and the glory of the Lord will be your reward. Heavenly angels will break forth into singing as souls receive the great gift of God through Jesus

Christ. You may assure the sick and afflicted that Christ is the healer. They may believe on Him, and trust in His Word; for it will never fail."

* * * * *

God Invests with Holy Dignity Those Who Go Forth in His Power to Heal the Sick

(General Instruction)

K. 203'05 (July 18, 1905)

Advantage should be taken of these opportunities to establish and extend gospel medical missionary work; for time is short, and we must sow the seeds of health reform principles.

I have been instructed that we are not to delay to do the work that needs to be done in health reform lines. Through this work we are to reach souls in the highways and byways. I have been given special light that in our sanitariums many souls will receive and obey present truth. In these institutions men and women are to be taught how to care for their own bodies, and at the same time how to become sound in the faith. They are to be taught what is meant by eating the flesh and drinking the blood of the Son of God. Said Christ, "The words that I speak unto you, they are spirit and they are life.

Our sanitariums are to be schools in which instruction shall be given in medical missionary lines. They are to bring to sinsick souls the leaves of the tree of life, which will restore to them peace and hope and faith in Christ Jesus. Forbid not those who have a desire to extend this work. Let the light shine forth. All worthy health productions will create an interest in health reform. Forbid them not. The Lord would have all opportunities to extend the work, taken advantage of...

[53] By means of such an institution hundreds would become enlightened in regard to present truth. We need to give all the publicity we possibly can to the work God desires to have done. The seeds of truth are to be sown beside all waters. Let the Lord's work go forward. Let the medical missionary and the educational work go forward. I am sure that this is our great lack,—earnest, devoted, intelligent, capable workers.

In every large city there should be a representation of true medical missionary work. The principles of genuine health reform are to be brought out in clear lines, in our health publications and in lectures delivered to the patients in our sanitariums. In every city there are men and women who would go to a sanitarium were it near at hand, who would not be able to go to one a long way off. There are many who will be convicted and converted, who now appear indifferent. I look at this matter in a very decided light.

Let many now ask, "Lord, what wilt Thou have me to do? It is the Lord's purpose that His method of healing without drugs shall be brought into prominence in every large city through our medical institutions. God invests with holy dignity those who go forth farther and still farther, in every place to which it is possible to obtain entrance. Satan will make the work as difficult as possible, but divine power will attend all true-hearted workers. Guided by our heavenly Father's hand, let us go forward, improving every opportunity to extend the work of God.

We shall have to labor under difficulties, but because of this, let not our zeal flag. The Bible does not acknowledge a believer who is idle, however high his profession may be. There will be employment in heaven. The redeemed state is not one of idle repose. There remaineth therefore a rest to the people of God, but it is a rest found in loving service. Some among the redeemed will have laid hold of Christ in the last hours of life, and in heaven instruction will be given to these ones, who when they died, did not understand perfectly the plan of salvation. Christ will lead the redeemed ones beside the river of life, and will open to them that which while on this earth they could not understand. "He showed me a pure river of water of life, clear as crystal, proceeding out of the throne of God and of the Lamb.

In the midst of the street of it, and on either side of the river, was there the tree of life, which bare twelve manner of fruits, and yielded her fruit every month; and the leaves of the tree were for the healing of the nations. And there shall be no more curse; but the throne of God and of the Lamb shall be in it; and they shall see His face; and His name shall be in their foreheads."

Thank God, thank God! Let us improve every opportunity to

reach poor, suffering, sinsick souls with the message of salvation. Let the precious light of truth be shed abroad.

*****

In the Early Days, The Workers Were Medical Missionaries, and the Power of God was Manifest in the Healing of the Sick

H. 191'05 (July 5, 1905)

The end of all things is at hand. The signs foretold by Christ are fast fulfilling. The nations are angry, and the time of the dead has come, that they should be judged. There are stormy times before us, but let us not utter one word of unbelief or discouragement. Let us remember that we bear a message of healing to a world filled with sinsick souls.

You will remember the poverty that we met when starting the work in New England, in Boston, New Bedford, and other places. But the difficulties we encountered only made us unite in pushing forward the harder, and we have not forgotten what wonderful victories the Lord gave us. How many times there came upon us trials that almost overpowered us. In every place, heresies came in, and every conceivable error strove for entrance. What were our weapons? Faith and prayer. We were medical missionaries, and we realized the fulfillment of the promise, "Lo I am with you alway, even unto the end of the world." How manifest was the power of God in healing the sick! What rejoicing, What thanksgiving was heard!

We never thought in those days that we should have institutions for healing the sick. We did not suppose that time would last long enough for us to build meeting houses. But all over the United States we now have sanitariums, and a large corps of intelligent physicians are working earnestly to present the principles of health reform, and to point souls to Christ.

In those early days, how many seasons of fervent prayer were held! A holy, submissive, Christlike spirit was breathed upon us; for we knew that the Saviour was with us. No one was instructed to spend years in preparation for the work to be done. Practical, earnest knowledge was imparted. There was seen the faith that works by love and purifies the soul. Few today are better armed and equipped for service than were the workers of that time. Christianity was seen to be the exemplification of the Holy Spirit's working on human hearts. God's wonderful, miracle-working power was exercised according to our faith. The manifest revealing of the grace of Christ carried a deeper conviction to souls than the logic of man could possibly have carried.

* * * * *

Medical Missionaries and Ministers to Meet Together to Study Bible [55]

K. 23 '04 (Dec., 1903)

A Bible institute should be held in some place where medical missionary workers and ministers may meet together to study the Scriptures. Let the Bible explain its own statements. Accept it just as it reads, without twisting the words to suit human ideas. "What is the chaff to the wheat?"

* * * * *

To be a Medical Missionary, Means to be a Laborer Together with God

MS. 139'02 (Sept. 15, '02)

The Lord has given me these words to speak and write over and over again, until a decided adherence to the principles of truth shows that men have been called to repentance. A grand side of the word of God is revealed by the words, "Medical Missionary". To be a medical missionary means to be a laborer together with God. Medical missionary work, a work that is to be a great help and strength to the cause, is to be carried forward in all carefulness and wisdom. Into this work not one thread is to be drawn that will spoil the beautiful pattern that God designs shall be worked out.

The medical missionary work is God's own work, and it is to be controlled by no human power. Human agencies are to act as the Lord's helping hand, guided and controlled by the power of the Holy Spirit. Not one act is to be done that will dishonor the work.

Mistakes will be made. But let men be very careful how they bear down upon those who have made mistakes. Sometimes the one who treats the erring with little mercy has made mistakes far more grievous in the sight of God than those made by the one whom he so unsparingly condemns.

Under the Lord's special guidance, some things have been done that are contrary to the specified directions laid down by men. Unseen agencies were guiding in another way than that marked out by human wisdom. Then let men be careful how they call their brethren to account, as though they were in God's place.

The Lord has heard the humiliating censure that had been given to those who had not rebellion in their hearts, who thought they were doing just what they were told to do. The Lord saw that His work would be marred if the directions given by men were followed, and He guided the minds of the workers to do the work in the very way that He wished it done. The workers did not follow the plan laid out by men, because God had a better plan for them. The divine guiding produced the right result...

I am instructed to say to our ministers and medical missionary workers, Be careful what spirit you manifest to one another.

*****

The Training of Medical Missionaries, Not Properly Understood

B. 210'03 (Sept. 21 '03)

The Lord calls upon our young people to enter our schools and quickly fit themselves for service. In various places, outside of the cities, schools are to be established, where our youth can receive an education that will prepare them to go forth to do evangelical work and medical missionary work.

The Lord must be given an opportunity to show men their duty, and to work upon their minds. No one is to bind himself to serve for a term of years under the direction of one group of men or in one specified branch of the Master's work; for the Lord Himself will call men, as of old He called the humble fishermen, and will Himself give them instructions regarding their field of labor and the methods they should follow. He will call men from the plow and from other occupations, to give the last note of warning to perishing souls. There are many ways in which to work for the Master, and the great Teacher will open the understanding of these workers, enabling them to see wondrous things in His Word.

I have repeatedly been instructed that no one should be advised to pledge himself to spend two, three, four, five, or six years under any one man's supervision. Let students stand where they can follow the will of God. Their service belongs to Him. Their capabilities and talents are to be refined, purified, ennobled. In this lower school—the school of earth—they are to be prepared for translation into the school of heaven, where their education will be continued under the personal supervision of Christ, the great Teacher, who will lead them beside the living waters, and open to them the mysteries of the kingdom of God.

* * * * *

The Training of Medical Missionaries

Medical missionary work is yet in its infancy. The meaning of genuine medical missionary work is known by but few. Why?—Because the Saviour's plan of work has not been followed. God's money has been misapplied. In many places practical evangelistic medical missionary work is not being done; but many of the workers who should go forth as did the disciples are being collected together and held in a few places, as they have been in the past, notwithstanding the Lord's warning that this should not be.

Many of the men and women who should be out in the field, working as medical missionary evangelists, helping those engaged in the gospel ministry, are collected in Battle Creek, acting over the same program that has been acted over in the past, confining the forces, binding them up in one place. God has spoken against this by sending His judgments upon the institutions in Battle Creek but notwithstanding this, every movement on the part of those striving to heed the warnings by laboring to change the order of things, has been made very hard because of the misconception of some regarding the way in which the medical missionary work should be carried forward.

God has not given us the work of erecting immense sanitariums, to be used as health resorts for all who may come. Neither is it His purpose that medical missionary workers shall spend a long term of years in college before they enter the field. To build up a school in Battle Creek, as some of our people there desire, would tend to counterwork the influence that God has declared should be exerted on His people in these last days of this earth's history.

The interests that the Lord has declared should not remain in Battle Creek are not now to be brought back and reestablished there. Much of the force that would be needed to carry forward there, amidst many disadvantages, the work of these interests, should be used in doing gospel medical missionary work in the large cities still unworked.

"Break up the large centers," has been the word of the Lord. "Carry the light to many places." Those who are desirous of receiving a training for effective medical missionary work, should understand that large sanitariums will be conducted so much like institutions of the world, that students laboring in such sanitariums cannot obtain a systematic training for Christian medical missionary work.

The proclamation of the truth in all parts of the world calls for small sanitariums in many places, not in the heart of cities, but in places where city influence will be as little felt as possible.

I am obliged to say that the making of so large a plant in Battle Creek, and the calling together of those who should be engaged in medical missionary work in many places, is doing just what God has specified should not be done.

The fact that many patients are coming to the new sanitarium at Battle Creek is not to be read as a sign that the planning for so large a work there was for the best. To this large institution will come many men and women who are not really sick. Workers will be required to wait on them; our nurses will become the servants of worldly men and women who are not inclined to piety or religion. But this is not the work that God has given to His medical missionaries. Our charge has been given us by the greatest Medical Missionary that this world has ever seen. Standing but a step from His Father's throne, Christ said to His disciples:—

"All power is given unto Me in heaven and in earth. Go ye therefore, and teach all nations, baptizing them in the name of the Father, and of the Son, and of the Holy Ghost." "Go ye into all the world," He said, "and preach the gospel to every creature," "teaching them to observe all things whatsoever I have commanded you; and, lo, I am with you alway, even unto the end of the world."

Let our ministers who have gained an experience in preaching the Word, learn how to give simple treatments, and then labor intelligently as medical missionary evangelists.

Workers—gospel medical missionaries—are needed now. We cannot afford to spend years in preparation. Soon doors now open to the truth will be forever closed. Carry the message now. Do not wait, allowing the enemy to take possession of fields now open before you. Let little companies go forth to do the work to which Christ appointed His disciples. Let them labor as evangelists, scattering our publications, and talking of the truth to those they meet. Let them pray for the sick, ministering to their necessities not with drugs, but with nature's remedies, and teaching them how to regain health and avoid disease.

Let the workers remember always that they are dependent on God. Let them not trust in human wisdom, but in the wisdom of the One who declares, "All power is given unto Me in heaven and in earth... Lo, I am with you alway, even unto the end of the world." Let them go forth two and two, depending upon God, not on man, for wisdom and success. Let them search the Scriptures, and then present the truths of God's Word to others. Let them be guided by the principles that Christ has laid down.

*****

Privileges and Opportunities of a Gospel Medical Missionary

J. 228 '03 (Oct. 19, '03)

God's purpose for us is that we shall ever move upward. Even in the smaller duties of common life, we are to make continual growth in grace, supplied with high and holy motives, powerful because they proceed from the One who gave His life to furnish us with the incentive to be wholly successful in the formation of Christian character...

[59] You are to be strong in the strength of God, grounded in the hope of the gospel. You are acquainted with God's requirements and I beg of you not to remain a weakling. You possess qualifications that if rightly used would make you a blessing in the world. Arise in your God-given dignity, living the truth in its purity. Christ is ready to pardon you, to take away your sins, and make you free. He is ready to purify your heart, and give you the sanctification of His Spirit. As you commit yourself to His service, He will be at your right hand to help you. Day by day you will be strengthened and ennobled. Looking to the Saviour for help, you will be a conqueror, yes, more than a conqueror over the temptations that beset you. You will become more and more like Christ. The angels of heaven will rejoice to see you standing on the Lord's side, in righteousness and true holiness.

I am very hopeful that you will become all that the Lord desires you to be,—a gospel medical missionary. You are to be not only an increasingly skillful physician, but one of the Lord's appointed missionaries, in all your work placing His service first. Let nothing mar your peace. Give your heart's best and holiest affections to Him who gave His life that you might be among the redeemed family in the heavenly courts. Striving for the crown of life will not make you dissatisfied or less useful. The great Teacher desires to acknowledge you as His helping hand. He calls for your cooperation. Will you not now give Him all that you have and are? Will you not consecrate your talents to His service?

* * * * *

Medical Missionaries to Unite with Ministers

MS. 46 '04 (May 18 '04)

My brethren, the Lord calls for unity, for oneness,.. We are to be one in the faith. I want to tell you that when the gospel ministers and the medical missionary workers are not united, there is placed on our churches the worst evil that can be placed there. Our medical missionaries ought to be interested in the work of our Conferences, and our Conference workers ought to be as much interested in the work of our medical missionaries.

* * * * *

Every One to Work as Christ Worked

Ms. 94 '03 (Copied Aug. 27 '03)

Our youth... are not to be bound about, so that they cannot develop. They should daily be given the highest motives to advance. They should attend our schools, and the teachers should work with them, and pray with them. They should leave these schools true medical missionaries, firmly bound up with the gospel ministry.

Our churches who have a deep interest in the children and youth, and in the work of training workers to carry forward the work essential for this time, need not blunder; for God will open ways before all who are perfecting Christian characters. He will have places ready for them in which to begin to do true missionary work. It was to prepare workers for this work, that our schools and sanitariums were established...

I say to our people, Let not those on whom we must depend to do gospel missionary work in places where the truth should be represented, be drawn away by any pretense from their work. The cause of God needs the very best workers. God's workers are ever to cherish a clear idea of what is constituted by pure and undefiled religion. In the cities where the truth is to be established, there will be needed workers of Bible faith and practise. The work of God is to be carried forward in the South, and the youth whose talents make them most desired in Battle Creek are to be ready to step into the places prepared for them in institutions where they can obtain a training for work without being thrown into the companionship of worldly people, who know not God and whose wrong sentiments will leaven the minds of those with whom they are brought in contact. We cannot afford to allow the minds of our youth to be thus leavened; for it is on these youth that we must depend to carry forward the work in the future.

I call upon the presidents of our conferences to exert their God-given influence to open the fields that have never yet been worked. These fields stand as a reproach to our people. Organize your work intelligently, and then proceed to action. Let your simplicity of speech, and your simplicity and neatness of dress speak of your work as missionaries. Educational advantages will be provided, and the Lord will go before those who will take up the work in the spirit of self-sacrifice.

Study the life and teachings of Christ. Men may bid for your services, offering large inducements. Remember that Christ paid for you the price of His own life, and that you are not your own. You are to glorify God in your body and in your spirit, which are His.

* * * * *

Every One to Work as Christ Worked

C. 117 '03 (Copied June 24 '03)

Christ stood at the head of humanity in the garb of humanity. So full of sympathy and love was His attitude that the poorest was not afraid to come to Him. He was kind to all; easily approached by the most lowly, He went from house to house, healing the sick, feeding the hungry, comforting the mourners, soothing the afflicted, speaking peace to the distressed. He took the little children in His arms and blessed them, and spoke words of hope and comfort to the weary mothers. With unfailing tenderness and gentleness He met every form of human woe and affliction. Not for himself, but for others did He labor. He was willing to humble Himself, to deny Himself. He did not seek to distinguish Himself. He was the servant of all. It was His meat and drink to be a comfort and a consolation to others, to gladden the sad and heavy laden ones with whom He daily came in contact.

[61]

Christ stands before us as the pattern Man, the great Medical Missionary,—an example for all who should come after. His love, pure and holy, blessed all who came within the sphere of its influence. His character was absolutely perfect, free from the slightest stain of sin. He came as an expression of the perfect love of God, not to crush, not to judge and condemn, but to heal every weak, defective character, to save men and women from Satan's power. He is the Creator, Redeemer, and Sustainer of the human race. He gives to all the invitation, "Come unto Me, all ye that labor and are heavy laden, and I will give you rest. Take My yoke upon you, and learn of Me; for I am meek and lowly in heart, and ye shall find rest unto your souls. For My yoke is easy and my burden is light."

What, then, is the example that we are to set to the world? We are to do the same work that the great Medical Missionary undertook in our behalf. We are to follow the path of self-sacrifice trodden by Christ.

As I see so many claiming to be medical missionaries, the representation of what Christ was on this earth flashes before me. As I think of how far short the workers today fall when compared with the divine example, my heart is bowed down with a sorrow that words cannot express. Will men and women ever do a work that bears the features and character of the great Medical Missionary? ...

Is there not woe enough in this sin-stricken, sin-cursed earth to lead us to consecrate ourselves to the work of proclaiming the message that "God so loved the world that He gave His only begotten Son, that whosoever believeth in Him should not perish, but have everlasting life?" This earth has been trodden by the Son of God. He came to bring men light and life, to set them free from the bondage of sin. He is coming again in power and great glory, to receive to Himself those who during this life have followed in His footsteps.

Oh, how I long to see those who claim to be medical missionaries honoring the great Exemplar, whose life declares what is comprehended in the claim to be a medical missionary! I would that they were learning the Saviour's meekness and lowliness. My heart aches to think that Christ is so greatly disappointed in His followers. They bear a name that their daily life does not give them the right to bear.

We must be sanctified, soul and body, through the truth; then we shall honor the name, Medical Missionary. Oh, this name means so much! It calls for a representation altogether different from the representation given by many who bear it. Soon these will understand how far they have departed from the principles of heaven, and how greatly they have grieved the heart of Christ.

* * * * *

Every One to Work as Christ Worked

K. 181 '03 (Sept. 2 '03)

The real end of the gospel is to develop in human beings supreme, sanctified love for God and unselfish love for one another. This love is not a fitful impulse; it is not merely the exercise of benevolence, or philanthropy; it is the fruit of a heart purified from all defilement.

The gospel was made known by God to raise human beings from sin to righteousness. He who receives the gospel constantly reaches out for the divine, perseveringly taking hold of the strength of the Saviour. His heart is an abiding place for the Holy Spirit. Day by day He shows forth the praises of Him who has called Him out of darkness into His marvelous light.

Does not this help you to see the full significance of being a gospel medical missionary? Every one who bears the name of medical missionary is to work as Christ worked. The love of Christ in his heart is to make him an example to others. He is to serve the Lord with all humility of mind, doing his appointed work, to accomplish, not his own ends, but God's purpose.

* * * * *

Medical Missionaries to be Thoroughly Educated in Bible Lines

J. 178'03 (Aug. 2 '03)

The very same reasons that were given for the removal of the old Battle Creek College from Battle Creek, should now lead our brethren to decide to train in other places the youth who now expect to prepare themselves for medical missionary work. Those who expect to become medical missionary workers must be thoroughly educated in Bible lines. They should have the very best spiritual advantages, in order that they may be fitted to teach and to train others.

My brother, I am surprised that you are found asleep on this point. I declare unto you, in the name of the Lord, that the arrangements being made for the training of medical missionaries in Battle Creek are not right. A great work is to be done in a short time, and God forbids that we should encourage so many of our youth to bind themselves up for three, or four, or six years of training, before engaging in active work,.. Men and women should gain an education by working along practical lines in different places, in accordance with the light that God has given, and under the instruction of experienced leaders.

* * * * *

Medical Missionary Work as a Door to Large Cities

K. 233 '05 (Aug. 9 '05)

May the Lord increase our faith, and help us to see that He desires us all to become acquainted with His ministry of healing and with the mercy-seat. He desires the light of His grace to shine forth from many places. We are living in the last days. Troublous times are before us. He who understands the necessities of the situation arranges that advantages should be brought to the workers in various places, to enable them more effectually to arouse the attention of the people. He knows the needs and the necessities of the feeblest of His flock, and He sends His own message into the highways and byways. He loves us with an everlasting love.

There are souls in many places who have not yet heard the message. Henceforth medical missionary work is to be carried forward with an earnestness with which it has never yet been done. This work is the door through which the truth is to find entrance to the large cities, and sanitariums are to be established in many places...

The Lord speaks to all medical missionaries, saying, Go work today in My vineyard to save souls. God hears the prayers of all who seek Him in truth. He has the power that we all need. He fills the heart with love, and joy, and peace, and holiness. Character is constantly being developed. We can not afford to spend time working at cross purposes with God.

There are physicians who because of a past connection with our sanitariums find it profitable to locate close to them; and they close their eyes to the great fields neglected and unworked in which unselfish labor would be a blessing to many. Missionary physicians can exert an uplifting, refining, sanctifying influence. Physicians who do not do this, abuse their power, and do a work that the Lord repudiates.

* * * * *

The Purpose of Medical Missionary Work

H. 305 '05 (Oct. 27 '05)

[64] Sanitarium work is one of the most successful means of reaching all classes of people. Our sanitariums are the right hand of the gospel, opening ways whereby suffering humanity may be reached with the glad tidings of healing through Christ. In these institutions the sick may be taught to commit their cases to the great Physician, who will cooperate with their earnest efforts to regain health, bringing to them healing of soul as well as healing of body.

Christ is no longer in this world in person, to go through our cities and towns and villages healing the sick. He has commissioned us to carry forward the medical missionary work that He began and in this work we are to do our very best. Institutions for the care of the sick are to be established, where men and women suffering from disease may be placed under the care of God-fearing physicians and nurses, and be treated without drugs.

* * * * *

Labor in Connection with the Gospel Ministry

K. 21 '04 (Jan. 2 '04)

I am glad that you see the evil influence of division. Had you put yourself where you should have been, there would long ago have been a united company, and a medical missionary Work, in connection with the gospel ministry, would have had a far-reaching influence for good. This I know; for the truth has been represented to me too clearly for me to turn away from it.

* * * * *

Make the Bible Your Man of Counsel. Your Acquaintance with it Will Grow Rapidly If You Keep Your Mind from Rubbish

B 241 '03 (Oct. 17 '03)

The one book that is essential for all to study is the Bible. Studied with reverence and godly fear, it is the greatest of all educators. In it there is no sophistry. Its pages are filled with truth. Would you gain a knowledge of God and Christ, whom He sent into the world to live and die for sinners? An earnest diligent study of the Bible is necessary in order to gain this knowledge.

Many of the books piled up in the great libraries of earth confuse the mind more than they aid the understanding. Yet men spend large sums of money in the purchase of such books, and years in their study, when they have within their reach a book containing the words of Him who is the Alpha and Omega of wisdom. The time spent in a study of these books might better be spent in gaining a knowledge of Him whom to know aright is life eternal. Those only who gain this knowledge will at last hear the words, "Ye are complete in Him."

[65] Study the Bible more, and the theories of the medical fraternities less, and you will have greater spiritual health. Your mind will be clearer and more vigorous. Much that is embraced in the medical course is positively unnecessary. Those who take a medical training spend a great deal of time in learning that which is merely rubbish. Many of the theories that they learn may be compared in value to the traditions and maxims taught by the scribes and Pharisees. Many of the intricacies with which they have to become familiar are an injury to their minds.

These things God has been opening before me for years. In our medical schools and institutions we need men who have a deeper knowledge of the Scriptures, men who have learned the lessons taught in the Word of God, and who can teach these lessons to others, clearly and simply, just as Christ taught His disciples the knowledge that He deemed most essential.

If, during the remainder of this year, our medical missionary workers would follow the great Physician's prescription for obtaining rest, a healing current of peace would flow through their souls. Here is the prescription:—

"Come unto Me, all ye that labor and are heavy laden, and I will give you rest. Take My yoke upon you, and learn of Me: for I am meek and lowly in heart, and ye shall find rest unto your souls. For My yoke is easy and My burden is light."

When our medical missionary workers follow this prescription, gaining from the Saviour power to reveal His characteristics, their scientific work will have a greater soundness. Because the Word of God has been neglected, strange things have been done in the medical missionary work of late. The Lord cannot accept the present showing.

Study the Word, which God in His wisdom and love and goodness has made so plain and simple. The sixth chapter of John tells us that (what) is meant by a study of the Word. The principles revealed in the Scriptures are to be brought home to the soul. We are to eat the Word of God, that is, we are not to depart from its precepts. We are to bring its truths into our daily lives, grasping the mysteries of godliness.

Pray to God. Commune with Him. Prove the very mind of God, as those who are striving for eternal life, and who must have a knowledge of His will. You can reveal the truth only as you know it in Christ. You are to receive and assimilate His words; they are to become part of yourselves. This is what is meant by eating the flesh and drinking the blood of the Son of God. You are to live by every word that proceedeth out of the mouth of God,—that is, what God has revealed. Not all has been revealed, we could not bear such a revelation. But God has revealed all that is necessary for our salvation. We are not to leave His Word for the suppositions of men.

Obtain an experimental knowledge of God by wearing the yoke of Christ. He gives wisdom to the meek and lowly, enabling them to judge of what is truth, bringing to light the why and wherefore, pointing out the results of certain actions. The Holy Spirit teaches the student of the Scriptures to judge all things by the standard of righteousness and truth and justice. The divine revelation supplies him with the knowledge that he needs.

And the needed knowledge will be given to all who come to Christ, receiving and practising His teachings, making His words a part of their lives. Those who place themselves under the instructions of the great Medical Missionary, to be workers together with Him, will have a knowledge that the world, with all its traditionary lore, cannot supply.

Make the Bible the man of your counsel. Your acquaintance with it will grow rapidly if you keep your mind free from the rubbish of the world. The more the Bible is studied, the deeper will be your knowledge of God. The truths of His word will be written in your soul, making an ineffaceable impression.

Not only will the student himself be benefited by a study of the Word of God. His study is life and salvation to all with whom he associates. He will feel a sacred responsibility to impart the knowledge that he receives. His life will reveal the help and strength that he receives from communion with the Word. The sanctification of the Spirit will be seen in thought, word and deed. All that he says and does will proclaim that God is light and in Him is no darkness at all. Of such ones the Lord Jesus can indeed say, "Ye are laborers together with God."

* * * * *

Nurses as Missionary Evangelists

Ms. 71 '03 (June 18 '03)

Christ the great Medical Missionary, is our example- Of Him it is written, that He "went about all Galilee, teaching in their synagogues, and preaching the gospel of the kingdom, and healing [all manner of sickness and disease among the people." He healed] the sick [and preached the gospel.] In His service, healing and teaching were linked closely together. Today they are not to be separated.

The nurses in this institution (St. Helena San.) are to be fitted up to go out as medical missionary evangelists, uniting the ministry of the Word with their ministry of physical healing...

We must let our light shine amid the moral darkness. Many who are now in darkness, as they see a reflection of the light of the world, will realize that they have a hope of salvation. Your light may be small, but remember that it is what God has given you, and that He holds you responsible to let it shine forth. Some one may light his taper from yours, and his light may be the means of leading others out from the darkness. [67]

All around us are doors open for service. We should become acquainted with our neighbors, and seek to draw them to Christ. As we do this, He will approve and cooperate with us...

Often the inhabitants of a city where Christ labored wished Him to stay with them and continue to work among them. But He would tell them that He must go to cities that had not heard the truths that He had to present. After He had given the truth to those in one place, He left them to build upon what He had given them, while He went to another place. His methods of labor are to be followed today by those to whom He has left His work. We are to go from place to place, carrying the message. As soon as the truth has been proclaimed in one place, we are to go to warn others.

* * * * *

Physicians and Nurses to Unite with Ministers in Soul-Saving Work

p. 220 '03 (Oct. 14 '03)

If right principles had been followed the relation existing between the physicians and their brethren would be exactly what the Lord designed it to be; but for years an effort has been put forth to make the medical missionary work the body. God designs that the medical missionary work shall be bound up with the gospel ministry.

God has chosen a people out of the world, and has instructed them to remain forever separate from the world. While living in the world they are not to be of the world. Dr. Kellogg has bound himself with worldlings by inviting them into his councils; and he has been dishonoring the sacredness of the truth by bringing worldly lawyers into connection with the work of God's people. The Lord has signified that it is His purpose to keep His people free from the contaminating influence of the world but the leaders of the medical work at Battle Creek have been working in a way altogether different from the way marked out by the Lord. The first and the second chapters of 1 Peter are full of instruction in regard to the manner in which we should labor.

[68] I would not now speak so plainly, were it not for the intense desire I feel that our medical workers shall be molded and fashioned after the similitude of Christ, in order that all their work and their relation to God's cause may be in harmony with His purpose. God calls upon every physician and every other medical missionary worker to take his stand on the platform of truth, where he shall not be influenced by any man's false theories and wrong devising. The pure, living principles of the gospel are to be respected. God has a people in His church who are laboring just as disinterestedly to save sinners, as the medical missionary workers have been laboring. He calls upon His medical missionary workers to labor unitedly with His church, and not to allow any physician to control their efforts by his authority.

The Lord now calls upon His people to unify. Let all our medical missionaries unite with our ministers in soul-saving work.

Nothing should be allowed to stand in the way of perfect, complete unity between the medical missionary workers and the gospel ministry. God has not empowered Dr. Kellogg with spiritual grace to be a lord over all our physicians and other medical missionaries. It is time that the teachings of the great Medical Missionary should be brought into the life-practices of our Medical Missionary workers. It is time that God's voice should be heard; for His words, spoken in truth, are spirit and life. He never makes a mistake.

If Dr. Kellogg would unite with His ministering brethren and give them his confidence, believing that they will work as Christ works through them, then he himself could see that others should be granted the privilege of standing in their God-given lot and place, and that he should respect all whom God has called as gospel missionaries to work in His cause. Working as Christ worked, our brethren would not be divided at all. But so long as our brother determines to carry things in his own way, irrespective of the Lord's workers, as if he were the only man whom heaven could acknowledge as a leader, God is displeased. If he were to occupy his proper place, he would be respected; but never is he to be regarded as he has regarded himself,—as chief of all the medical missionary workers; as one who has the privilege of consulting only those who exalt him, and of ignoring as not worthy of acting a part in the great medical missionary work, all the gospel ministers who disapprove of some of his ideas.

✶ ✶ ✶ ✶ ✶

Companies Organized and Educated Most Thoroughly to Work as Nurses, as Evangelists, as Ministers, as Canvassers

Ms. 25 '03 (Copied April 9 '03)

No arrangements should be made to gather a large number of students at any one place. For just as surely as this is done, the stamp of the educator's mold will be imparted to the student's mind and character. If the mind of the teacher is radical, or if it is not complete, where it ought to be perfect through Christ Jesus, the students will show the defective stamp.

[69]   There should be companies organized, and educated most thoroughly to work as nurses, as evangelists, as ministers, as canvassers, as gospel students to perfect a character after the divine similitude. To prepare to receive the higher education in the school above, is now to be our purpose.

* * * * *

MS. 125, '03 (Copied Oct. 16, 1903)

In the gospel medical missionary work there are noble men who bear aloft the banner upon which is inscribed, the commandments of God and the faith of Jesus. Consideration should be given to these faithful missionaries. They are not to be left to the caprice of men who are neither cold nor hot, and who because of their lukewarm condition are an offense to God...

* * * * *

Plans for Medical Missionary Work

Young men who have a practical knowledge of how to treat the sick, are now to be sent out to do gospel medical missionary work, in connection with more experienced gospel workers. If these young men will give themselves to the study of the Word, they will become successful evangelists. The ministers with whom these young men labor are to give them the same opportunity to learn that Elijah gave Elisha. They are to show them how to teach the truth to others. Where it is possible these young men should visit the hospitals, and in some cases they may connect with them for awhile, laboring disinterestedly. The purest example of unselfishness is now to be shown by our medical missionary workers. With the knowledge and experience gained by practical work, they are to go out to give treatment to the sick. As they go from house to house, they will find access to many hearts. Many will be reached who otherwise would never have heard the gospel message.

Much good can be done by those who do not hold diplomas as fully accredited physicians. Some are to be prepared to work as competent physicians. Many, working under the direction of such ones, can do acceptable work without spending so long a time in study as it has been thought necessary to spend in the past.

Many will go out to labor for the Master who have not been able to take a regular course of study in school. God will help these workers. They will obtain knowledge from the higher school, and will be fitted to take their position in the rank and file of workers as nurses. The great medical missionary sees every effort that is made to find access to souls by presenting the principles of health reform.

Decided changes are taking place in our world. The Lord has declared that He will turn and overturn. Humble men, who hitherto have been in obscurity, must now be given opportunity to become workers.

To those who go out to do medical missionary work, I would say, Serve the Lord Jesus with sanctified understanding, in connection with the ministers of the gospel and the great Teacher. He who has given you your commission will give you skill and understanding as you consecrate yourselves to His service, engaging diligently in labor and study, doing your best to bring relief to the sick and suffering.

To those who are tired of a life of sinfulness, but who know not where to turn to obtain relief, present the compassionate Saviour, full of love and tenderness, longing to receive those who come to Him with broken hearts and contrite spirits. Take them by the hand, lift them up, speak to them words of hope and courage. Help them to grasp the hand of Him who has said, "Let him take hold of My strength, that he may make peace with Me, and he shall make peace with Me."

"Behold," Christ declares, "I come quickly; and My reward is with Me, to give every man according as his work shall be." God calls upon us to voice the words, "Even so, come Lord Jesus." God will do much more for His people if they will have faith in Him. Infidelity is stalking abroad through the land. Satan has laid his plans to undermine our faith in the history and the cause and work of God. I am deeply in earnest as I write this. Satan is working with men in prominent positions to sweep away the foundations of our faith. Shall we allow this to be done, brethren?

My soul is stirred within me. I shall trust in God with heart and soul. I shall proclaim the messages that He has given me to proclaim. I testify in the Lord that our youth should not be encouraged to go to Battle Creek to be made infidels. God will help us to see what can be done to prevent this. We are now to work earnestly and intelligently to save our youth from being taken captive by the enemy.

* * * * *

MS. 139 '03 (Copied Oct. 23 '03):

Then they will be able to see with anointed eyes how closely the medical missionary work is to be bound up with the proclamation of the message for this time.

The Lord has presented before me the dangers that are threatening His people who have the sacred work of proclaiming the third angel's message with clearness and distinctness. God's people must beware lest they be ensnared by unsanctified propositions. Our young people must not be placed where they will be misled by wrong sentiments. The truth is not to be blanketed. The message for these last days is to be given in no indistinct utterance.

* * * * *

MS. 141 '03 (Copied Aug '03) [71]

Medical Missionary work is yet in its infancy. The meaning of genuine medical missionary work is known by but few. Why?— Because God's money has been misapplied. Practical evangelistic work is being done (should be: "is not being done") in many places, but the workers who go (should be: "who should go forth") forth as did the disciples are collected in one place, as they have been in the past, notwithstanding God's warning that this should not be.

The men and women who should be in the field as medical missionaries, helping those engaged in the gospel ministry, are collected in Battle Creek, acting over the same program that has been acted over in the past, confining the forces, and binding them up in one place. God has spoken against this by sending His judgments on the institutions in Battle Creek. But every movement on the part of those heeding the warnings, to change the order of things, has been made very hard by the misconception of some regarding the way in which the medical missionary work should be carried forward.

God has not given us the work of erecting immense sanitariums, to be used as health resorts for all who may come. Neither is it His purpose that medical missionary workers shall spend a long term of years in college before they enter the field. Let the young men and women who know the truth go to work, not in places where the truth has been proclaimed, but in places that have not heard the message, and let them work as canvassers and evangelists. Let the teachers of these youth take them away from the place where God has indicated by His judgments that they should not be...

Many men and women will come (to the new Sanitarium in Battle Creek) who are not really sick. Workers will be required to wait on them. But this is not the work that God has given His medical missionaries. Our charge has been given us by the greatest

Medical Missionary that this world has ever seen. Standing but a step from His Father's throne, Christ said to His disciples,—

"All power is given unto me in heaven and in earth. Go ye therefore, and teach all nations, baptizing them in the name of the Father, and of the Son, and of the Holy Ghost." He did not tell them to establish a seminary in Jerusalem, and to gather together students to be instructed in the higher classics. "Go ye into all the world," He said, "and preach the gospel to every creature," "teaching them to observe all things whatsoever I have commanded you; and, lo, I am with you alway, even unto the end of the world."

[72] Do not gather together those to whom God has given this commission, and make them believe that they have to spend years in college in order to obtain a training for the Lord's work. Christ's presence is of more value than years of training. Let our young people come under the yoke of Christ, and by faith go forth as gospel medical missionaries, taking with them the promise, "Lo, I am with you always, even unto the end of the world." Let them go forth two and two, depending on God, not on man, for their wisdom and their success. Let them search the Scriptures, and then present the truths of God's word to others. Let them be guided by the principles that God has laid down.

Let our ministers who have gained an experience in preaching the word learn how to give simple treatments, and then go forth as medical missionary evangelists.

Workers,—gospel medical missionaries—are needed now. We cannot afford to spend years in preparation. Soon doors now open to the truth will be forever closed. Carry the message now. Do not wait, allowing the enemy to take possession of fields now open before you. Let little companies go forth to do the work to which Christ appointed His disciples. Let them labor as evangelists, scattering our publications, talking of the truth to those they meet, praying for the sick, and if need by, treating them, not with drugs, but with nature's remedies. Let the workers remember always that they are dependent on God. Let them not trust in human beings for wisdom, but in the One who declares, "All power is given unto Me in heaven and in earth." Thus we labored in the early history of the message."

* * * * *

MS. 97 '02 (Copied July 8, 1902)

From the light that has been given me, the medical missionary work and the gospel ministry are never to be divorced. They are to be bound together as one work. Christ is the Head of the body—the Church, and we are to work unitedly with Him. Referring to our relation to Him, the apostle says, "We are laborers together with God."

[72A]

In the days of Christ there were no sanitariums in the Holy Land. But wherever He went, He Himself was a sanitarium. The Great Physician carried with Him the healing efficacy that was a cure for every disease, spiritual and physical. This He imparted to those who were under the afflicting power of the enemy, healing their diseases and infirmities....

In doing medical missionary work we shall meet the same opposition that Christ met. He declares: "Ye shall be hated of all men for My name's sake: but he that endureth to the end shall be saved. When they persecute you in this city, flee ye into another; for verily I say unto you, 'Ye shall not have gone over the cities of Israel, till the Son of Man be come."

We are to teach others how to obtain eternal life. And we should ever remember that the efficiency of the medical missionary work is in pointing sin-sick men and women to Jesus. We are to call upon them to "behold the Lamb of God, which taketh away the sin of the world."

The life of Christ and His ministry to the afflicted are inseparably connected. And today He is the same compassionate Physician. We should let all the afflicted understand that in Him there is healing balm for every disease, restoring power for every infirmity.

The world has departed far from true principles of restoration and health. Perverted appetite and base passion have taken control of the minds of many. Too often inclination to be irritable is strengthened by cultivation. Ill temper, cherished, destroys the delicate, pure, holy perceptions of the soul. Satan desires to cause us to be worried and harassed over mere trifles, so that we shall lose sight of the weighty matters pertaining to our eternal welfare.

The Lord desires every one to do his best. You may think that you can do very little; but remember that in the parable of the talents, Christ did not represent all the servants as receiving the same amount.

To one servant was given five talents; to another, two, and to still another, one. If you have but one talent, use it wisely, increasing it by putting it out to the exchangers. Do what you can to roll back the wave of disease and suffering that is sweeping over our world. Come up to the help of the Lord, to the help of the Lord against the mighty powers of darkness.

[72B] This medical dispensary work that Brother Sadler has outlined to us, is similar to the work that we did in Australia. While we were in Cooranbong, there was no physician within many miles of us; and my nurse, a woman of experience in treating the sick, took the place of a physician in our community. She responded to the many calls made, traveling from place to place and doing the work that God wants many others to do. In this line of work, some cannot do as much as others, but every one is to do what he can to relieve suffering. God desires every one of His children to have intelligence and knowledge, so that with unmistakable clearness and power His glory shall be revealed in our world.

* * * * *

MS. 14 '04 (Copied Feb. 3, '04)

Into the medical missionary work there must be brought more of a yearning for souls. It was this yearning that filled the hearts of those who established our first medical institution. Christ is to be present in the sick-room, filling the heart of the physician with the fragrance of His love. When his life is such that Christ can go with him to the bedside of the sick, there will come to them the conviction that he, the compassionate Saviour, is present, and this conviction will do much to restore them to health.

In word and deed the physicians and nurses in our medical institutions are to say, so plainly that it cannot be misunderstood, "God is in this place," to save, not to destroy. Christ invites our physicians to become acquainted with Him. When they respond to His invitation, they will know that they receive the things they ask for. Their minds will be enlightened by wisdom from above. Constantly beholding the Saviour, they will become more and more like Him, till at last it can be said of them in the heavenly courts, "Ye are complete in Him." Christ has pledged Himself to give His disciples what they ask for in His name. As they labor in harmony with Him, they can ask Him to aid them in every time of need.

* * * * *

MS. 62 '04 (Copied June 25, '04)

Read the eighth chapter of Matthew, and learn from it how Christ united the ministry of the Word with medical missionary work. Study the methods of the great Healer, and labor as He labored.

* * * * *

K. 180 '03 (Copied March 5, '03)

Those who profess to be medical missionaries are to be consecrated, working for the best interests of the world, yet not ensnared with the wiles of the world. The Lord desires you to be a vessel unto honor...

The following words outline true gospel missionary work,—the work in which all will engage who are truly converted: (See the MS. for many Scriptures.)

* * * * *

W. 202 '03 (Copied Sept. 11, '03)

Medical missionary workers are needed in the Southern field, who can engage in sanitarium work. Sanitariums are needed, in which successful medical and surgical work can be done. These institutions, conducted in accordance with the will of God, would remove prejudice, and call our work into favorable notice. The highest aim of the workers in these institutions is to be the spiritual health of the patients. Successful evangelistic work can be done in connection with medical missionary work. It is as these lines of work are united that we may expect to gather the most precious fruit for the Lord.

From the instruction that the Lord has given me from time to time, I know that there should be workers who make medical evangelistic tours among the towns and villages. Those who do this work will gather a rich harvest of souls, both from the higher and the lower classes. The way for this work is best prepared by the efforts of the faithful canvasser.

Many will be called into the field to labor from house to house, giving Bible readings, and praying with those who are interested.

It is of the utmost importance that harmony exist in our institutions. Better for the work to be crippled than for workers who are not fully devoted to be employed. It is unconsecrated, unconverted men who have been spoiling the work of God. The Lord has no use whatever for men who are not wholly consecrated to His service.

The hearts and interests of God's workers should be one. The workers should be bound up with Christ, and should esteem one another highly for their work's sake...

* * * * *

I. 42 '98 (Copied May 19, '98)

A most decided work need to be done in our churches in Michigan. There has been a lack of cooperation and harmonious action, but if you will all draw steadily in Bible lines, a change will be wrought in the churches.....

I hope that now, as never before, you will all,—ministers and church members—come up to the help of the Lord, to the help of the Lord against the mighty powers of darkness. But I have written so much matter that I need not write largely to you. I will inquire why some of our ministerial brethren are so far behind in proclaiming the exalted theme of temperance? Why is it that greater interest is not shown in health reform? There are many who nourish and keep alive a constant prejudice against Dr. Kellogg. He is doing a large work. Why do they not fill their places in the ministry as well, as zealously as he is filling his place? Why do not the ministers of our churches do the very work that ought to have been done years ago? I am glad that some one has taken up the work that has been so neglected.

The complaint comes, Dr. Kellogg has gathered up all the young men he can get, and therefore we have no workers. But this is the very best thing that could be done for the young men and the work. (At that time, about 1898, I think.) Let us check such dates carefully, that we be not confused by Satan. Soon after above was written, Sister White found it necessary to counsel against sending youth to Battle Creek because the work grew too large and Dr. Kellogg taught considerable error mixed with much light.—Copyist, ERP)

To you, (words missing from page) as President of the General Conference, and to Brother Evans, President of the General Conference Association, and to Brother Durland, as President of the Michigan Conference, I would say, Continue to work with tact and ability. Get some of these young men and young women to work in the churches. Combine medical missionary work with the proclamation of the third angel's message. Make regular, organized efforts to lift the churches out of the dead level in which they have been for years. Send out into the churches workers who will set the principles of health reform before every church in Michigan. See if the breath of life will not then come into these churches.

A new element needs to be brought into the work. God's people must receive the warning, and work for souls right where they are; for people do not realize their great need and peril. Christ sought the people where they were, and placed before them the great truths in regard to His kingdom. As He went from place to place, He blessed and comforted the suffering, and healed the sick. This is our work. God would have us relieve the necessities of the destitute. The reason that the Lord does not manifest His power more decidedly is because there is so little spirituality among those who claim to believe the truth.

There are in our world many Christian workers who have not yet heard the grand and wonderful truths that have come to us. These are doing a good work, in accordance with the light they have, and many of them are more advanced in knowledge, and practical work than are those who have had great light and great opportunities.

The indifference among our ministers in regard to health reform and medical missionary work, is surprising. Even those who do not profess to be Christians treat the subject with greater reverence than do some of our own people, and they are going in advance of us. The word given to me for you is, "Go forward." "All power is given unto Me in heaven and in earth. Go ye therefore, and teach all nations, baptizing them in the name of the Father, and of the Son, and of the Holy Ghost; teaching them to observe all things whatsoever I have commanded you; and, lo, I am with you always, even unto the end of the world...."

Bro. Irwin, take hold of the work of health reform. If any of the ministers have the idea that the medical missionary work is gaining preponderance, let them take the men who have been working in these lines with them into their fields of labor, two here and two there. Let the ministers receive these medical missionaries as they would receive Christ, and see what work they can do. I do not think they will find them dwarfs in religious experience. See if in this way, you cannot bring some of heaven's vital current into the churches. See if there is not a class who will grasp the education they need so much, and see if they will not bear the testimony, "But God, who is rich in mercy, for His great love wherewith He loved us, even when we were dead in sins, hath quickened us together with Christ, (not aside from Christ), (by grace ye are saved) and hath raised us up together, and made us sit together (not in independent atoms) in heavenly places in Christ Jesus."

* * * * *

B 17. '05 (Copied Jan. 11, '05)

In our Washington work, wise, competent physicians, efficient managers, and nurses with the very best qualifications will be needed. Earnest, devoted young people also will be needed, to enter the work as nurses. These young men and women will increase in capability as they use conscientiously the knowledge they gain, and they will become better and better qualified to be the Lord's helping hand. They may become successful missionaries, pointing souls to the Lamb of God, which taketh away the sin of the world, and whose healing efficiency can save both soul and body.

The Lord wants wise men and women, acting in the capacity of nurses, to comfort and help the sick and suffering. Through the ministrations of these nurses, those who have heretofore taken no interest in religious things will be led to ask, "What must I do to be saved?" The sick will be led to Christ by the patient attention of nurses who anticipate their wants, and who bow in prayer and ask the great Medical Missionary to look with compassion upon the sufferer, and to let the soothing influence of His grace be felt and His restoring power be exercised. O that all who are sick and afflicted could be ministered to by Christ-like physicians and nurses, who could help them to place their weary, pain-racked bodies in the care of the great Healer, in faith looking to Him for restoration.

The nervous timidity of the sick will be overcome as they are made acquainted with the intensive interest that the Saviour has for all suffering humanity. O the depth of the love of Christ! To redeem us from death, He died on the cross of Calvary.

Let our physicians and nurses ever bear in mind the words, "We are laborers together with God." Let every physician and every nurse learn how to work for the alleviation of mental as well as physical suffering. At this time, when sin is so prevalent and so violently revealed, how important it is that our sanitariums be conducted in such a way that they will accomplish the greatest amount of good. How important that all the workers in these institutions know how to speak words in season to those who are weary and sinsick.

Physicians and nurses should ever be kind and cheerful, putting away all gloom and sadness. Let faith grasp the hand of Christ for His healing touch...

As our nurses minister patiently to those who are sick in body and soul, let them ask God to work for the suffering ones, that they may be led to know Christ, and let them believe that their prayers will be answered. In all that is done, let the love of Christ be revealed.

Every sincere Christian bows to Jesus as the true physician of souls. When He stands by the bedside of the afflicted, there will be many, not only converted, but healed, He who declared, "I am the Way, the Truth, and the Life," will be with His faithful physicians and nurses as they strive to cooperate with Him. If through judicious ministration the patient is led to give his soul to Christ, and to bring his thoughts into obedience to the will of God, a great victory is gained.

* * * * *

B 29 '05 (Copied Jan. 1, '05)

O how I long to see the work going with power in New Bedford and Fairhaven, and in many other places just as greatly in need of the truth as these places. We hope that sometime a sanitarium may be established in New Bedford. Medical Missionary workers are needed in such cities. But, dear sister, it requires talent of no ordinary ability to manage a sanitarium. Men of experience, tried and tested must take hold of the work. That part of the workers who undertake to establish such an institution are experienced and qualified, is not sufficient. For their own sake, for the sake of the institution, and for the sake of the cause at large, it is important that a complete corps of well qualified men and women be found to enter upon the work. The Lord's eye is over the whole field, and when the time is ripe for an institution to be started in a certain field, He can turn toward that place the minds of the men and women best prepared to enter the institution.

There are many lines of work to be carried forward. There is an opening for well-trained nurses to go among families and awaken in households an interest in the truth. There is urgent need of many evangelists and Bible workers in such cities as Boston and New Bedford. Such workers would find many opportunities to sow the good seed. There is work for every energetic, thorough, earnest worker. The teaching of Christ, the simple truths taught by His parables, are just as much needed today as they were when He was in the world in person.

* * * * *

O, -55 '05 (Copied Jan 30, '05)

The Lord gave me great light on health reform. In connection with my husband I was to be a medical missionary worker. I was to set an example to the church by taking the sick to my home and caring for them. This I have done, myself giving the women and children most vigorous treatment. I was also to speak on the subject of Christian temperance, as the Lord's appointed messenger. I engaged heartily in this work, and spoke to large assembly on temperance in its broadest and truest sense...

While we were in Australia we worked as medical missionaries in every sense of the word. At times I made my home in Cooranbong, an asylum for the sick, and afflicted. My secretary, who had received a training in the Battle Creek Sanitarium, stood by my side, and did the work of a missionary nurse. No charge was made for her services, and we won the confidence of the people by the interest that we manifested in the sick and suffering. After a time the Health

Retreat at Cooranbong was built, and then we were relieved of this burden.

* * * * *

B. 59 '05 (Copied Feb. 4 '05) L.B. 38, p. 173.

The nurses connected with these institutions should be prepared to exert a soul-saving influence. Those who are not rooted and grounded in the truth should not be employed. Let them first become established in the truth. Then let them learn to be ever on guard, ever seeking to make the right impression on the minds of the sick...

Nurses should always be pleasant and cheerful, and should show thoughtful consideration. They are ever to strive to do their work wisely and well, realizing that they are serving the Lord, and that in the discharge of their duties they are to live out before unbelievers their faith in the truth for this time.

Great care should be shown in choosing young people to connect with our sanitariums. Those who have not the love of the truth in the soul should not be chosen. The sick need to have wise words spoken to them. The influence of every worker should make an impression on the minds in favor of the religion of Christ. Light has been given me that the young people chosen to connect with our sanitariums should be those who have evidence that they have been apt learners in the school of Christ...

Nurses should have regular Bible instruction, that they may be able to speak to the sick words that will enlighten and help them. Angels of God are in the rooms where the suffering ones are to take treatment, and the atmosphere surrounding the soul of the one giving treatment should be pure and fragrant. In the lives of the physicians and nurses the virtues of Christ are to be seen. His principles are to be lived. Then, by what they do and say, the sick will be drawn to the Saviour...

It is to save the souls, as well as to cure the bodies of men and women, that our sanitariums are at much expense established. God designs that by means of them, the rich and the poor, the high and the low, shall find the bread from heaven and the water of life...

An experienced Christian nurse in the sickroom will use the best remedies within her knowledge for restoring the sufferer to health.

And she will pleasantly and successfully draw the one for whom she is working to Christ, the Healer of the soul as well as of the body. The lessons given, line upon line, here a little and there a little, will have their influence. The older nurses, whether they be men or women, should lose no opportunity of calling the attention of the sick to Christ. Those who care for the sick should be prepared to blend spiritual healing with physical healing. Let the nurses in our sanitariums show that in the solemn work of caring for the sick, they do not rely on drug medication, but on the power of Christ, and the use of the simple remedies that He has provided,—the application of hot and cold water and simple, nourishing food, without intoxicating liquor of any kind, with judicious exercise, and a putting away of all injurious practices. In treatment such as this there is health for the sick.

*****

To Our Brethren and Sisters in Southern California [79]

Los Angeles, Cal.
Dec. 12, 1904.

I am instructed to bear a message to you. You have a great work to do in soul-saving, but you cannot accomplish this work by following man-made plans and human devisings.

Special light has been given me regarding the character and magnitude of the work to be done in Los Angeles. Several times messages have been given regarding the duty that rest (rests) upon us of proclaiming the third angel's message with power in that city.

And now, as we see that the Lord has blessed the labor of Brother Simpson and his faithful helpers, and that large additions have been made to the Los Angeles church, it is our duty to be wide-awake to the privileges and opportunity of the hour. Wherever such an interest is awakened as that which is now manifested in Los Angeles, men of the best ability should be called in to help with the work. They should enter heartily into the work of visiting and holding Bible-readings with those newly come to the faith, and with those interested, laboring to establish them in the faith. The new believers are to be carefully instructed, that they may have an intelligent knowledge of the various lines of work committed to the church of Christ. One or two men should not be left alone with the burden of such a work.

For a long time our people in Southern California have had messages from the Lord that there should be sanitariums near Los Angeles. For want of means the work has been delayed. But not long ago a building at Glendale, eight miles from Los Angeles was purchased, and is now being fitted up for the work. I have visited the building and can say that it is beautifully situated and is well adapted for sanitarium work.

Ample treatment rooms are being added to the building, which will soon be fully equipped. Between twenty and thirty rooms are being furnished, and as soon as money is provided for its purchase, a much-needed heating plant will quickly be installed.

We hope that our people in Southern California will come quickly and heartily to the support of this sanitarium, so providently placed in our hands, and that it may begin without delay to do its work.

The Lord has not been honored or glorified by the past showing of the sanitarium work in Southern California. This work has been greatly hindered because men have relied upon human devising, instead of following the Lord's leading. Dependence has been placed upon human wisdom, and failure has been the result. But we now see a united force of workers anxious to push the enterprise forward along right lines, and we are confident that if they will follow the Lord's instruction and rely upon His guidance, He will cooperate with them.

Elder J. A. Burden has been chosen as business manager of the institution, and Sister Burden is to be bookkeeper. Brother Burden has had a long experience in the St. Helena Sanitarium. He also spent about three years in Australia, acting an important part in the building of the Sydney Sanitarium. His self-denying efforts and unselfish labors in connection with this institution were greatly appreciated.

Sister Burden is an intelligent and successful bookkeeper. Gladly would we have had her take the place of matron, but we feel that she is in the path of duty in taking charge of the accounts; for this is a most important line of work.

We are very much encouraged as we see these self-denying laborers taking hold of the work at the Glendale Sanitarium. They have had a wide experience in sanitarium work, and they understand how sanitariums should be conducted in order to be successful.

Dr. Leadsworth is endeavoring to dispose of his treatment rooms in Riverside, that he may act a leading part in the medical staff of the Glendale Sanitarium. Dr. Abbey-Winegar-Simpson is to be the lady physician, and will stand at the head of the training school for nurses. She is fully capable of filling this position. Dr. Abbott, also, will assist in the medical work of the institution.

Bro. W. R. Simpson has been chosen to act as purchasing agent. In this work he will be brought into contact with many business men, and will have opportunity to reveal the high, ennobling principles of truth. He can speak words in season to some who will appreciate the light thus given them. He is constantly to be watching for souls as one who must give an account.

These workers, each doing a special line of work, are to harmonize and counsel together, seeking wisdom from Him who never makes a mistake. Each has an important place to fill. We feel that the approval of God will rest upon this company of workers. They are to seek help one (seek to help one) another as each takes up his important line of work.

One night we seemed to be in a council meeting, and the question being considered was, How can the sanitarium work in Southern California be best advanced? One present proposed one thing and still another proposed something entirely opposite.

One of dignity and authority arose and said, "I have words of counsel for you. Never, never repeat the mistakes of the past. Men have placed too much confidence in themselves, and have allowed cultivated and hereditary tendencies to wrong, which ought to have been overcome, to control and to bear away the victory. Various lines of work are to be earnestly carried forward, for the enlightenment of those who are in spiritual darkness. Evangelical work must receive first attention, and is to be intelligently carried forward, in all lines of your medical work.

"You have," said our Instructor, "come to an important place in the history of your work. Who shall be chosen to carry responsibilities in the sanitarium at the beginning of its work? No mistake must be made in this matter. Men are not to be placed in positions of trust who have not been tested and tried. Men and women who understand the will of the Lord are to be chosen,—men who can discern the work that needs to be done, and prayerfully do it, that the mistakes and errors of the past need not be repeated."

"The one who is placed in the position of business manager," he said, "must daily be managed by the Lord. He occupies a very important place and he must possess the necessary qualifications for the work. He should have dignity and knowledge, blended with a clear sense of how to use his authority. Christ must be revealed in his life. He must be a man who can give religious instruction and exert a spiritual influence. He must know how to deal with minds, and

[81]

he must allow his own mind to be controlled by the Spirit. Wisdom is to come forth from his lips in words of encouragement to all with whom he is connected. He must know how to discern and correct mistakes. He must be a man who will harmonize with his fellow-workers, a man who possesses adaptability. He should be able to speak of the different points of our faith, as occasion requires. His words and acts should reveal justice, judgment, and the love of God. He who gave the Israelites instruction from the pillar of cloud, and led them through the wilderness into the promised land, is our leader today. We are under divine guidance, and if we are obedient to God's commands, we shall be in perfect safety, and will receive distinguished marks of His favor.

The Israelites were often suggesting their own plans. Often they refused to follow God's plans, and this always led to failure and defeat. Christ led them through the wilderness that they might be separated from all that would tend to interfere with His purposes for them. During their journey, He gave them instruction through Moses. These truths are to be gathered up and cherished by His people today, and are to be sacredly obeyed.

[82] No imagination can present the rich blessings that come to those who learn diligently of God. These blessings are secured through the most diligent efforts to advance the work in every way possible.

The throne of God is arched by the bow of promise. Every Christian worker should keep ever before him the remembrance of this emblem. A covenant-keeping God holds the reins of guidance. He is to bear rule in every home, in every church, in every school, in every printing office, in every sanitarium.

Our medical missionary work is to be to the third angel's message as the right hand to the body. Our sanitariums are one great means of doing medical missionary work. They are to reach the people where they are. The workers in our sanitariums are to be sympathetic, kind, and straightforward in their dealings with one another and with the patients. Their words and acts are to be noble and upright. They are ever to receive from Christ light and grace to impart to those in darkness. By their efforts the sick, the sinful, the prodigals, who have left the Father's house, are to be encouraged to return. God's words to these workers is, "Lo, I am with you alway, even unto the end." "Fear not, neither be discouraged; for I am thy God."

We are now called upon to show an unselfish interest in establishing sanitarium work in Los Angeles, and in San Diego. Sanitariums and treatment rooms are greatly needed in these places. A work is to be done that will open the Bible to the sick and suffering, and point them to the great Medical Missionary.

My brethren and sisters, I ask you to remember that money is needed to advance the work at the Glendale Sanitarium. Do you wish to act a part in the important work that the Lord has given us to do in that Institution? Will you now do your best to help us to secure the necessary facilities for the advancement of its work? Intelligent, self-denying, self-sacrificing effort is now needed, effort put forth by those who realize the solemnity and importance of the Lord's work. The medical missionary work given us to do means much to every one of us. It is a work of soul-saving. Christian philanthropists should step forward just now to fulfill the commission of Christ.

Let our brethren send in their gifts with thanksgiving and with prayer, that they may be multiplied and blessed by the Lord, as was the food given to the disciples to give to the five thousand. If we make the best use we can of the means we have, God will enable us to reach the multitudes that are starving for the bread of life.

* * * * *

Elmshaven, Sanitarium, Calif.
Feb. 20, '05. B.-75-05

Dear Brethren Palmer and Ballenger,

We are well pleased with the reports that Brother Ballenger has sent us of the work of the Paradise Valley Sanitarium. What we see being accomplished there is a fulfillment of what I have been instructed we might expect. For this we thank the Lord, and take courage for the future, believing that the Lord will bless and guide.

The patronage you are receiving, even before you are fully prepared to accommodate patients, has exceeded my expectations. The Lord has been good to us, and we must ever bear in mind that this sanitarium is to be made a means of communicating truth to those who know it not.

Treatment rooms should be fitted up soon. Let them be, as suggested when we were there, outside the main building. Were they inside the sanitarium, the steam from them would make an unhealthful atmosphere, which would pervade the rooms of the patients. Let us take every precaution to make everything connected with the Paradise Valley Sanitarium, healthful and wholesome.

We are made sad as we see in many places so much left undone that should be done. But the Lord will use in the accomplishment of His work means that we do not now see. He will raise up from among the common people, men and women to do His work, even as of old He called fishermen to be His disciples. There will soon be an awakening that will surprise many. Those who do not realize the necessity of what is to be done, will be passed by, and the heavenly messengers will work with those who are called the common people, fitting them to carry the truth to many places. Now is the time for us to awake and do what we can.

I have received a letter from Brother Burrill of Canada, in which he speaks of the Sunday question that is soon to be met there. He says that they especially need Brother Robinson to help them in meeting this issue. He is a native-born Canadian, and can be a great help to them at this time.

Brother Burrill has written to me because he understood that I had encouraged Brother Robinson to come to San Diego. At first I could remember nothing in regard to the matter, but after I received Brother Ballenger's letter stating that Brother Robinson was expected in San Diego soon to act as business manager of the Sanitarium, I remembered that Brother Robinson was one whose name had been mentioned in some of our councils. I think he was presented as one who was not well, and who needed a change of climate. I asked if he were qualified to act as manager. When it was stated that he seemed to have the qualifications necessary for the place, I think I said, "Then by all means let him come." But I did not present this as light that had been given me by the Lord. It was merely my personal judgment, formed from your presentation of the case.

Brother Burrill also stated that Elder W. W. Simpson is a Canadian, and that such men as he are needed in Canada. He seems to think that it is not right that Elder Simpson should be held in Los Angeles. I know nothing in regard to Elder Simpson's case, except that he has been used by the Lord in His work in Los Angeles, and that he has been greatly blessed. Over one hundred have taken their stand for the truth as a result of his labors. At the close of his last series of tent-meetings he thought of changing his field of labor, but he received a petition signed by many of the citizens of Los Angeles asking him to remain and continue his meetings. The Lord has given Brother Simpson a spirit of adaptability with wisdom to plan and carry out his work, and He has blessed him in the bringing out of leaflets, notices, and charts that have aroused the interest of the people.

I would say, let Brother Simpson labor where his message is evidently accomplishing great good. Those who have come to his meetings have given freely of their means to sustain the work that he has carried forward. At this time, when there is such urgent need of workers in Los Angeles, when the brethren are seeking to establish a sanitarium there, I dare not say to Elder Simpson, you must go back to Canada. And besides, such a move might not be best for his health. For the present let him remain in Los Angeles for the Lord is giving him marked success in bearing the message to the people. Let him give the trumpet a certain sound, arousing those who have never heard the truth. May the Lord encourage him to remain in Los Angeles until the church members are aroused to gird on the armor, and show that they have a burden to give the message. Our ministers are not to hover over the churches. They are to proclaim the truth, as Elder Simpson is doing. Let these who know not the truth be given an opportunity to hear the reasons of our faith.

I believe that Brother Simpson is presenting the truth as God would have many others present it. Some of the brethren in Los Angeles felt that he should do more in the church there. When this was suggested to me, I thought of the answer that Christ gave when the priests and rulers reproached Him for eating with Publicans and sinners. "I came not to call the righteous, but sinners to repentance," he declared. Let the work now being accomplished for these who have never before heard the truth, lead our ministers and church members in Los Angeles to arouse. Let them take hold, as they see that God is working. Let them make diligent work in repenting of their coldness and indifference and selfishness. As the church is by repentance cleansed from this neglect, and the members are converted, they will heartily engage in laboring from house to house. By teaching those who are seeking for the light of truth, they themselves will receive a valuable education.

Let no one, by precept or example, seek to draw Elder Simpson from his God-appointed work. Let all take hold with him in an effort to carry the work in clear lines. The members of the Los Angeles church need to heed every message that comes to them bidding them arouse from their stupor. If they will earnestly seek the Lord, He will give them light and life, and the quickening power of the Holy Spirit.

The message that I have to bear to the church in Los Angeles is, "Awake, and put on the whole armor of God. There is selfishness in the church that must be rooted out. Seek the Lord earnestly. Reveal in your lives the sanctifying power of the truth. Cooperate with the evangelist that the Lord has placed among you. God would have you work as fishers of men.

Pray much, and practise self-denial, that you may help in establishing the sanitarium at Glendale, which is struggling to make a beginning. Seek to make it an institution after God's order. Some can do more than others, but all can do something. There are those who, if they will deny self, may do much more than they have done, and if all will take hold in earnest the Glendale Sanitarium may be made a praise in the earth.

In securing of buildings for Sanitarium work in Southern California, we see the gracious leading of God. These buildings have been secured at a very small cost, and the Lord would now have His people build up and strengthen the work.

The Glendale Sanitarium must be furnished and equipped. There is a great work to be done for that institution. Do not discourage those who are trying to do what they can to carry on the work. Help Brother Burden and those who are placed in charge of the Sanitarium work, that they may do all that needs to be done.

I make a special appeal to the church in Los Angeles. God expects you, as a church to be purified and refined. Put away all accusing and dissension, lay aside all fault-finding and jealousy, and let every one come up to the help of the Lord. You need to arise and trim your lamps, that they may give a clearer light. All should appreciate what is being done to bring the truth before unbelievers.

Let the older members be an example to those who have recently come into the truth. I entreat those who have been long in the truth not to hurt the new converts by living irreligious lives. Lay aside all murmuring, and do thorough work in your hearts. Break up the fallow ground of your hearts, and seek to know what you can do to advance the work in Los Angeles.

Temptations are being brought in by men who have been long in the truth. The truths that we received in 1841, '42, '43 and '44 are now to be studied and proclaimed. The messages of the first, second, and third angels will in the future be proclaimed with a loud voice.

The members of the Los Angeles church need to have a deep work of grace done in their own hearts. Let every one build over against his own house. The messages given by Elder Simpson, which convert sinners, should be sufficient to arouse you also. Awake, awake, and give to the unconverted evidence that you believe the truth of heavenly origin. Unless you do awake, the world will not believe that you practice the truth that you profess to hold.

Pray earnestly. Read and study the prayer of Christ, as given in the seventeenth chapter of John, and then seek to live lives that will answer that prayer. Read also the messages given in the third chapter of Revelation. God sent His angel from heaven to give these messages. The message to the Laodicean church belongs to the church in Los Angeles, and to our churches generally. Will they arouse, and do the work that God has given them to do?

Ellen G. White

* * * * *

To the Workers in the Glendale Sanitarium

Elmshaven, Sanitarium, Calif.
March 14, 1905 B.97 '05.

We are glad that notwithstanding some delay, the property at Glendale has been secured for a sanitarium. Years ago the Lord gave me instruction that there should be a sanitarium near the city of Los Angeles. Instruction was also given that we should find properties for sale on which there would be buildings suitable for sanitarium purposes, and that we might secure such properties at a very low cost. The location of the Glendale Sanitarium meets the representation given me of places God has reserved for us. The electric cars running close by the institution make access to it very convenient.

Let all connected with this sanitarium keep in mind the purpose for which the property has been secured. The institution is to act a special part in bringing souls to Christ, leading them to love God and keep His commandments. Unless the workers have a living connection with God, unless there is seen in the institution a spirit of kindness and compassion, which will recommend Bible truth and win souls to Christ, the establishment of the sanitarium will have been in vain. Spiritual as well as physical healing is to be brought to those who come for healing.

Brother and Sister Burden, I am glad that you have a part in the work of the Glendale Sanitarium. May the Lord increase your wisdom and courage and faith. I am glad that Dr. Simpson and her husband can unite with you. You and Dr. Abbott and the other workers may do a precious work in letting the light of present truth shine forth in clear rays. Remember that you are doing a work for time and for eternity. You should have an ever-increasing faith in the promises of God's word. It is your privilege to seek wisdom and help from God. Come to the Saviour in humility, confessing your sins, and asking for strength and grace.

The Holy Spirit enlightens the mind of the one who depends on the merits of a crucified and risen Saviour, and indites a prayer of confession and repentance that is acceptable to the Lord. "We know not what we should pray for as we ought; but the Spirit itself maketh intercession for us, with groanings that cannot be uttered." "He that searcheth the heart knoweth what is the mind of the Spirit, because he maketh intercession for the saints according to the will of God."

Let no man boast that he does not confess the sins that the Lord has pointed out to him. If he makes no confession, he receives not forgiveness and pardon from God. He must go forth in sorrow, to work in his own strength. The enemy finds him in this position, a subject to be deceived.

There are many, many of this class. May the Lord open their eyes, that they may see the danger of their self-sufficiency. A superficial work is always a snare to every professed Christian. Satan finds easy access to the heart of the one who is careless and slack in his experience, and beguiles him with seducing theories that will destroy his faith in God. "He that cometh to God must believe that He is," as He has declared Himself personally "and that He is a rewarder of those who diligently seek Him."

In every sanitarium there must be kept before all in the institution the principles of true service. From the institution is to go forth light and knowledge. All connected with it are to act their part intelligently, as representatives of the truth for this time. It is that they may be trained to do true missionary work, that young people are brought to our sanitariums.

If you will cooperate with God, He will go before you, and the glory of the Lord will be your reward. Heavenly angels will break forth into singing as souls receive the great gift of God through Jesus Christ. You may assure the sick and afflicted that Christ is the great Healer. They may believe on Him, and trust in His word; for it will never fail.

"Thus saith the Lord, Keep ye judgment, and do justice; for My salvation is near to come, and My righteousness to be revealed. Blessed is the man that doeth this, and the son of man that layeth hold on it; that keepeth the Sabbath from polluting it, and keepeth his hand from doing any evil."

What a representation is here given! "My salvation is near to come,"—that great salvation wrought out for each soul through Jesus Christ, the salvation for which the prophets have inquired and searched diligently. Our Lord is soon to come to us in mercy and compassion and love. We must go forth to receive Him as a welcome guest.

[88] The Lord Jesus calls upon every one to become interestedly engaged in the work of becoming a channel of light through which the grace of Christ may flow. Jesus has said, "Ye are the light of the world... Let your light so shine before men that they may see your good works, and glorify your Father which is in heaven." In the great salvation wrought through Jesus Christ, the unbelieving world is to be helped through the work of believers. In the work you do in the sanitarium, many may become convinced that you are indeed the children of God.

"Seek ye the Lord while He may be found, call ye upon Him while He is near; let the wicked forsake his way, and the unrighteous man his thoughts; and let him return unto the Lord, and He will have mercy upon him: and to our God, for He will abundantly pardon."

"For my thoughts are not your thoughts, neither are your ways My ways, saith the Lord. For as the heavens are higher than the earth, so are my ways higher than your ways, and my thoughts than your thoughts. For as the rain cometh down, and the snow from heaven, and returneth not thither, but watereth the earth, and maketh it bring forth and bud, that it may give seed to the sower, and bread to the eater; so shall my word be that goeth out of my mouth; it shall not return unto me void, but it shall accomplish that which I please, and it shall prosper in the thing whereto I sent it."

All the promises of God's word are made on gospel terms. If we on our part will fulfill the conditions, if we will seek the Lord, while He may be found, we may claim the promise:

"For ye shall go out with joy, and be led forth with peace; the mountains and the hills shall break forth before you into singing, and all the trees of the field shall clap their hands. Instead of the thorn shall come up the fir tree, and instead of the brier shall come up the myrtle tree; and it shall be to the Lord for a name, for an everlasting sign, that shall not be cut off."

Let this message be sounded to all people, Seek the Lord while He may be found. Seek Him against whom you have been in rebellion. Let us make every effort to check the seducing sentiments that would come into our ranks. Let every soul be wide-awake to close every avenue of the soul to the sophistry of Satan, as revealed in heaven and in Eden. Let us be armed with that vigilance that shall resist his enchantments.

Ellen G. White

* * * * *

Sanitarium, California.
B.-115-'05. April 12, 1905.

Dear Brother Burden,

I hear that plans are being laid for Elder W. W. Simpson to leave Southern California to labor elsewhere. If Elder Simpson feels it his duty to go, I have nothing to say against it but I had hoped to see him extend his work from Los Angeles to Redlands and Riverside. The condition of Brother Simpson's health is such that great care must be exercised in regard to the location of his field of labor. He should have suitable help, that he may be relieved from the burden of speaking so frequently. Would it not be well if Elder Corliss and Elder Simpson could labor together?

Redlands and Riverside have been presented to me as places that should be worked. These two places should not longer be neglected. I hope soon to see an earnest effort put forth in their behalf. Will you please consider the advisability of establishing a sanitarium in the vicinity of these towns, with treatment-rooms in each place to act as feeders to the institution?

We cannot afford to allow these places to go unwarned. Instead of Elder Simpson's going somewhere else to work, would it not be better to let a determined effort be put forth to make a success of the work in these places? There are other cities in Southern California in which a work similar to that carried on by Elder Simpson in Los Angeles should be conducted. The Lord would have His ministers working zealously for those who have never heard the truth. But Elder Simpson should have someone connected with him to help him in the work.

Our people in the churches of Southern California need to arouse to a work that is necessary within their own borders. Let them awake to prayer and labor. They need more spiritual vitality. They need to be converted, that they may labor for souls. Wherever there is spiritual life, there will be an imparting as well as a receiving of light and blessings. The nourishment from God's word will be received and earnest work will be done. The act of imparting keeps open the channel for receiving. This truth our Saviour ever sought to keep before the people."

I have a message to bear to the church members in Southern California. "Arouse and avail yourselves of the opportunities open to you. While Christ pleads in your behalf, plead for yourselves, that you may be purified from every unrighteous thought, every unholy action. Make an entire surrender to God of body, soul, and spirit. Be determined to do all in your power to learn the true science of soul-saving. While the light of God's mercy still shines, gather up every divine ray.

Are you prepared to sell all, that you may purchase the field that contains the treasure? Said the apostle Paul, "I count all things but loss for the excellency of the knowledge of Christ Jesus, my Lord... that I may win Christ, and be found in Him."

Give up the self-righteousness that you have been cherishing. If the Lord permits you to behold such work as has been done in Los Angeles, seek with all humility, to act your part. Not in your own strength, but in the strength of Christ you are to ascend the ladder heavenward round by round. Make diligent, thorough work in humbling yourselves, that the old habits and practices and all evil speaking may be put away. Draw nigh to God, and He will draw nigh to you. Die to self; live to God.

Brother Burden, say to the church that the Lord will manifest Himself to all who seek Him with humble hearts. The end of all things is at hand. Let your eyes be fixed upon Christ. As the called and chosen of God, we must represent truth in its purity. Our lives are to be such that the world will take knowledge of us that we have been with Christ, and that truth may seem to them more desirable than error.

If rightly conducted, our sanitariums may exert a refining, ennobling influence, and lead many souls to Christ. The religious principles maintained in these institutions will demonstrate that there is relief for the soul, weary and sick with sin. Many are weak and sick because of disease of the soul. Let Christ be held up before them as the great Healer, Who invites them to come to Him and find rest. Tell them that the heart of Christ is drawn out in compassion and love for His blood-bought heritage. He will heal the troubled heart that looks to Him in faith.

To the poor, sin-sick soul repeat the Saviour's invitation: "Come unto Me, all ye that labor and are heavy laden, and I will give you rest. Take my yoke upon you, and learn of me; for I am meek and lowly in heart, and ye shall find rest unto your souls. For my yoke is easy, and my burden is light." There is true joy in learning of Christ.

Tell the suffering ones of a compassionate Saviour. He is the only physician who can heal both body and soul. He has given His life for the world, that men should not perish, but have everlasting life. He looks with compassion upon those who regard their case as hopeless.

While the soul is filled with fear and terror, the mind cannot see the tender compassion of Christ. Our sanitariums are to be an agency for bringing peace and rest to the troubled minds. If you can inspire the despondent with hopeful, saving faith, contentment and cheerfulness will take the place of discouragement and unrest. Wonderful changes can then be wrought in their physical condition. Christ will restore both body and soul, and realizing His compassion and love, they will rest in Him. He is the bright and morning star, shining amid the moral darkness of this sinful, corrupt world, and all who give their hearts to Him will find peace and rest and joy.

The world is filled with sickness. Sin is increasing, especially in the large cities. Death is taking away large numbers. But the great Medical Missionary invites men to come to Him. "Come unto me," He says, "and I will give you rest." "Ask, and ye shall receive; seek, and ye shall find; knock, and it shall be opened unto you."

Our part is, by believing His word, to find rest in Christ Jesus. His words are spirit and life. In believing them there is rest and peace. "Knock, and it shall be opened unto you."

Our prayers will reach the ear of Christ, and He will open unto us the rich treasures of His grace. Through prayer we are brought into communion with the high and holy One who inhabiteth eternity. He opens the door to every one who will knock.

As I think of how the skillful Physician longs to heal every sin-sick soul, I feel so anxious that those who are drawn to our sanitariums may there find what they need for the cure of their physical and spiritual maladies.

"Come out from among them, and be ye separate, saith the Lord, and touch not the unclean thing; and I will receive you, and will be a Father unto you, and ye shall be My sons and daughters, saith the Lord Almighty." This invitation will be accepted by those who are burdened for souls. They will become members of the royal family, children of the heavenly King.

The law of God is to be obeyed. Obedience is the life of the soul. It brings health and peace and assurance. Seek the Lord in every necessity, and know that you have a friend in Jesus, one who loves you with an everlasting love. He will be as an anchor to the soul, both sure and steadfast. When men and women come just as they are, He cleanses them from their sins, and they become His sons and daughters.

Ellen G. White

* * * * *

Takoma Park, D. C.
May 14, 1905. B. 139'05.
Dear Brother Burden,

Your letter has just been read. I had no sooner finished reading it than I said, "I will consult no one; for I have no question at all about the matter." I advised Willie to send you a telegram without spending time to ask the advice of the brethren. Secure the property by all means, so that it can be held, and then obtain all the money you can and make sufficient payments to hold the place. This is the very property that we ought to have. Do not delay; for it is just what is needed. As soon as it is secured, a working force can begin operations in it. I think that sufficient help can be secured to carry this matter through. I want you to be sure to lose no time in securing the right to purchase the property. We will do our utmost to help raise the money. I know that Redlands and Riverside are to be worked, and I pray that the Lord may be gracious, and not allow any one else to get this property instead of us.

We had a very pleasant trip from San Francisco to Washington. Several times a song-service was held in the car and this took well. Many of the passengers outside of our party united in the singing.

I am recovering from the cold that I caught about three weeks before leaving home. On Thursday morning I spoke in the large tent, and on Sabbath morning I spoke again. The large tent was crowded, and I am told that my voice could be heard very distinctly even by those on the seats at the very back. I shall send you a copy of my talk when it is written out.

Today, Sunday, Elder Haskell spoke in the forenoon. The afternoon meeting was broken up by a thunderstorm. The rain came through the large tent, and people were obliged to hurry away to the small tents.

A good work is being done on the school and sanitarium land here. Money is coming in for the completion of the one-hundred thousand dollar fund. Last Friday morning, at a meeting held for this purpose, about six thousand dollars were handed in by the delegates for the Washington work. A great many Conferences had not at that time reported fully, and at the end of this week, there will be several thousand dollars more to hand in.

We hope that this meeting will be the means of accomplishing much good. If the Lord sees that we are in earnest in seeking Him, He will be found of us. Oh, it would be sad indeed to get above the simplicity of the work. When we are humble enough to receive wisdom, the Lord will certainly teach us His way. I have such a hungering and thirsting after God! I must have a strong faith, and I must bear a decided testimony, which will not be weakened. Bible truth will prevail, and oh, how my heart longs to see our church-members obtaining a deep experience, which will stand the test that is before us.

Let us seek the Lord while He may be found, and call upon Him while He is near. Let the wicked forsake his way, and the unrighteous man his thoughts; and let him return unto the Lord, and He will have mercy upon him; and to our God; for He will abundantly pardon."

Let us make straight paths for our feet. The Lord will not leave those who love Him and keep His commandments to be spoiled by the enemy. A short work will the Lord do upon the earth, and He will stir His people mightily. A great work is to be done. Let us read and study the fifty-fifth and fifty-sixth chapters of Isaiah; for they contain wonderful encouragement, and the Lord wants us to bring all the uplifting possible to His people.

"Thus saith the Lord, Keep ye judgment, and do justice; for My salvation is near to come, and My righteousness to be revealed. Blessed is the man that doeth this, and the son of man that layeth hold on it; that keepeth the Sabbath from polluting it, and keeps his hand from doing any evil...

"Also the sons of the stranger that hath joined themselves to the Lord, to serve Him and to love the name of the Lord, to be His servants, every one that keepeth the Sabbath from polluting it, and taketh hold of my covenant; even them will I bring to My holy mountain, and make them joyful in my house of prayer; their burnt-offerings and their sacrifices shall be accepted upon Mine altar; for Mine house shall be called a house of prayer for all people. The Lord God, which gathereth the outcasts of Israel, saith, Yet will I gather others to Him, beside those that are gathered unto Him."

Here is the word of the Lord. Open up every place possible. We are to labor in faith, taking hold of a power that is pledged to do large things for us. We are to reach out in faith in Los Angeles and in Redlands and Riverside.

Ellen G. White

* * * * *

Takoma Park, Washington, D. C. B. 143 '05 May 23, 1905.

Dear Brother and Sister Burden,

I have been waiting to hear from you again regarding the place near Redlands, about which you wrote not long ago. I hope that this place can be secured, because I think that the Lord has made it possible for us to obtain it. If you have anything further to tell us, please do so. We do not want this place to be a snare to us; for I feel impressed that it will be a great blessing. I hope that you will send me a line when you have come to a decision regarding the place.

Redlands and Riverside must be worked, and they could be worked from the place about which you have written us. If Brother and Sister Haskell can possibly get away from Nashville, I should like them to spend a little time in Southern California...

Ellen G. White

* * * * *

**Takoma Park, Washington, D. C.,
B.145 '05 May 24, 1905.**
Dear Brother Burden,

We received your letter today. I wish to say that I cannot ask the Conference to invest in a sanitarium at Redlands. They have enough responsibilities to carry without taking upon them others. If you in Los Angeles will do your best, we will do our best. If you will do nothing, say so, and we will do nothing. If you will work intelligently, as we know you can, then we will do what we can. But if you do nothing, waiting for the Conference you will lose your chances. If you are going to depend on the Conference purchasing it, I have no hope of your obtaining it.

Can you give us definite terms of payment? Then we shall know what to tell the people. I am anxious to secure the place for a sanitarium, but if you cannot state anything definite as to the terms of payment, we are left without any certain information.

Brother Burden, if you wait for Brother Santee to work out the plans, there will be no hope at all in the matter. I will not write more till I hear something further from you. Telegraph us at once the price of the property, and the best terms of payment you can obtain.

Ellen G. White

* * * * *

**Takoma Park, Washington, D. C.
B.-153-'05. May 28, 1905.**
Dear Brother Burden,

When you wrote to me about the advisability of purchasing the property known as Loma Linda, I did not consult with anyone, because I thought this would hinder us, and I believed that we could carry the matter forward without putting the burden on the Conference. We do not desire to bring perplexity upon the Conference regarding this matter. Be assured my brother, that I never advance anything unless I have a decided impression that it should be carried out, and unless I am firmly resolved to assist.

I am glad that means is in sight to make the first payment on the place; for we ought to have it. I do not know just where to look for the rest of the money needed. I have asked Brother Washburn to let me know of anyone who would be willing to lend me some money without interest. He thinks that I could get means on these terms.

We will appropriate the proceeds of the sale of a certain number of copies of "Ministry of Healing" toward the purchase of this property. The book will soon be on the market.

By all means secure the property, if you can; for I believe it to be the very place the Lord desires us to have. We do not desire to burden the Conference. We can as a company raise the required sum, I believe. I hope that we shall see you soon, and then we can talk these matters over. We shall have to stay here for a week after the meetings close, because Willie has some committee work to do ...

Ellen G. White

* * * * *

Takoma Park, Washington, D. C.
B.155 '05 May 31, 1905
Dear Brother Burden,

.... We hope to see you soon now, but in regard to the purchase of "Loma Linda" I will say, Go ahead. I hope to be able to help by giving the proceeds from a certain number of copies of "Ministry of Healing." I can do no more, except to borrow. I wish the place purchased. Do not neglect to tell me all I ought to know. I have been looking over your descriptive letter, and I am well satisfied that the place is one we ought to have. It is cheap at forty thousand dollars. We will not leave you, but will stand back of you, and help you to raise the means. In regard to the right man to manage the institution, I am confident that we shall find some one when the right time comes.

Ellen G. White

* * * * *

Takoma Park, Washington, D.C.
 B. 223, 1905. June 2, 1905.
Dear Brother Burden,

I am much encouraged by the letters that I have received from you regarding Loma Linda. From your descriptions of the place, I believe it meets the representation which I have seen of what we should seek for as sanitarium locations. Such a place was presented to me a few miles from an important city. The city has recently been built up.

I have tried to place before our people the representations given me regarding sanitariums in the country, and I have urged upon them the necessity of establishing our sanitariums outside of the cities. I have had repeatedly presented to me the advantages of securing locations some miles out of the cities. Those who follow the counsel of God in providing places where the sick and suffering can receive proper treatment will be guided to the right places for the establishment of their work.

Let our sanitariums be located where there is an abundance of land. I can see the advantage of such a place as Loma Linda. The Lord worked to help us to secure this property. The work of this institution is to be carried forward on pure, elevated lines. It can be conducted in such a way that the truth will be presented as the rock upon which to build.

In order that our institutions shall teach right lessons, there must be connected with them men of such simplicity that they are willing to learn of the great Teacher. "To you it is given," Christ said, "to the people who keep My commandments and do those things that I have presented in my word, "to know the mysteries of the kingdom of heaven."

We are to proclaim the truth to the world, for thus the great medical missionary has commanded us. "What ye hear in the ear, that preach ye upon the house-top; for there is nothing hid that shall not be made known." "The secret of the Lord is with them that fear Him, and keep His commandments." "As many as received Him, to them gave He power to become the sons of God."

The church of Christ is dependent on Him for her very existence. Only through Him can it gain continued life and strength. The members are to live constantly in the most intimate, vital relationship with the Saviour. They are to follow in His steps of self-denial and sacrifice. They are to go forth into the highways and byways of life to win souls to Him, using every possible means to make the truth appear in its true character, before the world.

The truth is to be presented in various ways. Some in the higher walks of life will grasp it as it is presented in figures and parables. As men labor to unfold the truth with clearness, that conviction may come to their hearers, the Lord is present as He promised to be. As they go forth on their mission, teaching all things whatsoever Christ has commanded, the promise will be fulfilled, "Lo, I am with you alway, even unto the end of the world." Those who are honest in heart will see the importance of the truth for this time, and will take their place in the ranks of those who are keeping and teaching the commandments.

All that can be done to make clear the mystery of godliness is to be done. The earthly has its place in illustrating the heavenly. All nature is a lessonbook, a teacher to every one who will learn.

In His wonderful sermon on the mount, Christ used the lilies of the field in their natural loveliness to illustrate a great truth. His language is adapted to the opening intellect of child-life. The great Teacher brought his hearers in contact with nature, that they might listen to the voice which speaks in all created things; and as their hearts became tender and their minds receptive, He helped them to interpret the spiritual teaching of the scenes upon which their eyes rested. The parables, by means of which He loved to teach lessons of truth, show how open His spirit was to the influence of nature, and how He delighted to gather spiritual teaching from the surroundings of daily life.

The birds of the air, the lilies of the field, the sower and the seed, the shepherd and the sheep,—with these Christ illustrated immortal truth. He drew illustrations from the facts of life, facts of experience familiar to the hearers,—the hid treasure, the pearl, the fishing net, the lost coin, the prodigal son, the house on the rock and on the sand. In His lessons there was something to interest every mind, to appeal to every heart. Thus the daily task, instead of being a mere round of toil, bereft of higher thoughts, was brightened and uplifted by constant reminders of the spiritual and the unseen...

Our medical workers are to do all in their power to cure disease of the body and also disease of the mind. They are to watch and pray and work, bringing spiritual as well as physical advantages to those for whom they labor. The physician in one of our sanitariums who is a true servant of God has an intensely interesting work to do for every suffering human being with whom he is brought in contact. He is to lose no opportunity to point souls to Christ, the great Healer of body and mind. Every physician should be a skillful worker in Christ's lines. There is to be no lessening of the interest in spiritual things, else the power to fix the mind upon the great Physician will be diverted. While the needs of the body are to be strictly attended to, while all efforts are to be made to break the power of disease, the physician is never to forget that there is a soul to be labored for.

God would draw minds from the conviction of logic to a conviction deeper, higher, purer, and more glorious, a conviction unperverted by human logic. Human logic has often nearly quenched the light which God would have shine forth in clear rays to convince minds that the God of nature is worthy of all praise and all glory, because He is the Creator of all things.

Christ illustrated character-building by a house built on a rock, against which storm and tempest were powerless, and the house built on the sand, which was swept away. We are living in perilous times...

Ellen G. White

* * * * *

**Glendale, Calif.,
June 23, 1905. B.-183 '05**

Dear Brother Butler,

Since leaving Washington, I have had much writing and speaking to do. I have spoken twice to the Los Angeles Church. The Lord gave me a message for the people before leaving San Diego.

On our way to Los Angeles, we stopped off at Loma Linda, and visited the property that we have purchased for sanitarium work. We were taken through the different buildings. There is one large main building, which was built for sanitarium work and is well adapted for that purpose. Some changes will have to be made regarding bath and treatment facilities, but otherwise, everything is in readiness for us to begin work at once.

[101] Until this recent visit, I have never before seen such a place with my natural eyes, but four years ago such a place was presented before me as one of those that would come into our possession if we moved wisely. It is a wonderful place in which to begin work for Redlands and Riverside. We must take decided efforts to secure helpers who will do most faithful medical missionary work. If God will bless the treatments given and Christ will let His healing power be felt, a wonderful work will be accomplished.

We shall need the very best physicians that can be secured, men and women who are faithful and true, and who will live in constant dependence upon the great Healer, men and women who will humble their hearts before God, and believe His word, men and women who will keep their eyes fixed on their leader and counselor, the Lord Jesus Christ.

This work must be carried on aright. In the past, decided failures have been made in the institutions established for the care of the sick because so much business has been crowded in that the main object for which our sanitariums are established has been lost sight of. Great loss has thus been sustained. I am to urge upon our people that the proclamation of the principles of truth must be kept prominent, as the main line of work for which our sanitariums were instituted.

The Lord calls for a solemn dedication to Him of the Sanitariums that shall be established. Our object in the establishment of these institutions is that the truth for this time may through them be proclaimed. In order that this may be done, they must be conducted on right lines. In them, business interests are not to be crowded in to take the place of spiritual interests. Every day devotional exercises are to be held. The work of God is in no case to be given a secondary place. Those who come to our sanitariums for treatment must see the word of God, which is the bread of life, exalted above all common, earthly considerations. A strong religious influence is to be exerted. It must be plainly shown that the glory of God and the uplifting of Christ are placed before all else.

Ellen G. White

* * * * *

**San Jose, Calif.,
June 25, 1905. B.-161- '05**

Dear Brother and Sister Burden,

It is just daylight, and I am seated on my couch, beginning a letter to you. Our meeting here began a day or two ago, and I think there will be a good attendance of our people. On Sabbath the brethren and sisters at Mountain View turned out well. On Sabbath morning at half past ten I spoke to a large number in the big tent.

I have an intense desire that this meeting shall be the very kind of meeting that the Lord desires us to have. I hope much for the revival of the Spirit of the Lord.

I have consented to remain here till the close of the campmeeting,—one week from Monday. We shall then return to our home at St. Helena.

There are many matters to be considered, and we will need the guidance of the Holy Spirit. I pray that a right impression may be made on the minds of those present at the meeting.

The school question will receive careful attention, and we hope that matters may be so adjusted that future work in educational lines will be of a more advanced and satisfactory character. The Lord can do much through the teachers and students of our schools, if they will carry the work steadily forward and upward....

In regard to Sister Burden continuing to hold her place as bookkeeper, I think that if she would take the exercise that she should, the evils I have feared might be avoided. She should not confine herself too closely. She can be a real help in teaching others how to keep books. This is a line of education that is greatly needed, and in no case should it be neglected. But Sister Burden should be left entirely free to take up the work that she chooses. She can help with her experience in many ways. She can give valuable counsel in regard to many matters that will come up for discussion.

I have a great desire that you may both be greatly blessed in your work in the new sanitarium. I hope that Brother Reaser will move understandingly in reference to the sanitariums already in operation and also in regard to the new sanitarium. I pray that the Lord may provide suitable people to connect with this institution, people who will be a genuine strength to the institution.

Do not be discouraged if in any wise there is some cutting across of your plans, and if you are somewhat hindered. But I hope that we shall never again have to meet the hindrance that we have met in the past because of the way in which things have been conducted in some lines in Southern California. I have seen the hold-back principles followed, and I have seen the displeasure of the Lord because of this. If the same spirit is manifested, I shall not consent to keep silent as I have done.

It is the most awful thing a man can do to dethrone God from his heart, refusing to take the Bible as his counselor. The man who does this debases whatever he has connection with. Christ does not abide in his heart. The law of God is to him an empty form. He may be supposed to be a Christian, but he debases whatever he touches.

The gospel of Christ has been dishonored by being handled with sin-stained hands. Professed Christians act and speak in a way that is no honor to God. What men and women need now is thorough conversion. Every part of their intelligence should go out to meet Christ, and every part of their spiritual nature should yearn for more of Him. The Father seeketh such to worship Him,—those who worship Him in spirit and in truth and in the beauty of holiness. Let us separate from the contaminating influences of the world, and hold communion with the Saviour. Let us bring ourselves, in thought, word and deed, into conformity with the will of Christ. The Redeemer is seeking for those whose highest aim is to serve and glorify God.

The message that the Lord has given me for the church in Los Angeles, is, Through faith and diligent service you are to become one with Christ. You are to eat His flesh and drink His blood, making

His words a part of the daily life. The great Teacher will accept only the purest integrity, the most distinct representation of His words and His Spirit. Spiritual-mindedness must not be allowed to become a strange thing among us. We are to become more and more nearly conformed to Christ. The joy of the Lord, the praise of God, is to be on our lips and in our hearts. The character is to be transformed from the mist and cloud of uncertainty into the radiance of the light proceeding from heaven. The world is to be eclipsed by the contemplation of heavenly things.

I ask the believers in Los Angeles to seek for a deeper, higher experience in the things of God. The Father seeketh such to worship Him. Arise, and brace your souls for action. Take an extensive survey of the work that is to be done. Read your Bibles with an increasing determination to have a larger experience in the things of God. Stand in the light of the Sun of Righteousness.

What could induce the pure, sinless Son of God to tabernacle with men in a world filled with crime and strife and wickedness? He did this that He might better reach the lost and perishing. He suffered, being tempted Proportionate to the perfection of His holiness, was the strength of the temptation. Because of the depravity so revolting to His purity, His residence in the world was a perpetual sorrow. On every hand He saw men and women destroying themselves by yielding to perverted appetite and passion.

Christ gave His life for the life of the world. He came to this earth in the likeness of man, to present before human beings an example of the character that all must form in order to be saved. He came to bring them power to overcome all the temptations of the enemy.

O, that every soul might be awakened, and led to become a subject of the heavenly kingdom, surrendering all to Christ. The word of God gives us no encouragement that a sinner is pardoned in order that he may continue in sin. He is pardoned on condition that he receives Christ, confessing and repenting of his sin and becoming renewed. Many who pass under the name of Christian are not converted. Conversion means renovation. The sinner must enter into the renovating process for himself. He must come to Jesus. He must give up the wrong habits in which he has indulged. He must bring his unsubdued, unchristlike tendencies under the control of

[104]

Christ, else he cannot be made a laborer together with God. Christ works, and the sinner works. The life of Christ becomes the life of the human agent. It is through the renewing power of the divine Spirit that man is fashioned into a perfect man in Christ.

By the character that he is forming, every man is deciding his future destiny. In the books of heaven is made the record. There the character is photographed. There is seen a picture of the unclothed soul.

The promise is given, "As many as received Him, to them gave He power to become the sons of God, even to them that believe on His name." It is the striving souls who receive the assistance of heaven and partake of its elements. It is by test and trial that the followers of Christ are fitted to dwell with Him in the heavenly courts.

M.H.

Ellen G. White

* * * * *

St. Helena, Calif.
July 10, 1905. B-197-'05
Dear Brother and Sister Burden,

On my way from San Jose to St. Helena, I met Dr. Stewart, from the Battle Creek Sanitarium, and had some conversation with him. He is one of Dr. Kellogg's lieutenants, and I hope that you will not be deceived by any flattering statements that may be made. I know that Dr. Kellogg is doing a work which is misleading. I am writing now to put you on guard. Dr. Kellogg is sending men all around to encourage those whom they visit to take sides. Do not give the least credence to their words or plans.

We know not what tactics Satan will adopt in his efforts to gain the control. I have confidence that you will hold the fort at Loma Linda. The Lord will work for us if we will carry the work forward without binding it up with the work at Battle Creek.

I wish I could see you and talk with you. Let nothing draw you to Battle Creek. It is presented to me that every effort is being made to draw to Battle Creek our young people and those who should be engaged in missionary work elsewhere. Men must be placed in charge of the educational branches of our work who are sound in the faith and as firm as a rock to principle.

I want you to keep me posted about the money coming in with which to make the payments on the Loma Linda property. I am writing to different ones, asking them to help us at this time, and I think that we shall obtain means to make every payment. Please write to me often, and tell me what you are doing, and what the prospects are for obtaining means.

We have been passing through some very hot weather. Yesterday I succumbed for a little while, but carefulness set me right again.

W. C. White has been at Mountain View most of the time since we parted from you, working on "Ministry of Healing." He will return to St. Helena tonight or tomorrow morning.

If the Lord will, I shall attend the camp-meeting in Southern California. I am anxious that this meeting should be held in the best place. Would it not be well to have the principal camp-meeting at Redlands, securing the best help for the work there, and then hold a smaller meeting at San Diego? What is your mind regarding this? You are on the ground, and I put great confidence in your judgment. To me, it seems as if we ought to make Redlands the center for the coming meeting.

Ellen G. White

* * * * *

(From MS. 92' 05—latter portion.)

July, 1905.

The Loma Linda Sanitarium

I wish to present before our people the blessing that the Lord has placed within our reach by enabling us to obtain possession of the beautiful sanitarium property known as Loma Linda. This property lies sixty miles east of Los Angeles, on the main line of the Southern Pacific Railway. Its name, Loma Linda,—"Beautiful Hill'—describes the place. Of the 76 acres comprised in the property, about thirty-five form a beautiful hill, which rises one hundred and twenty-five feet above the valley. Upon this hill the sanitarium building is situated.

The main building is a well-planned structure of sixty-four rooms, having three stories and a basement. It is completely furnished, heated by steam, and lighted by electricity. It is surrounded with large pepper trees and other shade trees.

About ten rods away and on the highest part of the hill there is a group of five cottages. The central cottage has nine beautiful living rooms and two bathrooms. In the basement is a heating plant for the five cottages.

[109]   Prettily grouped around this larger cottage are four smaller ones, having four rooms each, with bath and toilet. An interesting feature of three of these cottages is that each room has its veranda, with broad windows running to the floor, so that the beds can be wheeled right out on the veranda, and the patients can sleep in the open air.

Between these cottages and the main building, there is a recreation building, which can be used as a gymnasium, and for classrooms and meetings.

In all there are ninety rooms. The buildings are furnished throughout, and are ready for use.

There is a post office in the main building, and most of the trains stop at the railway station, about forty rods from the sanitarium.

The seventy-six acres of hill and valley land is well cultivated and will furnish much fruit and many vegetables for the institution. Fifteen acres of the valley land is in alfalfa. Eight acres are in good

Loma Linda Sanitarium

bearing orange orchard. Many acres of land round the cottages and the main building are laid out in lawns, drives, and walks.

There are horses and carriages, cows and poultry, farming implements and wagons. The buildings and grounds are abundantly supplied with excellent water.

This property is now in our possession. It cost the Company from who we purchased it about $140,000.00. They erected the buildings and ran the place for a time as a sanitarium. Then they tried to operate it as a tourist hotel. But this plan did not succeed, and they decided to sell. It was closed last April, and as the stockholders became more anxious to sell, it was offered to us for $40,000. and for this amount our brethren have purchased it.

We must now secure money with which to complete the payments. Ten thousand dollars have already been paid. Ten thousand more must be paid in September and December, and the remaining twenty thousand at the end of two years.

Until our recent visit, I had never before seen such a place as this with my natural eyes, but four years ago just such a place was presented before me as one of those that would come into our possession if we moved wisely. It is a wonderful place in which to work for the sick, and in which to begin our work for Redlands and Riverside. We must make decided efforts to secure helpers who will do most faithful medical missionary work. If Christ will bless the treatment given, and let His healing power be felt, a great work will be accomplished. We shall need to secure competent physicians and nurses,—men and women who are true and faithful; and who can be relied on; men and women who live in constant dependence upon the great Healer; men and women who humble their hearts before God and believe His Word, keeping their eyes fixed on their Leader and Counselor, the Lord Jesus Christ.

[110]

O, how I long to see the sick and suffering coming to this institution! It is one of the most perfect places for a sanitarium that I have ever seen, and I thank our heavenly Father for giving us such a place. It is provided with almost everything necessary for sanitarium work, and it is the very place in which sanitarium work can be carried forward on right lines, by faithful physicians and managers.

The buildings are all ready, and work must be begun in them as soon as we can secure the necessary physicians and nurses. I am anxious to see the work started. For some time I have been looking for just such a place as this, with good buildings, all ready for occupancy, surrounded by shade trees and orchards. When I saw Loma Linda, I said, Thank the Lord. This is the very place we have been hoping to find.

The character of the buildings, the terraced hill, covered by graceful pepper trees, the profusion of flowers and shrubs, the tall shade trees, the orchards and fields,—all combine to make this place meet fully the descriptions that I have given in the past of the place presented to me as the most perfect for sanitarium work. Everything at Loma Linda is fresh and wholesome and attractive. The patients could live out of doors a large part of the time. The land will serve as a school for the education of patients. By out-door exercises and working in the soil, men and women will regain their health. Rational methods for the cure of disease will be used in a variety of ways. Drugs will be discarded.

Out of the cities, has been my constant advice. But it has taken years for our people to become aroused to an understanding of the situation. It has taken years for them to realize that the Lord would have them leave the cities and do their work in the quiet of the country, away from the turmoil and noise and confusion. We are thankful to God for Loma Linda. It is one of the best locations for sanitarium work that I have ever seen. At this place the sick can be given every natural advantage for regaining health and strength.

Forty years ago the Lord began to give us instruction in regard to the establishment of sanitariums, as one of His chosen ways for proclaiming the third angel's message. Men and women bring disease upon themselves by transgressing the laws of God. The laws of nature, as truly as the precepts of the decalogue, are divine, and only in obedience to them can health be recovered or preserved. Many are suffering as the result of hurtful practises, who might be restored to health if they would do what they might for their own restoration. They need to be taught that every practice which destroys the physical, mental or moral energies is sin, and that health is to be secured through obedience to the laws that God has established for the good of all mankind.

[111] Our sanitariums are to be schools in which people of all classes shall be taught the way of salvation. In them the sick are to be

taught to overcome the appetite for tea coffee, fleshmeat, tobacco, and intoxicating liquor of all kind.

In every one of our medical institutions the sick and suffering are to be pointed to the Saviour as their only hope. In the Christian life there is strength and joy and courage. Turning away from the injurious fashions of this degenerate age brings peace of mind and the assurance of the love and friendship of the heavenly Father. Receiving the Lord in simplicity places men and women where they know the meaning of the words, "As many as received Him, to them gave He power to become the sons of God."

Out of the cities, is my message. Those who have had the light, but have neglected to follow the instruction that the Lord has given regarding the location of our health institutions and our schools, will one day see the folly of clinging to the cities. They will realize how kind the Lord was to point out the right way.

Let your schools, the high and the lowly, be out of the cities. If your desire to live a heavenly life in this world, place yourselves in right relation to God. Let your aspirations be Christlike. Christ lived much in contact with nature. God's missionaries are to form their lives after the divine similitude. They are to have a close connection with Christ. His life is to be their example.

For the past twenty years the Lord has been giving the message that plants are to be made in many places. He will greatly bless us as we endeavor to carry out His will. Out of the city into the country, is the word that has been given, and this word is to be obeyed. Our sanitariums are to be established in the most healthful surroundings. We have tried to follow closely the Lord's directions in this matter, and he has let light shine on our pathway, as we have endeavored to establish sanitariums where sin-sick souls may be led to the great Healer. God declared that we should find buildings suitable for our work, and that these buildings would be offered to us at a very low price. Has not our recent experience in Southern California proved this true?

I could not but weep for joy as I saw how plainly the providence of God had been revealed in our selection of places for sanitarium work in San Diego, Los Angeles, and Redlands and Riverside districts.

Money is needed with which to establish the work in places outside of the cities, from which the cities can be worked. We must have means with which to meet the payments on Loma Linda. I ask our brethren who have means to awake to the responsibilities resting upon them, and to do what they can to help us. Those who have the Lord's money in trust should regard it as a privilege to give of their means to help to pay for a place so well adapted for sanitarium work. Gifts, and loans at a low rate of interest, will be gladly received. My brethren, it is the Lord's money that you are handling, and you cannot invest it better than by putting it into the Lord's work. Thus you will lay up treasure in heaven. I beseech you, by the mercies of God, "That ye present your bodies a living sacrifice, holy, acceptable unto God, which is your reasonable service. And be not conformed to this world, but be ye transformed by the renewing of your mind, that ye may prove what is that good and acceptable and perfect will of God."

I have had much to write in regard to the shortness of time. Our work is soon to close, and we are now to place ourselves in working order in God's way. We are not to link ourselves up with those who are not wise to discern what is the will of God."

I have had much to write in regard to the shortness of time. Our work is soon to close, and we are now to place ourselves in working order in God's way. We are not to link ourselves up with those who are not wise to discern what is the will of God. We are to come out from among them and be separate. The end of all things is at hand, and the message of warning must be given. A spirit of anger is stirring the nations, and it will soon be too late to work for the Lord. Every conceivable deception will be brought in, and the enemy will work with masterly power. Stronger and stronger will be his efforts, until in heaven it is said, "It is finished."

Ellen G. White

* * * * *

"Elmshaven", Sanitarium, Calif.
K. 233'05 August 9, 1905.
Dear Brother and Sister Kress,

....I wish to say to you that if God opens the way for the brethren in other parts of Australia to purchase property that may be used for sanitarium work, such as the place that Brother Semmens has written about, forbid them not. Utter not one word of remonstrance. There are many cities to be worked, and medical missionary work is not to be confined to a few centers.

For a long time the Battle Creek Sanitarium was the only medical institution conducted by our people. But for many years light has been given that sanitariums should be established near such cities as Melbourne and Adelaide. And when opportunities come to establish the work in still other places, never are we to reach out the hand and say, No, you must not create an interest in other places, for fear that our patronage will be decreased. If sanitarium work is the means by which the way is to be opened for the proclamation of the truth, encourage and do not discourage those who are trying to advance this work.

May the Lord increase our faith, and help us to see that He desires us all to become acquainted with His ministry of healing and with the mercy-seat. He desires the light of His grace to shine forth [113] from many places. We are living in the last days. Troublous times are before us. He who understands the necessities of the situation arranges that advantages should be brought to the workers in various places, to enable them more effectually to arouse the attention of the people. He knows the needs and the necessities of the feeblest of His flock, and He sends His own message into the highways and the byways. He loves us with an everlasting love.

There are souls in many places who have not yet heard the message. Henceforth medical missionary work is to be carried forward with an earnestness with which it has never yet been done. This work is the door through which the truth is to find entrance to the large cities, and sanitariums are to be established in many places.

Since we returned from Australia, the Lord has opened the way for the establishment of the sanitarium work in Southern California. The brethren there have found opportunity to buy several properties at a price very much below the original cost. The first of these was an opportunity to purchase the Fernando school buildings...

Not long ago a building at Glendale, eight miles from Los Angeles, was purchased and fitted up for sanitarium work. Originally this building was an expensive one, costing the owners about forty thousand dollars. There are seventy-five rooms, many of which are arranged in suites, a small one for a bedroom, and a larger one for a sitting-room. There were two bathrooms on each floor. but they were not such as would be needed in giving treatments, and new treatment-rooms have been added.

The rooms in the buildings are pleasant, and the location of the building is very good. The place is a sightly one. When Brother Burden first went to see the agent about purchasing this place, twenty thousand dollars was asked for it. Brother Burden then told the agent something of the purpose for which those desirous of purchasing the building wished to use it. He told him about our medical missionary work, and assured him that this work was carried on without any thought of making money except for missionary purposes. The agent was much interested, and was inclined in favor of the idea, and he named a sum considerably lower than the sum first mentioned. But Brother Burden told him that it would be impossible for us to pay that price, and he then said, "You can have it for twelve thousand five hundred dollars and you may consider the remainder of the price a gift to the institution."

Recently we have purchased what is known as the Loma Linda property. This property is sixty miles from Los Angeles, and is on the main railway line from Los Angeles to New Orleans. It was owned by a corporation of one hundred and fifty people, seventy of whom were physicians. But the physicians did not agree among themselves, and the place lost money instead of making it; and it was decided to sell. It continued to be a loss financially and the stockholders became anxious to sell. It was offered for forty thousand dollars, and for this price our brethren have purchased it, paying down five thousand dollars. They will make three other payments of five thousand each, and after that will have two years in which to pay the remainder, at six percent interest.

The property is a most beautiful one. There are seventy-six acres of land, twenty-three of which are set out to fruit and ornamental trees. There are twelve acres of oranges, and eight acres of plums, apricots, lemons, and grapefruit. The rest of the land is garden, alfalfa, and pasture-land.

There is one large building and five cottages, four of which have four rooms each, and one nine rooms. In all there are ninety rooms. The buildings are all furnished throughout, and are ready for use.

There are several good carriages, five horses, four cows and one hundred and thirty-five chickens.

There is an ample water supply, the property having two good wells.

I know that it was in the providence of God that we had an opportunity to purchase this property.

I wrote the foregoing last night, and this morning I am roused up to repeat the instructions that the Lord has given me in regard to establishing sanitariums. Again and again this matter has been presented to me, and one case especially has been urged upon my notice. At great cost a sanitarium was erected at Boulder, Colorado. It has been a very difficult matter to make this sanitarium what it should be, and yet meet all expenses. The effort to do this has meant a great deal of hard work and much careful study.

During the past four years one of our doctors established himself in the city of Boulder, just a little distance from our sanitarium, and began to build up a private sanitarium. This was not right, and has been to the injury of our sanitarium, which has always had a struggle to make a success and to accomplish the work which the Lord designed it to do. The action of the one who established this private sanitarium was neither just nor righteous. Were he to continue to do as he has done in the past, constant difficulties would arise. He draws patients away from the sanitarium established in the order of God. More than this, he allows his patients to have meat, while the workers in our sanitariums have always endeavored to show their patients that they would be better off without meat.

The question is, what shall be done? Here are two institutions, one endeavoring to hold up and follow the principles of health reform, and the other allowing its patients to indulge in the use of flesh-meat, and because of this, drawing patients away from the first institution. The matter is to be treated in a fair, Christlike manner. When the one who has established himself so close beside the Lord's institution, is converted in heart and mind, he will see the necessity of carrying out the principles of the word of God, and will harmonize with his neighbors. If he cannot blend with them, he will go to some other place. There are many other places to which he could go.

The question has been asked, should we sell the Boulder Sanitarium to the one who has set up practice so close to it? I answer No, No! The one who has offered to buy it is not keeping up the standard of health reform, and the Lord would not be pleased to have the institution sold to him. The Boulder Sanitarium is to do its appointed work. From it the truth for this time is to shine forth, and the great message of warning be given...

Ellen G. White

* * * * *

Loma Linda Meeting

Loma Linda, near Redlands, Calif.
M. 247, '05. Aug. 24, 1905.
Dr. John F. Morse
Dear Brother,

I write to invite you to connect with our sanitarium work in Southern California. We now have three sanitariums in the southern part of the state. Loma Linda, the one most recently purchased, is the most desirable place I have ever seen for a sanitarium. We realize that the Lord has been very gracious to us in opening the way for us to secure this plant, which was originally constructed as a sanitarium.

Upon this property there has been made an investment of about one hundred and fifty thousand dollars. Several months ago our brethren spoke to me of the place as a beautiful location with grand buildings; but they supposed that it would be valued so high that we could not possibly secure it.

Until I saw Loma Linda, I could not feel that I had seen a place that seemed in every respect to correspond with the representations I had seen of what a sanitarium should be. I had been instructed to say to our brethren that we should have a sanitarium situated near Redlands and Riverside. This institution is about five miles from Redlands, and twelve from Riverside. But I had no idea that we would be able to purchase Loma Linda, though we had heard that the owners were very anxious to sell the property.

While I was at Takoma Park attending the General Conference, I received a letter from Brother Burden describing the property at Loma Linda, and informing me that the place was offered for sale for forty thousand dollars. There were others who desired to secure the property, but we were given an option till the brethren could communicate with us. The description given by Brother Burden answered in every respect to that of places that I had been instructed would be offered far below their original cost.

This letter from Brother Burden I received one Friday afternoon. I asked W. C. White to telegraph immediately to Brother Burden that he should by all means secure the property. Some of our brethren connected with the Conference advise other-wise, fearing that the conference would be more deeply involved in debt. But I followed my telegram with a letter saying distinctly that the place should be purchased without delay. I considered that the advantages of this location authorized me to speak positively regarding this matter. I said, There is sufficient money in the hands of God's people, and if we seek the Lord, He will make their hearts willing to help in this time of need.

After writing to Brother Burden, the uncertainty so affected me that for several nights I was unable to sleep. I lifted my heart to God in prayer. With great anxiety I waited till at last word came that a deposit of one thousand dollars had been made, and the way was opened for us to secure the place.

We now have possession of this valuable property. All the negotiations have been pleasant and agreeable. Brother Burden has been a man in the right place. The former owners have every confidence in him, and seem pleased that we have purchased the place. We thank the Lord for this.

We have just been attending the Los Angeles camp-meeting and before going home I am spending a few days here, and expect to stop for a few days at the Paradise Valley Sanitarium.

Owing to a weakness in my hip, I was unable to go over the building when I was here last spring, but I could see something of the advantages of the place, and the beauty of the seventy-six acres. There are many lovely pepper trees, and other varieties of trees, the names of which I have not learned. Hundreds of happy birds sing in the branches. There is a large orchard set out to orange trees, grapefruit, plums, peaches, nectarines, lemons, pears, etc.

[120] In the cellar I see a large quantity of jellies that have been put up. Shelf after shelf is laden with jars of rich fruit. The work of fruit canning is now going on, superintended by those who thoroughly understand the business. Some of the fruit will be sent to the Sanitarium at San Diego.

The buildings here are completely furnished with nearly every essential necessary to conduct a sanitarium. Every room is furnished with a bed, and elegant and substantial furniture. The mattresses and pillows are excellent. The chairs are well selected. Many of them are very expensive. The buildings are lighted with electricity. The main building has four stories. Everything is in first-class condition. There are many articles of furniture that we could not have furnished if we had been fitting up the building. We thank the Lord for His providence that has brought us to this beautiful place.

We have also a beautiful property near San Diego. We thank the Lord for such a beautiful location and such excellent buildings at so low a cost. We must put forth every effort to fulfill the purpose of God in this institution. Suitable bath-rooms are needed there and we are asking the people to help us in making the necessary additions.

We are to take advantage of every blessing within our reach. Above all things let us seek for the excellency of the knowledge of Christ. The apostle Paul, who had received abundant revelation from God, whose judgment had been formed under the special intuition of the Holy Spirit, says, "Yea, doubtless, I count all things but loss for the excellency of the knowledge of Christ Jesus my Lord." That knowledge we must impart to others.

The knowledge of Jesus Christ is obtained through correct views of our Lord. Through the work of our sanitariums, the light of truth may shine forth to the world. To these institutions we may invite all classes of people, men and women of every denomination. We must have physicians who will reveal Christ in knowledge and in speech. We want well qualified physicians, who have a well-grounded hope in Jesus Christ.

It is through the love of Christ that we receive spiritual food, that we may break the bread of life to others. His blessings, which have gladdened our hearts, are to be communicated to those who know not Christ. We must make every provision possible to lead others to become acquainted with the Saviour.

The highest and most noble work we can do in this world is to reflect the glory of God as seen in the face of Jesus Christ. Let Christ appear through those who love the truth. Let him be seen as the desire of all ages.

How can we prepare the way of the Lord? We will present our reasonable request that He may open the way before us; then we will walk and work and act our faith. "Faith is the substance of things hoped for, the evidence of things not seen." Christ is all and in all, and we need an increase of faith.

[121]   Brother Morse I feel impressed to ask you to come to California, and connect with the Sanitarium at Loma Linda. Your talent is needed here. If you but have faith in our Lord and Saviour Jesus Christ, your health will improve physically and spiritually.

Ellen G. White

* * * * *

**Loma Linda, Calif.,
B 251-1905 Aug. 27, 1905.
Dr. Patience Bourdeau.**
Dear Sister,

We have come to this beautiful place from the Los Angeles camp-meeting, where I spoke six times in the large tent to a congregation of about two thousand. The last Sabbath of the meeting the tent was especially crowded. In order to speak so that all could hear I was obliged to take very deep inspirations, and that night I suffered with severe pain in my chest and around my heart, caused by inhaling the impure air of the crowded tent.

The Lord greatly sustained me in my work at the camp-meeting. In some of the business meetings, I sat on the platform, that I might know what questions would come up for consideration by the Conference. I was fearful lest some ill-advised moves might be made. When a resolution was brought in to change the constitution in such a way as might lead to confusion, I arose and told them that such moves should not be made so hastily. The resolution was finally laid on the table.

Brother and Sister Burden have just come in with beaming faces to tell me that they have just attended an excellent meeting on the lawn below. Brethren from Redlands, Riverside, and other smaller churches were present. One man bore a testimony saying that he had been convicted of the truth at the recent camp-meeting. He had been a Methodist, but he is in full sympathy now with our people and wishes to join with us. He handed Brother Burden one hundred dollars to be used in purchasing this place.

I was not told beforehand that this meeting was to be held; for the brethren thought I would be unable to attend. I was not very strong, but I think that had I understood what the nature of the meeting was to be, I should have been present.

Some of the brethren have promised to give of their time in helping to do the things that need to be done to put everything in order so that the institution may soon be opened for patients. We are glad to see the means coming in to lessen the debt on this grand place. I have never before seen a sanitarium in a situation of such natural beauty.

I am sure that you and your mother would be happy here and I hope that you may come just as soon as you can, to connect with this institution. We want you present to counsel with us in getting everything in working order. I believe the questions concerning your work and wages can be adjusted satisfactorily.

I can not write much now, but I invite you to come, and we will all give you a hearty welcome. We do not wish you to be separated from your mother. You will be happier in each other's society. There are concrete walks leading to all the buildings, and your mother will enjoy walking around the beautiful premises. Dr. Bourdeau, your mother could not be in a better place than right here, where she can walk around, viewing the flowers and trees and the grand mountain scenery. I hope to spend considerable time here, but just how long before I will leave this time I do not know.

W. C. White was with us for two days, but he left Sunday morning in great haste for Los Angeles, Mountain View, and St. Helena.

Ellen G. White

* * * * *

Loma Linda, Calif.,
K-253, '05 Aug. 29, '05.
Dear Brother and Sister Kress,

I have just enjoyed the pleasure of reading your good letters...

Brother H. W. Kellogg from Battle Creek spent Sabbath and Sunday with us here at Loma Linda. He was astonished that such beautiful premises and such a complete equipment could be purchased at so low a price as that for which we have secured this property.

We regard this place as one especially provided for us by the Lord. Some of the brethren had spoken to me of Loma Linda as a popular health resort, conducted as a hotel, but it was not considered possible that we would be able to pay so much as it was supposed they would ask. I had supposed we would be obliged to erect buildings for sanitarium work in the vicinity of the beautiful cities of Redlands and Riverside.

Last spring I asked Brother Burden to look carefully for an opening to secure property suitable for a sanitarium in this vicinity. While I was in Washington, he wrote to me describing the beauty of Loma Linda, and stated that everything connected with the place was offered to us for forty thousand dollars.

When I read the description of the property as written by Brother Burden I recognized it as answering fully to an ideal sanitarium property such as had been presented to me. I received the letter on Friday afternoon, and I told W. C. White to telegraph Brother Burden immediately that he should secure the place. One of our brethren sent another telegram contrary to this. Some of the men connected with the conference thought that such a large place would be like an elephant on their hands. I was so burdened that for several nights I could not sleep. I feared lest the enemy might, through unbelief, keep this property out of our hands.

In the meanwhile Brother Burden had been obliged to tell the men that we would be unable to purchase the property. But when he received from me a letter of good cheer and hope, and an assurance that this was the place for which I had long been looking to correspond with places such as the Lord had shown me would be offered to us at a small part of their original cost, Brother Burden, in fear and trembling, returned to the agent, and told him we would purchase the place. Had he been an hour later, the opportunity might have been lost; for they were sending men to offer the property to other parties.

The main building contains four stories. In its entrance is a most beautiful sun-parlor. There is also a large parlor, carpeted with the very best body Brussels. The furniture in the house is of first class quality,—not fancy but durable and very handsome. We could not have furnished the building as expensively as it has been furnished by others. In this main building the furniture cost twelve thousand dollars, and has been in use less than two years.

The long halls are carpeted with fine Brussels carpet, and there are carpets and rugs for the various rooms throughout the building. There is a large roll of rubber carpet that can be used wherever it is thought best. The mattresses on the beds look like new ones. There are two feather pillows, sheets, blankets, quilts, and spreads for every bed. Every room contains chairs, substantial but very comfortable.

Besides the main building, in which there are about sixty rooms that can be used by patients, there are four-roomed cottages sitting back on higher ground. Some of these are so arranged that each room is connected with a private veranda, where in warm weather, a bed can be rolled from the room through the large windows. Besides the four cottages with four rooms each, there is a two-story cottage with nine beautiful rooms, splendidly furnished. This of itself is quite a large building.

Between the cottages and the main building is what they called the amusements building. This has been used for a bowling alley and a billiard hall. The billiard table will be sold; and with a few alterations the building may be made into a good meeting-house.

There are seventy-six acres of land in this property, quite a portion of it is set out in orchard. They raise oranges, lemons, grapefruit, peaches, apples, plums, pears, etc. I am having strawberries from the second crop, and they are very nice.

Five horses, three cows, about a hundred hens and a few turkeys were purchased with the place. There were also a number of hogs, which have since been sold.

About a hundred and fifty thousand dollars has been expended in making the property what it is at present, and forty thousand dollars seems very reasonable for such a complete equipment as we find here. It would be a heavy tax if we had to pay interest on such an amount, but we believe that our brethren will raise the money, and that we shall soon be free from debt. Every dollar is to be expended with great care. Something must be done to furnish treatment-rooms, but this need not incur great expense.

[124]

The city of Redlands is five miles from the institution. This city is one of the most beautiful cities in America. When President Roosevelt visited Redlands about two years ago, he expressed the thought that it was as near like heaven as any place he had ever seen. The purchase of Loma Linda will help to give us an influence with the people of this city.

The more we realize of the advantages of this location, the more certain we feel that we are in the line of duty. We shall now endeavor to secure the very best help possible to conduct the work of this institution. Some of the outside stairways need to be painted, and other work must be done before we are ready to open the institution.

For a time we had to work against fearfulness and unbelief in the minds of some of our brethren. There are some who will always be found holding back when any advance move is to be made.

Last June a meeting was called at Los Angeles to consider the question of purchasing Loma Linda. I was very glad that Elder Irwin was present. When some expressed themselves as thinking it was unwise for the Conference to incur further indebtedness, by such a heavy investment, Elder Irwin spoke right to the point, urging them to follow the manifest leadings of God.

I also bore my testimony that the Lord would bless us if we would act in faith. There are some who seem to consider it a virtue to talk unbelief and to hold back when there should be an advance. We are hoping that there may be connected with the work in Southern California men who will act in faith.

Only a few were present at this meeting, but they expressed themselves as favoring the purchase of the property, and they pledged eleven hundred dollars as a gift to start the enterprise.

Last Sunday afternoon quite a number of our brethren from neighboring churches met on the lawn under the trees just back of the main building, and Brother Burden says they had an excellent meeting. One man said he had gone to the camp-meeting in Los Angeles, as an unbeliever, but had been convicted of the Sabbath truth. He seemed very happy, and made a donation of one hundred dollars to Loma Linda. We shall now endeavor to secure the necessary means, so that we shall not have to carry a heavy burden of interest on borrowed money.

Let us praise the Lord that He is making it possible for us to obtain such advantages, where we can help the sick to take their minds away from themselves, and delight in the beauty of God's handiwork.

Ellen G. White

* * * * *

Glendale, Los Angeles, Calif.
W.-239-'05. Sept. 4, 1905.

We have recently purchased another sanitarium property, known as Loma Linda. I am most grateful to the Lord for making it possible for us to secure this property. It lies sixty miles east of Los Angeles, on the main line of the Southern Pacific Railway. Its name, Loma Linda,—"Beautiful Hill"—describes the place. Of the 76 acres comprised in the property, about thirty-five form a beautiful hill, which rises one hundred and twenty-five feet above the valley. Upon this hill the sanitarium building is situated.

The main building is an imposing structure of sixty-four rooms, having three stories and a basement. It is completely furnished, heated by steam, and lighted with electricity. It is surrounded with large pepper trees and other shade trees.

The entrance steps broaden as one ascends, and from them is entered the glass parlor, a large, beautiful room, three sides of which are of glass. In this room there are ten rocking chairs, and more can be supplied if necessary. At appropriate distances, there are two decorative pillars, which look something like bowls turned upside down, and round these pillars are seats. This room opens into another large parlor, carpeted with excellent body Brussels. In this room there are three lounges, ten rockers, and some upholstered chairs.

The second parlor opens into a spacious hall, which is furnished with easy chairs. At the right of the hall, double doors open into a large dining-room. Ascending a few steps, one enters an office room, and this room opens on to a beautiful grove of pepperwood trees.

About ten rods away, on what is known as Summit Hill, there is a group of fine cottages. The central cottage has nine beautiful rooms and two bathrooms. In the basement is the heating plant for the five cottages. Prettily grouped around this large cottage are four small ones, having four rooms each, with bath and toilet. An interesting feature of these cottages is that each room has its veranda, with broad windows running to the floor, so that the beds can be wheeled right out on to the veranda, and the patients can sleep in the open air.

There is another building, which was known as the Recreation Building. In this is a billiard table, which must have cost several hundred dollars. This, of course will be disposed of. A partition runs through this building, and we have thought that one side could be used for meetings, and other side for classrooms.

[126]

The land is well cultivated, and will furnish much fruit and many vegetables for the institution. Fifteen acres of the valley land is in alfalfa hay. Eight acres of the hill in apricots, plums, and lemons. Ten acres are in good bearing orchard. Many acres of land around the cottages and the main building are laid out in lawns, drives, and walks.

There are horses and carriages, cows and poultry, farming implements and wagons. The building and grounds are abundantly supplied with water.

This property is now in our possession. It cost the company from whom we purchased it about one hundred and forty thousand dollars. They erected the buildings, and ran the place for a time as a sanitarium. Then they tried to operate it as a tourist hotel, but this plan did not succeed, and they decided to sell. It was closed last April, and as the stockholders became more anxious to sell, it was offered to us for forty thousand dollars, and for this amount our brethren have purchased it.

O, how I long to see the sick and suffering coming to this institution. It is one of the most perfect places for a sanitarium that I have ever seen. I thank our Heavenly Father for giving us such a place. It is provided with almost everything necessary for sanitarium work, and it is the very place in which sanitarium work can be carried forward by faithful workers.

The buildings are all ready, and work must be begun in them as soon as we can secure the necessary physicians and nurses. For some time I have been looking for just such a place as this, with good buildings, all ready for occupancy, surrounded by shade trees and orchards. When I saw Loma Linda, I said, Thank the Lord. This is the very place that I have been hoping to find.

Ellen G. White

* * * * *

(From a sermon by Mrs. E. G. White, MS 27, 1906. Los Angeles, Calif. Sept. 9, 1905.)

We are so thankful that God has opened the way for us to secure such favorable locations for our institutions in Southern California. He brought first to our notice the buildings now occupied by the Fernando School. When some one wrote and told me of the buildings that were offered for sale at such reasonable prices, I replied, "Lose no time in securing the property." The instruction given was obeyed and for two or three years a school has been conducted there. God calls upon you to take a greater interest in this school than you have in the past.

The Lord has wonderfully opened up the way for us to establish sanitariums. These institutions should be centers of education. They should be conducted by men and women who have the fear of God in their hearts, and who can speak words in season, bringing to troubled souls the comfort of the grace of God. This is the work that should be done in every sanitarium.

For a long time we have desired to see a work begun in Redlands. Now, in the providence of God, we have come into possession of Loma Linda. This will give us an influence in Redlands and Riverside, enabling us to find openings for the proclamation of present truth. This beautiful property was offered to us at a very low price. It is completely furnished. We have only to take possession. We trust that our people will rally to the support of this institution, that it may not be burdened with a large interest bearing debt.

[127]

A Reform Needed

At this time, when Satan is rallying his forces, shall the people of God lay off the armor, and go to sleep? Shall we do nothing, or shall we remember that there is One who says, "All power is given unto Me in heaven and in earth, Go ye therefore, and teach all nations, baptizing them in the name of the Father, and of the Son, and of the Holy Ghost; teaching them to observe all things whatsoever I have commanded you; and, lo, I am with you alway, even unto the end of the world."

Many have so little faith in God that He is unable to work for them. Elder Simpson has labored diligently and faithfully in Los Angeles, and the Lord has given him success. But his success would have been far greater had the church rallied to his support, and every member been consecrated to God. Some have thought that Elder Simpson should labor for the church. The church-members should rather have assisted Elder Simpson by going to their neighbors and telling them of the truth, inviting to attend the meetings.

There is now a large number of believers in Los Angeles. Many of these should be fitting themselves to work for the Master, that the truth may go forth as a lamp that burneth. Read the fifty-eighth chapter of Isaiah. Read it over many times, and you will receive a deeper impression each time.

I have always felt a deep interest in the work in Southern California. For more than twenty years this part of the State has been represented to me as an important field. Our people should be ready to meet those who come and go, and speak to them the words of life. They should scatter the publications containing present truth. The Lord will do great things for those who cooperate with Him.

Ellen G. White

* * * * *

To the Executive Committee of the Southern California Conference

[128]

Sanitarium, National City, Calif.
B-261-1905 Sept. 14, 1905.

Dear Brethren,

I am instructed to say that where an effort is made to open the gospel work in a new field, there should be not less than two speakers, to labor together in the ministry. When Christ sent forth His disciples on their missionary tour, He sent them out two by two. This is the Lord's plan.

In opening up the work in San Diego, Elder Simpson should not be left to stand alone. There should be associated with him some one who is fitted to share these responsibilities. Elder Owen should be freed from other work that he may unite with Elder Simpson in presenting the truth to the people of San Diego.

That this may be accomplished, another Bible teacher must be selected for the school at Fernando, But it will be easier to find a suitable Bible teacher than to secure the service of one who has the wisdom and tact necessary to deal with an interest in the important city of San Diego. I ask you to unite in an effort to make such changes that Elder Owen may be released from the school work, to unite with Elder Simpson.

Elder Healey may consider that he is fitted to share this burden with Elder Simpson. But this would be a mistake. Elder Healey has neither the necessary physical strength, nor the tact and ingenuity that should be manifested by those who are engaged in a large public effort.

The Lord designs that His work shall be carried solidly. To enter a new field involves large expenses. But the extra expense of a second man to help Brother Simpson will be an investment that will bring returns. I feel to urge this matter, because so much is at stake. I pray the Lord to impress your minds to carry out His will.

I will now leave the matter with you, but I cannot free myself from the conviction that it is God's will that Elder Owen and Elder Simpson shall unite in the important work that is to be undertaken in San Diego. I entreat of you to secure some one else to give instruction in Bible at Fernando, that Elder Owen may be free to unite with Elder Simpson.

Ellen G. White

* * * * *

Sanitarium, National City, Calif.
P-265-1905. Sept. 14, 1905.
Dear Sister Peek,

During our conversation this morning, I felt greatly perplexed to know what to say in reference to your work. I love you, and I want to see you in a position where you can best serve the Master.

I do not know what would be your own choice of work. Many of our people desire and urge you to enter the educational work. If you feel that this is your duty, I am willing to release you from my employ. I know of no one who is better fitted than yourself to undertake educational work. In regard to your connection with me, I can not say very much, because you have in the past been called to so many other lines of work.

One thing I must say: If you choose to remain with me, the school work must be laid aside. If you prefer to labor in educational lines, then you must be free so that you can give your undivided attention to that work. I leave the matter entirely with you, that you may follow your own choice. I dare not decide for you. The great necessity for your efficiency as a teacher is the only consideration that leads me to be willing to release you. So many have spoken to me of your efficiency and talent as an educator that I dare not hold you. If at any time in the future you shall choose to connect with me again you will not have become less efficient.

I write this that you may not be left in uncertainty. Seek the Lord for yourself. If you feel impressed that you prefer to remain with me, I have abundance of work that you can do. If it seems to be the will of God for you to remain with me, we must take hold of the work in earnest, and not allow others to come in and give you a double burden to bear.

Now, my sister, I feel anxious that if you take up the school work, you shall not load yourself down with too many responsibilities. Make that your work, and carry it as you did the school in St. Helena. If I should act a part in the work at Redlands and Loma Linda, we may be more or less connected in preparing students for time and for eternity.

May the Lord bless you and give you much of His Holy Spirit, wherever you may labor. If it be your lot to educate students that they may impart to others the heavenly intelligence, I shall be pleased. I have always loved and respected you, and I have not been disappointed in you. The form of sound words is to be prized above every earthly thing. God is glorified by every word that leads to right action. I respect you highly, and desire you to have every advantage possible that you may make continual progression in the service of God.

In love,

D.R. Ellen G. White

* * * * *

Paradise Valley Sanitarium, National City, Calif.
W. 291, 1905. Sept. 14, 1905.
Dr. Julia A. White:
Dear Sister,

I write to urge you to connect with our sanitarium work at Loma Linda. In the providence of God, this property has passed into our hands. The securing of this sanitarium, thoroughly equipped and furnished, is one of the most wonderful providences that the Lord has opened before us. It is difficult to comprehend all that this transaction means to us.

The Lord has signified that the time has come for us to work Redlands, San Bernardino, Riverside, and the neighboring towns. I am filled with a solemn joy at the thought that these places are soon to be entered by our workers.

We need your services, my Sister, just as soon as you can come. We are hoping that we may secure the services also of Dr. Holden. Sister Sara Peek may undertake some of the lines of educational work. We are now anxious to see the work started, and we hope to see you just as soon as you can come.

I have recently spent two weeks at Loma Linda. I am sending you a booklet that will give you some idea of the property. The large main building is furnished in an expensive manner. There are also five cottages, one having nine rooms, the others four each. In some of these, the verandas are so arranged that beds can be rolled out from the rooms. The grounds are beautifully laid out. There are concrete walks between all the buildings. These walks are bordered with flowers. There is a good orchard, and ample grounds for garden. There are many eucalyptus, pepper trees, and many other varieties of ornamental trees and shrubbery. Meetings can be held in the open air on the beautiful lawns. There is also another building that has been used as a bowling alley and billiard hall. This can be utilized as a meeting-house.

We hope that you can see your way clear to connect with this sanitarium as lady physician. Your services will be greatly appreciated, and I hope that you may soon be on the ground.

Ellen G. White

* * * * *

Elm Haven, St. Helena Sanitarium,
B-272 Sept. 27, 1905

Dear Brother and Sister Burden,

We are very much pleased that you have secured the help of Miss Doctor White. It is as I hoped it would be, and I thank the Lord.

I received a letter from Dr. Holden very similar to the one he wrote to you, and I have not responded to the same yet. You know what this will mean to the Sanitarium. The man asks much, and as far as his requirements to have vacation is concerned it is right for every physician to have, yourself and wife also to have the same privilege, but I cannot see yet the true position we shall take in this matter, just how the arrangements should be made. I have written a letter to him but have not sent it as yet. I will look it over carefully today.

We have not a physician yet for St. Helena. We have no use for Dr. Sanderson and shall not give him another call. His wife is sufficient objection to his coming to St. Helena. Dr. Bush is promised to spend Sabbath and Sunday and to come to the call in an emergency. We dare not plant Dr. Sanderson and his wife on the hillside. We are afraid of the result. The Lord will send us a physician we believe, and we will watch and pray lest we enter into temptation. We see no call for Dr. Sanderson until he is a converted man.

Sister Dr. Margaret Evans has accepted an offer to accompany a wealthy lady to Europe. We would have you call for Dr. White at once. Sister Bourdeau is married and can not leave her present position until next year sometime, but she has written to Dr. White she had better go to Washington, but secure her if you have not done so. I am just about used up with continued writing.

September 6: I just came across this letter unfinished. You can read it and act I think. Dr. Holden better be secured and you prepared to work. I will send you copies of letters today if I can, if not, the first of the week. I shall not send the letter I had written to Dr. Holden. Make your terms with him for we must have someone to educate nurses for our Sanitariums. Please do your best. I have written early and late without rest and now this morning am admonished that I must rest. Be sure and call Dr. White without delay. I hope you have done this, and that her capabilities may be secured. Keep up good courage in the Lord, Brother and Sister Burden.

Ellen G. White

* * * * *

Sanitarium, Calif.,
B.-271-'05. Sept. 27, 1905.
Dear Brother and Sister Burden,

I cannot express the relief that your letter has brought to us. I thank the Lord that you are able to secure the services of Dr. Julia White. I believe she will do well. I think it well for you to ask Dr. Abbott to connect with the Loma Linda Sanitarium for the present.

While I was in Los Angeles, I spoke to you of inviting Dr. Gibbs to connect with the work in our sanitariums. What I said would not lead you to understand that he is to act as chief physician, but he can come in on trial. I hardly feel clear before God in giving him no further opportunity to be proved.

Have you learned how much Dr. Holden proposes to charge for his services? If a physician does his work skillfully, his talent should be recognized, but there is danger of our being brought into perplexity. If we introduce a new system of paying our surgeons high wages, there may be a hard problem to settle after a time. Other physicians will demand high wages, and our ministers will require consideration also.

I very much wish that Brother and Sister Haskell might be with the family at Loma Linda, and inaugurate in Redlands, Riverside, and San Bernardino a work similar to the work they conducted in Avondale and in Nashville.

I am glad that you are taking steps to have the water supply at Loma Linda pure and good. Very much depends upon having good water. We must be sure that the representations given in the books descriptive of this place are true in every sense of the word.

Last week we had an important gathering at the sanitarium here of our health food workers. I spoke to them on Sabbath, and on Sunday I addressed them for about an hour on the subject of our restaurant work. I told them that there must be a thorough reformation in the health food business. It is not to be regarded so much as a commercial enterprise. At present but little is seen as the result of this work to lead us to recommend the establishment of more places to be conducted as our restaurants have been in the past. But few have been converted by this work in Los Angeles and in San Francisco. Many of the workers have lost the science of soul-saving.

Please read carefully what is published in Testimonies, Vol. 7, regarding the health food work and the evangelical work. I feel more and more impressed that we must make diligent efforts to present the truth. I need not now write much regarding these lines of work, for the light has been in print for some time. But since these testimonies were published, circumstances have arisen that reveal the necessity for the cautions that have been given. Health reform needs a reformation, before it shall stand as God designs it should.

We need to practise true godliness in every undertaking. In all the restaurants in our cities there is danger that the combination of many foods in the dishes served shall be carried too far. The stomach suffers when so many kinds of food are placed in it at one meal. Simplicity is a part of health reform. There is danger that our work shall cease to merit the name which it has borne.

If we would work for the restoration of health, it is necessary to restrain the appetite, to eat slowly, and only a limited variety at one time. This instruction needs to be repeated frequently. It is not in harmony with the principles of health reform to have so many different dishes at one meal. We must never forget that it is the religious part of the work, the work of providing food for the soul, that is more essential than anything else.

Our young men and women should be encouraged to attend schools away from the cities, that under intelligent teachers, they may receive a training that will fit them to stand on vantage ground. How can our young people advance spiritually, while working as servants simply to prepare food for and serve worldlings? They often do unnecessary work in the preparation of foods that are not even wholesome. Shall our youth be encouraged to rest satisfied with such an education?

The Lord does not design that His denominated people shall exhaust their strength to carry on restaurants in the manner in which they are now conducted. The many complicated combinations of food that are not wholesome tend to make of the health reform a health deform.

There is great necessity for decided reforms to be made in regard to our dealings with the workers in our sanitariums. Faithful, conscientious workers should be employed, and when they have performed a reasonable amount of work in a day, they should be relieved that they may secure needed rest.

Only a reasonable amount of labor should be required, and for this the worker should receive a reasonable wage. If helpers are not given proper periods for rest from their taxing labor, they will lose their strength and vitality. They cannot possibly do justice to the work, nor can they represent what a sanitarium employee should be. More helpers should be employed if necessary, and the work should be arranged that when one has performed a day's labor, he may be freed to take the rest necessary to the maintenance of his strength.

Let no man consider it his place to judge of the amount of labor a woman should perform. A competent woman should be employed as matron, and if any one does not perform her work faithfully, the matron should deal with the matter. Just wages should be paid, and every woman should be treated kindly and courteously, without reproach.

And let those who have charge of the men's work be careful lest they be too exacting. The men should have regular hours for service, and when they have worked full time, they are not to be begrudged their periods of rest. A sanitarium is to be all that the name indicates.

Every worker should seek to educate himself to perform his work expeditiously. The matron should teach those under her charge how to make quick, careful movements. Train the young to perform the work with tact and thoroughness. Then when the hours of work are over, all will feel that the time has been faithfully spent, and the workers are rightfully entitled to a period of rest.

Educational advantages should be provided for the workers in every sanitarium. The workers should be given every possible advantage consistent with the work assigned them.

Ellen G. White

* * * * *

Sanitarium, Calif.,
H. - 305,'05 Oct. 27, 1905.

Sanitarium work is one of the most successful means of reaching all classes of people. Our sanitariums are the right hand of the gospel, opening ways whereby suffering humanity may be reached with the glad tidings of healing through Christ. In these institutions the sick may be taught to commit their cases to the great Physician, who will cooperate with their earnest efforts to regain health, bringing to them healing of soul as well as healing of body.

Christ is no longer in this world in person, to go through our cities and towns and villages healing the sick. He has commissioned us to carry forward the medical missionary work that He began; and in this work we are to do our very best. Institutions for the care of the sick are to be established where men and women suffering from disease may be placed under the care of God-fearing physicians and nurses, and be treated without drugs.

Mr. E. G. White

* * * * *

**Elmshaven, St. Helena, Calif.
B. - 309- '05. Nov. 1, 1905.**
Dear Brother and Sister Burden,

Were deeply interested in your letter in regard to the prospect of having patients almost as soon as you are ready for them. I am very much pleased with your report..

I am so thankful to our heavenly Father that for a long time He has kept before me that there were buildings that we could obtain at a greatly reduced price. This instruction kept me from trying to purchase land on which to erect buildings at large cost. The Lord has certainly prepared the way for us, and He wants us to work interestedly in securing sanitariums

I feel thankful for the school property at Fernando. And I do thank the Lord for the property at Paradise Valley. And now you can see that the Lord designs that these places should be worked. It may be that there will have to be another building secured at a distance from Los Angeles; for thus it had been presented to me. But we cannot yet reach out for more, unless the Lord should make it known that the time has come. If we consecrate our individual service to the Lord, we shall have that wisdom which will enable us to move intelligently...

I thank the Lord with heart and soul and voice that He has brought Loma Linda to our notice, that we might obtain it. I thank the Lord that He has sent you to help me carry out in determined effort that which He designed should be a great blessing to us. Redlands will be a center, and so also will Loma Linda. A school will be established as soon as possible, and the Lord will open the way. I could not but think, as I read the notice of the people flocking into Los Angeles, if Loma Linda had not been sold to us, there would now be a ready sale for it. With all the buildings in connection with the main building, we have large advantages. If we will walk humbly with God, and do according to that which He has prospered us, we will have Christ as our friend and our helper. "If any man will come after Me, let him deny himself, and take up his cross, and follow Me." These are the terms of our discipleship. Will we comply with them?

Christ was the Prince of heaven, but He made an infinite sacrifice, and came to a world all marred with the curse brought upon it by the fallen foe. He lays hold of the fallen race. He invites us, "Come unto me, all ye that labor and are heavy laden, and I will give you rest. Take My yoke upon you, and learn of Me; for I am meek and lowly in heart, and My burden is light." The offer is ours, and every advantage is ours if we will accept the terms. I am trying to do this most earnestly. We can be an example to others by our cheerful obedience to the will of God. Let us comply with the conditions, and in complying we shall find the rest we crave.

In regard to the proposition made by Brother Holden, I look at the matter as you do. We cannot afford to start out on the high wage plan. This was the misfortune of the people in Battle Creek, and I have something to say on this point. We have before us a large field of missionary work. We are to be sure to heed the requirements of Christ, who made himself a donation to our world. Nothing that we can possibly do should be left undone. There is to be neatness and order, and everything possible is to be done to show thoroughness in every line. But when it comes to paying twenty-five dollars a week, and giving a large percentage on the surgical work done, light was given me in Australia that this could never be, because our record is at stake. The matter was presented to me that many sanitariums would have to be established in Southern California; for there would be a great inflowing of people there. Many would seek that climate.

We must stand in the counsel of God, everyone of us prepared to follow the example of Jesus Christ. We cannot consent to pay extravagant wages. God requires of His under-physicians a compliance with the invitation, "Take My yoke upon you, and learn of Me; for I am meek and lowly in heart, and ye shall find rest unto your souls. For My yoke is easy, and My burden is light..

Ellen G. White

H.-245-'05.
Glendale, Los Angeles, Calif.
Dr. _____ Holden, Portland, Oregon.

Dear Brother and Sister Holden,

I have been disappointed and sorry that you did not feel that you could unite with us in our sanitarium work. If you knew how much we need you, I think you would change your mind. I know you have the ability to act a part in the work in more than one line of work. You can do good work as a teacher and as a surgeon. I ask you to come and help us here in Southern California. Sister Sarah Peck, who has been connected with my work for several years, has been telling me a little of your experience. We are sorry that you have been so disappointed. If you will come to Southern California I can assure you that you will receive a hearty welcome. We are in great need of a thoroughly trained man to act as surgeon and teacher. Come, and we will treat you as the son of the Prince of Life, your wife as the daughter of the King, and your little one as the Lord's child.

I will send you a booklet describing Loma Linda, the institution with which we wish you to connect. For sanitarium work, this place is in advance of any other place that I have yet seen.

Dr. Abbie Winegar-Simpson, with who you were associated in Battle Creek, is here in the Glendale Sanitarium. I have been talking with her about our work at Loma Linda. She holds you and your wife in the highest esteem, and is anxious that you should come to our help here in Southern California. We need the aid of your talents. We need help that you can give us a physician and a teacher.

I highly esteem your wife's mother, Sister Harris. She was one of our best and truest friends.

I think that Dr. Patience Bordeau will come to Loma Linda to act as lady physician. I am told that she is an excellent physician.

Brother and Sister Burden, my dear and faithful friends, will be connected with the institution. Brother Burden will be general manager. He is well qualified for the position. His wife will act as accountant. We hope to carry forward the work of the institution in accordance with the will of the Lord.

Dr. Holden, I write you to come and see Loma Linda. It is a grand place for sanitarium work. It is the Lord's doing that this place has come into our possession, and we praise His holy name. We realize that we are highly favored in having been able to obtain possession of this property. We are greatly pleased with it.

[140] Right around the Loma Linda Sanitarium there is a wide field for missionary effort. Redlands is only five miles from the institution, San Bernardino about the same distance, and Riverside a little further away. These cities are all important places. Elder Simpson has done some work in Redlands and River- side, and in each a neat little meeting house has been erected. But the Lord has a larger work to be done in those places. In the future I expect to spend a portion of my time at Loma Linda.

By placing Loma Linda in our hands, the Lord has opened the way for us to work these places. We are to regard the district in which these towns are situated as our special field of missionary work. We are anxious to become known to the people living in those places, and especially to those whom we can help in spiritual and physical lines. Through the power of Jesus Christ our Lord, we may lift them out of suffering, and bring them to health of body and soul. You know what joy there is in taking the weak and suffering by the hand and raising them up. You have rejoiced in this work in the past, and there is much for you to do in the future. It will bring you lasting joy and satisfaction.

A great battle must be fought. Time is short. Let us keep step with Christ. Let us by faith clasp His hand and hold it fast. He will never repulse us.

My brother, turn your mind away from your disappointment, and believe that the Lord is leading you. Trust in the Lord God, and let Him be your helper. Use your talents in advancing the most important interests. Let it be your one desire to please God and do His will. Then you will have courage in the Lord. We must all be determined to make a success of our life work, even though some have no appreciation of our efforts. If any man love God, the same is known of Him. Then make the Lord Jesus your trust always.

God sees our dangers, and knows the weight of our burdens. He remembers that we are in need of His strength, and those who make Him their trust will be enabled to resist every temptation. We shall have enemies who will plot against us because they know not the value that God places on those whom He has chosen. But the Lord God knoweth them that are His. However misrepresented and misjudged these may be, if they walk humbly before Him, He will give them help in time of need. They may be compassed with discouragements, but He who knows what is the mind of the Spirit knows all who love Him, and He will honor them.

In the work in Southern California, we need men of earnest, determined faith, and unshaken courage in the Lord. Our time to work is short, and we are to labor with unflagging zeal. I earnestly hope that you will decide to come to our assistance. Please consider this matter carefully, because we need your help. Please respond to this letter, addressing me at Sanitarium, Napa Co., California.

Ellen G. White

* * * * *

Sanitarium, Napa Co., California. [141]
H.-277'05

Dear Brother and Sister Haskell,

I thank you for your letter telling me about your movements and plans.

I think I have kept before you my expectation that you would spend a part of the winter in California. By unmistakable representations, the Lord has given evidence that a great work is to be done in Southern California.

Elder Simpson has been holding tent-meetings in Los Angeles with good results. Many souls have been converted to the truth. We thank the Lord that we have a good sanitarium at Paradise Valley, seven miles from San Diego; a sanitarium at Glendale, eight miles from Los Angeles; and a large and beautiful place at Loma Linda, sixty-two miles east from Los Angeles, and close to Redlands, Riverside, and San Bernardino. The Loma Linda property is one of the most beautiful sanitarium sites I have ever seen. There has been expended on the place more than one hundred and fifty thousand dollars, and it was purchased by our people for forty thousand. Of the seventy-six acres of land comprised in the property, about one half forms a hill which stands one hundred and twenty-five feet above the valley. On this hill the buildings are situated.

Loma Linda is about five miles from Redlands, five miles from San Bernardino, four miles from Colton, and nine miles from Riverside.

Redlands and Riverside are places which the Lord has shown me should be thoroughly worked. Elder Simpson has done some evangelical work in these places, and in each of them a company of believers has been raised up, and a meeting house built. But more work must be done there, and a work must be done in San Bernardino.

I have wished that you and your wife could come to Loma Linda, and carry on a work similar to that which you have done in other places. You could make your home at the sanitarium, and drive back and forth to Redlands and Riverside and other surrounding places. The roads are level and well oiled.

By the securing of Loma Linda, the Lord has opened the way for a work to be done in the neighboring cities and towns. The securing of this property at such a price as we paid for it, is a miracle that should open the eyes of our understanding. If such manifest workings of God do not give us a new experience, what will? If we cannot read the evidence that the time has come to work in the surrounding cities, what could be done to arouse us to action?

That you should receive an invitation to go to Battle Creek and give Bible lessons to the nurses and medical students, is not a surprise to me. I have been instructed that an effort would be made to obtain your names as teachers to the nurses at Battle Creek, so that the managers of the sanitarium can say to our people that Elder and Mrs. Haskell are to give a course of lessons to the Battle Creek Sanitarium nurses, and use this as a means of decoying to Battle Creek those who otherwise would heed the cautions about going there for their education.

I warn you against doing anything which would help those who are working directly contrary to the counsels of God, to carry out any of their deceptive plans. I know you would not willingly place yourself in any such position, and I warn you because I know the men and the plans better than you do.

If you should be drawn into such a plan, it would bring much perplexity upon me, and I should have another hard battle to fight. You must take no part in healing "the hurt of the daughter of my people slightly." Should the word go forth that Elder and Mrs. Haskell were to take part in teaching the nurses in the Battle Creek Sanitarium, it would be my duty to send forth testimonies that I do not wish to be called upon to bear.

Elder and Mrs. Farnsworth have been requested to spend some time in Battle Creek laboring for the church. I encouraged them to do so, and shall counsel them how to labor. It will be well for Elder Farnsworth and Elder A. T. Jones to stand shoulder to shoulder, preaching the word in the Tabernacle for a time, and giving the trumpet a certain sound. There are in Battle Creek precious souls who need bracing up. Many will gladly hear and distinguish the note of warning. But Elder Farnsworth should not remain in Battle Creek long. I write these things to you because it is important that they should be understood.

God would have men of talent, who will not deviate from the principles of righteousness, to stand in defense of the truth, in the Tabernacle at Battle Creek. One man should not be stationed in Battle Creek for long at a time. After he has faithfully proclaimed the truth for a time, he should leave to labor elsewhere, and some one else be appointed who will give the trumpet a certain sound.

We should understand by experience word for word the message the Lord gave to Isaiah, and from this message there is to be no deviation. The Holy Spirit's meaning will be understood. This meaning is not to be changed a hair's breadth to harmonize with any new doctrine.

We know that in the past the truth has been demonstrated by the Holy Spirit. Not one word of human devising is to be permitted to subvert minds or to add unto or to take from the message that God has given.

There must be connected with our sanitariums in various places ample facilities for the training of workers, and great care should be taken in the selection of young people to connect with our sanitariums. We cannot afford to accept every one who is willing to come. Great injury is done to our medical institutions when we con-

[143]

nect with them inexperienced youth, who do not understand what it means to do faithful service for God.

Every soul connected with our institutions is to be tested and tried. If self is not hid with Christ in God, the workers will blindly do many things that will hinder the precious work of God.

"Sanctify the Lord of hosts Himself; and let Him be your fear, and let Him be your dread. And He shall be for a sanctuary; but for a stone of stumbling, and for a rock of offense to both the house of Israel, for a gin and for a snare to the inhabitants of Jerusalem. And many among them shall stumble, and fall, and be broken, and be snared, and be taken." "Bind up the testimony, seal the law among my disciples."....

Those who have crowded into Battle Creek, and are being held there, see and hear many things that tend to weaken their faith, and engender unbelief. They would gain a more practical knowledge in an effort to impart to others that which they receive of the word of God. They should scatter out, and be working in all our cities under the training of men who are sound in the faith. If those who teach these workers are true and loyal, a great work will be accomplished.

There is to be a working of our cities as they never have been worked. That which should have been done twenty, yes, more than twenty years ago, is now to be done speedily. The work will be more difficult to do now than it would have been years ago; but it will be done.

Our work is made exceedingly hard because of many false theories that have to be met, and because of a dearth of efficient teachers and willing helpers.

It is not the work of the Lord that so many are gathered in Battle Creek, receiving a mold which unfits them for the work of the Lord, till they are thoroughly converted.

The Lord is to do a strange work very soon. A representation has been given me that I have not yet had strength to trace upon paper. I must know when to speak and when to keep silent. When the Lord bids me speak, I cannot keep silent.

The Lord will work. Great facts will be revealed in the Word. There are rich experiences to be received from the great Medical Missionary. The knowledge of salvation through faith and a full trust in a personal God and a personal Saviour, will be manifest.

Those who have held the beginning of their confidence firm unto the end will have the proof of the things which they have learned by personal experience.

The gospel will be revealed and verified. The experience of the day of Pentecost will surely be repeated. Some will receive the Holy Spirit of truth; yes, some who are now in uncertainty. The Lord has given His word. For years He has been sending messages of warning, but by many they have been unheeded. Notwithstanding the repeated urgent warnings God has given, many have been turned away from their original faith, and are lost in the fog of error. They have refused to follow the light that God has given to point out the true path.

Christ is the same Christ that He has ever been. He is our Redeemer. Those who have been striving to quench their thirst at broken cisterns, which can hold no water, need to be born again, that Christ may be formed within, the hope of glory.

There are those who will never receive the gospel message in its fullness. They will never see the greater light and working of the Holy Spirit. There is a depth of depravity in unbelieving human nature that will never be healed, because the true light has been misinterpreted and misapplied. The Lord has given His Spirit in abundance of assurance to enable men and women to understand the fallacies and errors of Satan, and to guard against them.

Some will soon turn from their deceptive errors and calculations. To these who will be born again, the Bible will become a new book. There is a higher elevation to reach. True faith is to take the place of unbelief. The living springs of the word of God, with all their rich treasure, are to flow into the soul. The truth of the Christian religion depends upon the divine authority of the word of God. The authority of the word is Yea and Amen.

Jesus Christ is the Way, the Truth, and the Life. Our great need is to have Him formed within, the hope of glory. He is to come into our individual experience, as a personal Saviour. He is the foundation of our faith, the Rock of Ages. "Blessed is the man to whom the Lord imputeth not iniquity."

When Christ shall come in His glory and all the holy angels with Him, then will all men be convinced of the truth that God hath set apart Him that is godly for Himself. But the words of Isaiah will

[144]

come to many minds. "Cry aloud, spare not, lift up thy voice like a trumpet, and show my people their transgression, and the house of Jacob their sins." The fifty-eighth chapter of Isaiah gives a wonderful presentation of truth.

I wish you could make me a visit at my home. I should indeed be pleased to see you and talk with you. Do nothing that will lead others to make of no account the long, determined resistance which has been shown to the messages sent by the Lord.

We do not want the impression left on minds that our nurses should be educated and trained in Battle Creek. You are not to remove the impression that I have been trying to make, that our people are to be drawn away from Battle Creek.

[145] I have light regarding the impression that your going to Battle Creek would make on our people who have had placed before them many falsehoods regarding the work and influences there. Your going to Battle Creek in answer to the call you have received, would not be in harmony with the light God has given me.

If you cannot understand this, I can, and I will make every effort possible to save our people from being mixed up with the methods followed by some of the Battle Creek Sanitarium managers.

The Lord would have Dr. Morse leave Battle Creek, and labor where the light of truth has not been taught, and that he may break every thread of sophistry. The sophistry that there is no personal God and no personal Christ has been set forth, and still lives, to be brought forth and fastened upon human minds. I have seen satanic agencies leading and controlling the minds of those who have taught these theories. Unless the snare is broken, ruin will result as surely as to the house built upon the sand.

Great trials are right upon us, to test every soul. The end of the world is near at hand. We are not to consent to have our workers, God's workers, tied up in Battle Creek. Out of Battle Creek, is my message. I understand perfectly the meaning of the invitation that has been sent you. You have not a sense of what it means, but I am to tell you that God has not given you the work of teaching nurses in Battle Creek, or in any way encouraging our youth to go there for their training.

We must soon start a nurses' training school at Loma Linda. This place will become an important educational center, and we need the efforts of yourself and your wife to give the right mold to the work in this new educational center, and in Los Angeles, where there are many converts.

If you see your way clear to labor a portion of this winter in Southern Calif., I think I could be with you and I will help you all I can to open up the work. If you will gather about you a group of workers, and do for a time in Southern Calif., a work similar to that which you have done in New York and Nashville, praying and working and doing the will of the Lord, God will not fail to show Himself your Helper; for you will be following where He has marked out the way.

I do not propose that you divorce yourself permanently from the work in the cities of the Southern States, but I ask you to come and help us start the work of training true medical missionaries in this very fruitful field, Southern California.

If we turn unto the Lord with full purpose of heart, teaching in the places He indicates, all things that He has commanded, we may be assured of the promise, "Lo, I am with you alway, even unto the end of the world." God is able and waiting to be gracious.

[146]

Ellen G. White

* * * * *

St. Helena Sanitarium, Calif.
B-325-'05. Dec. 10, 1905.
Dear Brother and Sister Burden,

I have received a letter from each of you. I was glad to hear the good news of $5,000 being raised, and the interest amounting to $300 being cut out. This is very favorable. I am so much pleased that Sister Burden is in the very place that will be beneficial to her healthwise. I am continually thankful to our heavenly Father that in His providence we have been favored to secure this beautiful location for a health resort. It answers perfectly to the representation that was given me, a main building and cottages so well fitted with windows. The surroundings are very attractive. Praise the Lord for His goodness and mercy expressed to us amidst the difficulties we have to meet. The Lord is our helper, our keeper and our constant guide. We may expect that everything will not move as encouragingly as we wish in our connection with the work of God, but we will praise the Lord with heart and soul and voice. I say to you, my brother and sister, Jesus will be to us a present help in every time and need...

I think Elder Haskell is on his way to Loma Linda. I have received a letter from Sister Haskell, stating that they would leave South Lancaster Dec. 7. They are precious help in Bible lines. Loma Linda is just the climate for them, and the whole place will be a delight to their senses.

Do not be disappointed if we do not come just now. I do not know of a place where I should be more pleased to be for a time than in Loma Linda. I could enjoy every bit of the scenery and all the advantages. The reason my coming may be doubtful is that I do not wish to leave my workers just at this stage of my work. I am in good health for me; better than I have been in for years, and while my mind is clear, I want nothing to interpose as an extra burden. I want every jot and tittle of my strength to reproduce the representations the Lord has given me, and to make them as vivid as possible while I can do so. This is the only reason I plead not to leave my workers... We have all the multitudinous productions of the pen to be placed in the best order to handle, and I am more than pleased with the care that is manifested in arranging everything so that it may be well prepared for me to use.

In regard to the school, I would say, Make it all you can in the education of nurses and physicians. What about Dr. Holden? Will he not become an educating force in the Sanitarium? Brother and Sister Haskell are versed in the Scriptures; and after a few weeks I may meet my son at Loma Linda. But at present I wish to advance a little more decidedly in the writings I am preparing.

We are having beautiful weather. It is almost like summer.

Ellen G. White

* * * * *

Sanitarium, Napa Co., Calif.
B.-329-'05 December 11, 1905.
Dear Brother Burden,

I have been conversing with you in the night season in regard to some matters that I will write to you about. We were conversing in reference to Brother Hansen and his manufacturing health foods. In regard to the family, you understand that Sister Hansen must be carefully cared for; because she has had lung trouble. It would be well for them to be provided with a home by themselves. They can be so located that burdens shall not come upon Sister Hansen too heavily, and where she can care for their own family. She may entirely recover from her lung difficulty, but it will be well to take every precaution. Matters can be managed so that those who need to be connected with the institution may not in any way be exposed. You and your wife may be wise on this subject and a word to the wise is sufficient...

We were conversing in regard to erecting a store, and One of authority who was in our midst, speaking to several present, suggested the propriety of erecting such a building at a distance from the main building and all other buildings that are now standing there, so that there will be no danger to them from fire. He suggested that changes would need to be made after thorough study, and that the building should be placed where the wind would not carry the smoke or sparks to the main building. Great care is to be exercised in regard to this matter, and intelligence is to be shown in the movements made...

The Speaker said, "You can all be a blessing to one another, if you open your hearts to receive the precious love of Christ. Let all keep diligent guard over their own disposition, and then pleasant words will be spoken. Let not those who are connected with the Sanitarium as helpers think that they have liberty to exercise authority over others. God will help the ones who are chosen to act a part in the duties connected with the Sanitarium, to labor as workers together with God. Let them be sure to take charge of their own individual selves. Those who come to the Sanitarium as patients are to see that Christian love and kindness are shown to all who are connected with the institution. Let every one stand in his lot and place, refusing to go out of his way to assume authority as a dictator. The Lord calls upon every man to be courteous and to discipline himself. He is not to exercise authority that is not given him. Let every one learn daily his lesson of preparing his own heart for the heavenly inspection, for the record is written in the books of heaven. Let souls be emptied of self. Then invite Christ to come in, and open the door of the heart to His knock. He says, "If any man hear My voice, I will come in and will sup with Him, and He with me." This divine companionship is what is needed in every home, in every church, in every sanitarium. There is need of strong, spirited men, men who will be sure to do special honor to the Lord Jesus Christ. We must be preparing to become members of the royal family in the heavenly mansions Christ is preparing for every one who through the grace received will wear His yoke.

Christ invites us, "Learn of Me; for I am meek and lowly in heart, and ye shall find rest unto your souls. For my yoke is easy and My burden is light." In our character-building give encouragement to every divine, sacred influence. The blessing from Jesus makes everything good and profitable. Have His praise in your heart and in your voice and in your words, and your hearts will become fit temples for the Holy Spirit of God. Your success depends upon constant watchfulness and earnest prayer. "Ye are My friends, if ye do whatsoever I have commanded you." Depending upon the Lord, you can do the very things that are to be done, without murmuring and without disputing.

Satan is watching to secure every soul possible, to do him service by careless work and careless words. He desires to impress the minds of the converted and the unconverted that those connected with the sanitarium are lacking in piety and the meekness of Christ, that they are not Christians. Jesus will help you to prevent this impression being made.

Christ would have every one possess in abundance, the grace of heaven. He desires that His joy may be in you, and that your joy may be full. Every soul is to discipline himself in strict, faithful service, just as verily out of meeting as in meeting. You are in full view of the heavenly angels, and every faithful disciple may be, if he will as was Ezra before the king. The hand of God is upon all these for good who seek Him, but His power and His wrath are against those who forsake Him, and who trust in the help and friendship of the world, going to the God of Ekron to inquire, and heeding not the Counsel of the living God.

The children of God will know who is their helper. They will know in whom they can trust implicitly, and with Christ's help, they may, without presumption have a holy confidence. Yes His servants may safely trust in Him alone, without fear, looking unto Jesus, pressing on in obedience to His requirements, leaving everything that is joined to the world, whether the world opposes or favors. Their success comes from God, and they will not fail because they have not the wealth and influence of wicked men. If they fail, it will be because they do not obey the Lord's requirements and the Holy Spirit is not with them.

I am instructed that our only safety is in being joined to the Lord Jesus Christ. We can afford to lose the friendship of worldly men. Those who join themselves to worldly men, that they may carry out their unsanctified purposes, make a fearful mistake; for they forfeit the favor and blessing of God. I am to urge upon the attention of our people that the Lord Himself has placed a wall of separation between the world and that which He has established on the earth. God's people are to serve Him; for Christ has called them out of the world, and sanctified and refined them, that they may do His service. He has been given all power in heaven and in earth.

There is no such thing as maintaining concord between the profane and the Holy. There can be no concord between Christ and Belial. But "the Lord hath set apart him that is godly for Himself." And this consecration to the Lord, this separation from the world, is plainly declared and positively enjoined in both the Old and the New Testament.

Brother Burden, before closing my letter, I will finish what I intended to say about the building of the food factory. This work requires much wisdom and genuine good sense. If you can bring it about do so. Make the best possible use of "Ministry of Healing" to aid you in your work. I believe that you can accomplish that which seems to be a necessity. I think that if we all walk humbly with God, we shall always have grateful hearts.

There will be those who will invest their means in our Sanitariums, with the understanding that they shall be given a home there as long as they shall live. These should receive kind, Christian treatment...

Ellen G. White

* * * * *

Sanitarium, California
B. 329-1905 December 11, 1905.
Dear Brother Burden,

....

Later. This morning, Dec. 14, I could not sleep after one o'clock, so I arose and dressed, and have come to my office to complete the letter that I began writing to you two or three days ago. We are interested in every movement made at Loma Linda.

Did not the Lord have oversight, I should not care to live another day. But this is a question settled in my mind,—that we are under a power which is beyond human control, and in that power we can trust. The Lord is good to us, and if we will walk carefully before Him, He will ever reveal His power in our behalf. He will save to the uttermost all who love and obey Him.

[150] I long daily to be able to do double duty. I have been pleading with the Lord for strength and wisdom to reproduce the writings of the witnesses who were confirmed in the faith in the early history of the message. After the passing of the time in 1844, they received the light and walked in the light, and when the men claiming to have new light would come in with their wonderful messages regarding various points of Scripture, we had, through the moving of the Holy Spirit, testimonies right to the point, which cut off the influence of such messages as Elder A. F. Ballenger has been devoting his time to presenting. This poor man has been working decidedly against the truth that the Holy Spirit has confirmed. When the power of God testifies as to what is truth, that truth is to stand forever as the truth. No after suppositions contrary to the light God has given are to be entertained.

Men will arise with interpretations of Scripture which are to them truth; but which are not truth. The truth for this time, God has given us as a foundation for our faith. He himself has taught us what is truth. One will arise, and still another with new light, which contradicts the light that God has given under the demonstration of

His Holy Spirit. A few are still alive who passed through the experiences gained in the establishment of this truth. God has graciously spared their lives to repeat and repeat, till the close of their lives, the experiences through which they passed, even as did John the apostle till the very close of his life. And the standard-bearers who have fallen in death are to speak through the reprinting of their writings. I am instructed that thus their voices are to be heard. [They are to bear] their testimonies as to what constitutes the truth for this time.

We are not to receive the words of those who come with a message that contradicts the special points of our faith. They gather together a mass of scripture, and pile it as proof around their asserted theories. This has been done over and over again during the past fifty years. And while the Scriptures are God's word, and are to be respected, the application of them, if such application moves one pillar of the foundation that God has sustained these fifty years, is a great mistake. He who makes such an application knows not the wonderful demonstration of the Holy Spirit that gave power and force to the past messages that have come to the people of God.

Elder Ballenger's proofs are not reliable. If received, they would destroy the faith of God's people in the truth that has made us what we are. We must be decided on this subject; for the points he is trying to prove by scripture are not sound. They do not prove that the past experience of God's people was a fallacy. We had the truth; we were directed by the angels of God. It was under the guidance of the Holy Spirit that the presentation of the sanctuary question was given. It is eloquence for every one to keep silent in regard to the features of our faith in which they acted no part.

God never contradicts Himself. Scripture proofs are misapplied if forced to testify to that which is not true. Another and still another will arise, and bring in supposedly great light, and make their assertions. But we stand by the old landmarks.

"That which was from the beginning, which we have heard, which we have seen with our eyes, which we have looked upon, and our hands have handled of the word of life; (for the life was manifested, and we have seen it, and bear witness, and show unto you that eternal life, which was with the Father, and was manifested unto us) that which we have seen and heard declare we unto you that ye also may have fellowship with us; and truly our fellowship is with the Father, and with His son Jesus Christ. And these things write we unto you, that your joy may be full. This then is the message which we have heard of Him, and declare unto you, that God is light, and in Him is no darkness at all.

"If we say that we have fellowship with Him, and walk in darkness, we lie, and do not the truth; but if we walk in the light, as He is in the light, we have fellowship one with another, and the blood of Jesus Christ His Son cleanseth us from all sin. If we say that we have no sin, we deceive ourselves, and the truth is not in us. If we confess our sins, He is faithful and just to forgive us our sins, and to cleanse us from all unrighteousness. If we say that we have not sinned we make Him a liar, and His word is not in us."

I am instructed to say that these words we may use as appropriate for this time; for the time has come when sin must be called by its right name. We are hindered in our work by men who are not converted, who seek their own glory. They wish to be thought originators of new theories, which they present, claiming that they are truth. But if these theories are received, they will lead to a denial of the truth that for the past fifty years, God has been giving to His people, substantiating it by the demonstration of the Holy Spirit.

Let all men beware what is the character of their work. They would better be falling into line; for their own soul's sake and for the sake of the souls of others. "If we walk in the light as He is in the light, the blood of Jesus Christ His Son cleanseth us from all sin." It is nothing to the credit of any man to start on a new track using scriptures to substantiate theories of error, leading minds into confusion, away from the truths that are to be indelibly impressed on the minds of God's people, that they may hold fast to the faith.

Ellen G. White

* * * * *

Sanitarium, Calif.
C.-337, 1905. Dec. 19, 1905.
Mrs. Jessie Christiansen, Sebastapol, Calif.
My dear Sister,

I am trying to do all I possibly can to urge the work forward in new places. The Lord has signified that in different places there are buildings which would be offered to us at a very low price, which we could use in our work. His word to us regarding this has been verified in our experience in opening up medical missionary work in Southern California. Recently the Lord has placed a great blessing within our reach by enabling us to obtain a beautiful sanitarium property known as Loma Linda. This property is sixty miles from Los Angeles, and it is a wonderful place in which to work for the sick, and in which to begin work for Redlands and Riverside.

Its name—Loma Linda—"beautiful hill", describes the place. Of the 76 acres comprised in the property, about 35 form a beautiful hill, which rises one hundred and twenty-five feet above the valley. Upon this hill the sanitarium building is situated.

The main building is a well-planned structure of sixty-four rooms, having three stories and a basement. It is completely furnished, heated by steam, and lighted by electricity. It is surrounded with large pepper trees and other shade trees.

About ten rods away and on the highest part of the hill there is a group of five cottages. The central cottage has nine beautiful living rooms and two bath rooms. In the basement is the heating plant for the five cottages.

Prettily grouped around this larger cottage are four smaller ones, having four rooms each, with bath and toilet. In all there are ninety rooms. The buildings are furnished throughout, and are ready for use.

[154]

The seventy six acres of hill and valley land are well cultivated and will furnish much fruit and many vegetables for the institution. Fifteen acres of the valley land are in alfalfa hay. Eight acres of the hill are in apricots, plums, and almonds. Ten acres are in good bearing orange orchard. Many acres of land round the cottages and main building are laid out in lawns, drives and walks.

This property cost the Company from whom we purchased it, about one hundred and forty thousand dollars. They erected the buildings, and ran the place for a while as a sanitarium. Then they tried to operate it as a tourist hotel. But this plan did not succeed, and they decided to sell. It was closed last April, and as the stockholders became more anxious to sell, it was offered to us for forty thousand dollars, and for this amount our people purchased it.

This property came into our possession in such a way that we know the hand of the Lord was in the matter. Loma Linda is one of the most perfect places for a sanitarium that I have ever seen, and I thank our heavenly Father for giving us such a place. It is provided with almost everything necessary for sanitarium work, and it is the very place in which sanitarium work can be carried forward on right lines by faithful physicians and managers.

Not far away are the cities of Redlands and Riverside and San Bernardino. These places are to be thoroughly worked. Something has already been done in Redlands and Riverside, and a neat house of worship has been erected in each place. But as soon as possible a thorough evangelistic effort must be made.

Ellen G. White

* * * * *

Sanitarium, Calif.
B.-34-'06 January 19, 1906.
Dear Brother and Sister Burden,

I received your letter yesterday, and was very glad to hear from you. I have been very busy of late. The Lord has sustained me in preparing matter to meet the unbelief and infidelity expressed regarding the Testimonies He has given me to bear to His people. He has given me words to write. I may have to visit Battle Creek when the unsettled weather is over.

I think with great pleasure of the Loma Linda Sanitarium, and the advantages that it possesses. I sometimes wish that I could be with you in Southern California. But here everything for my work is ready to my hand, and to go away anywhere just now seems inconsistent; for I am getting out much matter that is very important.

The Lord understands all things, and He is my only dependance. I need His power back of every effort I shall henceforth make, as it has been back of the efforts I have made in the past. I wish to be prepared to meet the falsehoods that are coming in. The Lord is good, and He is my stronghold. He understands the situation, and He will never leave me as long as I cling to Him. He will guide me in judgment.

We have had a good visit from Brother and Sister Haskell. It has seemed like a revival of old times. I think that Elder Haskell is anxious to return to Loma Linda, but they wish first to visit Sister Haskell's sister, Mrs. Grey. After that they will be free to begin work at Loma Linda.

Elder Haskell has suffered a great deal from boils. He has taken treatment at the Sanitarium several times, but most of his treatment he has taken in his room in our house. Our home has been his sanitarium. He has been afflicted continuously, and has kept to his bed most of the time. Pulverized charcoal poultices have been used with good results. His wife is a good nurse, and she has taken faithful care of him. He has thought several times that he had overcome the affliction, and that he would recover rapidly, but as soon as he began to stir around, boils would again appear. His countenance looks clear and wholesome for a man of his age.

I am glad that Brother and Sister Haskell could stay with us for a while. We have tried to make them feel at home. They have been perfectly free to do as they wished. They seem to appreciate this advantage.

You speak of the sunshine at Loma Linda. It is indeed a blessing. I am glad that you have so much of it. We have hardly seen the sun for two weeks. For two weeks we have had continuous rain, day and night. The rain has fallen gently but continuously, in soft showers, until the ground is full of water. The water in the canyon is up to our bridge, and if there is much more rain, will overflow into the orchard.

The rain was certainly needed; for thus far this winter we have only had one short rain. This present rain is making up in quantity for what was lacking in the earlier rain.

This morning at three o'clock the stars were shining, and the last quarter of the moon was plainly visible in the sky. But as daylight comes, I can see that the atmosphere is hazy, and the rain may begin again. I am so thankful that the drought has broken. The ground has seemed to absorb a great deal of the gently falling rain.

The Lord is good and greatly to be praised. I will not complain. I feel very sad over the state of things in Battle Creek. I am trying to do all that is possible to guard the flock of God from falling into error. God alone can keep them, and through them work out

His good pleasure. I am satisfied with the working of the Lord. If unbelief is multiplied, through the exercise of unbelief in the testimonies, having done all we can do, we will talk faith, and work on the affirmative side of the question. If my name is cast out as evil, I am in excellent company. Those who would not receive Christ were dead in trespasses and sins. As they looked upon the evidences that He presented, by curing disease and making the suffering ones rejoice in health, why did they not yield their unbelief? Because by such an action they would have confessed themselves to be sinners. In the place of receiving the evidence offered them, in the place of recognizing in Christ's works the endowment of heaven, they held right on to their wicked purposes, and said, He performed this wonderful work through the devil.

This was the sin against the Holy Ghost. They had not forgiveness in this world, nor in the world to come.

What reason had Christ given them for making this statement? None at all. The Prince of life was seeking the lost sheep. At last the leaders of Israel put Him to death. What had He done? He had expressed to a rebellious world the love of God. And His death was the great freewill offering for sin. By it a fountain of mercy was opened to a world yet to be convinced of the wonderful sacrifice made in order that whoever believed in Christ should not perish, but have everlasting life. The preaching of the gospel gives sinners opportunity to receive the greatest gift ever proffered human beings. Those who refuse this gift reveal the highest contempt for God.

It is our privilege to be partakers of the divine nature. If we be falsified, if men give to the world a mis-statement of the work that God has done through the humble instrument, dishonoring Christ by making a misrepresentation of Him, they are partakers of the shame and reproach brought upon me.

We understand the present feebleness and smallness of the work. We have had an experience. In doing the work God has given us, we may go trustingly forward, assured that He will be our efficiency. He will be with us in 1906, as He was with us in 1841, 1842, 1843, and 1844. Oh, what wonderful evidences we had then of the presence of God with us. In the earlier stages of our work, we had many difficulties to meet, and we gained many victories.

If the Lord is leading us, we may go forward courageously, assured that He will be with us as He was with us in past years, as we labored in feebleness, but under the miracle working power of the Holy Spirit. He will be with us as He was with us when we had to meet the opposing influences of erroneous theories.

Many of the most successful undertakings made in behalf of the truth have at the beginning been small, and have cost many tears and prayers. At the beginning of our work, some brought in grave errors, and meeting these placed upon us much hard labor, and such difficulties as God's help alone could enable us to overcome. We prayed a great deal; often we wrestled whole nights in prayer. Then the light, precious light on Bible truth, would come upon the whole company assembled. All could understand the difficulties, and the truth of the Bible was comprehended and substantiated.

[157]

Thus we worked and thus we prayed. Errors were continually being brought in, but we went to God in prayer, and searched the Scriptures diligently. Year after year, after the passing of the time, many false theories were presented, but we collected our forces in favorable places, and continued in prayer, watching, and praying, and searching the Scriptures. Then light was given to the very youngest of those assembled, and the truth of the Word of God in regard to position we were occupying, was plainly specified.

The time of respite granted us seemed short, too short, to open to the world the great and wonderful things of God's law. The promises of God—how we laid hold upon them! We could not bear all the glory! Our physical strength left us, and the power of God, like a halo of glory was over us. What praises went up to God! "Yet a little while, and he that shall come will come, and will not tarry." There was a tarrying time for us, but He, our Lord, knew the end from the beginning. It was no delay, and from year to year we worked and prayed and believed. The errors that were rushing in upon us, we met in the power of God, and explained them. And the glory filled the room where we were assembled.

We had thought that the work would have been accomplished before this. But the light came from the Lord regarding the extension of the work. "Jesus came and spake unto them, saying, All power is given unto me in heaven and in earth." This power we needed then in the early history of our work. "Go ye therefore and teach all nations, baptizing them in the name of the Father, and of the Son, and of the Holy Ghost." Then we understood that there was a world to be warned. "Teaching them to observe all things whatsoever I have commanded you; and, lo, I am with you always, even unto the end of the world." Here is our work, our commission. The truth was to go to every city in America, and we were to gather up our forces to proclaim the message in the "regions beyond."

Had the work been done that God designed should be done, the condition of things in our world would now be very different. But the professing followers of Christ are asleep. The churches have not fulfilled the solemn charge laid upon them. Men placed as watchmen have been asleep at their post, and many refuse to wake up. They are not fulfilling the gospel commission.

After Christ had risen from the dead, the angels said to the women, "Go quickly, and tell his disciples that he is risen from the dead; and, behold, he goeth before you into Galilee, there shall ye see him; lo, I have told you. And they departed quickly from the sepulcher with fear and great joy; and did run to bring his disciples word. And as they went to tell his disciples, behold, Jesus met them, saying, All Hail. And they came and held him by the feet, and worshiped Him. Then said Jesus unto them, Be not afraid; go tell my brethren that they go into Galilee; and there shall they see me."

"Then the eleven disciples went away into Galilee, into a mountain where Jesus had appointed them. And when they saw him, they worshiped Him; but some doubted." They doubted that He had risen from the dead, in spite of the most powerful facts in proof of it. The Jews did not deny the resurrection of Christ for want of evidence to prove it, nor did they hire soldiers to tell a lie because they believed the falsehood or could substantiate it. They did it to keep the people from knowing the truth. False teachers are always afraid to have the truth come before the people. This knowledge they wish to hide, to keep the people from becoming acquainted with the facts. They desire preeminence, and the truth would spoil their history and their character.

There are many ways in which the truth has been withheld from the world that Christ has purchased with the price of His blood, But Christ has supreme authority over all, and power to give knowledge to all who desire it, and who seek it from God in His word.

The sacred commission given us is to work for all nations. To turn sinners from iniquity is to be the great object of the followers of Christ. In various ways this work is to be done. In our campmeetings, a much more decided effort is to be put forth to accomplish this work. Short discourses right to the point are to be given, and those who hear are to be called to make a decision. The laborers are to be fervent in spirit. During the meeting our periodicals are to be distributed and sold.

Let all strive together to reach the object Christ has set before us. The gospel is to be translated into every tongue, and is to be preached to every creature. The divine presence of Christ will ever be with the true workers, enlightening their minds as they open the Scriptures to others. All who reach out for the Lord Jesus in their prayers, seeking for wisdom and efficiency, will be given success in their endeavors to win souls to righteousness. They will be God's light-bearers, shining amidst the darkness of the world.

Ellen G. White

* * * * *

Sanitarium, California
McP.-94, 1906 March 1, 1906.

My dear Niece Addie,

..... Loma Linda has a large, beautiful lawn, which is encircled with pepper trees; and on it there are comfortable benches. I once spoke on this lawn to quite an audience, a number not of our faith being present. But the tops of the pepper trees met over the stand, and the odor of these trees, which I thought would be most beneficial to me, was too strong. I find that we must live to learn....

Soon we shall begin evangelistic work in Redlands, a town about four miles from Loma Linda. Elder Haskell and his wife have come from the East to help us start this work. They spent a month with us here, and then visited Sister Haskell's sister at Armona. They are now at Loma Linda....

A few miles from Redlands there are cities that have never been worked. Riverside is eight miles from Loma Linda. We have treatment-rooms there. They are not extensive, but are large enough

[159]

to accommodate the people of that city. While we were in Redlands last year, we drove to Riverside, a distance of eleven miles, and I spoke in our church there. At this place our people have a very nice meeting house. We drove over in order to see the country. We passed through acres of orange groves. It was a beautiful and interesting sight; for the trees were loaded with fruit. I never saw anything like it before. We returned to Redlands on the trains, and again we passed through miles of orange land, the trees laden with their beautiful, golden fruit. We saw also large groves of grapefruit and lemon trees.

Our future effort must be to reach the people of these cities with the truth. At Fernando, ... we have a school. This school is not far from Loma Linda and Redlands.

President Roosevelt, on a journey through Southern California, when he first got a view of the city of Redlands and its surrounding, took off his hat, and said, "This is glorious. I never imagined such a sight." The scenery is indeed charming.

In Redlands we have a splendid opening for work. Some time ago Elder Simpson held a series of tent-meetings here, and a company of believers was raised up. They built a small but very neat house of worship, and in this church I spoke when I was in Redlands, a year ago.

It was in the providence of God that we obtained possession of Loma Linda. This property comprises one large building, five cottages, and seventy-six acres of land, in a most beautiful location. The land was purchased and the building erected and equipped by a company of one hundred and fifty physicians, at a cost of one hundred and fifty thousand dollars. Under their management the institution did not succeed financially, and not long ago we bought it, furnished throughout with durable, high-grade furniture for forty thousand dollars. Twenty thousand dollars of the purchase price was to be paid in several payments at stated times with the balance in two years. But the former owners found themselves in need of money, and agreed to take off two hundred dollars interest, were a certain payment made at a date before the time agreed upon. Brother Burden raised the money and thus saved two hundred dollars.

Once more these men found themselves in a strait place and they said that if we would pay the remaining amount of indebtedness, they would throw off nine hundred dollars. Brother Burden paid the whole amount, some of our people taking stock in the institution, and some making gifts. This means to the institution a saving of eleven hundred dollars, which otherwise would have had to be paid. This was a great advantage.

In enabling us to obtain possession of this property, the Lord has certainly brought to the cause a most wonderful opportunity. We praise God with heart and soul and voice. There are five cottages, well fitted up, besides the large building. These are all furnished in the best of style. The smaller cottages are made with wide piazzas running around the four sides, and the windows are so arranged that the beds can be wheeled out on to the veranda. In each cottage there is a bathroom. The larger cottage has two stories, and is furnished throughout with solid red and black mahogany furniture.

All the mattresses, blankets, sheets, pillow-slips, couch-pillows, and bedding in general were in excellent condition when we took over the property. There were about eighty towels besides those in the rooms, and about one hundred and thirty-five small linen towels. There are table napkins in abundance, and silverware of all description, as well as chinaware.

There is one room in which sun baths may be taken, and a large parlor, two sides of which are of glass. This is the most beautiful room I was ever in in my life. There is also another large, well-furnished parlor. Two rooms above this have in them twenty rocking chairs and reclining chairs, which are very comfortable.

Besides these buildings, there is another building, which was used as a recreation building. This will serve for a time as a meeting-house. Both lower and upper stories are fitted up with rocking chairs. Those in charge seemed to have a passion for rocking chairs.

There are two barns and some carriages, somewhat worn, several horses, four cows, and a large calf, a good number of chickens and some turkeys. There were some hogs, but these have been disposed of.

Ten acres of the land is in oranges and apricots. The apricots are the largest I have ever seen. We only tasted the oranges when we were there, but Brother Burden has recently sent us several boxes of oranges and grapefruit, which we find most excellent. The apples grown there do not amount to much. We secured the place last summer before the fruit was ripe, and more was put up during the season than they will be able to use this summer. We had to buy peaches for canning. I helped to pick some of them. We bought the fruit on the trees, and it was delicious. They are now setting out more grape vines and orange trees and other kinds of fruit, but these will not come into bearing for some time.

The main building stands on an eminence, and one must climb a long flight of steps to reach the front door. About two hundred rods from the building there is a little railway station. From here there is a drive of easy and gradual ascent which encircles the rise of ground upon which stand the main building, the nine-roomed cottage, and the four smaller cottages. The hill is set out to ornamental and fruit trees. On it there is still another cottage, which has been used for the laborers.

The Loma Linda Sanitarium will be dedicated in four or five weeks. I hear that the institution is filled with patients. Every one who has gone there is delighted with the place.

Now I have given you the fullest description of Loma Linda that I have written to any one, as I thought you would like to hear about the place. I have never lost my interest in you; for you are one of my children, a member of my family. If you will love and serve the Lord I shall be grateful that in your childhood I consented to take charge of you. You are the purchase of the blood of Christ, and I do want you to find entrance into the city whose builder and maker is God. Let us all strive together to secure the immortal inheritance...

Ellen G. White

Notes Of Travel (E. G. W.)

Review, June 21, 1906
Dedication of the Loma Linda Sanitarium

Sunday, April 15, 1906, the beautiful buildings and ground of the Loma Linda Sanitarium were solemnly dedicated to the service of God.

The exercises of the day meant much to those who had made many personal sacrifices in order to help secure the institution and set it in operation...

During the exercises the people were told of the remarkable providences that had attended every step taken to secure the property. The purpose we have in view in the establishment of many sanitariums was also dwelt upon. I was present at the meeting only a portion of the time, and spoke with freedom for nearly half an hour on the advantages of outdoor life in the treatment of disease.

I tried to make it plain that the sanitarium physicians and helpers were to cooperate with God in combating disease, not only through the use of the natural remedial agencies He has placed within our reach, but also by encouraging their patients to lay hold on divine strength through obedience to the commandments of God.

... Physicians and ministers are to unite in an effort to lead men and women to obey God's commandments. They need to study the intimate relationship existing between obedience and health. Solemn is the responsibility resting upon medical missionaries. They are to be missionaries in the true sense of the term. The sick and the suffering who entrust themselves to the care of the helpers in our medical institutions, must not be disappointed. They are to be taught how to live in harmony with heaven. As they learn to obey God's law, they will be richly blessed in body and spirit.

The advantage of outdoor life must never be lost sight of. How thankful we should be that God has given us beautiful sanitarium properties at Paradise Valley and Glendale and Loma Linda. "Out of the cities! Out of the cities!"—this has been my message for years.

And yet how slow some are to realize that the crowded cities are not favorable places for sanitarium work.

Even in Southern California not many years ago, there were some who favored the erection of a large sanitarium building in the heart of Los Angeles. In the light of the instruction God has given we could not consent to the carrying out of any such plan. In the visions of the night, the Lord had shown me unoccupied properties in the country, suitable for sanitarium purposes, and for sale at a price far below the original cost.

It was some time before we found these places. First, we secured the Paradise Valley Sanitarium, near San Diego. A few months later, in the good providence of God, the Glendale property came to the notice of our people, and was purchased and fitted up for service. But light came that our work of establishing sanitariums in southern California was not complete; and on several different occasions Testimonies were given that medical missionary work must be done somewhere in the vicinity of Redlands.

April 6, 1905. "On our way to Redlands, as our train passed through miles of orange groves, I recognized this section of southern California as one of the places that had been presented to me with the word that it should have a fully equipped sanitarium...

"As I looked from the car window, and saw the trees laden with fruit,... there arose before me a vision of what the spiritual harvest might have been had earnest, Christlike efforts been put forth for the salvation of souls.

"The Lord would have brave, earnest men and women take up His work in these places. The cause of God is to make more rapid advancement in southern California than it has in the past. Every year thousands of people visit S. Calif. in search of health, and by various methods we should seek to reach them with the truth. They must hear the warning to prepare for the great day of the Lord which is right upon us...

"We are called upon by God to present the truth for this time to those who year by year come to S. Calif. from all parts of America. Workers who can speak to the multitudes are to be located where they can meet the people, and give them the warning message...."

These words were written before I had learned anything about the property at Loma Linda. Still the burden of establishing another sanitarium rested upon me. In the fall of 1903 I had a vision of a sanitarium in the midst of beautiful grounds, somewhere in S. Calif., and no property I had visited answered to the presentation given in this vision. At the time I wrote about this vision to our brethren and sisters assembled at the Los Angeles campmeeting early in Sept. 1903.

While attending the General Conference of 1905, at Washington, D. C., I received a letter from Elder J. A. Burden describing a property he had found four miles west of Redlands, five and one-half miles southeast of San Bernardino, and eight miles northeast of Riverside. As I read his letter, I was impressed that this was one of the places I had seen in vision, and I immediately telegraphed him to secure the property without delay. He did so, and as the result, Loma Linda is in our possession.

Later, when I visited this property, I recognized it as one of the places I had seen nearly two years before in vision. How thankful I am to the Lord our God for this place, which is all prepared for us to use to the honor and glory of His name.........

The extensive view of valley and mountain is magnificent. One of the chief advantages of the institution at Loma Linda is the pleasing variety of charming scenery on every side.

But more important than magnificent scenery and beautiful buildings and spacious grounds, is the close proximity of this institution to a densely populated district, and the opportunity thus afforded of communicating to many, many people a knowledge of the third angel's message. We are to have clear spiritual discernment, else we shall fail of understanding the opening providences of God that are preparing the way for us to sound the warning message, by the agencies that God has given us for this purpose. Let us remember that one most important agency is our medical missionary work. Never are we to lose sight of the great object for which our sanitariums are established,—the advancement of God's closing work in the earth.

Loma Linda is to be not only a sanitarium, but an educational center. With the possession of this place comes the weighty responsibility of making the work of the institution educational in character. A school is to be established here for the training of gospel medical missionary evangelists.

Much is involved in this work, and it is very essential that a right beginning be made. The Lord has a special work to be done in this part of the field. He instructed me to call upon Elder and Mrs. S. N. Haskell to help us in getting properly started a work similar to that which they had carried on in Nashville and at Avondale. They came, and are now laboring with all the powers of their being to do a solid work. They conduct classes regularly in the institution, and have established a Bible training school at San Bernardino, from which center is extending an influence throughout this district.

November 1, 1905. B-309-'05

"I thank the Lord with heart and soul and voice that He has brought Loma Linda to our notice, and that we might obtain it. I thank the Lord that He has sent you to help me carry out in a determined effort that which He designed should be a great blessing to us. Redlands will be a center, and so also will Loma Linda. A school will be established as soon as possible, and the Lord will open the way."

December 10, 1905.

"I am certainly thankful to our heavenly Father that in His providence we have been favored to secure this beautiful location as a health resort. It answers perfectly to the representation that was given me. Praise the Lord for His goodness and mercy expressed to us amidst the many difficulties we have to meet. The Lord is our helper, and constant guide. I say to you, my brother, Jesus will be to us a present helper in every time of need. In regard to the school, I would say, Make it all you possibly can in education of nurses and physicians."

"Make the school especially strong for nurses and physicians. Thousands of workers are to be qualified with all the ability of physicians, to labor not as physicians, but as medical missionary evangelists."

* * * * *

To Ministers and Physicians

Loma Linda Calif,
MS. 37, 1906.
May 1, 1906

I am now charged to write out the straight testimony which was given to me Monday night. I am to withhold none of it. I am to say to ministers and physicians, We must have a work done among us who bear the gospel message. We need the power of the truth in the soul. The close of this Earth's history is drawing near, and our work has not extended into the highways and byways as it should have done. In very many places the gospel message must be given in all its power, and in such a way that souls will be aroused. A spirit of self-sacrifice must take possession of ministers and physicians; every one must do a self-denying work. Souls are perishing in their sins.

Sanitariums must be established in various places away from the cities. Schools must be established in connection with the sanitariums. As far as possible, these organizations must be blended, each helping the other, and yet each doing its special work.

No longer should our people go to Battle Creek as they have been doing. Infidelity has been sown there in words in false statements, in unsanctified influence of mind over mind. God is dishonored, we are to prepare to accept the situations God may prepare for us. Never before did the matter appear as the Lord presents it today. False theories, repeated again and again, appear as falsely inviting today as did the fruit of the forbidden tree in the Garden of Eden. The fruit was very beautiful, and apparently desirable for food. Through false doctrines many souls have already been destroyed. Some will never see the light and come to their senses. The Lord God of Israel now declares, "If the Lord be God, serve Him; and if Baal, serve him. Choose ye this day whom ye will serve."

The light of truth must be held up in Battle Creek. Faithful watchman must be stationed there. The truth must go forth by the exposition of the Word, to saints and to sinners. Laborers are now needed there, who will distinguish the difference between eating of the fruit of the forbidden tree, and the eating of the fruit of the tree bearing the gospel message.

I am instructed to say, Prepare places where will be given true education free from deceptive theories. Let the plain words of Christ, uncontaminated by false science, be taught. It will require no elaborate preparations to engage sincerely, humbly, prayerfully in this work.

Will we now make thorough work for eternity? We have no time to criticize another soul. Do not consider it your duty to chastise another. See that your own soul is right with God.

Ellen G. White

* * * * *

Mountain View, Calif.
B.-140,'06 May 6, 1906.
Dear Brother Burden,

I must write you words of counsel. I am instructed to say, Move guardedly, and be careful not to take upon yourself too many responsibilities. Your mind is to be left free as possible from matters of secondary importance.

The Lord has instructed me that it would be a mistake for us to plan for the production of a large quantity of health foods at Loma Linda, to be distributed through commercial channels. Loma Linda is a place that has been especially ordained of God to make a good impression upon the minds of many who have not had the light of present truth. Every phase of the work in this place, every movement made, should be so fully in harmony with the sacred character of present truth as to create a deep spiritual impression.

Everything connected with the institution at Loma Linda should, so far as possible, be unmingled with commercialism. Nothing should be allowed to come in that would in any wise lessen the favorable impression you are striving to make. If we manifest a genuine faith in eternal realities, this will have a far-reaching effect on the minds of others. We must allow nothing to hinder our efforts for the saving of souls. God requires us to leave impressions that will help awaken unbelievers to a realization of their duty. Let us use voice and pen in helping those who need clear discernment.

Many are now inquiring, What shall I do to inherit eternal life? We cannot answer this question satisfactorily by connecting with our sanitarium the production of health foods for commercial gain. By our example we are to leave upon the minds of our patients the impression that we are sustained and guided by the grace of God, and that we are keeping constantly in view the glory of the Lord.

It is not rank, or wealth, or learning, or power that lends influence to a Christian; but a willing mind, and a heart consecrated to the cause of Christ. In the service of God there is a place for every one; and He is glorified when everyone is satisfied in filling the place appointed him. To His servants He imparts grace sufficient for every duty. However humble may be their sphere of service, they may by His grace reveal that they are Christian gentlemen and Christian ladies.

In the visions of the night, these principles were presented to me in connection with the proposal for the establishment of a bakery at Loma Linda. I was shown a large building where many foods were made. There were also some smaller buildings near the bakery. As I stood by, I heard loud voices in dispute over the work that was being done. There was lack of harmony among the workers, and confusion had come in.

Then I saw Brother Burden approach. His countenance bore a look of anxiety and distress as he endeavored to reason with the workmen, and bring them into harmony. The scene was repeated, and Brother Burden was often drawn away from his legitimate work as manager of the sanitarium, to settle variances. He was carrying too heavy a load, and he looked careworn and perplexed.

I then saw patients standing on the beautiful sanitarium grounds. They had heard the disputes between the workmen. The patients did not see me, but I could see them and hear them, and their remarks were brought to my ears. They were expressing words of regret that a food factory should be established on these beautiful grounds, in such close proximity to an institution for the care of the sick. Some were disgusted, and a most unfavorable impression was being made. How sorry I felt! All these buildings had cost money that

[167]

should have been used in fitting up bathrooms, which would involve considerable expense.

Then One appeared on the scene, and said, "All this has been caused to pass before you as an object-lesson, that you might see the result of carrying out certain plans. Sanitariums must help those who come to them by calling attention to the work to be done. This beautiful place came to us in the providence of God, and it should be kept as a restful desirable, healthful retreat, to which we may call the sick, where they shall be greatly blessed physically, and where they can hear the evidences of present truth and the reasons for our faith."

And then, lo, the whole scene changed. The bakery building was not where we had planned it, but at a distance from the sanitarium buildings, on the road toward the railway. It was a humble building, and a small work was carried on there. The commercialism idea was lost sight of, and in its stead, a strong spiritual influence pervaded the place. A suitable helper was given Brother Hansen at such times as he required help. The management of this small bakery did not bring a heavy responsibility upon Brother Burden. The patients were favorably impressed by what they saw.

Brother and Sister Burden, you are to unite in being a blessing in spiritual lines. The Lord will bless you, and make you a blessing. You must not be encouraged to take upon yourselves the responsibility of conducting a large business in the health food line. We must all fill our appointed places, and become like-minded with God. Then we shall not fail nor be discouraged. The strength and power and influence of the Word will be revealed in Christ-like tenderness, through the softening subduing influence of the Holy Spirit of God.

Nothing of a commercial nature, as a means of lessening the debt on the sanitarium, should be brought in to burden the mind. There are many considerations in connection with this matter that I fear I shall not be able to define plainly to you. Improvements on the Loma Linda property will need to be made; but your work is not to gather in perplexities that will tax brain and nerve.

My brother, you and your wife are to be a special help to the sick and the afflicted. You can take them out to ride, and in many other ways show a genuine interest in their behalf while acting as manager of the Sanitarium and as religious instructor.

The manager and the pastor have their appointed work to do. The Lord calls upon His servants to attain unto perfection of Christian character in every line of effort. We are to see that our hearts are under the control of the Holy Spirit,—under the control of a power out of and above ourselves. Let every soul take hold of the work earnestly, because he is thoroughly converted; because he discerns the methods and ways of the Lord.

[168]

The manager of a sanitarium bears important responsibilities. Let his associates who are engaged in continuous hard labor in the various handicrafts, keep their souls searched as with a lighted candle. Unity of action in diversity of labor must be maintained. The workers are to live out the prayer of Christ, who declares, "I sanctify myself, that they also may be sanctified through the truth." Let them read the word of the Lord, in order that they may have the wisdom that is unto salvation. The richest treasures are to be found by searching for them in the Word. Some minds will be so impressed to seek these hidden treasures as to sell all that they have in order to buy the field and come into possession of the priceless jewels of truth. Of times the most lowly are in possession of the hidden treasure, which they may impart to others.

The truths of the word of God, applied to the heart and carried out with humility in the daily life-practise, will make Christians strong in the strength of Jehovah, and happy in His peace. Christian kindness and earnest consecration are constantly to be manifested in the life. We are not always engaged in special duties connected with sacred service; but the common, daily round of duties may be done in His Spirit, and such labor will commend itself to every man, even to the unconverted who know not the doctrine. We may let our light so shine in good works that the truth which we cherish shall be, to unbelievers, spirit and life.

Loma Linda is to be not only a sanitarium, but an educational center. With the possession of this place comes the weighty responsibility of making the work of the institution educational in character. The school that is to be established at Loma Linda is to stand in the freedom of the truth.

We shall have a work to do at Loma Linda in supplying health foods, in a limited way, to the surrounding cities; but it has been presented to me that in the establishment of a large food factory, you would be disappointed in your expectations. The influence connected with its management would not make a favorable impression upon the people. The Lord is able to make the proper impression upon human minds, when we cooperate with Him and follow the plans that He outlines.

The light given me is that in a food business large enough to supply Southern California, it would be difficult to avoid commercialism; and if the perplexing details were not attended to most carefully, there would be more expense than income. You can ill afford to spend the time that would be required to make the business a success. The Lord calls upon us to ascend a higher platform. Our example must exert a decided influence in favor of the doctrines we profess. Let us cling close to the teaching of the Word. Let us make the Word our counselor. The truths of the Word, carried out in our daily lives, will keep the soul pure and refined, noble and elevated. Walking in the light of the truth, self will be hid in constant love and fear of God. Before the world, the truth is to become majestic; for it reveals God in word, in spirit, in character.

The words were spoken by my instructor: "The influence to be constantly going out, is that which is created by the light shining forth with clear, convincing power from every soul who claims to believe the truth. The Lord would have you exalt the truth in language, in faith, in practice. Those who are connected with you are in no wise to be permitted to become deficient in tenderness, in mercy, in refinement of speech. The heart is ever to be obedient unto God. Cling to your heavenly Helper."

Talk these things, Brother Burden, and you will be a laborer together with God. By beholding you become changed into the likeness of His image; through His grace you become a partaker of His divine nature. You can glorify God by writing helpful, encouraging letters; by engaging in conversation with the patients; and by placing select reading-matter in the hands of those with whom you become acquainted. The life of Christ was a life of incessant labor to prepare human beings to be members of the royal family in the mansions above.

How shall the people be convinced of their great need of a preparation for the future life, which measures with the life of God, except by wisely-given appeals and warnings, as well as by the example of uprightness and of earnest, abiding faith which they see in the Christian life of believers? You and your helpers are laboring together with God to relieve the suffering sick, and to reclaim the wandering. You are also to edify the believers, in advice, in counsels, and in the daily workings of a training school.

A word in season is to be spoken to every one in need. To the unbelievers, we must be as the light of the world, as a city set on a hill, which cannot be hid. Our time and our intelligence are to be spent in revealing the sanctification that comes through love and obedience. In this lower school the truth of the Word will prepare men for the heavenly school. All are to be learners, and in the humble walks of life are to exemplify the mighty power of God.

In humility all are to become living, eloquent commentaries on the words that God hath spoken: "God hath chosen the weak things of the world to confound the things which are mighty; and base things of the world, and things which are despised, hath God chosen, yea, and things which are not, to bring to nought things that are." There is power for all who will seek it. Let us yield our God given faculties to Him who is our sanctification and our redemption. We shall have faith, if we have strong confidence in God.

[170]

Our faith in eternal realities is to become stronger and firmer with exercise. In every sanitarium, in every school, an upward, spiritual influence needs to be exerted. I am instructed to say to all physicians, Awake, awake, and take hold of the real issues that are for the uplifting of men and the magnifying of present truth. Let not your sense of individual responsibility become feeble. Let not your mind grow weary, while there remain your talent of speech, your pen, and the privilege of service. Let the truth, eternal truth, be brought into action to impress, to convince, to convert minds. Let us proclaim that the day of the Lord is upon us.

Many are now perishing for want of knowledge. Shall we not give mind and soul and voice to proclaiming the truth as it is in Christ Jesus? To every worker I would say, Show to unbelievers that there is strength in God. Communicate your ideas in regard to what is required, by the words of warning, "Prepare to meet thy God." Sow the seeds of truth by all waters. Wake up the watchmen, and, with them, bear the message in words of power. "Cry aloud, spare not, lift up thy voice like a trumpet, and show My people their transgression, and the house of Jacob their sins." The increase of your own experience will be proportionate to your individual trust and confidence in God.

There are many, many to be converted through the instrumentality of men who will be taken from the plow and from the common vocations of life to engage in the great, grand work of giving soul-saving [truth] to the people.

There are all classes to be reached. Those who have been called to labor in hygienic restaurants where thousands are fed but are not given the bread of life, should inquire, What is the way of the Lord? There are some who are laboring in hygienic restaurants, who should be breaking away, and be giving themselves to the grand work of carrying the last gospel message to multitudes. They must make sure that the truth for this time is implanted within their own hearts by the Holy Spirit of God. Then with minds cleansed from all sin, they will be able to feed the flock of God with pure provender, thoroughly winnowed from all fanciful and fatal delusions.

"Ye shall not surely die," the enemy declared in the beginning; "ye shall be as Gods." Our first parents yielded to the sophistry of the tempter, and fell.

We are now to awaken the men who have known the truth, and have lost from their hearts the love of it. Let us not cease our warning, day nor night. With tenderness even unto tears and with prayers of faith, let us lay hold of souls for whom Christ has died. Let us not wait for some costly arrangement before we work out Christ's plan. Some will be reached by the provisions the Lord has made to reach souls in the highways as well as in the byways. He has furnished us with buildings in which a good work may be done. There are dangers of consuming and not producing; but the evidence is given us that buildings have been provided that will enable us to reach the higher classes and present to them the truths of the Word.

There is a large work to be done. Sanitariums are to be carried on in many lands. When facilities are added to sanitariums that have been set in operation, let the additions be most thoroughly and firmly constructed; but there should be no large expenditure of means to secure every advantage at the beginning.

While at Loma Linda it is necessary to add some treatment rooms and other rooms, yet I would counsel you not to add anything that would greatly increase the labor and expense of operating the institution. Build no more than is positively necessary.

To the managers of all our sanitariums, I would say, Let no large debts be created. Make no unnecessary move. Set aside your desire for full equipments at once. Let the best possible use be made of fewer facilities, rather than to increase debts. All that is needed may in time be obtained, but all the furnishings and facilities need not be provided at once. Let reason, calm thought, and wise calculation be the rule of action. If success attends our institutions established for the care of the sick, it will be because the managers have preferred to get along with the most essential things, rather than to pile up debts.

The Lord calls upon us to do a work in many places. We shall have sanitariums that can be carried on without involving our cause heavily in debt. A word to the wise is sufficient. Let none think they must invest in the most costly conveniences. There is a more humble way of working successfully. Provide first the simpler appliances necessary for giving treatments. We need not now go to the expense of providing swimming pools and other costly facilities.

Our sanitarium work at Loma Linda may be carried on with simplicity, without incurring a heavy debt. Let our people be wise and true, and do their work in a humble way, in order that means may be saved in every line possible. This will facilitate the establishment of sanitariums in other places. My brethren, study to show yourselves approved unto God. We are laborers together with God, to save the souls and the bodies of many, to the glory of Christ Jesus.

Ellen G. White

* * * * *

Sanitarium. Calif.
N. 148 05 May 14, 1906.

Dr. C. C. Nicola. Dear Brother Nicola,

I was very much pleased to receive a letter from you regarding the sanitarium at Melrose. I have not been situated so that I could respond sooner. Early in April we were called upon to attend the dedicatory exercise of two of our S. Calif. sanitariums,—at Loma

Linda, near Redlands, and at Paradise Valley, near San Diego. We also visited the Glendale Sanitarium, near Los Angeles, and have just returned home.

At Loma Linda, arrangements were made for an out-of-door service. During the forenoon, the friends of the institution began to come in, and at noon a lunch was served to all. Early in the afternoon the people gathered together for the dedication. Seats had been placed on the lawn, under the shadow of a beautiful grove of pepper trees. In front was a large platform, on which were seated the speakers and the singers. I was present only a portion of the time. There were several speakers, and the time was limited. I spoke with freedom for nearly half an hour.

Now I wish, Brother Nicola, that you and your wife could have been present to enjoy this occasion with us, and to look over the Loma Linda property. I cannot describe the place; for I have but little strength for writing. I will send you an illustrated booklet giving some idea of the buildings and surroundings.

Loma Linda cost us forty thousand dollars. The original cost was nearly three times this sum. There were seventy-six acres of land in the tract, and thirty have been added since. As a sanitarium site, the property is a valuable one. The grounds have been carefully laid out at great expense to the original owners, and are beautified by well-kept lawns and flower-gardens. The surrounding scenery varies, in many respects from that seen from the grounds of the New England Sanitarium; but the extensive view is fully as magnificent as the Melrose view. There is more improved land about Loma Linda, including many square miles of bearing orange groves. Like Melrose, one of the chief advantages of situation at Loma Linda is the pleasing variety of charming scenery. We believe that both places have come into our possession to be used to the very best advantage possible for sanitarium purposes.

But more important than magnificent scenery and beautiful buildings and spacious grounds, is the close proximity of these institutions to densely populated districts, and the opportunity thus afforded of communicating to many, many people a knowledge of the third angel's message. We are to have clear spiritual discernment, else we shall fail to understanding the opening providences of God that are preparing the way for us to enlighten the world. The great crisis is just before us. Now is the time for us to sound the warning message, by the agencies that God has given us for this purpose. Let us remember that one most important agency is our medical missionary work. Never are we to lose sight of the great object for which our sanitariums are established,—the advancement of God's closing work in the earth.

Loma Linda is in the midst of a very rich district, including three important cities,—Redlands, Riverside, and San Bernardino. This field must be worked from Loma Linda, as Boston must be worked from Melrose.

When the New England Sanitarium was removed from South Lancaster to Melrose, the Lord instructed me that this was in the order of His opening providence. The buildings and grounds at Melrose are of a character to recommend our medical missionary work, which is to be carried forward not only in Boston, but in many other unworked cities in New England. The Melrose property is such that conveniences can be provided that will draw to that sanitarium persons not of our faith. The aristocratic as well as the common people will visit that institution to avail themselves of the advantages offered for restoration of health.

Boston has been pointed out to me repeatedly as a place that must be faithfully worked. The light must shine in the outskirts and in the inmost parts. The Melrose Sanitarium is one of the greatest agencies that can be employed to reach Boston with the truth. The city and its suburbs must hear the last message of mercy to be given to our world. Tent-meetings must be held in many places. The workers must put to the very best use the abilities God has given them. The gifts of grace will increase by wise use. But there must be no self-exaltation. No precise lines are to be laid down. Let the Holy Spirit direct the workers. They are to keep looking unto Jesus, the author and finisher of their faith. The work for this great city will be signalled by the revelation of the Holy Spirit, if all will walk humbly with God.

We hear that something is now being done in Boston. We are rejoiced to learn, through a report in a recent "Review" of Elder L. S. Wheeler's work as pastor of the Boston church, and of the work of his faithful co-laborers. We are also pleased to learn that Elder F. C. Gilbert has been laboring in Everett, a suburb. We hope that those in charge of the work in New England will cooperate with the Melrose Sanitarium managers in taking aggressive steps to do the work that should be done in Boston. A hundred workers could be laboring to advantage in different portions of the city, in varied lines of service.

The terrible disasters that are befalling great cities, ought to arouse us to intense activity in giving the warning message to the people in these congested centers of population, while we still have an opportunity. The most favorable time for the presentation of our message in the cities, has passed by. Sin and wickedness are rapidly increasing; and now we shall have to redeem the time by laboring all the more earnestly.

The medical missionary work is a door through which the truth is to find entrance to many homes in the cities. In every city will be found those who will appreciate the truths of the third angel's message. The judgments of God are impending. Why do we not awaken to the peril threatening the men and women living in the cities of America? Our people do not realize as keenly as they should the responsibility resting upon them to proclaim the truth to the millions dwelling in these unwarned cities.

There are many souls to be saved. Our own souls are to be firmly grounded in a knowledge of the truth, that we may win others from error to the truth. We need now to search the scriptures diligently, and as we become acquainted with unbelievers, we are to hold up Christ as the anointed, the crucified, the risen Saviour, witnessed to by prophets, testified of by believers, and through whose name we receive the forgiveness of our sins.

We need now a firm belief in the truth. Let us understand what is truth. Time is very short. Whole cities are being swept away. Are we doing our part to give the message that will prepare a people for the coming of their Lord? May the Lord help us to improve the opportunities that are ours.

Ellen G. White

* * * * *

Sanitarium, Calif.

B-142-'06 May 17, 1906.

Dear Brother and Sister Burden,

I have no apology to make for not sending you, sooner, this matter regarding the bakery at Loma Linda. The delay has been occasioned by illness and traveling. On my journey to Mountain View, I had a peaceful, restful night on the cars; but I had not been able to throw off a cold that I contracted in S. Calif. When I reached Mountain View Thursday morning, my throat was suffering considerably. We had expected to stop only two or three hours, and then go on to St. Helena, but the brethren urged us to stop longer; and as we considered the needs of the work there, in view of the disaster to the Pacific Press, we consented to remain over the Sabbath.

Thursday morning we were driven over a portion of Mountain View, and shown the ruins of several buildings, including the post office and some two-story brick buildings, that were completely wrecked by the earthquake. I was made sad to see the ruins of the sides of the "Signs" Office. The building has been repaired temporarily, and the chapel was repaired sufficiently to make it safe and comfortable for Sabbath services. We have reason to thank the Lord that no greater damage was done. Thursday afternoon I met with the brethren in council, and spoke a short time.

Nearly every morning we were there, the sky was overcast with fog. I rode out a short distance on Friday. That day I was quite sick, and very weak, and I hardly dared hope to be able to speak on the morrow. However, I ventured to allow the brethren to make an appointment for me to address the people Sabbath afternoon. I made the Lord my entire dependence; for I knew that unless He should be my helper, I could not speak more than a few words. I was afflicted with the influenza, and my throat and head were greatly troubled. I was so hoarse that I could scarcely talk.

When the appointed hour came, I went over to the usual place of meeting, and was surprised to find the Chapel crowded. I feared I should fail, but began talking about the last prayer of Christ, as recorded in the seventeenth of John. The moment I began to speak, strength was imparted, and I was relieved of my hoarseness, and spoke without difficulty for nearly an hour. My illness seemed to disappear and my mind was clear. As soon as I finished speaking,

[175]

the hoarseness came upon me again, and I am still under difficulty, coughing and sneezing.

To me, this experience was marked evidence of divine help. I am so grateful to my heavenly Father for this special miracle of His power, which gave me no chance for any doubt. In the afternoon I had a very strange movement of the bowels, which cleansed my system but left me prostrated. I was so very weak; but I praise the Lord for His goodness, and for evidence of His special power upon me in such a way that I could not entertain a doubt but that He had a message for me to bear to the people. I was very sick in the afternoon, and restless during the night; but Sunday I was able to sit up in bed, and trace some of the lines that I am sending to you.

Monday noon we started home, by the way of San Francisco. In Palo Alto we saw the ruins of the beautiful stone entrance of the Leland Stanford Jr. University. Many of the magnificent buildings of this great university are badly wrecked.

At the Valencia St. Station, we secured a cab, and spent an hour and a half riding through the streets of the stricken city. Terrible were the sights that met our eyes. The situation there can scarcely be exaggerated. Our church on Laguna Street was not burned. The chimney is down, and the building has been damaged otherwise, to the extent of about a thousand dollars, we are told. The beautiful park close by is a safe retreat for many refugees. All of these scenes were a very solemn import to me.

Since coming home, I have taken quite thorough treatment, but my cough has been coming on mornings, and sometimes at night. Hot baths have relieved me considerably. Still, I am not well. I feel very weary, and have been able to do but little writing. I have finally completed this that I am now sending you; and as I have been writing it out. I have thought, how pleased I would be to converse with you!

Brother Burden, we appreciate your ability as a manager and as a spiritual instructor, and we feel anxious that you should not be harassed with so many perplexing details of business that the spiritual work shall take a secondary place. I pray that you may preserve your capabilities, and constantly increase in talent and spiritual power.

Sister Burden, you need to get out often, and ride. This is the prescription I give, in the name of the Lord. We hope you will both have health and strength and vitality, and that your spiritual growth shall not decrease, but increase.

From various sources I have been receiving letters containing statements regarding supposed inconsistencies in the Testimonies and reasons why they can not be regarded as reliable. As soon as I am able, I plan to take up these matters; but I cannot expect to do anything before I recover from the effects of the influenza.

Be of good courage in the Lord. Trust fully in His power to strengthen and uphold you.

In faith and love,

Ellen G. White.

* * * * *

C. Later:- I have just had an interview with Dr. Preston S. Kellogg. He has a knowledge of surgery, and has made a success in this line. For his spiritual good, he needs to be connected with some one of our sanitariums. Will you please favor me by giving him a close looking over, to see if he would not be one who could be used at Loma Linda to do the work that we once thought Dr. Holden would do.

I have urged Brother Kellogg to go to Loma Linda, and see the place. May the Lord give you wisdom to know how to handle this case. I have had only a few minutes talk with him, and now leave the matter to your judgment. Elder Behrens says that he and his wife are having a good religious experience.

Ellen G. White

* * * * *

**Sanitarium, Calif.,
K. 164 '06 May 28, '06.**

Melrose and Loma Linda are both very beautiful places. Each has excellent advantages, and these two places near the cities, will open the way for the truth to find access to many people who have never heard it.

Elder Haskell and wife have begun work at San Bernardino, and they are sparing no pains. They are doing their best. They labor earnestly to keep the workers all alive and interested to sell the literature, and the work is certainly taking hold. Some souls have already taken their stand.

We feel deeply interested to see our cities worked. We hope that our workers in Boston will have courage in the Lord. The Lord is soon to come, and there is need that every talent shall be improved.

I have seen the city of San Francisco, and what a scene of devastation it presents. We were an hour and a half riding through the ruins. As we looked at such complete destruction, we could hardly realize that the largest city in California was in ruins.

We shall do all we possibly can to get the truth before the people now. The special number of the "Signs" is a medium through which much good will be accomplished.

If I were twenty-five years younger, I would certainly take up labor in the cities. But I must reach them with the pen.

Looking at the tall buildings in San Francisco, some of them having one side still standing, it seemed to say, The touch of the Lord's finger will lay in ruins the most costly and the highest of buildings. One of the standing walls of these high structures came down with a crash as we were looking at it. The completeness of the ruin cannot be described ...

We know not what may come next to arouse the people to investigate Bible truth. The day of the Lord will come unlooked for, as a thief in the night. If these awful calamities do not make an impression on our minds, what will?

"Be ye also ready, for in such a day as ye think not the Son of man cometh."

Ellen G. White

* * * * *

Elmshaven, Sanitarium, Calif.
B.-204-'06 June 17, 1906.

Dear Brother Burden,

For several days I have thought of writing you, but could not because so many things demanding immediate attention have come in. I may have written to you regarding the equipment of your treatment rooms, but fearing that I have not. I will come right to the point.

When we were at the Paradise Valley Sanitarium, we were conducted through the new treatment rooms. One room was elaborately fitted up with electrical appliances for giving the patients treatment. That night I was instructed that some connected with the institution were introducing things for the treatment of the sick that were not safe. The application of some of these electrical treatments would involve the patient in serious difficulties, imperiling life.

One was conversing with the doctors, and with great earnestness was saying, "Never, never carry out your wonderful plans. There have been various mechanical devices brought into the treatment rooms that are expensive, and the men who make a specialty of treating certain cases are liable to make grave mistakes."

There are men who make a specialty of treating the rectum, and some feel that they have been greatly benefitted. But I have been instructed that this treatment, as well as many surgical operations, leaves with many a serious weakness.

Several things were mentioned that have been brought into the Paradise Valley Sanitarium, which were not necessary, and which should not have been purchased without consultation with other physicians. The amount of money which some of these machines cost, and the salary which must be paid to the one who operates them, should be taken into consideration. I felt impelled to talk with Brother Robinson in reference to these matters, although we were driving with a number of people, and it was not a favorable place to converse about such matters.

Now I am certain that great care should be taken in purchasing electrical instruments and costly mechanical fixtures. Move slowly, Brother Burden, and do not trust to men who suppose that they understand what is essential, and who launch out in spending money for many things that require experts to handle them.

Several times I have been instructed that much of the elaborate, costly machinery used in giving treatments, did not help in the work

[178]

as much as is supposed. With it we do not get so good results as with the simple appliances we used in our earlier experiences. The application of water in the various simple ways is a great blessing.

I have been instructed that the x-ray is not the great blessing that some suppose it to be. If used unwisely, it may do much harm. The results of some of the electrical treatments are similar to the results of using stimulants. There is a weakness that follows...

Keep the patients out of doors as much as possible, and give them cheering, happy talks in the parlor, with simple reading and Bible lessons easy to be understood, which will be an encouragement to the soul. Talk on health reform, and do not you, my brother, become burden-bearer in so many lines that you cannot teach the simple lessons of health reform. Those who go from the Sanitarium should go so well instructed that they can teach others the methods of treating their families.

There is danger of spending far too much money on machinery and appliances which the patients can never use in their home lessons. They should rather be taught how to regulate the diet, so that the living machinery of the whole being will work in harmony. Let them become intelligent in regard to the importance of laying aside corsets and shortening their skirts. Such lessons will be to the women more valuable than they can estimate.

Ellen G. White

* * * * *

Elmshaven", Sanitarium, California
June 24, 1906 H-192-'06 " June 8, 1906.
Dear Brother and Sister Haskell,

We have received and read your interesting letter, also the enclosures from Sister Burgess. Thank you for sending these communications. The experiences they relate are very encouraging.

The recent developments in Battle Creek have caused me a great amount of writing. I have been kept under a constant strain to meet the emergencies as they arise. Through the day, and by lamplight in the early morning hours, I have worked, until, with congested brain and weakened eyes, I have been obliged to call a halt. But the Lord has graciously blessed me this morning, and I have some relief.

Elder Taylor has left Battle Creek and has returned to California. He says that he went to Battle Creek, hoping that he might help the brethren spiritually, but he now feels that the conditions there are such that it is impossible for him to benefit them, so he has left.

Yesterday I had a long visit as I rode out with Brother and Sister Howell. Brother Howell is very desirous of knowing how to plan for the educational work with which he is connected, so that no mistakes may be made. I tell him that the Lord will lead all who are willing to be led. The Bible is our safe guide book. Said Christ, "He that will come after me, let him take up his cross and follow Me." We cannot mark out a practice line to be followed unconditionally. Circumstances and emergencies will arise for which the Lord must give special instruction. But if we begin to work, depending upon the Lord, watching, praying, and walking in harmony with the light He sends us, we shall not be left to walk in darkness.

I am glad that you are carrying forward the work you have undertaken in San Bernardino. I believe that you are working in harmony with the light that has been given to me. In your work you come in contact with people who need to feel a hunger and thirst after righteousness. The Lord's blessing will be with all who work in harmony with His plans.

It has often been presented to me that there should be less sermonizing by ministers acting merely as local pastors of churches, and that greater personal efforts should be put forth. Our people should not be made to think that they need to listen to a sermon every Sabbath. Many who listen frequently to sermons, even though the truth be preached in clear lines, learn but little. Often it would be more profitable if the Sabbath meetings were of the nature of a Bible class study. Bible truth should be presented in such a simple, interesting manner that all can easily understand and grasp the principles of salvation.

We should seek to follow more closely the example of Christ the great Shepherd, as He worked with His little company of disciples, studying with them and with the people the Old Testament Scriptures. His active ministry consisted not merely in sermonizing, but in educating the people. As He passed through villages, He came in personal contact with the people in their homes, teaching and ministering to their necessities. As the crowds that followed Him

[180]

increased, when He came to a favorable place, He would speak to them, simplifying His discourses by the use of parables and symbols.

"The Word was made flesh, and dwelt among us," that we may understand the character we may possess if we eat His flesh and drink His blood. "Whoso eateth My flesh, and drinketh My blood," He declares "Hath eternal life." And He further says, "The flesh profiteth nothing, the words that I speak unto you, they are spirit and they are life."

The infinite sufficiency of Christ is demonstrated by His bearing the sins of the whole world. He occupies the double position of offerer and of offering, of priest and of victim. He was holy, harmless, undefiled, and separate from sinners. "The prince of this world cometh," He declares, "and findeth nothing in Me." He was a Lamb without blemish, and without spot. As we look to Him we see our work exemplified.

How can the sinner be redeemed? When the conscience has been awakened to a sense of an intolerable burden of guilt, what will give a hope that outweighs all discouragement and despair? "It is Christ that died." O, price above all price!! Rejoice, sinful one; sin is not infinite. However aggravated its character, however oppressive the guilt of conscience, there is blessed hope. "Though your sins be as scarlet," repentant one, despair not. "They shall be as white as wool; though they be red like crimson, they shall be as wool." "If we confess our sins, He is faithful and just to forgive us our sins, and to cleanse us from all unrighteousness."

What shall turn us from the love of God? Shall we not earnestly endeavor to point sinners to the matchless love of Christ?

Ellen G. White

* * * * *

[181] **Elmshaven, Sanitarium, California**
H - 192 - '06 June 8, 1906.
Dear Brother and Sister Haskell,

I am glad that you are carrying forward the work you have undertaken in San Bernardino. I believe that you are working in harmony with the light that has been given to me. In your work you come in contact with people who need to feel a hunger and thirst after righteousness. The Lord's blessing will be with all who work in harmony with His plans.

It has often been presented to me that there should be less sermonizing by ministers acting merely as local pastors of churches, and that greater personal efforts should be put forth. Our people should not be made to think that they need to listen to a sermon every Sabbath. Many who listen frequently to sermons, even though the truth be presented, in clear lines, learn but little. Often it would be more profitable if the Sabbath meetings were of the nature of Bible Class study. Bible truth should be presented in such a simple, interesting manner that all can easily understand and grasp the principles of salvation.

We should seek to follow more closely the example of Christ, the great Shepherd, as He worked with His little company of disciples, studying with them, and with the people the Old Testament Scriptures. His active ministry consisted not merely in sermonizing, but in educating the people. As He passed through villages, He came in personal contact with the people in their homes, teaching, and ministering to their necessities. As the crowds that followed Him increased, when He came to a favorable place, He would speak to them, simplifying His discourse by the use of parables and symbols...

Ellen G. White

* * * * *

To Elders Reaser, Burden, and the Executive Committee of the Southern California Conference

Oakland, Calif.
B. - 274- '06 August 19, 1906.
Dear Brethren,

I am very anxious that Brethren Reaser and Burden, and their associates shall see all things clearly. God has given to every man a certain work to do, and He will give to each the wisdom necessary to perform his own appointed work.

To Brethren Reaser and Burden I would say, In all your counsels together, be careful to show kindness and courtesy toward each other. Guard against anything that has the semblance of domineering spirit.

[182]   Be careful not to do anything that would restrict the work at Loma Linda. It is in the order of God that this property has been secured, and He has given instruction that a school should be connected with the sanitarium. A special work is to be done there in qualifying young men and young women to be efficient medical missionary workers. They are to be taught how to treat the sick without the use of drugs. Such an education requires an experience in practical work.

The work at Loma Linda demands immediate consideration. Preparations must be made for the school to be opened as soon as possible. Our young men and young women are to find in Loma Linda a school where they can receive a medical missionary training, and where they will not be brought under the influence of some who are seeking to undermine the truth. The students are to unite faithfully in the medical work, keeping their physical powers in the most perfect condition possible, and laboring under the instruction of the great Medical Missionary. The healing of the sick and the ministry of the Word are to go hand in hand. There is to be a thorough education in Bible truth. The Word of God is spirit and life. We need constantly to look to Jesus. The efficiency of every worker is largely determined by the education and training he receives. In our educational institutions there is to be a higher class of education than can be found elsewhere. The students are to be treated kindly, tenderly, and interestedly.

In order properly to fit the sanitarium and the school at Loma Linda to carry on the work that the Lord has plainly directed should be carried on, means must be raised. And let no one act a part in influencing our brethren and sisters in S. Calif. not to do that which needs to be done.

The Lord has blessed Elder Burden, and He will continue to bless him, as he continues to move in the fear of God, and plans wisely and economically with his associates for the fitting up and management of the institution. If any of his brethren act arbitrarily in an effort to restrain him in this, they would be hindering the very work that the Lord has signified should be done. He is not to be forced to turn aside from his convictions as to the way in which the work under his charge shall be carried on.

In the carrying forward of the educational work at Loma Linda, our brethren must constantly guard against the efforts of the enemy to bring in a spirit of criticism and of alienation between brethren.

There are times when certain sanitariums will have to pass through a close, severe struggle for means in order to do a special work which the Lord has particularly designated should be done. In such emergencies, they are to be free to receive gifts and donations from our churches. Some who receive the truth have means and they will aid in sustaining the good work which should be done in our sanitariums.

My brethren, I am praying that the Lord will guide you in the very best methods of reaching hearts. Let no one, whatever his official position, decide matters fully on his own judgment, or he may make mistakes that will have to be corrected. One thing is certain, we have a short work before us. We are living very near the end of this earth's history.

[183]

For years we have wrestled to see the work of God advanced in S. Calif. At one time we found such narrow, prescribed plans that the work could not move forward. Then when an effort was made to advance, it resulted in large outlay, and in extravagant plans that were altogether out of order. Then followed a pressure for money, and the work was held back.

Still the light kept coming to me that the work should be conducted after a different order, that many plans and devisings of men needed to be changed. Of late some moves have been made. The Lord has wrought in the securing of properties at Fernando, at Paradise Valley, and at Glendale.

A sanitarium has been established at Loma Linda, and this is in the providence of God. Some know how difficult it has been to accomplish the work that has been done. But the work at Loma Linda is not yet perfected. More money must be raised in order to make this place a center for the training of medical missionary evangelists.

As the president and executive committee of the S. Calif. Conference unite with Brother Burden and his associates in planning for the thorough accomplishment of the sanitarium and school work at Loma Linda, they will find strength and blessing. Brother Burden is not to be bound about in his work.

Pray to the Lord, my brethren, counsel together, and then labor unitedly to help in establishing the work which we all so greatly desire shall not be hindered.

The work of higher education has been greatly hindered because men and women have not discerned spiritual things as they should. We should know the facts that are of weight in making decisions.

All our brethren are to be sober-minded and cautious. Those who hold office need the ability to view every matter wisely. We are all to be workers together with God.

Ellen G. White

* * * * *

Sanitarium, Calif.
L.-286-'06 Sept. 3, 1906.
Roy Logan:
Dear Brother,

Sister King has spoken to me of you as a young man desiring advice in regard to entering a school of Osteopathy, conducted by unbelievers.

I would caution you to be on your guard. You cannot be too careful how you place yourself in a position where you will be surrounded by students who are unbelievers, and receive instruction from teachers who are not taught by the great Teacher, the Lord Jesus Christ.

It has frequently been seen that what seemed to be favorable opportunities for obtaining an education in worldly institutions, were snares of the enemy. The time of the student has been occupied, to the exclusion of the study of God's word. They have completed the course of study, but they were not fitted to take up the study of the work of the Lord.

It is not necessary for you to go to a worldly school to obtain an education; for there are excellent opportunities before you in schools conducted by those who understand the truth, and where you can receive an education in Bible knowledge. If you desire to fit yourself for medical missionary work, you can find at Loma Linda the very best opening. If you need preliminary work, this you can obtain at the college in Healdsburg. Would it not be wisdom for you to attend one of these schools, rather than to place yourself in the company of those who neither teach nor obey the commandments of God?

You will have severe enough battles to fight, even when you place yourself under the best influences possible. Would it not be presumption to place yourself unnecessarily in a school where the teachers do not have respect to the Lord's commandments, where the Sabbath is not recognized as His sign? ...

Our young men need, above all else, to be thoroughly instructed that they may teach the way of the Lord to perishing souls. "The words that I speak unto you," says Christ, "they are spirit, and they are life." Study the word. The strictest fidelity is to be cherished. The love of the truth, and a genuine desire for improvement in the understanding of the Word, will make you that ye shall neither be barren nor unfruitful in the service of God. As you learn, you should seek for opportunities to explain the truth to others.

The tempter is watching you, in your uncertainty. He will make a determined effort to secure you to serve his purposes. How few understand Satan's great power to deceive. Close every door where he might enter. Surrender yourself, body, soul, and spirit to God.

Place yourself under those who teach and obey the truth and learn all you can from them. When you place yourself under the influence of the Holy Spirit, then you can see light in God's light, and you will rejoice in His truth. Keep yourself in the circle of His light, where His light is cherished, and then "let your light so shine before men that they, by seeing your good works, may glorify your Father which is in heaven."

Ellen G. White

* * * * *

[185] **Sanitarium, Calif.**
Oct. 3, 1908.-6- B-304-'06 Sept. 14, 1906.
Dear Brother and Sister Burden,

I cannot sleep after one o'clock. We left St. Helena on Friday morning to spend Sabbath and Sunday in Oakland. I spoke both afternoons in the tent. On Sabbath afternoon the tent was filled, mostly with our own people; and all present were interested. I had special freedom in speaking from the seventh chapter of Revelation. This is a most interesting chapter.

The only place that could be obtained for the tent was a lot of ground close by the car line, where the cars are coming all the time. You can see that this would not be the most favorable place for speaking. The interest was good; but I would not dare to attempt to speak in so high a key as would be necessary in this tent, and shall not venture to do this. Apart from this disadvantage the location is excellent. After a while we may get a better location. The Lord has graciously strengthened me to stand before the people. Souls are becoming interested in the truth.

I am in good health now, and I praise the Lord with heart and soul and voice. I would like to see you and to converse with you. Be of good courage in the Lord. I received your letter, and although it was short, I was glad to have it.

September 28, 1906

I have been writing from two this morning until six, when W. C. White left for his journey to Washington I had written eighteen pages of letter paper for him to take with him. I could not get the matter copied at so early an hour, but thought he could take it with him in the original writing. After he had gone I wrote eighteen pages more. Before he left we had a season of prayer, and the Lord gave us His peace.

Brethren Burden and Howell, the work of the school and the sanitarium will be a blessing, the one to the other. Each must act its individual part, but both must blend together; then the interests of both will be advanced. If there is cooperation between the educational work and the work of the sanitarium, we can heartily recommend that the higher education be carried on in the sanitarium grounds for this is the Lord's plan. If the men at the head of this enterprise plan for the usefulness of these institutions, each helping the other, there is nothing to hinder the operations of the school. As the work grows, buildings may have to be prepared.

Brother Burden, I have written a great deal of late in regard to the subject of food manufacture. We are not to allow Dr. Kellogg's plans in regard to the corn flakes cause a large investment of money that should be invested in less expensive preparations of food. We will deal in foods that will require such an outlay of means in order to secure the privilege of using them. I will send to you copies of some things I have written on this subject. (These will be sent soon. D.E.R.")

Time is very short; and cities and towns are to be visited with judgment. Fire and water will work with their destructive forces. We should not make the food business a straining for high profits. We should work in connection with the great food manufacturer, Jesus Christ, who fed five thousand people with five loaves and two small fishes.

"When Jesus then lifted up his eyes, and saw a great company come unto Him, He said unto Philip, Whence shall we buy bread, that these may eat?" This question was asked simply to see what Philip would say; for Jesus knew what He would do. Philip answered, "Two hundred pennyworth of bread is not sufficient for them, that every one of them may take a little."

Christ might have said to Philip, "Have I been so long time with you, and yet hast thou not known Me, Philip? or, as the Lord answered Moses in a similar case, "Is the Lord's hand waxen short?" In our feeble faith we are likely to distrust God's power, and believe no farther than we can see. After seeing the miracles of Christ, Philip could readily have answered, "Lord, if Thou wilt, Thou canst exert Thy power for this hungry multitude;" but now He asked, "What are they among so many?"

"Bid the men sit down," Christ commanded; for the grass was abundant in that place. A blessing was asked upon the food, and thanks were offered for it; and never did food taste sweeter. The seemingly meager supply was passed from the hand of Christ to the disciples, and the disciples to them that were set down; and likewise of the fishes as much as they would.

There might have been questioning among the multitude how they might entertain their benefactor and His disciples; for many of the people were rich, and they knew that Christ and His disciples were poor. But Christ would give these men a lesson; He entertained the hungry crowd by working a miracle. In this way He teaches that spiritual gifts are not to be bought, but are the free gift of God. Having fed their souls with the precious word, the Bread of Life, He supplied their temporal necessities, and thus encourages a manifestation of the grace of thankfulness.

When all had eaten, the word went forth from lips that had blessed the bread, "Gather up the fragments, that nothing be lost." "Therefore they gathered them together, and filled twelve baskets with the fragments of the five barley loaves, which remained over and above to them that had eaten." Then leading the minds of the miracle-fed men from the temporal to spiritual food, Christ represented Himself as Bread of eternal life.

[187] The food provided was not especially inviting, and by many would be considered coarse. This does not signify that we should confine ourselves to a coarse fare, when Providence supplies us with better. But when necessity demands, and the blessing of the Miracle worker is upon the food, even the coarsest fare will become palatable. To those hungry men, the meal composed of barley bread and fish was the most palatable they had ever eaten.

Ellen G. White

* * * * *

Sanitarium, Calif.
B.-304-'06 Sept. 14, 1906.
Dear Brother and Sister Burden,

...

To Elders Reaser, Burden, and the Executive Committee of the Southern California Conference

The work of the school and the sanitarium (Loma Linda) will be a blessing, the one to the other. Each must act its individual part, but both must blend together; then the interests of both will be advanced. If there is cooperation between the educational work and the work of the sanitarium, we can heartily recommend that the higher education be carried on in the sanitarium grounds; for this is the Lord's plan. If the men at the head of this enterprise plan for the usefulness of these institutions, each helping the other, there is nothing to hinder the operations of the school. As the work grows, buildings may have to be prepared.

* * * * *

Ellen G. White

Sanitarium, Calif.
MS. 81, 1906. Sept. 27, 1906

... In many places, in different sections of the country, an effort should be made to utilize natural products for healthful foods. A good work along this line may be done at Loma Linda. Our brethren there should make a beginning soon, even if all the arrangements regarding this work cannot be definitely decided upon at this time. As our brethren at Loma Linda study how to make the health food work a means of bringing the truth for this time before the minds of unbelievers, the Lord will add His blessing, and will make plain the course they should pursue in the conduct of the business.

A similar work is to be carried forward in the Southern States. Men and women who embrace the truth in the South will often need to be helped to find employment. Many will find opportunity to engage in evangelistic work; and these should learn, in connection with this work, to teach worldlings how to prepare simple, palatable food.

Outside the city of Nashville there are advantages that should be utilized in providing wholesome food for the people...

[188]

Ellen G. White

* * * * *

Sanitarium, Calif,
Nov. 2, 1906. B.280'07

Elder J. A. Burden,

I have words to speak to you. The Lord has laid upon you the responsibilities of no ordinary nature. At the time of the meeting held before you were settled at Loma Linda, when I was so sick, the Lord showed me what was to be your work as director of the Sanitarium, and that if you would connect yourself with divine wisdom, you would be taught of God. You need a clear mind in order to settle wisely the many questions that come to you for decision. The Lord would have you taught of Him.

My Brother, do not allow men of limited experience to come in, as Elder Reaser has done, and assume a controlling power. Brother Reaser has placed himself as teacher and adviser and ruled in many matters, and unless you work and watch carefully, such an influence will retard the work. Brother Reaser should learn that he is not qualified to do the work he supposes he is to do.

Brother Reaser supposes that if it were not for his watching of the finances, there would be serious losses, whereas, if he had nothing to do and say in these matters, it would save many perplexities. He has taken upon himself burdens that the Lord has not laid upon him. He has learned some of his lessons of Elder Healey who has done much to retard the work in the South. If he would attend to his work of ministry, and keep his hands off the work of directing, he would save himself and others many burdens. From the light that has been given me, I know that it is a mistake for him to be connected with our sanitariums; he should not be a manager.

In regard to the health food business, I would urge you to move slowly. Dr. Kellogg's proposition to sell the corn flakes rights to our people for twenty years has just been considered by our brethren here; and I fear, if I had not been on the ground, this matter would have been carried through to the loss of our food business. When a thing is exalted, as the corn flakes has been, it would be unwise for our people to have anything to do with it. It is not necessary that we make the corn flakes an article of food.

I would advise you, my brother, to keep away from the influence of Dr. Kellogg's ingenious plans. Let us use our own ingenuity to invent the best kinds of food possible. We are living in the closing days of the earth's history; souls are starving for a knowledge of the word of God and of healthful living. Let us seek to carry our work solidly, giving all possible instruction regarding the principles of health reform, praying with the sick, and teaching the people how to care for themselves in sickness and health.

The Lord has sent us valuable help in Dr. White, who is studying to know how to follow the way of the Lord. Let there be much earnest prayer on the part of the workers, each depending on the great Physician to carry the work according to His purpose "For we are laborers together with God; ye are God's husbandry; ye are God's building." In our efforts to build up the cause of God in the earth, we are to make sure work for eternity.

Many workers who are bearing responsibilities are embracing too much authority; and they will certainly confuse the human judgment by their dictatorial authority. I must warn my brethren to be on their guard against this. The cause of God is imperiled when the workers become self-confident, and seek to embrace more than the Lord has laid upon them. Hindrance instead of advancement is the result of such a spirit.

Brother Burden, carry your work intelligently, ever consulting the word of God; for this word is very precious to the worker in the cause. Study the messages that God has sent to His people for the last sixty years through the Spirit of Prophecy. Do not seek the counsel of men, but by earnest prayer seek the wisdom of God. A mistake has been made in the past by leaning upon the guidance of men. Seek to correct this mistake....

Yesterday was a strange day for me. I was compelled to leave letters and other writings unfinished.

The Lord has been working with Elder Simpson, teaching him how to give to the people this last warning message. His method of making the words of the Bible prove the truth for this time, and his use of the symbols presented in Revelation and Daniel, are effective. Let the young men learn as for their lives what is truth, and how it should be presented. We are living in the last days of the great conflict; the truth alone will hold us securely in this time of trouble. The way should be prepared for Elder Simpson to give the message, and our young men should attend his evening meetings.

Those who have considered themselves qualified to bear responsibilities in the churches, should seek to obtain light and a knowledge of how to prosecute their work at this time in the cities, north and south, east and west, that are calling for a knowledge of the truth for this time. Our campmeetings should do a more thorough work in preparing the laborers for the work that is to be done in every place.

The campmeetings which my husband attended were made special seasons of seeking the Lord. Every morning at an early hour the ministers assembled in the large tent, where we sought to become of one mind. The question would be asked, Have we any personal difficulties to settle? If so, let us settle them. Let us not pass one day on this ground cherishing hard feelings against a brother. Let there be no evil speaking one of another; for this will greatly dishonor God. Let us by every means in our power seek to remove the alienation and differences that exist.

[192] Then we would have a season of prayer, and these were times of confession and breaking of heart before God. Often the workers, and especially the ministers, would state their true feelings, relating their temptations, and confessing their loss of confidence in their brethren. These confessions tended to clear away any ill feeling that existed, and brought in a very different atmosphere.

At these campmeetings, no one man carried the burden of deciding who should speak, but those were chosen who were experienced in the message and in conducting campmeetings. We used then the very arguments that are now given why the young men should not be brought to the front while the aged workers were passed by.

God speaks through the men who understand the guiding of the Holy Spirit. When thousands come out to attend our meetings, they desire to get the greatest benefit possible, and it is poor policy to place as speakers men who are not fully adapted to meet the needs of the situation. The word should be spoken by men who have felt the deep moving of the Spirit upon their hearts, and who feel the burden of the message that God has given them for the people. The old soldiers of the cross are not to be passed by.

Men who have been placed in office for the first time and who are just gaining their experience, need to move carefully and in humility of mind; for often they are not apt to judge wisely. When Elder Reaser was placed in a position of responsibility, he did not

To Elders Reaser, Burden, and the Executive Committee of the Southern California Conference 247

~~see his need to learn all that he could from the experience of others~~ who had a knowledge of the history of the work in S. Calif., and who had burdens laid upon them for that work by the Lord. At the first assuming of his new responsibilities, Elder Reaser should have considered that these persons understood the situation better than he did. By his officious attitude, he has made the work much more perplexing than it otherwise would have been. If he will be taught, the Lord will teach Elder Reaser that He has men on the ground who are fully as capable of planning and devising for the interests of the work as himself.

The Lord has given you your work, Brother Burden. He has not appointed Elder Reaser to tell you what your duty is, as superintendent of the sanitarium, your work is an important one. Elder Reaser is not to intrude himself upon that which God has given you to do. That there shall be no more money in the sanitarium until the institution shall have earned that amount required, is not for Elder Reaser to decide. Hire money, if this is necessary in order to perfect the work.

Ellen G. White

* * * * *

The Workers in the Paradise Valley Sanitarium

Sanitarium, Napa Co.,
Calif. B.-56-'07 Feb. 12, 1907.

Dear Brethren and Sisters,

The past night has been one of wakefulness and prayer. I am anxious to understand the ways of the Lord, and to know what words I should speak to those who are in charge of the Paradise Valley Sanitarium.

I heard One of authority speaking to a company of workers, including every one who has a part to act in the sanitarium. These were the words He said.

"Let not your hearts be troubled: ye believe in God, believe also in Me. In My Father's house are many mansions; if it were not so I would have told you. I go to prepare a place for you, and if I go and prepare a place for you, I will come again, and receive you unto Myself, that where I am there ye may be also."

When Jesus spoke these words to His disciples, He was about to leave them. He had just given them a portion of His parting address, and in that He had foretold the work of Judas in betraying his Lord for thirty pieces of silver. When Judas left the presence of Christ to perform this terrible work, Jesus said to His disciples, "Now is the Son of Man glorified, and God is glorified in Him. If God be glorified in Him, God shall also glorify Him in Himself, and shall straightway glorify Him. Little children, yet a little while I am with you. Ye shall seek Me, and as I said unto the Jews, Whither I go ye cannot come; so now I say unto you. A new commandment I give unto you, that ye love one another. By this shall all men know that ye are my disciples, if ye have love one for another."

"Simon Peter said unto Him, Lord, whither goest Thou? Jesus answered him, Whither I go thou canst not follow me now; but thou shalt follow Me afterwards. Peter said unto Him, Lord, why cannot I follow Thee now? I will lay down my life for Thy sake? Jesus answered him, Wilt thou lay down they life for My sake? Verily,

verily I say unto thee, the cock shall not crow, till thou hast denied Me thrice.

The workers in our sanitariums should understand that each has an individual work. Each should realize his duty to keep his soul and body under discipline to the great Physician, who gave His life to rescue us from the control of a powerful foe. After He had burst the fetters of the tomb, He said to His disciples, "I am the resurrection and the life." And before He ascended to heaven, He declared, "All power is given unto Me in heaven and in earth. Go ye therefore and teach all nations, baptizing them in the name of the Father, and of the Son, and of the Holy Ghost, teaching them to observe all things whatsoever I have commanded you; and, lo, I am with you always, even unto the end of the world."

Here is your work. Teach the sick. Proclaim the gospel to them, persuading them to become Christ's disciples. The Father, the Son, and the Holy Spirit are pledged to be with you in every emergency. Act as Christians, having divine orders. God is to be trusted, believed, obeyed. His character is to be represented in every household.

A wonderful responsibility rests upon those connected with the sanitariums established in His name for the treatment of the sick. This is to be done without the use of poisonous drugs. Those who become workers in the sanitariums are to believe the words of Christ, "Lo, I am with you alway, even unto the end of the world." Those who have the fear of God in the heart will cultivate a sweet disposition. Forbearance and courtesy will be manifested in the life. Duties will be faithfully discharged and in a way that will not leave a disagreeable impression on the minds of the sick or the well.

In order to maintain a right influence, the workers must reveal that they are one in sentiment. Do not let it be seen that there is disunion among the helpers.

In your care of the sick, act tenderly, kindly, faithfully, that you may have a converting influence upon them. You have need of the grace of Christ in order to properly represent the service of Christ. And as you present the grace of truth in true, disinterested service, angels will be present to sustain you. The Comforter will be with you to fulfill the promise of the Saviour, "Lo, I am with you alway, even unto the end of the world."

[199] I have a charge to give, a message to bear to our sanitarium workers. Keep your souls in purity. Do a work that will have a winning influence on those placed in your charge. You can speak often to the sick of the great Physician, who can heal the diseases of the body as verily as He heals the sickness of the soul. Pray with the sick, and try to lead them to see in Christ, their healer. Tell them that if they will look to Him in faith, He will say to them, Thy sins be forgiven thee. It means very much to the sick to learn this lesson.

Ellen G. White

[200]
* * * * *

[201] **Sanitarium, Calif.,
Apr. 3, 1907. B. -120- '07.
Elder J. A. Burden, Loma Linda, Sanitarium.**
Dear Brother,

There are some things that I desire to write to you. Do not be in haste about the health food business. There is a possibility of entering into a work that will bring gain of means but which would result in spiritual loss to the sanitarium.

[202] Commercial enterprises often work to a large degree counter to the purpose for which our institutions are established. They detract from the influence which God desires shall attend the work. The condition brought about is sometimes the condition in which Christ found the barren fig-tree. Searching for fruit with which to satisfy His need, the Saviour found nothing but a show of leaves. In visions of the night I have seen Christ searching in our institutions for fruit, for that virtue revealed in the lives of His workers that tells in the saving of the soul unto eternal life. You have a noble work to do in praying with the sick, and in feeding their souls with the bread of life. You are to be God's medical missionary, teaching souls what it means to eat the flesh and drink the blood of the Son of God. Christ explains the meaning of these words, "The flesh profiteth nothing," He said; "the words that I speak unto you, they are spirit, and they are life." You have the ability to speak in a pleasant, intelligent, interesting way to the sick. It is your privilege to inspire them with hope and courage, and lead them to a knowledge of the truth of the word.

Many of the patients who come to the sanitarium are children in their understanding of the word. If you will take hold of these cases, and seek to lead them to the truth, One who is your righteousness will go before you, and the glory of the Lord will be your reward."

Your mind must be a treasure house, full of good things. Keep the patients cheerful. Pleasant words of instruction may be given to them that will be a blessing to them while they are at the sanitarium; and when they return to their homes, the message of truth they have heard will be constantly repeating itself to them. We do not appreciate how far greater are the results for good when we bring cheerfulness and the joy of the Lord into our work.

I am very desirous that you shall feel as free as possible to do this gospel work. Your strength for it, and your success in it, will depend largely on the time and strength you reserve for this work. You should not allow yourself to be overwhelmed with responsibilities, so that you cannot have the realization in your own soul that you are in the right place.

It is necessary that you share your responsibilities with others. Those who are spiritually minded, and whom you can trust with the work should be employed to help carry out your plans. You will find that you accomplish much more in the end if you will allow others to bear burdens. Your perceptions are good, but they must be worked in order to be improved. This is also true of your fellow-workers.

In no place in the world can our influence tell on the Lord's side with such power as in the position to which He calls us. The most useful thing we do in the service of God is to encourage the souls that are distressed, and lead them to Christ. Keep the lives of the patients constantly refreshed by the example of a Christlike example. You will have success if you will be a self-denying Christian. An earnest desire to be obedient to the will of your heavenly Father will bring you to the place where you will wear Christ's yoke. Those who are great in the sight of the Lord will, like John the Baptist, have humility of heart. Then good works will follow. Your example may be such that others will wish to emulate it. Your obedience and humbleness of mind will make obedience and humility a desirable thing to those who are associated with you.

The words of truth were so simple as Christ explained them that the disciples could comprehend them. The word of God is our spirit and life. It is the weapon by which we are to resist the attacks of Satan. Those who are much with God in prayer and consent to wear, the yoke of Christ, will be meek and lowly in heart. They will be one with Christ.

You and your wife can be a source of help and strength to each other, and a blessing to the sanitarium. Prayer is the key that will unlock the treasure of heaven to you. Let your faith increase. Increased faith and sanctification of the spirit, will qualify you to be a wise counsellor. Words spoken in season and in the spirit of tenderness, accompanied by the silent working of the Holy Spirit, will make the right impression. Do not think that you are accomplishing nothing because you cannot see definite results for your work. You are to sow the seed, knowing not which shall prosper, this or that.

May the Lord help and strengthen and bless you in your work, is my prayer.

Ellen G. White

* * * * *

**National City, California,
W.-164-'07 May 7, 1907.
Elder J. E. White:**
Dear Son Edson,

...

In many places I see a great need for the investment of means in the cause of God. Next week I expect to return to Loma Linda, and while there I will do what I can to help forward the work in the surrounding cities. I desire to invest some means in the work in these places. I hope to find opportunity to speak to our people in that locality, and to arouse them to a sense of their responsibility to hold up the light of truth. If, before I leave Loma Linda, I can see the right work begun, I shall not then feel pressed as a cart beneath sheaves, after I return home.

Mrs. Dr. Starr has been doing a good work in San Bernardino. She has been giving education in health principles, and has found access to many fine homes. I hope to strengthen her hands, and given her encouragement to continue the work in Redlands and Riverside

...... *Ellen G. White*

* * * *

[204]

An Open Letter

**Loma Linda, Calif.,
B.-174-'07. May 19, 1907.**

Dear Brethren and Sisters,

The Lord has greatly blessed our people in Southern Calif., in enabling them to secure at very low cost valuable sanitarium properties. Through the institutions that are established here, the Lord desires to reach a class that can be reached in no other way. Therefore I would urge upon our people to whom the Lord has entrusted the talent of means, that they make loans and gifts to place these institutions in a position where they can do without embarrassment the work that will be to the honor and glory of God.

For forty thousand dollars our brethren secured at Loma Linda buildings and land that cost originally one hundred and fifty thousand dollars. These buildings were furnished completely, far more elegantly than we would have furnished them.

The Lord has worked wonderfully in bringing us into possession of this place. Here is a center from which light is to shine into the surrounding cities of Redlands, Riverside, San Bernardino, Colton, and other places near by.

It has been found necessary to provide additional bathroom facilities at Loma Linda, and to make some changes greatly needed, and a small bakery should be added. We are in need of means to accomplish that which must be done, and we pray the Lord to put it into the heart of our brethren and sisters to help in this time of necessity.

For years the Lord has instructed us that we should have a sanitarium in the vicinity of San Diego, where many thousands of tourists come every year. A valuable property was secured at National City at a very small part of its original cost.

There an important work is to be done in caring for the sick, and in reaching many with the light of truth. At the Paradise Valley Sanitarium also it was found necessary to add to the original building, and obligations have been made that must soon be met. The Lord has blessed this institution, and some have been converted to the truth as the result of the work already done.

At Glendale, a few miles from Los Angeles, we purchased a sanitarium at about one fourth its real value. This institution is at the present time full of patients. It is well equipped for work, and is in a position of influence. Its need is not so pressing as that of the sanitariums at Loma Linda and National City.

The establishment of these three institutions has brought a heavy financial burden to our people in Southern Calif. Yet they have cheerfully responded to the calls for means that have been made. Brother Burden, Dr. White, and others connected with these sanitariums have invested all they could spare, that the work might not be hindered.

We have none too many sanitariums. There is need for every one that has been established. In these institutions we are endeavoring to carry the work earnestly and solidly, in harmony with the instruction the Lord has given in regard to sanitarium work. They are to stand as a means of teaching the truth in these great centers of tourist resort.

At our request, Brother Burden is going East to attend some of our campmeetings, where he may come in contact with many of our brethren and sisters, and lay before them the opportunities for assisting these important branches of the Lord's work. We unite in asking those who have means to spare, to consider the matter of investing some of their money in these institutions, thus helping to provide necessary facilities, that a thorough work may be done in caring for the sick who are coming to S. Calif. in search of health.

May the Lord give ability to help, and a willing mind.

Ellen G. White

* * * * *

Glendale, Calif., H.-176-1907. May 20, 1907.

Dear Brother and Sister Haskell,

We left home on our visit to S. Calif. April 18th. On our way to San Diego, we stopped off at Fernando, and we spent a few days at Loma Linda. At the Paradise Valley Sanitarium we found a very small patronage. Twice I spoke to the helpers and guests. On Sabbath and Sunday, May 4 and 5, I spoke to the church in San Diego. I bore a very plain testimony. Sunday afternoon, I followed an earnest appeal with a prayer. This was followed by a social meeting, at which some confessions were made...

I remained at Loma Linda nearly a week, during which time I spoke to the students twice. Sabbath forenoon I spoke to a large number who had assembled from the surrounding churches. The meeting was held on the lawn. Among those present were some who have recently begun the observance of the Sabbath in Redlands, where Elder Hare and Elder Whitehead have been conducting a series of meetings.

Seats were arranged under the pepper trees at the back of the Sanitarium. It was an interesting occasion. The Lord blessed me in speaking from the fifty-eighth chapter of Isaiah. Before I closed, I made a strong appeal to those who had means to help in the Lord's work, and I presented the needs of the Loma Linda Sanitarium. I urged them not to spend all their efforts merely in commercial lines, but to lay up treasure beside the throne of God.

In the evening, Brother Nichols came to my room, his face aglow with happiness, and said, "I want to tell you what your words today have accomplished. A sister came to Brother Burden and gave him ten dollars, and a gentleman has offered to lend him a thousand dollars for a year without interest." I thank the Lord for this response.

From Brother Burden I learned that the one who had offered to lend him a thousand dollars is a patient who had been in the sanitarium for some time. He had a serious stomach difficulty, and for some time his life was hanging in the balance. The crisis safely passed, he has begun to study the truth, and is deeply interested.

After the morning service, a lunch was provided by the sanitarium, on the lawn, for the visitors. Brother Burden felt that the sanitarium would not be a loser by doing this, and I agreed with him for I remember the experiences we have had in the past in making similar provision. Such actions are sometimes the means of sowing seed in the hearts of those who are inquiring after the truth.

In the afternoon, Elder Luther Warren gave an excellent discourse. Brother Warren is an able worker, and we hope he may labor for a time in this needy field. Now is a favorable time to work Redlands. The Women's Christian Temperance Union recently held an important convention in Redlands, and Dr. Starr attended their meetings. She was introduced to the convention, and by invitation spoke to them on the subject of healthful dress. She was well received, and has received many invitations to give lectures at various places. We trust that the Lord will open the way before her, and that she may be a help in removing the prejudice of some, that they may be willing to listen to the truth...

Ellen G. White

* * * * *

R.-182-'07. May 22, 1907.
Glendale, Calif.,
Elder A. T. Robinson:

Dear Brother Robinson,

At our request Brother Burden has consented to visit important gatherings of our people in the Middle West, and to endeavor to secure gifts or loans for some of our Southern Calif. Sanitariums. We desire that wherever he goes, he may be given opportunity to present the work and needs of the Paradise Valley and Loma Linda Sanitariums. We need help in both places. Both at Loma Linda and Paradise Valley it has been necessary to build additions to the main building for bathrooms. This had left us with debts that must be met shortly, and we greatly need financial assistance.

At Loma Linda, a school is being conducted for the training of medical missionary evangelists, and we want this school to be of the highest order. Both the sanitarium and the school can be a help one to the other.

Elder Burden has felt an earnest interest in the advancement of the Sanitarium work along right lines. He and Sister Burden have put their whole soul into an effort to make the work at Loma Linda a success. They have put into the institution all the means they could spare to keep the enterprise moving. We have the utmost confidence in the integrity of Brother Burden, and have no reason to doubt that the Lord selected him as the manager of the Loma Linda Sanitarium.

Will you, Brother Robinson, assist Brother Burden in his mission in behalf of these institutions? You may introduce him to some of our loyal brethren who have means, or you may permit him to speak before gatherings of our people, and raise donations or loans in your conference. We trust that our brethren in Nebraska may be able to assist in relieving the pressure for means that exists at present in these two sanitariums that the Lord has providentially placed in our hands.

Ellen G. White

* * * * *

B.-186-'07. May 29, 1907.
Sanitarium, Calif.,
Elder G. I. Butler, 24th Ave., North Nashville, Tennessee:
My dear Brother,

I received your letter, for which I thank you. I am always glad to hear from you.

For nearly six weeks I have been absent from St. Helena, traveling in S. Calif.... Sabbath and Sunday, April 20 and 21, I spent at Fernando. Our school this year at Fernando has been greatly blessed. Many of the students have offered themselves for service in the Master's vineyard. On Monday I left for Loma Linda. I remained there a little over a week, and returned again to Loma Linda after a visit to Paradise Valley, San Diego, San Pasqual, and Escondido.

On Sabbath, May 18th, the members of several churches gathered at Loma Linda, and we held meetings under the pepper trees on the lawn at the back of the sanitarium. In the forenoon I spoke for one hour, and the Lord helped me wonderfully. Before closing my remarks, I presented to those present the needs of the sanitarium, and expressed the desire that sufficient money might be received to complete the payments on the additions that have been made to the main building. Before we purchased the property, the main building had been used mostly as a hotel, and the bathroom facilities were limited. In order to do efficient work in the sanitarium, it was necessary to make additions to the buildings already standing. Dr. White, Brother and Sister Burden, and the sisters of Sister Burden, invested in the sanitarium at Loma Linda all that they could possibly spare, but there still remains an indebtedness that must be cleared off.

After the morning service, a lunch was provided by the sanitarium for the visitors, and served on the lawn. Brother Burden felt that the sanitarium would not be a loser by this entertainment and I agreed with him; for I remember the experiences we have had in the past in making similar provision. Such acts of hospitality are sometimes the means of sowing seed in the hearts of those who are inquiring after truth.

[208]

In the afternoon Elder Luther Warren gave an excellent discourse. Brother Warren is an able worker, and we hope that he may labor for a time in this needy field. At present he is resting somewhat on account of the condition of his own and his wife's health. After his service, the visitors left for their homes; and all were agreed that they had spent a pleasant day. and had been blessed by the discourses.

After the Sabbath, Brother Nichols came to my room, his face glowing with happiness, and said, "I want to tell you what your words today have accomplished." He then told me that one sister had come to Brother Burden and given him ten dollars, and that a gentleman had offered to lend him one thousand dollars for a year without interest. I felt to praise the Lord at this response.

Later, Brother Burden gave me some particulars concerning this man who has loaned the money. He was brought to the sanitarium in such a diseased condition that his case was thought to be hopeless, but he was carefully treated, and the crisis was safely passed. He is one of the most grateful patients they have had. He has become interested in the truth, and by his loan he has shown his appreciation of what has been done for him.

I had promised to speak at Los Angeles on Sunday afternoon, so it was necessary for us to hasten away by the early train from Loma Linda. We had about sixty miles to travel. On our arrival at Los Angeles, we went up to our restaurant and treatment rooms on Hill Street, and while waiting there before the service I prayed to the Lord for strength for the work before me.

At the church we found that a large crowd had gathered. Every foot of room was occupied, even the aisles being filled, and I was told that some were unable to find entrance to the building. Among those present were a large number not of our faith.

I presented the importance of obedience to the commandments of God, dwelling upon the instruction given in connection with the proclamation of the law from Mt. Sinai. Never before had these Scriptures appealed to me so forcibly. I spoke for a full hour, and the interest was marked throughout. As I felt my voice weakening, I paused to send a prayer to heaven for help. Then the power of the Holy Spirit strengthened me, and I knew that angels of God were by my side. At the last I became somewhat hoarse, but I felt very thankful that the Lord had permitted me to speak so long and so distinctly...

Ellen G. White

* * * * *

Individual Responsibility

MS-63'07
June 18, 1907 July 9, 1907.
Sanitarium,

I have a message to bear to our church in every place. There is a matter that should be clearly understood by all. Every soul who claims to be a Christian is to bear the responsibility of keeping himself in harmony with the guidance of the word of God. God holds each soul accountable for following for himself the pattern given in the life of Christ, and of having a character that is cleansed and sanctified.

I am bidden to say that the work of following the guidance and direction of men is a mistake, from beginning to end. God now calls for genuine conversion on the part of those who have taken up the work of telling other men just where they shall go and how they shall labor. No man has been delegated by God to act as a dictator to his fellow-laborers, telling them what is their duty; for this is assuming by weak and erring man that which belongs to God alone. Our brethren should refuse to accept such responsibility; for by taking such a course they are teaching men to seek the direction and guidance of man instead of the control and guidance of God. Our Christian activity is to be greatly increased, and in this work the Lord is to be the guide and counsellor of His servants.

[212]

One great object in the mission of Christ was to establish in every believer a sense of the guiding and controlling power of God. This lesson is to be repeated again and again. No greater injury can be done to our churches than for members to be taught to look to their fellowmen for guidance. And there is no man so humble in heart and so respectful of his brethren that he can safely take upon himself this work.

The grace of humility is rare in these times; but he who possesses it will reveal the grace of Christ in word and spirit and action. We need individually to seek the Lord until we find Him, and then to follow on to know the beauty of His character. Christ invites His believing people: "Come unto me, all ye that labor, and are heavy laden, and I will give you rest. Take my yoke upon you, and learn of Me; for I am meek and lowly in heart, and ye shall find rest unto your souls. For My yoke is easy, and My burden is light." The worker who responds to this invitation will have a correct estimate of his individual duty.

Ellen G. White

* * * * *

God's Wisdom to be Sought

August 15, 1907 (Organization) MS-75-'07. July 29, 1907. Sanitarium,

The Lord has given me a message for the laborers in the S. Calif. Conferences. The Lord Jesus wants us to believe that He is our Wisdom, and Sanctification, and Redemption. Influences are appearing among us that are decidedly opposed to the healthy development of the work which the Lord would have carried in straight lines.

[221]

God has instructed me to say to conference presidents and to ministers. Teach every church in the Conference to look to God for an understanding of present truth and duty. The Lord has not placed upon presidents or ministers the responsibilities of the position that He alone, as head of His church, can occupy. Church and conference organization do not give man any such responsibility.

Listen to the words of the Saviour, "Come unto Me, all ye that labor and are heavy laden, and I will give you rest. Take My yoke upon you, and learn of Me; for I am meek and lowly in heart, and ye shall find rest unto your souls. For my yoke is easy, and My burden is light." "My sheep hear My voice; and I know them; and they follow Me. And I give unto them eternal life; and they shall never perish; neither shall any man pluck them out of My hand."

The exercise of authority has been carried to such extremes that it is now time to call a halt; for church members are receiving a false education. A mistake has been made that should be corrected before it is too late. Those who dare to accept responsibilities that are contrary to the Gospel plan are in a dangerous place. They need to see its course of action in its true light. Their permissions and their forbiddings have fostered wrong ideas regarding the responsibility that individuals should carry, and have led believers to look to man instead of looking to God.

Brethren, the Lord will bless you in an effort to break up this wrong influence. Ministers will become weak and unChristlike if they continue to encourage this kind of work. God is to be the strength and wisdom of His people. Man power is not to rule the church of Christ.

A Change of Heart Needed

The men who have accepted kingly authority need to be converted; for the self-exaltation they have manifested is dishonoring to God. The word of God is to be exalted as the rule of faith and practice, for this word reveals the standard of character we are to reach and teaches us our duty to love as brethren. Its requirements are to be strictly obeyed. At this time, when God is calling every man to put away his natural and cultivated tendencies to wrong, and to rid himself of his preconceived opinions; at this time, when Satan's influences are coming into our ranks with such power, God's servants must understand the way of the Lord. The word of man is fallible, imperfect, unreliable; but the word of the Lord standeth sure, and is done in truth and uprightness.

The men bearing chief responsibility on our conference must not seek to embrace too much authority. I have been shown that men receive ideas from men, and follow their own judgment and the judgment of their fellows, and that the Lord is not always their counsellor. The work of setting up erring man to judge and dictate to their fellows is folly. When men suppose that they must watch God's laborers, and exercise over them their human judgment the sure result must be confusion and dishonor to God.

"The sweet Psalmist of Israel said, the Spirit of the Lord spake by me, and His word was in my tongue. The God of Israel said, the Rock of Israel spake to me, He that ruleth over men must be just, ruling in the fear of God. And He shall be as the light of the morning, when the sun riseth, even a morning without clouds; as the tender grass springing out of the earth by clear shining after rain."

The work of judgment has not been given to any minister or conference president. "Judge not," the Saviour says, "that ye be not judged; and with what measure ye mete, it shall be measured to you again. And why beholdest thou the mote that is in thy brother's eye, and considereth not the beam that is in thine own eye? Or how wilt thou say to thy brother, Let me pull out the mote out of thine eye; and, behold, a beam is in thine own eye."

The God of power and glory, the Strength of Israel, is being put out of sight by man's glorification of human capabilities. A change must be brought about. There is no need of so much of man's devising. We are nearing the close of this earth's history. God says I will overturn, overturn, until man stands in his appointed place. I am the true Shepherd of My flock. The voice and judgment of man is not to be the voice and judgment of My people. Church members are to be educated, line upon line, and precept upon precept, to look to God for wisdom and counsel.

"As every man hath received the gift, even so minister the same one to another," the apostle Paul exhorts, "as good stewards of the manifold grace of God. If any man speak, let him speak as the oracles of God; if any man minister, let him do it as of the ability which God giveth; that God in all things may be glorified through Jesus Christ." When the principles of the word of God are brought into the life practice of the workers, we shall have men of God's appointment.

There are those who, had they placed themselves in a position where the Spirit of God could lead them, would have been a great help and blessing to God's people; but they have hindered the work that God purposed to do through them by taking upon themselves responsibilities which God never required them to carry. To all who have thus exalted themselves, I am bidden to say, Let the principles of the word of God find a place in your work. Let the strong traits of character, that would eclipse the attributes of mercy and love and compassion, be put away. Every principle of the word of God is to stand magnified in the life of the servant of God.

Ellen G. White

* * * * *

N-242-'07 Aug. 6, 1907. August 7, 1907.
Sanitarium, Calif.,
Dr. M. Nicola, Hinsdale, Chicago, Ill. :
Dear Sister Nicola,

I read your letter yesterday, and I would say in response, I want you to make straight paths for your feet. I would not have your husband placed where he will be overtaxed. This you must carefully guard against. In writing to you, I did so for the good of both yourself and your husband. Your husband must not take too many burdens upon himself, and you can help in arranging his work, so that this shall not be.

My sister, you and your husband need at this time the words spoken to the church in Sardis: "These things saith He that hath the seven spirits of God, and the seven stars, I know thy works. Be watchful, and strengthen the things which remain, that are ready to die, for I have not found thy works perfect before God. Remember how thou hast received and heard; and hold fast, and repent. Thou hast a few names even in Sardis which have not defiled their garments. And they shall walk with me in white; for they are worthy. He that overcometh, the same shall be clothed in white raiment; and I will not blot out his name out of the book of life; but I will confess his name before My Father, and before His angels." It means very much to every soul at this time, what stand they shall take toward the work of God.

My brother and sister, I would urge you not to bind yourselves up with the work of the sanitarium at Hinsdale. Chicago is not the best place for you to live. Loma Linda is the place where you should be. I ask you, for reasons which I shall not now state, to accept the position at Loma Linda. Acceptable provision will be made for your children. I did not design to write you particulars.

I ask you now to connect with the sanitarium at Loma Linda, for I cannot have you go into peril unwarned. I fear that confusion will come to you as the result of your remaining where you are. I pray that you may be led to place yourselves on the right side. I have felt deeply over your affliction, and I have seen how important it is that your faith be firmly established in a plain "Thus saith the Lord." I hold you very near to my heart, and I desire that you both shall be placed where the Lord can lead you and abundantly bless you.

If Dr. Nicola will commit his case fully to God, to follow on to know His ways, the peace of God will come into his heart, and the light of heaven shine into his mind. We are living in perilous times, when the powers of darkness are constantly at work to overthrow our faith. "It is written" is to be our anchor. The assertions of men are of little value. Only He who makes the word of God his anchor will be secure.

Those who would be safe teachers of the truth, must first be learners in the school of Christ. You must recognize in Christ a personal Saviour if you would lead those whom you instruct to Him. Christ invites, "Come unto Me, all ye that labor, and are heavy laden; and I will give you rest. Take My yoke upon you, and learn of Me; for I am meek and lowly in heart; and ye shall find rest unto your souls; for My yoke is easy, and My burden is light. Learning the lessons of Christ you will find rest.

Christ is the great fountain head of all wisdom, the One who never makes a mistake. All the treasures of heaven were committed to Him that He might impart them to the persevering seeker after truth. The Son of God is made unto us wisdom, and righteousness, and sanctification and redemption. Teachers should bear in mind that He is the great standard for all teachers. Beholding Christ, and studying His teachings, you will learn to appreciate their originality, their authority, their spirituality, their tenderness, their benevolence, and their practicability. All who dig for the treasure of truth will be imbued with the spirit of Christ. By beholding Him, they will be changed into the same image.

Those who make the word of God their counsellor, will realize the weakness of the human heart; but they will find courage in the assurance that the power of the grace of God is sufficient to subdue every unsanctified, unholy impulse. When the enemy comes in like a flood, the Spirit of the Lord will lift up a standard against him. And when the Spirit of the Lord lifts up for His blood-bought heritage a standard against the enemy, the principles of the word of truth will bear sway in the life. Having surrendered themselves to the will of God, they reveal a faith that works by love, and purifies the soul.

Ellen G. White

* * * * *

B-244-'07 Aug. 6, 1907. August 7, 1907.
Sanitarium, Calif.,

Eld. J. A. Burden, Loma Linda, Calif.:

Dear Brother and Sister,

Yesterday I sent you a copy of the letter I wrote to Brother and Sister Nicola. Having written thus to them, I think I have done my duty in that respect.

I felt that we ought to make way for them to come to the Loma Linda Sanitarium, but it was not my thought that they should be placed in charge of the training of the workers. From the light that God has given me, I know that they have had great confidence in Dr. Kellogg, and this has influenced them to some extent. Their spiritual experience is not what it should be, and the Melrose Sanitarium has not maintained the high spiritual standing that it ought. They have been carrying the work there too much as worldlings would conduct it. Our sanitariums were instituted for a special work, and God cannot prosper them unless they maintain a high standard in religious matters. The truth for these times is to be revealed in every department of the sanitarium work.

In desiring that Brother and Sister Nicola be given an opportunity to connect with the Loma Linda Sanitarium, I have no wish that you should concede in any way to any ideas and practices that are not in harmony with the principles that God has told us must be maintained. Do not open the way for them to become rulers, but give them an opportunity to be with those who teach the truth in its purity. They have been lost in the fog, and I desire that they shall be fully recovered.

Satan often finds a powerful agency for evil in the power which one human mind is capable of exerting on another human mind. This influence is so seductive, that the person who is being molded by it is often unconscious of its power. God has bidden me speak warning against this evil, that His servants may not come under the deceptive power of Satan. The enemy is a master worker, and if God's people are not constantly led by the Spirit of God, they will be snared and taken.

For thousands of years Satan has been experimenting upon the properties of the human mind, and he has learned to know it well. By his subtle workings, in these last days, he is linking the human mind with his own, imbuing it with his thoughts, and he is doing this work in so deceptive a manner that those who accept his guidance know not that they are being led by him at his will. The great deceiver hopes so to confuse the minds of men and women, that none but his voice will be heard.

When Christ revealed to Peter the time of trials and suffering that was just before Him, and Peter replied, "Be it far from thee, Lord; this shall not be unto Thee," the Saviour commanded, "Get thee behind Me, Satan." Satan was speaking through Peter, making him act the part of the tempter. Satan's presence was unsuspected by Peter, but Christ could detect the presence of the deceiver, and in His rebuke to Peter He addressed the real foe.

One occasion, speaking to the twelve, and referring to Judas, Christ declared, "One of you is a devil." Often in the days of His earthly ministry the Saviour met His adversary in human form, when Satan as an unclean spirit took possession of men. Satan takes possession of the minds of men today. In my labors in the cause of God, I have again and again met those who have been thus possessed, and in the name of the Lord I have rebuked the evil spirit.

It is not by force that Satan takes possession of the human mind. While men sleep, the enemy sows tares in the church. While men are spiritually sleeping, the enemy accomplishes his work of iniquity. It is when his subject "understandeth it not" that he catcheth away the good seed sown in the heart. When men and women are in this condition, when their spiritual life is not being constantly fed by the Spirit of God, Satan can imbue them with his spirit, and lead them to work his works.

[229] I will not write more on this subject at this time. But I entreat that there may be a putting away from the life every action which does not bear the approval of God. We are drawing near to the close of earth's history; the battle is growing daily more fierce. There is a day appointed when men who have bowed to the mandates of Satan will find themselves the subjects of the wrath of God, when the Judge of all the earth shall pronounce the sentence against Satan and his adherents, 'Depart from Me, ye cursed, into everlasting fire, prepared for the devil and his angels."

Now, my dear friends, we have a peculiar work before us in the case of Brother and Sister Nicola. As Christ's messengers, we have a special work to do to save these people. This is a test case. I have sent you the letter I wrote them, that you may understand how the matter stands.

Ellen G. White

Jehovah is Our King

MS. 73-'07 August 15, 1907.

God has revealed many things to me which He has bidden me give to His people by pen and voice. Through this message of the Holy Spirit, God's people are given sacred instruction concerning their duty to God and to their fellow-men.

A strange things has come into our churches. Men who are placed in positions of responsibility that they might be wise helpers, to their fellow workers, have come to suppose that they were set as kings and rulers in the churches, to say to one brother, Do this, to another, Do that, and to another, Be sure and labor in such and such a way. There have been places where workers have been told that if they did not follow the instruction of these men of responsibility, their pay from the conference would be withheld.

It is right for the workers to counsel together as brethren; but that man who endeavors to lead his fellow-workers to seek his counsel and advice regarding the details of their work, and to learn their duty from him, is in a dangerous position, and needs to learn what responsibilities are really comprehended in his office. God has appointed no man to be conscience for his fellow-man, and it is not wise to lay so much responsibility upon an officer that he will feel that he is forced to become a dictator.

A Constant Peril

For years there has been a growing tendency for men placed in positions of responsibility to lord it over God's heritage, thus removing from church members their keen sense of the need of divine instruction and an appreciation of the privilege to counsel with God regarding their duty. This order of things may be changed. There must be a reform. Men who have not a rich measure of that wisdom which cometh from above, should not be called to serve in positions where their influence means so much to church members.

In my earlier experience in the message I was called to meet this evil. During my labors in Europe and Australia, and again at the San Jose campmeeting I had to bear my testimony of warning against it, because souls were being taught to look to man for wisdom, instead of looking to God who is our wisdom, our sanctification, and our righteousness. Recently the same message has again been given me, more definite and decisive, because there has been a deeper offense to the Spirit of God.

An Exalted Privilege

God is the teacher of His people. All who humble their hearts before Him, will be taught of God. "If any man lack wisdom, let him ask of God, that giveth to all men liberally, and upbraideth not, and it shall be given him." The Lord wants every church member to pray earnestly for wisdom, that he may know that the Lord would have him do. It is the privilege of every believer to obtain an individual experience, learning to carry his cares and perplexities to God. It is written, "Draw nigh to God, and He will draw nigh to you."

Through His servant Isaiah God is calling His church to appreciate her exalted privilege in having the wisdom of the Infinite at her demand: "O, Zion, that bringest good tidings, get thee up into the high mountain; O Jerusalem, that bringest good tidings, lift up thy voice with strength, lift it up, be not afraid; say unto the cities of Judah, Behold your God: Behold the Lord will come with a strong hand and His arm shall rule for Him. He shall feed His flock like a shepherd: He shall gather the lambs with His arm, and carry them in His bosom, and shall gently lead those that are with young. (Isaiah 40:12-17, 28-31)

In the forty-first to the forty-fifth chapters of Isaiah, God very fully reveals His purpose for His people; and these chapters should be prayerfully studied. God does not here instruct His people to turn away from Him and look to finite man for wisdom. (Isaiah 44:21-23; 45:21-25)

I write thus fully because I have been shown that ministers and people are tempted more and more to trust in finite man for wisdom, and to make flesh their arm. To conference presidents and men in responsible places I bear this message: Break the bands and fetters that have been placed upon God's people. To you the word is spoken, "Break every yoke." Unless you cease the work of making man amenable to man, unless you become humble and yourselves learn the way of the Lord as little children, the Lord will divorce you from His work. We are to treat one another as brethren, as fellow-laborers, as men and women who are, with us, seeking for light and understanding of the way of the Lord, and who are jealous for His glory.

God declares, "I will be glorified in My people": but the self-confident management of men has resulted in putting God aside, and accepting the devisings of men. If you allow this to continue, your faith will soon become extinct. God is in every place, beholding the conduct of the people who profess to represent the principles of His word. He asks that a change be made. He wants His people to be molded and fashioned, not after man's ideas, but after the similitude of God. I entreat of you to search the Scriptures as you have never yet searched them, that you may know the way and will of God. O that every soul might be impressed with this message, and put away the wrong!

Paul's Experience

We would do well to study carefully the first and second chapters of First Corinthians. "We preach Christ crucified," the apostle declared, "unto the Jews a stumblingblock, and unto the Greeks foolishness; but to them which are called, both Jews and Greeks, Christ the power of God, and the wisdom of God." (1 Corinthians 1:24-28; 2:16.)

Read also the third chapter of this book, and study and pray over these words. As a people our faith and practice need to be energized by the Holy Spirit. No ruling power, that would compel men to obey the dictates of the finite mind, should be exercised. "Cease ye from man, whose breath is in his nostrils," the Lord commands. By turning the minds of men to lean on human wisdom, we place a veil between God and man, so that there is not a seeing of Him who is invisible.

In our individual experience we are to be taught of God. When we seek Him with a sincere heart, we will confess to Him our defects of character; and He has promised to receive all who come to Him in humble dependence. The one who yields to the claims of God will have the abiding presence of Christ, and this companionship will be to him a very precious thing. Taking hold of divine wisdom, he will escape the corruptions that are in the world through lust. Day by day we will learn more fully how to carry his infirmities to the One who has promised to be a very present help in every time of need.

This message is spoken to our churches in every place. In the false experience that has been coming in, a decided influence is at work to exalt human agencies, and to lead some to depend on human judgment and to follow the control of human minds. This influence is diverting the mind from God. God forbids that any such experience should deepen and grow in our ranks as Seventh-day Adventists. Our petitions are to reach higher than erring man, to God ... God does not confine Himself to one place or person. He looks down from heaven upon the children of men, He sees their perplexities, and is acquainted with the circumstances of every issue of life. He understands His own work upon the human heart, and He needs not that any man should direct the workings of His Spirit.

"This is the confidence that we have in Him, that if we ask anything according to His will, He heareth us. And if we know that He hears us, we know that we have the petitions that we desire of Him." God has appointed the angels that do His will to respond to the prayers of the meek of the earth, and to guide His ministers with counsel and judgement. Heavenly agencies are constantly seeking to impart grace and strength and counsel to God's faithful children, that they may act their part in the work of communicating light to the world. The wonderful sacrifice of Christ has made it possible for every man to do a special work. When the worker receives wisdom from the only true source, he will become a pure channel of light and blessing; for he will receive his capability for service in rich currents of grace and light from the throne of God.

Ellen G. White

Extracts from Letters to Mrs. S. M. I. Henry.

MS. 77-'07 Aug. 15, 1907. -8-
Showing the relation that may be sustained toward the Woman's Christian Temperance Union by Seventh-day Adventist women of ability who have influence among the members of this organization.
"Sunnyside," Cooranbong, Australia
Dec. 1, 1898.
Dear Sister Henry,

* * * * *

 I am thankful that the Lord is leading you. I believe that the Lord has appointed you to do His work in His way. Let us in our work have faith in God, and trust Him. While we may take pleasure in counseling with our brethren, an individual work is to be done which is beyond the power of any mind to comprehend.

 I thank the Lord with heart, and soul, and voice that you have been a prominent and influential member of the Woman's Christian Temperance Union. In the providence of God you have been led to the light, to obtain a knowledge of the truth... This light and knowledge you need to bring into your work, as you associate with women whose hearts are softened by the Spirit of God, and who are searching for the truth as for hidden treasure. For twenty years I have seen that the light would come to the women workers in temperance lines. But with sadness I have discerned that many of them are becoming politicians, and that against God. They enter into questions and debates and theories that they have no need to touch. Christ said, "I am the light of the world; he that followeth Me shall not walk in darkness, but shall have the light of life."

 The Lord, I fully believe, is leading you that you may keep the principles of temperance clear and distinct, in all their purity in connection with the truth for these last days. They that do His will shall know of the doctrine. The Lord designs that women shall learn of Him meekness and lowliness of heart, and cooperate with the greatest Teacher the world has ever known. When this is done, there will be no strife for the supremacy, no pride of opinion; for it will be realized that mind, and voice, and every jet of ability, are only lent talents, given by God to be used in His work, to accumulate for Him, and to be returned to the Giver with all the increase. We are expected to grow in capability, in influence, and in power, ever looking unto Jesus. And by beholding, we shall be changed into His likeness.

The women's work is a power in our world, but it is lost when, with the Word of God before her, she sees a "Thus saith the Lord" and refuses to obey. The great and difficult thing for the soul to do is to part with its own supposed works of merit. It is not an easy matter to understand what it means to refuse self the least place of honor in the service of God. All unconsciously we act out the attributes of our own character and the bias of our own mind in the very presence of God, in our prayer and worship, in our service, and fail to see that we are absolutely dependent upon the leading of the Holy Spirit. Self is expected to do a work that is simply out of its power to do. This is the great peril of women's work in Christian temperance lines.

The Lord does not bid you separate from the Women's Christian Temperance Union. They need all the light you can give them. You are not to learn of them, but of Jesus Christ. Flash all the light possible into their pathway. You can agree with them on the ground of the pure, elevating principles that first brought into existence the Women's Christian Temperance Union. "Behold," said Christ, "I send you forth as lambs among wolves." If He sends His disciples on such a mission, will He not work through you to open the Scriptures to those who are in error? Cherish the fragrance of that love that Christ has revealed for fallen humanity, and by precept and example teach the truth as it is in Jesus.

The Holy Spirit alone is able to develop in the human agent that which is acceptable in the sight of God. The Lord has given you capabilities and talents to be preserved uncorrupted in their simplicity. Through Jesus Christ you may do a good work. As souls shall be converted to the truth, have them unite with you in teaching these women who are willing to be taught, to live and labor intelligently and unitedly.

* * * * *

**"Sunnyside," Cooranbong, Australia,
March 24, '99**
Dear Sister Henry,

* * * * *

... I am so glad, my sister, that you did not sever your connection with the Women's Christian Temperance Union. You may have to sever this connection, but not yet, not yet. Hold your place. Speak the words given you by God, and the Lord will certainly work with you. You may see many things you do not approve of, but do not fail nor be discouraged. I hope and pray that you may be clothed daily with the righteousness of Christ.

* * * * *

"Sunnyside," Cooranbong, Australia,

June 21, 1899.
Dear Sister Henry,

* * * * *

My sister, let your heart repose in confidence in God. The Lord will be to you a present help in every time of need. He does not need to work through other minds in order to lead His Chosen ones. He is desirous of communicating through those who seek Him with all the heart. While we put our entire trust in our Redeemer, we are perfectly safe. We have a large work to do, and we are to have respect unto the recompense of reward. And more than this we are to use every God-given faculty, that others, through our influence and Christlike example, may have the same respect that we have.

I hope, my sister, that you will have an influence in the Woman's Christian Temperance Association to draw many precious souls to the standard of truth. The Lord is drawing many to an examination of the truth, and you need not fail nor be discouraged. Sow beside all waters. These are good waters in which you can sow the seeds of truth, even if you do not dwell publicly upon the prominent features of our faith. It would not be wise to be too definite. The oil of grace revealed in your conscious and unconscious influence will make known that you have the light of life. This will shine forth to others in your direct, positive testimony upon subjects on which you can all agree, and this will have a telling influence.

* * * * *

"Sunnyside," Cooranbong, Australia, Dec., 1899.

Dear Sister Henry,

* * * * *

I was greatly pleased with your letter, in which you give me the history of your experience with the W.C.T.U. When I read it, I said, "Thank the Lord. That is seed-sowing which is of value." I am pleased, so much pleased. The Lord has certainly opened your way. Keep it open, if possible. A work can be accomplished by you. Preserve your strength for such efforts. Attend important gatherings when you can. These occasions will be very trying seasons, but when the Lord gives His loved ones a special work to do, He sends His angels to be round about them.

There are very many precious souls whom the Lord would have reached by the light of truth. Labor is to be put forth to help them to understand the Scriptures. I have felt an intense interest in the W.C.T.U. workers. These heroic women know what it means to have an individuality of their own. I desire so much that they shall triumph with the redeemed around the great white throne. My prayers shall rise in your behalf that you may be given special opportunities to attend their large gatherings, and that your voice may be heard in defense of the truth.

I dare not give you advice in this important matter. You are on the ground and Christ is on the ground. Be assured that He will work with you and through you and by you.

It ought to be a great encouragement to you in your work to think of the compassion and tender love of God for those who are seeking and praying for light. We should hold convocations for prayer to ask the Lord to open the way that the truth may enter the strongholds where Satan has set up his throne, and dispel the shadow which he has cast athwart the pathway of those he is seeking to deceive and to destroy. We have the promise, or rather, the assurance, "The effectual fervent prayer of a righteous man availeth much."

Ellen G. White

The Work to be Done for the W.C.T.U

MS. 91-'07 Aug. 15, 1907. April 18, 1900.
"Sunnyside," Cooranbong, Australia,

Dear Brother _____,

Light has been given me that there are those with most precious talents and capabilities in the W.C.T.U. Much time and money has been absorbed among us in ways that bring no returns. Instead of this, some of our best talent should be set at work for the W.C.T.U., not as evangelists, but as those who fully appreciate the good that has been done by this body. We should seek to gain the confidence of the workers of the W.C.T.U. by harmonizing with them as far as possible. We are to let them see and understand that the foundation of the principles of our doctrine is the Word of God.

The necessity of working for the women of the W.C.T.U. has never been fully and squarely met. The problem has never received the consideration it ought to have received. If the workers in the W.C.T.U. can obtain the true faith, and set their feet in the right path, what a work will be done. But there is to be no driving on our part, no warfare, no use of the two-edged sword, which cuts every way. This people have been rich in good works. When the light of present truth is given them through carefully prepared methods, when the golden oil is received into the willing hearts of our workers, the treasures of truth and grace will be communicated from one to another. By the women of the W.C.T.U. the law of God is misunderstood. If they can be enlightened in regard to this point, we shall see that their educated ability will do much more than it is now doing to create working forces for the advancement of truth and righteousness.

The Lord asks us, my brother, to seek His face. The work of the Holy Spirit must be felt in our hearts. Many who are standing aloof from Seventh-day Adventists are living more in accordance with the light they have received than are many Seventh-day Adventists. This may seem strange to you, but strange things will have to be demonstrated to show the foolishness of the wisdom of those who judge others who have not seen the light.

Much good would be done if some of the W.C.T.U. women were invited to our camp-meetings to take part in the meetings by teaching our sisters how to work. While at the meeting they would be hearing and receiving as well as imparting. There is a great work to be done, and instead of presenting the features of our faith which are objectionable to unbelievers, let us say to them as Philip said to Nathanael, "Come and see." We have had great light, great knowledge, and continual instruction, yet the word is given me for many of our people, "You are weighed in the balances, and are found wanting."

There are many ways in which we can work to reach those not of our faith. It would be well to return to the methods of presenting health and temperance that were adopted nearly thirty years ago. We need to trim our lamps and receive in them the holy oil from the two olive-branches. When the power of the Spirit of God rests upon us, there will be a showing for our labors altogether different from that now seen.

Let us not represent truth and the situation of things as so formidable that those belonging to the W.C.T.U. will turn away in despair. There are vital truths upon which they have had very little light. They should be dealt with in tenderness, in love, and with respect for their good work. We are to guard against approaching them in such a way as to close doors whereby some, yes, many might be reached. Instead of condemning them, let us strive to reach their hearts,—not through the learned arguments of ministers, but through the wise efforts of women of influence and tact who can devote time and thought to this line of work.

The Lord wants His people to follow other methods than to condemn wrong, even though their condemnation be just. He wants them to do something more than to hurl at their adversaries charges which do not convict, but only send those at whom they are made, farther from the truth,—charges which make those in error point to the words written, and say, "You see, it is impossible to have any union with Seventh-day Adventists, for they will give us no chance to connect with them unless we believe just as they believe."

Let us remember that there is need of sanctified pens and sanctified tongues. When we as a people live as God would be pleased to have us live, we shall see the deep movings of His Spirit. Much will then be done for those who have never heard the truth. In our work for unbelievers we may expect to hear much that is not ordered by God. But let us remember that those who speak these words do not know any better. Let us pray for them, and approach them in discretion and with Christlike tenderness. Those who oppose the counsel of God against themselves need gentle dealing. God can at any time so move upon hearts by His Holy Spirit that they will be prepared to receive the truth and unite with His commandment-keeping people.

Ellen G. White

The Temperance Work

MS. 79-'07 Aug. 16, '07-8-
Extracts from printed Testimonies and from unpublished MSS., outlining work done thirty years ago, and in more recent years; also, the work that should be done today.

[237] Soon after my husband and I returned from Calif. to Michigan in the spring of 1877, we were earnestly solicited to take part in a temperance mass-meeting, a very praiseworthy effort in progress among the better portion of the citizens of Battle Creek. This movement embraced the Battle Creek Reform Club, six hundred strong, and the W.C.T.U., two hundred and sixty strong. God, Christ, the Holy Spirit, and the Bible were familiar words with these earnest workers. Much good had already been accomplished, and the activity of the workers, the system by which they labored, and the spirit of their meetings, promised greater good in time to come. It was on the occasion of the visit of Barnum's great menagerie to this city on the 25th of June, that the ladies of the Women's Christian Temperance Union struck a telling blow for temperance and reform by organizing an immense temperance restaurant to accommodate the crowds of people who gathered in from the country to visit the menagerie, thus preventing them from visiting the saloons and groceries, where they would be exposed to temptation. The mammoth tent, capable of holding five thousand people, used by the Michigan Conference for campmeeting purposes, was tendered for the occasion. Beneath this immense canvas temple were erected fifteen or twenty tables for the accommodation of guests.

By invitation, the Sanitarium set a large table in the center of the great pavilion, bountifully supplied with delicious fruits, grains, and vegetables. This table formed the chief attraction, and was more largely patronized than any other. Although it was more than thirty feet long, it became so crowded that it was necessary to set another about two-thirds as long which was also thronged.

By invitation of the Committee of arrangements, Mayor Austin, W. H. Skinner, cashier of the First National Bank, and C. C. Peavey, and I spoke in the mammoth tent, Sunday evening, July 1, upon the subject of Christian Temperance. God helped me that evening; and although I spoke ninety minutes, the crowd of fully five thousand persons listened in almost breathless silence.

(Testimonies for the Church 4:274-275)

*****

On Sunday, June 23, 1878, I spoke in the Methodist Church of Salem, Oregon, on the subject of temperance. The attendance was unusually good, and I had freedom in treating this, my favorite subject. I was requested to speak again in the same place on the Sunday following the campmeeting, but was prevented by hoarseness. On the next Tuesday evening, however, I again spoke in this church. Many invitations were tendered me to speak on temperance in various cities and towns of Oregon, but the state of my health forbade my complying with these requests.

(Testimonies for the Church 4:290-291)

*****

Early in August, 1878, we visited Boulder City, Colorado, and beheld with joy our canvas meeting-house, where Elder Cornell was holding a series of meetings. The tent had been loaned to hold temperance meetings in, and, by special invitation, I spoke to a tent full of attentive hearers. Though wearied by my journey, the Lord helped me to successfully present before the people the necessity of practising strict temperance in all things.

(Testimonies for the Church 4:297)

*****

[238]   Monday morning, June 2, 1879, while in attendance at a campmeeting held at Nevada, Missouri, we assembled under the tent to attend the organization of a temperance association. There was a fair representation of our people present. Elder Butler spoke, and confessed that he had not been as forward in the temperance reform as he should have been. He stated that he had always been a strictly temperance man, discarding the use of liquor, tea, and coffee, but he had not signed the pledge being circulated among our people. But he was now convinced that in not doing so he was hindering others who ought to sign it. He then placed his name under Col. Hunter's, I wrote mine next, and Brother Farnsworth's followed. Thus the work was well started.

My husband continued to talk while the pledge was circulating. Some hesitated, thinking that the platform was too broad in including tea and coffee; but finally their names were given, pledging themselves to total abstinence.

Brother Hunter, who was then called upon to speak, responded by giving a very impressive testimony, as to how the truth found him and what it had done for him. He stated that he had drank liquor enough to float a ship, and that now he wanted to accept the whole truth, reform and all. He had given up liquor and tobacco, and this morning he had drank his last cup of coffee. He believed the testimonies were of God, and he wished to be led by the will of God expressed in them.

As a result of the meeting, one hundred and thirty-two names were signed to the teetotal pledge, and a decided victory was gained in behalf of temperance. R & H. July 10, 1879.

* * * * *

In our public meetings in Australia, we took special pains to present clearly the fundamental principles of temperance reform. Generally, when I spoke to the people on Sunday, my theme was health and temperance. During some of the campmeetings, daily instruction was given on this subject. In several places, the interest aroused over our position on the use of stimulants and narcotics, led the friends of temperance to attend our meetings and learn more of the various doctrines of our faith.

During a series of meetings held late in the year 1899, at Maitland, New South Wales, I was requested by the president of the Maitland branch of the W.C.T.U. to speak to them one evening. She said that they would be very glad to hear me, even if I should speak only ten minutes. I asked her if the ten minutes that she proposed for me to speak was all the time that was allowed, because sometimes the Spirit of the Lord came upon me, and I had more than a ten minutes' talk to give. "Oh," she said, "your people told me that you did not speak in the evening, and I specified ten minutes as the time, thinking that I would not get you at all if I made it longer. The longer you can speak to us, the more thankful we shall be."

I asked Mrs. Winter, the president, if it was her custom to read a portion of Scriptures at the opening of the meeting. She said that it was. I then asked for the privilege of praying, which was gladly granted. I spoke with freedom to them for an hour. Some of the women present that night afterward attended the meetings in the tent. (Unpublished MS.)

* * * * *

In our work more attention should be given to the temperance reform. Every duty that calls for reform, involves repentance, faith, and obedience. It means the uplifting of the soul to a new and nobler life. Thus every true reform has its place in the work of the third angel's message. Especially does the temperance reform demand our attention and support. At our camp meetings we should call attention to this work, and make it a living issue. We should present to the people the principles of true temperance, and call for signers to the temperance pledge. Careful attention should be given to those who are enslaved by evil habits. We must lead them to the cross of Christ.

Our campmeetings should have the labors of medical men. These should be men of wisdom and sound judgement, men who respect the ministry of the Word, and who are not victims of unbelief. These men are the guardians of the health of the people, and they are to be recognized and respected. They should give instruction to the people in regard to the dangers of intemperance. This evil must be more boldly met in the future than it has been in the past. Ministers and doctors should set forth the evils of intemperance. Both should work in the gospel with power to condemn sin and exalt righteousness. Those ministers or doctors who do not make personal appeals to the people are remiss in their duty. They fail of doing the work which God has appointed them.

In other churches there are Christians who are standing in defense of the principles of temperance. We should seek to come near to these workers, and make a way for them to stand shoulder to shoulder with us. We should call upon great and good men to second our efforts to save that which is lost.

If the work of temperance were carried forward by us as it was begun thirty years ago; if at our campmeetings we presented before the people the evils of intemperance in eating and drinking, and especially the evil of liquor drinking; if these things were presented in connection with the evidences of Christ's soon coming, there would be a shaking among the people. If we showed a zeal in proportion to the importance of the truths we are handling, we might be instrumental in rescuing hundreds, yea thousands, from ruin.

Only eternity will reveal what has been accomplished by this kind of ministry,—how many souls, sick with doubt, and tired of worldliness and unrest, have been brought to the Great Physician, who longs to save to the uttermost all who come unto Him. Christ is a risen Saviour, and there is healing in His wings.

(Testimonies for the Church 6:110-111)

Ellen G. White.

* * * * *

To Elder Geo. W. Reaser and the Ministers in Southern Calif

R. 290-'07. Aug. 29, '07.
Sanitarium, Calif.,
Dear Brother Reaser,

The Lord has revealed to me that in your work as president of the Southern Calif. conference, you are in danger of embracing too much responsibility. Some time ago the Lord showed me that if you were placed in office, you would attempt to rule in every branch of the work, but that this was not to be permitted, because you have not the judgment to deal with all lines of work and because God has chosen especially qualified workers for certain lines of His work.

Because of a wrong comprehension of the duties of your office, the work in your field has become sadly confused in the past two years. You have accepted responsibilities that should not have been placed upon you. Because you were president of the Conference, you considered yourself to be in a certain sense the manager of the work of the Loma Linda Sanitarium, and that it was your duty to see that matters there were conducted according to your ideas. I am bidden to say to you that you are not qualified to take the control of the sanitarium work.

Elder Burden has been given this work, and he has good helpers and advisers in the workers who are associated with him. The Lord appointed Elder Burden to the position he occupies, and he is to bear his responsibilities in that position without interference. He is fully capable of doing the work that has been given him to do. The Lord has not told you to watch and criticize, and interfere with his work. He bids you, my brother, to stand out of the way. Elder Burden has proved in the past that he can do his work acceptable. He is to stand in his lot and place, exercising his God-given right to ask wisdom of Him who giveth to all men liberally and upbraideth not.

It is a mistake for a conference to select as president one who considers that his office places unlimited power in his hands. The

Lord has instructed me to tell you that you do not know when to use authority, and when to refrain from using it unwisely. You have much to learn before you can do the work of a conference president intelligently. You are to bear in mind that in the cause of God there is a chief Director, whose power and wisdom is above that of human minds.

God will have nothing to do with the methods of working where finite men are allowed to bear rule over their fellow-men. He calls for a decided change to be made. The voice of command must no longer be heard. The Lord has, among his workers men of humility and discretion; from these should be chosen men who will conduct the work in the fear of God.

It would be well if Elder Cottrell and at least one other worker of broad experience should be called upon to consult together and consider your plans that affect the medical work. God designs that His servants shall carry the responsibilities of that conference in a spirit of humility and dependence on Him.

It is dangerous work to invest men with authority to judge and rule their fellow-men. Not to you nor to any other man has been given power to control the actions of God's people, and the effort to do this must be no longer continued. God has been dishonored by the education that has been given to the churches in Southern Calif. in looking to one man as conscience and judgment for them. God has never authorized any man to exercise a ruling power over his fellow-workers; and those who have allowed a dictatorial spirit to come into their official work, need to experience the converting power of God upon their hearts. They have placed man where God should be.

When men engage in labor for the souls of others, they are not to be made amenable to the will of their fellow-laborers. God is well able to direct the course of action of those who work for Him. But when His laborers, instead of calling upon Him, seek first and regard as of first importance the counsel and advice of human minds, He is dishonored. The method of sending one minister to another minister to learn his duty is a plan of working that should not be encouraged. Greater evils will result from such a course than finite and erring man can foresee.

My brother, God lives and reigns. Let your brethren have the right of way to the footstool of Christ. Encourage them to carry their burdens to the Lord, and not to any human being. Never take the responsibility of becoming conscience for another. As brethren, you can counsel together, and pray together, and seek instruction from the source of all wisdom; but you are not to seek to direct another regarding his duty. Let all work of this character be done away. God forbids that this spirit shall again come into His work while time shall last.

Ellen G. White

Arise Shine

MS-95-'07 August 29, 1907.

A message has been given me for our people in S. Calif. God bids you, "Arise and shine." Now, just now, let every believing soul study to comprehend the words of Christ. "Ye are the light of the world." It is no time now to become weakened and discouraged. This is a time for every soul to humble his heart before God in confession of mistakes and sins, and to wait upon the Lord that His spiritual strength may be renewed.

Day by day God's faithful, commandment-keeping people are to become better prepared to let their light shine forth amid the moral darkness of a world that is rapidly filling up its cup of apostasy, and becoming as it was in the days of Noah. Knowing the time, we are to set in operation every agency that can be employed in doing missionary work for Christ. The great aim of those who profess to believe the third angels' message, should be to bring all their powers into active service in the cause of God.

[242] Not all are called to engage in the same line of labor, but to every man and woman who enters the service of Christ, are given responsibilities to bear, and a special work to do. My brethren and sisters, Christ sends you this message, "Search the Scriptures; for in them ye think ye have eternal life; and they are they which testify of Me." Humble your hearts before God, and seek counsel of Him who never makes a mistake. Under His guidance you will never go astray. You need to seek as you have never sought before for an understanding of the word of God. Pray that the Lord will open your understanding, and turn your whole heart to the One who has bought you with an infinite price. You are Christ's purchased possession. Ask Him to tell you what He would have you do.

Letters come to me from near and from far, asking for definite instruction in regard to individual duty. I gladly refer these inquirers to the words of Christ, spoken just before His ascension to heaven. "And Jesus came and spake unto them, saying, All power is given unto Me in heaven and in earth. Go ye therefore and teach all nations baptizing them in the name of the Father, and of the Son, and of the Holy Ghost; teaching them to observe all things whatsoever I have commanded you; and lo; I am with you alway, even unto the end of the world."

Before leaving them, the Saviour outlined to His disciples the work in which they were to engage. They did not yet fully comprehend the mission to which, as the followers of Christ, they had given themselves. Then opened He their understanding, that they might understand the Scriptures, and said unto them. Thus it is written, and thus it behooved Christ to suffer, and to rise from the dead the third day; and that repentance and remission of sins should be preached in His name among all nations, beginning at Jerusalem. And ye are witnesses of these things. And, behold, I send the promise of My Father upon you; but tarry ye in the city of Jerusalem until ye be endued with power from on high."

As the Lord's missionaries, a great work was before the disciples; but they were to be witnesses for Christ first in Jerusalem where His enemies thought to extinguish the torch of truth that had been lighted. In their cruel murder of the Saviour, and by the false reports they had circulated regarding His resurrection, they thought to remove all witness to the truth. But these falsehoods were to be met by the positive testimony of the disciples. They had talked with Christ after His resurrection; they had been eye-witnesses of His ascension.

The enemies of Christ had supposed that the disciples would be intimidated by the events that had taken place, and would give up their faith in the Messiah. They were astonished when they saw with what boldness these humble followers took up the work where Christ had laid it down. Multitudes from many parts of the world were gathered at Jerusalem at the time of the crucifixion of Christ, and these had heard the false reports regarding the Messiah. Before these multitudes the disciples, with the power of the Holy spirit resting upon them, bore witness to the truth of the words of Christ, "I am the Resurrection and the Life." The gospel message heard by these representatives of other nations, was carried by them to their homes; the scenes they had witnessed at the crucifixion of Christ and on the day of Pentecost were related; and the message of repentance and remission of sins preached in Christ's name, was carried to many places.

In the words of the Saviour, "Go ye therefore, and teach all nations," the work of the followers of Christ in every age was outlined. There is a promise for us in His assurance, "All power is given unto Me in heaven and in earth." Brethren, shall we not take up our work, not seeking to carry burdens which the Lord has not committed to us, but doing that to which we are called, with a spirit of thoroughness, earnestness, and willingness? If we do our work faithfully, the Lord will complete His part of the contract, fulfilling the promise of His presence, "Lo, I am with you alway, even unto the end of the world." Let us not allow our faith to waver, but putting our dependence in God, let us teach all things whatsoever He has commanded. Day by day we need to receive divine instruction. I pray that every laborer may ask, and believe, and receive, the promise, "Lo, I am with you alway."

O, how much less we are doing as a people than we should be doing! Even those in responsible positions do not realize their privileges and duties. And how weak seem my words, how inadequate to set before God's people what He requires of them. I am distressed as I see the work developing, and note how difficult it is to support the agencies appointed for the diffusion of the light of the gospel. The Lord demands more of His people than they are doing.

The invitation is given to all, "Come unto Me, all ye that labor and are heavy-laden, and I will give you rest. Take My yoke upon you, and learn of Me; for I am meek and lowly in heart; and ye shall find rest unto your souls. For My yoke is easy and My burden is light."

Those who have a part in the work and cause of God should be careful that they strike no discordant notes. There are some who have been laboring in the S. Calif. Conference who need to lay off the armor for a while until they learn Christ's method of working. They need to be converted; for they give the impression to others that they consider all the other workers out of harmony with them. Thus the seeds of dissension and strife are sown. When these workers take upon them the yoke of Christ, and learn of Him who is meek and lowly in heart, they will return to God in acceptable service the talents He has lent them, and in doing this they will find rest unto their souls. They will hunger and thirst after righteousness, and their desire will be satisfied in a new and living experience. They will become daily students of the word of God; and guided by the light shining from that word, they will follow on to know the Lord, whose going forth is prepared as the morning.

No worker is to consider it his duty to administer reproof, to point out existing evils, and stop with this. Such work does not accomplish any good, but only disheartens and discourages. Plain, sensible, intelligent discourses should be preached to the churches, that will show the need of seeking the Lord in Prayer, and of opening the heart to the light of life, and that will lead churchmembers to engage in humble work for God. To every man God has given a work; to each worker who engages in service for Him, He gives a part to act in communicating light and truth. [244]

The appointed leaders of our churches need themselves to seek the Lord with humble, broken hearts; then they will discern their own defects of character. They need to present their cases before the Lord, asking, what shall I do that I may comprehend my individual duty? What shall I do that I may meet the mind and will of God? And when you have asked this question, my brethren, do not yield the point until you have surrendered soul, body, and spirit to God. Then God can stamp His image on your soul.

God placed His church in the earth that it might be the light of the world. But the self-indulgent course of many churchmembers, and the rising up of self to take the lines of control, have resulted in diffusing darkness rather than light. God's professing people need to seek Him in sincere sorrow of heart, because there is so little life in the church, so little effort put forth to let the light shine in good works. We are laborers together with God, "The apostle Paul declares: 'Ye are God's husbandry; ye are God's building." God designs that life-giving beams shall, through the individual members of the church, shine forth to the world. Receiving that light from the Source of all light, they are to reflect that light to others. But this can be done only as the church draws near to God and lives in close connection with the giver of life and light. The purity and simplicity of Christ, revealed in the lives of His humble followers will witness to the possession of genuine piety. The believer who is imbued with a true missionary spirit, will be a living epistle, known and read of all men. He is a partaker of the divine nature and therefore escapes the corruptions that are in the world through lust.

The field is the world. Christ declares, "Go ye into all the world, and preach the gospel to every creature." My brethren you would increase your pleasure in the Lord if you would practise self-denial. If you would resolve to love God truly and keep His commandments, you would discern the duties that devolve upon you as laborers together with God. You would willingly bring Him your offerings. You would faithfully and joyfully tithe your income, that His work in home and foreign fields might be advanced. The truth would go forth from your lips in no feigned words. Your zeal and piety would be greatly increased, and the unbelieving world would see that you have been in communion with God, and have learned of Him.

[245] When this is your experience, no words of censure or blame will fall from your lips for those who are your fellow-workers, because you are taught of God, and are learning to speak the words of Christ. Your earnest prayers for pardon for your own defects, and for the blessing of God upon your efforts, will show that your lips have been converted. And this will touch the cold hearts of unbelievers. They will distinguish between the human and the divine.

.....

We read that on the day of Pentecost, when the Holy Spirit descended upon the disciples, no man said that aught that he possessed was his own. All they owned was held for the advancement of the wonderful reformation. And thousands were converted in a day. When the same spirit actuates believers today and they give back to God His own with the same liberality, a wide and far-reaching work will be accomplished.

The Spirit of the Lord has been working with His people, and many have given liberally for the upbuilding of the kingdom of God on the earth. Brethren, let us take hold anew, holding ourselves and all that we have in readiness to meet the demands of the cause of God upon us.

Ellen G. White

* * * * *

B.-260-'07. August 29, 1907.

Dear Brother and Sister Burden,

I have been very anxious to learn something of the meetings you have been holding; W. C. White had written us no particulars. I should be glad if you would bear in mind that I am intensely interested in this meeting, and desire to know about it. Has it meant victory or defeat?

One night this week, I think it was Sunday, I did not sleep any through the entire night; and again on Wednesday I had a wakeful night. I slept for a short time before three o'clock. While I lay awake, I spent the time in prayer that God would give to His people sanctified and converted minds, that individually they might comprehend their duty, and learn to reveal the power of the truth in sound speech that cannot be condemned.

The talent of speech is a precious talent. The riches of the grace of Christ, which He is ever ready to bestow upon us, we are to impart in true, hopeful words. "Rejoice in the Lord alway, and again I say, Rejoice." If we would guard our words, so that nothing but kindness shall escape our lips, we will give evidence that we are preparing to become members of the heavenly family. In words and works we shall show forth the praises of Him who has called us out of darkness into His marvelous light. O, what a reformative influence would go forth if we as a people would value at its true worth the talent of speech and its influence upon the human souls.

The Sabbath meetings, the morning and evening worship in the home, the services held in the chapel,—all should be vitalized by the Spirit of Christ. Each member of the sanitarium family should confess Christ openly and with gladness, expressing the joy and comfort and hope that is written in the song. Christ is to be set forth as the Chiefest among ten thousand, and the One altogether lovely. He is to be set forth as the Giver of every good and perfect gift, the One in whom our hopes of eternal life are centered. If we would do this, all narrowness must be set aside, and we must call into exercise the love of Christ. The joy we experience in this love will be a blessing to others.

I am bidden to say to the sanitarium family, Let your social meetings, and all your religious exercises be characterized by a deep earnestness and a joy that expresses the love of God in the soul. Such meetings will be profitable to all; for they will bind heart to heart.

Let there be earnest seasons of prayer; for prayer will give strength to the religious experiences. Confess Christ openly and bravely, and manifest at all times the meekness of Christ.

The Lord would have the family of workers at Loma Linda be channels of light. If we will keep the heart and mind opened heavenward, cherishing the comfort of His grace in the heart, the presence of Christ will be revealed. Let earnestness and zeal come into your lives. Make no backward movements. The Lord is our helper, our guide, our shield, our exceeding great reward. Do not allow levity to come into your experience, but cultivate cheerfulness; for this is an excellent grace. We cannot afford to be unmindful of our words and deportment.

During the past night I seemed to be standing before a large congregation, speaking to the people the words of life. I long to understand more perfectly about this meeting that was presented to me. I seemed to hear the sweet melody of praise to God, and expressions of gratitude were coming from souls that were the recipients of the grace of Christ. The voice of praise and thanksgiving was heard, and countenances were aglow with the light of the love of God. It seemed that angel's voices united with those in the meeting who were offering praise to God.

My father was a very cheerful Christian. No doleful testimony was ever suffered to go forth from his lips. When those about him were giving mournful testimonies, his voice would be heard, "What doth much increase the store? When I thank Him, He gives me more."

We all have very much to be thankful for; let us open our lips in praise and thanksgiving to God. Let us come nearer to the Lord Jesus, and acknowledge our daily obligations to Him. He has made it possible for us to secure for ourselves a very happy life even in this world of sin, and holds out the hope of being continually in His presence in the kingdom He is preparing for His people. Should not these thoughts call forth from us praise and thanksgiving? May the Lord bless you, and bless the sanitarium family, is my prayer.

Ellen G. White

Extracts with Explanatory Notes on the Training of Medical Students

(Sept. 1907)

In all the instruction given through the Spirit of Prophecy regarding the training of medical students, the necessity of spiritual consecration and of faithfulness in Bible study is constantly emphasized. The students are directed to search the Scriptures, and to establish themselves thoroughly on all phases of the third angel's message.

In a manuscript dated August 1885, and published in a leaflet entitled, "Counsel to Physicians and Medical Students," the spiritual side of the training of our youth is constantly kept uppermost. Note the following: MS-2a-1885 July 27, 1885.

"We greatly need godly physicians; we need men who have high and holy principles. I have been shown that young men will accept the responsibility of obtaining a medical education, and enter upon their course of study, designing to be right and maintain their Christian principles; but do they do this? No, they fall into temptation, and evil influences affect their morals. Among our own people who profess to believe the most solemn truths ever committed to mortals, there is a tarnishing of virtue, a sacrificing of principle. They do not, like Joseph and Daniel, preserve their integrity of morals, much less their Christian principles. The habits and customs of associates who claim to be respectable men and women have a molding influence upon them. Not only the youth, but those of mature age are inclined to conform to the worldling's standard in order not to be considered singular."

This was written about ten years before the founding of the American Medical College. The perils to be met by the youth in a worldly medical school were described in the following words:

"We are in need of physicians; but the plan of sending young men to a medical college to learn to treat the sick, is questionable; for many of them have no root in themselves, and as in sending out children to the other colleges in our land, they are brought in contact with every class of minds, and are thrown into a sink of iniquity, the companionship of skeptics, infidels and the profligate; where not one out of one hundred escape from being contaminated. They do not come forth like Joseph and Daniel uncorrupted, firm as a rock to principles...

"These students who intend to deal with suffering humanity will find no graduating place this side of heaven. Every bit of knowledge that is termed science should be acquired, while the seeker daily acknowledges that the fear of the Lord is the beginning of wisdom. Every item of experience and everything that can strengthen the mind, should be cultivated to the utmost of their power, while at the same time they should seek God for His wisdom from above, (lest) they become an easy prey for the deceptive power of Satan." And again,

"I wish I could set before the medical student the true responsibility which rests upon him in his work. There is not one in one hundred who has a just sense of his position, his work, his accountability to God, and how much God will do for him if he will make Him his trust. The very first lesson that he should learn is dependence upon God. Make God your counselor at every step. The worldly and the nominal Christian may insinuate that in order for you to be successful you must be a policy man—you must at times depart from the strictest rectitude; but be not deceived, be not deluded... Throw not open the door for the enemy to take possession of the citadel of the soul...

Like Enoch, the physician should be a man that walks with God. This will be to him an antidote to all the delusive, pernicious sentiments which make so many infidel physicians, or skeptics. The true antidote is truth, the truth of God revealed in His word, practised in the life, and constantly guiding in all that concerns the interests of others. Having the soul thus barricaded with heavenly principles you may humbly yet confidently say, I will not fear the face of man. God is not unmindful of your struggles, of your conflicts to maintain the truth and obtain a personal daily experience in walking in the ways of truth. When you appreciate every word that proceedeth out of the mouth of God, as revealed in His Word, higher than worldly policy, you will be guided into every good and holy way...

"Let not medical students be deceived by the wiles of the devil, or by any of his cunning pretexts which so many adopt to beguile and ensnare, by practices of the ungodly. Cling closely to your Bibles. Inquire, What saith the Lord? He has spoken and told me how to ennoble and purify my life. This light I will follow. The Majesty of truth I will respect and honor...

"It is the privilege of every student to enter college with the same fixed, determined principle that Daniel had when he entered the courts of Babylon, and to preserve his integrity untarnished. You all need a living religion, that you may stand as God's witnesses..."

These words were written at a time when there was no medical school operated by Seventh-day Adventists—ten years before the founding of the American Medical Missionary College; and at that time, when the only way for our youth to obtain a medical education was to enter a worldly college. Students were assured that so long as they chose to cling closely to their Bibles, and obey God, they would be kept from contamination while studying science in these medical schools.

This instruction is very similar to that found in "Testimonies for the Church 5:583, 584, where we read:

We would that there were strong young men, rooted and grounded in the faith, who had such a living connection with God that they could, if so counseled by our leading brethren, enter the higher colleges in our land, where they would have a wider field for study and observation. Association with different classes of minds, an acquaintance with the workings and results of popular methods of education, and a knowledge of theology as taught in the leading institutions of learning, would be of great value to such workers, preparing them to labor for the educated classes and to meet the prevailing errors of our times. Such was the method pursued by the ancient Waldenses; and, if true to God, our youth like theirs, might do a good work, even while gaining their education, in sowing the seeds of truth in other minds."

About the time this was written—early in the eighties, it was also written (Testimonies for the Church 5:446-8) that:

"Painstaking effort should be made to induce suitable men to qualify themselves for this work—the work of a physician. They should be men whose characters are based upon the broad principles of the word of God—men who possess a natural energy, force, and perseverance that will enable them to reach a high standard of excellence...

"In this age there is danger for every one who shall enter upon the study of medicine. Often his instructors are worldly-wise men and his fellowstudents infidels, who have no thought of God, and he is in danger of being influenced by these irreligious associations. Nevertheless, some have gone through the medical course, and have remained true to principle. They would not continue their studies on the Sabbath; and they have proved that men may become qualified for the duties of a physician, and not disappoint the expectations of those who furnished them the means to obtain an education. Like Daniel, they have honored God, and He has kept them...

"The young physician has access to the God of Daniel. Through divine grace and power, he may become as efficient in his calling as Daniel was in his exalted position. But it is a mistake to make a scientific preparation the all-important thing, while religious principles, that lie at the very foundation of a successful practice, are neglected... The man who is closely connected with the great Physician of soul and body, has the resources of heaven and earth at his command, and he can work with a wisdom and unerring precision, that the godless man can not possess."

In a letter dated February 19, 1893, over two years before the American Medical Missionary College was established, it was stated that, K-35-1893 (similar wording)

Devoted persons, both men and women, are wanted now to go forth as medical missionaries. Let them cultivate their physical and mental powers and their piety to the utmost. Every effort should be made to send forth intelligent workers. The same grace that came from Jesus Christ to Paul and Apollos, which caused them to be distinguished for their spiritual excellencies, can be received, now; and will bring into working order many devoted missionaries.

In October of the same year, two years before the AMMC was opened, there was written the following:

"God will surely advance the humble, trustful, praying whole-souled medical missionary, as He advanced Daniel and his fellows."

A study of the Testimonies sent from Australia to Battle Creek during the time when the AMMC was being founded and placed in running order, reveals the fact that while Sister White rejoiced to know that our youth would no longer be exposed to the perils of the worldly medical schools, yet she repeatedly brought to view the importance of daily Bible Study—in connection with the study of science.

December 1, 1895, a few weeks after the founding of the AMMC these words were written (as published in Testimonies for the Church 8:156-7.):

"If the medical students will study the Word of God diligently, they will be far better prepared to understand their other studies, for enlightenment always comes with an earnest study of the Word of God. Let our medical missionary workers understand that the more they become acquainted with Bible history, the better prepared they will be to do their work.

"The students in our schools should aspire to higher knowledge. Nothing will so help to give them a retentive memory as the study of the Scriptures. Nothing will so help them in gaining a knowledge of their other studies...

"Faithful teachers should be placed in charge of the Bible classes,—teachers who will strive to make the students understand their lessons, not by explaining everything to them, but by requiring them to explain clearly every passage they read. Let these teachers remember that little good will be accomplished by skimming over the surface of the Word. Thoughtful investigation and earnest, taxing study are required in order for this Word to be understood...

"The Bible is the great lesson-book for the student in our school... Those who consult the divine Oracle will have light. In the Bible every duty is made plain... Every lesson reveals to us the Father and the Son. The Word is able to make all wise unto salvation. In the Word the science of salvation is plainly revealed. Search the Scriptures; for they are the voice of God speaking to the soul.

In 1898, when God's purpose in the training of our youth for service as physicians was being lost sight of, a communication was written under date of February 3, 1898, cautioning against the tendency to separate the medical work from the evangelical line of work. Extracts from this Testimony, as printed in Testimonies for the Church 8:158-162, clearly point out conditions then existing:

"Remember, my brother, that medical missionary work is not to take men from the ministry, but is to place men in the field, better qualified to minister, because of their knowledge of medical missionary work. Young men should receive an education in medical missionary lines, and then go forth to connect with the ministers...

"Those who are receiving an education in medical lines hear insinuations from time to time that disparage the church and the ministry. These insinuations are seeds that will spring up and bear fruit. The student might better be educated to realize that the church of Christ on earth is to be respected. They need a clear knowledge of the reasons of our faith. This knowledge they must have, in order to serve God acceptably. Line upon line, precept upon precept, they must receive the Bible evidence of the truth as it is in Jesus.

"Do not, I beg of you, instill into the minds of the students ideas that will cause them to lose confidence in God's appointed ministers. But this you are most certainly doing, whether you are aware of it or not."

Thus, nearly eleven years ago, and less than three years after the AMMC was founded, it was pointed out through the Spirit of Prophecy that our medical students were from time to time hearing insinuations that disparaged the church and the ministry in their estimation; and it was again urged most emphatically that the students "needed a clear knowledge of the reasons of our faith. This knowledge they must have in order to serve God acceptably."

October 26, 1898, about nine months later than the date of the preceding communication, and just three years from the time the AMMC was founded, the following was written, as published in Testimonies for the Church 8:163-5. (See Vol. 8)

At the 1901 General Conference, in an article entitled "Instructions Regarding the School Work," read before the delegates April 22, 1901, it was pointed out that our medical students were not to receive their training at the one medical college in Battle Creek. Of our schools that were introducing reforms, Sister White read: G.C.B. p. 455, 1901.

"We are thankful that an interest is being shown in the work of establishing schools on a right foundation, as they should have been established years ago. If the proper education is given to students, it is a positive necessity to establish our schools at a distance from cities, where the students can do manual work...

"Although there may be few students at first, do not be discouraged. The school will win its way. Introduce the medical missionary work. Some of the students are to be educated as nurses and some as physicians. It is not necessary for our students to go to Ann Arbor for a medical education. They may obtain at our schools all the education that is essential to perform the work for this time.

"It will take some time to get a right understanding of the matter, but just as soon as we begin to work in lines of true reform the Holy Spirit will lead us and guide us if we are willing to be guided. It is a delicate matter to deal with human minds, and no one should engage in this work without the aid of the Holy Spirit. All must place themselves under the influence of the Spirit. When they place themselves under the direction of the Spirit, they will accommodate themselves to Bible lines. When the Word of God takes possession of the minds of teachers, then they are fitted to deal with the education of others...

"The Word of God is to stand at the foundation of all education. It is to be made the basis of all the schools we shall establish. Following "Thus saith the Lord," brings the schools into close connection with heavenly intelligences. The Lord has been greatly dishonored because His holy Word, which will accomplish so much, has been placed on the background, while books which do not contain the highest instruction in regard to practical life and true science of eternal things have been brought to the front...

"God's dealings with His people are to be our guide in all educational advancement. His glory is to be the object of all study. Those who are being trained as medical missionaries are to realize that their work is to restore the moral image of God in man by healing the wounds which sin has made"...

In 1903 some very plain letters were written, warning our medical students against the danger of losing sight of the lessons of the Word, and learning instead the sophistries of the enemy. The subtleness of this danger is clearly pointed out in a letter written in October, and copied on November 5, 1903, addressed, "To Medical Students and Nurses:" B-240-'03.

"There is a burden upon my mind in regard to the temptations and perils that surround medical students, and those in training for medical missionary work at our sanitariums, and especially for those who are studying at Battle Creek.

"There are teachers who do not daily bring the Word of God into their lifework. They have not a saving knowledge of God or of Christ. It is those who do not live the truth who are most inclined to invent sophistries, to occupy the time and absorb the attention that ought to be given to the study of God's Word.

"Christ, the Great Medical Missionary, came to this world at infinite sacrifice, to teach men and women the lessons that would enable them to know God aright. He lived in this world a perfect life, setting an example that all may safely follow. Let our medical students and other young people study the lessons that Christ has given. It is essential that we should have a clear understanding of these lessons. It would be a fearful mistake for them to neglect the study of God's Word for a study of theories that are misleading, diverting minds from the words of Christ to fallacies of human production.

"When our physicians and ministers are diligent students of the Scriptures, when they live in accordance with the teaching of the Word of God, making this Word their text-book, God will be able to bestow on them rich blessings.

"The teaching regarding God that is presented in 'Living Temple' is not such as our students need. Those who seek to define God are on forbidden ground. We are to enter into no controversy regarding God,—what He is and what He is not. He, the Omniscient One, is above discussion. Those who express such sentiments regarding Him show that they are departing from the faith...

"I will call upon our ministers, physicians and all church members to study the lessons that Christ gave His disciples just before His ascension. These lessons contain instruction that the people of God need. When our physicians understand this instruction, they will realize that the Holy Spirit will never lead them to speak or write that which is at variance with the teachings of the Word of God. Take the Bible as your study-book. It contains the Alpha and Omega of knowledge. All can understand the instruction that it contains...

"Human talent and human conjecture have tried by searching to find out God. Many have trodden this pathway. The highest intellect may tax itself until it is wearied out, in conjectures regarding God, but the effort will be fruitless; and the fact will remain that man, by searching, can not find out God. This problem has not been given us to solve. All that man needs to know and can know of God has been revealed in the life and character of His Son, the Great Teacher. As we learn more and more of what man is, of what we ourselves are, in God's sight, we shall fear and tremble before Him.

"To those who would represent every man as born a king; to those who would make no distinction between the converted and the unconverted; to those who are losing their appreciation of their need of Christ as their Saviour, I would say, Think of yourselves as you have been during the period of your existence. Would it be pleasant or agreeable for you to contemplate feature after feature of your life-work, in the sight of Him who knows every thought of man, and before whose eyes all man's doings are as an open book?

"I call upon all who are engaged in the service of God to place themselves fully on Christ's side. There are dangers on the right and on the left. Our greatest danger will come from men who have lifted up their souls unto vanity, who have not heeded the words of warning and reproof sent them by God. As such men choose their own will and way, the tempter, clothed in angel robes, is close beside them, ready to unite his influence with theirs. He opens to them delusions of a most attractive character, which they present to the people of God. Some of those who listen to them will be deceived, and will work in dangerous lines.

"The Lord calls. Will men and women hear His voice? He gives the warning. Will they heed it? Will they listen to the last message of mercy to a fallen world? Will they accept Christ's yoke and learn from Him His meekness and lowliness?"

In connection with the foregoing extracts, there was written, under date of October 17, 1903, a letter addressed, "To Our Medical Missionaries," in which is a summary of the instruction given during a long series of years regarding the training most essential for our medical students: B-241-'03. (Counsels on Health, 369)

"God would have all who profess to be gospel medical missionaries learn diligently the lessons of the Great Teacher. This they must do if they would find peace and rest. Learning of Christ, their hearts will be filled with the peace that He alone can give.

"The one book that is essential for all to study is the Bible. Studied with reverence and godly fear, it is the greatest of all educators. In it there is no sophistry. Its pages are filled with truth. Would you gain a knowledge of God and Christ, whom He sent into the world to live and die for sinners? And earnest, diligent study of the Bible is necessary in order to gain this knowledge.

"Many of the books piled up in the great libraries of earth confuse the mind more than they aid the understanding. Yet men spend large sums of money in the purchase of such books, and years in their study, when they have within their reach a book containing the words of Him who is the Alpha and Omega of wisdom. The time spent in a study of these books might better be spent in gaining a knowledge of Him whom to know aright is life eternal. Those only who gain this knowledge will at last hear the words, 'Ye are complete in Him.'

Study the Bible more, and the theories of the medical fraternity less, and you will have greater spiritual health. Your mind will be clearer and more vigorous. Much that is embraced in a medical course is positively unnecessary. Those who take a medical training spend a great deal of time in learning that which is merely rubbish. Many of the theories that they learn may be compared in value to the traditions and maxims taught by the scribes and Pharisees. Many of the intricacies with which they have to become familiar are an injury to their minds.

"These things God has been opening before me for many years. In our medical schools and institutions we need men who have a deeper knowledge of the Scriptures, men who have learned the lessons taught in the Word of God, and who can teach these lessons to others clearly and simply, just as Christ taught His disciples the knowledge that He deemed most essential.

"If during the remainder of this year, our medical missionary workers would follow the Great Physician's prescription for obtaining rest, a healing current of peace would flow through their souls. Here is the prescription:

"Come unto Me, all ye that labor and are heavy laden, and I will give you rest. Take my yoke upon you, and learn of Me; for I am meek and lowly in heart, and ye shall find rest unto your souls, for My yoke is easy and My burden is light."

"When our Medical Missionary workers follow this prescription, gaining from the Saviour power to reveal His characteristics, their scientific work will have greater soundness. Because the Word of God has been neglected, strange things have been done in the medical missionary work of late. The Lord can not accept the present showing.

"Study the Word, which God in His wisdom and love and goodness has made so plain and simple... The Holy Spirit teaches the student of the Scriptures to judge all things by the standard of righteousness and truth and justice. The divine revelation supplies him with the knowledge that he needs. And the needed knowledge will be given to all who come to Christ, receiving and practicing His teachings, making His words a part of their lives. Those who place themselves under the instruction of the Great Medical Missionary to be workers together with Him, will have a knowledge that the world with all its traditional lore cannot supply.

"Make the Bible the man of your counsel. Your acquaintance with it will grow rapidly if you keep your mind free from the rubbish of the world. The more the Bible is studied, the deeper will be your knowledge of God. The truths of His word will be written in your soul, making an ineffaceable impression.

"Not only will the student himself be benefited by a study of the Word of God, but his study is life and salvation to all with whom he is associated. He will feel a sacred responsibility to impart the knowledge that he receives. His life will reveal the help and strength that he receives from communion with the Word. The sanctification of the Spirit will be seen in thought, word, and deed. All that he says and does will proclaim that God is light, and in Him is no darkness at all. Of such ones the Lord Jesus can indeed say, "Ye are laborers together with God."

In the light of these extracts, and in the light of the fact that for the past eleven years there has been no change in the purpose of those who in 1898 were conveying to our medical students insinuations from time to time that disparage the church and the ministry,"'and who more recently have taught doctrines that undermine faith in the fundamental features of the third angel's message, it is not difficult to understand why of late the Lord has been counseling His people to establish several centers of medical training, where students can obtain thorough Bible instructions, and at the same time pursue a line of scientific study that will fit them to go forth into the field as physicians of the body as well as the soul. As consecrated young men and women associate daily with God-fearing teachers in these centers of training, they will be strengthened to withstand the influences that they must constantly meet while pursuing certain lines of scientific study.

* * * * *

To the Workers in Southern California

**B.343-'07 Oct. 20, 1907. Sept. 2, 1907.
Sanitarium, Calif.,**

This morning my prayers have ascended to God for spiritual grace and a clear comprehension of His will.

I have been instructed regarding the mistake that has been made in placing men in positions of responsibility to meet emergencies which they think it necessary to be met. [256]

Complaints of a grave character were made, to the effect that some of our ministers while drawing pay from the Conference were out of their place in taking the responsibility of going to various places and of spending means to pay their traveling expenses, when they had not been told to go to these places by the president of the conference. These complaints led to certain rules being laid down by which these ministers could not receive from the Conference the moneys expended, unless they had first, in taking up any line of work, gone to the Conference president to ask his consent. Thus these workers were put under the rule of their fellow minister.

The evils that will result from the adoption of such a course are not discerned by those who favor it. But the Lord has plainly revealed to me that this is not right, and that He is greatly dishonored when ministers are instructed to go to their fellow men for permission to do the work that He has pointed out was their duty to do.

Man is not to be made amenable to his fellow man. I am bidden to write decidedly regarding this matter. The work of exalting men as rulers is a dangerous work, for it educates the workers to look to human agencies instead of looking to God, and this spoils their religious experience. Their minds are diverted from the true source of their strength.

I have been shown that the evangelistic labors of the gospel minister are not to be directed by a fellow minister. The workers for God should inquire of Him, the fountain of wisdom, in regard to their labors. They are to follow the guidance of the Holy Spirit of

God. God is able to move upon their minds, and to guide them with judgment. "The meek will He guide with judgment, and the meek will He teach His way." God will work with those who will listen to His voice.

The word of God is to be the man of our counsel, and is to guide our experience. The lessons of the Old Testament history, if faithfully studied, will teach us how this can be. Christ, enshrouded in a pillar of cloud by day, and a pillar of fire by night, was the guide and the light of the children of Israel, in their wilderness-wandering. Here was an unerring guide. In all their experiences, God was trying to teach them obedience to their heavenly Guide, and faith in His power to deliver them. Their deliverance from affliction in Egypt, and their passage through the Red Sea, revealed to them His power to save. When they rebelled against Him, and went contrary to His will, God punished them. When they persisted in their rebellion, and were determined to have their own way, God gave them that for which they asked, and in this way showed them that that which He withheld from them He withheld for their own good. Every judgment that came as a result of their murmurings was a lesson to that vast multitude that sorrow and suffering are always the result of transgression of the laws of God.

The history of the Old Testament was recorded for the benefit of those who should live in the generations following. The lessons of the New Testament are as greatly needed. Here again Christ is the Instructor, leading His people to seek that wisdom that cometh from above, and to gain that instruction in righteousness that will mold the character after the divine similitude. Both Old and New Testament Scriptures teach the principle of obedience to the commandments of God as the terms of securing that life which measures with the life of God; for it is through obedience that we become partakers of the divine nature, and learn to escape the corruptions that are in the world through lust. Therefore its maxims are to be studied, its commands obeyed, its principles, which are more precious than gold, brought into the daily life.

The light that has been given at this time is only a repetition of the message that was sent in the past.

"Let every department of our work, every institution connected with our cause, be conducted on considerate, generous lines. Let every branch of the work, while maintaining its own distinctive character, seek to protect, strengthen, and build up every other branch. Men of varied abilities and characteristics are employed for carrying forward the various branches of the work. This has always been the Lord's plan. Each worker must give his own branch special efforts; but it is the privilege of each to study and labor for the health and welfare of the whole body of which he is a member.

"Not consolidation, not rivalry, or criticism, but cooperation, is the Lord's plan for His institutions, that 'the whole body fitly joined together and compacted by that which every joint supplieth, according to the effectual measure of the working in every part,' may make 'increase of the body unto the edifying (building up) of itself in love.'

"God desires to bring men into direct relation with Himself. In all His dealing with human beings, He recognizes the principles of personal responsibility. He seeks to encourage a sense of personal dependence, and to increase the need of personal guidance. His gifts are committed to men as individuals. Every man has been made a steward of sacred trusts; each is to discharge his trust, according to the direction of the Giver; and by each an account of his stewardship must be rendered to God.

"In all this, God is seeking to bring the human into association with the divine, that through this connection man may become transformed into the divine likeness. Then the principle of love and goodness will be a part of his nature. Satan, seeking to thwart this purpose, constantly works to encourage dependence upon man, to make men the slaves of men. When he thus succeeds in turning minds away from God, he insinuates his own principles of selfishness, hatred and strife.

"In all our dealings with one another, God desires us carefully to guard the principle of personal responsibility to and dependence upon Him."—See Vol. VII, pp. 174-176.

When Christ sent out His disciples, He sent them out two and two, and commanded them saying, "Go not into the way of the Gentiles, and into every city of the Samaritans, enter ye not, But go rather to the lost sheep of the house of Israel." Why was this restriction made? This was their first trial, the first time that they should attempt to labor without the personal presence of their Lord.

They were not to go into the way of these caviling religionists who would draw them into controversy. "Go rather unto the lost sheep of the house of Israel. And as ye go, preach, saying, The kingdom of heaven is at hand. Heal the sick, cleanse the lepers, raise the dead, Cast out devils; freely ye have received, freely give." Matthew 10:10, 17.

It was those who claimed to be religious, whom Christ declared would do this work of persecution. Ministers today need to look carefully to their own hearts, that they may understand where they really stand. The gospel of Christ is to be carried to all nations and people, but it is to be carried in meekness and lowliness of spirit, long suffering, forbearing one another in love; endeavoring to keep the unity of the Spirit in the bonds of peace."

"There is one body," the apostle says, "and one Spirit, even as ye are called in one hope of your calling; one Lord, one faith, one baptism, one God and Father of all, who is above all, and through all, and in you all. But unto every one of us is given grace according to the measure of the gift of Christ."

"And He gave some apostles, and some prophets, and some— (Ephesians 4:11-16.)

Ellen G. White

* * * * *

B.-274-'07 Sept. 2, 1907.
Sanitarium, Calif.,

Dear Brother Burden,

I received your letter, and read it with much interest. The work you speak of that has been done for the W.C.T.U. is in harmony with the work that, before the Loma Linda property came into our hands, I was shown must be entered into. A grand work is to be done by our people for the W.C.T.U. The Lord has in that association precious souls, who will accept the truth and become one with our labors. These workers will be a great help to us in our efforts in temperance lines. And the education of our people have had in Bible truth and in a knowledge of the requirements of the law of Jehovah, they will impart to those who come in among us. Thus a union and sympathy will be created where in the past prejudice has existed.

We need the help that these women workers can give us, they need the help we can give them in a knowledge of the gospel Sabbath. By holding ourselves aloof from the workers of the W.C.T.U. our people have lost much; and the members of the W.C.T.U. have also been on losing ground. If every possible effort is now made to reach these people, prejudice will be removed, and souls will be reached when our people have thought would never accept present truth.

I have been instructed that no hindrance should be placed in the way of Sister Starr's work for the W.C.T.U. While I was in Australia, Elder A. T. Jones, by an unwise course of action, nearly knocked us out of all opportunity to work for this people. At that time I was shown that no obstacle should be placed in the way of those who are seeking to teach these temperance workers. In some matters they are far in advance of our leaders on the important question of temperance.

Give Sister Starr the right of way. Let no hand be stretched out to hinder her work. Give her an opportunity to bring this message before the temperance organization. Every possible ray of light that we can shed upon the W.C.T.U. should be given. If we had one hundred soundly converted workers from this body, the cause of present truth would be greatly helped. Many of our own laborers would be taught wherein they might come up on to higher ground, and our sisters would learn how they might exert a wider and more uplifting influence than they have in the past.

We need to have the temperance question revived among our own people. It would be a good thing if at our campmeetings we should invite the members of the W.C.T.U. to take part in our exercises. This will help them to become acquainted with the reasons of our faith, and will open the way for us to unite with them in temperance work. If we will do this, we will come to see that the temperance question means more than many of us have supposed. And we in turn can teach these workers many things. They will hear the truth, and many will be converted to the faith.

In his labors, my husband, whenever he had opportunity, invited the workers in the temperance cause to his meetings, and gave them an opportunity to speak. And when invitations were given to us to attend their gatherings, we always responded. I have had some opportunity to see the great advantage to be gained by connecting with the W.C.T.U. workers, and I have been much surprised as I have seen the indifference of many of our leaders to this organization. I call on my brethren to awake. The Lord gave the best gift of heaven to the world that He might win men back to their allegiance to Him. We should do all in our power to cooperate with heavenly agencies for the promulgation of truth and righteousness in the earth. We cannot do a better work than to unite, so far as we can do so without compromise, with the W.C.T.U. workers.

Years ago we regarded the spread of temperance principles as one of our most important duties. It should be so today. Our schools and sanitariums are to reveal the power of the grace of Christ to transform the life. They should be important factors in the temperance cause.

[260] In choosing men and women for His service, God does not measure them according to the standard of the world. He asks, "Do they walk in such humility that I can teach them my way? Can I put My words in their lips, and trust them to speak those words? Will they represent Me in meekness and lowliness of heart? Will they receive My Spirit, learn My ways, and wear My yoke? All who truly follow Me will represent in their characters the immortal principles of Truth."

God's commandment-keeping people are to stand distinguished from the world because He has placed His seal upon them. Christ has healing power for every soul. He will manifest in His believing ones His own character, and cover them with the robe of His righteousness.

(Signed)

Ellen G. White.

* * * * *

B.-276-'07

Dear Brother Burden,

I have read with much interest your letter regarding the camp-meeting.

I have a message to bear to some who hold positions of responsibility in the Southern Calif. Conference. They have lost from their experience that true fervor which the presence of the Holy Spirit gives, and which would teach them to subdue self and walk humbly in the way of Christ. The responsible worker who will not become a humble follower of Christ will do a great harm to the cause of God, by molding and fashioning the experience of the conference to a common, cheap standard. The sacred work that we handle will never, if performed in a spirit of consecration, cheapen the experience of a single soul.

That man is unfit to be the president of a conference or a leader among God's people, who has not broad ideas and views. It is the privilege and duty of those who bear responsibilities in the cause to become learners in Christ's school. The professed follower of Christ must not follow the dictates of his own will; his mind must be trained to think Christ's thoughts, and enlightened to comprehend the will and way of God. Such a believer will be a learner of Christ's methods of work.

A mistake was made in the methods that were adopted to clear the schools in Calif. from debt. The book "Christ's Object Lessons" was given to relieve the indebtedness of our schools. But this plan has not been presented in our schools as it should have been; the students and teachers have not been educated to take hold of this book and push its sale for the benefit of the educational work. The plan that has been followed of calling on our people to support these schools must not be continued; for this is giving to our teachers and students, and to our people in general, a wrong education. They must not be so instructed that they will forget the needs of other fields outside their own.

In the cities of Riverside, Redlands, and San Bernardino a mission field is open to us that we have as yet only touched with the tips of our fingers. A good work has been done there as far as our workers have had encouragement to do it; but there is need of means to carry the work successfully. It was God's purpose that by the sale of "Ministry of Healing" and "Christ's Object Lessons" the necessary means would be raised for the work of our sanitariums and schools, and thus our people be left free to donate of their means for the opening of the work in new fields. If our people had engaged in the sale of these books as God purposed they should, we would now have the means to carry the work in the way the Lord designed.

Wherever the work of selling "Christ's Object Lessons" has been taken hold of in earnest, the book has had a good circulation. And the lessons that have been learned by those who have engaged in this work have well repaid their efforts. Our people should all be encouraged to take a part in this missionary effort. Light has been given me that in every possible way instruction should be given to our people in the best methods of presenting this book to the people. We have been instructed that at our large gatherings, workers should be present who will teach our people how to sow the seeds of truth. This means more than instruction how to sell the Signs of the Times and other periodicals. It includes such books as "Christ's Object Lessons" and "Ministry of Healing." These are books which contain precious truths, and from which the reader can draw lessons of highest value.

At your recent campmeeting, was anyone appointed to present the interests of this line of work to our people? If this was not done, you lost a precious opportunity of placing large blessings within the reach of the people and an opportunity of raising means for the relief of our institutions. My brother, let me encourage our people to take up this work without further delay. Let those who have had experience in the sale of health foods interest themselves in the sale of "Christ's Object Lessons" and "Ministry of Healing;" for here is food unto eternal life. Los Angeles has been presented to me as a very fruitful field for the sale of these books. I know that every household in the land would be benefited by their presence in the home.

Those who bear responsibilities in our sanitariums and schools should act wisely in this matter, encouraging all by this means to gather the money required to meet the expense of the different institutions. We have need of workers in Southern Calif. who have clear spiritual eyesight, men who will weigh matters wisely, and can see afar off. If our workers were more fully consecrated to the cause of God, a much more effective work would be done.

God's Spirit is grieved because His people are so slow to understand that which the Lord requires of them. Our workers should present these books to our people at our large and small gatherings, and call for volunteers who will engage in the sale of them. When this work is entered into with the earnestness which the times in which we live demand, the indebtedness that now rests upon our schools and sanitariums will be wiped out, and the people who are now being called on to give of their means to support these institutions, will be free to donate their offerings to missionary work in other needy places.

Great good will result by bringing these books before the women of the W.C.T.U. Invite these workers to your meetings, and give them an opportunity to become acquainted with our people. Place these books in their hands, and tell them the story of their gift to the cause and its object. Explain how by the sale of "Ministry of Healing" patients will be brought to the Sanitarium for healing who could never get there unaided, and how through this means also sanitariums are managed wisely by men and women who have the fear of God before them; the workers in the temperance cause will not be slow to see the advantage of this branch of the work. If you will in earnestness and faith work out the plan that God has laid down, angels of God will attend your steps, and the blessing of heaven will be upon your efforts.

I send you these lines because I see that there is need of a deeper intuition, a wider perception, on the part of our sanitariums that God intends shall come to them through these books. I ask you, Brother Burden, to read these words to our people, that they may learn to show the wisdom of a sound mind. The Lord gave me His Holy Spirit to enable me to write the manuscript for this book, the Review and Herald and the Press donated the labor required to prepare it for the public; and God now calls upon our people, men and women and youth, to make the most of this gift to His cause. Let the students, under wise directors, be set to work to sell the books, and let all understand why they are engaged in this missionary enterprise. The blessing and approval of God will rest upon those who make the effort.

Ellen G. White

* * * * *

S.-278-'07 Sept. 5, 1907
Sanitarium, Calif.,

Dr. Lillie Wood-Starr Loma Linda. Calif.:

Dear Sister Starr,

Be of good courage in the Lord. I pray that you will look constantly to God, and trust fully in Him. He will be your helper in every emergency.

I am deeply interested in the W.C.T.U. It is the Lord's pleasure that you should feel free to act in concert with them. It is by uniting with them in their labors that we shall be able to bring to these people an understanding of the claims of the fourth commandment. I believe there are many honest souls in this organization, who, when they are convinced of the claims of the Bible Sabbath, will obey the dictates of conscience.

In our earlier labors in the message, our campmeetings were held in out-of-the-way places. Of late years, a change has been brought about in this respect and for this I am grateful. In our labors together, my husband and I always felt that it was our duty to demonstrate in every place where we held meetings, that we were fully in harmony with the workers in the temperance cause. We always laid this question before the people in plain lines. Invitations would come to us to speak in different places on the temperance question, and I always accepted these invitations, if it was possible. This has been my experience not only in this country, but in Europe and Australia, and other places where I have labored.

I am sorry that there has not been a more lively interest among our people of late years to magnify this branch of the Lord's work. We cannot afford to lose one opportunity to unite with the temperance work in any place. Although the cause of temperance in foreign countries does not always advance as rapidly as we could wish, yet in some places decided success has attended the efforts of those who engaged in it. In Europe we found the people sound on this question. On one occasion, when I accepted an invitation to speak to a large audience on the subject of temperance, the people did me the honor of draping above the pulpit the American flag. My words were received with the deepest attention, and at the close of my talk a hearty vote of thanks was accorded me. I have never in all my work on this question, had to accept one word of disrespect.

We need at this time to show a decided interest in the workers of the W.C.T.U. None who claim to have a part in the work of

God should lose interest in the grand object of this organization in temperance lines. I am not afraid that you will lose your interest, or backslide from the truth because you interest yourself in this people who have taken such a noble stand for the temperance question, and I shall urge our people, and those not of our faith, to help us in carrying forward the word of Christian temperance.

I am being aroused anew on this subject. We have a work to do along this line besides that of speaking in public. We must present our principles in pamphlets and in our papers. We must use every possible means of arousing our people to their duty to get into connection with those who know not the truth. The success we have had in missionary work has been fully proportionate to the self-denying, self-sacrificing efforts we have made. The Lord alone knows how much we might have accomplished if as a people we had humbled ourselves before Him, and proclaimed the temperance truth in clear, straight lines. A large work of seed-sowing is yet to be done. The light of truth has flashed upon many minds who have not yet fully taken their stand, and these souls are waiting to see what next. The Lord's workers are to draw nigh to Him, and He will give them keener perceptions and broader views of His purpose and of their individual duty.

Look not to human agencies to learn your duty. Seek the Lord to know His will, and He will give you light. He is the One who can truly estimate character. Christ bids His workers, "If any man lack wisdom, let him ask of God, that giveth to all men liberally, and upbraideth not; and it shall be given him. But let him ask in faith, nothing wavering; for he that wavereth is like a wave of the sea, driven with the wind and tossed. For let not that man think that he shall receive anything of the Lord." God bids us carry our difficulties and perplexities to Him. He presents for the acceptance of the believing soul the virtues of Christ's character. A way is opened for him to receive the truth as it is in Jesus, and to have that faith which works by love and purifies the soul ...

Sister Starr, look to Jesus, and make Him your Counselor, go forward in faith with the work the Lord has pointed out to you. If wisely labored for, many of these women who have taken such a noble stand for the cause of temperance, will go still farther, and will yield themselves to obedience to the commandments of God. A true missionary spirit will lead our workers to welcome these women to our meetings, that they may hear the truth for this time.

We need to put away our narrowness of vision. We need to search the Scriptures, studying the works of Christ in His efforts to reach every class of people. Again and again, Christ was charged with receiving sinners, and eating with them. But He said, "I came not to call the righteous, but sinners to repentance." This is the answer we may give to those who would criticize your works because they cannot reason from cause to effect.

Be encouraged to continue your work for the W.C.T.U. Unite with them in their good work as far as you can do so without compromising any principle of truth. Lead them to see that there is more light for them in the word of God. God has shown you that it is your privilege to unite with these workers that you may give them a more intelligent understanding of the principles of His word.

Ellen G. White

To Ministers, Physicians and Teachers in Southern California

B.-294-'07. Sept. 23, 1907. Sept. 12, 1907.
Sanitarium, Calif.,
Dear Brethren,

I have a message to bear to some who hold positions of responsibility in the Southern Calif. Conference. They are losing from their experience that true fervor which the presence of the Holy Spirit gives, and which would teach them to subdue self and walk humbly in the way of Christ. The responsible workers who will not become a humble follower of Christ will do great harm to the cause of God by molding and fashioning the experience of the conference to a common, worldly standard. The sacred work that we handle, if performed in a spirit of consecration, will never cheapen the experience of a single soul.

The men who stand as presidents of conferences, or as leaders in any part of the solemn work of giving the last gospel message must cultivate and cherish broad views and ideas. It is the privilege of all who bear responsibilities in the work of the Gospel, to be apt learners in Christ's school. The professed follower of Christ must not be led by the dictates of his own will; his mind must be trained to think Christ's thoughts, and enlightened to comprehend the will and way of God. Such a believer will be a follower of Christ's methods of work.

A mistake has been made in the course that has been followed to clear the San Fernando school from debt. When the school property was first purchased, and the minds of our people were upon it, only a feeble effort was made to raise the money spent in its purchase. But after the sanitariums were purchased and the sympathy and financial strength of the people were needed to put them in working order, there were some who made the school debt the matter of first consideration, and who by criticism of the Sanitarium work and management, discouraged the brethren from giving them the full support that they needed.

The Lord did not call upon the president of the conference to make it his first work to gather up the gifts of our people for the school. There was necessity just then of giving first attention to the requirements of the sanitariums.

Provision for our Schools

Our brethren should not forget that the wisdom of God has made provision for our schools in a way that will bring blessing to all who participate in the enterprise. The book "Christ's Object Lessons" was donated to the educational work that the students and other friends of the schools might handle these books, and by their sale raise much of the means needed to lift the school indebtedness. But this plan has not been presented to our schools as it should have been; the teachers and students have not been educated to take hold of this book and courageously push its sale for the benefit of the educational work. Long ago, the teachers and students in our schools should have learned to take advantage of "Christ's Object Lessons." In selling these books the students will serve the cause of God, and while doing this by the dissemination of precious light, they will learn invaluable lessons, in Christian experience. All our schools should now come into line, and earnestly endeavor to carry out the plan presented to us for the education of the workers, for the relief of the schools, and for the winning of souls to the cause of Christ.

In the cities of Riverside, Redlands, and San Bernardino a mission field is open to us that we have as yet only touched with the tips of our fingers. A good work has been done there as far as our workers have had encouragement to do it; but there is need of means to carry the work forward successfully. It was God's purpose that by the sale of "Ministry of Healing" and "Christ's Object Lessons" much means should be raised for the work of our sanitariums and schools, and that our people would thereby be left more free to donate of their means for the opening of the work in new missionary fields. If our people will now engage in the sale of these books as they ought, we shall have much more means to carry the work in the way the Lord designed.

Wherever the work of selling "Christ's Object Lessons" has been taken hold of in earnest, the book has done good. And the lessons that have been learned by those who have engaged in this work, have well repaid their efforts. And now our people should all be encouraged to take part in this special missionary effort. Light has been given me that in every possible way instruction should be given to our people in the best methods of presenting these books to the people.

I have been instructed that at our large gatherings, workers should be present who will teach our people how to sow the seeds of truth. This means more than instructing them in how to sell "The Signs of the Times" and other periodicals. It includes thorough instruction in how to handle such books as "Christ's Object Lessons" and "Ministry of Healing." These are books which contain precious truths, and from which the reader can draw lessons of highest value.

Why was not someone appointed at your recent campmeeting to present the interests of this line of work to our people? In your failure to do this, you lost a precious opportunity for raising means for the relief of our institutions. My brethren, let us encourage our people to take up this work without further delay.

There are some who have had experience in the sale of health foods who should now interest themselves in the sale of our precious books; for in them is food unto eternal life. Los Angeles has been presented to me as a very fruitful field for the sale of "Christ's Object Lessons" and "Ministry of Healing". The thousands of transient residents and visitors would be benefited by the lessons they contain, and those who bear responsibilities in our sanitariums should act wisely in this matter, encouraging all, nurses, helpers, and students, to gather by this means as much as possible of the money required to meet the expenses of the different institutions. We have need of workers in Southern Calif. who have clear spiritual eyesight, men who will weigh matters wisely, and who can discern what is needed both nigh and afar off. If our workers were more fully consecrated to the cause of God, a much more effective work would be done.

Why are our people so slow to understand what the Lord would have them do? Our leading workers should prepare before-hand to use their opportunities at our large and small gatherings to present these books to our people, and call for volunteers who will engage in their sale. When this work is entered into with the earnestness which our times demand, the indebtedness which now rests upon our schools will be greatly lessened. And then the people who are now being called upon to give largely of their means to support these institutions, will be free to turn a larger part of their offerings to missionary work in other needy places, where special efforts have not yet been made.

Great good will result by bringing these books to the attention of the leaders of the Women's Christian Temperance Union. We should invite these workers to our meetings, and give them an opportunity to become acquainted with our people. Place these precious books in their hands, and tell them the story of their gift to the cause, and its results. Explain how that by the sale of "Ministry of Healing" patients may be brought to the sanitarium for healing who could never get there unaided, and how through this means assistance will be rendered in the establishment of sanitariums in places where they are greatly needed. If our sanitariums were wisely managed by men and women who have the fear of God before them, they will be the means of bringing us in connection with workers in the W.C.T.U., and these workers will not be slow to see the advantage of the medical branch of our work. As a result of their contact with our medical work, some of them will learn truths that they need to know for the perfection of Christian character.

One point that should never be forgotten by our workers is that the Lord Jesus Christ is our Chief Director. He has outlined a plan by which the schools may be relieved of their indebtedness; and He will not vindicate the course of those who lay this plan aside for lack of confidence in its success. When His people will come up unitedly to the help of His cause in the earth, no good thing that God has promised will be withheld from them.

In a place like Los Angeles, where the population is constantly changing, a wonderful opportunity is presented for the sale of our books. A great loss has been sustained because our people have not more fully embraced this opportunity. Why should not teachers and students from the San Fernando school make Los Angeles a special field for the sale of "Object Lessons." If with earnestness and faith they will work out the plan that has been given us for the use of this book, angels of God will attend their steps, and the blessing of heaven will be upon their efforts.

It would have been an excellent thing if the teachers of the San Fernando school during the vacation had availed themselves of this opportunity to push the work with "Christ's Object Lessons." They would have found a blessing in going out with the students and teaching them how to meet the people, and how to introduce the book. The story of the gift of the book and its object, would lead some to have a special interest in the book, and in the school for which it is sold. Why have not the teachers in our schools done more of this work? If our people would only realize it, there is no more acceptable work to be done in the home field than to engage in the sale of "Christ's Object Lessons"; for while they are thus helping to carry out the Lord's plan for the relief of our schools, they are also bringing the precious truths of the word of God to the attention of the people.

[270] The indifference that has been manifested by some toward this enterprise is displeasing to God. He desires that it shall be recognized by all our people as His method of relieving our schools from debt. It is because this plan has been neglected, that we now feel so keenly our lack of means for the advancing work. Had the schools availed themselves of the provision thereby made for them, there would be more money in the school treasury, and more money in the hands of His people to relieve the necessities of other needy departments of the cause; and best of all, teachers and students would have received the very lessons that they needed to learn in the Master's service.

I send you these lines because I see that there is need of a deeper intuition, a wider perception, on the part of our sanitarium and educational workers, if they would get all the benefit that God intends shall come to them through the use of "Object Lessons" and "Ministry of Healing." I ask you, my brethren, to read these words to our people, that they may learn to show the spirit of wisdom, and of power, and of a sound mind.

Ellen G. White

* * * * *

From a newsy letter of Sept. 17, 1907, the following is taken:

As to the bakery and my "indomitable perseverance," I have no argument to make. I suppose my convictions as to what should be done are somewhat like other people's: I try to see that it is done.

However, the Lord will have to settle this matter like many other problems too great for human wisdom. I am sure that many of the Conference Committee feel as clear as I do that it should be; perhaps they are not so willing to face problems and therefore do not say much about it, but personally a number have talked to me, and said that they felt clear that it was a part of the work, and in time would come about.

J. A. Burden

MS.-97-'07. (Testimonies for the Church 8:270)

Sept. 19, '07.

In Humility and Faith

Special instruction has been given me for God's people, for perilous times are upon us. In the world, destruction and violence are increasing. In the church, man power is gaining the ascendency, those who have been chosen to occupy positions of trust think it their prerogative to rule.

Men whom the Lord calls to important positions in His work are to cultivate humble dependence upon Him. They are not to seek to embrace too much authority; for God has not called them to a work of ruling. But to plan and counsel with their fellow laborers. Every worker alike is to hold himself amenable to the requirements and instructions of God.

To our brethren in Southern California I bear this message: The president of your Conference has the lesson to learn that he is not to endeavor to rule his fellow-laborers who have occupied positions of trust under God in the work; neither is he to consider himself capable of carrying all things after his own ideas. He has thought that it was his right to rule in every branch of the conference work, and this has led him to judge and criticize fellow-laborers who were better able than he to do the work. He must first rule himself before he can hope, to rule others wisely, or to plan wisely, for the advancement of the work. Position will not give to any man an all-round education.

Because of the importance of the work in Southern Calif., and the perplexities which now surround it, there should be selected, no less than five men of wisdom and experience to consult with the presidents of the local and union conference regarding general plans and policies. The Lord is not pleased with the disposition some have manifested to rule those of more experience than themselves. By this course of action, some have revealed that they are not qualified to fill the important positions which they occupy. Any human being who spreads himself out to large proportions, and who seeks to have the control of his fellows, proves himself to be a dangerous man to be entrusted with religious responsibilities.

Upon the Union Conference President should rest the greater responsibilities, and I am instructed that he needs other helpers to advise him in his work. He should not cling to the idea that unless money is in hand no move should be made that calls for the investment of means. If in our past experience we had always followed this method, we would often have lost special advantages such as we gained in the purchase of the Fernando School property, and in the purchase of the sanitarium properties at Paradise Valley, Glendale, and Loma Linda.

To make no move that calls for the investment of means unless we have the money in hand to complete the contemplated work, should not always be considered the wisest plan. In the upbuilding of His work, the Lord does not always make everything plain before His servants. He sometimes tries the confidence of His people by having them move in faith. Often He brings them into straight and trying places, bidding them go forward when their feet seem to be touching the waters of the Red Sea. It is at such times, when the prayers of His servants ascend to Him in earnest faith, that He opens the way before them, and brings them out into a large place.

The Lord wants His people in these days to believe that He will do as great things for them as He did for the children of Israel in their journey from Egypt to Canaan. We are to have an educated faith that will not hesitate to follow His instructions in the most difficult experience. "Go forward," is the command of God to His people.

Faith and cheerful obedience are needed to bring the Lord's designs to pass. When He points out the necessity of establishing the work in the places where it will have influence, the people are to walk and work by faith. By their godly conversation, their humility, their prayers and earnest efforts, they should strive to bring the people to appreciate the good work that the Lord has established among them. It was the Lord's purpose that the Loma Linda Sanitarium should become the property of our people, and He brought it about at a time when the rivers of difficulty were full and overflowing their banks.

The working of private interest for the gaining of personal ends is one thing. In this, man may follow their own judgment. But the carrying forward of the Lord's work in the earth is entirely another matter. When He designates that a certain property should be secured for the advancement of His cause and the building up of

His work, whether it be for sanitarium or school work, or for any other branch, He will make the doing of that work possible, if those who have experience will show their faith and trust in His purposes, and will move forward promptly to secure the advantages He points out. While we are not to seek to wrest property from any man, yet when advantages are offered, we should be wide awake to see the advantage, that we may make plans for the upbuilding of the work. And when we have done this, we should exert every energy to secure the free-will offerings of God's people for the support of these new plants.

Often the Lord sees that His workers are in doubt as to what they should do. At such times, if they will put their confidence in Him, He will reveal to them His will. God's work is now to advance rapidly, and if His people will respond to His call, He will make the possessors of property willing to donate of their means, and thus make it possible for His work to be accomplished in the earth. "Faith is the substance of things hoped for, the evidence of things not seen." Faith in the word of God will place His people in the possession of property which will enable them to work the large cities that are waiting for the message of truth.

The cold, formal, unbelieving way in which some of the laborers do their work is a deep offense to the Spirit of God. The apostle Paul says, "Do all things without murmurings and disputings; that ye may be blameless and harmless, the sons of God in the midst of a crooked and perverse nation, among whom ye shine as lights in the world; holding forth the word of life, that I may rejoice in the day of Christ, that I have not run in vain, neither labored in vain. Yea, and if I be offered on the sacrifice and service of your faith, I joy and rejoice with you all."

We are to encourage in one another that living faith that Christ has made it possible for every believer to have. The work is to be carried forward as the Lord prepares the way. When He brings His people into strait places, then it is their privilege to assemble together for prayer, remembering that all things come of God. Those who have not yet shared in the trying experiences that attend the work in these last days, will soon have to pass through scenes that will severely test their confidence in God. It is at the time when His people see no way to advance, when the Red Sea is before them, and the pursuing army behind, that God bids them "Go forward." Thus He is working to test their faith. When such experiences come to you, go forward, trusting in Christ. Walk step by step in the path He marks out. Trials will come, but go forward. This will give you an experience that will strengthen your faith in God, and fit you for truest service.

A deeper and wider experience in religious things is to come to God's people. Christ is our example. If through living faith and sanctified obedience to God's word, we reveal the love and grace of Christ, if we show that we have a true conception of God's guiding providences in the work, we shall carry to the world a convincing power. A high position does not give us value in the sight of God. Man is measured by his consecration and faithfulness in working out the will of God. If the remnant people of God will walk before Him in humility of faith, He will carry out through them His eternal purpose, enabling them to work harmoniously in giving to the world the truth as it is in Jesus. He will use all, men, women, and children, in making the light shine forth to the world, and calling out a people that will be true to His commandments. Through the faith that His people exercise in Him, God will make known to the world that He is the true God, the God of Israel.

"Let your conversation be as becometh the gospel of Christ, the apostle Paul exhorts, "That whether I come and see you, or else be absent, I may hear of your affairs, that ye stand fast in one spirit, with one mind striving for the faith of the gospel; and in nothing terrified by your adversaries; which is to them an evident token of perdition, but to you of salvation, and that of God. For unto you it is given in the behalf of Christ, not only to believe on Him, but also to suffer for His sake." (Philippians 2:1-13)

I have been instructed to present these words to our people in Southern Calif. They are needed in every place where a church is established; for a strange experience has been coming into our ranks. It is time now for men to humble their hearts before God, and to learn to work in His ways. Let those who have sought to rule their fellow-workers study to know what manner of spirit they are of. They should seek the Lord by fasting and prayer, and in humility of soul. Christ in His earthly life gave an example that all can safely follow. He appreciates His flock, and He wants no power set over them that will restrict their freedom in His service. He has never placed man as a ruler over His heritage. True Bible religion will lead to self control, not to control of one another. As a people we need a larger measure of the Holy Spirit, that we may bear the solemn message that God has given us without exaltation.

Brethren, keep your words of censure for your individual selves. Teach the flock of God to look to Christ, not to erring man. Every soul who becomes a teacher of the truth must bear in his own life the fruit of holiness. Looking to Christ and following Him, He will present to the souls under His charge an example of what a living, learning Christian will be. Let God teach you His way. Inquire of Him daily to know His will. He will give unerring counsel to all who seek Him with a sincere heart. Walk worthy of the vocation wherewith you are called, praising God in your daily conversation as well as in your prayers. Thus holding forth the word of life, you will constrain other souls to become followers of Christ.

Ellen G. White

* * * * *

S.-302 -'07 September 19,'07
Sanitarium, Calif.
Dr. Lillie Wood Starr, Loma Linda, Calif.:

Dear Sister Starr,

I feel very thankful that you have had the privilege of becoming better acquainted with the workers of the Women's Christian Temperance Union. Our workers should make special efforts to come in touch with this organization, and to connect with the workers in the temperance cause. This will prove a great help to our own people, and also to these women workers. If the present truth is presented to them in the simplicity of godliness, they will see and accept it. We must keep close to the Lord. If we are imbued with His Spirit, the light will shine forth. It is Christ in the life that will make the truths we advocate forcible, and will lead souls to accept Him.

While many of the workers in the W.C.T.U. have heard the truth of the third angel's message, there are many more who have never had it presented to them in its fullness. These women will not be condemned for not receiving that which they have not heard. I have been shown that if the Sabbath truth is presented to these, many will accept it. We should not neglect them, or treat them as if they were opposed to the cause of present truth. By showing ourselves interested in their work of temperance, we shall open the way to give them the light we have.

We need so much to study Christ's methods of labor. He traveled continually from place to place, ministering to the temporal and spiritual needs of the multitudes that followed Him. He grasped every opportunity of presenting truth to the people, and the seeds of truth he dropped into the hearts of His hearers sprang up and brought forth fruit ...

I have been shown that we have not labored as we should for the women of the W.C.T.U. They need patient, wise, Christ-like efforts made for them. We can never do for them what God expects of us by standing apart from them to condemn. We need to give them the truth as it was revealed in the life of Jesus.

Let no one hinder you from putting forth efforts to get the Sabbath truth before this class. Show them that you desire to connect with them in their work of temperance. Draw near to them, and in your association together, show them that you have a practical faith. And they, by coming to our meetings, and being permitted to have a part in them, will learn the reasons of our faith.

At our campmeetings we should make special efforts to reach the unbelieving, and to let the light shine forth amid the moral darkness. Consecration meetings should be held as well as discourses given. The living truths for this time should be preached. At the Los Angeles campmeeting, opportunities should have been improved to make special efforts for the workers in the temperance cause. The tame way in which the temperance question is being handled by our people is not in harmony with the necessities of the times. The work of making known our belief in matters of temperance should now be entered into most heartily. When the W.C.T.U. workers see that we are in harmony with their temperance principles, they will be willing to listen to other points of our faith. As we present our principles on health reform, they will see that there is further light for them on the temperance question. We can bring the Sabbath truth before them.

[275]

I cannot at this time write as fully as I desire, but I urge you, my sister, to let the light of health reform shine forth in clear, bright rays. The Lord will bless you in this work as He makes your knowledge of the truth a blessing to others. Lean hard upon God; trust fully in Him; walk in humility, realizing that the Lord is your helper, and your deliverer, your front guard and your rearward.

Ellen G. White

* * * * *

**Sanitarium, Calif.,
N.-306-'07 Sept. 30, 1907.
Dr. C. C. Nicola, Hinsdale, Ill.:**
Dear Brother and Sister Nicola,

Brother Burden has informed me that you have been considering again going to Loma Linda. I thank the Lord for this, for I know that Loma Linda is the place where you should go. I trust that the snare of the enemy is broken.

A message has been given me for you. I am charged to say to you, Do not go to Battle Creek. You do not understand how the enemy is working to place you in opposition to the truth and the work of God.

A. T. Jones, Dr. Kellogg, and Elder Tenney are all working under the same leadership. They are classing themselves with those of whom the apostle writes, "Some shall depart from the faith, giving heed to seducing spirits and doctrines of devils." In the case of A. T. Jones, I can see the fulfillment of the warnings that were given me regarding him.

I want this message to come to you before you shall make a wrong move. I do not want you to imperil your souls. Heed the message that the Lord sends, and have nothing to do with those at Battle Creek who are opposing the messages of the Spirit of God. Clear light has been given me regarding those who are thus departing from the faith.

I want you to understand that you are both in positive danger. I plead with you to break this influence that would lead you into wrong paths. It proceeds from the one who, if it were possible, would deceive the very elect. Free yourselves from the influence prevailing at Battle Creek, and place yourselves fully on the Lord's side. I do not want you to lose your souls. I beg of you to resist the devil. Make your calling and election sure. Christ gave His precious life for you. Do not let Him make this sacrifice in vain.

My brother and sister, this is a life and death question with you. As the Lord's messenger, I urge you to free yourselves from the snare of Satan, and place yourselves on the platform of eternal truth. I cannot let you take this step without warning you of your danger. If I should do this, I could not be clear before God.

The world is fast becoming as it was before the flood. Wickedness of every description is abroad in the land. Very soon the earth will be ripe for destruction. It is the time now for those who believe that Jesus is soon coming to take their stand fully on the Lord's side. I have an earnest desire that you shall stand with God's people.

I believe, Brother and Sister Nicola, that you will heed these words, and decide to connect with the Loma Linda Sanitarium. Will you not write to me as soon as you receive this, and set my mind at rest. May the Lord give you His Holy Spirit to guide and direct you, is my prayer.

Ellen G. White

* * * * *

B.-312-'07 Oct. 2, 1907
Elder J. A. Burden, Loma Linda, California:

Dear Brother and Sister Burden,

I have just written a letter to Brother Nicola. I have sent you a copy of this. We should use every opportunity we have to save these souls.

The apostle Jude writes, (Jude 3, 4, 20-23)

We shall have more decided opposition to meet from those who have departed from the faith. Those who were once strong teachers, but who have forsaken the way of the Lord, will be just as strong in their opposition of the truth. There is need now that our people be educated to put their trust in God alone. They must learn that their trust is not to be placed in any human voice or arm of flesh. We need ever to keep in mind the experiences of the children of Israel, and learn the lesson that the record of their failures is intended to teach us...

The Lord wants you to understand your individual responsibility for the salvation of your soul. With the word of God as your guide and instructor, you are to personally work out your own salvation. You are to strive to secure eternal life, when you may dwell forever with the Lord. In studying how you may gain this, seek for that wisdom which God alone can impart. Accept the invitation, "If any man lack wisdom, let him ask of God that giveth to all men liberally, and upbraideth not; and it shall be given." "My brethren," the apostle James writes, "count it all joy." (James 1, 2-8)

There is an individual work for all to do before our labors can accomplish anything for others. Blessed is the man who endures temptation, who when he is tried, takes the word of life as his own, brings the promises to the Lord, and claims them as his. This man relies not on any human power, but on the strength of the Lord.

Faith in the word of God will bring to us the fulfillment of His promises. "Whatsoever ye shall ask in My name, that will I do," the Saviour declares. "And all things whatsoever ye shall ask in faith, believing, ye shall receive." When we learn to place our reliance, not on the words of man, but in God, He will make that word yea and amen to us in Christ Jesus.

Brother and Sister Burden, study the Word. You are not to go to any man to learn your duty. Take the Bible as your guide, live its teachings. "Ask, and ye shall receive." We all need a deeper spirituality; we should each seek God for ourselves. Let us ever remember that while we seek to follow one pattern Christ Jesus, we are to maintain our individuality. (James 1:16-20)

When the Word of God is received and obeyed, your light will shine forth in good works. (James 1:22-27)

Ellen G. White

To the Workers in Southern California

B-340-'07 Oct. 3, 1907

This morning I cannot rest. My mind is troubled over the situation in Southern California. God has given to every man his work; but there are some who are not prayerfully considering their individual responsibility.

When a worker is selected for an office, that office of itself does not bring him any power of capability that he did not have before. A high position does not give to the character Christian virtues. The man who supposes that his individual mind is capable of planning and devising for all branches of the work, reveals a great lack of wisdom. No one human mind is capable of carrying the many and varied responsibilities of a conference embracing thousands of people and many branches of work.

But a greater danger than this has been revealed to me in the feeling that has been growing among our workers that ministers and other laborers in the cause should depend upon the mind of certain leading workers to define their duties. One man's mind and judgment is not to be considered capable of controlling and molding a conference. The individual and the church have responsibilities of their own. God has given to every man some talent or talents to use and improve. In using these talents he increases his capability to serve. God has given to each individual judgment, and this gift He wants His workers to use and improve. The president of a conference must not consider that his individual judgment is to control the judgment of all.

In no conference should propositions be rushed through without time being taken by the brethren to carefully weigh all sides of the question. Because the president of a conference suggested certain plans, it has sometimes been considered unnecessary to consult the Lord about them. Thus propositions have been accepted that were not for the spiritual benefit of believers, and which involved far more than was apparent at the first casual consideration. Such movements

[279]

are not in the order of God. Many, very many matters have been taken up and carried by vote, that have involved far more than was anticipated and far more than those who voted would have been willing to assent to, had they taken time to consider the question from all sides.

We cannot at this time afford to be careless or negligent in the work of God. We must seek the Lord earnestly every day, if we would be prepared for the experiences that come to us. Our hearts are to be cleansed from every feeling of superiority, and the living principles of the truth are to be planted in the soul. Young and aged and middle-aged should now be practising the virtues of Christ's character. They should daily be making spiritual development, that they may become vessels unto honor in the Master's service.

"And it came to pass, as He was praying in a certain place when He ceased, one of His disciples said unto Him, Lord, teach us to pray, as John also taught his disciples." The prayer that Christ gave to His disciples in answer to this request is not made in high-flown language, but expresses in simple words the necessities of the soul. It is short, and deals directly with the daily needs.

Every soul has the privilege of stating to the Lord his own special necessities, and to offer his individual thanksgiving for the blessings that he daily receives. But the many long and spiritless, faithless prayers that are offered to God, instead of being a joy to Him, are a burden. We need, O so much! clean, converted hearts. We need to have our faith strengthened. "Ask, and ye shall receive," the Saviour promised; "Seek, and ye shall find; knock, and it shall be opened unto you." We need to educate ourselves to trust in this Word, and to bring the light and grace of Christ unto all our works. We need to take hold of Christ, and to retain our hold of Him until we know that the power of His transforming grace is manifested in us. We must have faith in Christ if we would reflect the divine character.

Christ clothes His divinity with humanity, and lived a life of prayer and self-denial, and of daily battle with temptation. He is our efficiency and power, He desires that through the appropriation of His grace humanity shall become partakers of the divine nature, and thus escape the corruption that is in the world through lust. The word of God in the Old and New Testaments, if faithfully studied and received into the life, will give spiritual wisdom and life. This word is to be sacredly cherished. Faith in the word of God and in the power of Christ to transform the life will enable the believer to work His works, and to live a life of rejoicing in the Lord.

Again and again I have been instructed to say to our people, Let your faith and trust be in God. Do not depend on any erring man to define your duty. It is your privilege to say, "I will declare Thy Name unto my brethren; in the midst of the congregation will I praise Thee. Ye that fear the Lord, praise Him. All ye the seed of Jacob, glorify Him; and fear Him, all ye the seed of Israel. For He hath not despised nor abhorred the affliction of the afflicted; neither hath He hid His face from him; but when he cried unto Him He heard. My praise shall be of thee ... I will pay my vows before them that fear Him. The meek shall eat and be satisfied; they shall praise the Lord that seek Him; your heart shall live forever.

These scriptures are right to the point. Every church member should understand that God is the One to whom to look for an understanding of individual duty. It is right that brethren counsel together; but when men arrange just what their brethren shall do, let them answer that they have chosen the Lord as their counselor. Those who will humbly seek Him will find His grace sufficient. But when one man allows another to step in between him and the duty that God has pointed out to him, giving to man his confidence and accepting him as guide, then he steps from the true platform to a false and dangerous one. Such a man, instead of growing and developing, will lose his spirituality.

There is no power in any man to remedy the defective character. Individually our hope and trust must be in One who is more than human. We need ever to remember that help has been laid on One who is mighty. The Lord has provided the needed help for every soul who will accept it.

Ellen G. White

* * * * *

R-324-'07 Oct. 3, 1907. 257
Sanitarium Calif.,
Elder Reaser S. Hill St., Los Angeles, Calif.:

My Brother,

I have read your letters, but cannot possibly answer them fully now. You would misunderstand me if I should write. If I attend the Los Angeles meeting, I can then communicate to you and to others. I have much to say. Until then make no decided move.

In the last few days I have written many letters to Australia, to Washington, and to other places. Not all that I have written has been sent. I am not able to sleep for the burdens I carry for the many places where souls are in peril. The cases of some have been especially urged upon me. Satan is playing the game of life for their souls. I cannot let them make decisions that will place them in the power of Satanic agencies. By giving them a plain and decided message, God may use my words to save them.

For a long time I have seen the danger that was coming into our ranks in the tendency to look to human wisdom and to depend on human guidance. This will always prove a snare to souls, and I am bidden to lift the danger signal, warning my fellow-workers against it, and pointing them to the Lord Jesus. The man or woman who leans upon the wisdom of the human mind, leans on a broken reed.

I am instructed to point those who are in need of wisdom to the Lamb of God which taketh away the sin of the world. "He was in the world, and the world was made by Him; and the world knew Him not. He came unto His own, and His own received Him not. But as many as received Him, to them gave He power to become the sons of God, even to them that believe on His name." "If any man lack wisdom, let him ask of God, that giveth to all men liberally and upbraideth not, and it shall be given him. But let him ask in faith, nothing wavering; for he that wavereth is like a wave of the sea, driven with the wind and tossed; for let not that man think that he shall receive anything of the Lord. A double minded man is unstable in all his ways... Blessed is the man that endureth temptations, for when he is tried, he shall receive the crown of life, which the Lord hath promised to them that love Him."

"Ask and it shall be given you," the Saviour declared; "seek and ye shall find; knock, and it shall be opened unto you; for everyone that asketh receiveth, and he that seeketh findeth, and to him that knocketh, it shall be opened. Or what man is there, if his son ask bread, will he give him a stone? Or if he ask a fish, will he give him a serpent? If ye then being evil, know how to give good gifts unto your children, how much more shall your Father which is in heaven, give good things to them that ask Him? Therefore whatsoever ye would that men should do to you, do ye even so to them: for this is the law and the prophets.

"Enter ye in at the strait gate: for wide is the gate, and broad is the way, that leadeth to destruction, and many there be that go in thereat: because strait is the gate, and narrow is the way, which leadeth unto life, and few there be that find it."

[282]

Never should a worker encourage one who is in need of instruction and help to go first to human agencies for an understanding of his duty. It is our privilege as laborers to pray together and to counsel together; but we are individually to seek God to know what He would have us do. When the Lord impresses the mind of one of His servants that he is to go to a certain place to labor, that man is not under obligation to go to a human being to know if it is right for him to do this.

It is a wrong education to teach our people to lean on human aids, instead of going to the Lord in prayer. The enemy of souls has been the instigator of this, that minds might become obscured. The people are now to be instructed differently. God's people are to meet together in counsel, but no leader or worker is to take the position that God's children are to make no move until he is first consulted. Those who bear responsibilities in the work are to cooperate with heavenly angels in teaching men and women to look to God as the source of their strength.

Wherefore "as the Holy Ghost saith, Today if ye will hear His voice harden not your hearts, as in the provocation, in the day of temptation in the wilderness, when your fathers tempted Me, proved Me, and saw my works forty years. Wherefore I was grieved with that generation, and said, They do always err in their heart; and they have not known my ways. So I sware in my wrath, They shall not enter into my rest. Take heed, brethren, lest there be in any of you an evil heart of unbelief, in departing from the living God. But exhort one another daily, while it is called today; lest any of you be hardened through the deceitfulness of sin. For we are made partakers of Christ, if we hold the beginning of our confidence steadfast unto the end; while it is said, Today, if ye will hear His voice, harden not your hearts as in the provocation. For some, when they had heard, did provoke; howbeit not all that came out of Egypt by Moses. But with whom was He grieved forty years? Was it not with them that had sinned, whose carcasses fell in the wilderness? and with whom sware He that they should not enter into His rest, but to whom they believed not? So we see that they could not enter in because of unbelief."

"God who at sundry times and in diverse manners spake in times past unto the fathers by the prophets, hath in these last days spoken unto us by His Son, whom He hath appointed heir of all things; by whom also He made the worlds; who being the brightness of His glory, and the express image of His person, and upholding all things by the word of His power, when He had by Himself purged our sins, sat down on the right hand of the Majesty on high. Being made so much better than the angels, as He hath by inheritance obtained a more excellent name than they... But to which of the angels said He at any time, Sit on my right hand, until I make thine enemies thy footstool? Are they not all ministering spirits, sent forth to minister to them that shall be heirs of salvation?"

The ministration of Christ is ever to be kept before the minds of the people; His efficiency is that to which they should ever be directed. Ministers in word and doctrine are not to seek in human wisdom to supply the necessities of these souls; they are not to direct and guide. By doing this they educate the flock of God to depend on human beings who are liable to err. "If any man lack wisdom, let him ask of God, that giveth to all men liberally and upbraideth not; and it shall be given him. But let him ask in faith nothing wavering." Here is marked out a straight path to the world's Redeemer, which every soul may take. Christ tasted death that every man might be partaker of the blessings of the gospel. Then let all, experienced and inexperienced, be directed to the source of all efficiency and power. Christ has promised to be our wisdom, our righteousness, our sanctification and redemption.

Elder Reaser, my message to you is, Consecrate yourself to the Lord Jesus Christ. Seek the One who understands your every weakness, and who never makes a mistake. He is able to impart to you His rich grace. Looking unto Jesus, studying His word, learn to humble your soul before God and to wrestle in prayer with Him.

It is not the position you may hold in the work that determines your efficiency. A high position will not change the character or increase the moral worth. It is written, "Thou madest him a little lower than the angels; thou crownedst him with glory and honor, and didst set him over the works of Thine hands: Thou hast put all things in subjection under his feet. For in that He put all things in subjection under him, He left nothing that is not put under him... But we see Jesus, who was made a little lower than the angels crowned with glory and honor; that He by the grace of God should taste death for every man. For it became Him for whom are all things, and by whom are all things, in bringing many sons unto glory, to make the captain of their salvation perfect through suffering. For both he that sanctifieth and they that are sanctified, are all of one; for which cause he is not ashamed to call them brethren; saying, I will declare Thy name unto My brethren, in the midst of the church will I sing praise unto Thee."

The all-sufficiency of the Saviour is brought to view in this Scripture. He experienced in His human nature all that we can possibly experience. Taking our nature, and in the strength that his humanity received from God, He coped successfully with the powers of Satan and fallen angels. He bids His servants learn of Him. "Come unto Me, all ye that labor and are heavy-laden," He invites, "and I will give you rest. Take my yoke upon you and learn of Me; for I am meek and lowly in heart, and ye shall find rest unto your souls. For My yoke is easy, and My burden is light." Learn of Christ. As you study His personal life, and practise His works, you will find rest to your soul.

I am bidden to say to every professing child of God, Go not to human agencies to learn your duty. Take your case to the one who has tasted death for every man. "In all things it behooved Him to be made like unto His brethren, that He might be a faithful and merciful high priest in things pertaining to God to make reconciliation for the sins of the people. For in that He Himself hath suffered, being tempted, He is able to succor them that are tempted."

The worker who considers himself in a position of such high responsibility that he allows the members of the churches to look to him to voice their decisions and control their actions, is educating men and women to wear a human yoke. They are not learning of the divine teacher. To the one who is being led to have such an experience I would say, "Go to Christ; ask Him to give you an experience; learn to emulate His faultless character, and do not look for experience of guidance to any human being, who is as liable to err as yourself.

There are reasons why we should not put our trust in men who are placed in positions of large responsibility. It is often difficult for them to maintain a humble and teachable spirit. They suppose that their position gives them the power to control their fellows, and they flatter themselves, as did Peter, that they will not fall under temptation. When in the hour of His trial Christ declared to His disciples that they would all forsake Him, Peter answered, "Lord, why cannot I follow Thee now? I will lay down my life for Thy sake. Jesus answered him, Wilt thou lay down they life for My sake? Verily, verily I say unto thee, The cock shall not crow till thou hast denied me thrice." Throughout His trial Christ preserved His humility. Peter's self-confident assertion was tested, and he failed to endure the test. He denied his Lord in the hour of temptation.

I am instructed to present these words before the workers in Los Angeles and at Paradise Valley. Man is not to be depended on as a model in speech or in plans.

If it is possible, there should be chosen to fill the responsible positions in a conference, men who will not lead others to depend upon them, but who will lead all to make the life of Christ their study, and their pattern. Christ ever manifested a heavenly courtesy in dealing with human souls. His life was a life of constant self-denial and self-sacrifice. Those who are numbered with the overcomers will be those who have practised the virtues of Christ. My heart has been made sick and sore when I have seen the example set by those who have loved to dictate and control; and I have said, If this wrong continues in spite of the warnings that have been given, I shall have no courage regarding their meeting successfully the great conflict that is before us.

Ellen G. White

* * * * *

The Responsibilities of a Conference President

MS. -105-'07. October 10, 1907.

(Interview on Southern California Conference Matters.—Part 1.)

Report of an interview, Sabbath afternoon October 5, 1907, at the home of Mrs. E. G. White, Sanitarium, California. Present: Mrs. E.G. White, Elders G.W. Reaser, J.A. Burden, and W.C. White, and C.C. Crisler.

J.A. Burden: Brother Reaser and I came here to talk over some matters. The communications that have been sent us by you have been very stirring, very touching, and Brother Reaser, it seemed to me, was taking a somewhat wrong view of them, and I felt that others were influencing him in wrong ways concerning them. Of course, in his position, when leading men talk to him in the line that he is inclined to feel like following, it even urges him on' and so I advised him to come and talk with you. But he did not want to come, unless I should come along with him. I had all confidence to come to headquarters, and that you would meet him here, and tell him whether there was any further light for him.

Now this is the position that is taken by a great many, concerning the communications that you have recently sent to Southern California: That the communications were written with reference to a situation that had been set before you by Brother W. C. White—that you had written communications to meet the situation, as it was represented to you by him. Now this thing has gone all through Southern California. Many brethren have taken the same position. But I said, I do not believe that is the right position at all, and so I thought that Brother Reaser could come and see you, and have the matter cleared up in his mind, so that he might know of a surety that the Lord was speaking directly, and not on a false view of a situation.

Although he and I have differed, I have confidence in Brother Reaser, that when he sees a thing right, he will take a right stand;

but I have felt that he was seeing things wrong, and taking a wrong stand.

Sister White: During the past few days, I have been looking over my old diaries, and in them I find written out principles very similar to those outlined in the Testimonies sent recently to brethren in Southern California. The same dangers of centralizing the work, and of binding about and restricting the laborers of our fellow workers, are brought to view. Southern California is not the only field where there is a tendency to restrict and bind about.. In several other fields the same evil has to be met.

J.A. Burden: You will pardon me, if I speak of definite points. All the brethren that have met this, agree on a certain line, namely, that a situation is laid before you by Brother White, and you, from your knowledge, write on that representation, and not because you have received light apart from that.

Sister White: He will tell you himself that it is I that presents the situation to him.

J.A. Burden: That is what I say.

Sister White: He does not seem to want to tell me anything about the Southern California meeting. Scarcely anything has he told me,—only some points that he knows would not trouble my mind. He does not feel like opening things to me, but I come to him with manuscripts, and I tell him, This must be copied, and sent out just as quickly as it can be. Now I have light, mostly in the night season, just as if the whole thing was transacting, and I viewed it, and as I am listening to the conversation, I am moved to get up and meet it. This is the way it is, and then in the morning I tell him about it. Often he doesn't say a word,—not a word; but after awhile, when I have written and written, then he acknowledges that it is so. He is quite sure that it is so, because he was there; but he did not tell me.

J.A. Burden: But what I feel so anxious about is that our brethren shall know these things; for they are in the dark about them.

Sister White: They shall know them, if God gives me strength to go to the next meeting; and I expect to have strength to go. you were not up to the camp-meeting in St. Helena, were you? Well, I had a message for them at St. Helena, but I did not give it. For a long time I labored under a depression, fearing I had neglected my duty, but recently I had light that I was not under condemnation, because the circumstances did not belong to me; they belonged to others.

W.C. White: Mother continued in a weak and discouraged condition until about ten days before the Los Angeles Camp-meeting and then when the Lord opened up to her the conditions there, and what she must write, she told me about the burden that had been given to her for the work there, and she told me that the Lord would give her strength.

G.W. Reaser: Now, Sister White, may I make a few statements to you concerning why I came up here especially?

Sister White: Certainly.

G.W. Reaser: You know, of course, as well as I do, that the Testimonies that you sent down there were directed largely to me and concerning my work, and it brought in such an intense situation that I felt as if I could not go on and have anything further to do with the health work, without having some understanding; and I did not want to come up here alone, because Brother Burden represents one side of the situation there; and if I, who have represented another side, should have come up here alone, and carried back a report, it would not have been so well as for two to carry it. So we are here together.

The situation is this: There have been some extremely heavy burdens for some of us to bear in Southern California, and apparently but few to bear the burdens. It is all too true that we have not trusted the Lord enough to bear our burdens. I am not here to speak of these burdens, but I want to have an understanding as to just what to do, and what not to do. Now, of course, we have had, as you know, several heavy burdens to bear down there. The matter about our going into debt, was practically the only thing that has been between Brother Burden and me. The only material difference of opinion was about the matter of going into debt at Loma Linda after we took over the property; and I felt as if I was strengthened by almost everybody in the Conference, and in the Union Conference as well, in trying to prevent a heavy debt coming; and I really thought, Sister White, I was strengthened, too, by your writings along that line.

Sister White: How long have you been in the position as President of the Conference?

G.W. Reaser: Two and a half years.

Sister White: Were these debts accumulating all this time?

G.W. Reaser: We took Loma Linda after I was called to the presidency of the Conference, and the debts were accumulated at the time of the purchase of this property, and afterward. We set to work to reduce the Fernando debt, and it is now reduced from $24,000 to $4,000; but the indebtedness has been increased on Loma Linda by making good investments, and, with my understanding of the situation, I could hardly grasp all of that.

Sister White: The raising of money was for the school particularly?

G.W. Reaser: With the blessing of the Lord, we have reduced the indebtedness of Fernando Academy from $24,000 to $4,000 in round numbers. It would not take long to cancel the remaining indebtedness. My whole nature and education were against going into debt heavily, and that was what caused the whole issue down there; and yet when I came up to this camp-meeting, I told Brother Burden that hereafter I was not going to take such strong ground as I had in the past. I confessed to the brethren that I had taken too strong ground, and asked them to forgive me; and I asked the Lord to forgive me, because I was radical in my position, and thought we ought not to go into debt. Sometimes I did not say right things to Brother Burden. But each of us hold nothing against the other.

Now the question is, when the Testimonies have come, saying what they have, does the Lord want me to cut loose entirely from the Sanitarium work, and not have anything to do with it? Or, does the Lord want me to have something to do with it, and try always to manifest grace,—to manifest the right spirit? That is the question I want light upon.

Sister White: If you continue as president of the Conference, that responsibility should be carried in perfect accord with your brethren. Here is one who has the chief burden of one enterprise, and another the chief burden of another enterprise. Now if one has been placed by the Lord in a position where he carries the burden of a sanitarium enterprise, it is perfectly right that you should counsel with him, but to keep agitating, all the while, the minds of your brethren, by criticizing the work that he is doing, is not right. He has his appointed work; and there are others, in other positions of responsibility, who have their appointed work, as in Bible times.

The Scripture says, "He gave some, apostles; and some, prophets; and some, evangelists." Thus it goes on to tell what the work of different ones is.

I have felt very much burdened over the responsibilities connected with the opening of the Loma Linda Sanitarium, because there were so many things to be done at once. And I could not see how I could help the situation. I have felt burdened very much; and I kept all the time planning how we could reach out, and get hold of something that would relieve some of their indebtedness. In the night, the thought came to me, "Well, what are you worried about? The Lord has made known your duty, and you have done it, by offering the sanitarium the privilege of selling "Ministry of Healing," and applying the proceeds to the reduction of their indebtedness. You have paid your workers; you have paid your typewriters, and then you have given away all that would otherwise have come to you from the book."

So also with regard to "Christ's Object Lessons," given for the relief of our schools. To my certain knowledge, $200,000 has been brought in from the sale of "Object Lessons," to help relieve the school of indebtedness...

W.C. White: About 20,000 copies of "Ministry of Healing" have been put out, and there is so little being done in the relief way, that now we are planning to get out a subscription edition at the beginning of the year, to be sold by the agents in the regular way. Still, those who wish will have the privilege of using "Ministry" as a relief book wherever they desire to do so.

G.W. Reaser: A good work has been done by these books, but it ought to go further. Now this, Sister White: I do not want to tire you this evening, I want to make this little statement to you, that ever since I have been a Conference President, in different parts of the country, I have had an interest in the medical work, and have always been anxious that wherever I was located, in every Conference, that there might be perfect harmony between the medical work and the Conference work; and I felt anxious about that in Southern California.

During the past two years I have tried to use whatever influence and prestige that went with the Conference Office, to get strong workers for the institutions, and, of course, I have gotten considerable funds, too. When these last Testimonies came, within the past few weeks, and especially the one that pointed it out as being a mistake for me to be connected with the Sanitarium work, I thought I ought to drop that work, and let someone else carry it; and yet we are very short of men.

Sister White: It is not that you are not to be connected with the work, but that you are not to be connected with it to discourage. Brother Burden has enough to carry. He had to put up some improvements, we know. I do not know just how far Bro. Burden has gone in the matter of improving the property. But there is a kind of authority that you feel at liberty to use, that the Lord does not give you,—a kind of domineering, that is not in harmony with the Lord's work, and our relation one with another. I have felt that I ought to be very careful about presenting things, in order to prevent the exercise of a domineering power. This was so distinctly laid out before me, that I felt as if I must write you...

W.C. White: As you expressed it to me the day you were writing about, it was a movement to get the work into a shape where two or three men could control all lines of work.

Sister White: Yes; and I wrote them at once.

G.W. Reaser: I was so perplexed over the situation in Southern California, that I thought best to come here to get right, and to get into perfect line. We want perfect harmony down there between the medical work and the Conference work, and the work will be crippled, unless we have it. I want to know what light there is for me, that I may relate myself just right to the work there, and overcome all objectionable traits.

Sister White: Well, here is your danger—of considering that the whole responsibility of the Conference, the sanitarium work, and all other lines of work, rests upon you, to run them... I know that unless there is a change in your manner of carrying matters, a condition of things will come in that it will be very difficult to undo. You cannot afford it, nor can I afford it. In the matter of your raising the money for the school as you have done, you are thereby placed in a relation before that Conference, where they think certainly that you are the man that can carry things through. But the Lord did not mean that it should go in that way. He had provided these books, He had given me the privilege of dedicating those books to the schools and to the sanitariums. Then He desired that every soul should come in and act a part in making the most of that gift. Every one should learn how to handle these books, and if each one does this, rich experiences will be gained, and blessings will fall upon the workers.

G.W. Reaser: One more question, and then perhaps I ought not to tax your strength further this evening; and that is this: It seemed to us, with our many medical institutions in Southern California, that there ought to be perfect understanding, perfect accord, between the Conference and the medical workers.

Sister White: Certainly there ought.

G.W. Reaser: And the question is, should I, as Conference President, be in any way officially connected with the Sanitariums, and use the prestige of the Conference and the influence of the Conference to gather workers, as strong workers as we can, to the work, and to get money? Now, those things have been in my mind, whether I ought to drop that line, and give attention to what we call purely conference work, or whether I ought to keep on.

Sister White: Well, I can not tell you. This is what I was saying: In the visions of the night, in a meeting, I said: "Brother Reaser, why did not you feel an interest in that sanitarium, to create a fund so that it should not have so large a debt? Which was of the greatest consequence,—was it of the greatest consequence to take up that school, in which the parents and so many friends were interested and could all exert an influence,—which was of the greatest consequence?" Thus I was talking right to you in the meeting. "Now," said I, "which is of the greatest consequence, Brother Reaser? Is it a sanitarium that is to stand as a constant voice and influence, that shall bring in all classes of minds, and all kinds of persons, some in poverty and some with influence? Or is it a school?" I thought, Brother Burden, you were present also...

We have been altogether too delicate, in our sanitariums, never to call upon men of means, and ask them for a donation. There are wealthy men outside of the institution, who would help. Tell them that we are in a strait place, and we want help. We have to fit up the place at Loma Linda, because, when we bought the property we had everything that was wanted but the very thing that was most wanted. The very thing that was wanted the most, was treatment-rooms. We had to have more room, and appliances with which to carry on the work. Those who sold you the sanitarium, did not really know what was needed the most for the successful operation of a sanitarium...

J.A. Burden: Now may I state what Brother Reaser has referred to? I have felt this way: I would like to stand shoulder to shoulder with Brother Reaser, carrying what I can in the medical line; but I feel that to make a perfect unit, he, as President of the Conference, should use his office to encourage the medical people, to associate with the medical people, encourage people to help in the work, and they would then feel that the Conference was morally and financially interested. And it would seem as if the sanitarium was a part of the Conference work.

Sister White: If, in the beginning, he had taken hold of those things that were of such large consequence and far-reaching importance to the community all around there; if he had done all he could do to help set that sanitarium in working order, it would have been more in harmony with the ideas that God has given me, than is the course that has been pursued. The sanitarium work at Loma Linda must stand among things of first importance. The sanitarium work is that which is going to bring in and reach the highest class of people everywhere...

J.A. Burden: Then if he can see that situation, and can feel to throw his influence that way, would you see any objection to his being on the Board with us?

Sister White: Why, no, you need to counsel together, just as brethren need to counsel together, but not in an authoritative way.

G.W. Reaser: No; that is right.

Sister White: Now here is a thought—if I can get it out so you can understand it: There is all the difference in the world between a school where they are educating students, and a sanitarium that is to reach the highest classes, and that must show a prosperity in the work; for God has selected that place for us, and as He has selected it, we must harmonize with Him, and take right hold, and work for its prosperity; and yet we must guard everything so as not to have an unnecessary outlay of means.

There is a point I desire to mention before I forget it; I want to bring it out before you both, as it is this: We shall have to take a position in regard to the health food business. They are gathering in, and have gathered in, some of the very persons that are wanted to work in the cause of God. They very persons that should take hold and unite with us and become missionaries, are now bound up in the manufacture of foods; and what do they gain? How many are they converting? How many are receiving the truths of the third angel's message? Now the light that I have from God, is that, we must not encourage our people to make too much of the business of manufacturing foods; we must not do it; because it is taking, in some instances, the very flower of our youth to keep up an appearance in an establishment for the manufacture of food to set upon many tables, to feed worldlings—and how much do they gain by it?

W.C. White: As that is presented to you, do you see the factory and the workers in the factory, or the workers that have gone out to sell the foods, or the workers in the Restaurant?

Sister White: It is the whole business; it relates to the whole; some of the very persons that we ought to have in the work, as Bible missionaries, are doing a work that does not bring souls to an acquaintance with soul-saving truth.

J.A. Burden: But the simple method that you have outlined for a small plant, in connection with our institutions, to make foods for our institution, and the surrounding neighborhood—do you refer to that?

Sister White: No: you want to educate the neighbors in health reform; you want the Sanitarium workers to have a proper education also. There are foods, you know, that the people are ignorant about, and they ought to be educated. Many can hardly make a good loaf of bread. But to enter into the business of manufacturing largely, is not best—only for cities or settlements around where you want your influence to tell, where you want them to see what good cookery is, etc...

The people would learn much regarding health reform, if "Ministry of Healing" were circulated widely. You can have the "Object Lessons" to use in relief work for the school, right where you are, and also the "Ministry of Healing" as a help for the sanitariums. There is to be no bondage, no territorial lines drawn, in this matter of trying to place these institutions at Loma Linda on vantage-ground.

J.A. Burden: If the brethren can all see light in the right, it is wonderful what will come. But when some are lifting up and others are pushing down, it goes hard.

Sister White: Well, that is the devil's work. He came to Christ, while the Saviour was fasting. The enemy thought that if he could take advantage of Him in His weakness, he would obtain a wonderful victory. But Christ answered him in the words of Scripture.

J.A. Burden: It throws our people into an uncertainty when our leading brethren represent, Sister White, that some one has come and talked with you; that is the influence that comes in.

Sister White: Well, it shows that they do not have much confidence in the work that God has given me to do.

J.A. Burden: In Loma Linda, and elsewhere, there are some who feel that some of the things you wrote back from Washington, two years ago, about the necessity of securing Loma Linda, were inspired by an interview that I had with you on the train as you were passing through, en route to the Conference.

Sister White: I wondered that you did not write more to me; but I knew how it was, and I feel that we should move intelligently, so that God can accept our work. The work at Loma Linda is to be carried on a high religious plane.

Ellen G. White

* * * * *

The Management of Conference Affairs

MS.-109-'07

(Interview on Southern California Conference Matters,—Part 2.)

Report of an interview, Sunday morning, Oct. 6. 1907, in the office room of Mrs. E.G. White. Present: Mrs. E.G. White, Elders G.W. Reaser, J.A. Burden, W.C. White and C.C. Crisler.

J.A. Burden: In your communication to us, you mention that there should not be less than five men of wisdom selected to act with the Union Conference President and the Local Conference President, to lay out a policy and plan for the work. We were not clear what was meant by this—whether men outside should come in and meet with us, or whether men there should come in with us. It seemed to us that five men outside were to come in and act with us.

Sister White: The five men should act a part in carrying the larger responsibilities. One man is not wise enough, in any place, in any situation, to be a complete whole. This you might as well understand. There must be several minds who will, in the fear of God, act a part in carrying responsibilities.

J.A. Burden: In our Conference Committee there are seven members; namely, Elder Reaser, myself, Elder Healey, Elder Owen, Elder Ford, Dr. Leadsworth, and Professor Lucas of Fernando. Did your statement have reference to these men?

Sister White: No, no; it is men who can bear more especially the religious responsibilities. And when the religious responsibilities are kept in the fear of God, everything else will be easily carried. We do not want any human power to dominate his fellowman as regards to religious duties.

Years ago, my husband and I used to study how we should manage perplexing matters in the office, and deal with men of peculiar temperaments... "Well," my husband used to say, "let us pray about it." And so we would kneel down, often in the night season, and we would pray the Lord to pen the way, so that we could approach men wisely, and give them the right instruction. Afterward, when we would try to talk kindly with them, and yet plainly, they would almost always yield. They did not always remain steadfast in their determination to pursue a right course; and because they returned to their former ways, we often had the same battle to fight over and over again. But whatever the matters might be, we felt that the Lord knew all about them, that He could tell us how to act, and that He could move on hearts...

From the light I have had, the elements in the Southern California Conference have been sadly lacking with regard to a religious experience, a spirit of Christian unity and harmony of action. Some seem too ready to advocate this man or that man, or the other man. Such a spirit has been revealed by many. You know there are different sentiments, and different temperaments, and all these peculiar conditions have made it difficult for those in responsibility to know how to manage; and yet it would be a very unwise thing, Brother Reaser, for you to feel free to question certain things, and give to the people a feeling of uncertainty regarding matters over which they should have no doubt. When doing such work, you are sowing seeds. You may not realize any fruit just at present, but you are sowing seeds that will bear fruit. We must cultivate a spirit of unity. We must strive for unity in following the gospel pattern—Christ Jesus. There is nothing, nothing, that we can present to the people, that will be of greater value than to present Christ, and to study what He would do under like circumstances. And if we present Christ, and strive to labor in the bonds of Christian unity, one party will not be set up against another. Thus grave evils will be avoided.

Brother Reaser has felt that he was perfectly competent in all these matters, but he doesn't understand as much in regard to himself as he thinks he does. A course that he would take, would lead to certain sure results, and he would not know that what he said at a certain time, had blossomed out and developed into objectionable fruit. But if we try to keep in unity, and humble ourselves before God, He will bless our efforts. You remember that when Solomon was exalted to be king, he humbled himself before God. Realizing that he was taking upon himself responsibilities that he had never carried before, he acknowledged to the Lord, before all the people, that he was but a little child. And so he was, in management. In after years, he was spoiled by his association with idolatrous wives.

Oh, I have thought, often have I thought, if we only could once get thru with these difficulties, and know we tried to do our best in the fear of God. Shall we not have a crown of life?

J.A. Burden: We shall feel that it is a joy to be relieved of the things we have suffered.

Sister White: Well, we shall feel strong, with our life hid with Christ in God. (Sister White referred, at some length, to the sufferings of Christ)...

Sister White: There is one other point that I want Brother Reaser to keep in his mind,—perhaps he does not understand it fully. He has thought that Willie tells me. Now I am up in the morning, you know, before any one else is up,—at one o'clock, two o'clock, three o'clock, and seldom ever after four—more often by three. Recently, for nights and nights and nights, I have seldom been able to sleep after two o'clock, but have been up, writing. I write out the presentations that the Lord has given me in the night season; and when, later on in the morning, Willie comes in to see me, I have already written many pages. Often the manuscript has been placed in the hands of one of my copyists, and is being written out, before he knows that I have written anything, or what I have written. After it is typewritten, a copy is often placed in his hands. It is not he that comes with things to me, but I give to him the light that I have received.

W.C. White: Sometimes, you know, you propose to read to me what you have written. Sometimes you tell me a little about it, but there is not more than one-twentieth part that I really know anything about before it is passed on by you into the hands of the copyist, to be typewritten.

Sister White: Yes; I know that.

W.C. White. But the real point in the minds of the brethren is: Do I, after seeing how things are going in the field,—do I come to you with my representations of how things look to me, and keep presenting them so as to stir you up to write out principles which are good, true principles, but principles which may not be needed at that time, and which do not exactly apply at that time, but which

[298]

you think apply at that time because of the representations I have made to you of the conditions of the field?

Sister White: I have not been able to get from Willie full particulars regarding perplexing matters; he is careful to tell me only of victories gained, or anything that will encourage me. When he attends meetings, he does not make it a point to tell me of the difficulties that he encounters in these meetings. Instead of going into particulars regarding the matters that perplex the brethren, he presents those things that he thinks will not disturb my mind. Sometimes letters come, giving me information that I should never gain from him because he won't tell me.

W.C. White: Tell the brethren who told you most about the Southern California camp-meeting,—I, in all the times I have been with you, or Brother Cottrell, in his one visit of two hours and a half here?

Sister White: Elder Cottrell told me much that I had not heard at all from W.C. White, you know. There were only a few items referred to that had been told me before. Elder Cottrell entered into the particulars. I told him that I wanted to know something about conditions in Southern California, and about his impression of the meeting recently held there; for I had written out some things, and I wanted to know how matters stood; and so he told me some things about the Los Angeles meeting. Of course, our interview was not so very long, and we could not cover the whole ground.

W.C. White: Now with reference to Paradise Valley Sanitarium, and the proposed transfer of the institution to the California Conference: That was a perplexing thing for me to present to Mother. I will tell you what I did. I insisted that Brother Ballenger should write us a letter, giving an official statement from the president. He did so. Mother has read it, and we now have this statement on file. Now with reference to my own report. Instead of telling Mother about it, I sat down and wrote to Eld. Daniells, and let her read my letter to him. Now what she has gotten from me regarding Paradise Valley, is from the reading of Brother Ballenger's letter, giving his statement as president of the Board, and also what she learned from the letter that I wrote to Eld. Daniells. Both of these letters are on file in my office. Now if any one wants to know what I have presented to

Mother about Paradise Valley, they can see these letters that she has read.

You may know how the brethren felt, and why they excluded Prof. Ballenger and me from the committee meeting when they considered our propositions and made other propositions. So up to the present day I have never heard any of the reasons why the brethren rejected our propositions, nor the reasons for the propositions which they made. It was voted that I should present these matters before the stockholders. I cannot do it, because I was excluded from that council meeting. Now why was I excluded? Was it the fear of some members that I was going to make representations of what was done in the committee to Mother, and that they were going to be censured?

G.W. Reaser: I did not hear that.

W.C. White: Well, of course, if the brethren ever get around to tell me the reasons why they excluded me from the council, it would be very interesting.

G.W. Reaser: You may know that Dr. P. S. Kellogg is at Paradise?

E.G. White: Is he there now? Well, I am glad they have secured a doctor, but I wish they had secured one who is inclined to take more active part in religious matters.

G.W. Reaser: He is not inclined that way, much—

W.C. White: There is a physician by the name of Eastman, who has been working in Santa Barbara. He has some money. He has recently visited Paradise Valley, along with Brother Ballenger. They have talked up a plan of his taking his money, and buying out some of the present stockholders, and then with the other stockholders, forming a new association, in which he will be the manager and the physician.

J.A. Burden: His proposition is to buy the property, as Brother White has said, taking in some of the old stockholders who would be congenial with him; and he would run the place as a private institution, a private corporation, in harmony with the conference— or aim to run it in harmony with the Conference. This plan, of course, our brethren realize, would give them a permanent physician, and would relieve them of financial pressure.

G.W. Reaser: And he proposes that this new corporation have in it the same magnanimous features stipulated by the original incor-

[299]

porators—to let all the surplus, above the sum necessary for interest and other running expenses, go to missionary work, and for the upbuilding of the institution.

Sister White: it will be necessary for our brethren to find out what the religious principles of the man are.

G.W. Reaser: So far as we know him, he is an excellent spiritual-minded man. He has been an elder of the church at Santa Barbara. We do not know anything wrong concerning him. He is a rather young physician, but he seems to be thoroughly in harmony with the organized work.

Sister White: Well, why can not he come in now?

J.A. Burden: I asked that question,—why, if he is such a magnanimous man and a missionary? The answer was, He would want more wages than they felt like paying—a hundred and fifty dollars a month, and his board and room, and his wife's board and room.

G.W. Reaser: If he goes in as the manager and physician, he wants a hundred and fifty dollars a month for himself, besides board and room for himself and wife.

W.C. White: Can this matter rest until we go down there at the time of the meeting, or is it something that must be decided now?

Sister White: How much did Dr. Holden ask?

J.A. Burden: One hundred dollars a month, and thirty-three and a third percent of his surgical fees.

Sister White: And you thought that was too much, did you?

J.A. Burden: We would have been glad to pay him one hundred dollars, or even one hundred and fifty a month, but we did not feel that it was right to pay him a percentage on the surgical fees.

Sister White: Well, I do not know; I do know that one of the evils that crept in at Battle Creek, and spoiled the spirituality of men in responsibility, was the desire for higher and still higher wages. I have forgotten just how high they did climb.

W.C. White: Thirty dollars a week.

Sister White: The setting of a high price upon a man's labors, by the man himself, does not give a right representation of the self-denial of Jesus Christ; and He is our Pattern. I wrote to Dr. Kress recently regarding the matter of wages, and counselled him to be careful to set before his associates, at the very beginning of his work in Washington, an example of self-denial, so that others whose wages were not high, would not feel as if they were being wronged. The evil of high wages is liable to crop out almost anywhere; and we must keep before our brethren the self-denying example of our Pattern, Christ Jesus; for we are to be a missionary people, and many laborers are to be set at work and supported in the Lord's vineyard.

*****

*****　　　　　　　　　　　　　　　　　　　　[301]

The Work Hindered by Lack of Faith

Sanitarium, Calif.
MS. 117'07 Oct. 22, 1907. Oct. 11, 1907.

How shall we obtain means for our sanitariums, is a question that must be solved. Some of our institutions are prospering; some seem to have come to a standstill; and others are running behind. As I present our perplexities to the Lord, there comes to my mind with considerable force this scripture, "Although the fig-tree shall not blossom, neither fruit be in the vine; and the labor of the olive shall fail, and the flock shall be cut off from the fold; and there shall be no herd in the stall; yet will I rejoice in the Lord, and joy in the God of my salvation."

In the word of God I find these promises, "Behold, the days come, saith the Lord of hosts, that I will make a new covenant with the house of Israel, and with the house of Judah. Not according to that which I made with their fathers when I took them by the hand to bring them out of the land of Egypt; which my covenant they brake, although I was an husband unto them, saith the Lord. But this shall be the covenant that I will make with the house of Israel; After those days, saith the Lord, I will put My law in their inward parts, and write it in their hearts; and will be their God, and they shall be My people. And they shall teach no more every man his neighbor; for they shall all know Me, from the least of them even unto the greatest, saith the Lord; for I will forgive their iniquity, and I will remember their sin no more."

I thank the Lord for these words of comfort and encouragement. I will put my trust in the Lord, and will wait patiently for Him. He will work in our behalf, and make us to rejoice in His mercies. He will surely be the help of His people.

Unbelief is finding an entrance in our churches, in our sanitariums, and in our publishing houses. There are some who have committed the error of turning away from the source of their strength to follow devices and plans of men,—plans that are not after the order of the Lord; and because of this, they are weak when they should be strong. This is the reason that God has not wrought more mightily for His people. Had He done more for us, human beings would have taken to themselves the glory that should be given to God.

God has a purpose in leaving men in their weakness when they turn from Him to follow the dictation of human minds. He wants them to learn where only true light and wisdom dwells. The Lord pities our weakness; He is grieved because of the error that has come in, because of the education that has been given to believers to look to men for wisdom and help. He wants His people to learn lessons of faith and trust in Him, and to stand in the strength of Israel's God...

* * * * *

Our Sanitariums should all be in running order, so that they may act their part in influencing that class of people who can be reached in no other way than by the work of the sanitarium. Our physicians are to rebuke in decided terms the sins which are the cause of sickness and disease. We have need of men who, under the inspiration of the Holy Spirit, will rebuke gambling and liquor-drinking, which are such prevalent evils in these last days. We need men who will bear their message against the selfishness that is eating out the very vitals of godliness. God calls for men of faith and prayer. "Pray ye therefore the Lord of the harvest that He will send forth laborers into His harvest."

Tremendous responsibilities are ours; and men are called for who will not misinterpret their responsibilities, but will do their appointed work in a spirit of humility and in the fear of God. We should ever be afraid of a spirit that would lead us to place restrictions on the work of others, lest we hinder the advance of the message of truth. Those who have in the past allowed such a spirit to control them have sadly hurt the work. They need to repent and be converted; for the Holy Spirit can not work with them as an oppressive power to close the lips that He has opened.

This age demands that the servants of God be men of faith and prayer, who realize the responsibilities that rest upon them as bearers of the last message of mercy to a perishing world. "Ye are the light of the world," Christ declared. "Let your light so shine before men, that they may see your good works, and glorify your Father which is in heaven." Many, many souls will be brought to a knowledge of the truth if intelligent labor is put forth in their behalf...

Ellen G. White

* * * * *

Report of the committee on Suggestive Plans and Resolutions Pacific Union Conference Medical Convention

From talk given by Mrs. E. G. White, Loma Linda, Oct. 30, 1907.

Here (at Loma Linda) we have ideal advantages for a school and for a sanitarium. Here are advantages for the patients. I have been instructed that here we should have a school, conducted on the principles of the ancient schools of the prophets. It may not be carried on, in every respect, as are the schools of the world, but it is to be especially adapted for those who desire to devote their lives, not to commercial pursuits, but to unselfish service for the Master.

We want a school of the highest order,—a school where the word of God will be regarded as essential, and where obedience to its teachings will be taught. For the carrying forward of such a school, we must have carefully selected educators. Our young people are not to be wholly dependent on the schools where they are told, "If you wish to complete our course of instruction, you must take this study, or some other study,"—studies that perhaps would be of no practical benefit to those whose only desire is to give to the world God's message of health and peace. In the education that many receive there are not only subjects that are non-essential, but much that is decidedly objectionable. We should endeavor to give instruction that will prepare students quickly for service to their fellow-men.

We are to seek for students who will plow deep into the word of God, and who will conform the life practice to the truths of the word. Let the education given be such as will qualify consecrated young men and women to go forth in harmony with the great commission, "Go ye therefore, and teach all nations, baptizing them in the name of the Father and of the Son and of the Holy Ghost; teaching them to observe all things whatsoever I have commanded you."

Elder Burden: I want to ask a question. Is this school that you [304] have spoken of simply to qualify nurses, or is it to embrace also the qualifications for physicians?

E.G. White: Physicians are to receive their education here. Here they are to receive such a mold that when they go out to labor, they will not seek to grasp the very highest wages, or else do nothing.

* * * * *

**Loma Linda, Calif.,
W. 360'07 Oct. 30,'07.
Mrs. Mable Workman:**

My dear Granddaughter,

I have just read a letter that you wrote to your father, and will now begin a letter to you...

Last Sunday night we were on the cars, and I was unable to sleep well. The next night we spent at Loma Linda. I had a good bed, but was wakeful, and had but a short period of rest. At the early morning meeting on Tuesday, I spoke to the people. After breakfast I rode out for an hour.

Tuesday afternoon I met with the stockholders of the Paradise Valley Sanitarium. Their council meeting was held in the bowling alley. In coming out we had to pass through the assembly room, where there was a large audience. Brother Burden asked me to stay, as they were speaking of the work of higher education that should be carried on in medical lines, but I thought it best not to do this. After I had climbed the long flight of stairs to my room on the third floor, which was the third time for that day, I found an article that I had written about a year ago, in reference to the establishment of a school of the highest order, in which the students would not be taught to use drugs in the treatment of the sick. With this I went down stairs again, and returned to the meeting.

Elder Burden was reading some extracts from letters that I had written about the school work. When he had finished I read the article I had with me, which was right to the point. It spoke of the school that should be operated here at Loma Linda. Here there are wonderful advantages for a school. The farm, the orchard, the pasture land, the large buildings, the ample grounds, the beauty,—all

~~are a great blessing. If all will now take hold intelligently of the~~ work that should be done here, there will be success.

For some weeks before this meeting I had been feeling very poorly. But the Lord has greatly blessed me here, and for this I am very thankful. The Lord has imparted to me strength as the occasion has demanded.

Thursday morning, Sara came to my room, and told me it was time to go to the early meeting. I had been writing since three o'clock. I attended the meeting, and spoke for about three-quarters of an hour, and then there was a testimony meeting. I could not hear what was said, but I was told that it was an interesting meeting. In all my talks I have tried to present Christ as our wisdom, our sanctification, and our righteousness.

Ellen G. White

* * * * *

The Work In Southern California

MS.-127-'07 Nov. 3, 1907.
Loma Linda, Calif.,

I have passed a wakeful night; for there have been presented to me some things connected with the past, present, and future of the work in Southern California.

I have now no hesitation in speaking plainly, and in calling things by their right names. For three nights in succession, the message has been given to me that Elder Reaser, as president of this Conference, is out of his place. He should not occupy such a position in any of our conferences. He is leading some of his brethren to ignore the messages that the Lord is sending to His people. He has refused to accept the testimonies that have not harmonized with his own mind and judgement.

The results of his administration will be further developed in the future. Why should men be entrusted with such grave responsibilities before they have been sufficiently proved? Elder Reaser has made the work of Elder Burden exceedingly difficult. He has worked in an underhanded manner to thwart the efforts of Brother Burden to do the work that should be done at Loma Linda. The influence of Brother Reaser has been counter to the messages of instruction that the Lord has given concerning this sanitarium. For two years this work of opposition has been carried forward.

The word of the Lord in unmistakable language is that Elder Reaser should not occupy the position of a Conference president. He needs to learn some of the first lessons of what God requires of His people who are living amid the perils of the strong temptations of these last days. He needs to be converted, heart, soul, and mind to the truth. Self has borne rule in his plans, and he has endeavored to convert others to his own ideas. As yet there has been but a part development of his character, but if he continues in his present course it will not be long before there will be a more open opposition to the work that we have, under the direction of God, endeavored to accomplish in Southern California.

The authoritative utterances of our brother, in their commands and their forbiddings, bear not the heavenly impress. They are not inspired by the Holy Spirit of God. Unless he becomes thoroughly convinced that his mind is not infallible, his future life will be characterized by a spirit of exalting whomsoever he will, and of hindering those who are not in harmony with him. In his present state of mind, he should not be entrusted with responsibilities that would give him the power to dictate to any church.

I have borne the testimony that Brother Reaser should have no control over Bro. Burden. I have borne a testimony, even in the meeting that has just been held here, that the Lord's servants are to seek their counsel from God. It is contrary to God's plan that men shall exercise arbitrary authority over their brethren. God will convince those who have felt called upon to exercise a wrong authority over their brethren, that He has not authorized them to take upon themselves such responsibilities. He has not appointed a man to take the place of God in this Conference.

The Saviour bids us pray, "Lead us not into temptation." Our heavenly Father will lead us not into temptation. Our heavenly Father will lead His people in the paths of righteousness. The word of the Lord to the churches in this conference is: "Watch and pray, lest ye enter into temptation. Be on your guard against the efforts of the powers of darkness to resist the testimonies of God's Spirit, that are to be understood." Actions spring from desires and purposes. God alone can discern the thoughts and intents of the heart. He weighs with unerring accuracy the very motives of the mind.

The president of the Southern California Conference needs the power to see himself as he is in the sight of God. He is as a man lost in the woods, blinded by a dangerous confidence in himself. A humbling of the soul, with earnest prayer, and a diligent study and reception of the word of God, are the means by which to overcome these peculiar temptations. The armor of truth is to be found in the word of God. Clothed in this armor, a man will be humble, not dictatorial, but a learner from the Great Teacher.

The Lord has witnessed the unnecessary hardships that have been brought upon Brother Burden. Avenues of assistance have been hedged up, and it has been made well nigh impossible to raise the money that has been needed at Loma Linda for the addition of bathrooms, and other needed facilities. There must be a change in these conditions. Relief must be given to this institution, which by the working of God in our behalf, has been brought within our reach.

[312] Influences have been brought to bear upon minds and hearts to lead men away from God, that they should obey men, and show to men the honor that belongs alone to God. He alone is to be honored and glorified. Men placed in positions of trust may be a help to the churches, but they are not to lord it over God's heritage. Neither are they to show favors to certain ones, with the expectation that they will in return receive certain favors from these persons.

During the past night there has passed before me scene after scene, where men in positions of trust were bearing rule over their fellow men. There seemed to be with them but little burden for the sacred truth for this time, that would sanctify the heart, the thoughts, the speech, and the actions.

One stood by my side, and said, "These men are becoming too wise to follow a plain 'Thus saith the Lord.' They are departing from God."

A Bible lay upon the stand, and the heavenly messenger held it to view, saying in solemn tones: "The Holy Scriptures of the Old and the New Testament. Together they are to act a more important part in presenting before the people God's saving truth. The Word is to be carefully studied, but not to present theories that will lead away the minds of the people, diverting them from the warnings sent to prepare a people to stand in the day of the Lord."

God has a message to be proclaimed in all the world. By every teacher in our schools, every minister, every medical missionary, the only true God is to be uplifted. But some of the watchmen are asleep. They are as the blind leading the blind. The time to labor is fast passing away, and Satan is leading some to stand as the accuser of their brethren who are bearing heavy burdens.

Who of our ministers are awake, giving the trumpet a certain sound? The trumpet of some in official positions has been sounding their own exploits. The spirit that has characterized their work has borne the disapproval of God. Who of those that have been appointed to office in the work of God understand what that office embraces? Where are the faithful watchmen?

Some who should be watchmen, are seeking to gain advantage for themselves in commercial lines. For the sake of financial profit they are becoming tainted with the spirit of commercialism. This spirit has so blinded the eyes of their understanding that they have not a clear scriptural understanding of Bible principles. At times when they have not been guided by the Spirit of God, they have dictated to their brethren, and have considered that any proposition that they might make should be accepted without question. Their position has been such that many of their brethren have been deceived and deluded.

The word of the living God is to be our lesson-book. Here, in both the Old and New Testaments, is a statement of the mistakes made by ancient Israel. Shall we, as did they, fail to improve the most precious opportunities for doing the work of God? If, during the three years past, the opportunities had been truly improved to meet the requirements of this time, some who are now lost to the cause of God, would stand ready to serve as genuine missionaries.

Awake, awake from your stupor, you who have been under the control of other human minds. No longer allow yourselves to treat with indifference subjects that need to be presented to the people with clearness. Your president does not realize where he stands in the sight of God. Influences have been brought in that have turned his mind away from the preparation that is essential for these last days. And as he has turned away from Christ, the spirit of commercialism has absorbed his mind. The light of the world has been eclipsed. There is a profession to know God, but there is even a denial of Him in words and in action.

God permitted Christ, the Sun of Righteousness, to come to our world to seek and to save perishing souls. But today some who have been entrusted with the care of these blood-bought souls are denying Him in word, in method, in action. Darkness covers the earth and gross darkness the people.

Where are the earnest calls that should be given to arouse the people to that preparation of heart that will purify, refine, and ennoble characters to shine as lights amid the moral darkness? The soul is never safe, save under divine guidance. The word of God coming from sanctified hearts and lips will soften and break hard hearts. And if ever there was a period of time when the words of Christ should be heard, it is now.

None but He who created man can effect a change in the human heart. Every teacher is to realize that he must be moved by divine agencies. The mind and judgment must be submitted to the Holy Spirit. Through the sanctification of the truth, we may bear a decided testimony for righteousness both before believers and before unbelievers.

We are far behind what we should be in our experience. We are backward in pronouncing the testimony that should flow from sanctified lips. Even when sitting at the table, Christ taught truths that brought comfort and courage to the hearts of His hearers. Whenever it is possible, we are to present the words of Christ. If His love is in the soul, abiding there as a living principle, there will come forth from the treasure-house of the heart, words suitable to the occasion, not light, trifling words, but uplifting words, words of truth and spirituality.

Let teachers and students watch their opportunities whenever possible to confess Christ in their conversation, speaking of their experiences in following Christ, praying with their brethren for the Holy Spirit. Confessing Christ openly and bravely, exhibiting in the choice of words the simplicity of true godliness, will be more effective than many sermons. There are but few who give a true representation of the meekness of Christ. Oh, we need, and we must have, His meekness! Christ is to be formed within, the hope of glory.

[314]   We are preparing for translation to the heavenly world. Our conversation should be in heaven, from whence we look for the Lord Jesus. He is to be acknowledged as the Giver of every good and perfect gift, the Author of all our blessings, in whom is centered our hope of eternal life.

Angels of heaven are taking note of all our works, and watching to see how they can minister to our needs. With intensity of spirit, all heaven stands ready to lend aid to us in our divine progress. Shall we improve our present opportunities, and receive the impress of the divine image?

I am instructed that those who believe in the present truth, and who are set as guides to the people of God, are not to become engaged in commercial pursuits. Their minds must not become so absorbed that they cannot distinguish between the sacred and the common. A strife for victory in business deals will develop a pugilistic spirit, a spirit that is spoiling the record of some of our brethren in Los Angeles. Such a course will develop in these brethren characters that may not now be clearly discerned. We are to educate the mind in pleasant considerations of divine things. But those who suppose that they are to guide other minds, must in a most earnest manner seek the Lord.

The only way that temptation may be overcome is through watchfulness and prayer. The trial of the faith must come. Satanic agencies are busy, endeavoring to spoil the record of many souls. Those who are neglectful of Bible study, are in danger of disregarding the Testimonies. Those who seem to feel that position and influence places them above temptation, are under a strong delusion of the enemy. In this conference there is a strong temptation to consider that position makes the man. Men placed in positions of responsibility are to honor that position, by a most earnest determination to be like Christ, as He gave us example in His earthly life. His life testified that the strongest of temptations are no excuse for yielding to sin.

"In the last day, that great day of the feast, Jesus stood and cried, saying, If any man thirst, let him come unto Me, and drink. He that believeth on Me, as the scripture hath said, Out of His belly shall flow rivers of living water. (But this spake He of the Spirit, which they that believe on Him should receive.)"

"Come unto Me, all ye that labor and are heavy laden, and I will give you rest. Take My yoke upon you, and learn of Me; for I am meek and lowly in heart; and ye shall find rest unto your souls, For My yoke is easy, and My burden is light."

Ellen G. White

* * * * *

Elder J.A. Burden and Others Bearing Responsibilities at Loma Linda

(Page 652, B-90-'08—March 24, '08)
Loma Linda, Calif.
Nov. 3, 1907

[315] *Dear Brethren,*

I feel a deep interest that careful study shall be given to the needs of our institutions at Loma Linda, and that the right moves may be made. In the carrying forward of the word at this place, men of talent and of decided spirituality are needed.

We may, in the work of educating our nurses, reach a high standard in the knowledge of the true science of healing. That which is of the most importance is that the students be taught how to truly represent the principles of health reform. Teach the students to pursue this line of study faithfully, combined with other essential lines of education. The grace of Jesus Christ will give wisdom to all who will follow the Lord's plan of true education.

Let the students follow closely the example of the One who purchased the human race with the costly price of His own life. Let them appeal to the Saviour, and depend upon Him as the One who heals all manner of diseases. The Lord would have the workers make special efforts to point the sick and suffering to the great Physician who made the human body. He would have all become obedient children to the faith, that they may come with confidence and ask for bodily restoration. Many who come to our sanitariums will be blessed as they learn the truth concerning the word of God, many who would never learn it through any other medium.

It is well that our training-schools for Christian workers should be established near to our health institutions, that the students may be educated in the principles of healthful living. Institutions that send forth workers who are able to give a reason for their faith, and who have that faith that works by love and purifies the soul, are of great value.

I have clear instruction that wherever it is possible, schools should be established near to our sanitariums, that each institution may be a help to the other. But I dare not advise that steps be taken at this time to branch out so largely in the educational work at Loma Linda that a large outlay of means will be required to erect new buildings. Our faithful workers at Loma Linda must not be overwhelmed with such great responsibilities that they will be in danger of becoming worn and discouraged.

I am charged to caution you against building extensively for the accommodation of students. It would not be wise to invest at this time so large a capital as would be required to equip a medical college that would properly qualify physicians to stand the test of the medical examinations of the different States.

A movement should not now be inaugurated that would add greatly to the investment upon the Loma Linda property. Already there is a large debt resting upon the institution, and discouragement and perplexity would follow if this indebtedness were to be greatly increased. As the work progresses, new improvements may be added from time to time as they are found necessary. An elevator should soon be installed in the main building. But there is need of strict economy. Let our brethren move cautiously and wisely, and plan no larger than they can handle without being overburdened.

[316]

In the work of the school maintain simplicity. No argument is so powerful as is success founded upon simplicity. And you may attain success in the education of students as medical missionaries without a medical school that can qualify physicians to compete with the physicians of the world.

Let the students be given a practical education. And the less dependent you are upon worldly methods of education, the better it will be for the students. Special instruction should be given in the art of treating the sick without the use of poisonous drugs and in harmony with the light that God has given. Students should come forth from the school without having sacrificed the principles of health reform.

The education that meets the world's standard is to be less and less valued by those who are seeking for efficiency in carrying the medical missionary work in connection with the work of the third angel's message. They are to be educated from the standpoint of conscience; and as they conscientiously and faithfully follow right methods in their treatment of the sick, these methods will come to be recognized as preferable to the methods of nursing to which many have become accustomed, which demands the use of poisonous drugs.

We should not at this time seek to compete with worldly medical schools. Should we do this, our chances of success would be small. We are not now prepared to carry out successfully the work of establishing large medical institutions of learning. Moreover, should we follow the world's methods of medical practice, exacting the large fees that worldly physicians demand for their services, we would work away from Christ's plan for our ministry to the sick.

There should be at our sanitariums intelligent men and women, who can instruct in Christ's methods of ministry. Under the instruction of competent, consecrated teachers, the youth may become partakers of the divine nature, and learn how to escape the corruptions that are in the world through lust. I have been shown that we should have many more women who can deal especially with the diseases of women, many more lady nurses who will treat the sick in a simple way and without the use of drugs.

There are many simple herbs which, if our nurses would learn the value of, they could use in the place of drugs, and find very effective...

I write these things that you may know that the Lord has not left us without the use of simple remedies which when used will not leave the system in the weakened condition in which the use of drugs so often leaves it. We need well-trained nurses who can understand how to use the simple remedies that nature has provided for restoration to health, and who can teach those who are ignorant of the laws of health, how to use these simple but effective cures.

He who created men and women has an interest in those who suffer. He has directed in the establishment of our sanitariums and in the building up of schools close to our sanitariums, that they may become efficient mediums in training men and women for the work of ministering to suffering humanity. In the treatment of the sick, poisonous drugs need not be used. Alcohol or tobacco in any form must not be recommended, lest some soul be led to imbibe a taste for these evil things. There will be no excuse for the liquor-dealers in that day when every man shall receive according to his works. Those who have destroyed life will by their own life have to pay the penalty. God's law is holy and just and good.

We have seen the poor wrecks of humanity come to our sanitariums to be cured of the liquor habit. We have seen these who have ruined their health by wrong habits of diet, and by the use of flesh-meats. This is why we need to lift up the voice like a trumpet, and show "My people their transgressions, and the house of Jacob their sins."

The Lord will judge according to their works those who are seeking to establish a law of the nations that will cause men to violate the law of God. In proportion to their guilt will be their punishment. The Lord would have us lift up the Sabbath of the Lord our God. We have a sacred work to do in opening blind eyes in regard to the day that the Lord has set apart and sanctified as the rest day of mankind. He declares, "The seventh day is the Sabbath of the Lord thy God." He has placed His own signature upon that day that He has set apart to be observed as long as time shall last. We should have much to say upon this subject just now.

Let Seventh-day Adventist medical workers remember that the Lord God omnipotent reigneth. Christ was the greatest Physician that ever trod the sin-cursed earth. The Lord would have His people come to Him for their power of healing. He will baptize them with His holy Spirit, and fit them for a service that will make them a blessing in restoring the spiritual and physical health of those who need healing.

Ellen G. White

* * * * *

H.-358-'07 Nov. 3, 1907.
Loma Linda, Cal.,
Dear Brother and Sister Haskell,

We thank you for your letters and for the news that they contain...

For more than a year the light has been coming to me that here at Loma Linda we should have a school of the highest order, and that the very best talent should be obtained, in order to prepare young men and young women for medical missionary work. This work we are desirous of seeing accomplished. It should not be necessary for students to be placed under the influence of teachers who do not obey the law of God.

[318] I wish that you might have been present at this meeting. I think it would be well for you to be here as soon as possible. The instruction you might give would just now be very timely. You should be here with us to help in molding and fashioning the work. We are all doing the best we can to take advanced steps in the right direction.

There should be a different mold placed upon the work in this Southern Calif. Conference. The president of this field has not had the experience that one should have who occupies such an important position. He seems to be unable to understand the Lord's plans for the carrying forward of the work.

A man lives unto God when he continually recognizes Him as a present Helper. When there is a recognition of the Lord Jesus Christ, there will be a holy fear lest he shall make mistakes. The soul will be drawn out continually in earnest prayer as he realizes his needs. As he draws nigh to God, God will draw nigh unto him, the love of God will be kindled in his heart, and he will be able to speak the words of God. The language of the heart will then be, "Whom have I in heaven but Thee, and who on earth do I desire beside Thee?"

We must give evidence of a spiritual relationship to God, in all our ways acknowledging Him. Others will be able to detect whether we make ourselves a center; or whether we regard Christ as all and in all. When we have the fear of the Lord ever before us, our experience will not be tame and spiritless. Christ formed within will be the hope of glory.

The fear of the Lord is the beginning of wisdom. In Him there is a hope that "maketh not ashamed." The joy of the Lord will break forth from lips that are sanctified. We must now receive rich experiences in the service of God.

Our faith is to be expressed in thanksgiving. "Whoso offereth praise glorifieth God." "In everything give thanks." "Bless the Lord, O my soul, and all that is within me, bless His holy name." Let expressions of praise flow forth from human lips. We are to rejoice in the Lord more than we have done. Let not the heart remain cold and dull and unimpressive.

There are some who think that in matters of practical Christianity, they have a superior intelligence. Whether or not this is so, will be demonstrated by the life-actions. Are they self-centered, or are they moved by the Holy Spirit of truth and righteousness. Religion is to become a living, active principle. The one all-absorbing motive of the true Christian is to give an expression of the goodness and love of Christ.

We need you here, Brother Haskell, to exert your influence against the presumption of men who feel that their brethren must ask permission of them, before engaging in the Lord's service where and in the manner that He indicates. Such presumption should find no place in the cause of God. We hope that there may be such changes here that the work of the Lord may move on more smoothly.

The Lord sends His messages to correct the erring, however highly they may regard themselves. He asks that they submit their judgment to His control. Every soul must be under discipline to God. To occupy an exalted position is not always evidence that the Lord has placed an individual in that position. It is the works, not position, that testify to the value of a man. Hereditary traits of character need to be overcome. A man cannot safely be entrusted with the control of others, unless he himself is under the sanctification of the Holy Spirit.

In the spirit of meekness and lowliness of heart, all methods and plans should be submitted to wise counselors for their prayerful consideration and their endorsement. Otherwise, a restless, speculative energy and ambition may make an evil mark upon the cause of God, and subvert and hinder the very work that the Lord has declared should be done in this Conference.

In order that the great work of sanctification that needs to be carried forward in the churches of Southern California may be accomplished, the minds and wills of our ministers, physicians, and teachers should be united, their hearts blending in one Spirit to give the trumpet a certain sound. Let every voice proclaim [distinctly the third angel's message. In word and act let those who are proclaiming] the message, reveal that they are numbered among those "that keep the commandments of God, and the faith of Jesus."

If this had been done faithfully, with the word of the living God as the great lesson-book, the third angel's message would have gone with greater power. Had all God's ministers, as faithful stewards of the grace of God, called upon the world to hear the last note of warning, giving the trumpet a certain sound, thousands more might have been converted, and added their voices in proclaiming the message to the world. In distinct notes of solemn warning is to be given the closing message that will prepare a people to receive the seal of the living God.

Satan is working to fill minds with the spirit of ambition and of commercialism. Those whose minds are thus diverted, will lose their opportunity of giving the last message to the world.

If faithful work had been done during the last few years that have gone into eternity, thousands of souls would now be found with Bibles in their hands, reading the Word of God, and praying for light and guidance. Many of these would be engaged in the work of hunting for souls, and fitting up a people to stand in the great day of God. But some who ought to be missionaries, are filled with the spirit of commercialism, and with an ambition to secure for themselves certain advantages. The truth becomes to them a dead letter, not practiced nor obeyed.

Jehovah is the true God. Let Him be feared and reverenced.

Ellen G. White

* * * * *

Loma Linda, Calif.
H. 364-'07 Nov. 10, '07.
Dear Brother and Sister Haskell,

We feel that you are needed in the Southern California field at this time. W. C. White thinks that you may be planning to labor for a time in Nashville. But I feel that your labors are very essential right here at Loma Linda and I hope that you will not delay coming longer than seems necessary. If ever such help as you can give was needed, it is now.

We have found that some things are not as they should be, and I have borne a decided testimony concerning the workings of a one-man power. I wrote a very decided testimony regarding the course of Elder Reaser, and read it to Elders Daniells, Irwin, Cottrell, -and a few others. A copy was sent to Elder Reaser, and I think he has decided to resign his position as president of the conference. He has sown seed that will bear evil fruit. By his words and by his actions, he has disseminated doubts regarding the Testimonies.

Yesterday I spoke in the assembly Hall here at Loma Linda, and the Lord gave me a decided message. Elder Reaser opened the meeting with prayer, and I followed him with an earnest prayer for the presence of the Holy Spirit. I then spoke for one hour, and the Lord greatly helped me.

Now I hope that you can soon be here. The spirit of doubt and uncertainty that has been implanted in the minds of many in this conference demands that a strong testimony be borne in the churches...

Ellen G. White

* * * * *

To the Leading Men in the Southern California Conference

Loma Linda Calif.,
Nov. 18,-'07. B.-378-'07 Nov. 11, 1907.
Dear Brethren,

God's messengers are to sense their grave responsibility. They are to trust humbly in God. The Lord calls now for conscientious, humble minute-men. He invites them, "Take My yoke upon you, and learn of me; for I am meek and lowly in heart; and ye shall find rest unto your souls." The Lord Jesus came to our world as its Redeemer. He came as an example to all men. The world was in need of a correct representation of the future inhabitants of the city of God.

Every one who has responsibilities to bear will reveal by his daily life whether or not he is fitted for the office that he holds. Ministers of the gospel will be tempted to strive for worldly and commercial advantages; but worldly interests must be laid aside. The glory of God must be kept in view. The saving of souls is to be their all-important burden.

Men who live in the atmosphere of Christ's presence will communicate the principles of heaven in conversation, in spirit, in tenderness, because they are learning of Christ. They will set a right example to their associates.

There are many who may be saved, if their prejudiced ideas can be removed, and if they consent to take upon them the yoke of Christ. All should bear in mind the words of Christ: "Ye are the salt of the earth; but if the salt have lost his savor, wherewith shall it be salted? it is thenceforth good for nothing, but to be cast out, and to be trodden under foot of men.

"Ye are the light of the world. A city that is set on a hill cannot be hid. Neither do men light a candle, and put it under a bushel, but on a candlestick; and it giveth light unto all that are in the house. Let your light so shine before men, that they may see your good works, and glorify your Father which is in Heaven."

The special work of the leaders is to let the light so shine as to glorify God. As God's messengers, they must have a thorough knowledge of Bible truth. Through watchfulness and prayer they must maintain such a connection with God that they may be the light of the world, and that prejudice may be removed from those who behold their consistent walk, and hear their teachings, in regard to the word of God. As a result of their influence and teachings, many will joyfully accept the present truth.

By kindness, by graceful behaviour, the messenger of the Lord is to give to the world an evidence of what the truth has done for his soul. The very grace of his words will be a convincing evidence; for the Lord will impress the human mind, and many will submit to the sweet influence of the Spirit of God. Angels of God will impress the minds with sacred truths.

If believers fall in love with the truth in its purity, if they become free from all worldliness and self-exaltation, if they are all agreed, the influence of their lives will make an impression on unbelievers. Their reward may not always come in this life, but even in this world they will possess a peace and quietude, a rest in God, that passeth all understanding. Many will take knowledge of them, that they have been with Jesus and have learned of Him. In the future will come their exceeding great reward. In the heavenly courts they will hear the words, "Well done, good and faithful servant; enter thou into the joy of thy Lord." In their purity, their humility, and their meekness, they have represented Christ, and they are now entering into their eternal riches. They are washed and made white in the blood of the Lamb. The joy of Christ is their exceeding great reward.

I write these things to you, my brethren, although all of you may not fully comprehend them. If I did not believe that God's eye is over His people, I could not have the courage to write the same things over and over again. But I am bidden to say to the messengers, that no commercial spirit should be permitted to enter into their messages or into any part of their work. Said the Angel, "Be ye clean that bear the vessels of the Lord." These words were twice repeated during the representation that was given me.

Reformation Needed in the Churches

There is a work to be done in all our churches. The criticizing, the condemning, and the arbitrary forbiddings of men, whatever their position, is displeasing to God. During the past two years, the churches have had in some lines a wrong education.

God has a people whom He is leading and instructing. And the man who exercises the power to permit or to forbid, as his judgment may indicate, has given a representation of an unsanctified disposition.

[324] The churches will be left powerless, if they are educated to obey the dictates of finite men instead of obeying the leadings of God. They must not be made to feel that before they can engage in any enterprise, they must first obtain permission of men. God bids me say, Cease from man, whose breath is in his nostrils, for wherein is he to be accounted for? Am not I to be consulted? Are finite, impulsive human agencies to have the control of My chosen ones?

Our minds must be stayed on God, not on men who have lost their bearings, and who do not discern that position can not give a man unerring judgment. Every man is to fear and honor God. All are to reverence Him, and to show their interest in His people. There must be a constant seeking for divine instructions. The Lord has not appointed one man to exercise his conscience for another man.

The Conference President

When a man is placed as president of a conference, it is not to be supposed that he is to mold and fashion the minds of the workers in that conference after his own human ideas; and that if men do not follow his ideas, they may be brought to terms by his saying to them, "You cannot receive wages from this conference unless you do as I tell you."

It is the duty of the presidents of our conferences to deal kindly and impartially with all the workers under their charge. They should counsel with their fellow laborers, regarding the wisest course of action to be followed in their labors. In meekness and humility they should set an example of earnest zeal and integrity. But never should they assume the responsibilities that belong to other workers.

In the minds of many there is a false idea regarding the duties of a conference president. By a faithful example, it is his privilege to be a help spiritually to all the other workers, encouraging them to come into such relation to God that He can direct them in their appointed work. The first qualification for the president of a conference is that he himself has learned to seek and to receive counsel from God. "He hath showed thee, O man, what is good; and what doth the Lord require of thee, but to do justly, and to love mercy, and to walk humbly with thy God?"

I am instructed to say that when a man swells to large undue proportions, the people should assemble and in the name of the Lord release that man from office, and put some one in who will not suppose that he is sufficient in wisdom to define how every branch of the work shall be conducted, but one who will seek to find out what is his duty. It is the privilege of the conference president to say, "I have this responsibility. If I lose the sweet spirit of Jesus Christ, with its softening, subduing influence, that is to constitute me a light amid the moral darkness, then I must no longer hold this sacred office."

I now call upon all our churches in Southern California to awake, before it is everlastingly too late. The self-competent men who do not humble their souls before God, will unless they repent, certainly be lost.

In some lines, the work must now be remedied, and the all sufficiency of men must be outlived, by a diligent turning to the word of God. Oh, I am so sad, because of the example that has been given of a superiority, a dictatorial authority, that has been born of self!

[325]

A real converting, reformatory change should now take place. Every one who fears God should search the Scriptures, and carry with him into his day's work a sense of his privileges under a Ruler who understands the purity of his motives. Minds must not be diverted from God to man. We must not fear the fear of the wicked, and allow our consciences to be manipulated by men. Satan has been bearing rule in many minds. He will work through those who can be easily exalted and led to exercise their capabilities to repress or exalt others. The time has come when we must keep firm hold of the strong arm of Jehovah; for every species of delusion is being exercised. The prince of darkness is working through the minds of men who, in their lack of spiritual discernment, suppose that they are to rule the experience of the Lord's little children, who are to look to God in a living, simple working faith.

Satan is working to captivate the world. We have entered the last great conflict. But holy angels will guard the people of God, so long as they put their trust in His infinite power. Could our eyes be opened, we should see holy angels guarding the humble followers of Jesus, and evil angels working upon human minds to intercept the rays of light from the word of God that should come to the people.

"Cry aloud, spare not, lift up thy voice like a trumpet, and show My people their transgression, and the house of Jacob their sins. Yet they seek Me daily, and delight to know My ways, as a nation that did righteousness, and forsook not the ordinance of their God: they ask of Me the ordinances of justice; they take delight in approaching to God."

Read and study carefully the whole of the fifty-eighth chapter of Isaiah. If positions of responsibility are entrusted to men who are distrustful of self, and fear the Lord God, they will understand that it is a matter of great importance that they walk humbly before God, and that they do not become careless, or inattentive to His word.

I am to say to the people of God, Take heed that ye be not deceived. "Seek ye the Lord while He may be found, call ye upon Him while He is near: let the wicked forsake his way, and the unrighteous man his thoughts: and let him return unto the Lord, and He will have mercy upon him; and to our God, for He will abundantly pardon."

Ellen G. White

* * * * *

[326] **Paradise Valley Sanitarium**
W.-392-1907.
National City, California,
December 1, 1907.
Elder and Mrs. J. E. White:
Dear Children,

I thank the Lord that He has sustained me on this journey. I have done much important writing. On Sabbath a week ago, and again last Sabbath, I spoke in the church at San Diego...

I am hoping and praying that I may understand my duty. It seems to me that I must remain in this section of the country until after Elder Haskell arrives, and then I may not be able to leave for some weeks to come. An important work has been begun in the vicinity of Riverside. The third year class of students at Loma Linda went over to Riverside a few weeks ago, and did their first practical work in canvassing for "Ministry of Healing." There were eight in the class, and their object in visiting the homes of the people was more to become acquainted, and to talk of the work at Loma Linda, than it was to sell books for profit. However, in the course of their conversation, they would usually introduce "Ministry of Healing," tell the story of the book, and then offer to sell it as a volume that contained the principles taught in the school at Loma Linda. In this way, about seventy copies of the book were placed in the homes of the people, in a little over one week; and the students made many, many friends for the work at Loma Linda. Wherever they went, they sought to leave a good impression. We believe they did a good work. They were wide awake, and full of courage in the Lord, and seem to have met with success.

The second-year class will undertake a similar work soon while the third-year class continue their studies at Loma Linda. Later on, it is hoped that some members of the first-year class can go out. Thus each of the several students in the school will assist in working Riverside. I suppose you have seen that place. It is a grand city, and the managers of Loma Linda Sanitarium are seeking to gain a foothold there by introducing, first, the "Ministry of Healing." Afterward, they will send out students with "Christ's Object Lessons." They will earnestly endeavor to handle these books wisely.

A similar work is to be carried on in other places besides Riverside. We are all praying that the Lord may abundantly bless these first working forces going out from the school. It means much to our Loma Linda Training School and Sanitarium, not only with regard to the good impression that they hope to make on the minds of the people, but in a financial way as well. Many new students have come in, and considerable money will be needed to care for them all, and at the same time keep up the other running expenses of the school and sanitarium. At Loma Linda there are now over a hundred under training for medical missionary work.

Oh, how anxious I am to have a small press in operation at Loma Linda, so as to print the discourses that shall be given in the surrounding cities! I have mentioned the matter to Brother Henry W. Kellogg; for he has a special interest in this line of work. We need a small press for printing notices, and for bringing out in printed form, for use in surrounding cities, discourses that will be given from time to time. Now is our time to work. We expect to connect with the W.C.T.U. in some lines of service.

I can not feel free to return to St. Helena until I see the work fully in running order. The Lord has given light that these cities in the San Bernardino Valley should be worked. The time has come to do this, and we are to have wise managing forces to carry the work forward intelligently ...

There never was a time when we needed more to encourage faith, than at the present time; for there are perplexities on the right hand and on the left.

Ellen G. White

The Work in Southern California

MS—3—'08

Southern Calif. is a field that should depend more than it has upon its own resources. It should have more facilities, and should not be cramped as it has been in some respects.

Southern Calif. is a missionary field, a large part of which has received but little missionary effort. Henceforth it should receive more attention. The various lines of work that can be carried on should be diligently studied, and the advantages of such cities as Redlands and Riverside, and the need of putting forth decided effort for them, faithfully investigated.

Los Angeles demands constant labor because of its changing population. San Bernardino calls for earnest missionary effort. The work for all these places needs to be done by those who can adapt themselves to the needs of the field. In our work we miss the labors of Elder Simpson; but we must not leave the work undone because some of the faithful workers fall by the way.

In Loma Linda we have an advantageous center for the carrying on of various missionary enterprises. We can see that it was in the providence of God that this sanitarium was placed in the possession of our people. We should appreciate Loma Linda as a place which the Lord foresaw we should need, and which He gave.

The cities in the San Bernardino Valley were presented before me as places where the truth should go with power. The small printing press that Brother H. W. Kellogg has furnished should prove a blessing to the work in that part of the field, by printing publications that will be needed for the furtherance of the work in the Southern California Cities. Our publications must now be greatly multiplied. Papers and leaflets containing the best discourses preached by our ministers are to be published and scattered widely throughout the regions where meetings are being held.

It was the Lord who placed in our possession the sanitariums at Loma Linda, Glendale, and Paradise Valley... [328]

We have been indolent in regard to our duty to Southern California. The many tourists who visit the cities in this conference should be given opportunity to hear the truth for this time. Let us do all in our power to enlighten the people in this large field. It is the privilege of every believer to let the light shine forth. We are drawing near to the close of this earth's history; we have not one hour to devote to needless matters. Our ministers in the Southern California Conference should now devote their best efforts to proclaiming the message of truth in all these large resorts. The Lord will impart His grace to all who will work in Christ's lines. And hope and faith will strengthen as the workers for God put their trust in Him.

Ellen G. White.

* * * * *

Elmshaven, Sanitarium, Calif.
Jan. 5, 1908. B.-12-'08 Jan. 5, 1908.

Dear Brother Burden,

I have received and read your letter. I have written a letter in response to the one which Elder Reaser wrote me, and sent the same to Elder Haskell to deliver. Today I sent Elder Haskell a telegram, telling him to hold the letter until later.

Brother Reaser's letter touched my heart, and I replied in the hope that he might be helped in just the right way. If this is possible, we shall accomplish much. If Elder Reaser will see himself as he is and acknowledge his mistakes, he can unite his strength with ours to save others from going over the same ground that he has traveled. Much will be gained if he learns to stand. not in his own strength, but in the strength of God. I was so thankful for the acknowledgements that Brother Reaser made in his letter, that I could not refrain from weeping; for I knew that they would mean much to such a man as he. I know also that if he will turn his strength of purpose on the right side, he will be a power for good in the work of God. And the strength that he can give is needed.

I accepted his statements in sincerity, and wrote at once. Christ's lessons of forgiveness were in my mind. It was not I who had been hurt, but the precious cause of truth; for he in his self-confidence had taken a wonderfully bold stand. I thought that if the man was sincere, this acknowledgment and evidence in his life of the transforming grace of Christ, was all that we need ask. I can not express to you the gladness I felt as I thought that Elder Reaser had indeed come to see matters in the same light with his brethren. I hope he has done so; it seemed to me that as I read his letter I could see the work in Southern Calif. standing on a better and surer foundation, strengthened by the unity of the workers and the churches. But if this is only supposition, and his has not been a true conversion, then my burden comes back to me with grievous force.

I send these lines to you and to Elder Haskell: Truth will triumph, and bear away the victory. I am so full of thanksgiving when one soul who has lost his bearings is recovered; I know not how to express my gratitude. If this soul can be saved, do all in your power to save him.

I was so sorry when I heard that Elder Reaser was undermining the confidence of the people in the testimonies God had been giving to His people for the past sixty years. I thought, He certainly could not have studied them and received them as from God, or he could not make them of no account in the minds of the people. Then when his letter came, acknowledging his belief in the messages, I was filled with joy. The Lord would not now be dishonored; Brother Reaser would not now be so taken up with his own ideas that he could turn away from the testimonies.

There are many, many who are not studying the testimonies as they should. Some read them casually, or make some reference to them, but they are not presented in the spirit of assurance of the Spirit of truth. Many of those who profess the truth for this time turn from the messages and accept their own opinions and ideas as verity and truth.

I have never in all my experience met a man who felt so fully competent to carry all lines of the work as Brother Reaser. The Lord has shown me that he felt himself sufficient for this work, that he needed no others to advise or counsel him. How to reach him, how to open his eyes to see his true condition, seemed a very difficult thing. But this letter to me was of such a character that I could see that a change was taking place. If he continues to humble himself before God, Elder Reaser will become a little child to learn his lessons of the great Teacher, I have waited for this change to come, and I have felt sad indeed that it has been so long delayed. Let us see if our brother is not changed; let us look for a spirit of humility and meekness in him. Unless he has this spirit he is not safe.

God help him, is my prayer.

Ellen G. White

* * * * *

**Sanitarium, Calif.,
Feb. 2, 1908 B.-58-'08 Jan. 12, '08.
Elder J. A. Burden, Loma Linda, Calif.:**
Dear Brother and Sister Burden,

I have just written a short letter to Elder Reaser. When a man exalts himself as Elder Reaser has done, he is in great peril. He is in danger of losing his soul; and the enemy will endeavor to take advantage of his influence and his capabilities, and use them to deceive others, and lead them into false paths.

But I have been shown that if Elder Reaser will humble his heart, and make a decided change in his attitude toward the work and toward his brethren, then we should come close to him to help him. It will not help him to treat him coldly. Let us not risk the chance of losing his soul, but let us help and strengthen him, and forgive as Christ forgives.

Brother Reaser needs help. If he sees the changes he should make, and casts away the false confidence he has had, putting his trust in the One who gave His life for man, he can have power to overcome.

Elder Reaser is seeking to keep the better world in view, and he wants us to trust him. How tenderly my heart went out toward him as I read his letters. I desire to help him over this hard place. I believe that if we can tenderly help him at this time, that he will respond to our efforts in his behalf. I feel that we should not make it known to the churches that we feared he would have to resign his position. I would not take a step that would mar his life record. Let us try to help him to put his heart and soul and strength on the Lord's side, for the upbuilding of His church.

I would not willingly do anything that would show a spirit of coldness or lack of Christian forgiveness. I have told our brother where he has erred, and that the Lord was grieved with his course of action. We have many dangers to encounter in our Christian experience, but that which seems to me would be the most serious error just now would be to withdraw from one who needs our help while struggling to get on safe footing.

I have felt a deep yearning for the soul of Brother Reaser, and the mere thought that he may retain his position as president of the conference, and work in unison with his brethren, fills me with thankfulness. I shall rejoice greatly if he need not pass through the embarrassment of being separated from the work.

I have sought no counsel in this matter but the Lord's, and He has shown me that Brother Reaser, with the help and sympathy of his brethren, and working unitedly with them, can serve another year. Brethren Cottrell and Reaser should blend in their work, and give you the help you must have in your sanitarium work. This the Lord calls them to do.

[333]

Brother Reaser will have many difficulties to overcome; for he has misjudged the way in which the work of soul-winning should be done. He will need now, more than ever before, faithful, sympathizing friends,—those who will help him to do justice, to love mercy, and to walk humbly with God. He will be ennobled to do this if he will allow his heart to be worked by the Holy Spirit of God. And we are to watch, not only this soul, but other souls that may have been in the wrong way, and help them to place their feet in the right way. With the help of his brethren, Brother Reaser may learn his lesson and find the path that Jesus traveled, and become a representative of Him.

Let Brother Reaser help you in every possible way, and seek to strengthen him in every right purpose. Tell him the Lord says, "Be not discouraged; for I am thy God." When I think of any other course being taken, I am filled with sorrow. Christ would have us united in Christian fellowship,—a tie more binding than the ties of human kinship. Let us take our stand on a higher platform. Christ has pledged Himself to work for us if we will take hold of Him by faith.

Jesus does not willingly give sorrow to a single soul. Let us learn of Him how to manifest a tender affection. His promises will never fail; in Him we have an unchanging friend. Let us now take hold to glorify, not self, but Christ; then the light of His presence will shine upon us, illuminating all the way.

I am very desirous, Brother Burden, that you should help Elder Reaser wherever you can. As he shall come into right relation to God, you will be encouraged to help him in many ways. If Brother Reaser will come into harmony with the work, he can be a help to you, and you to him. There are many who have received wrong impressions. There are many church members who need to feel the converting power of God upon mind and heart and character. There are many in Los Angeles who if they would move out of the city and find homes in more retired places, would have an experience of a higher character. There is a great work to be done for the city of Los Angeles.

Ellen G. White

* * * * *

Sanitarium, Calif.,
B.-46-'08 Jan. 15, 1908.
Elders Burden and Reaser:
Dear Brethren,

I have words to speak to you. The Lord has a great work to do for His cause in the earth, and He will do it through those workers who will unite with Him.

I plead with you, Elder Reaser, to take your stand wholly on the right side. We cannot change the presidency without feeling a deep regret. If you will take your position firmly to counterwork the influence you have exerted against the Testimonies of the Spirit of God, then the Lord can accept you. But while you remain in an unsettled condition, having more confidence in your own judgment than you have in the counsel of the Lord, you are doing a work to undermine the confidence of the people in the work of the Lord. I must say to you, Elder Reaser, that there is need for much searching of self, for you have much prejudice to overcome. One seed of unbelief sown in the heart, will change the atmosphere of the soul. There is a far-reaching work to be done in counterworking the work of unbelief that has been done. If you will place yourself under the control of the Spirit of God, the Lord will help you to do this. Angels of God are by the side of those who choose to be taught of the Lord and who seek His counsel. Our workers need to counsel often together, that they may know what spirit is controlling them.

The workers in the Southern California Conference need to be minute men. No one is to exalt his own judgment or entertain the thought that he can carry the work in his own way. My brethren, when difficulties arise, do not leave the Lord out of your councils. Self-ruling will bring no strength to the church. A worker may magnify self to large proportions, but in doing so he will bring embarrassment to the work, and give an example to the church that God never designed it should have.

The work that was done in collecting money to lift the school debt in Southern Calif. was not a work of God's ordering. He gave our schools the precious book "Christ's Object Lessons" and He wants that book to be appreciated. The students have lost precious lessons because they have not taken up the work of pushing the sale of these books. There is a most valuable experience to be gained by those who will aid in doing this work for the benefit of our educational institutions. If teachers and students will act their part in this missionary enterprise, angels of God will open the way before them.

In this new year let new methods be recommended. Let parents encourage their children to act a part in the circulation of "Christ's Object Lessons." This will instruct the children in acts of self-denial. The work of selling "Christ's Object Lessons" is a work that Christ would have the children engage in and they themselves will be blessed in the work. Light, precious light, is contained in the book, which every family should follow.

"Ministry of Healing" is another book containing valuable instructions. It is also a gift to the work; its teachings will do good to those who receive them, as its title suggests. The sale of "Ministry of Healing" is one way in which the sanitarium is to receive help. Let us take a personal interest in this matter. These two books can be handled separately or together, as may be deemed advisable. And those who read them will see in them precious light. Angels will be beside those who study them to impress minds and hearts.

[335] The Loma Linda Sanitarium needs help. It was the Lord Who placed this institution in our possession, that we might carry forward His work through its instrumentality. It should have every convenience necessary to make it a blessing to the sick. In the efforts made to build up this work, Satan has tried in every way to discourage; but we must not be discouraged, but arouse to the task of carrying this work successfully. Los Angeles can help to meet the emergency by loaning means or making gifts to provide for the present necessities.

There is need of an elevator at the sanitarium; it is also necessary that some other improvements be made, and that, as far as possible, the indebtedness be decreased. Let all who possibly can, help in the circulation of "Ministry of Healing" that means may come in for the doing of the work. If at the beginning of this new year, we will take hold of this work, the blessing of the Lord will be upon us. The pushing of this enterprise is included in the missionary work to be done for this time. Let all plan to see what can be done.

We each need to arouse and be a benefit to the world in which we live. We are to act a part in the saving of souls. The spirit we reveal in words and character will live again in those for whom we labor as their ideal of what a Christian believer should be. When the will and desires are held subservient to the will and plans of the Lord, the soul will be as the garden of God, filled with all manner of pleasant flowers and fruits.

The first chapter of 2 Peter contains valuable instruction for every worker. Read this chapter, and understand it for your individual selves. It is your privilege to secure the everlasting life insurance policy there brought to view.

* * * * *

Jan. 19, 1906. B.-34-'06.
Sanitarium, California
Jan. 19, 1906.
Dear Brother and Sister Burden,

... (Note and deletion by copyist, ERP, March 19, 1960. Letter deleted here covering original pages 594, through 600 may be found on pages 96, 97, 98, 99 of this edition, 1960, of Loma Linda Messages, paged in original as 266 through 273.)

* * * * *

(594 through 600) Repetition of pages 266 through 273 found on pages 96-99, this edition (1960).

* * * * *

(601) Not for Publication

[336] (Note) This compilation has been made with the thought that it would serve as material from which our ministers and physicians could use extracts when making up some lessons regarding the medical missionary work, for presentation at our camp-meetings and among the churches.

*****

A Collection of Extracts from the Testimonies on the Medical Missionary Work

1. Our Work—To Preach the Everlasting Gospel. Matthew 28:19, 20. Revelation 14:6-11

The commission given to the disciples is given also to us. Today, as then, a crucified and risen Saviour is to be uplifted before those who are without God and without hope in the world. The Lord calls for pastors, teachers, and evangelists,—

The words, "Go ye into all the world, and preach the gospel to every creature," are spoken to each one of Christ's followers. All who are ordained into the life of Christ are ordained to work for the salvation of their fellow men. The same longing of soul that He felt for the saving of the lost is to be manifest in them. Not all can fill the same place, but for all there is a place and a work. All upon whom God's blessing have been bestowed are to respond by actual service; every gift is to be employed for the advancement of His kingdom. - Testimonies for the Church 8:15, 16.

It is essential that men be raised up to open the living oracles of God to all nations, tongues, and peoples. Men of all ranks and capacities, with various gifts, are to stand in their God-given armor, to cooperate harmoniously for a common result. They are to unite in the work of bringing the truth to all nations and people, each worker fulfilling his own special appointment,—The General Conference Daily Bulletin, March 2, 1899, Art. B, par. 5.

The truth for this time, the third angel's message, is to be proclaimed with a loud voice, (meaning with increasing power), as we approach the great final test. This test must come to the churches in connection with the true medical missionary work, a work that has the great Physician to dictate and preside in all its comprehends... The present truth for this time comprises the messages, the third angel's message succeeding the first and second. The presentation of this message, with all it embraces, is our work ... The third angel's message, in its clear, definite terms, is to be made the prominent warning; all that it comprehends is to be made intelligible to the reasoning minds of today. Unpublished MS... (H. 121-1900).

2. To Every Man His Work. Ephesians 4:11-13

The Lord has need of all kinds of skillful workmen. "He gave some, apostles; and some, prophets; and some, evangelists, and some pastors and teachers; for the perfecting of the saints, for the work of the ministry, for the edifying of the body of Christ; till we all come in the unity of the faith, and of the knowledge of the Son of God, unto a perfect man, unto the measure of the stature of the fullness of Christ.

[337] Every child of God should have sanctified judgment to consider the cause as a whole and the relation of each part to every other part, that none may lack. The field is large, and there is a great work of reform to be carried forward, not in one or two lines, but in every line. The medical missionary work is a part of this work of reform, but it should never become the means of separating the workers in the ministry from their field of labor. The education of students in medical missionary lines is not complete unless they are trained to work in connection with the church and the ministry, and the usefulness of those who are preparing for the ministry would be greatly increased if they would become intelligent on the great and important subject of health. The influence of the Holy Spirit is needed that the work may be properly balanced, and that it may move forward solidly in every line. "Test for the Church," Vol. VI, pp. 291. (Note: See chapter on Testimonies, Vol. VI, entitled, "The Medical Missionary Work and the Third Angel's Message.")

Let those who are laboring in the ministry or in the medical missionary work wear the yoke of Christ, walking in humility of mind before God, and using their varied gifts to bless humanity. Then God will use them as His helping hand. All are to be united in one Body under Christ. All parts of the work are to be controlled and guided by the wisdom which God gives. There is to be harmony in every action. There is to be no jealousy of Paul or Apollos or Cephas. All are to draw in even cords, without a sign of friction.—Unpub. MS. (B-107'01) (Note: See "Testimonies," Vol. VIII, p. 170.)

3 Medical Missionary Work a Part of the Gospel. Mark 16:17, 18

The rich and wonderful provisions of the gospel embrace the medical missionary work. This work is to be to the third angel's message as the right arm is to the body. Some have endeavored to make it the head, but this is not right.

The Lord reproves those who do not watch unto prayer, those who forget that they are wholly dependent upon Him and amenable to Him. He reproves those who misrepresent the great Medical Missionary, those who do not keep the way of the Lord, doing their utmost to prepare a people to become members of the family of the redeemed. He is dishonored by those whose course leads away from Christ and the truth for this time. The Lord desires that our medical workers shall proclaim the last warning message of the gospel. When they leave out the principles of present truth, skepticism runs through their work, and God can not endorse it.

The principles of present truth are to be studied and practiced by our people, that the line of demarcation between him that serveth God and him that serveth Him not may be kept unmistakably distinct. A close examination of God's word will reveal the riches of the grace of Christ, which are to be received by God's people, and by them imparted to those in need.—Unpub. MS. (B. 256 '03).

Christ, the great Medical Missionary, is our example. Of Him it is written, that He "went about all Galilee, teaching in their synagogues, and preaching the gospel of the kingdom, and healing all manner of sickness and disease among the people." He healed the sick, and preached the gospel. In His service, healing and teaching were linked closely together. Today they are not to be separated.

We are to teach others how to obtain eternal life. And we should ever remember that the efficiency of the medical missionary work is in pointing sin-sick men and women to Jesus. We are to call upon them to "Behold the Lamb of God, which taketh away the sin of the World." Unpub. MS. (MS. 97'03)

Christ understood the work that needed to be done for suffering humanity. As He was sending out the twelve disciples on their first missionary tour, He said to them, "As ye go, preach, saying, The kingdom of heaven is at hand. Heal the sick, cleanse the lepers, raise the dead, cast out devils; freely ye have received, freely give." The fulfillment of this commission by the disciples made their message the power of God unto salvation.

It is the divine plan that we shall work as the disciples worked. Connected with the divine healer, we may do great good in the world. The gospel is the only antidote for sin. As Christ's witnesses we are to bear testimony to its power. We are to bring the afflicted ones to the Saviour. His transforming grace and miracle-working power will win many souls to the truth. His healing power, united with the gospel message, will bring us success in emergencies. The Holy Spirit will work upon hearts, and we shall see the salvation of God.

In a special sense the healing of the sick is our work. But in order to do this work we must have faith,—that faith which works by love and purifies the soul.—Unpub. MS. (B. 134-'03).

In ministry to the sick, we have before us the work that Christ would have us do in behalf of our fellow men in every place where we can teach and practice the true principles of healing for both soul and body. Our time for work is short, and we must be more in earnest. There is a great work to be done, and we need means with which to do this work. Said Christ, "If any man will come after me, let him deny himself, and take up his cross, and follow Me." Shall we not follow Him in self-denial and sacrifice, laboring with all our power to prepare men and women, physically and spiritually, for the coming of Christ? For the Son of man is coming in His glory, with all the holy angels, and then will He fulfill the promise made to His disciples: "And if I go and prepare a place for you, I will come again, and receive you unto Myself, that where I am, there ye may be also."—Unpub. MS. dated August 3, 1905. (MS- 144-'05)

4. Medical Missionary Work to Prepare the Way for Gospel Workers

Our Saviour never used His power to make His own life less taxing. He went about doing good, healing the sick and preaching the gospel. In our work today the ministry of the Word and medical missionary work are to be combined.

Luke is called the "Beloved Physician." Paul heard of his skill as a physician, and he sought him out as one to whom the Lord had entrusted a special work. He secured his cooperation in his work. After a time he left him at Philippi. Here Luke continued to labor for several years, doing double service as a physician and a gospel minister. He was indeed a medical missionary. He did his part, and then besought the Lord, to let His healing power rest upon the afflicted ones. His medical skill opened many doors for Him, giving him opportunity to preach the gospel among the heathen.—Unpub. MS. (B. 134-'03).

Our sanitariums are established to break down the prejudice which exists in the world against the truth for this time. How important, then, that those connected with such an institution be free from reproach in any lines.—Unpub. MS. (B. 69"01).

The purest example of unselfishness is now to be shown by our medical missionary workers. With the knowledge and experience gained by practical work, they are to go out to give treatment to the sick. As they go from house to house, they will find access to many hearts. Many will be reached who otherwise would never have heard the gospel message.—Unpub. MS. (MS- 125-'03)

5. Union of Medical Missionary and Gospel Work

Both home and foreign missions should be conducted in connection with the ministry of the Word. The medical missionary work is not to be carried forward as something apart from the work of the gospel ministry. The Lord's people are to be one. There is to be no separation in His work. Time and means are being absorbed in a work which is carried forward too earnestly in one direction. The Lord has not appointed this. He sent out His twelve apostles and afterward the seventy to preach the Word to the people, and He gave them power to heal the sick and to cast out devils in His name. The two lines of work must not be separated. Satan will invent every possible scheme to separate those whom God is seeking to make one. We must not be misled by his devices. The medical missionary work is to be connected with the work of the third angel's message, as the hand is connected with the body; and the education of students in medical missionary lines is not complete unless they are trained to work in connection with the church and the ministry...

The medical missionary work is not to take men from the ministry, but to place them in the field. Wherever camp-meetings are held young men who have received an education in medical missionary lines should feel it their duty to act a part. They should be encouraged to speak, not only on these special lines, but also upon the points of present truth, giving the reasons why we are Seventh-day Adventists. These young men, given an opportunity to work with older ministers, will receive much help and blessing.—"Gen. Conf. Bulletin." 1899, p. 129.

[340] To our physicians and ministers I send the message, "Lay hold of the Lord's work as if you believed the truth for this time. Medical missionary workers and workers in the gospel ministry are to be bound together by indissoluble ties. Their work is to be done with freshness and power. Throughout our churches there is to be a reconversion, and a reconsecration to service. Shall we not, in our work in the future, and in the gatherings that we hold, be of one accord? "Test. for the Church." Vol. VIII, p. 46.

Let us now consecrate ourselves to the proclamation of the message, "Prepare ye the way of the Lord, make straight in the desert a highway for our God." "Review," Nov. 26, 1903.

The nurses in our sanitariums are to be fitted up to go out as medical missionary evangelists, uniting the ministry of the Word with their ministry of physical healing.—Unpub. MS. (MS. 71-'03)

No line is to be drawn between the genuine medical missionary work and the gospel ministry. These two must blend. They are not to stand apart as separate lines of work. They are to be joined in an inseparable union, even as the hand is joined to the body. Those in our institutions are to give evidence that they understand their part in the genuine gospel medical missionary work. A solemn dignity is to characterize genuine missionaries.—Unpub. MS. (B. 102'00)

Many are asking me how I regard the ministry of the gospel with reference to medical missionary work. These two lines of work should blend. They should both help to compose the body. The genuine medical missionary work should not be exalted above the gospel ministry. Some are in danger of regarding the medical missionary work as the body when it is only the arm and the hand.—Unpub. MS. (MS. 125-'03)

To those who go out to do medical missionary work, I would say serve the Lord Jesus Christ with sanctified understanding, in connection with the ministers of the gospel and the great Teacher. He who has given you your commission will give you skill and understanding as you consecrate yourselves to His service, engaging diligently in labor and study, doing your best to bring relief to the sick and suffering.

To those who are tired of a life of sinfulness, but who know not where to turn to obtain relief, present the compassionate Saviour, full of love and tenderness, longing to receive those who come to Him with broken hearts and contrite spirits. Take them by the hand, lift them up, speak to them words of hope and courage. Help them to grasp the hand of Him who has said, "Let him take hold of My strength, that He may make peace with Me, and he shall make peace with Me." "Review," Nov. 19. 1903. (MS-125-'03)

In the gospel medical missionary work there are noble men who bear aloft the banner upon which is inscribed, "The commandments of God, and the faith of Jesus." ...

Young men who have a practical knowledge of how to treat the sick, are now to be sent out to do gospel medical missionary work, in connection with more experienced gospel workers. If these young men will give themselves to the study of the Word, they will become successful evangelists. The ministers with whom these young men labor are to give them the same opportunity to learn that which Elijah gave Elisha. They are to show them how to teach the truth to others. Where it is possible, these young men should visit the hospitals, and in some cases they may connect with them for a while, laboring disinterestedly.—The Review and Herald, November 19, 1903.

Many will go out to labor for the Master who have not been able to take a regular course of study in school. God will help these workers. They will obtain knowledge from the higher school, and will be fitted to take their position in the rank and file of workers as nurses. The great Medical Missionary sees every effort that is made to find access to souls by presenting the principles of health reform.—The Review and Herald, November 19, 1903. See also, Testimonies for the Church 8:168.

6. High Calling of Medical Missionaries

Christ came to this world as the great Medical Missionary. When His example is followed, medical missionary work will be carried forward on a much higher plane than it is at the present time. God calls for a reconversion among gospel teachers, and especially among physicians and other medical missionary workers, that Christ may not be misrepresented and put to shame. The cleansing must begin in the heart and mind, and flow in the actions. The characters of our medical missionary workers need to be refined and ennobled. This result can be brought about only as these are made partakers of the divine nature, having escaped the corruption that is in the world through lust.—Unpub. MS. (MS. 78'03)

Should we not see in the world today medical missionaries who in all the features of their work are worthy of the name they bear? who aspire to the doing of deeds worthy of valiant soldiers of Christ? We are living near the close of the great conflict, when many souls are to be rescued from the slavery of sin. We are living in a time when to Christ's followers the promise especially belongs, "Lo, I am with you always, even unto the end of the world." He who commanded the light to shine out of darkness, He who has called us out of darkness into His marvelous light, bids us let our light shine brightly before men, that they may see our good works, and glorify our Father who is in heaven. In such rich measures has light been given to God's people that Christ is justified in telling them that they are to be the light of the world.—Unpub. MS. (MS. 134'03)

True sympathy between man and his fellow man is to be the sign distinguishing those who love and fear God from those who are unmindful of His law. How great the sympathy that Christ expressed in coming to this world to give His life a sacrifice for a dying world. His religion led to the doing of genuine medical missionary work. He was a healing power; "I will have mercy and not sacrifice," He said. This is the test that the great Author of truth used to distinguish between true religion and false.

God wants His medical missionaries to act with the tenderness and compassion that Christ would show were He in our world. Is it not time that we understood that not a sparrow falls to the ground without the notice of our heavenly Father?—Unpub. MS. (MS. 117'03)

7. Every Church Member to Engage in Medical Missionary Work

We have come to a time when every member of the church should take hold of medical missionary work. The world is a lazar-house filled with victims of both physical and spiritual disease. Everywhere people are perishing for lack of a knowledge of the truths that have been committed to us. The members of the church are in need of an awakening, that they may realize their responsibility to impart these truths. Those who have been enlightened by the truth are to be lightbearers to the world. To hide our light at this time is to make a terrible mistake. The message to God's people today is, "Arise, shine; for thy light is come, and the glory of the Lord is risen upon thee." "Test. for the Church." Vol. VII, p. 62. (Read further.)

The medical missionary work should be a part of the work of every church in our land. Disconnected from the church, it would soon become a strange medley of disorganized atoms.—Test. for the Church, Vol. VI. 289.

Much good can be done by those who do not hold diplomas as fully accredited physicians. Some are to be prepared to work as competent physicians. Many, working under the direction of such ones, can do acceptable work without spending so long a time in study as it has been thought necessary to spend in the past.—Unpub. Test. (MS. 125'03)

Workers—gospel medical missionaries—are needed now. We cannot afford to spend years in preparation. Soon doors now open to the truth will be forever closed. Carry the message now. Do not wait, allowing the enemy to take possession of fields now open before you. Let little companies go forth to do work to which Christ appointed His disciples. Let them labor as evangelists, scattering our publications, talking of the truth to those they meet, praying for the sick, and, if need be, treating them, not with drugs, but with nature's remedies. Let the workers remember always that they are dependent on God.

8. The Training of Physicians and Nurses

Great care should be exercised in the training of young people for the medical missionary work; for the mind is molded by that which it receives and retains. Too much incomplete work has been done in the education given. The most useful education is that gained by study in connection with practical work.

[343] Our institutions are not to be so overgrown that the most important points in education do not receive the proper consideration. Instruction should be given in medical missionary work. The teachings given in medical lines should be blended with a study of the Bible. And physical training should not be neglected.

Great care should be exercised in regard to the influences that prevail in the institution. The influences under which the nurses are placed will mold their character for eternity.—Unpub. MS. (MS. 115'03).

In every sanitarium established, preparation must be made to train young men and young women to be medical missionaries. The Lord will open the way before them as they go forth to work for Him.—Unpub. MS. (B.128'03).

We must provide educational advantages in the different conferences. All our medical workers must not receive the stamp of one man's mind. In different places, there should be sanitariums of a high order, where our young people can receive a thorough training. We are not to countenance the carrying on of sanitariums of an inferior order, in which incompetent instructors will do slipped work and call it educational work. The instructors in our medical missionary training-schools must be picked men and women of ability.

(To the question, "Should such an educational center be established in every one of our Union Conferences?" Sister White gave the following reply): In one sense yes. A beginning should be made in every Conference, and these schools can gradually attain to perfection. In every Conference educational advantages should be provided for young people."—Unpub. MS. (MS. 169'02).

All our denominational colleges and training-schools should make provision to give their students the education essential for evangelists and for Christian business men. The youth and those more advanced in years who fell it their duty to fit themselves for work requiring the passing of certain legal tests should be able to secure at our Union Conference training-schools all that is essential, without having to go to Battle Creek for their preparatory education...

If there are legal requirements making it necessary that medical students shall take certain preparatory course of study, let our colleges teach the required additional studies in a manner consistent with Christian education... They should arrange to carry their students to the point of literary and scientific training that is necessary. Many of these requirements have been made because so much of the preparatory work done in ordinary schools is superficial. Let all our work be thorough, faithful, and true.

In our training-schools, the Bible is to be made the basis of all education. And in the required studies, it is not necessary for our teachers to bring in the objectionable books that the Lord has instructed us not to use in our schools. From light that the Lord has given me, I know that our training-schools in various parts of the field should be placed in the most favorable position possible for qualifying our youth to meet the tests specified by State Laws regarding medical students. To this end the very best teaching talent should be secured that our schools may be brought up to the required standard...

[344]

Let me repeat: It is not necessary for so many of our youth to study medicine. But for those who should take medical studies our Union Conference training-schools should make ample provision in facilities for preparatory education.—"Review," Oct. 15, 1903.

A great work is to be done in a short time, and God forbids that we should encourage so many of our youth to bind themselves up for three, or four, or six years training, before engaging in active work. Men and women should gain an education by working along practical lines in different places, in accordance with the light that God has given, and under the instruction of experienced leaders.—Unpub. MS. (J. 178-1903).

Let not our young men be deterred from entering the ministry. There is danger that through glowing representations some will be drawn out of the path where God bids them walk. Some have been encouraged to take a course of study in medical lines, who ought to be preparing themselves to enter the ministry. The Lord calls for more men to labor in His vineyard.—"Gen. Conf. Bulletin," 1899, p. 129.

We have a work to do in securing the best talent, and in placing these workers in positions where they can educate other workers. Then when our sanitariums call for physicians, we shall have young men who, through their experience gained by practical work, have become fitted to bear responsibilities. We have failed, decidedly failed, in allowing so much to be done in one place. Everything is not to be brought under the control of one institution.—Unpub. MS. (D. 190'03).

All who desire to enter the medical missionary work, and who are worthy should be given an opportunity to learn. Giving the common treatments to the sick will accomplish much, and will give opportunity to those who administer these hygienic treatments to labor with earnestness for the spiritual recovery of their patients. Let the hearts of all who are working along these lines be softened and subdued. Let the workers learn to consult the great Physician in prayer much more than they have done. Pray, watch, wait, believe. - Unpub. MS (D. 190'03).

In training workers to care for the sick, let the minds of the students be impressed with the thought that their highest aim, should always be to look after the spiritual welfare of their patients. To this end they should learn to repeat the promises of God's word, and to offer fervent prayers daily, while preparing for service. Let them realize that they are always to keep the sweetening, sanctifying influence of the great Medical Missionary before their patients. If those who are suffering can be impressed with the fact that Christ is their sympathizing, compassionate Saviour, they will have rest of mind, which is so essential to the recovery of health.—Unpub. MS. (D.190'03.)

In new places where schools are being set in operation, arrange to have a treatment-room or rooms connected with the school. Let this place be outside the main school building, so that the sick will be where it is quiet. Let those who are qualifying to teach, give lessons on treating the sick. Soon much permanent fruit will be gathered, in physical improvement and in spiritual advancement, which, combined will be of great advantage.—Unpub. MS. (D. 190'03).

Over the medical missionary department, as well as over every other department of the school, there should be a head instructor to teach those under him. The beginning may be small. There may be only a few patients, but as the head instructor gives treatment to those, quite a number of students can look on to see how he does this work, and they can help him in many ways. Thus they will learn to do this kind of work themselves.—Unpub. MS (D.190'03).

We must certainly arouse from our passive position along these lines. Much may be learned by visiting the hospitals. In these hospitals not a few of our young people should be learning to be successful medical missionaries in caring for the sick intelligently. Observation, and the practice of that which has been learned, will result in consecrated youth becoming active, efficient medical missionary workers. But the surgical work must be done by faithful, skillful physicians.—Unpub. MS. (D. 190'03).

Those who expect to become medical missionary workers must be thoroughly educated in Bible lines. They should have the very best spiritual advantages, in order that they may be fitted to teach and train others.—Unpub. MS. (J. 178'03). See also, Testimonies for the Church 3:163-166.

* * * * *

Sanitarium, Cal.,
Feb. 11, 1908. B.72-'08. Feb. 6, 1908.
Elders Reaser and Burden, 257 So. Hill St., Los Angeles, Calif.:
Dear Brethren,

I was very glad to receive your letter telling of your experience in Los Angeles. Bless the Lord, O my soul, and praise His holy name. This is a good work, and one which the Lord would have go forward in every conference. I am more thankful than I can express that Elder Reaser is coming out of the perilous darkness into the light.

There is a special work to be done in clearing away the malarial atmosphere that has been coming into our churches. There is only one way in which this work can be accomplished, and that is by leading the believers fully into the light. Let special meetings be held in the churches that shall be seasons of humbling the heart before God, and of confession and cleansing of the soul. I pray that the believers in Southern California may improve this opportunity, and open the door of the heart to the Holy Spirit, that He may work through them without let or hindrance. If they will draw nigh to God, He will draw nigh to them.

I am so thankful that this work has begun. Let it not cease until the whole conference shall feel the converting power of God. The Lord is waiting to be gracious to all who will take up the work of clearing the King's highway. It is a work which should have been done in Oakland, but which a man ruling power has prevented from being accomplished.

I pray, Brother Reaser, that you may find an open door, that this may be made a pentecostal season in the churches. Encourage one another to put from the soul everything that would hinder the exercise of the grace of Christ. This precious privilege is now being presented that all may receive the assurance of the grace and love of Christ. The Lord will be the hope and strength of His commandment keeping people. Look for that grace that the Lord has in abundance for all who trust in him. Believe, and receive the special assurances of His grace. The blessing of God is more precious than silver and gold.

It was the unbelief of Israel, revealed in their repeated murmurings, that led Moses to plead with God, "Show my thy glory." And in response the Lord set his servant in the cleft of a rock, and caused all His glory to pass before Him.

"And Moses took the tabernacle, and pitched it without the camp, afar off from the camp, and called it the Tabernacle of the congregation. And it came to pass, that every one that sought the Lord went out into the tabernacle of the congregation, which was without the camp. And it came to pass, when Moses went out into the tabernacle, that every man rose up, and stood at his tent door, and looked after Moses, until he was gone into the tabernacle, the cloudy pillar descended, and stood at the door of the tabernacle, and the Lord talked with Moses. And all the people saw the cloudy pillar stand at the tabernacle door; and all the people rose up and worshiped, every man in his tent door. And the Lord spake unto Moses face to face, as a man speaketh unto his friend. And he turned again unto the camp:

but his servant Joshua, the son of Nun, a young man, departed not out of the tabernacle.

"And Moses said unto the Lord, See, thou sayest unto me, Bring up this people, and thou hast not let me know whom Thou wilt send with me. Yet thou hast said, I know thee by name, and thou hast also found grace in My sight. Now therefore, I pray Thee, If I have found grace in They sight, show my now Thy way, that I may know Thee, that I may find grace in Thy sight; and consider that this nation is Thy people. And He said, "My presence shall go with thee, and I will give thee rest. And he said unto Him, If Thy presence go not with me, carry me not up hence. For wherein shall it be known here that I and thy people have found grace in Thy sight? Is it not in that Thou goest with us? so shall we be separated, I and Thy people, from all the people that are upon the face of the earth.

"And the Lord said unto Moses, I will do this thing also that thou hast spoken: for thou hast found grace in My sight and I know thee by name. And he said, I beseech Thee, shew my thy glory. And He said, I will make all My goodness pass before thee, and I will proclaim the name of the Lord before thee, and will be gracious to whom I will be gracious, and will show mercy to whom I will show mercy. And he said, Thou canst not see My face; for there shall no man see My face and live. And the Lord said, Behold, there is a place by Me, and thou shalt stand upon a rock; and it shall come to pass while My glory passeth by, that I will put thee in a cleft of a rock and will cover thee with my hand while I pass by."

There is need for professing Christians to act like Christians if they would maintain their connection with God. I ask you to study also the thirty-fourth chapter of Exodus.

(Note by copyist, erp, 1960: The text of Exodus 34:1-14, included on photoprint copy of original, I have deleted here, as follows:)

".......... *Ellen G. White*

* * * * *

**Sanitarium, Calif.,
B.-82-'08. Feb. 20, 1908**

To the Physicians and Manager at Loma Linda, Calif.:
Dear Brethren,

My rest has been broken during the past night. I find myself considering the best course to be pursued toward our sanitariums and schools.

I have no clear light in regard to where Elder Owen should labor. There are so many places where educational talent is needed, that I would not dare to specify his duty unless God should give me special light concerning it.

We feel encouraged to believe that Elder Reaser has placed himself in right relation to the work, determined to labor harmoniously with his brethren. There are in Southern Calif. a goodly number of men of experience. But more, you have assurance from the highest Authority: "If any man lack wisdom, let him ask of God, that giveth to all men liberally, and upbraideth not; and it shall be given him." "Blessed is the man that trusteth in the Lord, and whose hope the Lord is; for he shall be like a tree planted by the waters, that spreadeth out her roots by the river; and shall not see when heat cometh; but her leaf shall be green, and shall not be careful in the year of drought, neither shall cease from yielding fruit." The whole of the seventeenth chapter of Jeremiah, which records, this precious promise, is worthy of your special study...

I dare not advise you in such large plans as you propose; you need to make the Lord your wisdom in these matters. I do not feel that you should plan for such large outlay of means without you have some certainty that you can meet your obligations. I would caution you against gathering a large load of indebtedness. There is the food factory to be completed and set in operation. I call your attention to this enterprise that you may not lay more plans than you can well carry out.

You are men of varied talents, and you are right on the ground. The Lord will be your instructor in all matters if you will seek His counsel in faith. Study every step, and pray that the Lord may lead you. If He gives you light in this matter, then you can move with assurance. Now is the time for you to ask of the Lord wisdom, and to submit your plans to Him. It is an excellent opportunity for you to receive an individual experience. Plan wisely; move guardedly; and the Lord will certainly be your helper.

I feel the deepest interest in the work at Loma Linda. The plans you suggest seem to be essential; but you need to assure yourselves that they can be safely carried. You should not make hasty moves that will involve heavy indebtedness.

The work which you propose will require wise business men and efficient physicians. If you had the talent and means to carry such responsibilities, we would be glad to see your plans carry. But the sanitarium must be your first consideration. May the Lord give you wisdom and grace to bear these responsibilities as He would have you. This institution must have all the talent that is needed to make it a success.

Clear light has been given that our educational institution should be connected with our sanitariums wherever this is possible. The work of the two institutions is to blend. I am thankful that we have a school at Loma Linda. The educational talent of competent physicians is a necessity to the school where medical missionary evangelists are to be trained for service. The students in the school are to be taught to be strict health reformers. The instructions given in regard to disease and its causes, and how to prevent disease, and the training given in the treatment of the sick, will prove an invaluable education, and one that the students in all our schools should have.

The blending of our schools and sanitariums will prove an advantage in many ways. Through the instruction given by the sanitarium, students will learn how to avoid forming careless, intemperate habits in eating. Let the instruction be given in simple words. We have no need to use the many expressions used by worldly physicians which are so difficult to understand that they must be interpreted by the physicians. These long names are often used to conceal the character of the drugs being used to combat disease. We do not need these.

Nature's simple remedies will aid in recovery without leaving the deadly aftereffects so often felt by those who use poisonous drugs. They destroy the power of the patient to help himself. This power the patients are to be taught to exercise by learning to eat simple healthful foods, by refusing to overload the stomach with a variety of foods at one meal. All these things should come into the education

[355]

of the sick. Talks should be given showing how to preserve health, how to shun sickness, how to rest when rest is needed.

There are many inventions which cost large sums of money which it is just as well should not come into our work. They are not what our students need. Let the education given be simple in its nature. In giving us His Son, the Father gave the most costly gift that heaven could bestow. This gift it is our privilege to use in our ministration to the sick. Let Christ be your dependence. Commit every case to the great Healer; let Him guide in every operation. The prayer offered in sincerity and in faith will be heard. This will give confidence to the physicians and courage to the sufferer.

I have been instructed that we should lead the sick in our institutions to expect large things because of the faith of the physician in the great Healer, who, in the years of His earthly ministry, went through the towns and villages of the land and healed all who came to Him. None were turned away; He healed them all. Let the sick realize that, although unseen, Christ is present to bring relief and healing.

After His resurrection, Christ met with His disciples, and for forty days instructed them concerning their future work. On the day of His ascension, He met with the disciples in a mountain in Galilee, where He had appointed them. And He said to them, "All power is given unto me in heaven and in earth; go ye therefore, and teach all nations; baptizing them in the name of the Father, and of the Son, and of the Holy Ghost; teaching them to observe all things whatsoever I have commanded you; and, lo, I am with you alway, even unto the end of the world." It is the privilege of every physician and every sufferer to believe this promise; it is life to all who believe.

Ellen G. White

* * * * *

The Medical Missionary Work [356]

Feb 23, 1908-6- MS. 5,-'08.

In all our sanitariums the work done should be of such a character as to win souls to Jesus Christ. We have a wide missionary field in our health institutions; for here people of all countries come to regain their health. The best helpers to have connected with our sanitariums are those men who desire to make the Bible their guide, those who will put forth their mental and moral powers to advance the work in correct ways.

Let the workers in the sanitariums remember that the object of the establishment of these institutions is not alone the relief of suffering and the healing of diseases, but also the salvation of souls. Let the spiritual atmosphere of these institutions be such that men and women who are brought to the sanitariums to receive treatment for their bodily ills, shall learn the lessons that their diseased souls need healing.

To preach the gospel means much more than many realize. It is a broad, far-reaching work. Our sanitariums have been presented to me as most efficient mediums for the promotion of the gospel message. Simple, earnest talks may be given in the parlors, pointing the sufferers to their only hope for the salvation of the soul. These religious meetings should be short and right to the point, and they will prove a blessing to the hearers. The word of Him who founded the world in six days, and on the seventh "rested and was refreshed," should be effectively brought before the mind. God has so clearly specified His claims upon the seventh day, that no soul need be in darkness. Jehovah regarded of such importance the knowledge of His law, of which the Sabbath commandment is a part, that He came down from heaven and on Mt. Sinai He proclaimed the ten commandments. God regards His law as a sacred thing, which it is the life of His people to obey.

Publications containing the precious truths of the gospel should be in the rooms of the patients, or where they can have easy access to them. There should be a library in every sanitarium, and it should be supplied with books containing the light of the gospel. Judicious plans should be laid that the patients may have constant access to reading matter that contains the light of present truth.

The work of the true medical missionary is largely a spiritual work. It includes prayer and laying on of hands; he therefore should be as sacredly set apart for his work as is the minister of the gospel. Those who are selected to act the part of missionary physicians, are to be set apart as such. This will strengthen them against the temptations to withdraw from the sanitarium work to engage in private practice. No selfish motive should be allowed to draw the worker from his post of duty. We are living in a time of solemn responsibility; a time when consecrated work is to be done. Let us seek the Lord diligently and understandingly. If we will let the Lord work upon human hearts, we shall see a great and grand work accomplished.

The medical missionary work done, in connection with the giving of the third angel's message, is to accomplish wonderful results. It is to be a sanctifying, unifying work, corresponding to the work which the great Head of the church sent forth the disciples to do. Calling these disciples together, Christ gave them their commission: "Go not into the way of the Gentiles, and into any city of the Samaritans enter ye not; but go, rather to the lost sheep of the house of Israel; and as ye go, preach, saying, The kingdom of heaven is at hand. Heal the sick, cleanse the lepers, raise the dead, cast out devils; freely ye have received, freely give.

"Provide neither gold nor silver, nor brass in your purses, nor scrip for your journey, neither two coats, neither shoes, nor yet staves; for the workman is worthy of his meat. And into whatsoever city or town ye shall enter, inquire who in it is worthy, and there abide till ye go thence... Behold I send you forth as sheep in the midst of wolves, be ye therefore wise as serpents and harmless as doves."

It is well for us to read this chapter, and let its instruction prepare us for our labors. The early disciples were going forth upon Christ's errands, under His commission. His spirit was to prepare the way before them. They were to feel that with such a message to give, such blessings to impart, they should receive a welcome in the homes of the people.

Some restraint was placed upon them in this their first experience. They were not to go in the way of the Gentiles, nor enter into any city of the Samaritans; for this would bring upon them trial and perplexity. This first offer of salvation was to be made to the lost sheep of the house of Israel. Their deeds of mercy and love, their message of truth, was first to be given to the Jewish nation. In the blessings that they were thus carrying to the people, they were to proclaim, "The Kingdom of God is come nigh unto you."

Through the first disciples a divine gift was proffered to Israel; the faithful evangelist today will do a similar work in every city where our missionaries enter. It is a work which to some extent we have tried to do in connection with some of our sanitariums, but a much wider experience in these lines is to be gained. Can not our Conference presidents open the way for the students in our schools to engage in this line of labor? Again and again it has been presented to me that "there should be companies organized, and educated most thoroughly to work as nurses, as evangelist, as ministers, as canvassers, as gospel students, to perfect a character after the divine similitude." There is a grand work to be done in relieving suffering humanity, and through the labors of students who are receiving an education and training to become efficient medical missionaries, the people living in many cities may become acquainted with the truths of the third angel's message. Consecrated leaders and teachers of experience should go out with these young workers, at first, giving them instruction how to labor. When favors of food or of lodging are offered by those who fear and honor God, these favors may be accepted. Thus opportunity will be found for conversation, for explaining the Scriptures, for singing Bible songs, and praying with the family. There are many to whom such labor as this would prove a blessing...

And each worker, as he goes forth to labor, should realize that he is as surely sent of God as were the first disciples. God's eye follows them; His Spirit goes with them. To those who accept His great commission He gives the assurance, "Lo, I am with you alway even unto the end of the world." "He that dwelleth in the secret place of the Most High shall abide under the shadow of the Almighty."

The Psalmist declares, "I will say of the Lord, He is my refuge and my fortress, my God, in Him will I trust. Surely He shall deliver me from the snare of the fowler and from the noisome pestilence; He shall cover thee with His feathers, and under His wings shalt thou trust; His truth shall be thy shield and buckler." Servants of God, you have great advantage, which you should appreciate.

I am thankful when I think of the advantages enjoyed by the schools that are established near our sanitariums, so that the work of the two educational institutions can blend. The students in these schools, while gaining an education in the knowledge of present truth, can also learn how to be ministers of healing to those whom they go forth to serve. The prayer of Christ includes such work as this: "Neither pray I for these alone," He said, "but for them also that shall believe on me through their word; that they all may be one; as thou, Father, art in Me, and I in Thee; that they also be one in us; that the world may believe that Thou hast sent Me. And the glory which Thou gavest Me, I have given them; that they may be one, even as We are One; I in them; and Thou in Me; that they may be made perfect in one: that the world may know that Thou hast sent Me; and hast loved them as Thou hast loved Me."

What a glorious request for all who hide their life with Christ in God. What a prospect it opens before the sincere believer. What privileges, what heights and depths of experience it assures to us. We are to become in every sense laborers together with God. Shall we through the perfection that there is in Christ, reach this high standard?

A good education in all phases of the truth means more than many of us realize. Yet with all the knowledge we may gain, we shall never realize the purpose of God for us, unless we become partakers of His divine nature. Where is our faith? ... We should be living each day as in the sight of God, becoming messengers of peace to those who need Him. We have only a little time now in which to receive from God light and wisdom for the souls who are in error. If we will exercise faith in God our faith will increase.

Again and again I am instructed to present to our churches the work that should be done for the cities. Let us encourage a spirit of consecration and earnest seeking after God in our schools and sanitariums. We need to feel the deep movings of the Spirit of God in our midst. Then humble workers will be encouraged to offer themselves in faith to the service of God. They will do this, not for the wages they receive, but out of sincere love for sinsick, suffering souls.

If ever there was a time when our work should be done under the special direction of the Spirit of God, it is now. Let those who are living at their ease, arouse. Let our sanitariums become what they should be—homes where healing is ministered to sinsick souls. And this will be done when the workers have a living connection with the great Healer.

Ellen G. White

* * * * *

Elder J.A. Burden and Others Bearing Responsibilities at Loma Linda

Sanitarium, Cal.,
B. 90'08. March 30, 1908.-7- March 24, 1908.
Dear Brethren,

I feel a deep interest that careful study shall be given to the needs of our institution at Loma Linda, and that the right moves may be made. In the carrying forward of the work at this place, men of talent and of decided spirituality are needed.

We may, in the work of educating our nurses, reach a high standard in the knowledge of the true sciences of healing. That which is of most importance is that the students be taught how to truly represent the principles of health reform. Teach the students to pursue this line of study faithfully, combined with other essential lines of education. The grace of Jesus Christ will give wisdom to all who will follow the Lord's plan of true education.

Let the students follow closely the example of the One who purchased the human race with the costly price of His own life. Let them appeal to the Saviour, and depend upon Him as the One who heals all manner of diseases. The Lord would have the workers make special efforts to point the sick and suffering to the great Physician who made the human body. He would have all become obedient children to the faith, that they may come with confidence and ask for bodily restoration. Many who come to our sanitariums will be blessed as they learn the truth concerning the word of God, many who would never learn it through any other medium.

It is well that our training schools for Christian workers should be established near health institutions, that the students may be educated in the principles of healthful living. Institutions that send forth workers who are able to give a reason for their faith and who have faith that works by love and purifies the soul, are of great value.

I have clear instruction that wherever it is possible, schools should be established near to our sanitariums, that each institution may be a help to the other. But I dare not advise that steps be taken at this time to branch out so largely in the educational work at Loma Linda that a large outlay of means will be required to erect new buildings. Our faithful workers at Loma Linda must not be overwhelmed with such great responsibilities that they will be in danger of becoming worn and discouraged.

I am charged to caution you against building extensively for the accommodations of students. It would not be wise to invest at this time so large a capital as would be required to equip a medical college that would properly qualify physicians to stand the test of the medical examinations of the different states.

A movement should not now be inaugurated that would add greatly to the investment upon the Loma Linda property. Already there is a large debt resting upon the institution, and discouragement and perplexity would follow if this indebtedness were to be greatly increased. As the work progresses, new improvements may be added from time to time as they are found necessary. An elevator should soon be installed in the main building. But there is need of strict economy. Let our brethren move cautiously and wisely, and plan no larger than they can handle without being overburdened.

In the work of the school maintain simplicity. No argument is so powerful as is success founded upon simplicity. And you may attain success in the education of students as medical missionaries without a medical school that can qualify physicians to compete with the physicians of the world.

Let the students be given a practical education. And the less dependent you are upon worldly methods of education, the better it will be for the students. Special instruction should be given in the art of treating the sick without the use of poisonous drugs, and in harmony with the light that God has given. Students should come forth from the school without having sacrificed the principles of health reform.

The education that meets the world's standard is to be less and less valued by those who are seeking for efficiency in carrying the medical missionary work in connection with the work of the third angel's message. They are to be educated from the standpoint of conscience; and as they conscientiously and faithfully follow right methods in their treatment of the sick, these methods will come to be recognized as preferable to the method of nursing to which many have been accustomed, which demands the use of poisonous drugs.

We should not at this time seek to compete with worldly medical schools. Should we do this, our chances of success would be small. We are not now prepared to carry out successfully the work of establishing large medical institutions of learning. Moreover should we follow the world's methods of medical practice, exacting the large fees that worldly physicians demand for their services, we would work away from Christ's plan for our ministry to the sick.

[366] There should be at our sanitariums intelligent men and women who can instruct in Christ's methods of ministry. Under the instruction of competent, consecrated teachers the youth may become partakers of the divine nature, and learn how to escape the corruptions that are in the world through lust. I have been shown that we could have many more women who can deal especially with the diseases of women, many more lady nurses who will treat the sick in a simple way and without the use of drugs.

There are many simple herbs which, if our nurses would learn the value of, they could use in the place of drugs, and find very effective. Many times I have been applied to for advice as to what should be done in cases of sickness or accident, and I have mentioned some of these simple remedies, and they have proved helpful.

On one occasion a physician came to me in great distress. He had been called to attend a young woman who was dangerously ill. She had contracted fever while on the campground, and was taken to our school building, near Melbourne, Australia. But she became so much worse that it was feared she could not live. The physician, Dr. Merritt Kellogg, came to me and said, 'Sister White, have you any light for me on this case? If relief can not be given our sister she can live but a few hours." I replied, "Send to a blacksmith's shop, and get some pulverized charcoal; make a poultice of it, and lay it over her stomach and sides." The doctor hastened away to follow out my instructions. Soon he returned, saying, "Relief came in less than half an hour after the application of the poultice. She is now having the first natural sleep she has had for days."

I have ordered the same treatment for others who were suffering great pain, and it has brought relief, and been the means of saving life. My mother had told me that snake bites and the sting of reptiles and poisonous insects could often be rendered harmless by the use of charcoal poultices. When working on the land at Avondale, Australia, the workmen would often bruise their hands and limbs, and this in many cases resulted in such severe inflammation that the worker would have to leave his work for some time. One came to me one day in this condition, with his hand tied in a sling. He was much troubled over the circumstances; for his help was needed in clearing the land. I said to him, "Go to the place where you have been burning the timber, and get me some charcoal from the eucalyptus tree, pulverize it, and I will dress your hand." This was done, and the next morning he reported that the pain was gone. Soon he was ready to return to his work

I write these things that you may know that the Lord has not left us without the use of simple remedies which when used will not leave the system in the weakened condition in which the use of drugs so often leaves it. We need well trained nurses who can understand how to use the simple remedies that nature provides for restoration to health, and who can teach those who, are ignorant of the laws of health how to use these simple but effective cures.

He who created men and women has an interest in those who suffer. He has directed in the establishment of sanitariums and in the building up of schools close to our sanitariums, that they may become efficient mediums in training men and women for the work of ministering to suffering humanity. In the treatment of the sick poisonous drugs need not be used. Alcohol or tobacco in any form must not be recommended, lest some should be led to imbibe a taste for these evil things. There will be no excuse for the liquor-dealers in that day when every man shall receive according to his works. Those who have destroyed life, will by their own life have to pay the penalty. God's law is holy and just and good.

[367]

We have seen the poor wrecks of humanity come to our sanitariums to be cured of the liquor habit. We have seen those who have ruined their health by wrong habits of diet, and by the use of flesh meats. This is why we need to lift up the voice like a trumpet, and show "My people their transgressions, and the house of Jacob their sins."

The Lord will judge according to their works those who are seeking to establish a law of the nations that will cause men to violate the law of God. In proportion to their guilt will be their punishment. The Lord would have us lift up the Sabbath of the Lord our God. We have a sacred work to do in opening blind eyes in regard to the day that the Lord has set apart and sanctified as the rest day of mankind. He declares, "The seventh day is the Sabbath of the Lord thy God." He has placed His own signature upon that day that He has set apart to be observed as long as time shall last. We should have much to say upon this subject just now.

Let Seventh-day Adventist medical workers remember that the Lord God Omnipotent reigneth. Christ was the greatest physician that ever trod the sin-cursed earth. The Lord would have His people come to Him for their power of healing. He will baptize them with His Holy Spirit, and fit them for a service that will make them a blessing in restoring the spiritual and physical health of those who need healing.

Ellen G. White

* * * * *

To the Brethren in Southern California

Sanitarium, Calif.,
April 28, 1908. B.-132-'08. Apr. 23, 1908.
Dear Brethren,

I am instructed to say to you, Let every soul earnestly seek the Lord. We all need to understand clearly what is our duty, that we may make no false moves. We need to hold fast the experiences which in the past the Lord has given us. I have a great desire to see success attend every movement we shall make.

There is a very precious work to be done in connection with the interests of the sanitarium and school at Loma Linda; and this will be done when we all work to that end. The word of God is to be our lesson book. In the unity that is coming in among our people we can see that God is working in our midst.

"Wherefore be ye not unwise, but understanding what the will of the Lord is." Let us walk and work circumspectly. Let humble prayers go up to God, and let us seek Him with the whole heart. Then the Lord will open the way for us to lay wise plans. My brethren, speak to yourselves in psalms, and hymns, and spiritual songs, "singing and making melody in your hearts to the Lord, giving thanks always for all things unto the Lord."

Ever bear in mind that heaven is interested in every question that agitates your mind in regard to your school and sanitarium. Both are to be strengthened. The Lord is our helper and our God; let us look to him to open the way for carrying out of our plans.

[376]

We must have a church at Loma Linda, that those in the sanitarium and school may have a suitable place in which to meet for worship; but this should not be an expensive building. We shall build a neat, modest, but roomy chapel, that will show that we believe we are living in the closing days of this earth's history, in a time when many of the cities because of their sins will be cast down and their lofty buildings destroyed.

In our school at Loma Linda many can be educated to work as missionaries in the cause of Health and Temperance. The best teachers are to be employed in this educational work,—not men who esteem highly their own capabilities, but men who will walk circumspectly, depending wholly upon the Lord.

Small cottages will have to be built at little cost to accommodate the teachers and students; for these are to gain all the advantages possible from the lectures given at the Sanitarium. This work should go forward as fast as means for it can be obtained.

If the teachers in medical lines will stand in their lot and place, we shall see a good work done. My soul is drawn out in earnest prayer to God that He will preserve the honest in heart from being led astray by those who are themselves in confusion and darkness.

Teachers are to be prepared for many lines of work. Schools are to be established in places where no efforts have been made. Missionaries are needed to go to other States where little work has been done. Truth, Bible truth, is to be presented in many places. Christ is represented as identifying Himself with all the needy upon earth when He said, "Inasmuch as ye have done it unto one of the least of these, My brethren, ye have done it unto Me."

All should put forth efforts to enlarge their experience. We are in a most critical situation; but Christ identified Himself with our necessities. Christians are to learn daily of Christ. Spiritual sinew and muscle are now needed to work out right principles in every city and town and village. Varied talents are to be appreciated and cultivated, and with all we need true wisdom. We may not see our need of counseling with God; but the true Christian in every place will inquire what is the will of the Lord concerning his individual work.

All heaven is interested in the work of preparation to be done in our schools. Let the talent that is among us be combined wisely for the accomplishment of the greatest good. "Ye are God's husbandry; ye are God's building." Then link up the powers that God has given for the doing of the special work He designs to have done. If self is kept humble, the transforming grace of Christ and His wisdom, will blend heart to heart. Let us make our gifts and offerings with a single heart. Let us draw upon our talents, remembering that for this purpose they were given. To every man God has given his work; and

He would have this work done intelligently. The Lord will make it possible for each to do a work that can be accepted by Him.

The Lord expects all, by acts of self-denial, to help in the upbuilding of His work. In the house of worship to be erected and the additional schoolrooms that will be needed, let all be willing to do their best, willing to deny themselves the unnecessary expenditures for display, that they may have means to give to the cause of God. The work in promulgating the principles of health reform, which the Lord has outlined to us, must be accomplished. When we study the self-denial of Christ, and make his life our example, truth and righteousness will prevail among us. We will esteem as of highest value the ornament of a meek and quiet spirit, which is in the sight of God of great value.

Ellen G. White

* * * * *

Deeper Consecration

May 17, 1908. MS. 31-'08.

The teachers employed in our schools should be men who are acquainted with God through an experimental knowledge. They know Him because they obey all the commandments He has given them. Jehovah engraved His ten commandments on tables of stone, that all the inhabitants of the earth might understand His eternal and unchangeable character. Those teachers who desire to advance in learning and proficiency, need to lay right hold of these wonderful revelations of God. But it is only as heart and mind are brought into harmony with God that they will understand the divine requirements.

None need concern themselves about those things which the Lord has not revealed to us.

In these days speculations will abound, but the Lord declares, "The secret things belong unto the Lord," The voice that spoke to Israel from Sinai is speaking in these last days to men and women, saying, "Thou shalt have no other gods before Me." The law of God was written with His own finger on tables of stone, thus showing that it could never be changed or abolished. It is to be preserved through the eternal ages, immutable as the principles of His government in heaven and in earth. Men have set their will against the will of God, but this will not silence His words of wisdom and command, though they may set their speculative theories in opposition to the teachings of revelation, and exalt human wisdom above a plain, "Thus saith the Lord."

It should be the determination of every soul who desires to enter the pearly gates, not so much to seek to understand all about the conditions that will prevail in the future state, as to know what the Lord requires of him in this life. It is the will of God that each professing Christian shall perfect a character after the divine similitude. By studying the character of Christ revealed in the word, by practicing His virtues, the believer will be changed into the same likeness of goodness and mercy. Christ's works of self-denial and sacrifice brought into the daily life, will develop in the soul the faith that works by love and purifies the soul. There are many who wish to evade the cross-bearing part, but the Lord speaks to all when He said, "If any man will come after Me, let him deny himself, and take up his cross daily, and follow Me."

A great work is to be accomplished by the setting forth of the saving truths of the Bible. This is the means ordained of God to stem the tide of moral corruption in the earth. Christ gave His own life to make it possible for man to be restored to the image of God. It is the power of His grace that draws men together in obedience to the truth. Those who would experience more of the sanctification of the truth in their own souls, should present the truth to those who are ignorant of it. Never will they find a more elevating, ennobling work.

The Teacher and Evangelist

The work of educating our youth, as outlined for us in the instruction given of God, is to be sacredly maintained. For this reason we must select as teachers those who will educate in right lines. Said my instructor: Let not teachers be chosen to educate and train the youth who will not maintain the simplicity of Christ's methods. His teachings contained the very essence of sanctified simplicity.

Those teachers who present matters to the students in an uncertain light are not fitted for the work of educating the youth. No man is qualified for this work unless he is daily learning to speak the words of the Teacher sent from God. Now is the time to sow the gospel seed. The seed we sow must be clean and pure, and that which will produce choicest fruit. We have no time to lose. The work of our schools is to become more and more in character like the work of Christ. Only the power of the grace of God working on human hearts and minds will make and keep the atmospheres of our schools and churches clean.

There have been teachers in our schools who could pass well in a worldly institution of learning, but were unfitted for the training of our youth because they were ignorant of the truths of the gospel of Christ. They were unable to bring the simplicity of Christ into their labors. It should be the work of every teacher to present those truths that have called us out to stand as a peculiar people before the world, and which are able to keep us in harmony with heaven's laws. In the messages that have been sent to us from time to time, we have truths that will accomplish a wonderful work of reform in our characters, if we will give them a place. They will prepare us for entrance into the holy city of God. It is our privilege to make continual advancement to a higher grade of Christian living.

One night I was awakened and instructed to write a straight testimony regarding the work of our school at Loma Linda. By that school a solemn and sacred work was to be done. The teachings of health reform were to stand out clearly and brightly that all youth in attendance might learn to practice them. All our educators should be strict health reformers. The Lord desires that genuine missionaries shall go out as pioneers from our schools. They are to be fully consecrated to the work, as laborers together with God daily enlarging their sphere of usefulness, and becoming more fully sanctified through the truth. The influence of a consecrated medical missionary teacher in our schools is invaluable.

I have been instructed to present these things before our teachers. We need to be converted from our faulty lives to the faith of the gospel. Christ's followers have no need to try to shine. If they will behold constantly the life of Christ, they will be changed in mind and heart into the same image. Then they will shine without any superficial attempt. The Lord asks for no display of goodness. In the gift of His Son He has made provision that our inward lives may be imbued with the principles of heaven. It is the appropriation of this provision that will lead to a manifestation of Christ to the world. When the people of God experience the new birth, their honesty, their uprightness, their fidelity, their steadfast principles, will unfailingly reveal it. Oh, what words were spoken to me. What gentleness was recommended through the grace abundantly given. The greatest manifestation that men and women can make of the grace and power of Christ, is when the natural man becomes partaker of the divine nature, and through the power that the grace of Christ imparts, overcomes the corruptions that are in the world through lust.

Ellen G. White

* * * * *

Instruction to Sanitarium Workers

June 3, 1908. MS. 63-'08.

I am very anxious that all those connected with our sanitariums shall be men whose lives are wholly devoted to God, free from all evil works. There are some who seem to have lost all sense of the sacred character of our institutions and the purpose for which they were established. A great dread has been upon my mind as to what the results will be of this lack of spirituality and clear discernment. There is great need of loyalty to principle. The Lord calls for young men to work in our sanitariums who will not yield to temptation. The lives of the young people connected with our sanitariums should be such as to exert a convicting and converting power upon those who have not received the message for this time.

Our sanitariums are to be conducted in such a way that God will be honored and glorified. They are not to become a snare. But unless the human instrumentalities are under the guidance of the Holy Spirit, the enemy will use them to carry out his devisings for the hindrance of God's cause and for the destruction of their own souls. Many have already lost their first love for the great, grand Bible truths concerning Christ's second coming.

It is only the Lord's working, believing people, who are full of faith and of the Holy Spirit, who will honor the truth they profess to believe. Their faith speaks out through their earnest belief of the truth. They render loyal obedience to their Leader. They rest upon the efficacy of His sacrifice for the race, knowing that it speaketh better things than the blood of Abel. They believe that to those who look for Him He will appear the second time without sin unto salvation.

In our sanitariums a pure religious influence should be paramount. Solemn impressions are to be made on the minds of those who come for treatment. The very highest interests are to be given the first attention. The accumulated light of the past, which has made us what we are,—Seventh-day Adventists,—is to shine forth through us to the world. The light of truth is to illuminate and irradiate all our sanitariums. The helpers are to be light-bearers to the world.

The truth is to be cherished, not banished or hidden from sight. The light is to shine forth in clear, distinct rays. These institutions are the Lord's facilities for the revival of pure, elevated morality. We do not establish them as a speculative business, but to help men and women to follow right methods of living. Christ, the great Medical Missionary, is no longer in our world in person. But He has not left the world in darkness. To His subjects He has given the commission, "Go ye into all the world, and preach the gospel to every creature," "teaching them to observe all things whatsoever I have commanded you; and, lo, I am with you alway, even unto the end of the world." The great questions of Bible truth are to enter into the very heart of society, to reform and convert men and women, bringing them to see the great necessity of preparing for the mansions that Christ told His disciples He would prepare for them that love Him. "If I go away," He declared, "I will come again, and receive you unto myself; that where I am, there ye may be also."

Satan will introduce every form of error in an effort to lead souls away from the work to be accomplished in these last days. There needs to be a decided awakening, in accordance with the importance of the subjects we are presenting. The conversion of souls is now to be our one object. Every facility for the advancement of God's cause is to be put into use, that His will may be done on earth as it is in heaven. We cannot afford to be irreligious and indifferent now. We must take advantage of the means that the Lord has placed in our hands for the carrying forward of medical missionary work. Through this work infidels will be converted. Through the wonderful restorations taking place in our sanitariums, souls will be led to look to Christ as the great Healer of soul and body.

God wants every one to stand with the whole armor on, ready for the great review. He wants us to do the work that He has given us. "In all thy ways acknowledge Him, and He shall direct thy paths." "The secret of the Lord is with them that fear Him."

The Lord will manifest Himself to all who seek Him with humble hearts. The end of all things is at hand. Let your eyes be fixed upon Christ. As the called and chosen of God, we must represent truth in its purity. Our lives are to be such that the world will take knowledge that we have been with Christ, and that truth may seem more desirable to them than error.

If rightly conducted, our sanitariums may exert a refining ennobling influence, and lead many souls to Christ. The religious principles maintained in these institutions will demonstrate that there is relief for the soul weary and sick with sin. Many are weak and sick because of the disease of the soul. Let Christ be held up before them as the great Healer who invites them to come to Him and find rest. Tell them that the heart of Christ is drawn out in compassion and love for His blood-bought heritage. He will heal the troubled heart that looks to Him in faith.

Great care should be exercised in regard to the influence that prevails in the institution. The influences under which the nurses are placed will mold their characters for eternity.

The influence of the sanitarium family should be a united influence, each member seeking to become a power for good in that department in which he labors. If this result is obtained, there must first be a weeding out of every lame principle; then the workers can hope to succeed in perfecting themselves as Christian workers. It is only as they place themselves under the discipline of God, conforming their daily lives to the pattern that they have in the Saviour's earthly life, that they can become partakers of the divine nature, and escape the corruption that is in the world through lust. As long as we are here in this world, we are on test and trial. We will be held accountable, not only for the working out of our own salvation, but for the influence for good or evil that we exert on other souls.

He who is meek in spirit, who is purest and most childlike, will be made strong for the battle. He will be strengthened with might by His Spirit in the inner man. He who feels His weakness, and wrestles with God as did Jacob, and like this servant of old cries, "I will not let thee go except Thou bless me," will go forth with the fresh anointing of the Holy Spirit. The atmosphere of heaven will surround him. His influence will be a positive force in favor of the religion of Christ.

These words point out what the workers in the sanitarium may be. I am so glad that we can come to God in faith and humility and plead with Him until our souls are brought into such close relationship with Jesus, that we can lay our burdens at His feet, saying, "I know in Whom I have believed, and am persuaded that He is able to keep that which I have committed to Him against that day". The Lord is able to do exceeding abundantly above all that we can ask or think. Our cold, faithless hearts may be quickened into sensibility and life, until we can say in faith, "The life that I now live in the flesh, I live by the faith of the Son of God." Let us seek for the fullness of the salvation of Christ. Let us follow in the footsteps of the Son of God, for the promise is, "He that followeth me shall not walk in darkness, but shall have the light of life."

Ellen G. White

* * * * *

June 1908

"Loma Linda is to be not only a sanitarium, but an educational center. A school is to be established here for the training of gospel medical missionary evangelists.

"Make the school especially strong for nurses and physicians. Thousands of workers are to be qualified with all the ability of physicians, to labor, not in professional lines, but as medical missionary evangelists.

"We need workers who will gain breadth of mind by studying the book God has opened before us of His created works. Angels cooperate with those who proclaim the truth represented by the things of nature."

—Loma Linda College of Medical Evangelists, Third Annual Announcement. 1908-1900

* * * * *

With the possession of this place comes the weighty responsibility of making the work of the institution educational in character. Loma Linda is to be not only a sanitarium, but an educational center. A school is to be established here for the training of gospel medical missionary evangelists.

In Loma Linda we have an advantageous center for the carrying on of various missionary enterprises. We can see that it was in the providence of God that this sanitarium was placed in the possession of our people. We should appreciate Loma Linda as a place which the Lord foresaw we would need and which He gave us. There is a very precious work to be done in connection with the interests of the sanitarium and school at Loma Linda, and this will be done when we all work to that end, moving unitedly in God's order.

At Loma Linda many can be educated to work as missionaries in the cause of health and temperance. Teachers are to be prepared for many lines of work. Schools are to be established in places where as yet no efforts have been made.

In regard to the school, I would say, make it especially strong in the education of nurses and physicians. In medical missionary schools, many workers are to be qualified with the ability of physicians to labor as medical missionary evangelists. This training, the Lord has specified, is in harmony with the principles underlying true higher education. We hear a great deal about the higher education. The highest education is to follow in the footsteps of Christ, patterning after the example He gave when He was in the world. We cannot gain an education higher than this, for this class of training will make men laborers together with God.

That which is of the most importance is that the students be taught how to represent aright the principles of health reform. Teach them to pursue this line of study faithfully, combined with other essential lines of education. The grace of Jesus Christ will give wisdom to all who follow the Lord's plan of true education. Let the students follow closely the example of the One who purchased the human race with the costly price of His own life. Let them appeal to the Saviour and depend upon Him as the One who heals all manner of diseases. The Lord would have the workers make special efforts to point the sick and suffering to the Great Physician who made the human body.

Let Seventh-day Adventist medical workers remember that the Lord God Omnipotent reigneth. Christ was the greatest physician that ever trod this sin-cursed earth. The Lord would have His people come to Him for their power of healing. He will baptize them with His Holy Spirit, and fit them for a service that will make them a blessing in restoring the spiritual and physical health to those who need healing.

The light given me is, We must provide that which is essential to qualify physicians, so that they may intelligently fit themselves to be able to stand the examinations required to prove their efficiency as physicians. And for the special preparation of our youth who have clear convictions of their duty to obtain a medical education that will enable them to pass the examinations required by law of all who practice as regularly qualified physicians we are to supply whatever may be required, so that these youth need not be compelled to go to medical schools conducted by men not of our faith. The medical school at Loma Linda is to be of the highest order, because those who are in that school have the privilege of maintaining a living connection with the wisest of all physicians, from whom there is communicated knowledge of a superior order.

—Second Annual Announcement, College of Medical Evangelists. 1910-'11.

* * * * *

A Plea for Medical Missionary Evangelists.
Importance of the Work

The end of all things is at hand. The signs foretold by Christ are fast fulfilling. The nations are angry, and the time of the dead has come, that they should be judged. There are stormy times before us, but let us not utter one word of unbelief or discouragement. Let us remember that we bear a message of healing to a world filled with sin-sick souls. May the Lord increase our faith and help us to see that He desires us all to become acquainted with His ministry of healing and with the mercy-seat. He desires the light of His grace to shine forth from many places.

We are living in the last days. Troublous times are before us. He who understands the necessities of the situation arranges that advantages should be brought to the workers in various places, to enable them more effectually to arouse the attention of the people. He knows the needs and the necessities of the feeblest of His flock, and He sends His own message into the highways and byways.

There are souls in many places who have not yet heard the message. Henceforth medical missionary work is to be carried forward with an earnestness with which it has never yet been done. This work is the door through which the truth is to find entrance to the large cities, and sanitariums are to be established in many places.

Sanitarium work is one of the most successful means of reaching all classes of people. Our sanitariums are the right hand of the gospel, opening ways whereby suffering humanity may be reached with the glad tidings of healing through Christ. In these institutions the sick may be taught to commit their cases to the great Physician, who will cooperate with their earnest efforts to regain health, bringing to them healing of soul as well as healing of body.

Christ is no longer in this world in person, to go through our cities and towns and villages, healing the sick. He has commissioned us to carry forward the medical missionary work that He began; and in this work we are to do our very best. Institutions for the care of the sick are to be established, where men and women suffering from disease may be placed under the care of God-fearing physicians and nurses, and be treated without drugs.

I have been instructed that we are not to delay to do the work that needs to be done in health reform lines. Through this work we are to reach souls in all the walks of life. I have been given special light that in our sanitariums many souls will receive and obey present truth. In these institutions men and women are to be taught how to care for their own bodies, and at the same time how to become sound in the faith. They are to be taught what is meant by eating the flesh and drinking the blood of the Son of God. Said Christ, "The words that I speak unto you, they are spirit, and they are life."

Our sanitariums are to be schools in which instruction shall be given in medical missionary lines. They are to bring to sin-sick souls the leaves of the tree of life, which will restore to them peace and hope and faith in Christ Jesus.

Let the Lord's work go forward, Let the medical missionary and the educational work go forward. I am sure that this is our great lack,—earnest, devoted, intelligent, capable workers. In every large city there should be a representation of true medical missionary work. Let many now ask, "Lord, what wilt Thou have me to do?" It is the Lord's purpose that His method of healing without drugs shall be brought into prominence in every large city through our medical institutions. God invests with holy dignity those who go forth farther and still farther, in every place to which it is possible to obtain entrance. Satan will make the work as difficult as possible, but divine power will attend all true-hearted workers. Guided by our heavenly Father's hand, let us go forward, improving every opportunity to extend the work of God.

The Lord speaks to all medical missionaries, saying, Go, work today in My vineyard to save souls. God hears the prayers of all who seek Him in truth. He has the power that we all need. He fills the heart with love, and joy, and peace, and holiness. Character is constantly being developed. We cannot afford to spend the time working at cross purposes with God.

* * * * *

There are physicians who, because of a past connection with our institutions, find it profitable to locate close to them; and they close their eyes to the great field neglected and unworked in which unselfish labor would be a blessing to many. Missionary physicians can exert an uplifting, refining, sanctifying influence. Physicians who do not do this, abuse their power, and do a work that the Lord repudiates.

The Training of Workers

If ever the Lord has spoken by me, He speaks when I say that the workers engaged in educational lines, in ministerial lines, and in medical missionary lines must stand as a unit, all laboring under the supervision of God, one helping the other, each blessing each.

Those connected with our schools and sanitariums are to labor with earnest alacrity. The work that is done under the ministration of the Holy Spirit, out of love for God and for humanity will bear the signature of God, and will make its impression on human minds.

The Lord calls upon our young people to enter our schools and quickly fit themselves for service. In various places, outside of cities, schools are to be established, where our youth can receive an education that will prepare them to go forth to do evangelical work and medical missionary work.

The Lord must be given an opportunity to show men their duty, and to work upon their minds. No one is to bind himself to serve for a term of years under the direction of one group of men or in one specified branch of the Master's work; for the Lord Himself will call men, as of old He called the humble fishermen, and will Himself give them instruction regarding their field of labor and the methods they should follow. He will call men from the plow and from other occupations, to give the last note of warning to perishing souls. There are many ways in which to work for the Master, and the great Teacher will open the understanding of these workers, enabling them to see wondrous things in His word.

* * * * *

Medical Missionary work is yet in its infancy. The meaning of genuine medical missionary work is known by but few, Why?—Because the Saviour's plan of work has not been followed. God's money has been misapplied. In many places practical, evangelistic medical missionary work is being done; but many of the workers who should go forth as did the disciples are being collected together and held in a few places, as they have been in the past, notwithstanding the Lord's warning that this should not be.

Many of the men and women who should be out in the field, working as medical missionary evangelists, helping those engaged in the gospel ministry, are collecting in a favored locality, acting over the same program that has been acted over in the past, confining the forces, binding them up in one place.

* * * * *

Nurses to be Evangelists

Christ, the Great Medical Missionary, is our example. Of Him it is written that He "went about all Galilee, teaching in their synagogues, and preaching the gospel of the kingdom, and healing all manner of sickness and all manner of disease among the people." He healed the sick and preached the gospel. In His service, healing and teaching were linked closely together. Today they are not to be separated.

The nurses who are trained in our institutions are to be fitted up to go out as medical missionary evangelists, uniting the ministry of the Word with that of physical healing.

We must let our light shine amid the moral darkness. Many who are now in darkness, as they see a reflection of the light of the world, will realize that they have a hope of salvation. Your light may be small, but remember that it is what God has given you, and that He holds you responsible to let it shine forth. Some one may light his taper from yours, and his light may be the means of leading others out from the darkness.

All around us are doors open for service. We should become acquainted with our neighbors, and seek to draw them to Christ. As we do this, He will approve and cooperate with us.

Often the inhabitants of a city where Christ labored wished Him to stay with them and continue to work among them. But He would tell them that He must go to cities that had not heard the truths that He had to present. After He had given the truth to those in one place, He left them to build upon what He had given them, while He went to another place. His methods of labor are to be followed today by those to whom He has left His work. We are to go from place to place, carrying the message. As soon as the truth has been proclaimed in one place, we are to go to warn others.

From the instruction that the Lord has given me from time to time, I know that there should be workers who make medical evangelistic tours among the towns and villages. Those who do this work will gather a rich harvest of souls, both from the higher and the lower classes. The way for this work is best prepared by the efforts of the faithful canvasser.

[387] Many will be called into the field to labor from house to house, giving Bible readings, and praying with those who are interested.

Let our ministers who have gained an experience in preaching the Word, learn how to give simple treatments, and then labor intelligently as medical missionary evangelists.

Workers—gospel medical missionaries—are needed now. We cannot afford to spend years in preparation. Soon doors now open to the truth will be forever closed. Carry the message now. Do not wait, allowing the enemy to take possession of the fields, now open before you. Let little companies go forth to do the work to which Christ appointed His disciples. Let them labor as evangelists, scattering our publications, and talking of the truth to those they meet. Let them pray for the sick, ministering to their necessities not with drugs, but with nature's remedies, and teaching them how to regain health and avoid disease.

* * * * *

Christ stood at the head of humanity in the garb of humanity. So full of sympathy and love was His attitude that the poorest were not afraid to come to Him. He was kind to all; easily approached by the most lowly. He went from house to house, healing the sick, feeding the hungry, comforting the mourners, soothing the afflicted, speaking peace to the distressed. He took the little children in His arms and blessed them, and spoke words of hope and comfort to the weary mothers. With unfailing tenderness and gentleness He met every form of human woe and affliction. Not for Himself, but for others, did He labor. He was willing to humble Himself, to deny Himself. He did not seek to distinguish Himself. He was the servant of all. It was His meat and drink to be a comfort and a consolation to others, to gladden the sad and heavy-laden ones with whom He daily came in contact.

Christ stands before us as a pattern Man, the great Medical Missionary,—an example for all who should come after. His love, pure and holy, blessed all who came within the sphere of its influence.

His character was absolutely perfect, free from the slightest stain of sin. He came as an expression of the perfect love of God, not to crush, not to judge and condemn, but to heal every weak defective character, to save men and women from Satan's power. He is the Creator, Redeemer, and Sustainer of the human race. He gives to all the invitation, "Come unto Me, all ye that labor and are heavy-laden, and I will give you rest. Take my yoke upon you, and learn of Me; for I am meek and lowly in heart: and ye shall find rest unto your souls. For My yoke is easy, and My burden is light."

What, then, is the example that we are to set to the world? We are to do the same work that the great Medical Missionary undertook in our behalf. We are to follow the path of self-sacrifice trodden by Christ.

Ellen G. White

* * * * *

Sanitarium, Cal.,
D.-196-'08. June 20, 1908.
Elder A. G. Daniells, Takoma Park St., Washington, D.C.:
Dear Brother,

I have been reading letters from you concerning the Bible Teacher needed at Union College.

I will say that Elder Owen is needed just where he is, and he is where the Lord would have him be. God has a work of special importance to be done in Southern California, and I know from the light given me that this work must now be perfected.

Loma Linda has been specified to me as a very important place and one which demands the best Bible teacher we can supply. There are promising youth here who are to be qualified to fill important positions in the work. They should have the best class of instructors, and capable Bible teachers who understand the truths of the Word. The truth and righteousness revealed in the Word of God is to be the stronghold of our workers.

There has been given me an outline of the work that must be done at Loma Linda, and I know that we must give to that place our best labors. The Lord wants the wisest talent there, for by means of our very best educational talent we are to train our ministerial laborers. The work is to be carried after the Lord's order, and not according to the suppositions of man.

The Lord has given us a wonderful advantage in enabling us to secure Loma Linda for the establishment of the work in progress there. A school is to be built up at Loma Linda that will train Bible workers and missionary nurses for efficient service. The Lord calls for the best talents to be united at this center for the carrying on of the work as He has directed, not the talent that will demand the largest salary, but the talent that will place itself on the side of Christ to work in His lines.

We must have medical instructors who will teach the sciences of healing without the use of drugs. If physicians refuse to give their services unless they can be paid the highest wage, we shall not bribe them. We are to prepare a company of workers who will follow Christ's methods.

There has been a dearth of means for our educational work because we have neglected to follow fully the Lord's directions. The Lord now asks that energy and zeal be given to the carrying out of His methods. The books "Christ's Object Lessons" and "Ministry of Healing" are the Lord's specified agencies for the financial aid of our institutions. By following the plan that He has laid down, a continual work of education may be carried on. I pray that God may teach us to understand His ways, and help us to learn daily of Christ.

Ellen G. White

* * * * *

[389] Sanitarium, Cal.,

Sept. 24, 1908. R. 270-'08. Sept. 23, 1908.

Dear Brother Reaser:

I hope that you will not again undertake the responsibilities connected with the Southern California Conference. It would be better for you to be in another field, and let new talent come into Southern California.

In some respects there are decided changes to be made in your character. Wherever you labor, you are to understand that while you are to stand as firm as a rock to principle, you are not to be a driver, but a fellow-laborer with our brethren. You are not to seek to rule, and dictate, and compel, but to be teachable in spirit, kind in disposition, and to be one with your brethren. It would be a serious mistake to place you again in a position which your past experience has shown that you have not wisdom to fill. The peculiar traits of your character lead you to desire to be a leader, but I have been shown that it would not be wisdom for you to occupy the position of the president of the Southern California Conference, another year.

I write this to you lest you should suppose that because there is some hindrance to the arrival of the one who was chosen for the Presidency of Southern Calif., you should retain the position. We need for the place a man who has less confidence in his own human judgment, one who will act as Christ acted, who, though Himself the prince of life, made Himself of no reputation, and coming to a world that was all seared and marred with the curse, placed Himself as one among the most needy and dependent. When He revealed Himself to the world as its Saviour, He said, "Learn of Me; for I am meek and lowly in heart; and ye shall find rest unto your souls."

The presidents of our conferences must be men who are not self sufficient and dictatorial. They must not give place to the idea that the office of president comprehends a vast amount of rulership. With such ideas they will leave impressions upon minds that will do injury to the work. Precious privileges will be lost to the people when presidents minutely define and direct the work of their co-laborers.

As a people we are to be purified from our natural habits and desires. Our hearts must be changed, or we cannot correctly represent the Lord Jesus who gave His life for us. The Son of God took humanity upon Him that He might make it possible for humanity to take hold upon divinity through the exercise of a perfect faith. Christ is our example for the development of a perfect character. Through the strength we receive from Him, we may be overcomers. In seeking Him for those things that we need, we must exercise faith that will not be denied. We must represent Him by following humbly in His footsteps. Through belief in His merits and practice of the truth, we shall receive of His grace, and this will be revealed in kindness of heart and action and singleness of purpose. Courtesy and sympathy will be revealed in our daily lives. By a daily opening of the heart to truth and righteousness as they are found in Jesus, we will be able to reveal that truth and that righteousness in our dealings with others.

The Spirit of Christ is grieved when any of His followers give evidence of possessing a harsh, unfair, or exacting spirit. As laborers together with God, each should regard the other as a part of God's great firm. He desires that they shall counsel together. There is to be no drawing apart, for the spirit of independence dishonors the truth we profess. One special evidence that the love of Christ is abiding in His church is the unity and harmony which exist among its members. This is the brightest witness to the possession of true religion; for it will convert and transform the natural man, and fashion Him after the divine similitude.

The converting power of Christ is to have a telling influence in all our institutions, and this power is the agency that will overcome our individual defects of character and make us laborers together with God. By the truth held in its purity, souls will be reached who could not otherwise be influenced to obey. The Holy Spirit is to be our counselor and guide in every branch of the work. The will of God made manifest in the life reveals the power of the word to overcome every natural trait of character, and to conduct the believer "from glory to glory, even as by the Spirit of the Lord."

I have a deep interest in you, my brother. I want you to receive the grace of our precious Saviour, that you may be sanctified soul, body, and spirit, through the belief of the truth. You are not required to set a standard of character for yourself, but to accept that standard, which if copied will lead you in the lowly steps of Jesus.

Ellen G. White.

* * * * *

Portion of a Letter from J. A. Burden to W. C. White, Nov. 18, 1908

I am studying most carefully the question of how our medical work should develop. I can see very plainly the wonderful help that has come to us by having the Bible work made strong. If we only had something better in the way of clinical work for advanced students it would be a great blessing. I have been taking up correspondence with the Medical Board of Examiners, also with the Board of Trustees of the American Medical Association of Colleges, to learn what I could in reference to the latter question. I can see clearly if we are to launch a fully accredited college to stand along side of other medical colleges, duplicating their work, that it will be a big proposition. But if we were to do, say, three solid years' work such as would be recognized with that of other schools, and fit workers for evangelistic work at home or in foreign fields, and at the same time would be counted for about two years in a recognized medical school, it seems to me it would open the way to the accomplishment of all that we want. It would give the student that which would enable him to stand when he entered these other Medical Colleges. I am going to correspond further, to see if such a plan can be worked out. If we could obtain a charter and incorporate our college in such a way as to carry out our plans, I believe it would be a step in the right direction.

I should be glad to receive any criticisms, counsel, or help on any of these points that I have suggested.

* * * * *

Nov. 26, 1908. B-332-'08.
Sanitarium, Calif., Nov. 25, 1908
Elder J. A. Burden, Loma, Linda, Calif.:
Dear Brother Burden,

Willie has permitted me to read your recent letter to him, in which you speak of Elder Andross' need of help, and suggest that Elder Healey be called to Los Angeles to unite with him.

There are wise reasons why this would not be for the best interests of the work in Southern California Conference. Elder Healey has not the physical strength to fit him to carry large responsibilities. Moreover, in the past his voice has sometimes been raised to counterwork moves that God has clearly indicated should be made. The Lord has in the Southern California Conference, men who can be trained to fill responsible positions and these men should be sought for.

The work of the Lord must be carried forward intelligently. Clear, well-defined plans must be laid for the spread of our message. Men are needed who will manifest the spirit and the mind of Christ. He calls for men who are consecrated to Him, body, soul, and spirit, who will carry out His will in meekness and humility, respecting the counsels given by His spirit. Let every man stand in his lot and place, looking to Christ as his Guide and Counselor, and yoking up with his brethren in service for the Master.

Christ will instruct those who manifest a teachable spirit. Among those who heed His instruction He will raise up men and women to act as His agents. But those who follow their (702) own wisdom, fearing to walk in harmony with the revealed plans of the Lord, can be but a hindrance to the work He desires to be performed. You, Brother Burden, have seen how the Lord has wrought when men have not placed themselves directly in the way of the working of His plans.

[392] We are engaged in an important and an essential work. We must carry on an aggressive warfare. We are to stand for the true Protestant principles; for the policies of the papacy will edge their way into every place possible, to proscribe liberty of conscience. Every eye must now be single to the glory of God. Those who have been seeking to undermine the confidence of our people in the testimonies that God has given for their benefit and in the leadings of Providence in our work, will some day be revealed as having acted a part similar to that acted by Judas.

Judas was tempted and tried, but not rising above his temptations and trials, he lost ground, and finally went so far as to betray his

Lord. Christ permitted him to go with the other disciples on their evangelistic tours, but he often manifested a spirit of superiority. He sought to exercise authority over his brethren. This spirit, unchecked and unrestrained, opened the way for the enemy to work upon his mind and heart, until at length he went so far as to betray his Lord and Saviour with a treacherous kiss. There are today, among the professed people of God, some who are walking in the same path as did Judas. Unless they are converted, they will some day be numbered among the open enemies of God's work for this time.

I will endeavor to write again when I have time, and feel stronger.

Ellen G. White

* * * * *

A Plain Statement of Facts Regarding the Establishment of the Paradise Valley Sanitarium

[395] During the thirty-third session of the General Conference of Seventh-day Adventists, held in South Lancaster, Mass., early in 1899, several communications were received from Mrs. E. G. White, then living in Australia. Among these was an appeal for means to be used in strengthening institutional work in the Australasian Union Conference. Particular reference was made to their need of a thoroughly equipped medical institution, suitably located. It was urged that such an institution might be made a center of training and of influence in that field.

It will be remembered by many that one of the principles brought out in the course of Sister White's plea for means, was that her continued presence in a field, is an indication that a special work is to be done there.

Here is a portion of the testimony read at the South Lancaster Conference, and published on pages 130 and 131 of the 1899 "Daily Bulletin:"

The Lord says to His people in America: "When I send my servants to establish My work in a new field, and build up the interests essential to give it character, I call upon My people to sustain that work with their prayers and with their means...

"When My servant whom I have called to make known My will was sent to Australia, you in America should have understood that you had a work to do in cooperation with her. Who was it that carried out My directions in laying the foundation of the institutions in America, which have grown to such large proportions? And when My servant was sent to establish the work in a new field, could you not see that He who owns all the gold and silver was calling for your cooperation? You had obtained a standing fully abundant and ample. And when the work was to begin in another field, I would be with My servant indicate the work; and you should have been ready to aid.

"Place your money where the work of God demands help, that the medical missionary work in that new field may be made a success. The work in Australia should have been placed on such a basis that after a time it might have become self-sustaining.

"When My servants were sent to Australia, you should have understood that God would work through them, and you should have exercised liberality in apportioning means to advance the work...

"Again the word of the Lord came to me, saying: 'I have spared your life to do My work, and wherever I send you, go, and I will send My angel with you. In no case should you be feeble in your request for the advantage of means. Wherever I send you, go, and speak My words. I will be thy mind, I will be thy judgment. All the advantages are mine. The means and facilities are Mine, and there should be no withholding. But selfishness, a desire to control, has kept the advantages in one place, so that everything is overbalanced. Call for the means God designed you to have long ago. Hold up My banner. Give honor to no human instrumentality, but to God, that My name may be a praise in the earth. The Lord, He is God, and before Him there is no other. My work in Australia has been greatly hindered... But go not forth in hesitancy. I will be with you. Ask of My people the means that should have gone to advance the work in the Australasian field, the new world to which I have sent you.'"

Sister White continues: "The work should be established in this country, and it will be; for thus the Lord has said. We might be years in advance if our brethren in America had stood unflinchingly to their duty, to hear and obey the word of the Lord. Let no more time be lost. You who have so many advantages, do your work unselfishly. It is God's work we are doing, and you will not find the work in your hands restricted, if you follow the will and word of God. Share your advantages, with us in the field, that the work may stand on a true basis, and have the influence and character it should possess. Your minds may not now be prepared to see the importance of surrendering yourselves to do what ought to have been done when we were appointed to come to this field. You may not be able to see all the particulars involved in this request of God to impart. But the special work has been laid out, and you are called upon to do your God-given duty in our onward march in this country by furnishing us with facilities for our work.

"Our brethren have not discerned that in helping us to do this work, they would be helping themselves. That which is given to start the work here will result in strengthening the work in other places. As your gifts free us from continual embarrassment, our labors can be extended; there will be an ingathering of souls, churches will be established, and there will be increasing financial strength. We shall have sufficiency, not only to carry on the work here, but to impart to other fields. Nothing is gained by withholding the very means that would enable us to work to advantage, extending the knowledge of God and the triumphs of truth in regions beyond."

In the above quotations, note particularly (1) The principle that wherever the servant of the Lord is sent to strengthen certain lines of work, God's people should stand ready to aid in bringing to pass that which is called for. Those who are familiar with Sister White's experience in Australia, and with the later development and prosperity of that which she was led to urge her brethren to establish in days of doubt and [severe] adversity, know that this principle is sound.

Note also (2) the principle that our minds may not be prepared to see the importance of surrendering ourselves to do that which ought to be done when God's servant is located for a time in a certain field. "You may not be able," she wrote, "to see all the particulars involved in this request of God to impart. But the special work has been laid out, and you are called upon to do your God-given duty."

And note further (3) the instruction that comes from a divine source to Sister White herself: "Wherever I send you, go, and I will send My angel with you. In no case should you be feeble in your request for the advantage of means. Wherever I send you, go, and speak My words. I will be thy mind, I will be thy judgment. All the advantages are Mine. The means and facilities are Mine, and there should be no withholding."

It is Plain from These Facts, That

1. There is a Providence over-ruling the movements of the servant whom God has called to make known His will.

2. Of this divinely-appointed servant, the Lord has said: "I have spared your life to do My work; and wherever I send you, go, and

I will send My angel with you.... I will be thy mind, I will be thy judgment."

3. When this servant of the Lord indicates that a certain work should be done, God's people should be ready to aid in an effort to do this work.

4. The minds of God's people may not be able to see all the particulars involved in these requests for aid in the accomplishment of a "special work" that "has been laid out," nevertheless, they are called upon to do their God-given duty.

5. That which the Lord says is to be established, will be established, notwithstanding the fact that years may be lost through a refusal to follow the leadings of God's providences. This is revealed in the statement regarding Australasia reading thus; "The work should be established in this country, and it will be; for thus the Lord has said. We might be years in advance if our brethren in America had stood unflinchingly to their duty, to hear and obey the word of the Lord. Let no more time be lost."

6. For the accomplishment of definite lines of work pointed out by the Spirit of Prophecy, the Lord's servant has been instructed: "In no case should you be feeble in your request for the advantage of means." And the people are instructed: "You may not be able to see all the particulars involved in this request of God to impart. But the special work has been laid out, and you are called upon to do God-given duty."

* * * * *

When applied to the entire situation at Takoma Park, D. C., these principles stand out very clearly. But few, if any, understood all that was involved in the appeals to our people for means to establish a school and a sanitarium at this place, in connection with the denominational headquarters. It required large faith to launch these enterprises; but the men in responsibility, while unable to "see all the particulars involved" in doing "the special work" that had been "laid out," went forward in faith. The reasons for establishing a school and a sanitarium in connection with the new center at the capital of the nation, are now beginning to be understood. Those who had the faith and the courage to advance in response to counsel given through the Spirit of Prophecy, are not rejoicing over that which has been accomplished.

When these principles are applied in a study of the history of our missions work in the countries of Continental Europe, it is evident that some of the foundations laid during the period when Sister White was stationed there—1885-1887—have had much to do with the building up of a substantial, solid work, in that field along right lines. There was a divine providence in Sister White's visit to Europe just at the time she did go there—when foundations were being laid for the magnificent superstructure that we behold today.

And when we turn to Australasia, we learn that those acquainted with the struggles of the men and women of faith who led out in the establishment of the Avondale School and the Wahroonga Sanitarium, in harmony with the direct leadings of the Spirit of Prophecy, are able to appreciate fully the divine providence connected with the sojourn of Sister White in that center of the Island field just at the time she was permitted to labor there.

*****

The time came when the servant of the Lord whom He had called to make known His will, was bidden to return from Australasia to America. Before leaving Australasia, she began to see the fruition of her hopes. The word of the Lord, as spoken through the human agent was being vindicated in a marked manner. And those who remained to carry on the work that had been set in operation, have with the passing years seen evidence upon evidence of the providential leadings of the Spirit of Prophecy during the formative period of the work in the Australasian Union Conference. God's promises, as spoken through His servant, are fulfilling; His word has been vindicated.

Medical Missionary Work in Southern California

That there are special providences connected with Sister White's sojourn in California, and with her continued burden in behalf of medical missionary work in Southern California, but few are prepared to gainsay. Whether beyond our feeble comprehension, or not, there is a special providence connected with the establishment of Sanitariums near San Diego, Los Angeles, and in the Redlands-Riverside-San Bernardino district. Year after year since her return to America, Sister White pointed out the importance of doing a strong work in Southern California, and of establishing in that field, not one mammoth sanitarium, but several smaller institutions. It seemed as if no one fully comprehended the import of her words. Repeatedly she pointed out, in this connection, the advantages to be gained by securing the Paradise Valley Sanitarium; and she urged the brethren in responsibility in Conferences (both State and Union), and also in our Medical Missionary and Benevolent Associations (both local and general) to act, and to act quickly. No one acted, apparently because of lack of faith in the proposed enterprise.

[399]

Sister White continued urging men in official positions to act, until, finally, she felt impelled to lead out herself, just as she had formerly led out in advancing the interests of the Avondale School at a time when many were disheartened over the prospect of founding a training-school there. But, unlike their Australasian brethren, who, reluctantly at first, and enthusiastically after some years of trial, assumed their full share of the financial burden and the burden of control,—unlike their Australasian brethren, the brethren in official responsibility in Southern California and in the Pacific Union Conference did not follow Sister White's leadings in this instance, and refused to take any financial responsibility what so ever. In fact, to this day, it is a matter of conjecture on the part of some who have been closely connected with the Paradise Valley enterprise, as to the real attitude that men in responsibility have taken, through the years, toward the plain instruction that came to them through Sister White to give serious consideration to the advantages that would be gained by securing possession of the Paradise Valley property.

When it came to the purchase of the Glendale Sanitarium property, it was in response to the repeated counsel of Sister White to secure a property near Los Angeles, suitable for a country sanitarium. This institution was to be one member of a sisterhood of sanitariums in the Southern California field, where extraordinary opportunities called for a special and an extraordinary work. In this instance, the Conference brethren—a few reluctantly, and many whole-heartedly—shouldered the entire responsibility of the enterprise. Nobly have the Conference officials stood by the Glendale institution.

When it came to the purchase of the Loma Linda property, Sister White again led out in urging that quick action be taken—exceedingly quick action, in fact. There were a few men whose faith led them to wish to act; but the greater portion of the men in responsibility in the Southern California Conference, and some counselors in the Pacific Union Conference, refused to act. The president of the Southern Calif. Conference, after consulting with some of his associates, even instructed the others not to act, save on their own individual responsibility. But, in this instance, the counsel of the Spirit of Prophecy to act, prevailed, after that memorable meeting in Los Angeles, when Elder Irwin held up before the Conference brethren the situation that the brethren in Australia had had to face when Sister White counseled them to persevere in an effort to build up a thoroughly-equipped training school for Christian workers, notwithstanding their inability to see light in all that was outlined before them. As Elder Irwin recounted the special providences connected with the establishment of the Cooranbong school, and how every specification that had been outlined regarding the future work and prosperity of that school, had been met, the hearts of the brethren in responsibility in Southern California gathered courage, and the Loma Linda enterprise was recognized as a Conference enterprise.

Afterward, it is true, when the servant of the Lord began to bear them message after message pointing out the necessity of inaugurating and developing an untried and difficult line of educational work at Loma Linda, the faith of many wavered, and for a time some in authority did much to hinder the carrying forward of this new line of training. But notwithstanding all the opposition of the wavering ones, the Loma Linda enterprise has ever remained a conference enterprise.

Why did not the men in charge of Conference affairs respond to Sister White's repeated appeals to consider the advantages to be gained by purchasing the Paradise Valley property? Plainly speaking, it was because they did not see light in the counsel given. For some reason, they seemed unable to understand the matter as portrayed in the Spirit of Prophecy, and evidently they were not prepared to move forward by faith in harmony with the repeated suggestions of the Lord's servant.

Why did the Conference brethren purchase the Glendale property?—Because they had turned resolutely from the long cherished dream of establishing something great and grand in the city of Los Angeles, and had recognized the wisdom of establishing, instead, smaller sanitariums in more retired locations. Accordingly, they acted in harmony with the counsel given through the Spirit of Prophecy—after a tedious delay, it is true, of two years and more; but they finally did act, and that right heartily.

Why did the Conference brethren respond to Sister White's appeals to purchase Loma Linda?—Because, after at first opposing this, they were visited by men of large faith in God's providential leadings, and were, in turn, inspired with faith through listening to a recital of providences connected with the establishment of large enterprises in other fields.

The Proposed Transfer

As to the proposed transfer of the Paradise Valley Sanitarium to Conference control: This was in harmony with Sister White's mind, provided the Conference wished to take over the property in the right spirit, and were ready to foster the enterprise whole-heartedly.

And why was the transfer not carried through?—Simply because, to all appearances at least, the Conference officials failed to recognize the providences connected with the purchase of the property originally, and proposed such terms of transfer as would have indicated to our own people, and to the world at large, that those who had led out in the enterprise, moved unadvisedly, and that it would have been better had they never secured the property in the first place. The impression was being left on the minds of many, that, inasmuch as the property had been purchased contrary to the judgment of the Southern California Conference officials, now the Conference would take over the enterprise as a matter of policy, and not because they even yet saw wisdom in the action taken by the original purchasers at a time when Conference officials refused to act.

Sister White was instructed, during the night season, that, under the existing circumstances, it would be wrong for the transfer to be made. There were providences connected with the purchase of the property, that should be recognized by those who take the management of the institution. Until such a time as the General Conference may be in a position to carry the burden of the Paradise Valley Sanitarium whole-heartedly and with freedom of spirit because of their conviction that the institution has been planted of God; until such time as they are prepared to act nobly and generously as men of faith in a heaven-born enterprise; until such time as those who assume control will have a desire to vindicate the reliability of the words that have been spoken regarding the work this institution is to do in the world,—until such time as the brethren in Southern California are prepared to take over the Paradise Valley Sanitarium on this basis, the present stockholders will in all probability be inclined to hold the property, and, as wise stewards, fulfill their God-given trust.

A Summary of Facts

There is every evidence that God has a wise purpose in view, in the presence of His appointed servant on the Pacific Coast, in placing on her a special and continuous burden in behalf of medical missionary work in the Southern California field.

We read in the extract quoted at the beginning, these words, that have been given us regarding the work of Sister White: "When My servant whom I have called to make known My will was sent to Australia, you in America should have understood that you had a work to do in cooperation with her." Again: "When My servant was sent to establish the work in a new field, could you not see that He who owns all the gold and silver was calling for your cooperation."

We read still further: "When the work was to begin in another field, I would be with My servant to indicate the work, and you should have been ready to aid."

What means the continued presence of the Lord's appointed servant in the California field?

What means the bearing of repeated messages to our people, messages in which are indicated definite lines of work to be carried forward in several places in Southern California?

What means the intensity of Sister White's burden in behalf of medical missionary work in San Diego County, prior to the establishment of the Paradise Valley Sanitarium?

What means the counsel, oft-repeated, that those in responsibility make advance moves in the San Diego field, as well as in the Los Angeles district and in the San Bernardino valley?

What means the fact that simultaneously with the plain instruction that was being given as to the advantages of establishing small sanitariums in country locations, repeated efforts were made to invest large sums of money in medical missionary work in the heart of the city of Los Angeles?

What means the personal action taken by the servant of the Lord, when, in anguish of spirit over the refusal of men in responsibility to step forward by faith and secure the Paradise Valley property, she herself and a few others assumed the responsibility?

What means the fact that those who thus advanced in faith made special provision for turning the property over to Conference control whenever a change of conducting might make it possible for a transfer to be made; in other words, whenever changed conditions would result in a willingness on the part of Conference officials to accept the property in the right spirit, and to conduct sanitarium work there in harmony with the divine plan?

What means the opportunity afforded the brethren in responsibility to take over the property, in the fall of 1907?

What means their action in proposing terms so exacting that the acceptance of these terms of transfer would have brought severe hardships upon the very ones who stepped forward in faith at a time when Conference officials refused to advance in the opening providence of God?

What means the counsel of the Lord through His servant, not to accept these terms—terms the acceptance of which would have made very difficult the vindication of His word concerning the wisdom of saving to the denomination the Paradise Valley property at a time when three days' longer delay would have made it well-nigh impossible to secure the property?

What means the attitude of many men in responsibility, even today, toward an enterprise, which, from the very beginning, might have been a Conference enterprise had Conference officials fulfilled their duty in the fear of God; but which, because of the inability of men in responsibility to discern the opening providences of God, has to this day remained in the hands of a few who acted quickly in a crisis to save to the denomination a passing opportunity to secure facilities for doing strong work in a needy field?

In Conclusion

There are men in responsibility who are keeping before their minds the noble purpose of making Sister White's declining years the brightest of all her long life of service in the cause of God. These men are doing all in their power to vindicate before a gainsaying world the reliability of the Spirit of Prophecy—the gift that has been preserved in our midst these many years.

In view of all that has been outlined in this "Statement of Facts," is it not apparent that there is something more involved in this problem of the status of the Paradise Valley Sanitarium, than simply the question as to whether the institution is technically a private enterprise or a Conference enterprise? When determining the status of the Paradise Valley Sanitarium, we are compelled, by the very fact of circumstances, to rise far above mere technicalities.

The facts herein set forth are abundantly sustained by documentary evidence, and by our own good judgment and our sense of justice and the right.

In view of these facts, in view of the strange and inexplainable attitude of men in responsibility toward this enterprise in former years, in view of our knowledge of the burden of anxiety and care resting on the heart of Sister White, because of the long-continued failure of her brethren to understand the messages regarding unusual opportunities for carrying on medical missionary work in the vicinity of San Diego, we can not afford to do otherwise than to rise above every technicality, and determine the status of the Paradise Valley Sanitarium, in the light of God's over-ruling providences and His far-reaching purposes.

Clarence C. Crisler

* * * * *

Jan. 14, 1909 K-94-'09
Bro. and Sr. D. H. Kress:

Soon after the Paradise Valley Sanitarium had been secured, the brethren at Los Angeles, after long search, decided to purchase a hotel property at Glendale, eight miles from the city. This property was offered at a price below its original cost, and within the reach of the Conference. As everything seemed favorable, it was secured, and has since been refitted and opened as the Glendale Sanitarium. Some additions have been made to the old building.

When we first saw the Glendale property, so unlike some other properties we had visited in the vicinity of Los Angeles, we believed that this was a place that had been providentially reserved for us, and we have had no reason since for changing our minds.

In less than a year after the establishment of the Glendale Sanitarium, the Loma Linda property was purchased. Thus within a comparatively short period of time, God wrought marvelously in the establishment of three sanitariums within the territory of the Southern California Conference.

M. 70 '09. April 12, '09.

Loma Linda, Calif.

Eliza Morton

* * * * *

We are about to leave Loma Linda for our journey to College View, Nebraska. I have spoken once while here. Last Sabbath the patients and church members assembled on the beautiful grounds of the sanitarium, and I spoke to them from the 58th chapter of Isaiah.

We hope that in the school established at Loma Linda many will be qualified to go forth and impart the knowledge of truth they have here received. A quick work will the Lord do in our world, for Satan is preparing his forces to seek to overcome the remnant people who love God and keep His commandments. He points to the smallness of their numbers, and flatters his followers that his larger army can out-number the believers. We know how powerful are the hosts of Satan; but God is more powerful than they. Our risen Saviour is all-sufficient for our needs.

* * * * *

To the Teachers in Union College

**Washington, D. C.,
May 10 '09 -6- B.84, - '09. May 7, 1909.**
Dear Fellow-Laborers,

Here are the words I spoke to you Monday morning, April 19, with a few paragraphs from a letter written upon the subject a few days before our visit to College View:—

[405] 'We then, as workers together with Him, beseech you also that ye receive not the grace of God in vain, (For He saith, I have heard thee in a time accepted, and in the day of salvation have I succored thee: behold, now is the accepted time, behold, now is the day of salvation). Giving no offense in anything, that the ministry be not blamed; but in all things approving ourselves as the ministers of God, in much patience, in afflictions, in necessities, in distresses, in stripes, in imprisonments, in tumults, in labors, in watchings, by the Holy Ghost, by love unfeigned, by the word of truth, by the power of God, by the armor of righteousness on the right hand and on the left, by honor and dishonor, by evil report and good report: as deceivers, and yet true, as unknown, and yet well known; as dying, and behold, we live; as chastened, and not killed; as sorrowful, yet always rejoicing; as poor, yet making many rich; as having nothing, and yet possessing all things.

"Be not unequally yoked together with unbelievers: for what fellowship hath righteousness with unrighteousness? and what communion hath light with darkness? and what concord hath Christ with Belial? or what part hath he that believeth with an infidel? and what agreement hath the temple of God with idols? for ye are the temple of the living God; as God hath said, I will dwell in them, and walk in them; and I will be their God, and they shall be my people. Wherefore come out from among them, and be ye separate, saith the Lord, and touch not the unclean thing; and I will receive you, and will be a father unto you, and ye shall be My sons and daughters, saith the Lord almighty."

There is constant danger among our people that those who engage in labor in our schools and sanitariums will entertain the idea that they must get in line with the world, study the things which the world studies, and become familiar with the things that the world becomes familiar with. This is one of the greatest mistakes that could be made. We shall make grave mistakes unless we give special attention to the searching of the Word.

The question is asked, What is the higher education? There is no education higher than that contained in the principles laid down in the words that I have read to you from the sixth chapter of Second Corinthians. Let our students study diligently to comprehend this. Through His own chosen messengers God has given us light and instruction as to what constitutes the higher education. There is no higher education to be gained than that which was given to the early disciples, and which is given to us through the word. May the Holy Spirit of God impress your minds with the truth that there is nothing in all the world in the line of education that is so exalted as the instruction contained in the chapters to which I have referred. Let us advance just as far as the word will take us. Let us work intelligently for this higher education. Let our righteousness be the sign of our understanding of the will of God committed to us through His messengers.

It is the privilege of every believer to take the life of Christ and the teachings of Christ as His daily study. Christian education means the acceptance, in sentiment and principle, of the teachings of the Saviour. It includes a daily conscientious walking in the footsteps of Christ, who consented to lay off His royal robe and crown and to come to our world in the form of humanity, that He might give to the human race a power that they could gain by no other means. What was that power? It was the power resulting from the human nature uniting with the divine, the power to take the teachings of Christ and follow them to the letter. In His resistance of evil, and His labor for others, Christ was giving to men an example of the highest education that it is possible for anyone to reach.

The Son of God was rejected by those whom He came to bless. He was taken by wicked hands and crucified. But after He had risen from the dead, He was with His disciples forty days, and in this time He gave them much precious instruction. He laid down to His followers the principles underlying the higher education. And when He was about to leave them and go to His Father, His last words to them were, "I am with you always, even unto the end of the world." Christ will not forsake us.

Strong temptations will come to many who place their children in our schools because they desire the youth to secure what the world regards as the most essential education. Who knows what the most essential education is unless it is the education to be obtained from that Book which is the foundation of all true knowledge. Those who regard as essential the knowledge to be gained along the line of worldly education are making a great mistake, one which will cause them to be swayed by individual opinions that are human and erring. To those who feel that their children must have what the world calls the essential education, I would say, bring your children to the simplicity of the word of God, and they will be safe. We are going to be greatly scattered before long, and what we do must be done quickly.

The light has been given me that tremendous pressure will be brought upon every Seventh-day Adventist with whom the world can get into close connection.

We need to understand these things. Those who seek the education that the world esteems so highly are gradually led farther and farther from the principles of truth until they become educated worldlings. At what a price they have gained their education! They have parted with the Holy Spirit of God. They have chosen to accept what the world calls knowledge in the place of the truths which God has committed to men through His ministers and prophets and apostles. And there are some who, having secured this world education, think that they can introduce it into our schools. But let me tell you that you must not take what the world calls the higher education and bring it into our schools and sanitariums and churches. I speak to you definitely; this must not be done.

[407]   Upon the mind of every student should be impressed the thought that education is a failure unless the understanding has learned to grasp the truths of divine revelation, and unless the heart accepts the teachings of the gospel of Christ. The student who, in the place of the broad principles of the word of God, will accept common ideas, and will allow the time and attention to be absorbed in commonplace,

trivial matters, will find his mind becoming dwarfed and enfeebled; he will lose the power of growth. The mind must be trained to comprehend the important truths that concern eternal life.

I am instructed that we are to carry the minds of our students higher than it is now thought by many to be possible. Hearts and mind are to be trained to preserve their purity by receiving daily supplies from the fountain of eternal truth. The divine Mind and Hand has preserved through the ages the record of creation in its purity. It is the word of God alone that gives to us an authentic account of the creation of our world. The Word is to be the chief study in our schools. Here we may hold converse with patriarchs and prophets; here we may learn what our redemption has cost. One who was equal with the Father from the beginning, and who sacrificed His life that a people might stand before Him redeemed from every common, earthly thing, and renewed in the image of God.

If we are to learn of Christ, we must pray as the apostles prayed when the Holy Spirit was poured upon them. We need a baptism of the Spirit of God. We are not safe for one hour while we are failing to render obedience to the word of God.

I do not say that there should be no study of the languages. The languages should be studied. Before long there will be a positive necessity for many to leave their homes and work among those of other languages; and those who have some knowledge of foreign languages will thereby be able to communicate with those who know not the truth. Some of our people will learn the languages in the countries to which they are sent. This is the better way. And there is One who will stand right by the side of the faithful worker to open the understanding and to give them wisdom. If you did not know a word of the foreign languages, the Lord could make your work fruitful. As you go among these people, and present to them the publications, the Lord will work upon their minds, giving them an understanding of the truth. Some who take up the work in foreign fields can teach the word through an interpreter. As the result of faithful effort there will be a rich harvest gathered that you do not now understand.

There is another line of work to be carried forward, the work in large cities. There should be companies of earnest laborers working in the cities. We should study what needs to be done in the places that have been neglected. The Lord has been calling our attention to the neglected multitudes in the large cities, yet little regard has been given to the matter.

[408] We are not willing enough to trouble the Lord, and to ask Him for the gifts of the Holy Spirit. And the Lord wants us to trouble Him in this matter. He wants us to press our petitions to the throne. The most valuable education that can be obtained will be found in going out with the message of truth to the places that are in darkness, just as the first disciples went out in obedience to the commission of Christ. The Saviour gave the disciples their directions in a few words. He told them what they might expect. "I send you forth," He said, "as sheep in the midst of wolves. Be ye therefore wise as serpents and harmless as doves." These workers were to go forth as the representatives of Him who gave life for the life of the world.

The Lord wants us to come into harmony with His spirit. If we will do this, His spirit can rule our minds. If we have a true understanding of what constitutes the essential education, and endeavor to teach its principles, Christ will stand by to help us. He promised His followers that when they should stand before councils and judges, they were to take no thought what they should speak. I will instruct you, He said, I will guide you. Knowing what it is to be taught of God, when words of heavenly wisdom are brought to our mind, we will distinguish them from our own thoughts. We will understand them as the words of God, and we will see in them life and power that is for us.

"I will give you tongue and utterance," Of all the precious assurances God has given me regarding my work, none has been more precious to me than this, that He would give me tongue and utterance wherever I should go. In places where there was the greatest opposition, every tongue was silenced. I have spoken the plain message to our own people and to the multitude, and my words have been accepted as coming from the Lord.

If we will look to Him, the Lord will help us to understand what constitutes true education. It is not to be gained by putting yourself through a long course of continuous study. In such a course you will get some things that are valuable, and many things that are not. The Lord would have us become laborers together with Him. He is our helper. He would have us come close to Him and learn of Him with all humility of mind.

We are to educate the youth to exercise equally the mental and the physical powers. The healthful exercise of the whole being will give an education that is broad and comprehensive. We had stern work to do in Australia in educating parents and youth along these lines; but we persevered in our efforts until the lesson was learned that in order to have education that was complete, the time of study must be divided between the gaining of book knowledge and the securing of a knowledge of practical work. Part of each day was spent in useful work, the students learning how to clear the land, how to cultivate the soil, and to build houses, in time that would otherwise have been spent in playing games and seeking amusement. And the Lord blessed the students who thus devoted their time to learning lessons on usefulness.

Do not regard as most essential the theoretical part of your education. Medical students will have to follow the prescribed studies. They will listen to many theories that are contrary to truth. The Lord would have our medical students connect closely with those who believe and teach the truth. And as helpers with them they can learn how to treat the sick, and how to become faithful ministers to the sick. There are many ways by which the Lord would have us connect with these who honor and teach His word, and He will give us through this connection, a most valuable education.

You may say, the world will not acknowledge us. What if the world will not acknowledge you? It is the power of God that makes the impress on the human mind. Let it be more and more deeply impressed upon every student that every one of us should have an intelligent understanding of how to treat the physical system. And there are many who would have greater intelligence in these matters if they would not confine themselves to years of study without a practical experience under the instruction of learned physicians and surgeons. The more fully you put yourself under the direction of God, the greater knowledge you will receive from God. As you keep yourself in connection with the Source of all power, and as you minister to the sick, suggestions will come to your mind how you can apply to the case in hand the principles learned in your student days. "Ye are laborers together with God." He is to be your chief instructor.

Ellen G. White

Passed by the Southern California Conference [410]

(This was omitted from the last Conference Committee Meeting's report. It should have been included under item concerning Loma Linda and the Gen. Conf.)

* * * * *

To The Delegates of the Thirty Seventh Session of the General Conference of Seventh-Day Adventists at Takoma Park Assembled.

We the members of the Conference Committee of Southern California, and, of the Board of Loma Linda Sanitarium, would respectfully submit the following memorial for your consideration:

At the 1901 General Conference, in an article entitled, "Instruction regarding the School Work," read before the delegates April 22, 1901, it was pointed out that all our medical students were not to receive their training at the one medical College in Battle Creek. Of our schools that were introducing educational reforms, Sister White read: (G.C.B. 455-1901) "We are thankful that an interest is being shown in the work of establishing our schools on a right foundation, as they should have been established years ago. If the proper education is given to students, it is a positive necessity to establish our schools at a distance from cities, where the students can do manual work." ...

Although there may be few students at first, do not be discouraged. The school will win its way. Introduce the medical missionary work. Some of the students are to be educated as nurses and some as physicians. It is not necessary for our students to go to Ann Arbor for a education. They may obtain at our schools all the education that is essential to perform the work for this time."

It will take some time to get a right understanding of the matter, but just as soon as we begin to work in the lines of true reform the Holy Spirit will lead us and guide us if we are willing to be guided.... All must place themselves under the influence of the Holy Spirit.

When they place themselves under the influence of the Spirit, they will accommodate themselves to Bible lines. When the word of God takes possession of the minds of teachers, then they are fitted to deal with the education of others.... The word of God is to stand as the foundation of all education. It is to be made the basis of all the schools that we shall establish."

Thus we see that eight years ago, God, foreseeing the calamity that would come upon the one medical school then in operation among us, counseled the establishment of other schools in which both nurses and physicians were to be educated. As pointing out the defectiveness of the American Medical College, and the necessity of giving the Bible its proper place in medical education, the following instruction was given,—which instruction should have been our guide in our school work.

Oct. 17, 1903, in a letter addressed "To our medical missionaries" (B-241-'03) we find the following: "God would have all who profess to be gospel medical missionaries, learn diligently the lessons of the great Teacher.... The one book that is essential for all to study is the Bible. Studied with reverence and Godly fear, it is the greatest of all educators... Study the Bible more and the theories of the medical fraternities, less, and you will have greater spiritual health. Your mind will be clearer and more vigorous. Much that is embraced in the medical course is positively unnecessary. Those who take a medical training, spend a great deal of time in learning that which is merely rubbish. Many of the theories that they learn may be compared in value to the traditions and maxims taught by the scribes and pharisees. Many of the intricacies with which they have to become familiar are an injury to their minds. These things God has been opening before me for many years. In our medical schools and institutions, we need men who have a deeper knowledge of the scriptures.... Because the word of God has been neglected, strange things have been done in our medical missionary work of late. The Lord can not accept the present showing."

During the years from 1901 to 1904, the mind of the servant of the Lord was directed in a special way to Southern California as a field in which the medical missionary work was to be given great prominence by the establishment of at least, four leading sanitariums with branches in various cities. One of these was to be located near the towns of Riverside and Redlands.

During the session of the General Conference four years ago, under the direction and imperative demand of the Spirit of Prophecy, Loma Linda was purchased, situated four miles from Redlands and about nine miles from Riverside. Soon sanitarium work was begun at this place. This was followed immediately by testimonies which have continued to come up to the present time, both guiding, and urging forward the work. Extracts from these testimonies are as follows:—

"Loma Linda is to be not only a sanitarium, but an educational center. With the possession of this place comes the weighty responsibility of making the work of the institution, educational in character. A school is to be established here for the training of gospel, medical missionary evangelists." "In regard to the school I would say, make it all you possibly can in the education of nurses and physicians." "Make the school especially strong for nurses and physicians." "Thousands of workers are to be qualified with all the ability of physicians, to labor, not as physicians, but as medical missionary evangelists."

"I have clear instruction that wherever it is possible, schools should be established near to our sanitariums, that each institution may be a help to the other."

[412]

Acting under the advice of these communications, steps were taken to establish the Loma Linda College of Evangelists. This was opposed by some and a communication was sent of which the following is an extract,—"Be very careful not to do anything that would restrict the work at Loma Linda. It is in the order of God that this property has been secured, and He has given instruction that a school should be connected with the sanitarium. A special work is to be done there in qualifying young men and young women to be efficient medical missionary workers. They are to be taught how to treat the sick without the use of drugs. Such an education requires an experience in practical work. The work at Loma Linda demands immediate consideration. Preparations must be made for the school to be opened as soon as possible. Our young men and young women are to find in Loma Linda a school where they can receive a medical missionary training, and where they will not be brought under the influence of some who are seeking to undermine the truth. The students are to unite faithfully in the medical work, keeping their physical powers in the most perfect condition possible, and laboring under the instruction of the great medical Missionary. The healing of the sick, and the ministry of the word, are to go hand in hand." In harmony with this instruction, the school was established with a three years' medical evangelistic course, supplemented by a strong three years' nurses course, designed to qualify workers with all the ability of physicians, in harmony with the testimonies given.

In connection with the opening of the school the following was sent:

* * * * *

"Much is involved in this work and it is very essential that a right beginning be made. The Lord has a special work to be done in this field. He instructed me to call on Elder and Mrs. Haskell, to help us in getting properly started, a work similar to that they had carried on at Avondale."

After the school was thus organized and our first class had nearly completed the second year in the medical course, testimonies came from which the following are extracts, dated April 23, 1908:

"There is a very precious work to be done in connection with the interests of the sanitarium and school at Loma Linda, and this will be done when all work to that end.... Ever bear in mind that heaven is interested in every question that agitates your mind in regard to your school and sanitarium. Both are to be strengthened... In our school at Loma Linda many can be educated to work as missionaries in the cause of Health and Temperance. The best teachers are to be employed in this educational work. Not men who esteem highly their own capabilities, but men who will walk circumspectly, depending wholly upon the Lord." (B - 132'08)

That this school is not to be patterned after worldly standards of medical education, is shown by the following:

* * * * *

"In the work of the school, maintain simplicity. No argument is so powerful as is success, founded upon simplicity. And you may attain success in the education of students as medical missionaries, without a medical school that can qualify physicians to compete with the physicians of the world. Let the students be given a practical education. And the less dependent you are upon worldly methods of education, the better it will be for the students. Special instruction should be given in the art of treating the sick without the use of poisonous drugs, and in harmony with the light that God has given. Students should come forth from the school without having sacrificed the principles of health reform.

"The education that meets the world's standard is to be less and less valued by those who are seeking for efficiency in carrying the medical missionary work in connection with the work of the third angel's message. They are to be educated from the standpoint of conscience, and as they conscientiously and faithfully follow right methods in their treatment of the sick, these methods will come to be recognized as preferable to the methods to which many have become accustomed, which demand the use of poisonous drugs." (B - 90 - '08)

That the school is designed of the Lord to be, not a local one, but general in its scope of influence and patronage, we would call attention to the following facts stated in the testimonies:—First, that thousands are to be trained. Second, that persons trained at this institution are to be sent to other states to conduct local schools of health and temperance. Both the school and sanitarium have been blessed of the Lord. And the school has now the endorsement and hearty cooperation of our local conference. During the last year the General Conference has assisted it by the payment of the salary of the Bible teacher employed.

Believing the school to be general in its character, the Conference Committee of Southern California, and the Board of management of the institution, desiring counsel and help in perfecting the work of the school in harmony with the light given, passed the following:—

We respectfully ask the General Conference to recognize the Loma Linda College of Evangelists, as an institution for the education and training of both nurses and physicians, in harmony with the testimonies above quoted. Second, that it assist the management in arranging the curriculum, and plans for the future development of the school.

* * * * *

Washington, D. C.
B.100 - '09. June 9, 1909.
Elder J. A. Burden:

In the night season I seemed to be conversing with you, and encouraging you to go forward in the name of the Lord, preparing your school to give the education most needed at this time. The education that is to be given by our people in the large cities of Southern California is set before me day and night. The people in these cities are to be made to understand what constitutes "higher education." Higher education means conformity to the plan of salvation.

Obtain facilities for your school work. Let the means that shall come to you be used very economically. Do not spend one dollar unnecessarily.

Endeavor to place yourself where you will not be confused by the representations and forbiddings of human agencies who would misinterpret the true meaning of the higher education. Lift up the Man of Calvary. By the work of teaching and by earnest prayer, endeavor to place the students where they will receive inspiration of heaven. Jesus Christ is to be presented before them as the Source of all light and knowledge. Let none dishonor Him by choosing to accept the world's interpretation of what the higher education means. Let us leave that to those who do not acknowledge the truths of the word of God as the source of all true knowledge.

Give to the teachers all the advantages possible, to secure a clear understanding of what constitutes the essential education.

Teach the students to look for wisdom to the One who gave His life for the salvation of the world. Now is your time to work. That same Jesus who walked with His disciples on earth, and who taught them from day to day, will teach His servants in this age.

I would call your attention to the eighth chapter of Acts, in which is related Philip's experience with the Ethiopian seeker after truth. The record states: - Acts 8:26-40 "And the angel of the Lord spake unto Philip, saying, Arise, and go toward the South unto the way that goeth down from Jerusalem unto Gaza, which is desert. And he arose and went; and, behold a man of Ethiopia, an eunuch of great authority under Candace queen of the Ethiopians, who had the charge of all her treasure, and had come to Jerusalem for to worship, was returning, and sitting in his chariot read Esaias the prophet.

Then the Spirit said unto Philip, Go near, and join thyself to this chariot. And Philip ran thither to him, and heard him read the prophet Esaias, and said, Understandest thou what thou readest? And he said, How can I, except some man should guide me? And he desired Philip that he would come up and sit with him.

The place of the scripture which he read was this, He was led as a sheep to the slaughter; and like a lamb dumb before his shearer, so opened he not his mouth: In His humiliation His judgment was taken away: and who shall declare His generation? for his life is taken from the earth. And the eunuch answered Philip, and said, I pray thee, of whom speaketh the prophet this? of himself, or of some other man?

Then Philip opened his mouth, and began at the same scripture, and preached unto him Jesus.

And as they went on their way, they came unto a certain water: and the eunuch said, See, here is water; what doth hinder me to be baptized? And Philip said, If thou believest with all thine heart, thou mayest. And he answered and said, I believe that Jesus Christ is the Son of God.

And he commanded the chariot to stand still: and they went down both into the water, both Philip and the eunuch; and he baptized him. And when they were come up out of the water, the Spirit of the Lord caught away Philip, that the eunuch saw him no more: and he went on his way rejoicing. But Philip was found at Azotus; and passing through he preached in all the cities, till he came to Caesarea."

The whole of the book of Acts should receive careful study. It is full of precious instruction; it records experiments in evangelistic work, the teachings of which we need in our work today. This wonderful history; it deals with the highest education, which the students in our schools are to receive.

* * * * *

MS. 53 - '09.

Talk by Mrs. E. G. White before the General Conference Committee, June 11, 1909

When Brother Burden was leaving for Southern California at the close of this Conference, he inquired of me, "What shall we plan to do for Loma Linda?" "Go straight ahead," I replied; "let the truth shine forth in every possible way. Continue to work with all your zeal in the territory surrounding your sanitarium. Help your students to learn how to labor, and keep sending them out into Redlands, and Riverside, and San Bernardino and the smaller towns and villages round about. Introduce our publications, and do thorough work. Let your light shine as a lamp that burneth. Encourage the students to greater activity in missionary labor while taking their course of study."

Our brethren at Loma Linda are in need of funds with which to carry on their work. But notwithstanding their present necessity, I have encouraged them not to falter, but to go forward in the name of the Lord. And now I appeal to my brethren in Washington not to allow them to suffer. While we are planning to support the educational work in such places as Washington, we must not forget the important work that must be done at Loma Linda, and in other centers of training.

The Relation of Loma Linda to Medical Institutions

MS. 71 - '09.

Report of interview between Mrs. E. G. White, J. A. Burden and W. C. White, Sanitarium, Calif., Sept. 20, 1909.

E. G. White: We want none of the kind of "higher education" that will put us in a position where the credit must be given, not to the Lord God of Israel, but to the God of Ekron. The Lord designs that we shall stand as a distinct people, so connected with Him that He can work with us. Let our physicians realize that they are to depend wholly upon the true God.

I felt a heavy burden this morning when I read over a letter that I found in my room, in which a plan was outlined for having medical students take some work at Loma Linda, but to get the finishing touches of their education from some worldly institution. I must state that the light that I have received is that we are to stand as a commandment-keeping people, and this will separate us from the world. The Sabbath is a great distinguishing line. As God's peculiar people we should not feel that we must acknowledge our dependence upon the transgressors of God's law to give us influence. He will give us advantages that are far above all the advantages we can receive from worldlings.

J. A. Burden: I know that these thoughts are what you have presented to us before. We do not want to cause you to carry a heavy burden. We simply wanted to be sure that we were moving in right lines. If the Lord gives you light, well and good, we will be glad to receive it, and if not, then we will wait.

E. G. White: If we follow on to know the Lord, we shall know that His going forth is prepared as the morning. There are some who may not be able to see that here is a test as to whether we shall put our dependence on man, or depend upon God. Shall we by our course seem to acknowledge that there is a stronger power with the unbelievers than there is with God's own people. When we take hold upon God, and trust in Him, He will work in our behalf. But we are to stand distinct and separate from the world.

I feel a decided interest in the work at Loma Linda, and I desire that it shall exert a powerful influence for the truth. Your success depends upon the blessing of God, not upon the views of men who are opposed to the law of God. When they see that God blesses us, then people will be led to give consideration to the truths we teach.

We need not tie to men in order to secure influence. We need not think that we must have their experience and their knowledge. Our God is a God of knowledge and understanding, and if we will take our position decidedly on His side, He will give us wisdom. I would that all our people might see the inconsistency of our being God's commandment-keeping people, a peculiar people zealous of good works, and yet feeling that we must copy after the world in order to make our work successful. Our God is stronger than is any human influence. If we will accept Him as our educator, we will make Him our strength and righteousness, He will work in our behalf.

These principles may result in a condition of things that is not just as we should like them to be. We may like to have certain conditions, that in the end would result in bondage which we do not anticipate.

Jesus Christ is our Saviour today, and He is willing to work in our behalf, if we will not put our dependence upon some other power. If we are sustained by the living God, the superiority of His Power will be manifested in His people. This is the testimony that I have borne all the way along.

J. A. Burden: We love to hear the truth over and over again, that we may be sure it is the truth.

E. G. White: You have the Word which tells you that God's commandment-keeping people are to have His special favor, and that they are to be sanctified through obedience to the truth. Shall we unite ourselves with those that are full of error, who have no respect for God's commandments, and shall our students go forth to obtain the finishing touches of their education from them?

W. C. White: What is to be the final outcome? Will all our medical missionaries be simply nurses? Shall we have no more physicians, or shall we have a school in which we can ourselves give the finishing touches?

E. G. White: Whatever plan you follow, take your position that you will not unite with those that do not respect God's commandments.

W. C. White: Does that mean that we are not to have any more physicians, but that our people will work simply as nurses, or does it mean that we shall have a school of our own to educate physicians?

E. G. White: We shall have a school of our own. But we are not to be dependent upon the world, we must place our dependence upon a power that is higher than all human power. If we honor God, He will honor us.

J. A. Burden: The governments of earth provide that if we conduct a medical school we must take a charter from the government. That in itself has nothing to do with how the school is conducted. It is required, however, that certain studies shall be taught. There are ten required subjects. Physiology is one. It is required that those who labor as physicians shall be proficient in these studies. In starting our sanitariums for the care of the sick, we must secure a charter from the government; our printing office must do the same. Would the securing of a charter for a medical school, where our students might obtain an education, militate against our dependence upon God?

E. G. White: No, I do not see that it would. Only see that you do not exalt men above God. If you can gain force and influence that will make your work more effective without tieing yourselves to worldly men, that would be right.

J. A. Burden: That is the vital point, where we have been hanging for three years. The only thing that we have asked for in this matter is to take advantage of the government provision that would give standing room for our students when they are qualified.

E. G. White: I do not see anything wrong in that, as long as you do not in any way lift men above the Lord God of Israel, or throw discredit upon His power.

J. A. Burden: In planning our course of study, we have tried to follow the light in the Testimonies, and in doing so it has led us away from the requirements of the world. The world will not recognize us as standing with them. We will have to stand distinct, by ourselves.

E. G. White: We shall always have to stand distinct. God desires us to be separate.

J. A. Burden: Now the proposition in this letter was to deviate from that, so that standing as we do, would enable us to stand with them, and to have their advantages. From the instruction that has come, it has seemed to me from the very first that we were to stand by ourselves in a distinct light, following the light that God has given with reference to physical healing, and that when we do that God will open the way before us, and give us prestige with the people. But if we deviate and connect with these other schools, we would find ourselves being thrown more and more into the very things that they are doing, and our students would be molded after their similitude instead of after the similitude of the truth.

E. G. White: That is what I am trying to guard against all the time. As we read the Bible we see that God is dishonored when His people go to any worldly power, or put their trust in a worldly power. That is where God's people spoiled their history. You must arrange the matter the best you can, but that which is presented to me is that you are not to acknowledge any power as above that of our God. Our influence is to be acknowledged of God, because we keep His commandments, and His commandments are not grievous.

W. C. White: Jesus said at one time, "The scribes and the Pharisees sit in Moses' seat: all therefore whatsoever they bid you observe, that observe and do; but do not ye after their works." Now the law says that a man shall not practice medicine unless he has a diploma from a college, and unless he has passed the examination of the state board, and has a certificate. The law would not recognize the diplomas of our physicians unless they have studied some things that we do not think are really essential. For instance, in their preparation they have to study a number of things that we think they might get along without, but we can teach them. We do not have to teach these subjects in their way; we can teach them in our way. When it comes to the study of drugs, they teach how to give them. We teach the dangers of using them, and how to get along without them. In some other schools they teach geology on the evolution basis. We can teach geology and show that evolution is false.

E. G. White: Well, you must plan these details yourselves. I have told you what I have received, but these details you will have to work out for yourselves.

J. A. Burden: It seems clear to me that any standing we can lawfully have without compromising, is not out of harmony with God's plan.

E. G. White: No, it is not. All I can say is that I have had very distinct light, however, that there is danger of our limiting the power of the Holy One of Israel. He is the God of the Universe. Our influence is dependent upon our carrying out the word of the living God. We weaken our powers by not placing our dependence upon God, and taking hold of His strength. This is our privilege. (MS-105-'09 very similar to MS-71-'09)

* * * * *

Medical Studies. Oct. 1, 1909.

The Medical Student

While seeking a preparation for his life-work, the medical student should be encouraged to attain the highest possible development of all his powers. His studies, taxing though they are, need not necessarily undermine his physical health, or lessen his enjoyment of spiritual things. Throughout his course of study, he may continually grow in grace and in a knowledge of the truth, while at the same time he may be constantly adding the store of knowledge that will make him a wise practitioner.

To medical students I would say, Enter upon your course of study with a determination to do right and to maintain Christian principles. Flee temptations, and avoid every influence for evil. Preserve your integrity of soul. Maintain a conscientious regard for truth and righteousness. Be faithful in the smaller responsibilities, and show yourselves to be close, critical thinkers, having soundness of heart and uprightness, being loyal to God and true to mankind.

Opportunities are before you; if studious and upright, you may obtain an education of the highest value. Make the most of your privileges. Be not satisfied with ordinary attainment; seek to qualify yourselves to fill positions of trust in connection with the Lord's work in the earth. United with the God of wisdom and power, you may become intellectually strong, and increasingly capable as soul-winners. You may become men and women of responsibility and influence, if, by the power of your will, coupled with divine strength, you earnestly engage in the work of securing a proper training.

Exercise the mental powers, and in no case neglect the physical. Let not intellectual slothfulness close up your path to greater knowledge. Learn to reflect as well as to study, that your minds may expand, strengthen, and develop. Never think that you have learned enough, and that you may now relax your efforts. The cultivated mind is the measure of the man. Your education should continue during your lifetime; every day you should be learning, and putting to practical use the knowledge gained.

In order for you to become men and women that can be depended upon, there must be a growth of the powers, the exercise of every faculty, even in little things; then greater power is acquired to bear larger responsibilities. Individual responsibility and accountability are essential. In putting into practice that which you are learning during your student days, do not shrink from bearing your share of responsibility because there are risks to take, because something must be ventured. Do not leave others to be brains for you. You must train your powers to be strong and vigorous; then the entrusted talents will grow, as a steady, uniform, unyielding energy is exercised in bearing individual responsibility. God would have you add, day by day, little by little, to your stock of ideas, acting as if the moments were jewels, to be carefully gathered and discreetly cherished. You will thus acquire breadth of thought and strength of intellect.

God will not require of man a more strict account of any thing than of the way in which he has occupied his time. Have its hours been wasted and abused? God has granted to us the precious boon of life, not to be devoted to selfish gratification. Our work is too solemn, our time to serve God and our fellow men too short, to be spent in seeking for fame. Oh, if men would stop in their aspirations where God has set the bounds, what different service would the Lord receive!

Students who are in training for medical missionary work, should be willing to learn under those of experience to heed their suggestions, to follow their advice. There are many who are in such haste to climb to distinction, that they skip some of the rounds of the ladder, and in so doing, lose essential experiences which they must have in order to become intelligent workers. In their zeal, the knowledge of many things looks unimportant to them. They skim over the surface, and do not go deep into the mine of truth, thus by a slow and painstaking process gaining an experience that will enable them to be of special help to others. We want our medical students to be men and women who are most thorough, and who feel it their duty to improve every talent lent them, that they may finally double their entrusted capital.

The light that God has given in medical missionary lines will not cause His people to be regarded as inferior in scientific medical knowledge, but will fit them to stand upon the highest eminence. God would have them stand as a wise and understanding people because of His presence with them. In the strength of Him who is the source of all wisdom, all grace, defects and ignorance may be overcome.

Let every medical student aim to reach a high standard. Under the discipline of the greatest of all Teachers, our course must ever tend upward to perfection. All whom are connected with the medical missionary work must be learners. Let no one stop to say, "I can not do this." Let him say instead, "God requires me to be perfect, He expects me to work away from all commonness and cheapness, and to strive after that which is of the highest order.

There is only one power that can make medical students what they ought to be, and keep them steadfast,—the grace of God and the power of the truth exerting a saving influence upon life and character. These students, who intend to minister to suffering humanity, will find no graduating place this side of heaven. That knowledge which is termed science should be acquired, while the seeker daily acknowledges that the fear of God is the beginning of wisdom. Everything that will strengthen the mind, should be cultivated to the utmost of their power, while at the same time they should seek God for wisdom; for unless they are guided by the wisdom from above, they will become an easy prey to the deceptive power of Satan. They will become large in their own eyes, pompous, and self-sufficient.

God-fearing physicians speak modestly of their work; but novices with limited experience in dealing with the bodies and souls of men will often speak boastingly of their knowledge and attainments. These need a better understanding of themselves; then they would become more intelligent in regard to their duties; and would realize that in every department where they have to labor, they must possess a willing mind, and earnest spirit, and a hearty, unselfish zeal in trying to do others good. They will not study how best to preserve their dignity, but by thoughtfulness and caretaking will earn a reputation for thoroughness and exactitude, and by sympathetic ministry will gain the hearts of those whom they serve.

In the medical profession there are many skeptics and atheists who exalt the works of God above the God of Science. Comparatively few of those who enter worldly medical colleges come out from them pure and unspotted. They have failed to become elevated, ennobled, sanctified. Material things eclipse the heavenly and eternal. With many, religious faith and principles are mingled with worldly customs and practices, and pure and undefiled religion is rare. But it is the privilege of every student to enter college with the same fixed determined principles that Daniel had when he entered the court of Babylon, and throughout his course, to keep his integrity untarnished. The strength and grace of God has been provided at an infinite sacrifice that men might be victorious over Satan's suggestions and temptations, and come forth unsullied. The life, the words, and the deportment are the most forcible argument, the most solemn appeal, to the careless, irreverent, and skeptical. Let the life and character be the strong argument for Christianity; then men will be compelled to take knowledge of you that you have been with Jesus and have learned of Him.

Let not medical students be deceived by the wiles of the devil or by any of his cunning pretexts which so many adopt to beguile and ensnare. Stand firm to principle. At every step inquire, What saith the Lord? Say firmly, I will follow the light. I will respect and honor the Majesty of truth.

Especially should those who are studying medicine in the schools of the world, guard against contamination from the evil influences with which they are constantly surrounded. When their instructors are worldly-wise men, and their fellow students infidels who have no serious thought of God, even Christians of experience are in danger of being influenced by these irreligious associations. Nevertheless, some have gone through the medical course, and have remained true to principle. They would not continue their studies on the Sabbath; and they have proved that men may become qualified for the duties of a physician, and not disappoint the expectations of those who have encouraged them to obtain an education.

It is because of these peculiar temptations that our youth must meet in worldly medical schools, that provision should be made for preparatory and advanced medical training in our own schools, under Christian teachers. Our larger Union Conference training schools, in various parts of the field, should be placed in the most favorable position for qualifying our youth to meet the entrance requirements specified by state laws regarding medical students. The very best teaching talent should be secured, that our schools may be brought up to the proper standard. The youth and those more advanced in years who feel it their duty to fit themselves for work requiring the passing of certain legal tests, should be able to secure at our Union Conference training-schools all that is essential for entrance into a medical college.

Prayer will accomplish wonders for those who give themselves to prayer, watching thereunto. God desires us all to be in a waiting hopeful position. What He has promised, He will do; and inasmuch as there are legal requirements making it necessary that medical students shall take a certain preparatory course of study, our colleges should arrange to carry their students to the point of literary and scientific training that is necessary.

And not only should our larger training schools give this preparatory instruction to those who contemplate taking a medical course but we must also do all that is essential for the perfecting of courses of study offered by our Loma Linda College of Medical Evangelists. As pointed out about the time this school was founded, we must provide that which is essential to qualify our youth who desire to be physicians so that they may intelligently fit themselves to stand the examinations required to prove their efficiency as physicians. They should be taught to treat understandingly the cases of those who are diseased, so that the door will be closed for any sensible physician to imagine that we are not giving in our school the instruction necessary for properly qualifying young men and young women to do the work of a physician. Continually the students who are graduated are to advance in knowledge, for practice makes perfect.

The medical school at Loma Linda is to be of the highest order because those who are in that school have the privilege of main- [432]

taining a living connection with the wisest of all physicians from whom there is communicated knowledge of a superior order. And for the special preparation of those of our youth who have clear convictions of their duty to obtain a medical education that will enable them to pass the examinations required by law of all who practice as regularly qualified physicians, we are to supply whatever may be required, so that these youth need not be compelled to go to medical schools conducted by men not of our faith. Thus we shall close a door that the enemy would be pleased to have left open; and our young men and young women, whose spiritual interests the Lord desires us to safeguard, will not feel compelled to connect with unbelievers in order to obtain a thorough training along medical lines.

The teachers in our medical college should encourage the students to gain all the knowledge they can in every department. If they find the students deficient in care-taking, in a comprehension of their responsibilities, they should lay the matter frankly before such ones, giving them an opportunity to correct their habits and to reach a higher standard.

The teachers should not become discouraged because some are slow to learn. Neither should they discourage the students when mistakes are made. As errors and defects are kindly pointed out, the students in turn should feel grateful for any instruction given. A haughty spirit on the part of the students should be discouraged. All should be willing to learn, and the teachers should be willing to instruct, training the students to be self-reliant, competent, careful, painstaking. As the students study under wise instructors, and unite with them in sharing responsibilities, they may, by the aid of the teachers, climb the topmost round of the ladder.

Students should go as far as possible in thought, training, and intelligent enterprise; but they should never infringe upon a rule, never disregard one principle, that has been interwoven into the upbuilding of the institution. The dropping down is easy enough; the disregard of regulations is natural to the heart inclined to selfish ease and gratification. It is much easier to tear down than to build up. One student with careless ideas may do more to let down the standard, than ten men with all their efforts can do to counteract the demoralizing influence.

Failure or success will be read in the course the students pursue. If they stand ready to question rules and regulations and order, if they indulge self, and by their example encourage a spirit of rebellion, give them no place. The institution might better close its doors than to suffer this spirit to leaven the helpers and break down the barriers that it has cost thought, effort and prayer to establish.

In training workers to care for the sick, let the student be impressed with the thought that his highest aim should always be to look after the spiritual welfare of his patients. He could learn to repeat the promises of God's word, and to offer fervent prayers, daily, while preparing for service. Help him to realize that he is always to keep the sweetening, sanctifying influence of the great Medical Missionary before his patients. If those who are suffering can be impressed with the fact that Christ is their sympathizing, compassionate Saviour, they will have rest of mind, which is so essential to recovery of health.

Importance of Bible Study

If medical students will study the word of God diligently they will be far better prepared to understand their other studies; for enlightenment always comes from an earnest study of the word of God. Nothing will so help to give a retentive memory as a study of the Scriptures. Let our medical missionary workers understand that the more they become acquainted with God and with Christ, and the more they become acquainted with Bible history, the better prepared will they be to do their work.

Faithful teachers should be placed in charge of the Bible classes, teachers who will strive to make the students understand their lessons, not by explaining everything to them, but by requiring them to explain clearly every passage they read. Let these teachers remember that little good is accomplished by skimming over the surface of the Word. Thoughtful investigation and earnest, taxing study are necessary to an understanding of this Word.

Christ the great Medical Missionary, came to this world at infinite sacrifice, to teach men and women the lessons that would enable them to know God aright. He lived a perfect life, setting an example that all may safely follow. Let our medical students study the lessons that Christ has given. It is essential that they have a clear understanding of these lessons. It would be a fearful mistake for them to neglect the study of God's word for a study of theories which are misleading, which divert minds from the words of Christ to the fallacies of human production. God would have all who profess to be gospel medical missionaries learn diligently the lessons of the great Teacher. This they must do if they would find rest and peace. Learning of Christ, their hearts will be filled with the peace that He alone can give.

Make the Bible the man of your counsel. Your acquaintance with it will grow rapidly if you keep your minds free from the rubbish of the world. The more the Bible is studied, the deeper will be your knowledge of God. The truths of His word will be written in your soul, making an ineffaceable impression.

These things God has been opening to me for many years. In our medical missionary training schools we need men who have a deep knowledge of the Scriptures, men who have learned the lessons taught in the Word of God, and who can teach these lessons to others clearly and simply, just as Christ taught His disciples that which He deemed most essential.

And the needed knowledge will be given to all who come to Christ, receiving and practising His teachings, making His word a part of their lives. The holy Spirit teaches the student of the Scriptures to judge all things by the standard of righteousness and truth and justice. The divine revelation supplies him with the knowledge that he needs. Those who place themselves under the instruction of the great Medical Missionary to be workers together with Him, will have a knowledge that the world, with all its traditionary lore, can not supply.

Ellen G. White

* * * * *

Memorial

To the General Conference Council, convened at College View, Nebr., Oct. 1909:

Dear Brethren,

We, the Faculty of the Loma Linda College of Evangelists, at the request of the Southern California Conference, hereby submit the following memorial.

In the great work of reform committed to us as a people, the necessity of capable workers in the line of the treatment of diseases and the general care of physical beings cannot be denied by any one who believes such statements as the following:

"The rich and wonderful provisions of the Gospel embraces the medical missionary work. This work is to be to the third angel's message as the right arm to the body. Some have endeavored to make it the head, but this is not right." Unpublished MS.

Again: "There are souls in many places who have not yet heard the message, henceforth the medical missionary work is to be carried forward with an earnestness with which it has never yet been carried. This work is the door through which the truth is to find entrance to the large cities. And Sanitariums are to be established in many places.

Again in speaking of the work of Luke we read:

"His medical skill opened the way for the Gospel message to find access to hearts. It opened many doors to Him giving him opportunities to preach the Gospel to the heathen."

That the departure from right principles is no less in the medical line than it is in the Educational and spiritual lines and that we need medical schools established upon Christian principles to prepare our physicians for their work in connection with the message just as certainly as such schools are needed to prepare our ministers and teachers for their work. Also the fact that the education to be obtained in schools of the world is so deeply dyed with false theories and skepticism that it utterly fails to qualify its recipient for a place in the work which is to be done, is clearly set forth in the following:

"Great care should be exercised in the training of young people for the medical missionary work, for the mind is molded by that which it receives and retains." Unpublished MS.

Again: "Study the Bible more, and the theories of the medical fraternities less, and you will have greater spiritual health. Your mind will be clearer and more vigorous. Much that is embraced in the medical course is positively unnecessary. Those who take a medical training, spend a great deal of time in learning that which is merely rubbish. Many of the theories that they learn may be compared in value to the traditions and maxims taught by the scribes and pharisees. Many of the intricacies with which they have to become familiar are an injury to their minds. These things God has been opening before me for many years." Instruction to Medical Missionaries, Oct. 17, 1903. (B-241-03)

"Their work should be more decidedly combined with the study of God's word. Ideas are inculcated that are not at all necessary, and the necessary things do not receive sufficient attention. While students are being educated in this way, they are being made less able to do acceptable work for the Master. The taxation that they undergo to obtain an extended knowledge in medical lines, unfits them for work as they should in ministerial lines...... Thus some are disqualified for the work that they might have done had they begun missionary work where it is needed, and let the medical line come in as an essential part connected with the work of the gospel ministry as a whole, as the hand is connected with the body."

That God has been endeavoring to lead us out into a position where we could work untrammeled by worldly influences is clearly shown in our past experiences and the instruction and reproof which have come to us in connection with these experiences. The need of medical missionary workers urged upon us by the Spirit of Prophecy led to the establishment of schools for training nurses in our sanitariums. This was a step in the right direction, but did not wholly supply the need. Still urged forward by the necessity of the situation and the Spirit of Prophecy we attempted to provide for the education of physicians by the establishment of the A.M.M.C. but when we came to receive our young people as students in this college, we found them deficient in many cases in preparatory work. The proposition to give them this preparatory work in outside schools was met by the Spirit of Prophecy in such words as the following:

If there are legal requirements making it necessary that medical students shall take a certain preparatory course of study, let our colleges teach the required additional studies in a manner consistent with Christian education... They should arrange to carry their students to the point of literary and scientific training that is necessary. Many of these requirements have been made because so much of the preparatory work done in ordinary schools is superficial.

It is not necessary for so many of our youth to study medicine. But for those who should take medical studies our Union Conference training-schools should make ample provision in facilities for preparatory education." The Review and Herald, October 15, 1903.

Acting under this advice, our schools introduced lines of study calculated to qualify students to enter the medical course. Thus by the Spirit of Prophecy we were prevented from making an improper alliance with the education furnished by the world.

In 1898 by the gift of Prophecy God pointed out the departure which was being made in the work of the A.M.M.C. by many Testimonies, of which the following is a sample.

"Remember now, my Brother, that medical missionary work is not to take men from the ministry, but is to place men in the field better qualified to minister because of their knowledge of medical missionary work. Young men should receive an education in medical missionary lines and then should go forth to connect with the ministry. Those who are receiving an education in medical missionary lines, (Referring to the students of the A.M.M.C.) hear insinuations from time to time that disparage the church and the ministry. These insinuations are seeds that will spring up and bear fruit. The student might better be educated to realize that the Church of Christ on earth is to be respected. They need a clear knowledge of the reasons of our faith. This knowledge they must have in order to serve God acceptably. Line upon line, precept upon precept, they must receive the Bible evidence of the truths that are hid in Jesus.

Do not, I beg of you, instill in the minds of the students ideas that will cause them to lose confidence in God's appointed ministers. But this you are certainly doing whether you are aware of it or not."

At the General Conference in 1901, in an article entitled, Instruction Regarding the School Work, read before the delegates in April 22, it was pointed out that all our medical students were not to receive their training at the one medical College at Battle Creek. Of our schools that were introducing educational reform, Sister White read: (G.C.B. 455-1901) "We are thankful that an interest is being shown in the work of establishing our schools on a right foundation, as they should have been established years ago. If the proper education is given to students, it is a positive necessity to establish our schools at a distance from the cities, where the students can do manual work.... Altho there be a few students at first, do not be discouraged. The school will win its way. Introduce the medical missionary work. Some of the students are to be educated as nurses, some as physicians. It is not necessary for our students to go to Ann Arbor for a medical education. They may obtain at our schools all the education that is essential to perform the work for this time. It will take some time to get a right understanding of the matter, but just as soon as we begin to work in the line of true reform, the Holy Spirit will lead us and guide us, if we are willing to be guided... All must place themselves under the influence of the Holy Spirit. When they place themselves under the influence of the Holy Spirit they will accommodate themselves to Bible lines. When the Word of God takes possession of the minds of the teachers, then they are fitted to deal with the education of others... The Word of God is to stand as the foundation of all education. It is to be made the basis of all the schools that we establish."

Thus we see that eight years ago, God foreseeing the calamity that would come upon the one Medical School, then in operation among us, counseled the establishment of other schools in which both nurses and physicians were to be educated. In pointing out the defectiveness of the A.M.M.C., and the necessity of giving the Bible its proper place in a medical education the following instruction was given; which instruction should have been our guide in our school work.

This instruction is contained in a letter dated Oct. 17, 1903, and addressed "To our Medical Missionaries," and is as follows: (B-241-'03)

"God would have all who profess to be gospel medical missionaries learn diligently the lessons of the Great Teacher... The one book that is essential for all to study is the Bible. Studied with reverence, and Godly Fear, it is the greatest of all educators... In our medical schools and institutions we need men who have a deeper knowledge of the Scriptures... Because the Word of God has been neglected, strange things have been done in the medical missionary work of late. The Lord cannot accept the present showing."

During the years 1901 to 1904 the mind of the Servant of God was directed in a special way to Southern California as a field in which the medical missionary work was to be given great prominence by the establishment of at least four sanitariums. One of these was to be located near the towns of Riverside and Redlands. During the session of the General Conference four years ago, under the direction and imperative demand of the Spirit of Prophecy, Loma Linda was purchased, situated four miles from Redlands and about nine miles from Riverside. Soon sanitarium work was begun at this place. This was followed immediately by Testimonies which have continued to come up to the present time, both guiding and urging forward the work. Extracts from these testimonies are as follows:

"Loma Linda is to be not only a sanitarium, but an educational center. With the possession of this place comes the weighty responsibility of making the work of the institution, educational in character. A school is to be established here for the training of gospel, medical missionary, evangelists. In regard to the school, I would say, make it especially strong in the education of nurses and physicians. In medical missionary schools, many workers are to be qualified with the ability of physicians to labor as medical missionary evangelists. Make the schools especially strong for nurses and physicians.

I have clear instructions that wherever it is possible schools should be established near to our sanitariums, that each institution may be a help to the other." Acting under the advice of these communications, steps were taken to establish the Loma Linda College of Evangelists. This was opposed by some, and a communication was sent of which the following is an extract:

* * * * *

Be very careful not to do anything that would restrict the work at Loma Linda. It is in the order of God that this property has been secured, and He has given instruction that a school should be connected with the sanitarium. A special work is to be done there in qualifying young men and young women to be efficient medical missionary workers. They are to be taught how to treat the sick without the use of drugs. Such an education requires an experience in practical work. The work at Loma Linda demands immediate consideration. Preparations must be made for the school to be opened as soon as possible. Our young men and young women are to find in Loma Linda a school where they can receive a medical missionary training, where they will not be brought under the influence of some who are seeking to undermine the truth. The students are to unite faithfully in the medical work, keeping their physical powers in the most perfect condition possible, and laboring under the instruction of the Great Medical Missionary. The healing of the sick, and ministry of the work, are to go hand in hand."

In harmony with this instruction, the school was established with medical evangelistic course designing to qualify workers with all the ability of physicians, in harmony with the testimonies given. In connection with the opening of the school the following was sent:

* * * * *

"Much is involved in this work and it is very essential that a right beginning be made. The Lord has a special work to be done in this field. He instructed me to call on Elder and Mrs. Haskell, to help us in getting properly started, a work similar to that they had carried on at Avondale."

After the school was thus organized, and our first class had nearly completed their second year in the medical course, testimonies came from which the following are extracts, dated April 23, 1908.

(B-132-08) "There is a very precious work to be done in connection with the interest of the sanitarium and school at Loma Linda, and this will be done when all work to that end. Ever bear in mind that Heaven is interested in every question that agitates your mind in regard to your school and sanitarium. Both are to be strengthened... In our school at Loma Linda many can be educated to work as missionaries in the cause of Health and Temperance. The best teachers are to be employed in this educational work not men who esteem highly their own capabilities, but men who will walk circumspectly, depending wholly upon the Lord."

That this school is not to be patterned after worldly standards of medical education, is shown by the following:

* * * * *

(B-90-'08) "In the work of the school, maintain simplicity. No argument is so powerful as is success founded upon simplicity. You may attain success in the education of students as medical missionaries without a medical school that can qualify physicians to compete with the physicians of the world. Let the students be given a practical education. The less dependent you are upon worldly methods of education, the better it will be for the students. Special instruction should be given in the art of treating the sick without the use of poisonous drugs and in harmony with the light that God has given.... In the treatment of the sick, poisonous drugs need not be used... Students should come forth from the school without having sacrificed the principles of health reform or their love for God and righteousness.

The education that meets the world's standard is to be less and less valued by those who are seeking for efficiency in carrying the medical missionary work in connection with the work of the third angel's message. They are to be educated from the standpoint of conscience and, as they conscientiously and faithfully follow right methods in their treatment of the sick, these methods will come to be recognized as preferable to the method of nursing to which many have become accustomed, which demand the use of poisonous drugs."

While the work of the school is largely to be the fitting up of many to labor as Medical Evangelists, yet, that some are to be prepared as fully qualified physicians is shown by the following, which was sent in the Fall of 1906 in response to a question as to the scope, and work, of the school.

"Make the school especially strong in the preparation of nurses and physicians."

"Much good can be done by those who do not hold diplomas as fully accredited physicians. Many working under their direction can do acceptable work without spending so long a time in study as it has been thought necessary to spend in the past."

Feb. 21, 1908, in a testimony addressed "The Work in Southern California," we find the following:

* * * * *

(MS-3-'08.) "Southern Calif. is a field that should depend more than it has upon its own resources. It should have more facilities, and should not be cramped as it has been in some respects. Southern Calif. is a missionary field, a large part of which has received but little missionary effort. Henceforth it should receive more attention. The various lines of work that can be carried on should be diligently studied, and the advantages of such cities as Redlands and Riverside and the need of putting forth decided effort for them, faithfully investigated... It was the Lord who placed in our possession the sanitarium at Loma Linda.... In Loma Linda we have an advantageous center for carrying on various missionary enterprises. We can see that it was in the providence of God that this sanitarium was placed in the possession of our people. We should appreciate Loma Linda as a place which the Lord foresaw we should need, and which He gave."

These testimonies coming to us as they did, after the purchase of the three sanitariums and the establishment of the school at Loma Linda, with classes organized and operating in at least two years of the medical work, led us to believe that we had not yet reached the standard in the mind of God. Consequently at the recent General Conference, an effort was made to bring about a proper consideration of the Loma Linda School.

A lack of time prevented this, altho it was given some attention. This resulted in a recommendation involving a plan whereby the Loma Linda school should give two years of a medical course, and provide by affiliation with outside schools for the recognition of this work, thus enabling the students of our school to complete the medical course in schools which already have state recognition.

This plan was laid before Sister White, and the result is seen in the following conversation which occurred in September 20, 1909:

(MS-105-'09) Mrs. E. G. White: "We want none of that kind of higher education, that will put us in a position where the credit must be given, not to the Lord God of Israel, but to the God of Ekron. The Lord designs that we shall stand as a distinct, sanctified and holy people, so connected with Him that He can work with us. Let our physicians realize that they are to depend wholly upon the true God. I felt a heavy burden this morning, when I read over the letter that I found in my room, in which a plan was outlined for having medical students take some work at Loma Linda, but to get the finishing touches of their education from some worldly institution. God forbid that such a plan should be followed. I must state that the light I have received is, that we are to stand as a distinct, commandment-keeping people. The Sabbath is the great distinguishing line, and its observance will separate us from the world. As God's peculiar people, we should not feel that we must acknowledge our dependence upon men who are transgressing God's law, to give us influence in the world. It is God that gives us influence. He is our exceeding great reward. He will give us advantages that are far beyond all the advantages that we might receive from worldlings by uniting with those who do not recognize the Law of God."

Elder J. A. Burden: "I know that these thoughts are what you have presented before. We do not want to cause you to carry a heavy burden. We simply wanted to know if we were moving in right lines. If the Lord gives you light, well and good, we will be glad to receive it, if not then we will wait."

E. G. White: "If we follow on to know the Lord, we shall know that His going forth is prepared as the morning. There are some who may not be able to see that here is a test, as to whether we shall put our dependence on man or depend upon God. Shall we by our course seem to acknowledge that there is a stronger power with unbelievers than there is with God's own people? When we take hold upon God, and trust in him, He will work in our behalf. But whatever the consequences may be, we are, in regard to our faith, to stand distinct and separate from the world. I feel a decided interest in the work at Loma Linda, and I desire that it shall exert a powerful influence for the truth. Your success depends upon the blessing of God, not upon

[444] the ideas and views of men who are opposed to the requirements of the law of God. When people see that God blesses us, and gives success to our work, as we make Him supreme, then they will be led to give consideration to the truth we teach. Many will be compelled to recognize that our methods are superior to those employed in the schools of the world, as they are commonly conducted. We need not tie to men in order to secure influence, we need not think that we are dependent upon the knowledge and experience of men who do not recognize the Lord as their Master. Our God is a God of knowledge and understanding, and if we will take our position decidedly on His side, to be wholly influenced by His spirit, He will give us wisdom. I would that all our people might see the inconsistency of those who profess to be God's Commandment-keeping people, a peculiar people, zealous of good works, thinking that they must copy after the world's pattern in order to make their work successful. Our God is stronger than any human influence. If we will accept Him as our educator, if we will make Him our strength and righteousness, He will work in our behalf. The following out of these principles, may result in a condition of things that is not just as we desire it to be. We might like to see certain conditions for the attainment of which we would be dependent on the world, but the result would be an experience that means weakness rather than strength. We should realize a bondage that we do not anticipate. Jesus Christ is our Saviour today, and He is willing to work in our behalf, if we will not put our dependence upon some other power. If we are sustained by the living God a superiority of His power will be manifest in His people. This is the testimony that I will continue to bear. We must exalt God, who is our wisdom, our sanctification, and our exceeding great reward.... Shall we unite ourselves with those who are full of error, who have no respect for God's commandments, and shall our students go forth to obtain the finishing touches of their education from men who unless they are converted, will not be honored with a place in the councils of Heaven?

W. C. White: "What is to be the final outcome? Will all our medical missionaries be simply nurses? Shall we have no more physicians? Or shall we have a school in which we can ourselves give the finishing touches?"

E. G. White: "Whatever plan you follow, take your position that you will not unite or be bound up with those that do not respect God's Commandments."

W. C. White: "Does that mean that we are not to have any more physicians? But that our people shall work simply as nurses? Or does it mean that we shall have a school of our own where we can educate physicians?"

E. G. White: "We shall have a school of our own. But we are not to be dependent upon the world. We must put our dependence upon a power that is higher than all human strength, if we honor God, He will honor us, because we observe His Commandments, which means eternal life.

J. A. Burden: "The governments of earth provide that if we conduct a medical school, we must take a charter from the Government. That in itself has nothing to do with how the school is conducted. It is required, however, that certain studies be taught. Physiology is one of these. It is required that those who labor as physicians shall be proficient in those subjects. In starting sanitariums for the care of the sick, we must secure a charter from the government. Our printing office must do the same. Would the securing of a charter for a medical school, where our students might obtain a medical education, militate against our depending upon God?

E. G. White: "No, I do not see that it would, if a charter was secured on right terms. Only be sure that you do not exalt men above God. If you can gain force and influence that will make your work more effective without tying yourselves to worldly men, that would be right. But we are not to exalt the human above the Divine."

Elder J. A. Burden: "That is the vital point where we have been hanging for three years. The only thing that we have asked for in this matter is to take advantage of the Government provision that would give standing room to our students when they are qualified."

Mrs. E. G. White: "I do not see anything wrong in that as long as you do not in any way lift men above the Lord God of Israel, or throw discredit upon His power. But enter into no agreement with any fraternity that would open a door of temptation to some weak soul to lose their hold on God."

We take this to be an unqualified statement that we are to have a chartered school for the education and training of physicians, as well as nurses. But in the conducting of this school, we are to recognize the power of God as superior to all earthly powers. And while thus relying upon Him, we have certain rights and privileges as citizens which we can use as did the apostle Paul to advantage for the truth, the right to charter our school being one of these.

We therefore solicit your endorsement and assistance in placing the school upon a successful working basis, so that it may accomplish what the Lord has designed that it shall.

We sincerely hope that you will give this question careful consideration, that the work that has now been hanging in the balance and retarded for four years, may be pushed forward with alacrity and certainty.

* * * * *

Condensed Memorial

Presented to the General Conference Council Convened at College View, Nebr. Oct., 1909

Loma Linda College of Evangelists

"With the possession of this place comes the weighty responsibility of making the work of the institution educational in character."

"Loma Linda is to be not only a sanitarium, but an educational center."

"A school is to be established here for the training of gospel medical missionary evangelists. Much is involved in this work, and it is very essential that a right beginning be made."

"In regard to the school, I would say, Make it especially strong in the education of nurses and physicians."

"Too much imperfect work has been done in the education given. The most useful education is that gained by study in connection with practical work."

"In medical missionary schools many workers are to be qualified with the ability of physicians to labor as medical missionary evangelists. This training the Lord has specified is in harmony with the principles underlying true higher education."

"Some of the students are to be educated as nurses, some as physicians. It is not necessary for our students to go to Ann Arbor for a medical education. They may obtain at our schools all that is essential to perform the work for this time."

"It will take some time to get a right understanding of the matter, but just as soon as we begin to work in the line of true reform, the Holy Spirit will lead us and guide us if we are willing to be guided."

"Much good can be done by those who do not hold diplomas as fully accredited physicians. Some are to be prepared to work as competent physicians. Many working under the direction of such ones can do acceptable work without spending so long a time in study as it has been thought necessary in the past."

We ought to have a school where women can be educated by women physicians to do the best possible work in treating the diseases of women."

To us, it seems clear from the foregoing testimonies that there are at least three classes of workers to be educated in medical lines,

* * * * *

[447]　First, Many well trained nurses to work as evangelists;

Second, A large number of persons qualified with the ability of physicians to labor as evangelists;

Third, a few fully accredited physicians with recognition to stand at the head of the work.

* * * * *

**Sanitarium, Calif.,
B.-132-'09. Oct. 11, 1909.
Elder J. A. Burden:**
Dear Brother,

I am instructed to say that in our educational work, there is to be no compromise in order to meet the world's standards. God's commandment-keeping people are not to unite with the world, to carry various lines of work according to worldly plans and worldly wisdom.

Our people are now being tested as to whether they will obtain their wisdom from the greatest Teacher the world ever knew or seek to the God of Ekron. Let us determine that we shall not be tied by so much as a thread to the educational policies of those who do not discern the voice of God, and who will not hearken to His commandments.

We are to take heed to the warning: "Enter ye in at the straight gate: for wide is the gate, and broad is the way, that leadeth to destruction, and many there be which go in thereat; because straight is the gate, and narrow is the way, which leadeth into life, and few there be that find it." Those who walk in the narrow way are following in the footprints of Jesus. The light from heaven illuminates their path.

Shall we represent before the world, that our physicians must follow the pattern of the world, before they can be qualified to act as successful physicians? This is the question that is now testing the faith of some of our brethren. Let not any of our brethren displease the Lord, by advocating in their assemblies the idea that we need to obtain from unbelievers a higher education than that specified by the Lord.

The representation of the great Teacher is to be considered an all-sufficient revelation. Those in our ranks who qualify as physicians are to receive only such education as is in harmony with these divine truths. Some have advised that students should, after taking some work at Loma Linda, complete their medical education in worldly colleges. But this is not in harmony with the Lord's plan. God is our wisdom, our sanctification, and our righteousness. Facilities should be provided at Loma Linda, that the necessary instruction in medical lines may be given by instructors who fear the Lord, and who are in harmony with His plans for the treatment of the sick.

[448]

I have not a word to say in favor of the world's ideas of higher education in any school that we shall organize for the training of physicians. There is danger in their attaching themselves to worldly physicians. Satan is giving his orders to those whom he has led to depart from the faith. I would now advise that none of our young people attach themselves to worldly medical institutions in the hope of gaining better success, or stronger influence as physicians.

When Israel was a child then I loved him, and called My son out of Egypt. As they called them, so they went from them: they sacrificed unto Baalim, and burnt incense to graven images. I taught Ephraim also to go, taking them by their arm; but they knew not that I healed them. I drew them with cords of a man, with bands of love: and I was to them as they that take off the yoke on their jaws, and I laid meat unto them."

The Lord gave to His people advantages which they failed to recognize. "My people," He says, "are bent to backsliding from Me; though they called them to the Most High, none at all would exalt Him. How shall I give thee up, Ephraim? How shall I deliver thee, Israel? how shall I make thee as Admah? how shall I set thee as Zeboim? Mine heart is turned within Me, My repentings are kindled together." Read also the promises of blessing to Israel on condition of their repentance, recorded in the fourteenth chapter of Hosea. These scriptures were written in times past, but they have also a present-day application.

The enemy has worked in Southern California, and has tried to thwart the purposes of God. Messages of reproof have been sent to leading men whose work was not done in righteousness. Reformations have been called for. What is now needed is that the leaders in the Lord's work shall be fully converted. It is time that the Lord's voice was heeded, and that men should put away the spirit of self-confidence and self-sufficiency. Should the ideas of some who are wise in their own estimation be carried out, there would result a condition of things that would demand a most thorough reformation.

Let none think that they can pass safely through the perils of these last days, while puffed up with self-sufficiency. Some would unsettle minds by urging the carrying out of false plans. False theories are taught as truth, and I am charged to meet these errors decidedly. We should heed the instruction found in the third and fourth chapters of second Timothy, especially the solemn charge given by Paul to Timothy:

"I charge thee, therefore, before God, and the Lord Jesus Christ, who shall judge the quick and the dead at His appearing; preach the Word; be instant in season, out of season; reprove, rebuke, exhort, with all long-suffering and doctrine. For the time will come when they will not endure sound doctrine, but after their own lusts shall they heap to themselves teachers, having itching ears; and they shall turn away their ears from the truth, and shall be turned unto fables. But watch thou in all things, endure afflictions, do the work of an evangelist, make full proof of thy ministry.

"I am now ready to be offered, and the time of my departure is at hand. I have fought a good fight, I have finished my course, I have kept the faith: henceforth there is laid up for me a crown of righteousness, which the Lord, the righteous Judge, shall give me in that day; and not to me only, but unto all them also that love His appearing."

I am intensely in earnest that our people shall realize that the only true education lies in walking humbly with God. The teachings of the word of God are opposed to the ideas of those who think that our students must receive the mold of an education that is according to human ideas. Some are departing from the faith, as the result of receiving from the world what they regard as a "higher education." The word of God just as it reads contains the very essence of truth. The highest education is the keeping of the law of God.

"Therefore, my brethren dearly beloved and longed for, my joy and crown, so stand fast in the Lord, my dearly beloved... Let your moderation be known unto all men. The Lord is at hand. Be careful for nothing; but in everything by prayer and supplication with thanksgiving let your requests be made known unto God. And the peace of God, which passeth all understanding, shall keep your hearts and minds through Christ Jesus.

"Finally, brethren, whatsoever things are true, whatsoever things are honest, whatsoever things are just, whatsoever things are pure, whatsoever things are lovely, whatsoever things are of good report; if there be any virtue, and if there be any praise, think on these things. Those things which ye have both learned, and received, and heard, and seen in me, do: and the God of peace shall be with you."

* * * * *

[450]

[451]

[452]

Sanitarium, Calif.,
B.-140-09. Nov. 5, 1909.
Elder J. A. Burden, Loma Linda, Calif.:
Dear Brother Burden,

Some questions have been asked me regarding our relation to the laws governing medical practitioners. We need to move understandingly, for the enemy would be pleased to hedge up our work so that our physicians would have only a limited influence. Some men do not act in the fear of God, and they may seek to bring us into trouble by placing on our necks yokes that we could not consent to bear. We cannot submit to regulations if the sacrifice of principle is involved; for this would imperil the soul's salvation.

But whenever we can comply with the law of the land without putting ourselves in a false position, we should do so. Wise laws have been framed in order to safeguard the people against the imposition of unqualified physicians. These laws we should respect, for we are ourselves by them protected from presumptuous pretenders.

Should we manifest opposition to these requirements, it would tend to restrict the influence of our medical missionaries.

[453] We must carefully consider what is involved in these matters. If there are conditions to which we could not subscribe, we should endeavor to have these matters adjusted, so that there would not be strong opposition against our physicians. The Saviour bids us be wise as serpents, and harmless as doves.

The Lord is our leader and teacher, He charges us not to connect with those who do not acknowledge God.

"Verily My Sabbaths ye shall keep, for it is a sign between Me and you throughout your generations." Connect with those who honor God by keeping His commandments. If the recommendation goes forth from our people that our workers are to seek for success by acknowledging as essential the education which the world gives, we are virtually saying that the influence the world gives is superior to that which God gives. God will be dishonored by such a course. God has full knowledge of the faith and trust and confidence that His professed people have in His providence.

Our workers are to become intelligent in regard to Christ's life and manner of working. The Lord will help those who desire to cooperate with Him as physicians, if they will become learners of Him how to work for the suffering. He will exercise His power through them for the healing of the sick.

Intemperance and ungodliness are increasing everywhere. The work of temperance must begin in our own hearts. And the work of the physician must begin in an understanding of the works and teachings of the Great Physician. Christ left the courts of heaven that He might minister to the sick and suffering of earth. We must cooperate with the Chief of Physicians, walking in all humility of mind before Him. Then the Lord will bless our earnest efforts to relieve the suffering of Humanity. It is not by the use of poisonous drugs that this will be done, but by the use of simple remedies. We should seek to correct false habits and practices, and teach the lessons of self-denial. The indulgence of appetite is the greatest evil with which we have to contend.

The truth brought to light by Christ teaches that humanity through obedience to the truth as it is in Jesus, may realize power to overcome the corruptions that are in the world through lust. Through living faith in the merits of Christ the soul may be converted and transformed into Christlikeness. Angels of God will be by the side of those who in humbleness of mind learn daily the lessons taught by Christ.

*****

B.168-09. Dec. 1, 1909.

Extracts from Testimony

To the Officers of the General Conference:
Dear Brethren,

In the night seasons I seem to be repeating the messages of warning and encouragement that I bore at the General Conference and I am instructed to urge upon our people that we, as the people of God, are not to follow the customs and fashions of the world. The world is following their leader, the great apostate; and we are to follow the Great Teacher, Jesus Christ.

I have endeavored to arouse our people to labor for the unworked portions of the great Missionary field, yet but few seem to respond to the appeals of the Spirit of God. We do not realize the extent to which Satanic agencies are at work in these large cities. The work of bringing the messages of present truth before the people is becoming more and more difficult. It is essential that new and varied talents unite in intelligent labor for the people. If the burden of these unworked cities rested upon the hearts of our people as it should, they would arouse to labor as they have not yet done for the souls that are perishing in sin...

The message that I am bidden to bear to our people at this time is, Work the cities without delay, for time is short. The Lord has kept this work before us for the last twenty years or more. A little has been done in a few places, but much more might be done. I am carrying a burden day and night, because so little is being accomplished to warn the inhabitants of our great centers of population of the judgments that will fall upon the transgressors of God's law...

It will be a great advantage to have our buildings in retired locations so far as possible. The healthfulness of the surroundings should be fully considered. Locations should be selected a little out from the noisy cities. Those who labor in the large cities need special advantages, that they may not be called to sacrifice life or health unnecessarily.

I write these things because it has been presented to me as a matter of importance that our workers should so far as possible avoid everything that would imperil their health. We need to exercise the best of judgment in these matters. Feeble or aged men and women should not be sent to labor in unhealthful crowded cities. Let them labor where their lives will not be needlessly sacrificed. Our brethren who bring the truth to the cities must not be obliged to imperil their health in the noise and bustle and confusion, if retired places can be secured.

Those who are engaged in the difficult and trying work in the cities should receive every encouragement possible. Let them not be subjected to unkind criticism from their brethren. We must have a care for the Lord's workers who are opening the light of truth to those who are in the darkness of error. We have a high standard presented before us....

Now is the opportune time to work the cities; for we must reach the people there. As a people, we have been in danger of centering too many important interests in a few places. This is not good judgment nor wisdom. An interest is now to be created in the principle cities. Many small centers must be established rather than a few large centers...

Let missionaries be laboring two and two in different parts of all our large cities. The workers in each city should frequently meet together for prayer and counsel, that they may have wisdom and grace to work together effectively and harmoniously. Let all be wide awake to make the most of every advantage. Our people must gird the armor on and establish centers in all the large cities. The agencies of Satan are active in the field, putting forth efforts to confuse the minds of men, and to fill them with vain imaginations, that they may not become interested in the truth.

The people of God have received many admonitions and encouragements to advance, and it is time that the purposes of God regarding His work shall be understood by them and carried out. By cherishing unbelief in the plans and directions that have been laid out for them to follow, and by exalting human judgment, much time and valuable experience have been lost. The Lord, He is God, and beside Him there is none else. Let all now search the word of the Lord, and walk in His ways. Let the prophecies of Isaiah be studied and heeded, and the Lord will perform His part. "Search the Scriptures; for in them ye think ye have eternal life."

While no one should be presumptuous, there is need that wise efforts be put forth to reach many who by the ordinary methods of labor are not reached. Let the leading men and women, chosen of God, unite in carrying forward the work intelligently and in faith. I am pained when I see with some a desire for the highest position, and to be honored of men. This is not the leading of the Holy Spirit. Angels of God are commissioned to labor with every company that will work humbly and intelligently. Truth and righteousness must go forth as a lamp that burneth...

Ellen G. White

* * * * *

To the Leading Ministers in California

**Sanitarium, Calif.,
B-178-'09. Dec. 6, 1909.**

Dear Brethren,

In the night watches of Nov. 22, I seemed to be bearing my testimony in a meeting where believers and unbelievers were assembled. I spoke to them in regard to the short work to be done in the earth, and our need of keeping before the world the evidences that the Lord is in our midst. This evidence may be given in words of praise and thanksgiving. Whoso offereth praise glorifieth God." The Lord calls for faithful witnesses. With our lips and in our works, we should praise Him. As a people we have received special advantages from the Lord, but we do not render to Him sincere thanksgiving. Daily His praise should be spoken by every one of us.

[462]

My attention was called to these words, which are profitable for our study:

"I am the Lord, and there is none else, there is no God beside Me: I girded thee, though thou hast not known Me; that they may know from the rising of the sun, and from the West, that there is none beside Me. I am the Lord, and there is none else; I form light, and create darkness; I make peace, and create evil: I the Lord do all these things. Drop down, ye heavens from above, and let the skies pour down righteousness: let the earth open, and let them bring forth salvation, and let righteousness spring up together. I the Lord have created it." (Isaiah 45:5-8)

"Thus saith the Lord, in an acceptable time have I heard thee, and in a day of salvation have I helped thee: and I will preserve thee, and give thee for a covenant of the people, to establish the earth, to cause to inherit the desolate heritage that thou mayest say to the prisoners, Go forth; to them that are in darkness, show thyselves. They shall feed in the ways, and their pastures shall be in all high places. They shall not hunger nor thirst; neither shall the heat nor sun smite them; for He that hath mercy on them shall lead them, even by the spring of water shall He guide them. And I will make all My mountains a way, and My highways shall be exalted. Behold these shall come from far; and lo, these from the north and from the west; and these from the land of Sinim.

"Sing, O ye heavens, and be joyful; and break forth unto singing, O mountains: for the Lord hath comforted His people, and will have mercy on His afflicted. But Zion said, the Lord hath forsaken me, and my Lord hath forgotten me. Can a woman forget her sucking child, that she may not have compassion on the son of her womb? yea, they may forget, yet will I not forget thee. Behold, I have graven thee upon the palms of My hands; thy walls are continually before me." (Isaiah 49:8-16)

"Ho, every one that thirsteth, come ye to the waters, and he that hath no money; come ye, buy and eat; yea, come buy wine and milk without money and without price. Wherefore do ye spend money for that which is not bread? and your labor for that which satisfieth not? hearken diligently unto Me, and eat ye that which is good, and let your soul delight itself in fatness. Incline your ear, and come unto Me; hear, and your soul shall live and I will make an everlasting covenant with you, even the sure mercies of David. Behold, I have given Him for a witness to the people, a leader and a commander to the people. Behold thou shalt call a nation that you knowest not; and nations that know not thee shall run after thee, because of the Lord thy God, and for the holy One of Israel; for He hath glorified thee." (Isaiah 55:1-5)

(Isaiah 55:6-13)

Let the instruction given in the fifty-eighth chapter of Isaiah be studied in connection with these Scriptures. Wonderful would be the results if ministers and church members would be converted, and adopt Christ's manner of witnessing to the power of the Lord.

In many places, and especially in Southern California plans and methods of labor have been followed that have hindered the Lord's work, so that those upon whom the Lord has laid special burdens could not do the work to which they were appointed. In some cases watchers were set to restrict the work and to hedge up the way of some who were laboring most earnestly for advancement (of the work. erp, 1960).

Unsanctified plans were laid that worked counter to the plans of God. All this was greatly displeasing to the Lord, and it was work which He repudiated. There were cities that might have been entered and a good work begun, but through lack of faith there developed a counter-working influence. With unbelief, jealousies arose, and with sacred missionary enterprises were linked up men who themselves needed to experience the converting power of God, and to learn to walk humbly before Him.

To those who had kept the way hedged up, I wrote out the instruction given me, and trusted the result with the Lord. The burden was heavy, and I feared I should not live to see the results of my efforts to break the yokes which men were placing upon their fellow-workers. The Lord presented before me in decided representations that it would take years to root out the evil resulting from placing in the hands of finite men the power to hinder and delay the work of God. Repeated messages of reproof and counsel were necessary, that capable men whom the Lord had specified as the ones to do a special work might be set free to follow the light that God was giving.

There were strong men in Southern California who stood decidedly against the light the Lord was giving His messenger regarding the work to be done. They were following their own counsel and judgment, and were imperiling the cause of God. I was instructed that the only way to counterwork this evil was to have placed in positions of trust men who would be guided by counsel of the Lord, and who would not be turned aside by those who were deficient in faith.

The Lord has wrought in a remarkable manner to uphold the messages sent to correct the strange work that was being done. The evil has been checked, but it has not yet been fully rooted out, and if there were not a continuation of the messages from the Lord to His people, the will and ways of men would yet prevail to bring in strife and contention, and a deformed work would be the result. I was shown that human power is constantly working to weave itself into the work of God. This brings in disjointed and inharmonious action. The messages of pure and unadulterated truth are in danger of being trampled under feet by self-willed unconverted men who work to destroy confidence in the warnings that God would speak to the hearts of His people to correct error, and to encourage righteousness.

A great many of the difficulties that have come into our work in California and elsewhere have come in through a misunderstanding on the part of men in official positions concerning their individual responsibility in the matter of controlling and ruling their fellow-laborers. Men entrusted with responsibilities have supposed that their official position embraced very much more than was ever thought of by those who placed them in office, and serious difficulties arose as the result.

Simple organization and church order are set forth in the New Testament Scriptures, and the Lord has ordained these for the unity and perfection of the church. The man who holds office in the church should stand as a leader, as an adviser and a counselor and helper in carrying the burdens of the work. He should be a leader in offering thanksgiving to God. But he is not appointed to order and command the Lord's laborers. The Lord is over His heritage. He will lead His people if they will be led of the Lord in the place of assuming a power God has not given them. Let us study the twelfth and thirteenth chapters of First Corinthians, and the fifteenth chapter of Acts.

Let the men carrying responsibilities treat those who labor with them with the same consideration that they would wish to receive, were they the helpers, and others the leaders. "All ye are brethren," the Saviour declares. Position does not give a man kingly authority. The meekness of Christ is a wonderful lesson given to the fallen world. Learning this meekness from the great Teacher, the worker will become Christlike.

For several years there have been leading men in the Northern California Conference who exercised an authority which they supposed was theirs by virtue of their office, to control the work according to their own disposition and judgment. The work was becoming confused, and the Lord gave me a message regarding the movements that should be made. Because of the strange conditions in the conference, Elder Haskell was to be called to take the presidency.

Elder Haskell and his wife have been engaged in the work for years, and their faith in the truth and in the Testimonies given by the Holy Spirit is strong. They have unitedly served according to the Lord's appointment, and we have sought to sustain them in their work. Conditions in the churches have changed decidedly, but the Lord has shown me that some in responsible positions are not yet converted, and without thorough conversion, they cannot conduct the work in right lines. Some who have been reproved and warned are not established and settled, and fully yielded to the guiding power of the Holy Spirit. Satan is not yet fully cast out of the minds of some, and it would take very little to produce again the conditions that existed ten years ago.

The cause of God in Oakland, San Francisco, and the surrounding places needs men of solid Christian character, who fear God and take counsel of God, or believers will be misled by those who attach themselves to the work, and who desire to guide and control according to human judgment and plans. The Lord desires to work through men of clean purposes and decided experiences, men who will learn from the Testimonies of His Spirit where they have not been in harmony with the Lord's will, and who will be converted. Then decided changes will be made. The perils threatening the work will be seen, conversions will be experienced, and our people will be preparing to stand firmly and unitedly with God to build up His kingdom in the earth.

Men who repudiate the teachings of the Spirit of God are not the proper persons to be placed in offices as leaders in the church. There is danger that the teachings of men who are not soundly converted may lead others into by and forbidden paths. In our efforts to secure consecrated leadership, we may expect to encounter opposition, for the enemy is seeking through unconverted men in positions of trust to mold the work, and he has too much at stake lightly to lose their influence.

Many have refused to see and adopt the light, because they would not humble themselves before God, and be daily converted to Christ. Yet this must be the experience of all who overcome by the blood of the lamb and the word of their testimony. When men humble their hearts, and are daily converted, following the example of the meek and lowly Jesus, then there is hope that they will become wise in their religious experiences....

I see a crisis before us, and the Lord calls for His workmen to come into line. Every soul should now stand in a position of deeper, truer consecration to God, than during the years that are past.

God corrects His people when they are in danger of being corrupted by those who obey not the truth. I have been charged to stand faithfully in the position in which the Lord has placed me among His people, that they might be instructed and counseled.

I have been shown that there are men helping to form committees, and men filling important positions in the churches, who are self-righteous, men walking after the counsel of their own hearts. Neither these self-righteous men nor those who have been influenced to hurt the work of God, should now be put in places of large responsibility; for the work of God will be marred by such steps. There are some who will always be deceived. We are living amid the perils of the last days. Let the Word of God teach righteousness. Let the chaff be separated from the wheat.

The work of Elder Haskell and others who have labored in Oakland and the nearby places might have been a much greater blessing, had they not been obliged to meet wrong influences in opposition to the counsels that God has given to build up and prepare a people for the final conflict that is before us.

It is not in harmony with the plan of God that men who are working counter to the spirit of the messages that the Lord gives to bless and strengthen His people, should be given places of large influence in our churches. Such men are not a help, but a hindrance. Their work is to unsettle minds, and they sow the seed which will spring up and bear its fruit to make of none effect the counsels that the Lord has so graciously given to His people.

* * * * *

* * * * *

A Message for Our Time on Medical Missionary Work

Isaiah 58, 55.

These two chapters describe in a special sense our condition, our work, and its possibilities under God in Southern California.

First, let us note the message to us describing our condition and the causes that have brought it. Isaiah 58:1-6. "Cry aloud and show my people their transgression, and the house of Jacob their sins. My people, even the faithful ones in the church are guilty, for all have sinned. The real trouble is between their way and God's way. The difference in the two ways is of such a nature that they cannot be united. Isaiah 58:8, 9. Our only hope is to give up our way and accept God's way. Isaiah 65:5-7.

God's way as compared with the results under our way. Isaiah 58:6-14; 55:10-13. The one is mercenary and disappointing in results, even to ourselves. The other is missionary and full of blessing to us and to others, and is crowned with everlasting success.

Such is the work to which God has called us in Southern California. The appeals to this people show that God would have us give to the world a living representation of Isaiah 58:6-14. He is calling for such a representation of medical missionary work in this field as the world has not seen since the days when Jesus of Nazareth walked among men and ministered to their necessity.

Here in this small territory, where the climate is so favorable, and where thousands are coming in search of health, Christ would have His people establish everywhere memorials for Him—institutions to which they may be drawn and learn of His healing power; places in which the laws of life and health shall be lived and taught in such simplicity that all may receive their benefit.

Shall we not at this time study most carefully the light that has been given upon this important subject that we may understand the mind of the Lord and be able to cooperate in His plan. Is it not time to put away our unbelief and go up and possess the goodly land? If the Lord delight in us, then He will bring us into this land. Numbers 14:8.

[474] That we may better understand the real purpose and plan of God for the medical work in Southern California, and may better appreciate its needs, we desire to bring to your minds a few of the many definite outlines for the work sent us by the spirit of prophecy, and rehearse to you a number of providential experiences that have attended the efforts put forth to carry out the instruction given. It may be that in the light of these experiences and the instruction given, our faith shall be strengthened, and our vision cleansed to forsake our way and walk in the Lord's.

Early in 1902, the following instruction came:

* * * * *

To Our Sanitarium Workers in Southern California

"I have a decided message for our people in Southern California ... for months I have carried on my soul the burden of the medical missionary work in Southern California. Recently much light has been given me in regard to the manner in which God desires us to conduct sanitarium work. We are to encourage the patients to spend much of their time out-of-doors. I have been instructed to tell our brethren to keep on the look-out for cheap, desirable property in healthful places suitable for sanitarium purposes. Soon the reputation of the health resorts in Southern California will stand even higher than it stands at present. Now is our time to enter that field for the purpose of carrying forward medical missionary work. As soon as possible sanitariums are to be established in different places in Southern California. Let a beginning be made in several places. If possible, let land be purchased on which buildings are already erected. Then, as the prosperity of the work demands, let appropriate enlargements be made.

"In Southern California there are many properties for sale on which buildings suitable for sanitarium work are already erected. Some of these properties should be purchased, and medical missionary work carried forward on sensible, rational lines. Several small sanitariums are to be established in Southern California, for the benefit of the multitudes drawn there in hope of finding health. Instruction has been given me that now is our opportunity to reach the invalids flocking to the health resorts of Southern California, and that a work may be done also in behalf of the attendants.

On the night of October 10, 1901, I was unable to sleep after half past eleven at night. Many things regarding the sanitarium work were presented to me in figures and symbols. I was shown a sanitarium near Los Angeles in running order. At one place I saw sanitarium work being carried on in a beautiful building. On the grounds surrounding the building there were many fruit trees.

"As in the visions of the night I saw this place, I said to our brethren: O, ye of little faith! You have lost much time. On the lawn were the sick in wheel chairs. On the grounds of this beautiful place that I saw in the visions of the night, there were many shade trees the boughs of which hung down in such a way as to form leafy canopies somewhat in the shape of tents. Underneath these canopies patients were resting. The sick were delighted in their surroundings. While some worked, others were singing. There was no sign of dissatisfaction.

"I awoke and for some time could not sleep. Many vivid scenes had passed before me, and I could not forget the words I had spoken to the helpers and patients. Again I lost consciousness, and other scenes passed before me. I was in another locality surrounded by different scenery. Again it seemed as it I were pleading with those who were sick to look unto Jesus, the great Healer.

"I then awoke, and began writing out some cautions that had been given me.

"In the night season I was given a view of a sanitarium in the country. The institution was not large, but it was complete. It was surrounded by beautiful trees and shrubbery, beyond which were orchards and groves. Connected with the place were gardens, in which the lady patients, when they chose, could cultivate flowers of every description, each patient selecting a special plot for which to care. Out-door exercise in these gardens was prescribed as a part of the regular treatment:

"Scene after scene passed before me. In one scene a number of suffering patients had just come to one of our country sanitariums. In another scene I saw the same company, but, O, how transformed their appearance! Disease had gone, the skin was clear, the countenance joyful; body and mind seemed to be animated with new life. God will work wonders for us if we will in faith cooperate with Him. Let us, then, pursue a sensible course, that our efforts may be blessed of heaven, and crowned with success."

This instruction led the brethren to make a forward move in medical missionary work. Plans were laid for the erection of a large sanitarium building in the city of Los Angeles. This move was contrary to the plain instruction given by the Spirit of Prophecy and called forth repeated counsel that the sanitarium should be outside the city as is shown by the following:

*****

In an article dated March 12, 1902 (MS-44-'02) I read: "Those who have true wisdom, will plan to establish our sanitariums in the country, where the patients can have the benefit of out-of-door life, where they can sit in the sunshine, or, when the sunshine is too warm, under the shade of the trees. The patients are to be given the advantage of the Lord's health-giving remedies to be found out-of-doors. And the treatments given them in other lines are to be conducted on the same natural, health-restoring principles."

Again, from manuscript dated March 17, 1902 (MS-43-'02) I read: "During the past three nights light has been given me that in the medical missionary work we have lost great advantages by failing to realize the need of a change in our plans in regard to the location of sanitariums. It is the Lord's will that our sanitariums shall be established outside the city... The surroundings of a sanitarium should be as attractive as possible. Out-of-doors life is a means of gaining health and happiness... In flower gardens and orchards, the sick will find health, cheerfulness, and happy thoughts.

"All these representations, and many more, passed as living reality before me. I felt grateful to God, as I realized what an influence an out-of-door life among the flowers and fruit-laden trees has upon those who are sick, both in body and in mind... "Let our medical institutions be established on extensive tracts of land, where the patients can have opportunity for out-of-doors exercise. This will prove to be one means for their restoration of health. Encourage the patients to live out-of-doors. Devise plans to keep them out-of-doors, where they will become acquainted with God through nature. As they take exercise in the open air, restoration will begin in body, mind, and soul... Jesus expects those who believe in Him to give the patients in our medical institutions the messages of God's word as healing leaves from the tree of life.

In another communication, dated March 14, 1902, (MS-41-'02) I read: "In the visions of the night I have been writing letters, and I dare not put off longer the work to be done. Night after night, I have been awakened at eleven, twelve, and one o'clock with a message from the Lord, and I arise at once, and begin to write, fearing that if I do not, I shall forget the instruction given me. Thus it was when I

[476]

was at Los Angeles. In the night season I was in a council meeting and the question under consideration was the establishment of a sanitarium in southern California. One brother urged that it would be best to have the sanitarium in the city of Los Angeles, and he pointed out the objections to establishing the sanitarium out of the city.

"There was among us One who presented this matter very clearly, and with the utmost simplicity. He told us it would be a mistake to establish a sanitarium within the city limits. A sanitarium should have the advantage of plenty of land, so that the invalids can work in the open air. For nervous, gloomy, feeble patients, out-of-door work is invaluable. Let them have flower beds to care for. In the use of rake and hoe and spade they will find relief for many of their maladies. Idleness is the cause of many diseases....

Life in the open air is good for body and mind. It is God's medicine for the restoration of health. Pure air, good water, sunshine, beautiful surroundings,—these are God's means for restoring the sick to health in natural ways... It is worth more than silver or gold to sick people to lie in the sunshine or in the shade of the trees.

"The time will come when God's people will have to move away from the cities, and live in small companies, by themselves. If our people regard God's instructions as of value, they will move out of the cities, so that they will not be corrupted by its revolting sights, and so that their children will not be corrupted by its vices. Those who choose to remain in the cities ... must share the disaster that will come upon them....

"Candid consideration is to be given to the matter of establishing a sanitarium in southern California. One thing is certain; this sanitarium is not to be established in the city. This I have said repeatedly, establish it where there is ground for cultivation, where the patients can have opportunity for healthful exercise. Out-of-door exercise, combined with hygienic treatment, will work miracles in restoring health to the sick....

"Grave mistakes have been made in establishing sanitariums in the cities. I was instructed that our sanitariums should be established in the most pleasant surroundings, in places outside the city, where by wise instruction the thoughts of the patients can be bound up with the mind of God. Again and again I have described such places, but it seems there has been no ear to hear. Last night in a most clear and convincing manner the mistakes now being made in our sanitarium work was presented to me.

In a communication dated March 17, 1902 (MS-43-'02), I read: "I am unable to sleep. My mind is much burdened in regard to the location of the sanitarium in southern California. There is a work to be done in California that has been strangely neglected. This work must now be done... Southern California is to be worked... Not half the energy has been brought into the management of the various lines of God's work that should be brought into them... The question of the location of the sanitarium in southern California is of great importance, and is not to be settled by the judgment of one man, or of several men who are all inclined to want the same thing...

"At the time when this matter was under consideration before, it was left unsettled because all did not agree. The delay has been long, but thus abrupt haste does not show wisdom. Many are to have the privilege of considering the subject of the location of the sanitarium in southern California. The Lord is interested in every line of His work. He understands when men are prepared to take hold of the work in the right spirit, when they are prepared to carry it forward wisely. His way is the best way.

"Last night the same scenes passed before me that passed before me thirty-five years ago, when the light was given to establish a sanitarium that would be the means of educating many souls in regard to right principles of living, and of bringing them to a knowledge of the truth. We must establish sanitariums for this purpose, and they must be so conducted that God can cooperate with the efforts made in them to relieve physical and spiritual suffering. God wants the sick and suffering to understand what it means to have the advantage of living in a sanitarium conducted in accordance with the principles of the gospel. Every worker connected with these institutions is to follow on to know the Lord, that He may know that his goings forth is prepared as the morning. If our missionary spirit were stronger, if the love of Jesus filled the hearts of those in service for Him, many of the sick and suffering would be drawn to Jesus, led to the tree of Life, to take of its health-restoring, life-sustaining power.

Again in a council meeting, dated April 13, 1902 (MS-86-'02) "Our sanitariums should not be established in the large cities. According to the light that the Lord has given me, in a little while from now, these cities will be terribly shaken. No matter how large or how strong the buildings may be, no matter how many safeguards against fire have been provided, if God touches it, in a few moments or in a few hours it is in ruins."

These repeated instructions from the Spirit of Prophecy stopped the erection of the large sanitarium in Los Angeles. Soon after the Los Angeles Medical Missionary Benevolent Association was organized to take charge of the medical work in southern California. Certain resolutions outlining plans and policies for the new organization were adopted. The history that followed I need not repeat.

Suffice it to say that the counsel from the spirit of prophecy continued the same as is shown by a communication to the directors of the Los Angeles Medical Missionary Benevolent Association, dated Oct. 13, 1902, from which I read: (B-157-'02)

"Dear Brethren,"

During my stay in southern California I was enabled to visit places that in the past had been presented to me by the Lord as suitable for the establishment of sanitariums and schools.... I have been instructed that the work in southern California should have advantages that it has not yet enjoyed. I have been shown that in southern California there were properties for sale on which buildings are already erected that could be utilized for our work,.. and that such properties will be offered to us at much less than their original cost... The work in southern California is to advance more rapidly than it has advanced in the past. The means lying in banks or hidden in the earth is now called for to strengthen the work in southern California. Every year many thousands of tourists visit southern California, and by various methods we should seek to reach them with the truth.

"Our medical missionary work in Los Angeles should be in a much more favorable condition than it is. The Lord designs that much more shall be done in this city than has been done there. But I cannot speak freely about this at present, for fear that men will take advantage of what I say, and will endeavor by my words, to vindicate wrong plans. Some of the brethren in Los Angeles have at times lacked spiritual discernment. They have not always been able to see what could be done by proper efforts on their part. A large work had been done in some lines, but the methods followed have not been such as to bring glory to God in the saving of souls." Various changes now came to the medical work in southern California, which resulted in opening a small sanitarium, not in the country, but in the city of Pasadena. Instead of prosperity, reverses come to the work which strained its credit and resulted in such heavy financial losses that the brethren were led to pass some very stringent measures against incurring further indebtedness in an effort to carry forward the medical missionary work.

All this time the spirit of prophecy was saying that sanitariums should be started in the country outside the city, as is shown by the following: (Similar to B-145-'04)

"Dear Brethren,

I wish to write you a few lines regarding the work in San Diego. We have long desired to see sanitarium work established in this place, not that we ourselves may be benefited, but that those who have never heard the truth may have an opportunity of hearing the last message of mercy to be given to the world....

I have always looked with great interest upon the work in Los Angeles and San Diego, hoping that right moves would be made, and that the sanitarium work might be established in these important places. Every year large numbers of tourists visit these places, and I have longed to see men moved by the Holy Spirit, meeting these people with the message borne by John the Baptist....

"The Lord has ordained that memorials for Him shall be established in many places. He has presented before me buildings away from cities, suitable for our work, which can be purchased at a low price. We must take advantage of the favorable openings for sanitarium work in southern California, where the climate is so favorable for this work.

"There are many other places in southern California, besides Los Angeles and San Diego, in which sanitarium work could be started. To sanitariums in southern California, people will come far and near, because the fame of the climate is world-wide. It is the Lord's purpose that sanitariums shall be established in southern California, and that from these institutions shall go forth the light of truth for this time. By them the claims of the true Sabbath are to be presented, and the third angel's message proclaimed.

Institutions in which medical missionary work can be done are to be regarded as a special essential to the advancement of the Lord's work. The buildings secured for this work should be out of the cities, in rural districts, so that the sick may have the benefit of out-of-door life. By the beauty of flower and field, their minds will be diverted from themselves, from their aches and pains, and they will be led to look from nature to the God of nature, who has provided so abundantly the beauties of the natural world. The convalescent can lie in the shade of the trees, and those who are stronger can, if they wish, work among the flowers, doing just a little at first, and increasing their efforts as they grow stronger. Working in the garden, gathering flowers and fruit, listening to the birds praising God, the patients will be wonderfully blessed. The angels of God will draw near to them. The fresh air and sunshine, and the exercise taken, will bring them life and vitality.

"At San Diego we have made an advance move by purchasing the Pott's Sanitarium in Paradise Valley. Three years ago light was given me that our people in Southern California must watch for opportunities to purchase such properties. I told our brethren that they would find already for use, and for sale at reasonable prices, just the buildings they would need for their work. And thus it has proved. In a most remarkable way the Lord is preparing the way for the advancement of His work in southern California.

"For two years I have been interested in the Pott's Sanitarium property and had advised and urged our people to secure it. I advised those having charge of the medical work in southern California, to purchase the building, and when they hesitated, because of a lack of funds, I persuaded Sister Gotzian and Brother Ballenger to join me, and we have purchased the Pott's sanitarium, and eight acres adjoining, for five thousand dollars.

"Something similar can be done in the neighborhood of Los Angeles, if wise plans are adopted for the carrying forward of the work, and if the men to whom God has entrusted His talent and means will put their money into use for the honor of God and the blessing of humanity.

"We have not purchased the Pott's Sanitarium to gain an advantage to ourselves, but to help in carrying forward the work which Christ has given us to do.

"From the light which was given me when I was in Australia, and which has been renewed since I came to America, I know that our work in southern California must advance. The people flocking there for health must hear the last message of mercy.

"God has not been pleased with the way in which this work has been neglected. From many places in southern California, the light is to shine forth to the multitudes. Present truth is to be as a city set on a hill which cannot be hid.

Southern California is world-renowned as a health resort. Every year thousands of tourists go there. These must hear the last warning message. We are called upon by God to explain the Scriptures to these people. We are not to build hotels for the accommodation of tourists, and we are not to establish sanitariums in the cities. We are to establish our work where we shall be able to do the most good to those who come to our sanitariums for treatment.

From the Review and Herald, dated March 16, 1905, I quote the following:

"During the spring of 1902 the attention of several of our brethren was called to the Paradise Valley Sanitarium building, which was erected for a sanitarium by Mrs. Mary L. Potts about twenty years ago....

"In September, 1902, after the Los Angeles camp meeting, we spent a week in San Diego, and visited several places that were offered us for sanitarium work. In the building offered us by Mrs. Potts, it seemed to me we found about all that we could ask...

"A year before, light had been given me that our people in southern California must watch their opportunity to purchase such properties, and it seemed plain to me and to those who were with me, that the opportunity of securing this place was a fulfillment of the encouragement given us....

"In December we learned that this place could be purchased, ... and I encouraged Dr. Whitelock to take steps to secure it. But our leading brethren in the southern California conference were not ready to cooperate in the matter, and nothing was done. In the summer of 1903 the property was offered us for eight thousand dollars, and again we found that our brethren were not in a position to act... In January, 1904, Dr. Whitelock wrote me that the mortgage could be bought for six thousand dollars, and perhaps less. Again I advised our brethren connected with the medical work in southern California to secure the place. But I learned that they were not prepared to act. Then I laid the matter before Sister Gotzian, and she consented to join me in securing the place. We then telegraphed an offer of four thousand dollars for the mortgage. Two days later a telegram was returned accepting the offer. Meanwhile a letter from other parties in San Diego was on its way to New York, offering six thousand dollars for the mortgage.

"When we visited the place in November 1, 1904, we found that much had been done during the summer.... Our great anxiety about the place was the matter of an ample supply of water.... The great question was, can we get plenty of water by digging? The well diggers had gone down eighty feet, and found a little water, but they wanted much more. O, how much depended upon our finding plenty of good pure water.... From the beginning I had felt the assurance that the Lord would open the way for our work to advance; but who could tell when and how? Our people were deeply desirous of seeing the sanitarium make a success, and as we met them, the question was, Have you found water? ... The next morning Brother Palmer came up early to tell me that there was fourteen feet of water in the well. The water is soft and pure, and we are greatly rejoiced to know that there is an abundant supply. This well is a treasure more valuable than gold or silver or precious stones....

"During the last three nights of my stay at this institution, much instruction was given me regarding the sanitarium which for years had been greatly needed, and which should long ago have been equipped and set in working order.... Our sanitariums are one great means of doing medical missionary work."

In a letter dated June 26, 1905, I read again: (B-335-'05)

"Dear Brethren and Sisters,

As we returned from the General Conference, we stopped ten days in southern California, and between the council meetings at Los Angeles, we made a short visit to San Diego, and spent four days at the Paradise Valley Sanitarium. I am much pleased to see the sanitarium fully furnished and in running order... My heart rejoices as I review the way in which the providences of God worked to help us to secure this property...

"More decided efforts are to be put forth in southern California. There is a great work to be done in this field. We have done all in our power to advance the work there, and now that this sanitarium property in San Diego County has been purchased, we call upon our brethren and sisters to aid us in properly equipping the institution that we may do successful work. I ask those who have been entrusted with the Lord's money to make gifts to this sanitarium, that it may be prepared to do the work that must be done for the sick and suffering.

"Brethren and sisters, I plead with you to help forward our sanitarium work. The Paradise Valley Sanitarium is in need of assistance... I ask you, my dear friends, to help us in this time of need, and I believe you will."

Such in brief is the instruction, the history, and the experience, in connection with the establishment of the sanitarium at San Diego. Had we lived in those days, what would have been our attitude?

* * * * *

To this letter, we received the following reply: (Almost identical with MS-7-1910).

"A Statement Regarding the Training of Physicians"

(The statement given below, was called forth by a question submitted to Mrs. E. G. White by Elders I. H. Evans, E. E. Andross, and H. W. Cottrell, reading as follows: "Are we to understand, from what you have written concerning the establishment of a medical school at Loma Linda, that, according to the light you have received from the Lord, we are to establish a thoroughly equipped medical school, the graduates from which will be able to take State Board examinations and become registered qualified physicians?)

"The light given me is, We must provide that which is essential to qualify our youth who desire to be physicians, so that they may intelligently fit themselves to be able to stand the examinations required to prove their efficiency as physicians. They should be taught to treat understandingly the cases of those who are diseased, so that the door will be closed for any sensible physician to imagine that we are not giving in our school the instruction necessary for properly qualifying young men and young women to do the work of a physician. Continually the students who are graduated are to advance in knowledge for practice makes perfect.

"The medical school at Loma Linda is to be the highest order, because those who are in that school have the privilege of maintaining a living connection with the wisest of all physicians, from whom there is communicated knowledge of a superior order. And for the special preparation of those of our youth who have clear convictions of their duty to obtain a medical education that will enable them to pass the examinations required by law of all who practice as regularly qualified physicians, we are to supply whatever may be required, so that these youth need not be compelled to go to medical schools conducted by men not of our faith. Thus we shall close a door that the enemy would be pleased to have left open;

and our young men and young women, whose spiritual interests the Lord desires to safeguard, will not feel compelled to connect with unbelievers in order to obtain a thorough training along medical lines.

Ellen G. White

* * * * *

A Statement Regarding the Training of Physicians

MS.-7-'10.
Jan. 27, 1910 -4-

> The statement given below, was called forth by a question submitted to Elder I. H. Evans, E. E. Andross and H. W. Cottrell, reading as follows:
>
> "Are we to understand, from what you have written concerning the establishment of a medical school at Loma Linda, that, according to the light you have received from the Lord, we are to establish a thoroughly equipped medical school, the graduates from which will be able to take State Board examinations and become registered, qualified physicians."

The light given me is, we must provide that which is essential to qualify our youth who desire to be physicians, so that they may intelligently fit themselves to be able to stand the examinations essential to prove their efficiency as physicians. They are to be prepared to stand the essential tests required by law, and to treat understandingly the cases of those who are diseased, so that the door will be closed for any sensible physician to fear that we are not giving in our school the instruction essential for the proper qualification of a physician. Continually the students who are graduated are to advance in knowledge; for practice makes perfect.

The medical school at Loma Linda is to be of the highest order, because we have a living connection with the wisest of all physicians, from whom there is communicated knowledge of a superior order. And whatever subjects are required as essential in the school conducted by those not of our faith, we are to supply so that our youth need not go to those worldly schools. Thus we shall close the door that the enemy would be pleased to have left open; and our young men and young women, whom the Lord would have us guard religiously, will not then need to connect with worldly medical schools conducted by unbelievers.

* * * * *

**Mountain View, Calif.,
January 27, 1910.**
Dear Brother,

....

No man's judgment is to be regarded as a safe and infallible guide. There is a certainty in sanctified submission to the will of God, and this is the only certainty that any man has the right to stand by. Any other position of certainty than this, of humble submission to the will of God, is unsafe, and is liable to lead a man to lose his hold on God, and mar his religious experience.

Many trials come to all who are called to engage in the work of God. Those who have the responsibility of locating and fostering our sanitariums and training schools, need the advice and counsel of men of sound judgment,—men who trust not in their own supposed wisdom, but who stand ready to advance by faith in the opening providences of God, and who constantly look to the Lord for wisdom and guidance...

In this our age of the world, we claim to be, in a special sense, the Lord's chosen people, as did Israel of old. And we are, indeed, the Lord's covenant-keeping people, pledged by our baptismal vows to walk in newness of life, and in obedience to all the commandments of Holy Writ. The Lord God of Israel is our God, whom we serve. Throughout the ages, the Sabbath of Jehovah has lost none of its meaning. It is still a sign between God and His people, and will ever remain a sign.

Those who have the responsibility of locating and keeping in operation our sanitariums and schools, are ever to bear in mind that those institutions are to be regarded as divinely appointed agencies for the restoration of the entire man,—physical, mental, and spiritual. In planning for the establishment of sanitariums in places where God has designated we should do a special work, we are to allow no selfishness, no personal ambition, to mar the work. Over and over again I have repeated that the establishment and maintenance

[488]

of sanitariums is ordained of God for the advancement of His cause in the earth. While Christ was on this earth, He ministered to the needs of suffering humanity. He is our example. We are to labor intelligently; and in planning for the extension of sanitarium work, we are to seek to secure the very places that God indicates are most suitable for carrying forward this line of our work.

In the providence of God, there come to this people, in time of need, favorable opportunities to secure valuable facilities that can be utilized wisely for the rapid advancement of the cause. At times, the Lord has specified that we should come into possession of properties in certain localities where we needed to obtain an entrance for the proclamation of the third angel's message. The idea that we are not to purchase any such properties, unless first the money is in hand, is not in accordance with the mind of God. Again and again, in years past, the Lord has tested our faith by opening the way for us to secure places possessing advantages, at a cost far below their real value and at a time when we had no money. We have at such times, met the situation by borrowing money on interest, and advancing in harmony with the command of our divine leader who bade us advance in faith. These experiences have been attended with many perplexing problems, but the Lord has helped us through them all, and His name has been glorified. Had we hesitated, the precious cause would have been retarded rather than advanced, and, in many cases, opportunity would have been given our enemies to triumph over our failures to secure these advantages placed within our reach. In such matters as these, we are to learn to walk by faith, when necessary, as some have walked in the past.

Light has been given that it is best to establish our sanitariums outside the cities. Some of our physicians have spoken in favor of locating our sanitariums in the cities. It is difficult to understand why any one would plan to establish a large sanitarium in a city. The very atmosphere of the cities is objectionable. We must conduct our sanitarium work in places suitable for the recovery of the sick. The more attractive the surroundings, the better. In the gardens of nature, the sick rapidly find something to please. Their thoughts are uplifted to the Creator. Let us thank God that so many of our sanitariums are established in pleasing country locations, and yet within easy reach of important centers of population where there are many people to whom we are to communicate a knowledge of saving truth.

It is the favorable situation of the property, that makes Loma Linda an ideal place for the recovery of the sick and for the warning of many who might otherwise never hear the truth for this time. It is God's plan that Loma Linda shall be not only a sanitarium, but a special center for the training of gospel medical missionary evangelists.

[489]

* * * * *

Interview Between Mrs. E. G. White and W. C. White

Thursday morning, January 27, 1910.

When I called to see how Mother was this morning, and to inquire if she was willing to attend the half-past eight meeting, she began to talk about her interview yesterday afternoon with Elder Evans. Then she inquired about the meetings—how they were progressing. I told her that one of the matters which was delaying the progress of the meeting, was the question which our brethren had submitted to her in writing, about the Loma Linda Medical school. And as the document was lying on her table, I handed it to her, and she read it again.

Then she began to repeat to me what she had said to Elder Evans regarding the work that must be done for the sick by nurses, and by intelligent people who are not physicians. Then I said to her, Mother, there is quite a general agreement on the part of our people that a great amount of work of this kind ought to be done, and that the Loma Linda School should train people to take a part in this work. But the question which perplexes many, is this: There are some among our young people who believe they ought to pursue a full line of studies that will enable them to receive diplomas, and take State examinations, and be prepared to meet all the requirements of a legalized physician. Shall the Loma Linda school undertake to furnish them the education they require, notwithstanding the large expense involved, or shall we permit the few who think they must qualify to be regular physicians, to get their education and qualification at the world's best colleges and universities, as they are doing at the present time?

The answer was: "Whatever education our young people preparing to be physicians, require, that we must give."

Afterward, she took pencil and paper, and wrote out a more complete statement, and sent it to Brother Crisler to be manifolded and placed in the hands of our brethren.

W. C. White

* * * * *

Words of Counsel

Sanitarium, Cal.,
B-132-'09
" Oct. 11, 1909.
"Elder J. A. Burden:
"Dear Brother,

I am instructed to say that in our educational work, there is to be no compromise in order to meet the world's standards. God's commandment-keeping people are not to unite with the world, to carry various lines of work according to worldly plans and worldly wisdom. "Our people are now being tested as to whether they will obtain their wisdom from the greatest Teacher the world ever knew, or seek to the God of Ekron. Let us determine that we shall not be tied by so much as a thread to the educational policies of those who do not discern the voice of God, and who will not hearken to His commandments.

"We are to take heed to the warning: 'Enter ye in at the strait gate: for wide is the gate, and broad is the way, that leadeth to destruction, and many there be which go in thereat: because strait is the gate, and narrow is the way, which leadeth unto life, and few there be that find it.' Those who walk in the narrow way are following in the footprints of Jesus. The light from heaven illuminates their path.

"Shall we represent before the world that our physicians must follow the pattern of the world before they can be qualified to act as successful physicians? This is the question that is now testing the faith of some of our brethren. Let not any of our brethren displease the Lord by advocating in their assemblies the idea that we need to obtain from unbelievers a higher education than that specified by the Lord.

"The representation of the great Teacher is to be considered an all-sufficient revelation. Those in our ranks who qualify as physicians are to receive only such education as is in harmony with these divine truths. Some have advised that students should, after taking some work at Loma Linda, complete their medical education in worldly colleges. But this is not in harmony with the Lord's plan. God is our wisdom, our sanctification, and our righteousness. Facilities should be provided at Loma Linda, that the necessary instruction in medical lines may be given by instructors who fear the Lord, and who are in harmony with His plans for the treatment of the sick.

"I have not a word to say in favor of the world's ideas of higher education in any school that we shall organize for the training of physicians. There is danger in their attaching themselves to worldly institutions, and working under the ministrations of worldly physicians. Satan is giving his orders to those whom he has led to depart from the faith. I would advise that none of our young people attach themselves to worldly medical institutions in the hope of gaining better success, or stronger influence as physicians....

Ellen G. White

"A Statement Regarding the Training of Physicians

The light given me is, We must provide that which is essential to qualify our youth who desire to be physicians, so that they may intelligently fit themselves to be able to stand the examinations required to prove their efficiency as physicians. They should be taught to treat understandingly the cases of those who are diseased so that the door will be closed for any sensible physician to imagine that we are not giving in our school the instruction necessary for properly qualifying young men and young women to do the work of a physician. Continually the students who are graduated are to advance in knowledge, for practice makes perfect.

"The Medical school at Loma Linda is to be of the highest order, because those who are in that school have the privilege of maintaining a living connection with the wisest of all physicians, from whom there is communicated knowledge of a superior order. And for the special preparation of those of our youth who have clear convictions of their duty to obtain a medical education that will enable them to pass the examinations required by law of all who practice as regularly qualified physicians, we are to supply whatever may be required, so that these youth need not be compelled to go to medical schools conducted by men not of our faith. Thus we shall close a door that the enemy would be pleased to have left open; and our young men and young women, whose spiritual interests the Lord desires us to safeguard, will not feel compelled to connect with unbelievers in order to obtain a thorough training along medical lines.

"Ellen G. White."

* * * * *

Talk to the Students at Loma Linda, Calif.
April 5, 1910.
By Mrs. E. G. White

Luke 13: "And behold there was a woman which had a spirit of infirmity eighteen years, and was bowed together, and could in no wise lift herself up. And when Jesus saw her He called her to him and said unto her, Woman, thou art loosed from thine infirmity. And he laid his hands on her, and immediately she was made straight and glorified God."

Thank God for this! That we can have such manifestations!

"And the ruler of the synagogue answered with indignation because that Jesus had healed on the Sabbath Day, and said unto the people, There are six days in which men ought to work; in them therefore, come and be healed and not on the Sabbath Day. The Lord then answered him and said. Thou hypocrite, doth not each one of you on the Sabbath Day loose his ox or his ass from the stall, and lead him away to the watering? And ought not this woman being a daughter of Abraham, be loosed from this bond on the Sabbath day?"

Consistency is a jewel and we all want it.

"And when he had said all these things his adversaries were ashamed"—and well might they be—"and all the people rejoiced for all the glorious things that were done by him.

Then said he, what is the kingdom of God like, and whereunto shall I resemble it? It is like a grain of mustard seed, which a man took and cast into his garden; and it grew and waxed a great tree; and the fowls of the air lodged in the branches of it. And again he said whereunto shall I liken the kingdom of God? It is like leaven which a woman took and hid in three measures of meal till the whole was leavened.

And He went thru the cities and villages teaching and journeying toward Jerusalem."

Talk to the Students at Loma Linda, Calif. April 5, 1910. By Mrs. E. G. White

We want to have just such a work that we shall take up after Christ's example. That is what we need. We need much more of the baptism of the Holy Spirit of God than we now manifest and it is our privilege to have it.

"And he went thru the cities and villages teaching and journeying toward Jerusalem. Then said one unto Him, Lord, are there few that be saved? And he said unto them, Strive to enter in at the straight gate; for many, I say unto you, will seek to enter in, and shall not be able."

Why? Why, because they trust to uncertainties. They do not read the Bible. They do not understand what the Word says. When they read the Bible and understand what the Word says, let me tell you, there will be a hundred fold more accomplished by our churches, by the ministers, and by those that are teachers, and by all men in office, and they will then see of the salvation of our God. What is the matter with us? We haven't a love from above. We do not make a business of serving God.

"And he went thru the cities and villages teaching and journeying toward Jerusalem."

Teaching on the way. He did not go right straight along. He was teaching on the way and when He saw persons who needed help he would take their cases and represent them in his teaching.

"Then said one unto him, Lord are there few that be saved? He said unto them, Strive to enter in at the straight gate for many I say unto you, will seek to enter in, and shall not be able."

What is the matter? Why, they are not living their faith. They seek to enter in but are not able because it requires earnest effort for every one of us to walk in the narrow path that leads to eternal life.

"When once the Master of the house is risen up and hath shut to the door, and ye begin to stand without, and to knock at the door saying, Lord, Lord, open unto us; and he shall answer and say unto you, I know ye not whence ye are; Then shall ye begin to say, we have eaten and drunk in thy presence, and thou hast taught in our streets, but he shall say, I tell you I know you not whence ye are; depart from me all ye workers of iniquity. And there shall be weeping and gnashing of teeth, when ye shall see Abraham and Isaac and Jacob, and all the prophets in the kingdom of God, and you yourself thrust out. And they shall come from East, and from

[534]

the West and from the North and from the South, and shall sit down in the kingdom of God. And behold there are last which shall be first, and there are first which shall be last.

[535] The same day there came certain of the Pharisees, saying unto him, Get thee out and depart hence for Herod will kill thee. And He said unto them, Go ye and tell that fox, Behold I cast out devils, and I do cures today and tomorrow, and the third day I shall be perfected. Nevertheless, I must walk today, and tomorrow, and the day following; for it can not be that a prophet perish out of Jerusalem."

"O Jerusalem, Jerusalem, which killest the prophets, and stonest them that are sent unto thee; how often would I have gathered thy children together, as a hen doth gather her brood under her wings and ye would not. Behold, your house is left unto you desolate, and verily I say unto you, Ye shall not see me, until the time when ye shall say, Blessed is he that cometh in the name of the Lord."

We see there is a great work to be done and we want everyone to be in the right position and do their part of the work. We are laborers together with God. Now, here God expects us to have a living experience as laborers together with God and he wants every one of us to be in working order. We are careless, we are too indifferent; we do not seem to know the plan being worked out. Now I see when I go on the cars, there is one comes thru with a great package of papers. We could read them, but what are they good for? We may find a little news in them, but what we need is the work of life and to have a missionary spirit wherever we are. The world will never be warned if we take it so easy. We know how it was with the schools of the prophets. We know that they were learning out of the scriptures and that they were praising God; because they understood the Scriptures, God was glorified. And as Saul was searching for David he came right up to the school of the Prophets and behold the first thing they knew he was prophesying right with the prophets. The school of the prophets was a special school to get the endowment of the Holy Spirit of God and then go forth into the dark places of the earth and seek for those who would listen to the testimony that they had to bring.

We are not half awake.... I was so astonished when I came back the first time after we had been gone nearly ten years in Australia, to see nothing being done scarcely at all in San Francisco and Oakland. There was so little being done! Well, I tried to inquire into it,—what it meant. "Oh, well" they said, they had men out. "How many have you?" "How many will it take in the manner you are doing the work?" Well, they said they had other duties to do, but they did not tell me what they were doing, and there the very work they ought to be doing—there was only one man going round and visiting, and he was not competent, he did not have the experience he needed and was a man of incompetency. But what right had that minister to do as he did, unless he would take a company and with them get out and hold meetings in different sections. God wants active men. He wants men that will work. He wants men that will understand that there is work for them to do. They can go in and give Bible readings. We know, because we have seen that accomplished. We have advised it and they have done it and the Spirit of the Lord has blessed their labors, but not one thousandth part has been done in these cities that ought to have been done. That is what is presented to me.

[536]

Now I want to tell our brethren that there is a work we are to do and they are to be interested in the cases of others. There are cities all around us, and when I was in Australia how glad I would have been, if we could have gone right around where the people were (as you can here). Christ said go everywhere preaching the word. It is the Word they must have. It is the Scriptures they must have. We do not need these papers that are coming into our parlors. Those who have never been used to our house sometimes don't know where to find their papers, but I say, "If you miss your papers, you must find them where you can. I do not take any charge of them whatever only to put them out of sight. We may want to know the news of the day and we may have some excuse to just run thru them and see what it is. But I want to tell you there is a great work to be done in our world and we feel intensely like doing our part.

Romans 14:1: "Him that is weak in the faith receive ye, but not to doubtful disputations.... Verse 11.

"For it is written, As I live saith the Lord every knee shall bow to me, and every tongue shall confess to God.

"So then every one of us shall give account of himself to God."

Are you prepared to do it? Are you preparing? Are you preparing to give an account of yourself before you shall go to rest in the night season? Have you called to mind what you can do to glorify God? Now, here is this institution and we are glad we have it. It is just what we wanted and now we want to act our individual part in it every one of us. We believe in Jesus Christ that He is our Saviour and that He will bear our sins and we want to glorify His name. But many who are coming into position just as soon as they consider that they are looked upon as those who can help—they grow into such large proportions that they cannot handle themselves nor anybody else. We want to be humble workers for Jehovah. We have to face the future of this work; we have to face it. We want those who come to this institution to obtain just as much blessing as they possibly can obtain. We want them to receive instruction, and light and physical health and understanding, so that when they return to their homes they can treat their own families and their own sick, and no doubt many consider this a great advantage.

[537] Now, every one of us can be workers with God and while we are here we can watch to see if we can not speak a word in season to this one and that one and the other one. And we shall have words enough to say. The blessing of the Lord will rest upon us just as surely as we try to bring ourselves in right relationship to God.

"In our campmeeting services there should be singing and instrumental music. Musical instruments were used in the religious services in ancient times. The worshippers praised God upon the harp and cymbal. Music should have its place in our services. It will add to the interest. And every day a praise meeting should be held, a simple service of thanksgiving to God. There would be much more power in our campmeetings if we had a true sense of the goodness and mercy and longsuffering of God, and if more praise went forth from our lips to the honor and glory of His name. We need to cultivate more fervor of soul. The Lord says whoso offereth praise glorifieth me.

"It is Satan's plan to talk about that which concerns himself. He is delighted to have human beings talk of his power, of his working thru the children of men, but by indulgence in such conversation the mind becomes gloomy and sour and disagreeable. We may become channels of communication for Satan thru which words bring no sunshine to the heart. But let us decide that this shall not be. Let us decide not to be channels thru which Satan shall send gloomy disagreeable thoughts. Let our words be not a savor of death unto death, but of life unto life, in the words we speak to the people and in the prayers we offer. God desires us to give unmistakable evidences that we have a spiritual life. We do not enjoy the fulness of the blessing which the Lord has prepared for us because we do not ask in faith. If we would exercise faith in the word of the living God, we should have the richest blessings. We dishonor God by our lack of faith; therefore we can not impart life to others unless we ourselves bear a living, uplifting testimony. We cannot give that which we do not possess. If we will walk humbly with God, if we will walk in the spirit of Christ, none of us will carry heavy burdens. We shall lay them on the great burden-bearer. Then we may expect triumphs in the presence of God, in the communion of His love. Every campmeeting may be a love feast from the beginning to the end because God's presence is with His people. All heaven is interested in our salvation. The angels of God, thousands upon thousands, and ten thousand times ten thousand are commissioned ministers to those who shall be heirs of salvation. They guard us against evil and press back the powers of darkness that are seeking our destruction. Have we not reason to be thankful every moment; thankful even when there are apparent difficulties in our pathway. The Lord Himself is our Helper."

"Sing, O daughter of Zion; shout, O Israel; be glad and rejoice with all the heart, O daughter of Jerusalem.

"The Lord hath taken away thy judgments, he hath cast out thine enemy; the King of Israel, even the Lord, is in the midst of thee; thou shalt not see evil any more.

"In that day it shall be said to Jerusalem, Fear thou not; and to Zion, Let not thine hands be slack.

The Lord thy God in the midst of thee is mighty; He will save, He will rejoice over thee with joy; He will rest in His love, He will joy over thee with singing." Zephaniah 3:14-17.

This is the testimony that the Lord desires to bear to the world. His praise should be continually in our hearts and upon our lips. Such testimonies will be an influence upon others as we seek to turn men from their self-indulgent efforts to secure happiness. We must show them that we have something better than that which they are seeking. When Jesus talked to the Samaritan woman he did not reprove her for coming to draw water from Jacob's well but he presented something of far greater value. In comparison with Jacob's well he presented the fountain of living waters."

If we prayed as much as we ought to pray, if we realized that there is an open communication between us and God, we should be in an altogether different position than we are. We should be cheerful, and we shall see that there are a hundred blessings all around no matter whether we belong to this institution or a different institution you will see that you can speak a word for Christ in the different places. We have a work to do, every one of us, and time is short. We have but a little time now! And we want that Satan shall not take the victory of the whole world. He is at work—the devil and the fallen angels. You remember that.

They too, rebelled in heaven with Satan and were turned out of heaven. Now, they have the highest efficiency and power. They have the highest efficiency and they want to hinder every one of you from obeying the Lord. They want to hinder every one of you that they can, in building up coldness and indifference between you. Now, we have work to do every one of us, and I need not tell you of it. But men may be doing all they can and still there are many on the lost side. In these books I have here—reads from Vol. 6:

"His praise should continually be in our hearts and upon our lips. Now, as I read, in comparison with Jacob's well He presented the fountain of living waters. "If thou knewest the gift of God, and who it is that saith to thee, Give me to drink thou wouldst have asked him, and He would have given thee living waters."

We had to work wonderfully hard before our institutions were established. We went from place to place giving treatments. There are a great many who cannot go to the sanitariums, but we may go right in where they are and see the sick and tell them how to treat themselves. That is the way my husband and I would do, and we took them right into our house, he would take the men and I the women and work that way. What is Satan doing? He links himself with every discordant spirit in the world. Satan and his vast, vast, numbers who are disobedient to the heavenly commands, and they will represent these things that are of great importance and give all to understand that they know all about it and that they can do thus and so. We are not building up what we should outside of our churches, and this is the very work the Lord wants carried forward. We have every endowment and capability and every facility provided for discharging the duties that devolve upon us. We should be grateful to God for these advantages.

When we went to Australia I cannot begin to tell you and you can't understand how little were the advantages there, compared with the darkest places around here. It was hard to gain a foothold for the work there. Here you are better situated. Here are the sick and you can go into their houses and take the Bible in your hand and take some of our books along and read some of the comforting things in these books and some of the encouraging things. We must not give ourselves right up to ourselves. This institution must spread as a great blessing.

This is a good school for children if you make it so; but if you do not make it so, why then it is worse than if they had not been here. We want to be in a position where we will honor and glorify God every day. Why are we here? What have we this institution for? To bring relief to the sick. This is according to our mission and just the work which should be carried on and the Lord wants every one of us to be in working order. And if we will come under discipline to God we will be as happy a people as you will wish to see. Why? We see the devil working on one side, and that is his side, and he can bring the most entrancing things of heaven that he is acquainted with. He brings these things into his work, but we can have a great deal more knowledge in these things than we possess and we can be the happiest people of any in the world. And right in this institution we can be continually at work on the right side. And do not let us look on the dark side. If you have children, here is a good place for you to learn how to bring them up and how to teach them and how to guide them. You can do this right here. But that is not enough. There are other places and other towns. We have seen these places being worked and we have felt thankful for it and we expect there is a work being done more or less, all around. What you want every one of you and every one of us is to keep the Saviour in view. Jesus told His disciples just before He left them, not to mourn about it, but he said "Let not your hearts be troubled; ye believe in God believe

[540] also in me. In my Father's house are many mansions; if it were not so I would have told you. I go to prepare a place for you and if I go and prepare a place for you, I will come again and receive you unto myself, that where I am there ye may be also."

Well, now He tells them just what He is going to do. We want to say we are a people now that have to have a religious experience for ourselves, and we can never enter heaven unless we have that experience. We may have our names on the church books, but have we a daily experience in the things of God? "Let not your hearts be troubled; ye believe in God believe also in me." And thus He comforts and encourages them with the cross right in view.

Our dear Saviour says again, "I am the true vine and ye are the branches and my Father is the husbandman. Every branch in me that beareth not fruit He taketh away; and every branch that beareth not fruit he taketh it away." Now we want to know what fruit we are bearing. We want our fruits shall be right before the world in the ministry of Christ on the earth, and they can be if we will. We have all these advantages and how thankful we should be. The Lord brought this place right into our hands. What advantages we have in this very place! But there are other places where they need help, and let every one who can, take his Bible in his hand and see what missionary work he can do; carry with him some of the little books that we have published, and if the people do not want to buy, leave the books with them, and tell them to read them whether they want to buy or not; and if any of you want to give some away, just do that. There is a chance to let our light shine and we want to do so. Now Satan has the advantage in many things. He can quote those glories that he had in the heavenly sanctuary just as though they belonged to him, and he will quote these things. He is working upon human minds and he will bring in all the sophistries that he can bring in, and mix it in with some of his wonderful learning and agency that he had in the heavenly courts. The world will certainly think that he is excellent. We want all that excellency and power, but we shall have the light of truth which is to shine. But Satan will present that light that he had in the heavenly courts, and many will think that it must be the truth, and they are intelligent men and good women, and he leads them right along to perdition.

But we have a Saviour who wants to make this institution a perfect success; He wants us to do the work intelligently, and He wants us to praise His holy name. We can do it if we will. Satan grasps the minds every time we come into a meeting where they have the love of the truth in its beauty and its charms. We want to be full of usefulness every one of us and God can make a success of this institution, but it depends upon us to make this all and in all.

"Cry aloud, spare not, lift up thy voice like a trumpet and show my people their transgressions, and the house of Jacob their sins. Yet they seek me daily and delight to know my ways as a nation that did righteousness and forsook not the ordinance of their God."

Well, now you see those who had not believed in the commandments of God. They did not believe in the Sabbath commandment. They did not obey this. We want to be in a situation where we can live these commandments; so that our lives will teach the people we believe just what we profess to believe. I want to say that it will be well for you to become acquainted with these books. (Vols. Test.)

We have seen the application. We have been placed where we had to see it. God meant we should see it.

A lady was passing by—one of our highest teachers in Battle Creek, and it was icy and she didn't know how to drive and neither did her husband, and the sleigh slipped and jerked the lines right out of their hands. "Jump, jump," said the husband, and she jumped and was caught right on the side of the sleigh and struck her head on the ice and the blood poured out of her ears and nose and eyes and they thought it would be impossible to save her, but we gathered her up and took her into the house. We said we will take care of her but it is a question of how long she can live. There must be no noise around anywhere. It may be possible we can save her life. The doctor was sent for and when he said, "What are you doing?" We said, giving her a hot foot bath right under the bed clothes. Well, he said, you know better than I, and he turned on his heel and walked off and that was the last we saw of the doctor. Well, we kept her for four weeks and we had all the roosters removed from the neighborhood and every bit of noise excluded. And we succeeded in saving her life. Five years later in passing a woman who looked like this same teacher, when she saw me she grasped me in her arms and said, "You saved my life and the life of this child, the only child I have, and I feel so grateful whenever I hear the name of Ellen White mentioned.

From this beginning they founded the institution in Battle Creek. It takes a great deal to break down prejudice. Tepid water will not melt cold tallow. We can not make much impression on cold tallow with warm water.

Well, now I have talked with you long enough. We are intensely interested. We have a grand review before us. People are watching us everywhere and they are watching to see how much higher our piety is than the piety of those who have no connection with an institution. We want to be in a position where we can let our piety pour over the outside when we can. There will be opportunities.

[542] You cannot neglect things here; you cannot do that; but you can find opportunities where you can let the light of this institution shine forth. God wants you to do it. I believe that you will try to do it. What we want is a greater work of faith that we may show forth the praises of God in what He is doing and what He will do for us. If we will show this faith, it will have as much influence as any treatment you can give to those who are looking on to see what we are doing. Let us get into the position where we will lay all on Jesus Christ, for there is a grand review to take place; only a little while and there is to be an examination of what we believe and what we are. Are we prepared to be transferred to higher grades? To a higher school where Christ will lead us to the tree of life and there will continue to teach us in regard to the ages of the eternal life. Are we prepared for that grand review? Are we fashioning our characters to that divine similitude? God help us that we may be Christians in every sense of the word. If we will obey God let me tell you the way is already open; the angels of God will be our representatives wherever we go. The angels of God are round about us. Every one is in communication with Jesus Christ; they are one with Him and we want to do the works of God. We want to be wide awake, full of zeal, and live for God and advance step by step heavenward. Are we prepared for the grand review? It is coming on. Satan is gathering all of his beautiful knowledge that he had when he was an angel of light and he is coming in to deceive the very elect with that very knowledge, and we want to be in a position where we can work intelligently,—where we can work in faith and bring souls to

a knowledge of the truth of the grand review that will take place when he tells them that he is going to have the whole world as his subjects and they will gather under his banner, but we must stand higher. Young men and young women, teachers, doctors, do not put on pompous (manners) positions, as tho you knew everything worth knowing, but act as little children coming to ask God to let His blessing rest upon you, that you may teach others; for if you do that the will of God will be revealed and it will follow you wherever you go. We have a whole Saviour. He is not a piece of a Saviour. He will save every soul that comes unto Him. Now, let us have that working faith, have that believing faith, have that intelligent faith that it is our privilege to have.

* * * * *

**Sanitarium, Calif.,
June 28, 1910 -6- B.-61-1910. April 27, 1910.
Elder J. A. Burden:**
Dear Brother,

I wish to express to you some thoughts that should be kept before the sanitarium workers. That which will make them a power for good is the knowledge that the great Medical Missionary has chosen them to this work, that He is their chief instructor, and that it is ever their duty to recognize Him as their teacher.

The Lord has shown us the evil of depending upon the strength of earthly organizations. He has instructed us that the commission of the medical missionary is received from the very highest authority; He would have us understand that it is a mistake to regard as most essential the education given by physicians who reject the authority of Christ, the greatest Physician who ever lived upon the earth. We are not to accept and follow the views of men who refuse to recognize God as their teacher, but who learn of men, and are guided by man-made laws and restrictions.

During the night of April 26, many things were opened before me. I was shown that now in a special sense we as a people are to be guided by divine instruction. Those fitting themselves for medical missionary work should fear to place themselves under the direction of worldly doctors, to imbibe their sentiments and peculiar prejudices, and to learn to express their ideas and views. They are not to depend for their influence upon worldly teachers. They should be "looking unto Jesus, the author and finisher of our faith."

The Lord has instructed us that in our institutions of education, we should ever be striving for the perfection of character to be found in the life of Christ, and in His instruction to His disciples. Having received our commission from the highest authority, we are to educate, educate, educate, in the simplicity of Christ. Our aim must be to reach the highest standard in every feature of our work. He who healed thousands with a touch and a word is our Physician. The precious truths contained in His teachings are to be our front guard and our rearward.

The standard set for our sanitariums and schools is a high one, and a great responsibility rests upon the physicians and teachers connected with these institutions. Efforts should be made to secure teachers who will instruct after Christ's manner of teaching, regarding this of more value than any human methods. Let them honor the educational standards established by Christ, and following His instruction give their students lessons in faith and in holiness.

Christ was sent of the Father to represent His character and will. Let us follow His example in laboring to reach the people where they are. Teachers who are not particular to harmonize with the teachings of Christ, and who follow the custom and practices of worldly physicians, are out of line with the charge that the Saviour has given us.

It is not necessary that our medical missionaries follow the precise track marked out by medical men of the world. They do not need to administer drugs to the sick. They do not need to follow the drug medication in order to have influence in their work. The message was given me that if they would consecrate themselves to the Lord, if they would seek to obtain under men ordained of God, a thorough knowledge of their work, the Lord would make them skillful. Connected with the divine Teacher, they will understand that their dependence is upon God and not upon the professedly wise men of the world.

Some of our medical missionaries have supposed that a medical training according to the plans of worldly schools is essential to their success. To those who have thought that the only way to success is by being taught by worldly men, I would now say, Put away such ideas. This is a mistake that should be corrected. It is a dangerous thing to catch the spirit of the world the popularity which such a course invites, will bring into the work a spirit which the word of God cannot sanction. The medical missionary who would become efficient, if he will search his own heart and consecrate himself to Christ, may by diligent study and faithful service, learn how to grasp the mysteries of his sacred calling.

At Loma Linda, at Washington, at Wahroonga, Australia, and in many other sanitariums established for the promulgation of the work of the third angel's message there are to come to the physicians and to the teachers new ideas, and a new understanding of the principles that must govern the medical work. An education is to be given that is altogether in harmony with the teachings of the word of God.

In the first chapter of Ephesians, beginning with vs. 2, we read: "Grace be unto you, and peace, from God our Father, and from the Lord Jesus Christ. Blessed be the God and Father of our Lord Jesus Christ, who hath blessed us with all spiritual blessings in heavenly places in Christ: according as He hath chosen us in Him before the foundation of the world, that we should be holy and without blame before Him in love: having predestinated us unto the adoption of children by Jesus Christ to Himself, according to the good pleasure of His will, to the praise of the glory of His grace, wherein He hath made us accepted in the beloved. In whom we have redemption through His blood, the forgiveness of sins, according to the riches of His grace; wherein He hath abounded toward us in all wisdom and prudence; having made known unto us the mystery of His will, according to His good pleasure which He hath purposed in Himself." Study the whole of this chapter, and grasp the assurances that are given again and again for your acceptance.

It is a lack of faith in the power of God that leads our physicians to lean so much upon the arm of the law, and to trust so much to the influence of worldly powers. The truly converted man and woman who will study these words of inspiration spoken by the apostle Paul may learn to claim in all their depth and fulness the divine promises.

I am charged to present these Scriptures to our people, that they may understand that those who do not believe the word of God can not possibly present to those who desire to become acceptable medical missionaries, the way by which they will become most successful. Christ was the greatest Physician the world has ever known; His heart was ever touched with human woe. He has a work for those to do who will not place their dependence upon worldly powers.

God's true commandment-keeping people will be instructed by Him. The true medical missionary will be wise in the treatment of the sick, using the remedies that Nature provides. And then he will look to Christ as the true Healer of disease. The principles of health reform brought into the life of the patient, the use of Nature's remedies, and the cooperation of divine agencies in behalf of the suffering, will bring success.

Satan will try to place barriers in the way of the true medical missionary. He will seek to bring discouragement upon those who recognize the commandments of God, and are determined to obey them. We must be careful not to carry our views of health reform to extremes, thus making it "health deform." Our food should be plain and free from all objectionable elements, but let us be careful that it is always palatable and good.

A time will come when medical missionaries of other denominations will become jealous and envious of the influence exerted by Seventh-day Adventists who are working in these lines. They will feel that influence is being secured by our workers which they ought to have. We should have in various places, men of extraordinary ability, who have obtained their diplomas in medical schools of the best reputation, who can stand before the world as fully qualified and legally recognized physicians. Let God-fearing men be wisely chosen to go through the training essential in order to obtain such qualifications. They should be prudent men who will remain true to the principles of the message.

These should obtain the qualifications, and the authority to conduct an educational work for our young men and our young women who desire to be trained for medical missionary work.

Now while the world is favorable toward the teaching of the health reform principles, moves should be made to secure for our own physicians the privilege of imparting medical instruction to our young people who would otherwise be led to attend the worldly medical colleges. The time will come when it will be more difficult than it is now, to arrange for the training of our young people in medical missionary lines.

* * * * *

A Statement Regarding the Training of Physicians

"The light given me is: We must provide that which is essential to qualify our youth who desire to be physicians, so that they may intelligently fit themselves to be able to stand the examinations required to prove their efficiency as physicians. They should be taught to treat understandingly the cases of those who are diseased, so that the door will be closed for any sensible physician to imagine that we are not giving in our school the instruction necessary for properly qualifying young men and young women to do the work of a physician. Continually the students who are graduated are to advance in knowledge, for practice makes perfect.

"The medical school at Loma Linda is to be of the highest order, because those who are in that school have the privilege of maintaining a living connection with the wisest of all physicians from whom there is communicated knowledge of a superior order. And for the special preparation of these of our youth who have clear convictions of their duty to obtain a medical education that will enable them to pass the examinations required by law of all who practice as regularly qualified physicians, we are to supply whatever may be required so that these youth need not be compelled to go to medical schools conducted by men not of our faith. Thus we shall close a door that the enemy would be pleased to have left open; and our young men and women, whose spiritual interests the Lord desires us to safeguard, will not feel compelled to connect with unbelievers in order to obtain a thorough training along medical lines.

"Ellen G. White."

* * * * *

In one of the most recent communications relative to this work, these words occur, "We are not to accept and follow the views of men who refuse to recognize God as their teacher, but who learn of men and are guided by man-made laws and restrictions. I was shown how that in a special sense we as a people are to be guided by divine instruction. Those fitting themselves for medical missionary work should fear to place themselves under worldly doctors, to imbibe their sentiments and peculiar prejudices, and to learn to express their ideas and views.... It is not necessary that our medical missionaries follow the precise track marked out by medical men of the world. They do not need to administer drugs to the sick. They do not need to follow the drug medication in order to have influence in their work. The message was given me that if they would consecrate themselves to the Lord, if they would seek to obtain under men ordained of God, a thorough knowledge of their work, the Lord would make them skillful.... Some of our medical missionaries have supposed that a medical training according to the plans of worldly schools is essential to their success. To those who have thought that the only way to success is by being taught by worldly men and by pursuing a course that is sanctioned by worldly men, I would now say, put away such ideas. This is a mistake that should be corrected. It is a dangerous thing to catch the spirit of the world; the popularity which such a course invites, will bring into the work a spirit which the word of God cannot sanction. It is a lack of faith in the power of God that leads our physicians to lean so much upon the arm of law, and to trust so much to the influence of worldly powers. The true medical missionary will be wise in the treatment of the sick, using the remedies that nature provides. And then he will look to Christ as the true healer of diseases. The principles of health reform brought into the life of the patient, the use of nature's remedies and the cooperation of divine agencies in behalf of the suffering, will bring success.

I am instructed to say that in our educational work there is to be no compromise in order to meet the world's standards. God's commandment-keeping people are not to unite with the world to carry various lines of work according to worldly plans and worldly wisdom.

"Our people are now being tested as to whether they will obtain their wisdom from the greatest Teacher the world ever knew, or seek to the God of Ekron. Let us determine that we shall not be tied by so much as a thread to the educational policies of those who do not discern the voice of God, and who will not hearken to His commandments.

"Shall we represent before the world that our physicians must follow the pattern of the world, before they can be qualified to act as successful physicians? This is the question that is now testing the faith of some of our brethren. Let not any of our brethren displease the Lord by advocating in their assemblies the idea that we need to obtain from unbelievers a higher education than that specified by the Lord.

"The representation of the great Teacher is to be considered an all-sufficient revelation. Those in our ranks who qualify as physicians are to receive only such education as is in harmony with these divine truths. Some have advised that students should, after taking some work at Loma Linda, complete their medical education in worldly colleges. But this is not in harmony with the Lord's plan. God is our wisdom, our sanctification and our righteousness. Facilities should be provided at Loma Linda, that the necessary instruction in medical lines may be given by instructors who fear the Lord, and who are in harmony with His plans for the treatment of the sick.

"I have not a word to say in favor of the world's ideas of higher education in any school that we shall organize for the training of physicians. There is danger in their attaching themselves to worldly institutions, and working under the ministrations of worldly physicians. Satan is giving his orders to those whom he has led to depart from the faith. I would now advise that none of our young people attach themselves to worldly medical institutions in hope of gaining better success, or stronger influence as physicians."

* * * * *

Pacific Union College, Calif.
B.-76-1910. Sept. 4, 1910
Elder J. A. Burden, Loma Linda, California:

Dear Brother Burden,

I am at the Pacific Union College, attending a council meeting of the church school teachers. Yesterday, Sabbath, I spoke in the chapel. The room was filled. A larger place will have to be provided in which to hold meetings. I spoke from the fifty-eighth chapter of

Isaiah. I had some very important instruction to give to those present regarding the necessity of our working intelligently, and the Lord gave me strength to speak.

Brother and Sister Burden, I am very anxious that you should work with the best of courage. Notwithstanding that there are those who do not speak to you the encouraging words that for their own souls' good the Lord would have them speak, yet I have this word for you: You are to press on; still bearing the Lord's message for this time. There is a great work that with the help of the Lord you can both do. I wish that all those connected with you were united heart and mind in assisting you in the right way by speaking words of encouragement. But so long as you keep the eye of faith fixed on your Leader, you are safe. Rest in his hands. I am bidden to charge you not to fail or become discouraged. Keep your hearts filled with courage. Talk faith. Some are ready to speak words of discouragement. The Lord says to you, Be of good courage. Walk humbly, and work out the will of God. I am to say to you, There are many words of an objectionable character spoken by some who suppose that thus they can bring in improvements. But go straight ahead, following the instruction of Christ.

* * * * *

To Those in our Sanitariums

Sanitarium, Napa Co., Calif.
B-77-1910, Sept. 10, 1910

I have decided words to speak to all who shall act a part in bearing responsibilities in our Sanitariums. We are intensely desirous that all connected with our Sanitariums shall give evidence that they are men and women who believe in Christ as the world's Redeemer. They are to show that they are laborers together with the Saviour, seeking to save the souls of those who are not truly converted, and working to save their own souls by striving to exert a correct example. Do not gather to your working forces men who, if they are tempted, give way to their feelings; men who will not understand that if they are influenced by wrong principles, they will be sure to sow seeds of distrust in other minds.

Christ came to our world to set his followers an example of perfection of character, that in his strength they might become Christlike, building for time and for eternity. I am bidden to give all our workers, men and women, a most solemn charge; if you are not truly converted, God can not use you. In word, in spirit, and in all your works you are to bear testimony to the truth, making straight paths for your feet lest the lame be turned out of the way by your walking in strange paths.

"Beloved, I wish above all things that thou mayest prosper and be in health, even as thy soul prospereth. I have no greater joy than to hear that my children walk in truth. Beloved, thou doest faithfully whatsoever thou doest to the brethren and to strangers which have borne witness of thy charity before the church, whom if thou bring forward on thy journey after a godly sort, thou shalt do well, because that for his name's sake they went forth, taking nothing of the Gentiles. We therefore ought to receive such, that we might be fellow-helpers to the truth."

Read slowly the whole of the first chapter of second Peter and grasp by faith the precious truths given for our encouragement.

Ellen G. White

* * * * *

Remarks of Mrs. E.G. White Regarding Aggressive Moves at Loma Linda

June 18, 1911. -5- MS. 9-1911.

At a Meeting in the Chapel, April 20, 1911

(Thursday afternoon, April 20, there was a council meeting in the Loma Linda Chapel, to consider the opportunity that had just been presented to purchase from Mr. Kelly a tract of land west of the Pepper Drive and south of the Colton road, consisting of about eighty-four acres.

After very brief remarks about the Vine and the Branches, and the benefits resulting from the disciplinary process of pruning, Sister White spoke of various phases of the work.)

Today with Sister McEnterfer, and again with my son, I rode around the Loma Linda grounds, and took more particular notice of them than ever before; and I feel very thankful that we have such a place. Surely we ought to be a grateful people because God has brought us into possession of this beautiful place.

In our meetings during this council, we have been speaking of the higher education. What is the higher education. It is to understand Christ's words and teachings, and to follow on to know the Lord. It is to know that His going forth is prepared as the morning.

Today, as I looked over the place more thoroughly than ever before, and saw the grounds, the drives, and the cottages that were standing before we came here, I felt gratitude in my heart toward God, that through His providences we had been brought into possession of Loma Linda. I felt thankful also to see the improvements that have been made since we had had the place, and I thought how important it is that we make every move in accordance with the will of God.

As the Lord prospers us, we should manifest our gratitude by a willingness to advance. We should see the advantage of adding to that which we already have. I feel a burden regarding the danger of letting anybody come into the neighborhood to spoil the place.

There is a piece of land across the railroad, lying next to a piece already purchased, which should be secured. One day we drove over it, and all around it. We wanted to see all about it. And I am sure from the representations that have been made to me, that this piece of land ought to come into our possession. If you are wise, the next time I come here, you will have that land. I will try to help you all I can. Let us work intelligently.

There are several reasons why you should have this land. You need the produce from it for your cattle to subsist upon; this piece is close at hand, and joins that which you already have.

Here we have our school, and here many important interests are centered. We must not permit elements to come in that will tend to hinder and retard the work. It will be pleasing to the Lord if we keep our eyes wide open, and are fully awake, ready to take advantage of every circumstance that will place us in right relation to the work we have to do. It would be a grievous error for us to allow to pass an opportunity to secure this property, for we might never again have such an opportunity. I advise you to secure it before it becomes so expensive that you could not afford to buy it.

There is danger of our becoming too narrow. Those many little houses close together across the railroad do not look well. If we can get land, and have room, so as not to build any more in that way, it will be better.

You need the land, and it will be a matter of regret by and by if it is not secured. Do not make any delay to take steps that will prevent its being taken up by those who would plan for unbelievers to crowd into it. We should keep them out. If we do this, we shall have reason to rejoice.

The Lord is well pleased with what you have already done here at Loma Linda. When one sees the prosperity that has attended the work, and the spirit of consecration that prevails, the conviction deepens that you are working in harmony with God.

I desire that all the work of this place shall be a correct representation of what our health institutions should be. Let everything that we lay our hands to, show the result of the moving of the Spirit of God upon the human heart. This will be evidence that we have the higher education. Workers whose hearts are in obedience to the movings of the Spirit of God will make this place what God desires it to be. I am surprised, happily surprised to see everything looking so well. It is beyond my expectations. And now let every one strive to keep it so, and labor for improvements.

I am highly gratified as I look upon the land we already have. This will be one of the greatest blessings to us in the future,—one that we do not fully appreciate now, but which we shall appreciate by and by. I hope that you will get the other land that I have spoken of, and join it to that which you already have. It will pay you to do this. As I have carried the burden of this place from the very beginning, I wanted to say this much to you. Now I leave the matter with you; and let us work in harmony.

Our Duty to Reach Out

Individually we should stand in freedom before God, serving Him intelligently. The Lord will work through every soul who is consecrated to Him. He will give them knowledge and spiritual understanding; and He will direct their steps. How shall we know that He is leading us? Because we act in accordance with the Holy Spirit and are in harmony with Christ.

You know how hard the enemy worked that we should not get this place. Now it is in our possession, and you have been working to the point of occupying and using and improving the place for the benefit of the sick and the honor of Christ's name. The Lord is pleased with this. He wants you to work His vineyard faithfully; and your faithful service appeals to the understanding of the patients and visitors. If it were not for this faithfulness, you never would have secured the favor and gained the advantages that you enjoy today in regard to the educational work taken up here. You stand in favor before the people. This advantageous position you could not have gotten if there had been a laxness in the work and a leaving things at loose ends.

"Wherefore, gird up the loins of your mind; be sober, and hope to the end for the grace that is to be brought unto you at the revelation of Jesus Christ."

Those who stand here are to be an example in humility, in steadfastness, in high standing, showing to the world what is the higher education, showing what it means to be linked up with Christ. If your will is united with Jesus Christ, we shall see the work of God advance steadily in this place. It will reach to Riverside; it will reach to other places that are all around. There is a work to be done in many little settlements round about here. There is no virtue in settling down in one place, and spending all your time and energies there. There are many towns and settlements where earnest work needs to be done for the saving of souls. You are to have an arm of strength in all these places. The word comes to you; Be wise; be vigilant.

We should feel a deep interest in those souls who are brought into connection with us. We are to labor for them, leaving unused no means that God has put in His world for our use in behalf of others. It was thus that Christ labored: Going from place to place, He preached the precious gospel, sowing the seeds of truth in the hearts of men and women who would listen to His testimony. And He wants every soul of us to appreciate the work that He has given us, and the example He has set.

Unity Among the Workers

Do not let division come in to destroy the spirit of unity. We want unity; and when we pray together, let faith lay hold upon the Mighty One. Christ is looking upon us in love. If we will walk in His footsteps, following on to know the Lord, we shall know that His going forth is prepared as the morning.

The blessed Saviour did not refuse to die for men, but for their sakes submitted to abuse and mockery from His enemies, His life was taken away in cruelty. As He hung upon the cross, His enemies, standing at the foot, divided His garments among them. Consider how much Christ endured that we might believe that no experience can come to us that He does not fully understand. We are to be led by a spirit entirely opposite to that which inspired the enemies of Christ. It is our privilege to help one another and sustain one another, thus showing that the Spirit of God is working in heart and mind and character.

I am glad there are sensible men and women here. I am pleased that there is a strong force of physicians and teachers. And I want to say to you all: work in harmony, "I beseech you, brethren, by the name of our Lord Jesus Christ, that ye all speak the same thing, and that there be no division among you; but that ye be perfectly joined together in the same mind, and in the same judgment." The Lord wants you to do this, and I believe you will. If you cannot possibly do it here; just go away where you can. We need to draw steadily with Christ, and to labor to glorify His holy name. And the responsible men and women in this place should give thanks to God for His manifold mercies. But do not complain or indulge in criticism, because this is all out of place. It will spoil the work.

Not Amusements but Consecrated Work

There are some who feel that if there is prosperity here it will be necessary to get up some amusement. Let us not cherish such thoughts as this. Rather let the people see that you have a mind for usefulness and duty, and that to the saving of the soul. The amusements that consume time just to gratify self, do not pay.

I have felt so thankful regarding the improvements that I see here. God has prospered you, and He will continue to prosper. And we must give ourselves to the education of those who do not appreciate these things. We must keep it before them in the living light. Regarding the securing of means for the development of the work, you must exercise the living faith that takes hold from above. Some here know what a battle we have had in order to secure harmonious action; and we thank the Lord that when the enemy comes in like a flood, then the Spirit of the Lord lifts up for us a standard against the enemy.

Some will think that by having amusements here we will gain more influence. But what we want is to go steadily forward, with our hands firmly holding the divine promises, believing that Christ will lead and guide and bless, and place a heavenly stamp upon our work. Do not feel that there is not enough in all that we have to do in this place for Christ and heaven, and that you must reach out for some amusement outside of your God-given work. Do not do it; for this will not harmonize with Christ's example. Stand solidly for God. Tell the students, here we have Riverside and other places. If you want to do a good work, take our publications, and carry them to these places. Hold meetings, and let the people see that you have a living connection with heaven. If you are a child of God, your prayers, and your work to strengthen and build up will have an influence, and God will bestow His blessing upon you. We need not feel that we must provide amusements to gratify the desires of some who come in here hoping to attract attention to themselves. It would be better that such ones should go elsewhere. We are here to give the last message of warning to a perishing world, and every jot of our influence is to be consecrated to God. It is not His will that frivolous, unsanctified amusements shall be instituted here. We have a heaven to win, a hell to shun; let us work solidly in behalf of ourselves and others for eternal life in the kingdom of God.

At Paradise Valley I told the workers that they must do all in their power to honor and glorify God. God makes the impression upon hearts; it is not we who make it. If we work faithfully to glorify God, he will make the impression upon the people. He will lift up and strengthen every soul that seeks Him in sincerity. He will teach us how to lay hold of His promises, so that His grace shall abound in the soul.

It is our privilege to be co-workers with God. Let no one feel that he must secure the highest place in order that he may do the greatest amount of acceptable service. Do not fear that you will lose patronage unless you enter into some of the world's fashions and amusements. Your eyes must be fixed on the pattern Christ Jesus. Imitate Him, in works, in conversation, in your deportment before the people. If you will follow in the footsteps of Jesus, you will have an everlasting reward. The way is open for you to work in unison with Christ; and He who gave His precious life for you will help and strengthen you, and guide you step by step, if you desire to be led.

* * * * *

Sanitarium, Calif.,
May 22, 1911.-5- B.-20-1911. April 30,'11.
Elder J. A. Burden, Loma Linda, Calif.:
Dear Brother and Sister Burden,

On Wednesday evening we took the train at Los Angeles. We had good accommodations, and nothing in particular transpired to cause any unpleasantness. It was a very long train of cars. We had a good lunch, and were all very comfortable.

My letter must be a short one, as my head is easily wearied. As soon as I begin to use it, I am troubled with disagreeable pains. I have not yet recovered from the severe affliction I suffered at Glendale. After our trip to Fernando my heart and arm were seriously painful. Sara gave me most thorough treatment, and after a long time relief came. I was urged to visit Long Beach, to see how they were situated in the work there; but I was in such pain that I had to refuse. I dared not venture to go.

In the afternoon of the day that we left for home, Elder Andross took us in an automobile to visit the several churches and the Bible workers' home in Los Angeles. We did not get out of the conveyance, but stopped and spoke to some of those engaged in the work. It was a very pleasant trip, and I was very glad to see so much of the work in Los Angeles. The automobile was an easy-riding machine that did not jolt me, so I was spared any increased suffering.

We reached home in safety, and on Friday I got relief from the pain I had endured for two days and nights. I felt that the Lord had blessed me; and on the next day, Sabbath, I consented to speak in the Sanitarium chapel. I was surprised to meet so large a congregation there, and was thankful for the opportunity of speaking to them.

My mind is settled in regard to the purchase of the land in front of the Loma Linda Sanitarium. We must have that piece of land. I will pledge myself to be depended upon for one thousand dollars. I hope to be favored with an opportunity to hire some money soon but I shall not worry in regard to this, or I shall not be able to do anything. The effort of speaking on Sabbath and of reading my letters today is all I have been able to do to the present time. But as soon as I can I will make some movement concerning the raising of the one thousand dollars. The piece of land we must have; for it will never do to have buildings crowded in there. Do not fail to carry through the purchase of it. Do your best, and I will do my best. The money from me you may depend upon. We shall be able to send it soon.

* * * * *

**Sanitarium, Calif.,
May 24, '11 -5- B.-22-1911. May 7, 1911.
Brethren Ruble, Burden, and Evans, Loma Linda, Calif.:**
Dear Brethren,

I have words of instruction for you and your co-workers who are ministers and physicians and counsellors at Loma Linda. During my visit to Southern California, light was given me that many of the leaders in our sanitariums were failing of meeting the requirements of God, and, more than this, they did not realize their lack. I was instructed that those who stand in positions of responsibility in these important institutions are engaged in a most sacred work, that they have little time in which to do the work committed to their trust, and that it was of the utmost importance that faithfulness and consecration mark their efforts in every line.

In a remarkable way God has brought into our possession some of the institutions through whose agency we are to accomplish the work of reformation to which we as a people are called. At this time every talent of every worker should be regarded as a sacred trust to be used in extending the work of reform.

The Lord instructed me that our sisters who have received training that has fitted them for positions of responsibility, are to serve with faithfulness and discernment in their calling, using their influence wisely, and, with their brethren in the faith, obtaining an experience that will fit them for still greater usefulness. The instruction of the apostle Peter, "Add to your faith virtue, and to virtue knowledge," they are to bring into their individual experience, and this work of daily sanctification through cooperation with the Spirit of God, will develop their knowledge and capabilities.

In ancient times the Lord worked in a wonderful way through consecrated women who united in his work with men whom He had chosen to stand as His representatives. He used women to gain great decisive victories. More than once, in times of emergency, He brought them to the front and worked through them for the salvation of many lives. Through Esther the queen the Lord accomplished a mighty deliverance for His people. At a time when it seemed that no power could save them, Esther, and the women associated with her, by fasting and prayer and prompt action, met the issue, and brought salvation to their people.

[570] A study of women's work in connection with the cause of God in the Old Testament times will teach us lessons that will enable us to meet emergencies in the work today. We may not be brought into such a critical and prominent place as were the people of God in the time of Esther; but often converted women can act an important part in more humble positions. This many have been doing and are still ready to do. It is a woman's duty to unite with her husband in the disciplining and training of her sons and daughters, that they may be converted, and their powers consecrated to the service of God. There are many who have ability to stand with their husbands in sanitarium work, to give treatments to the sick and to speak words of counsel and encouragement to others. There are those who should seek an education that will fit them to act the part of physicians.

In this line of service a positive work needs to be done, women as well as men are to receive a thorough medical training. They should make a special study of the diseases common to women, that they may understand how to treat them. It is considered most essential that men desiring to practice medicine shall receive the broad training necessary for the following of such a profession. It is just as essential that women receive such a training, and obtain their diplomas certifying their right to act as physicians.

Our institutions should be especially thorough in giving to women a training that will fit them to act as midwives. There should be in our sanitariums lady physicians who understand well their profession, and who can attend women at the time of childbirth. Light has been given me that women instead of men should take the responsibility in such cases. I was directed to the Bible plan, in which at such times women acted the part of the physician. This plan should be carried out by us; for it is the Lord's plan.

Again and again light has been given me that women should be chosen and educated for this line of work. Now the time has come when we should face the matter clearly. More women should be educated for this work, and thus a door of temptation may be closed. We should allow no unnecessary temptation to be placed in the way of physicians and nurses, or the people for whom they minister.

The Lord has greatly favored us in providing suitable buildings at Loma Linda for the carrying forward of the work as it should be carried. Let us be in earnest in following the counsel we have received.

I have been instructed to say to our leading sanitarium workers throughout our ranks; the work must move forward on a higher plane, and after a more sacred order than it has heretofore if it is to accomplish all that God designs should be accomplished by it in our churches and for the world. We need to pray, and to consider earnestly what is the great spiritual need of men and women in this age. Strange things are being done, which are not after the Lord's counsel, but after the devising of men. As wicked practices increase among those who are determined to do wickedly, there is a great need that our people bring into prominence before the world a pure, untainted work. The Lord says to us, Be ye clean that labor in the health institutions. Work under the influence of the Holy Spirit of God. Let the men holding positions of sacred trust view the work from a high standpoint.

I ask you who stand as leaders in this work to read prayerfully chapters four to eleven of the book of Deuteronomy; for there is instruction that all need who would understand God's dealings with His people. And I wish to impress upon all who read these chapters that they mean much to every soul who carries responsibilities in connection with sanitarium work. "Thou art a holy people unto the Lord thy God," the Lord declares, "and the Lord thy God hath chosen thee to be a peculiar people unto Himself above all nations that are upon the earth." All the directions He has given are to be carefully observed, from the greatest to that which may seem least.

The Lord says, to all, Purify your souls from all commonness. Set before your children and households an example in word and deportment that will lead them to desire above all things to render to God consecrated loving service. Pray for your home; instruct your family, sanctify the Lord God of Israel in your hearts and in your lives. I am deeply pained as I see with some a spirit of carelessness in speech and deportment. This is a hindrance to spirituality. The Lord declared to Israel. "What doth the Lord require of thee, but to fear the Lord thy God, and to walk in all His ways, and to love Him, and to serve the Lord thy God with all thy heart and with all thy soul, and to keep the commandments of the Lord, and His statutes, which I command thee this day for thy good. Behold the heaven and the heaven of heavens is the Lord's thy God, the earth also, and all that therein is. Only the Lord had a delight in thy fathers to love them, and He chose their seed after them, even you above all people, as it is this day." Read these words thoughtfully, and consider how great are the privileges of the people whom the Lord chose to serve Him. To all connected with sacred duties I am charged to say, Seek the Lord. Take heed to your conversation; lay off all cheapness of speech; for the Lord would have you become intelligent workers and wise counsellors. Let those with whom you associate see nothing of frivolity in your words and works. You have the knowledge of sacred truth, and you are to honor those truths as men and women who must give an account for the talents entrusted to them.

[572] God would have His honor exalted before men as supreme, and His counsels confirmed in the eyes of the people. The witness of the prophet Elijah on Mount Carmel gives the example of one who stood wholly for God and His work in the earth. The prophet calls the Lord by His name, Jehovah God, which He himself had given to denote His condescension and compassion. Elijah calls Him the God of Abraham and Isaac and Israel. He does this that he may excite in the hearts of his backslidden people humble remembrance of the Lord, and assure them of His rich free grace. Elijah prays, "Be it known this day that thou art the God of Israel." The honor of God is to be exalted as supreme, but the prophet asks further that his mission also may be confirmed. "Let it be known that Thou art God in Israel," he prays," and that I am Thy servant, and have done all things at Thy word." "Hear me, O Lord," he pleads, "Hear me." Elijah is intense. As he prayed the silence of death seemed to be about him. As the Amen was spoken, lo, the fire of heaven descended on the sacrifices in sight of the multitude.

The people were wonderfully affected by the scene. At the manifestation of God's power, they fell on their faces on the earth, and extolled the God of Abraham, and gave glory to the God of Israel. With a loud voice they shouted, "The Lord, He is the God; the Lord, He is the God."

But while the people acknowledged the God of heaven, the priests, with hardened hearts, refused to be convinced. They would remain still the prophets of Baal. Thus they showed themselves ripe for destruction. And Elijah said to the people, "Take the prophets of Baal; let not one of them escape." The time had come when delusion was unveiled. The people saw the false prophets, and when the word was spoken, they fell upon the prophets, brought them down to the brook Kishon, and took part in their slaughter. Thus was Elijah's faith crowned with victory, the priests of Baal put to shame, and the worshipers of false gods confounded.

Elijah's whole life was devoted to the work of reform. He was a voice crying in the wilderness to rebuke sin and press back the tide of moral evil. And while he came to the people as a reprover of sin, his message offered the balm of Gilead for the sinsick souls of all who would be healed. His zeal for God's glory and his deep love for the house of Israel present lessons for the instruction of all who stand today as representatives of God's work in the earth. Let the conductors of our institutional work catch the spirit of zeal felt by Elijah and learn its intensity. Let them seek for the grace of God that will give them an experience in advance of that which they have heretofore enjoyed. Let them love the work of God, and pray for its advancement in the world.

* * * * *

Sanitarium, Calif.,
May 22, 1911.-5- B. 18, 1911. May 18, 1911.
J. A. Burden:

....

I wish to say to Elder Burden that the money which I pledged to help purchase the eighty-five acres will be sent without fail. Please let me know if a couple of weeks' delay will trouble you seriously. I am truly glad that I gave my promise to help to purchase this land, under the influence of the Spirit of God. I felt that the land must be secured; otherwise that we should have reason to regret that we did not obtain it.

* * * * *

Sanitarium, Calif.,

June 7, 1911 -5- K.-32-1911. June 5, 1911.
Dr. D. H. Kress.:

I realize that a place like Loma Linda needs experienced men and women to conduct the work in its different departments. But the Lord is willing to work with all who will commit their ways to Him, and who will be led by the Holy Spirit. All are to be workers with Christ. He commits to His true followers the power of persuasion, the power of His grace and truth, a deep and constant love for His work in home and foreign fields. He gives them hearts that are in earnest in gathering with Christ. With helpers possessing such gifts as these, the medical missionary work cannot be without fruit.

The power of persuasion is a wonderful gift. It means much to those who would win souls to Christ. Let us keep our souls in the love of God. If Christ is working with His messengers, fruit will be seen as the result of their efforts.

* * * * *

Sanitarium, Calif.,
July 7, '11-5- B.-34-1911. June 7, 1911.
Elder J. A. Burden, Loma Linda, Calif.:

Dear Brother and Sister Burden,

I want to say to you both that I am thankful I was moved to speak as I did concerning the piece of land in front of the Loma Linda Sanitarium. I was urged by the Spirit of God to make the pledge of one thousand dollars; and I did so hoping that others, who were better able to give than I, would follow my example. I dared not leave the meeting without following the conviction I had; and now I feel that I have done my duty, showing my faith by my works.

I am glad that we were able to send you my part of the first payment a few days ago.

I would like to inquire what progress has been made in the raising of means for the purchase of the land. My investment was not made in order to lessen the responsibility of others who should help. Do what you can to encourage those who have money that they can use in the cause, to use it wisely and not let it slip away into speculation. Secure pledges from those who have not money in sight. We need special wisdom to move out at the right time. I thank the Lord that

He encouraged me to walk by faith, and I pray that He will help you to show others their privilege in this matter.

True faith is the substance of things hope for, and the evidence of things not seen. Thus far the Lord has led us as we have moved under the guidance of His Spirit. He will continue to work for us if we are careful to follow the counsel He gives.

Medical missionary work is the pioneer work of the gospel. Let us seek to understand the scope of the work to be done in our sanitariums for the saving of the souls and the healing of the bodies of those who come to us for relief. My soul is drawn out to encourage men and women to see in Christ the great Physician. If they will be drawn to Him, He will be their helper. He understands their every need. He stands ready to heal both body and soul. Let Physicians and nurses learn to tell of the One who has power and who is willing to do a marvelous work for human beings. Talk of His love, tell of His power to save every sinful soul who will cast himself upon Christ's merits. His power will save to the uttermost all who truly accept Him.

I am glad that your wife is wholeheartedly united with you in the work. Let her stand by you to give help and encouragement.

I have written to you the instruction that has been given me regarding the special work to be done by the lady physicians in our sanitariums. It is the Lord's plan that men shall be trained to treat men, and the women trained to treat women. In the confinement of women, midwives should take the responsibility of the case. In the Bible times it was not considered a proper thing for men to act in this capacity; and it is not the will of God that men should do this work today. Very much evil has resulted from the practice of men treating women, and women treating men. It is a practice according to human devising, and not according to God's plan. Long has the evil been left to grow, but now we lift our voice in protest against that which is displeasing to God.

Ellen G. White

* * * * *

Regarding the Purchase of Land Adjoining Loma Linda

Aug. 29, 1911.-5- Ms.-13-1911.

Loma Linda is an important center. We needed this place and all its advantages. We were successful in obtaining it, and we have had success in operating it, notwithstanding the opposition shown by some who should have been acting as helpers in the effort to equip the sanitarium properly. I have a deep interest in Loma Linda. It is a beautiful place. For sanitarium work, we could not have a more favorable situation. And it is well adapted for the other lines of work that we desire to see done there.

Recently the question arose about securing more of the nearby land that is for sale. One piece, a tract of 86 acres, has already been purchased, and there is another of 47 acres joining the Loma Linda property, which is now offered for sale. Because this piece of land is so near to our Loma Linda buildings, we do not want to see it sold to outsiders, who will divide it up, and sell it to those who may desire to crowd into this neighborhood. In the night season I was talking to our brethren, telling them that this must not be allowed, and pointing out what unfavorable results would follow. If this piece of land should be purchased by outsiders, and divided up and sold to those who would be no help to our work, the injury to Loma Linda would be serious and lasting. I cannot bear the thought of this. Cannot a group of individuals who are alive to the vital interests of the Lord's work, unite together and make this land our property? Then if we wish to sell any portion of it, let it be sold to our people. There is an orange orchard on the place, and this could be handled to advantage by the sanitarium. The institution is hardly complete without the control of this orange orchard.

Will not some of our brethren who thus far have invested but little in Loma Linda, help the Lord's cause by assisting in the purchase of this piece of land? I place this matter before you, feeling sure that you will not allow the land to pass into the hands of unbelievers. We ought not to place ourselves where we shall become unfavorably associated with those who could make it hard for us if they chose to do so, and restrict us to certain limits.

Families and institutions should learn to do more in the cultivation and improvement of land. If people only knew the value of the products of the ground, which the earth brings forth in their season, more diligent efforts would be made to cultivate the soil. All should be acquainted with the special value of fruit and vegetables fresh from the orchard and garden. As the number of patients and students increase, more land will be needed. Grape vines should be planted, thus making it possible for the institution to produce its grapes. The orange orchard that is on the place would be an advantage.

We must have room to keep ourselves distinct as a Sabbath-keeping people. The Lord has given directions that we are to make provision which will prevent our being harassed and inconvenienced by having to crowd in with unbelievers. I wish I might make on your minds the impression that has been made on mine regarding this matter.

If a portion of this land must be sold, we can sell it to the friends of the institution.

*****

An Appeal in Behalf of our Medical College

Sanitarium, Calif..
MS-15-1911 Aug. 29, 1911.

[581] The proper development of the work at Loma Linda calls for prayerful thought and planning, that the instruction which the Lord has given concerning the work there may be fulfilled. Our people in the Eastern and Middle States, as well as those on the Pacific Coast, should feel an intense interest that a special work be done at Loma Linda at the present time. It fills me with anxiety to think that any who seek to obtain the benefits of the education that Loma Linda can give, should be turned away because the buildings are insufficient to give them a place. That some patients have had to be turned away from the Sanitarium has caused me sorrow. The work of the Medical College at Loma Linda must not be crippled for lack of room. There must be some way devised to enlarge quickly the buildings for the rooming of students, so that those who seek a training may not be turned away.

The students at Loma Linda are seeking for an education that is after the Lord's order, an education that will help them to develop into successful teachers and laborers for others. When their education there is completed, they should be able to go forth and join the intelligent workers in the world's great harvest fields who are carrying forward the work of reform that is to prepare a people to stand in the day of Christ's coming. Everywhere workers are needed who know how to combat disease and give skillful care to the sick and suffering. We should do all in our power to enable those who desire to be thus fitted for service, to gain the necessary training. I am instructed that those among us who have means should become God's agencies in this work.

Our people should become intelligent in the treatment of sickness without the aid of poisonous drugs. Many should seek to obtain the education that will enable them to combat disease in its varied forms by the most simple methods. Thousands have been restored to health by simple methods of treatment. Let diligent study be united with faithful ministry. Let prayers of faith be offered by the bedside of the sick. Let the sick be encouraged to claim the promises of God for themselves. "Faith is the substance of things hoped for, the evidence of things not seen." Christ Jesus, the Saviour of men, is to be brought into our labors and councils more and more.

I am instructed that there are among us those who should become God's agents to labor for the advancement of this work. The Lord would be pleased to see our people who have means using it freely in opening the way for workers to get a training as medical missionaries. To those who have money we say, Make your donations. The Lord has given us great advantages in bringing into our possession such institutions as Loma Linda. Let us cooperate with Him in making these places a blessing to humanity. By liberal gifts let us say to the burden-bearers at Loma Linda, "Put up your men's dormitory quickly."

Elders Irwin and Corliss have been selected to visit our brethren in some of the larger conferences, and to ask for immediate help for Loma Linda. Others also are to be appointed to prepare the way for the work to go forward at Loma Linda. The Lord has made it possible for this place to stand as a training center for medical evangelists. A good beginning has been made, but the work must broaden. Help is needed at this time. Let us make room for the carrying forward of the grand work that

the Lord has specified should be done. Now, just now, let your means be invested to provide the buildings which the carrying on of this work demands. Do not delay. Encourage the brethren who call for means by revealing a spirit that is willing to do the work which greatly needs to be done.

I ask you, my brethren and sisters, to do what you can to help, and to do it now. Let your means be invested in this work that is so far-reaching. This is the work of God. He has given us great advantages for the carrying on of His work; He now calls for the advantage of your means, that many may be qualified to go forth to finish up His work in the earth. The Lord will reward all who come forward in emergencies, and do their best. Those who can help should be deeply interested in preparing the way for those who wish to be qualified as missionaries for God. My brethren, and sisters, work for God with your means while you have opportunity. In doing this, you will be using your talent to His name's glory.

Ellen G. White

* * * * *

Loma Linda

**Sept. 28, 1911.-5- H. 78-1911. Sept. 28, 1911.
Elder S. N. Haskell, Sanitarium, Calif.:**

I have made some investments for Loma Linda to enable that institution to secure land adjoining the sanitarium that was for sale. Had this land been sold to unbelievers, and they had crowded in, the institution would have been placed at a disadvantage. I felt that we could not afford to run this risk. The land is now purchased, and to that extent we are safe from elements that might work trouble and confusion to our medical school. I could not rest until I had the assurance that we were safe from this possibility. This purchase may mean the keeping away from the institution a class of people who might have proved burdensome. Now that we have this land a burden is rolled off my heart.

[587]

A Statement Regarding Some Interviews With Mrs. E. G. White

(Feb. 13, 1912.)

Shortly after I reached the office on Tuesday, February 13, 1912, Sister White came into my room, and told me that she had had a strange experience the night before, and experience somewhat similar to that which she passed through during the session of the Pacific Union Conference held at Mountain View in January 1910, when it had seemed as if she were being torn to pieces by the powers of darkness. She said that she had been struggling all night with unseen agencies that were striving to oppress and discourage and thus defeat the purposes of God. The struggle had been a long and wearing one, and at times had seemed as if the enemy might obtain the mastery; but finally, toward morning, the Lord had helped her to gain a decisive victory. The trying experience had left her, however, very weak, and she feared that during the day she would not be able to do much writing.

Sister White went on to say that it had seemed during the night as if some of the brethren were misrepresenting matters by placing unfair interpretations upon her writings. The counsels she had given, were being misapplied. Several times, in the course of our conversation, she used the words, misinterpret and misapply; and she brought out clearly the thought that some were making an unwise and an unwarranted use of isolated passages in her writings which, taken out of their original setting, seemed to vindicate and uphold their own policies, and to indicate that God's cause should be held back. She added that she had been instructed to meet these misinterpretations of her writings by preparing proper presentations, thus meeting the plans of the enemy, and bringing victory to the cause.

* * * * *

The Purchase of Land at Loma Linda

Sunday forenoon, February 25, Sister White again came into my office room, and after spending a few minutes in conversation over various matters pertaining to the manuscript work, she began to outline quite fully her experience in connection with the control of tracts of land adjacent to the Loma Linda Sanitarium. She spent fully half an hour in conversation on this one point, and emphasized the necessity of our being wide awake at times when we have opportunity to gain control of properties close by our leading institutions.

Sister White pointed out the advantages of our having control of certain farming lands close by Loma Linda, and even if we should not think best to have them owned always by the institution. She said that it is far better for us to have the deciding voice as to the future disposition of these lands, than allow speculators to come in and subdivide and sell to any one who may choose to buy.

She pointed out the fact that there are loyal men or large means who at some time may wish to settle close by Loma Linda, and that these brethren, if thought best, could be permitted to purchase portions of the land we are now seeking to control, and could stand as bulwarks against the invasion of the Loma Linda neighborhood by unfriendly parties.

Sister White also said that the growing needs of Loma Linda may make it advisable for the institution to control the farming lands in the future, so as to make suitable provision for the feeding of their stock, etc.

Over and over again she emphasized the importance of the opportunity we now have to reveal wisdom by keeping these properties under our own control, even if we could not immediately decide just what disposition ought finally to be made of them; for the interest on the investment required would be largely met by the annual crops that might be produced, and in the end we should not be the losers, even if we should some day decide to sell the lands to those who are favorable to the objects for which the institution has been founded. She said she was sure that our brethren who are gifted with wise discernment will appreciate the advantage of our handling these properties ourselves, thus conserving the interests of the institution, rather than to allow speculators to step in and handle the properties for selfish gain, regardless of the interests of the institution.

* * * * *

Wednesday morning, February 28, Sister White called me to her office room, and after going over some manuscript work relating to our cause in the Southern States, she dwelt on the importance of our preparing the publishing proper historical compilations on important missionary enterprises that have been undertaken and carried forward under the special guidance of the Holy Spirit, by workers of large faith. She referred particularly to the story of the work in the South, the story of the earlier experience of our workers in Europe, and the story of the rise and development of the third angel's message in Australia. During the course of our conversation along these lines, Sister White abruptly turned the conversation toward Loma Linda matters, and said that some of the brethren have thought it rather strange that she should take so active a part in the matter of our brethren at Loma Linda securing control of the farming lands lying close by the institutions.

Sister White said that when these lands were offered for sale, there were those who would have been glad to purchase them, to sell again as a matter of financial profit.

She told me that while at Loma Linda, she was instructed during the night season, "Beware." She awoke, and immediately fell asleep again, when she was further instructed that it was her duty to make proper presentation of the Loma Linda work before the people, just as she had thought of preparing histories of the early experiences of our workers in the South, in Europe, and in Australia, and in connection with the sanitarium and publishing enterprises.

Sister White said further that the angel instructed her that there are those who, because of their fear of the consequences of advancing by faith in the opening providences of God in connection with the development of the Loma Linda enterprise, might make a wrong use of her writings concerning the conduct of the work. She was also instructed that there are still others who, in their eagerness to press the work forward, might go too far, if left alone and unaided in their efforts to present to the people the encouraging counsels that have been given regarding the Loma Linda enterprise. In view of this situation, she was instructed that it was her duty to take an active part in the preparation of a correct presentation of the Loma Linda enterprise in all its general features, for publication at an early date.

Then Sister White began to speak again of the advantages we shall gain by making a wise use of the farming lands that have recently been secured by friends of the institution. I asked her particularly if she had been instructed to prepare some of her writings regarding Loma Linda, for publication, and she answered in the affirmative, and immediately began speaking again of the control of adjacent properties. She emphasized repeatedly the necessity of our being wide awake, at times when the enemy seeks to thwart the purposes of God concerning the advancement of His work in important centers.

Sanitarium, Calif.

Feb. 28, 1912.

Clarence C. Crisler

The Work Before Us

MS-11-1912.

Remarks by Mrs. E. G. White to those assembled at the annual meeting of the College of Medical Evangelists, Loma Linda Chapel, March 28 (or 23,. 1960), 1912.

As we were coming from Los Angeles, I thought of many things that should be considered at this meeting; but I did not expect to be the one to speak first. This, I say, however, I thank the Lord that we have this beautiful place. Last night I was considering this: We must always keep in mind that we are doing a work for time and for eternity.

In our Los Angeles meeting there was a unity of sentiment in the councils that gives me great encouragement; and here at Loma Linda we must strive to see, not how much we can differ from one another, but how closely we can come into the perfect unity of which the Word of God advises us.

Whenever I look at the buildings, the fields, and the orchards here at Loma Linda, I am thankful that we have this beautiful place, thankful for every foot of land that we control. By and by you will see, if you do not understand it now, that the securing of the land was essential. It may not appear to you now that it was necessary for us to secure so large a tract, but I am instructed that our work here must be carried forward on broad lines and in solid unity. That the will of the Lord may be done in this place, we must be in a position where we can understand His pleasure in regard to our words and actions, where we may be always helping forward that work which is most essential. During the night it was again impressed upon my mind that it was through the providence of God we obtained this place when we did. Also that the branching out and enlargement that we have done, and the development of the work as it stands today, is what the Lord would have us do.

As a people we cannot stand still. The work must grow as we move forward. We have now come to a time when there will be intensity of action on the part of some whose movements we do not now understand. How then shall we carry the work at such a time, when opportunities for advancement come unexpectedly and difficulties are constantly increasing? We must daily commit our ways to God in faith, and be learning continually of Christ Jesus. He will not leave us to walk in darkness, but will give us the enlightenment of the Holy Spirit.

Those who are bearing responsibilities in our institutions and in various branches of the Lord's work, need to be constant learners in the school of Christ. We must understand and know that the Lord is at the head of the work; although we do not always discern His overruling power. At all times it is our privilege to know that He is there, and to have the assurance that He will work with us if we will work with Him. But if one plans one thing and another plans another thing, and each endeavors to lead, we shall get things into confusion. We may avoid this if we will. We may carry this work intelligently, in the love and fear of God. If we will make up our minds to do this at any sacrifice, if we labor patiently, we shall not fail.

As I looked out of the window this morning after the fog had lifted, and saw the fields and the orchards in front of the institution, I felt thankful for all the land that is now in our possession. We are not to sell portions hastily to this one and to that; but we are to consider well who it is that we may sell to. Let every decision be made after prayer and faithful study. We need to cultivate the spirit of prayer, that all our plans may be laid wisely and in the fear of God.

The work to be carried on here at Loma Linda is a great work. To carry it forward successfully every one of us must stand in right relation to God, all striving to be learners in the school of Christ. We are not to stand in the position of persons looking for some opportunity to differ from one another. We are not to cherish differences of opinion and keep them to the front; but we are to seek to be of one mind, one heart, one spirit, because there is One who stands at the head, and it is His Character that we are to represent in our labors and association together.

When I was here last, representations were given to me showing what we as a people ought to be. We are to labor in perfect harmony, not trying to be as different as possible from our fellow-laborers, or to secure the leadership in some little matter; but striving to learn how to unify. The workers have come here from many different institutions, having different plans and methods of working, but no one is to put himself to the strain to bring in that which is new and odd, or something that nobody else has thought of or approves. Let us rather endeavor to come into harmony, that the blessing of God may rest upon us. We should know and understand that the Lord Jesus is our ruler, if we follow on to know the Lord, we shall know that His going forth is prepared as the morning. The righteousness and peace of God will be given to all who will follow on to know the Lord.

My brethren and sisters, harmonize, harmonize. Bring your minds into the right relation to God, and as your minds are sanctified, they will be refined. It cannot be otherwise, because the refining influence of the Spirit of God is upon you. It is for us to understand and appreciate that God has done great things for us. He has manifested such an intense interest in us, and worked so wonderfully in our behalf, that it is impossible for us to fully comprehend His goodness and His grace. He "so loved the world that He gave His only begotten Son, that whosoever believeth in Him should not perish, but have everlasting life."

Sometimes when I have seen brethren who do not appear to weigh carefully the influence of their words and actions upon those around them, I have felt an intense fear that they would miss the mark. We must talk humbly with God. We must learn to overcome difficulties through faith in the living God. "This is the victory that overcometh the world, even our faith."

We are here, a large company of workers, consecrated to the service of God. And when I have heard that this one wants to leave because something does not suit him, and another plans to go because he thinks something is going wrong, I have thought, Poor souls; it is you who must change. It is you who must come upon your knees to God, asking for the baptism of His Spirit. What we all need is a consecration and a faith that will stand the day of test and trial. We must have intelligence and confidence to look to God and say, We trust Thee, Our Saviour; and we will not be driven from our post of duty in order to gratify the enemy of the work.

What we need is a right hold on God; and if we have this, we shall come off victorious. Let us ask Him to bind us together in unity of mind, in an understanding of His guidance; and then He can work for us wonderfully. Then we shall see of the salvation of God.

I am thankful to see so many of my brethren here today—brethren whom I have not seen for a long time. The Lord will surely reveal Himself to His people in this place, that they may communicate the precious truth to all parts of the world. Let us bear in mind that it is faith that leads to perfection of character. I want to be in that position where I can hear the words of my Saviour to me. Let us each endeavor to keep our minds stayed upon God, and prove the Lord whether He will not give us wisdom and guidance at every step.

To the ministers assembled here I will say, Let every minister of the gospel give himself unreservedly to the work of God, laboring intelligently, patiently and with unflagging energy. Hold fast to the truth, as to hidden treasure, and advance constantly. As you advance you will find that you are not alone. You have the presence of Him who said,"Lo I am with you alway, even unto the end of the world." **MS-15-1912.**

You may ask "Why does Sister White read all this? (Matthew 6) I answer, "because there are lessons here that we have not yet learned." God wants us to recognize every gift we receive as coming from Him. When we do this, and gratitude for the goodness of God fills our hearts, a heavenly atmosphere will surround the soul. My brethren and sisters, shall we not strive to order our lives by the truth of God as it is found in His word? We need to be more diligent in the study of the Scriptures. They must be to us, not a make-believe story, but the truth of the living God, the foundation of our faith, the assurance on which we build our hope of eternal life in the kingdom of heaven.

I wish to bring before you this morning some things that have been presented to me, showing wherein some of us are making serious mistakes. The minds of many are occupied with the consideration of worldly matters, often to the exclusion of the religion of God's word. The thoughts are more often upon the matter of eating and drinking and dressing than upon the great and important duty of serving God with humility and prayer.

The Lord has shown me that in many families decided changes must be brought about it. They need to know what they must do to be saved. If they will inquire diligently the way of life, God will impart to them an understanding of His Word, and teach them to value at their true worth the things of eternity. Then the heart will no longer reach out covetously for worldly benefits and the pleasures of this life.

[602] Shall we not give diligent heed to the lessons that I have read? There is an individual work for us to do in union with Christ. We are to put on Christ, put on His qualities of character to represent Him in all our words and actions. When we are willing thus to follow on to know the Lord, walking in humility before Him and being taught of Him daily, the Holy Spirit will work through us, giving us power to represent to the world a better way.

"Therefore, I say unto you, Take no (anxious) thought for your life, what ye shall eat, or what ye shall drink; nor yet for your body, what ye shall put on. Is not the life more than meat, and the body than raiment?" While you do your best, weary not your body and mind with the cares of this life; do not spoil your religious experience by worry; but trust the Lord to work for you, and to do for you what you cannot do for yourself. The life is more than meat, and the body is more than raiment.

There is much needless worrying, much trouble of mind, over things that cannot be helped. The Lord would have His children put their trust fully in Him. Our Lord is a just and righteous God. His children should acknowledge His goodness and His justice in the large and the small things of life. Those who cherish the spirit of worry and complaint are refusing to recognize His guiding hand. Needless anxiety is a foolish thing; and it hinders us from standing in a true position before God. When the Holy Spirit comes into the soul, there will be no desire to complain and murmur because we do not have everything we want; rather, we will thank God from a full heart for the blessings that we have. There is great need of more thankfulness among our workers today; and until they have this spirit they will be unprepared for a place in the kingdom of heaven. There is a mighty work to be done for every one of us. We comprehend but little of what God desires to work out through us.

We should seek to realize the breadth of His plans, and profit by every lesson that He tried to teach us.

A great deal of mischief is wrought in the imagination of our own hearts and minds when we seek to carry our own way contrary to the law of kindness. Here is where many fail. We do not cultivate a disposition to kindness, we want everything to come in an easy way to ourselves. But the question of greatest importance to each one of us should be, not how we can carry our own plans against the plans of others, but how we can have the power to live Christ every day. Christ came to earth and gave His life that we might have eternal salvation. He wants to encircle each of us with the atmosphere of heaven, that we may give to the world an example that will honor the religion of Christ.

There is one blessing all may have who seek for it in the right way. It is the Holy Spirit of God; and this is a blessing that brings all others in its train. If we will come to God as little children, asking for His grace and power and salvation, not for our own uplifting, but that we may bring blessing to those around us, our petitions will not be denied. Then let us study the Word of God that we may know how to take hold of His promises, and claim them as our own. Then we shall be happy. The enemy will be unable to destroy our peace. As we come into right relation to God, we shall see of His salvation.

In our schools we do not see the mighty working of the Holy Spirit as we ought. Although we have worked hard that they might be conducted on right lines, and advance in the fear of God, we do not see that willingness to be guided by the Spirit of God that opens the way for its working in the fullness of its power. God desires that His rich blessing shall rest upon teachers and students. When they have the experience of being daily converted to God, the perverse disposition will be overcome; there will be no place for it. The converting power of God will come in to lead the students to act for Christ, to serve and glorify Him who by His infinite sacrifice has made it possible for them to be saved. We need to appreciate more than we do the wonderful condescension of Christ, that we may work out in our lives His gracious character.

The Lord has a very special work to do for all who shall become citizens of His kingdom. Here are many young people associating together day after day in labor and in study, and in all things their conduct should reveal that they are controlled by the Spirit of God. They are to receive an education that will result in full consecration to God. And their own conversion is not the end of this education; they are to learn how to win others to the truth. This they will best accomplish by a life that reveals the transforming power of truth. Christ is to be formed within the hope of glory.

To those having families I will say, there is a work to be done for your children in your homes. Speak kindly to them. They are the Lord's property; His heritage. You have no right to create unhappiness in their lives. In the home it is the privilege of these children to prepare for the heavenly mansions. By no better way than by their own example can parents help the youth to gain this preparation. They are to learn by example as well as by precept that there must be no coarseness, no unkindness where angels of God dwell.

In this life we are to be controlled by the Spirit that rules in the heavenly courts. Righteousness and truth are to go before us. And the glory of the Lord will be the reward of all who serve Him acceptably. They obtain Christ's righteousness.

We want our children to be saved; but we must save them in God's appointed way. They must be made to understand that they have something to do if they would win heaven. When I see so many of our children who are receiving no preparation to meet temptation, I feel that I cannot do enough in the line of helping to provide places where they can receive an education in the things of God. But unless, when we gather the youth into such places as this we give them the education that will fit them to be overcomers, we had better not gather them into our institutions. Do we want these children and youth to enter the courts of heaven and enjoy the blessings of eternal life? Then let us work to this end understandingly, and we shall see blessed results for our labors.

Great is our need of the saving grace of Christ. Everywhere we turn we see more or less clearly revealed the spirit of strife for place and position, a reaching out for honor and recognition. My brethren and sisters, if you desire honor, seek it in the right way. How shall you seek it, do you ask? in obedience to the word of truth. Our ambition in this life should be to honor Christ at every step. The hasty temper, the cruel speech, the unkind thought, are not to be indulged. It is not for us to exalt this one, and condemn that one. In right words, words that bless and encourage, we are to reveal the fruits of righteousness.

Have you determined to be rich? Then let these words recorded in the sixth chapter of Matthew impress your heart and direct your life. They will teach you to be content, and to yield your will to the control of the Holy Spirit. You will not then be elbowing your fellow-workers that you may make room for your plans. But your greatest desire will be to work in just the place that God assigned you, and where He can look upon you with approval. Shall we not come into right relation to God? Shall we not put away all strife, which is a manifestation of unconverted self? When you feel sore because you think that somebody else is getting ahead of you, take the matter to the Father in prayer. Ask Him to put the impress of His Spirit upon your mind and character. When you feel like complaining at your lot, look about you for some soul who does not have all the blessings that you enjoy. Speak to him words of hope and comfort and encouragement. Such ministry will be a blessing to him, and a greater blessing to yourself. We need to reach the place where as a people we shall reveal in word and work that the Spirit of God is dwelling within; that we are over-comers by the blood of the Lamb and the word of our testimony. It is our privilege to make the battle of life easier for those with whom we associate. Shall we not endeavor to do this? If we will partake of Christ's labors for the uplifting and redemption of souls, we shall hear His words of benediction, "Well done, good and faithful servant; enter thou into the joy of thy Lord."

Pure and undefiled religion,—this is our great need. When the religion of Christ is permitted to hold sway in our lives, there will be advance moves made that will reveal to all in this place the working of divine power. Our lives will be unselfish thoughtful lives, as we unitedly follow heavenward the path of self-denial and cross-bearing.

There is a great work for our people to do in this place. You have great advantages here,—advantages that have cost much labor and prayer to secure. I remember how hard we labored to secure this property. Now additional property has come to us. We are glad of this addition, for we need every foot of this land. Our duty in regard to this matter is very clear to my mind; and I mean to work in harmony with the light given to me. We are talking of enlarging our facilities, of adding more buildings; but I would not urge that this work go forward unless a different spiritual atmosphere shall pervade the institution. There is a spirit of strife for position with some. This must be overcome. When the soul is truly converted, all questions of promotion will be decided in the light of eternal interests.

It has been presented to me that unless changes are wrought in the dispositions of many who are here, they will never enter the kingdom of heaven. With some, self is uppermost. Contention and emulation are being cherished, the Spirit of God cannot control, but the enemy comes in to suggest and advise. My brethren and sisters, you cannot afford to permit this condition to continue. You cannot afford to make self-service first. This will destroy our work. It must not be that we have taken all these large responsibilities upon us for naught. We must do our work intelligently, and to the very best of our ability, if we would bring glory to God. His Spirit must come in and abide.

The Lord wants us to be Christlike, to represent to the world the beauties of Christian character. This has not always been done in this place by all the workers. When the character of Christ is reflected in God's professed people, they will desire, not the place of greatest honor, but the place that God chooses for them. "Learn of Me", the great Teacher said, "for I am meek, and lowly in heart; and ye shall find rest unto your souls." Christ wants us to work out the dispositions that He will work in, as we yield our lives to His fashioning.

My brethren and sisters, let us stand where Heaven can cooperate with us, where the grace of God and His Holy Spirit can rest upon us, and work through us. I was going away today, but I felt that before departing I must lay before you the great need of the converting power of God if the workers in this institution are to obtain the experience that was in His purpose in the establishing of this institution. All this seeking for the highest place, all this determination to carry our individual ideas and desires should stop right now. It does not please the Master. God wants us to be converted from our ways to His way.

As a people we are being watched by the world, and we should conduct ourselves in such a way that men and women will be convinced that we have something that they have not. We need the help of all who are located here. If any have concluded that they cannot throw their energies into this work, there is the world before them. God bids His people order their lives by the living principles that moved Christ to sacrifice Himself for the saving of the lost. The Son of God gave His life to redeem the youth. What shall we do for them? What shall we do for those older in years? My brethren, you need first to order your own lives by the plan of salvation, then gather with Christ with all the powers of your being. Then the Lord will work through your efforts.

When I consider how hard we have worked in different places to establish health institutions, I feel it my duty to impress upon the workers connected with them that they have a great responsibility to act in a way that will rightly represent the principles that are the foundation of this message. They should be righteous in word and deed. Strife and contention, which is of the devil, should find no place in their experience.

We may inherit the things prepared for God's people from the foundation of the world, if we will live in harmony with the righteous life of Christ. Let there be no contention, no strife. There is room enough in the world; there is opportunity for all to perfect a Christian character. Let us take hold of this work intelligently. Then when any change takes place in the working of the cause here, it will be seen, in the course taken by the workers, that their dispositions are being molded by the Spirit of God, that the grace of Christ is sanctifying character.

I do not want to weary you; I have spoken long enough, but, my brethren, I want you to understand how greatly I appreciate everything that is for the advantage of this place. I pray that from this institution an army of workers may go forth to glorify the One who gave His life for us. Oh, that we might all show in our daily lives that we appreciate this gift. May God bless you every one, is my prayer.

*****

Be of Good Cheer

MS. 71, 1912.

By Ellen G. White

Words addressed to board of directors of the College of Medical Evangelists, Loma Linda, Calif., Nov. 9, 1912.

I feel very thankful that it is our privilege to believe in God, and to walk carefully in accordance with the instruction He has given us in His Word. If we do this, our hearts will respond to the impressions of the Spirit of God, and we shall follow on to know the Lord, whose going forth is prepared as the morning, so we are to expect the revelations of His grace as we advance.

But if we keep silent, if we do not feel the importance of moving in harmony with His will, we shall not have His blessing attending us. We cannot afford, brethren and sisters, to be without His help and guidance. We need to be in a position where we can talk with God. We are to commune with Him. He who is our sanctification, our righteousness, has given us the privilege of being in a position where we may have a continually increasing faith. We must ever live by faith, and follow on to know the Lord.

God's promises to us are so rich, so full, that we need never hesitate or doubt: we need never waver or backslide. In view of the encouragements that are found all through the Word of God, we have no right to be gloomy or despondent. We may have weakness of body; but the compassionate Saviour says: "Ask, and it shall be given you; seek, and ye shall find; knock, and it shall be opened unto you: for every one that asketh receiveth; and he that seeketh findeth; and to him that knocketh it shall be opened."

Will you believe these assurances? Will you say, "Yes, Lord, I take Thee at Thy word. I will begin where I am, to talk an increase of faith; I will take hold of the promises; they are for me"? O brethren and sisters, what we want is a living, striving, growing faith in the promises of God, which are indeed for you and for me.

Words of Encouragement

Many, many times I have been instructed by the Lord to speak words of courage to His people. We are to put our trust in God, and believe in Him, and act in accordance with His will. We must ever remain in a position where we can praise the Lord and magnify His name. Then we shall see light in His Word, and follow on to know Him, whose going forth is prepared as the morning. Read 1 Peter 1:1-5.

These words are all-sufficient evidence that God desires us to receive great blessings. His promises are so clearly stated that there is no cause for uncertainty. He desires us to take Him at His word. At times we shall be in great perplexity, and not know just what to do. But at such times it is our privilege to take our Bibles, and read the messages He has given us; and then get down on our knees, and ask Him to help us. Over and over again He has given evidence that He is a prayer-hearing and a prayer-answering God. He fulfills His promises in far greater measure than we expect to receive help.

Perplexities

So long as Satan continues to live, we shall have perplexity; and if we choose to follow the counsel of the enemy, we shall have constant difficulty; but if we refuse to yield to satanic influences, choosing rather to lay hold on God and on the promises of His Word, we shall be able to help and strengthen and uphold one another. Thus we shall bring into the work with which we are connected a spirit of courage.

Never are we to utter a word that would arouse doubt or fear, or that would cast a shadow over the minds of others. I am determined not to permit myself to speak discouraging words; and when I hear criticism and complaint, or an expression of doubt and fear, I know that he who thus speaks has his eyes turned away from the Saviour. I know every such person does not appreciate Him who at infinite sacrifice left the royal courts and came down into the world that was lost, and lived among the children of men in order that He might speak words of hope and good cheer to the discouraged and desponding.

[613] Wherever we are, we are under obligation, as disciples of our Lord and Master, to anchor our faith in the promises of God. Individually we are to believe. We are not to cast about for a possible doubt, or imagine that sometime we may have to stand beneath the shadow of a cloud that seems to be gathering. We are chosen of God to be His children. We have been bought with an infinite price, and we have no occasion for placing the suggestion of the enemy before the assurances of the Lord Jesus Christ.

The Lord desires us to act sensibly. We shall have trials; we need never expect anything else; for the time has not yet come when Satan is to be bound. Wherever we may be, we shall continue to have trials. But if we give up to the suggestions of the enemy, we lose the battle. Can we afford to yield to the arch-deceiver? Oh, no! We are to turn for help and deliverance to Him who "according to His abundant mercy hath begotten us again unto a lively hope by the resurrection of Jesus Christ," even the hope of an eternal inheritance reserved for those "who are kept by the power of God through faith unto salvation."

I was here at Loma Linda when this place was purchased. As I spoke to the people the power of God came into our midst, again and again. On the occasion of my first visit to look over the property, I knelt right down with our brethren and the representatives of the owners of the place who were here; I knelt right down in the midst of them and prayed to God about the work that should be undertaken and carried forward in Loma Linda. When I got up, some of those who were not of our faith seemed to be deeply moved. From that time I have ever felt under bounden duty to God to make of this place just what it should be. I know that there are men here who have wrestled in the cause of God, and I know that they have passed through an experience that they never would have had if Satan had not had the power to oppress them.

Let us all strive to make of Loma Linda just what God means it should be. This is the principle thing I have to say—make of this place what God would have you make of it. Every one of you is under bounden duty to God to labor in harmony, and press the battle to the gate. (Note: This article, except last two paragraphs, above, in N. L.)

If unbelievers come in and talk their doubts and fears, remember that Satan is not dead. He has agencies through whom he works. But shall we become discouraged because of this? Oh, no! Christ, our Saviour, lives and reigns. Let us not look on the dark side. As soon as we yield to the temptation to do this, we shall have plenty of company. But there is nothing to be gained by looking on the dark side. What we want is courage in the Lord; and we want to follow on to know the Lord, that we may know that His going forth is prepared as the morning. This is not going back into darkness. You know how the morning is prepared. If you follow on to know the Lord every day, you will increase in brightness, in courage, in faith, and the Lord Jesus will be to you a present help in every time of need.—MS, 71, 1912.

[614]

* * * * *

An Important Interview Regarding Physicians' Wages

(On the morning of Dec. 4, 1913, the leading brethren of the Pacific Union Conference conferred with Mrs. E. G. White at her Elmshaven home in regard to the remuneration of our sanitarium Physicians. A stenographic report of the interview was made and the ribbon copy bears a handwritten note of endorsement by Mrs. White in these words: "This is correctly presented, and I repeat this for the benefit of others. May the Lord help us and teach and guide us at every step in our difficulties." Essential portions of the report of this Interview follow.—Compilers of Selected Messages 2:202.)

Present: Ellen G. White, Elders F. M Burg, G. W. Reaser, W. M. Adams, J. H. Behrens, C. L. Taggart, A. G. Christiansen, W. C. White; Also C. C. Crisler.

After introductions and greetings, Elder W. C. White said in part:

All day yesterday we were considering the interests of our various schools in the Pacific Union Conference. In these schools located at Angwin, Lodi, Fernando, Armona, and Loma Linda, there are between six and seven hundred students in training. We were encouraged as we took counsel together regarding these schools.

Today we must enter into consideration of sanitarium problems, particularly the question of the wages we should pay to physicians and surgeons. We have in our _____ Sanitarium a God-fearing physician who has won the confidence of all his associates—a man whom God has blessed greatly in his ministry to the sick. He wants to remain, and everybody wants him to remain, and he feels that it would be right for him to remain if his brethren could grant him a wage about twice as large as that paid to our average workers. He loves to give freely, and he wishes to have funds with which to live and to use for this purpose. We are much perplexed, and we would be glad to know if you have any light on this matter.

Sister White: If he is granted considerably more than other physicians, they will come to believe they are not treated right unless they have more also. We must move cautiously and understandingly, and not allow wages to creep up so high that many will be tempted. There may have to be a coming down rather than a going up, in physicians' wages; because there is a great work to be done. Unless you have some clear light from the Lord, it is not advisable to pay one man considerably more than another doing similar work. For, if you do, the other will think it perfectly proper to expect similar high wages. We must look at things on all sides, and it is of no use for us to think that we can offer a successful worker a high wage simply because he may demand it. We must rather, consider what we can afford to do at the present time, when the fields are opening upon which we shall henceforth have to expend much more means than we have spent hitherto. These are matters that will test the faith of our people.

[615]

W. C. White: They do test our faith, Mother,—especially when a group of workers have labored with a man until they have learned to love him and adore him and they believe that he can do better work than any other man. Then it is natural for them to think that it is wrong for the brethren to withhold from him that which he might use to advantage. They think, "What is a thousand dollars, or fifteen hundred dollars, extra, when life is involved?" They say, "Here is such and such a case that he has just brought through, and there is another whose life he has saved;" and they feel as if it would be awfully mean of us not to meet his requirements. They say, "There is no one who has to work and suffer as does a surgeon. Think of the hours of arduous labor, of anxiety, of mental anguish they have to endure, when a precious life is hanging by a slender thread."

But on the other hand, in considering this matter, we must remember that other institutions are influenced by our action. We see a poor struggling sanitarium situated in a beautiful place, in a position to do a large business, and with every prospect of making money if only they can have a brilliant physician; and they can get a good physician if they are encouraged to pay only three to five hundred dollars more than the wage scale recommended. They say, "If you will only let us pay a few hundred dollars more than you have advised, we can gain five thousand dollars to cover this small additional expense for wages." And thus it seems—when we look at it from a business point of view.

Sister White: You see there is a selfishness that underlies that, that the Lord is not pleased with. We must work harmoniously. It is through harmonious action that our work is to be carried forward, and some will have a very hard time. Some will have an easier time. But all these things will have to be taken just as they come, and the workers must remember what Jesus gave in coming to our world. I think of it over and over and over again, and it seems to me that we can do an excellent work, if we set a right example. But if we desire that which the most of our brethren can not receive, this injures our influence. One brother says, "Such and such a brother has a certain wage, and I must have a wage to correspond." And so the wages will climb, and keep climbing, higher and still higher. The fact is, that the wage of some may have to be lower and still lower in order that we may meet the extensive requirements of the work that is before us in warning the world.

O, I am so thankful that the Lord has given me a little strength that I may use in completing my books! I have not gotten through yet. I have not completed all that I desire to see done. I mean to take just as good care of myself as possible, that I may complete intelligently the work the Lord has entrusted to me. And in all this I desire to share with my brethren in self-denial. What we want, brethren, is to be an example in all matters, whether man sees it or not. Let us remember, brethren, that the Lord sees every sacrifice we make individually for the spread of the truth. But if you encourage some to receive a wage considerably higher than that which their brethren are receiving, others will desire to climb just as high; and if they are not allowed to do so, they will become dissatisfied.

Brethren, we cannot afford to lay a stumbling-block in the path of any soul simply because they think they must have matters arranged so and so. The Lord desires us to be consistent in everything. He desires us to follow the self-sacrificing example of Christ, and when we do that, His blessing rests upon us. When we go to various places and our brethren know that we have been tempted to ask for higher pay but that we have overcome this temptation, He will give us influence with the people. It is not the higher pay that brings success. Success comes through following in the footsteps of the Saviour, in self-denial and self-sacrifice. When we do this, the Lord pronounces His blessing upon us. He discerns the hidden motives, and when the work that is to be done is especially difficult and taxing, His grace will be sufficient for our every need.

Even if we as laborers of God go beyond that which seems to be for the good of our health and strength, we may look to Him in confidence, casting our helpless soul upon Him, and realizing that He who Himself led a self-sacrificing life of toil on this earth will acknowledge our faithfulness, and will help us marvelously. When we come to hard places, the angels of God will be right impressions upon those with whom we are associated, and to whom we are ministering.

Some may think that I ought to be in the field, at work, and brethren, it is in my heart to do public labor at general meetings. But at my age if I should undertake to travel from place to place, I would soon use up the little remnant of strength I still have, and would be unable to do the special work the Lord has called me to do. In former years I was strengthened to labor early and late, both in writing for the press and in public speaking. Now I am spending my chief energies in gathering up the fragments, and in preparing for publication that which should be placed in the hands of the people. If I had the strength, I should be very willing to go anywhere and to bear heavy burdens,—not that I desire to lift up myself, but that I might do some one some good.

[617]

Those who have the cause of God at heart, must realize that they are not working for themselves or for the small wage they may be receiving, and that God can make the little they do receive, go farther than they may think it can. He will give them satisfaction and blessing as they go forward in self-sacrificing labor. And He will bless every one of us as we labor in the meekness of Christ. And when I see some seeking for higher wages, I say to myself, "They are losing a precious blessing," I know this to be a fact. I have seen it worked out again and again.

Now brethren, let us take hold and do the very best that we possibly can, without asking for higher wages except as we find that it is an impossibility to do the work given us without more; but even then let others see this necessity as well as ourselves, for God puts it into their hearts to see it, and they will speak the word that will have more influence than for us to speak a thousand words. They will speak words that will give us a proper standing before the people. The Lord is our helper and God, our frontguard, and our rearward.

As we bring ourselves into right relationship with God, we shall have success wherever we go; and it is success that we want, not money—living success, and God will give it to us because He knows all about our self-denial. He knows every sacrifice that we make. You may think that your self-denial does not make any difference, that you ought to have more consideration, and so on. But it makes a great difference with the Lord. Over and over again I have been shown that when individuals begin to reach out after higher and still higher wages something comes into their experience that places them where they stand no longer on vantage ground. But when they take the wage that carries on the face of it the fact that they are self-sacrificing, the Lord sees their self-denial and He gives them success and victory. This has been presented to me over and over again. The Lord that seeth in secret will reward openly for every sacrifice that His tried servants have been willing to make.

The brethren often leave their families and make many other sacrifices in behalf of the cause that they love more than anything else in life. They may be tempted to think that in return for this self-denial they ought to receive more remuneration; but the more they might receive would not always bring them a blessing. If they go forward in a spirit of cheerfulness, others will follow their example; and as they go forward, following on to know the Lord more perfectly, they will know that His going forth is prepared as the morning. The Lord guards the men that are willing to brave hardship and danger in order to reach precious souls in out-of-the-way places. He regards their determination to make His cause first. He honors those who are willing to endure hardness as good soldiers of Christ. He sees every sacrifice that is made; He sees the end from the beginning, and He will care for every one of His servants who remain faithful. There have been times when I have thought that my brethren might have done better than they did do in my behalf. But I have been careful about criticizing. I have thought of the great sacrifice Christ made in giving His life for a lost world. God gave His only begotten Son to save fallen man, and the offering that was made was prompted by the spirit of self-sacrifice.

In years past, when this subject of wages has been under consideration, I have told my brethren that the Lord knows all about the spirit that prompts us to action, and that He can turn matters in our favor at times we do not expect it. As we set a right example the blessing of the Lord will rest upon us. I have seen the Lord work in many ways and in many places to help the very ones that view these matters in the right light and set a self-sacrificing example. And, brethren, as you labor earnestly, prayerfully, humbly, in the spirit of Christ, God will open doors before you. The people will see your self-denial.

At times when my brethren have come to me, seeking advice as to whether they should demand a higher wage, I have told them they might gain a little means by asking for higher waves, but that the blessing of God will accompany those who follow a different course. God sees the self-denial; the Lord God of Israel sees every motive; and when you come into a hard place, the angels of God are there to help you, and to give you victory after victory.

I have been very clear in counselling my brethren not to demand large wages, for this is not the impelling motive that leads us to spend our energies in the work of soul-saving. We are not to let the wage question stand in the way of our responding to the call of duty, wherever our services may be required. The Lord can bring matters around so that a blessing will attach to our labors far exceeding any compensation we may or may not receive; and He will give to His servants words to speak that are of the highest consequence to perishing souls.

The people are hungering and thirsting for help from heaven. I have tried to put in practice these principles of self-sacrifice, and I know whereof I speak when I say that the blessing of God will rest upon you when you make the call of duty first. I am glad for this privilege of testifying before you this morning that the Lord has turned matters, over and over again, in such a way as to give us more than we could possibly ask for. The Lord will prove His servants; and if they prove true to Him, and leave their cases with Him, He will help them in every time of need.

[619]

We are not laborers together for God for the wages we may receive in His service. True brethren, you must have wages with which to support your families; but if you should begin to stipulate as to just how much you shall receive, you may prove a stumbling-block to some one else who does not have the disposition, perhaps, that you have to be liberal; and the result will be confusion. Others will think that all are not dealt with on an equality. You will soon find that the cause of God will become cramped; and this result you do not desire to see. You wish to see the cause of God placed on vantage ground. By your example, as well as by your words, the people are to have a living assurance that the truth received into the heart begets a spirit of self-denial. And as you go forward in this spirit, there are many that will follow.

The Lord desires His children to act in that self-denying self-sacrificing way that will bring to us the satisfaction of having performed our duty well because it was duty. The only Begotten Son of God gave Himself to an ignominious death on the cross, and should we complain at the sacrifice we are called upon to make?

During my wakeful hours through the night season, I have been pleading with the Lord to guard our brethren against the tendency to promise to go here or there on the stipulation that they are to have a little higher wage. If they go in a spirit of self-sacrificing, trusting in Him, the Lord will grant sustaining power to mind and character, and success will be the result.

In the future, our work is to be carried forward in self-denial and self-sacrifice even beyond that which we have seen in past years. God desires us to commit our souls to Him, that He may work through us in manifold ways. I feel intensely over these matters. Brethren, let us walk in meekness and lowliness of mind, and put before our associates an example of self-sacrifice. If we do our part in faith, God will open ways before us now undreamed of.

W. C. White: How shall we meet this condition? Some of our physicians, like Dr. _____ and Dr. _____ and others, who are big-hearted and generous, are brought into contact with sickness and poverty and distress, and they feel intensely the importance of advance moves in the church and in the institutions with which they are connected, and they feel that they must give. They love to give. They make big donations, and they keep making big donations, and they say, "We need money so that we can keep on giving." How ought we to meet such proposals? Shall we put the money into their hands in the form of wages, or ought our institutions that have a surplus be willing to respond liberally to the requests to these men to do things for the poor and needy who greatly desire help?

Sister White: Yes, that is the way the matter should be handled. The institution should do what it can to help.

W. C. White: Sometimes the brethren call the attention of the management to certain needy cases, and they are met with the response, "We cannot afford it; there are lots of poor people in the world, and we cannot help them all." Then the physicians say, "We must have money to use in urgent cases, and the surest way to get it is to demand a liberal wage."

Sister White: That is not the best way. If matters are arranged so that the cause of God will be served to the best account, angels of God will work, and a right influence will be exerted. As those connected with the institutions share in sacrifice, the minds of the people will be impressed and all will be inspired to do the utmost of their ability. But if men feel that they cannot labor in our institutions unless they have large wages, they will meet with disappointment. This has been presented to me over and over again.

Let us not forget the infinite sacrifice Christ has made in our behalf. That He might obtain for us heaven, He hung on the cross and suffered death—a most shameful death. If He were willing to give Himself freely in order that we might have life everlasting, how glad we should be for the privilege of service, and how eager we should be to follow His example of self-sacrifice.

Many nights, when I think of these matters, I am unable to sleep. I keep saying to myself, O if I could only go before the public as I used to and set before them the self-sacrificing Saviour as our divine Pattern, how glad I would be! But my age does not permit me to do this at present.

W. C. White: Mother often mourns that she cannot go out as in former years to attend general meetings; but I try to encourage her that she can do more for the cause of God by sending out her writings for others to use in all parts of the field, than by attempting to attend meetings in a small portion of the field.

Sister White: In former years God blessed me as I went from place to place, preaching the Word. He gave me some remarkable experiences in temperance work, near Boston, where I was permitted to address thousands of people. During these meetings when I spoke in response to the invitation of those not of our faith, I usually refused to accept any remuneration for such labor, so that they might not misinterpret my motives.

W. C. White: May I tell the brethren of the things you said to me at New Castle, N. S. W., about the reform that we as a people must stand for in the matter of high charges? There are many others things you have said we should stand for, like men nursing men, and women nursing women; and some of these matters have been written out and printed. But I am not sure that this that you told me at that time has ever been written out, and I should like to repeat it to these brethren in your presence, so that you can testify as to whether I have told it correctly or not.

In New Castle, you remember, we were down there one time when Brother Starr and others were holding meetings. One Friday afternoon you and I were walking out by the creek, and you said that there was a reformation that we must stand for, in medical practice that was just as important as the discarding of drugs, and that was, the matter of very high charges for medical service.

E. G. White: I have some things written regarding this, but have not brought them before the public. I have not had a chance to prepare all the matter that I would like to prepare. But I mean to give myself to it.

W. C. White: Well, we are getting past our meeting's hour before we knew it. It seems to me, Mother, as if the Lord gave you thoughts this morning to help us in our present perplexities.

(Voices: Yes, Amen, True.) And we thank Him for it. Before we go may we kneel down and thank Him for these words of counsel, and pray for guidance today. And we will also ask your prayers that we may be guided today while we are considering many very perplexing matters.

E. G. White: Well brethren, if some one proposes something that is not in accordance with self-sacrificing principles on which our work is based, let us remember that one stroke of God's Hand can sweep away all seeming benefit because it was not to His Name's glory.

www.ingramcontent.com/pod-product-compliance
Lightning Source LLC
Chambersburg PA
CBHW080857010526
44118CB00015B/2179